Numerical Techniques and Computer Programming

for Engineering Problems

Numerical Techniques and Computer Programming
for Engineering Problems

N Krishna Raju

BE, MSc (Engg), PhD, MIE, MI (Struct Engg)
Emeritus Professor
Department of Civil Engineering
National Institute of Technology
Surathkal, Karnataka
MS Ramaiah Institute of Technology
Bengaluru, Karnataka

CBS

CBS Publishers & Distributors Pvt Ltd

New Delhi • Bengaluru • Chennai • Kochi • Kolkata • Mumbai
Hyderabad • Jharkhand • Nagpur • Patna • Pune • Uttarakhand

Numerical Techniques and
Computer Programming
for Engineering Problems

ISBN: 978-93-89688-07-8

First Edition: 2021

Published by Satish Kumar Jain and produced by Varun Jain for

CBS Publishers & Distributors Pvt Ltd
4819/XI Prahlad Street, 24 Ansari Road, Daryaganj, New Delhi 110 002, India.
Ph: 23289259, 23266861, 23266867   Fax: 011-23243014   Website: www.cbspd.com
e-mail: delhi@cbspd.com; cbspubs@airtelmail.in.
Corporate Office: 204 FIE, Industrial Area, Patparganj, Delhi 110 092
Ph: 4934 4934   Fax: 4934 4935   e-mail: publishing@cbspd.com;
publicity@cbspd.com

Branches

- **Bengaluru:** Seema House 2975, 17th Cross, K.R. Road,
  Banasankari 2nd Stage, Bengaluru 560 070, Karnataka
  Ph: +91-80-26771678/79   Fax: +91-80-26771680   e-mail: bangalore@cbspd.com
- **Chennai:** 7, Subbaraya Street, Shenoy Nagar, Chennai 600 030, Tamil Nadu
  Ph: +91-44-26680620, 26681266   Fax: +91-44-42032115   e-mail: chennai@cbspd.com
- **Kochi:** 42/1325, 1326, Power House Road, Opp KSEB, Power House, Ernakulam 682 018, Kochi, Kerala
  Ph: +91-484-4059061-67   Fax: +91-484-4059065   e-mail: kochi@cbspd.com
- **Kolkata:** 6/B, Ground Floor, Rameswar Shaw Road, Kolkata-700 014, West Bengal
  Ph: +91-33-22891126, 22891127, 22891128   e-mail: kolkata@cbspd.com
- **Mumbai:** 83-C, Dr E Moses Road, Worli, Mumbai-400018, Maharashtra
  Ph: +91-22-24902340/41   Fax: +91-22-24902342   e-mail: mumbai@cbspd.com

Representatives

| • Hyderabad | 0-9885175004 | • Jharkhand | 0-9811541605 | • Nagpur | 0-9421945513 |
| • Patna | 0-9334159340 | • Pune | 0-9623451994 | • Uttarakhand | 0-9716462459 |

Printed at: Rashtriya Printers, Dilshad Garden, Delhi, India

to
the pioneers and research workers
Richard Southwell, Nathan Newmark, Hardy Cross,
Newton-Raphson, Regula-Falsi, Runge-Kutta, John Backus,
Gauss, Jordan, Jacobi, Crout, Cramer, Taylor, Simpson, Cholesky, and
a host of others who toiled incessantly for the development and widespread
use of numerical methods and computer programming techniques

Preface

Numerical methods were developed as early as 1930 by pioneers like Richard Southwell, Hardy Cross, Nathan Newmark and several other investigators for solving engineering problems for which direct methods were either not suitable or not directly applicable. However, the numerical methods were not popular in the early period from 1930 to 1960 due to the monotony of tedious and repetitive computations using limited computational devices like slide rules and mechanical calculators.

The advent of the computer in the latter half of the 20th century revived the importance of the numerical techniques and in the recent past, phenomenal developments have taken place in this field resulting in the widespread use of numerical methods in conjunction with electronic computers to solve complex engineering problems.

This monograph is a compendium of lectures delivered by the author to the senior undergraduate and postgraduate students of civil and structural engineering streams over a period of several years.

The subject material of the book is arranged in such a way that the applications of numerical techniques are given more importance with a limited theory presented wherever essential. The book amply covers the syllabus requirements of undergraduate and postgraduate students in civil and structural engineering courses of various universities in India.

The subject material has been arranged in eight chapters covering the basic principles of various numerical methods relevant to the problems associated with civil and structural engineering domain alongwith a variety of numerical examples to illustrate the use of the numerical methods.

Chapter 1 deals with various direct methods of solving linear system of simultaneous equations, the prominent methods being the matrix inversion, Gaussian elimination, Cramer's rule and Cholesky's procedures.

In **Chapter 2**, the iterative procedures of Gauss–Seidal and Southwell's relaxation methods are outlined with examples. The methods of numerical solution of nonlinear equations comprising Newton–Raphson's method, Regula–Falsi method, Graeff's method and the method of iteration are presented in **Chapter 3**.

The solutions of ordinary differential equations by Euler, Runge–Kutta and Taylor's series are included in **Chapter 4**. The various numerical iteration techniques such as trapezoidal and Simpson's rule, Newmark's method and their applications in problems of different types of beams and columns are discussed in **Chapter 5**.

The powerful techniques of finite difference methods and their application for statically determinate and indeterminate beam problems, buckling of columns, vibrations of beams, bending of plates, beams on elastic foundations, membrane and torsion problems are comprehensively covered in **Chapter 6**.

Chapter 7 deals with the principles of optimization and the solution of linear programming problems using the graphical method and Simplex algorithms are illustrated with a variety of practical problems encountered in engineering industry.

Chapter 8 is devoted to computer programming dealing with the different programming languages and their application to the solution of engineering problems. Programming solutions are presented using mainly the FORTRAN language for a variety of engineering problems associated with the numerical techniques. A few computer programmes in the C language are also included at the end of the chapter.

In each chapter, the application of the numerical methods is illustrated by a large number of practical examples encountered in the civil and structural engineering domain. SI units have been adopted throughout the book. Several examples for practice are included at the end of every chapter to help students preparing for university examinations.

Each chapter is provided with relevant references to help students for further reading. Both review and objective type questions provided at the end of each chapter will help students for a deeper understanding of the subject matter and also in preparing for competitive examinations.

The author gratefully acknowledges the help rendered by his wife Pramila, late Dr KU Muthu and his colleagues at MSRIT, for the successful completion of this book writing project.

Finally, the author welcomes constructive criticisms and suggestions which will immensely help in updating the contents of the monograph.

N Krishna Raju

Contents

List of Symbols and Notations

A	Square matrix of order n
a_{ij}	Element in the ith row and jth column of matrix A
A^{-1}	Inverse of matrix A
A^T	Transpose of matrix A
$\mid A \mid$	Determinant of A
I	Unit matrix
U	Upper triangular matrix
L	Lower triangular matrix
$adj\ A$	Adjoint of the matrix
E	Modulus of elasticity of material
I	Second moment of area
EI	Flexural rigidity
W	Concentrated load
w	Uniformly distributed load
G	Rigidity of shear modulus
τ	Shear stress
M	Moment
V	Shear force
M_t	Torsion moment
ϕ	Slope
k	Spring constant
L	Length
t	Thickness of the plate
y	Deflection
P	Axial force
θ	Angle
β	Non-dimensional parameter
g	Acceleration due to gravity
P_{cr}	Critical or buckling load
f	Natural frequency of vibration
ω	Circular frequency of vibration
m	Mass of the beam per unit length
∇^4	Operator
D	Stiffness of the plate
μ	Poisson's ratio

1

Direct Methods for the Solution of Linear System of Equations

1.1 GENERAL ASPECTS

Complex engineering problems involving several parameters are generally expressed in the form of linear simultaneous equations. Most of the structural engineering problems like the determination of moments and deflections in simply supported and continuous beams can be reduced to a system of linear simultaneous equations. Several numerical methods have been developed by various authors[1,2,3] for the solution of linear simultaneous equations. These methods are classified under the following categories.

1. Cramer's rule or method of determinants[4]
2. Method of leading coefficients[5]
3. Gaussian elimination method[6]
4. Gauss–Jordan method[7]
5. Factorization and Cholesky's methods[8]
6. Matrix inversion method[9]
7. Solution of Eigen problems[10]

1.2 CRAMER'S RULE OR METHOD OF DETERMINANTS

The given set of simultaneous equations is arranged in the form of a matrix as shown below.

$$\begin{bmatrix} a_{11}x_1 + a_{12}x_2 + a_{13}x_3 = k_1 \\ a_{21}x_1 + a_{22}x_2 + a_{23}x_3 = k_2 \\ a_{31}x_1 + a_{32}x_2 + a_{33}x_3 = k_3 \end{bmatrix}$$

These equations can be expressed in the matrix from

$$\begin{bmatrix} a_{11} & a_{12} & a_{13} \\ a_{21} & a_{22} & a_{23} \\ a_{31} & a_{32} & a_{33} \end{bmatrix} \begin{Bmatrix} x_1 \\ x_2 \\ x_3 \end{Bmatrix} = \begin{Bmatrix} k_1 \\ k_2 \\ k_3 \end{Bmatrix}$$

$$[A]\,\{X\} = \{K\}$$

The determinant of A is expressed as the array.

$$D = \begin{bmatrix} a_{11} & a_{12} & a_{13} \\ a_{21} & a_{22} & a_{23} \\ a_{31} & a_{32} & a_{33} \end{bmatrix}$$

To determine x_1, replace the first column of the matrix A by the RHS vector and evaluate the determinant D_1 given by

$$D_1 = \begin{bmatrix} k_1 & a_{12} & a_{13} \\ k_2 & a_{22} & a_{23} \\ k_3 & a_{32} & a_{33} \end{bmatrix}$$

Similarly evaluate the determinants D_2 and D_3 expressed as

$$D_2 = \begin{bmatrix} a_{11} & k_1 & a_{13} \\ a_{21} & k_2 & a_{23} \\ a_{31} & k_3 & a_{33} \end{bmatrix}$$

$$D_3 = \begin{bmatrix} a_{11} & a_{12} & k_1 \\ a_{21} & a_{22} & k_2 \\ a_{31} & a_{32} & k_3 \end{bmatrix}$$

Then the values of x_1, x_2 and x_3 are obtained as

$$x_1 = \left(\frac{D_1}{D} \right), \quad x_2 = \left(\frac{D_2}{D} \right) \text{ and } x_3 = \left(\frac{D_3}{D} \right)$$

Example 1.1

Solve the following equations using Cramer's rule.

$$2x_1 + x_2 + 4x_3 = 4 \tag{1}$$
$$x_1 - 3x_2 - x_3 = -5 \tag{2}$$
$$3x_1 - 2x_2 + 2x_3 = -1 \tag{3}$$

Solution

$$D = \begin{bmatrix} 2 & -1 & 4 \\ 1 & -3 & -1 \\ 3 & -2 & 2 \end{bmatrix} = 2(-6-2) -1(2+3) + 4(-2+9) = 7$$

$$D_1 = \begin{bmatrix} 4 & 1 & 4 \\ -5 & -3 & -1 \\ -1 & -2 & 2 \end{bmatrix} = 4(-6-2) -1(-10-1) + 4(10+3) = 7$$

$$D_2 = \begin{bmatrix} 2 & 4 & 4 \\ 1 & -5 & -1 \\ 3 & -1 & 2 \end{bmatrix} = 2(-10-1) -4(2+3) + 4(-1+15) = 14$$

$$D_3 = \begin{bmatrix} 2 & 1 & 4 \\ 1 & -3 & -5 \\ 3 & -2 & -1 \end{bmatrix} = 2(3-10) - 1(-1+15) + 4(-2+9) = 0$$

Therefore, the values of x_1, x_2 and x_3 are obtained as

$$x_1 = \left(\frac{D_1}{D}\right) = \left(\frac{14}{7}\right) = 1$$

$$x_2 = \left(\frac{D_2}{D}\right) = \left(\frac{0}{7}\right) = 2$$

$$x_3 = \left(\frac{D_3}{D}\right) = \left(\frac{0}{7}\right) = 0$$

Check: By considering Eq. (1)

$$2(1) + 2 + 4\,(0) = 4$$

Example 1.2

Solve the following set of equations by the method of determinant.

$$2x_1 + 2x_2 - x_3 + x_4 = 4 \tag{1}$$
$$4x_1 + 3x_2 - x_3 + 2x_4 = 6 \tag{2}$$
$$8x_1 + 5x_2 - 3x_3 + 4x_4 = 12 \tag{3}$$
$$3x_1 + 3x_2 - 2x_3 + 2x_4 = 6 \tag{4}$$

Solution

Using the properties of determinants, the given array of (4 × 4) determinant is reduced to a (3 × 3) determinant by the following process.

$$D = \begin{bmatrix} 2 & 2 & -1 & 1 \\ 4 & 3 & -1 & 2 \\ 8 & 5 & -3 & 4 \\ 3 & 3 & -2 & 2 \end{bmatrix} \begin{bmatrix} -2\,(\text{Row 1}) & + & \text{Row 2} \\ -4\,(\text{Row 1}) & + & \text{Row 3} \\ -1.5\,(\text{Row 1}) & + & \text{Row 4} \end{bmatrix}$$

$$= \begin{bmatrix} 2 & 2 & -1 & 1 \\ 0 & -1 & 1 & 0 \\ 0 & -3 & 1 & 0 \\ 0 & 0 & -0.5 & 0.5 \end{bmatrix} = 2 \begin{bmatrix} -1 & 1 & 0 \\ -3 & 1 & 0 \\ 0 & -0.5 & 0.5 \end{bmatrix}$$

$$= 2[-1\,\{(1 \times 0.5) - 0\} - 1\,\{(-3 \times 0.5) - 0\}] = 2$$

$$D_1 = \begin{bmatrix} 4 & 2 & -1 & 1 \\ 6 & 3 & -1 & 2 \\ 12 & 5 & -3 & 4 \\ 6 & 3 & -2 & 2 \end{bmatrix} \begin{bmatrix} -1.5\,(\text{Row 1}) & + & \text{Row 2} \\ -3\,(\text{Row 1}) & + & \text{Row 3} \\ -1.5\,(\text{Row 1}) & + & \text{Row 4} \end{bmatrix}$$

$$= \begin{bmatrix} 4 & 2 & -1 & 1 \\ 0 & 0 & 0.5 & 0.5 \\ 0 & -1 & 0 & 1 \\ 0 & 0 & -0.5 & 0.5 \end{bmatrix} = 4\,[(0 - 0.5)\,(-0.5) + 0.5\,(0.5)] = 2$$

$$D_2 = \begin{bmatrix} 2 & 4 & -1 & 1 \\ 4 & 6 & -1 & 2 \\ 8 & 12 & -3 & 4 \\ 3 & 6 & -2 & 2 \end{bmatrix} \begin{bmatrix} -2\,(\text{Row 1}) & + & \text{Row 2} \\ -4\,(\text{Row 1}) & + & \text{Row 3} \\ -1.5\,(\text{Row 1}) & + & \text{Row 4} \end{bmatrix}$$

$$= \begin{bmatrix} 2 & 4 & -1 & 1 \\ 4 & -2 & 1 & 0 \\ 0 & -4 & 1 & 0 \\ 0 & 0 & -0.5 & 0.5 \end{bmatrix} = \begin{bmatrix} -2 & 1 & 0 \\ -4 & 1 & 0 \\ 0 & -0.5 & 0.5 \end{bmatrix} = 2$$

$$D_3 = \begin{bmatrix} 2 & 2 & 4 & 1 \\ 4 & 3 & 6 & 2 \\ 8 & 5 & 12 & 4 \\ 3 & 3 & 6 & 2 \end{bmatrix} \begin{bmatrix} -2\,(\text{Row 1}) & + & \text{Row 2} \\ -4\,(\text{Row 1}) & + & \text{Row 3} \\ -1.5\,(\text{Row 1}) & + & \text{Row 4} \end{bmatrix}$$

$$= \begin{bmatrix} 2 & 2 & 4 & 1 \\ 0 & -1 & -2 & 0 \\ 0 & -3 & -4 & 0 \\ 0 & 0 & 0 & 0.5 \end{bmatrix} = 2 \begin{bmatrix} -1 & -2 & 0 \\ -3 & -4 & 0 \\ 0 & 0 & 0.5 \end{bmatrix}$$

$$= 2[-1\,(-2) + 2\,(-1.5 + 0)] = -2$$

$$D_4 = \begin{bmatrix} 2 & 2 & -1 & 4 \\ 4 & 3 & -1 & 6 \\ 8 & 5 & -3 & 12 \\ 3 & 3 & -2 & 6 \end{bmatrix} \begin{bmatrix} -2\,(\text{Row 1}) & + & \text{Row 2} \\ -4\,(\text{Row 1}) & + & \text{Row 3} \\ -1.5\,(\text{Row 1}) & + & \text{Row 4} \end{bmatrix}$$

$$= \begin{bmatrix} 2 & 2 & 4 & 1 \\ 0 & -1 & -2 & 0 \\ 0 & -3 & -4 & 0 \\ 0 & 0 & 0 & 0.5 \end{bmatrix} = 2 \begin{bmatrix} -1 & -2 & 0 \\ -3 & -4 & 0 \\ 0 & 0 & 0.5 \end{bmatrix}$$

$$= 2[-1\,(-2) + 2\,(-1.5 + 0)] = -2$$

Using the above values, we can evaluate the values of x_1, x_2, x_3 and x_4 using the expressions defined.

$$x_1 = \left(\frac{D_1}{D}\right) = (2/2) = 1$$

$$x_2 = \left(\frac{D_2}{D}\right) = (2/2) = 1$$

$$x_3 = \left(\frac{D_3}{D}\right) = (-2/2) = -1$$

$$x_4 = \left(\frac{D_4}{D}\right) = (-2/2) = -1$$

Check: By considering Eq. (3)

$$8x_1 + 5x_2 - 3x_3 + 4x_4 = 1$$
$$8(1) + 5(1) - 3(-1) + 4(-1) = 12$$

1.3 METHOD OF LEADING COEFFICIENTS

The following steps are adopted to solve a set of equations using this method.

Step 1: The leading coefficients are rendered +1 or –1

Step 2: The number of unknowns is reduced from n to $(n - 1)$

Step 3: The leading coefficients are again reduced to +1 or –1

Step 4: The number of unknowns is further reduced from $(n - 1)$ to $(n - 2)$

The process is repeated until only one unknown is left and its value is determined.

The remaining unknowns are evaluated by back substitution. The method is illustrated by the following examples.

Example 1.3

$$2x - y + 3z = 8 \tag{1}$$
$$-x + 2y + z = 4 \tag{2}$$
$$3x + y + 4z = 4 \tag{3}$$

Solution

Step 1: Make the leading coefficients as +1 or –1 by dividing Eq. (1) by Eq. (2) and Eq. (3) by 3.

$$x - 0.5y + 1.5z = 4 \tag{4}$$
$$-x + 2y + z = 4 \tag{5}$$
$$x + 0.33y - 1.33z = 0 \tag{6}$$

Step 2: Reduce the unknowns from n to $(n - 1)$

Reduce the number of equations from 3 to 2

$1.5y + 2.5z = 8$	[Eq. (1) + Eq. (2)]	(7)
$2.33y - 0.33z = 4$	[Eq. (2) + Eq. (3)]	(8)

Step 3: Make the leading coefficients as +1 or –1

$y + 1.67z = 5.33$	[Eq. (4)/(1.5))]	(9)
$y - 0.14z = 1.72$	[Eq. (5)/2.33]	(10)

Step 4: Reduce the equations to one equation

$$y + 1.67z = 5.33$$
$$-y + 0.14z = 1.72$$
$$\overline{1.81z = 3.61}$$

Hence $z = 2$

From Eq. (10), $y = 2$

From Eq. (6), $x = 2$

Check: By considering Eq. (1), we have

$$2x - y + 3z = 8$$
$$2(2) - (2) + 3(2) = 8$$

Example 1.4

Solve the following equations by the method of leading coefficients.

$$w + x + y = 3 \tag{1}$$
$$-3w - 17x + y + 2z = 1 \tag{2}$$
$$4w + 8y - 5z = 1 \tag{3}$$
$$-5x - 2y + z = 1 \tag{4}$$

Solution

Step 1: Reduce the leading coefficients to +1 or −1

$$w + x + y = 3 \tag{5}$$
$$-w + 5.67x + 0.33y + 0.67z = 0.33 \tag{6}$$
$$w + 2y - 1.25z = 0.25 \tag{7}$$
$$-5x - 2y + z = 1 \tag{8}$$

Step 2: Reduce the unknowns from n to $(n-1)$

$$6.67x + 1.33y + 0.67z = 0.33 \qquad \text{Eq. (5) + Eq. (6)} \tag{9}$$
$$5.67x + 2.33y - 0.58z = 0.58 \qquad \text{Eq. (6) + Eq. (7)} \tag{10}$$
$$-5x - 2y + z = 1$$

Step 3: Reduce the leading coefficients to +1 or −1

$$x - 0.285y - 0.143z = -0.713 \tag{11}$$
$$-x + 0.41y - 0.102z = 0.1023 \tag{12}$$
$$x + 0.4y - 0.2z = -0.2 \tag{13}$$

Step 4: Reduce the number of unknowns n to $(n-1)$

$$0.125y - 0.245z = -0.6107 \tag{14}$$
$$0.81y - 0.302z = -0.0977 \tag{15}$$

Step 5: Reduce the leading coefficients to +1 or −1

$$y - 1.96z = -4.8856 \tag{16}$$
$$\underline{-y + 0.37z = +0.1206} \tag{17}$$
$$-0.159z = -4.765$$

Therefore $z = 3$

From Eq. (17), $y = 0.9894 = 1$

From Eq. (12), $x = 0$

From Eq. (5), $w = 2$

1.4 GAUSSIAN ELIMINATION METHOD

In this method, the unknowns are gradually eliminated by combining the given set of equations. Basically, the method involves the reduction of n equations with n unknowns to an equivalent rectangular set, which is then easily solved by the process of 'back substitution'. The elimination procedure is started from the equation which has the largest coefficient for the first unknown x_1. The value of x_1 is expressed in terms of the other unknowns, i.e. $x_2, x_3, ...$, etc. is substituted in other equations. The elimination procedure is repeated until only one unknown remains in the last equation and its value determined. The other unknowns are evaluated by back substitution. The method is illustrated through the following practical examples.

Example 1.5

Solve the following set of equations by Gaussian elimination method.

$$3x_1 + x_2 + x_3 = 4 \tag{1}$$
$$x_1 + 4x_2 + x_3 = -5 \tag{2}$$
$$x_1 + x_2 - 6x_3 = -12 \tag{3}$$

Solution

Step 1

Consider Eq. (1) having the largest coefficient of x_1 and divide it by 3 and rewrite the equation as

$$x_1 = (1.33 - 0.33x_2 - 0.33x_3) \tag{4}$$

Step 2

Substitute Eq. (4) in Eqs. (2) and (3)

$$(1.33 - 0.33x_2 - 0.33x_3) + 4x_2 - x_3 = -5$$
$$3.67x_2 - 1.33x_3 = -6.33 \tag{5}$$
$$(1.33 - 0.33x_2 - 0.33x_3) + x_2 - 6x_3 = -12$$
$$0.67x_2 - 6.33x_3 = -13.33 \tag{6}$$

Step 3

Consider Eq. (5) has the largest coefficient of

$$3.67x_2 - 1.33x_3 = -6.33$$
$$\frac{3.67x_2 = -6.33 + 1.033x_3}{x_2 = -1.72 + 0.362x_3} \tag{7}$$

Step 4

Substitute Eq. (7) in Eq. (6)

$$0.67(-1.72 + 0.362x_3) - 6.33x_3 = -13.33$$
$$\text{Therefore } x_3 = 2$$

Step 5

By back substitution, evaluate x_1 and x_2
From Eq. (7), $x_2 = -1.72 + 0.362(2) = -1$
From Eq. (4), $x_1 = 1.33 + 0.33(-1) - 0.33(2) = 1$
Therefore $x_1 = 1, \quad x_2 = -1, \quad x_3 = 2$

Example 1.6

Solve the following set of equations by the Gaussian elimination method.

Solution

$$w + x + y = 3 \tag{1}$$
$$-3w - 17x + y + 2z = 1 \tag{2}$$
$$4w + 8y - 5z = 1 \tag{3}$$
$$-5x - 2y + z = 1 \tag{4}$$

Step 1

Considering Eq. (3) having the largest coefficient of w

$$4w + 8y - 5z = 1$$
$$w = 0.25 + 1.25z - 2y \tag{5}$$

Step 2

Substitute Eq. (5) in Eqs. (1) and (2)

$$0.25 + 1.25z - 2y + x + y = 3$$
$$x - y + 1.25z = 2.75 \tag{6}$$
$$-0.75 - 3.75z + 6y - 17x + y + 2z = 1$$
$$17x - 7y + 1.75z = -1.75 \tag{7}$$

Also from Eq. (4), we have

$$5x + 2y - z = -1 \tag{8}$$

Step 3

Considering Eq. (7) having the largest coefficient of x

$$17x - 7y + 1.75z = -1.75$$
$$x = -0.103 + 0.411y - 0.1029z \tag{9}$$

Step 4

Substituting Eq. (9) in Eqs. (6) and (8)

$$-0.103 + 0.411y - 0.103z - y + 1.25z = 2.75$$
$$\therefore\ 0.589y - 1.147z = -2.853 \tag{10}$$
$$-0.515 + 2.055y - 0.5145z + 2y - z = -1$$
$$4.055y - 1.5145z = -0.485 \tag{11}$$
$$\text{or}\quad y = -0.1196 + 0.373z \tag{12}$$

Step 5

Substituting Eq. (12) in Eq. (10)

$$0.589(-0.1196 + 0.373z) - 1.147z = -2.853$$

Therefore $z = 3$

From Eq. (12), we have

$$y = -0.1196 + 0.373(3) = 1$$

From Eq. (9)

$$x = -0.103 + 0.411(1) - 0.1029(3) = 0$$

From Eq. (5)

$$w = 0.25 + 1.25(3) - 2(1) = 2$$

Hence, the values of the unknowns are

$$w = 2, \qquad x = 0, \qquad y = 1, \qquad z = 3$$

1.5 GAUSS–JORDAN METHOD

In the Gauss–Jordan method, the given set of equations are expressed in matrix form which is diagonalized by row operations so that the solution is directly obtained. The process of diagonalization eliminates the necessity using back substitution process used in Gauss's method. In contrast to the Gaussian elimination, where the unknown is eliminated from all equations except the pivotal equation, in the Gauss–Jordan method, the unknown is eliminated from all the equations.

The diagonalization process is implemented by the following stepwise procedure.

1. In the first step, the elements in the first column and first row is reduced to unity and subsequently the remaining elements in the first column are reduced to zero.

2. In the second step, the element in the second row and second column is reduced to 1 and the remaining elements in the second column are subsequently reduced to zero.

3. In the last step, the element in the third row and third column is reduced to unity followed by zero in the third column.

4. In this way, the diagonalization is done in a sequential manner and only row operations are performed to reduce the diagonal elements to unity and all other elements to zero.

The method is illustrated by the following numerical example.

Example 1.7

Solve the following set of equations by the Gauss–Jordan method

$$2x_1 + x_2 + 4x_3 = 4$$
$$x_1 - 3x_2 - x_3 = -5$$
$$3x_1 - 2x_2 + 2x_3 = -1$$

Solution

The given equations are written in the matrix form as

$$\begin{bmatrix} 2 & 1 & 4 \\ 1 & -3 & -1 \\ 3 & -2 & 2 \end{bmatrix} \begin{Bmatrix} x_1 \\ x_2 \\ x_3 \end{Bmatrix} = \begin{Bmatrix} 4 \\ -5 \\ -1 \end{Bmatrix}$$

By successive row operations, the original matrix is reduced to a coefficient matrix by the following procedure.

$$\begin{vmatrix} 2 & 1 & 4 & \vdots & 4 \\ 1 & -3 & -1 & \vdots & -5 \\ 3 & -2 & 2 & \vdots & -1 \end{vmatrix} \ldots\ldots 0.5R_1$$

$$= \begin{vmatrix} 1 & 0.5 & 2 & \vdots & 2 \\ 1 & -3 & -1 & \vdots & -5 \\ 3 & -2 & 2 & \vdots & -1 \end{vmatrix} \ldots\ldots (R_2 - R_1)$$

$$= \begin{vmatrix} 1 & 0.5 & 2 & \vdots & 2 \\ 0 & -3.5 & -3 & \vdots & -7 \\ 0 & -3.5 & -4 & \vdots & -7 \end{vmatrix} \ldots\ldots (R_2 / -3.5)$$

$$= \begin{vmatrix} 1 & 0.5 & 2 & \vdots & 2 \\ 0 & 1 & 0.857 & \vdots & 2 \\ 0 & -3.5 & -4 & \vdots & -7 \end{vmatrix} \begin{matrix} (-0.5R_2 + R_1) \\ (3.5R_2 + R_3) \end{matrix}$$

$$= \begin{vmatrix} 1 & 0 & 0 & \vdots & 1 \\ 0 & 1 & 0 & \vdots & 2 \\ 0 & 0 & 1 & \vdots & 0 \end{vmatrix} \begin{matrix} (R_1 + 1.5715R_3) \\ (R_2 + 0.857R_3) \\ \\ \end{matrix}$$

where R_1, R_2 and R_3 refer to the first, second and third row respectively.
The final matrix reduces to the required diagonal matrix expressed as

$$= \begin{bmatrix} 1 & 0 & 0 \\ 0 & 1 & 0 \\ 0 & 0 & 1 \end{bmatrix} \begin{Bmatrix} x_1 \\ x_2 \\ x_3 \end{Bmatrix} = \begin{Bmatrix} 1 \\ 2 \\ 0 \end{Bmatrix}$$

Therefore $x_1 = 1$, $x_2 = 2$ and $x_3 = 0$

Check: $x_1 - 3x_2 - x_3 = -5$

$$[1 - 3(2) - 0] = -5$$

Example 1.8

Using Gauss–Jordan method, solve the following equations.

$$2x_1 + 2x_2 - x_3 + x_4 = 4 \tag{1}$$

$$4x_1 + 3x_2 - x_3 + 2x_4 = 6 \tag{2}$$

$$8x_1 + 5x_2 - 3x_3 + 4x_4 = 12 \tag{3}$$

$$3x_1 + 3x_2 - 2x_3 + 2x_4 = 6 \tag{4}$$

Solution

The equation is written in matrix form as

$$\begin{bmatrix} 2 & 2 & -1 & 1 & \vdots & 4 \\ 4 & 3 & -1 & 2 & \vdots & 6 \\ 8 & 5 & -3 & 4 & \vdots & 12 \\ 3 & 3 & -2 & 2 & \vdots & 6 \end{bmatrix} = \begin{bmatrix} 1 & 1 & -0.5 & 0.5 & \vdots & 2 \\ 4 & 3 & -1 & 2 & \vdots & 6 \\ 8 & 5 & -3 & 4 & \vdots & 12 \\ 3 & 3 & -2 & 2 & \vdots & 6 \end{bmatrix} \quad \dots\dots0.5R_1$$

$$= \begin{matrix} \vdots 1 & 1 & -0.5 & 0.5 & \vdots & 2 & \vdots \\ \vdots 0 & -1 & 1 & 0 & \vdots & -2 & \vdots \dots\dots(R_2 - 4R_1) \\ \vdots 0 & -3 & 1 & 0 & \vdots & -4 & \vdots \dots\dots(R_3 - 8R_1) \\ \vdots 0 & 0 & -0.5 & 0.5 & \vdots & 0 & \vdots \dots\dots(R_4 - 3R_1) \end{matrix}$$

$$= \begin{matrix} \vdots 1 & 0 & 0.5 & 0.5 & \vdots & 0 & \vdots \dots\dots (R_1 + R_2) \\ \vdots 0 & 1 & -1 & 0 & \vdots & 2 & \vdots \dots\dots(-R_2) \\ \vdots 0 & 0 & -2 & 0 & \vdots & 2 & \vdots \dots\dots(-3R_2 + R_3) \\ \vdots 0 & 0 & -0.5 & 0.5 & \vdots & 0 & \vdots \end{matrix}$$

$$= \begin{array}{cccccc}
\vdots 1 & 0 & 0.5 & 0.5 & \vdots & 0 & \vdots \\
\vdots 0 & 1 & -1 & 0 & \vdots & 2 & \vdots \\
\vdots 0 & 0 & 1 & 0 & \vdots & -1 & \vdots \quad ....(-0.5R_1) \\
\vdots 0 & 0 & -0.5 & 0.5 & \vdots & 0 & \vdots
\end{array}$$

$$= \begin{array}{cccccc}
\vdots 1 & 0 & 0 & 0.5 & \vdots & 0.5 & \vdots \quad ....(-0.5R_3 + R_1) \\
\vdots 0 & 1 & 0 & 0 & \vdots & 1 & \vdots \quad ....(R_2 + R_3) \\
\vdots 0 & 0 & 1 & 0 & \vdots & -1 & \vdots \\
\vdots 0 & 0 & 0 & 0.5 & \vdots & -0.5 & \vdots \quad ....(0.5R_3 + R_4)
\end{array}$$

$$= \begin{array}{cccccc}
\vdots 1 & 0 & 0 & 0.5 & \vdots & 0.5 & \vdots \\
\vdots 0 & 1 & 0 & 0 & \vdots & 1 & \vdots \\
\vdots 0 & 0 & 1 & 0 & \vdots & -1 & \vdots \\
\vdots 0 & 0 & 0 & 0.5 & \vdots & -0.5 & \vdots \quad ....(2R_4)
\end{array}$$

$$= \begin{array}{cccccc}
\vdots 1 & 0 & 0 & 0 & \vdots & 1 & \vdots \quad ....(0.5R_4 - R_1) \\
\vdots 0 & 1 & 0 & 0 & \vdots & 1 & \vdots \\
\vdots 0 & 0 & 1 & 0 & \vdots & -1 & \vdots \\
\vdots 0 & 0 & 1 & 1 & \vdots & -1 & \vdots
\end{array}$$

The matrix finally reduces to the unit diagonal form given by

$$= \begin{array}{cccccc}
\vdots 1 & 0 & 0 & 0 & \vdots & x_1 & \vdots & \vdots 1 & \vdots \\
\vdots 0 & 1 & 0 & 0 & \vdots & x_2 & \vdots = & \vdots 1 & \vdots \\
\vdots 0 & 0 & 1 & 0 & \vdots & x_3 & \vdots & \vdots 1 & \vdots \\
\vdots 0 & 0 & 0 & 1 & \vdots & x_4 & \vdots & \vdots 1 & \vdots
\end{array}$$

Therefore $x_1 = 1, x_2 = 1, x_3 = -1$ and $x_4 = 1$

Check: By considering Eq. (3), we have

$$8x_1 + 5x_2 - 3x_3 + 4x_4 = 12$$

$$8(1) + 5(1) - 3(-1) + 4(1) = 12$$

1.6 FACTORISATION AND CHOLESKY'S METHODS

1.6.1 Factorisation Method

In this method of solving the general linear system $AX = b$, the coefficient matrix $[A]$ is factorised into the product of two lower and upper triangular matrices. The matrix $[A]$ is represented in the form

$$[A] = [L][U]$$

where L is the unit lower triangular matrix and U is the upper triangular matrix. The triangular matrices are represented as

$$\begin{bmatrix} 1 & 0 & 0 \\ L_{21} & 1 & 0 \\ L_{31} & L_{32} & 0 \end{bmatrix} \begin{bmatrix} U_{11} & U_{12} & U_{13} \\ 0 & U_{22} & U_{23} \\ 0 & 0 & U_{33} \end{bmatrix} = [A]$$

The matrix representation shown above is termed as factorisation. The diagonal non-zero entry of L matrix is the ith pivot of factorisation. Multiplying L and U, we can evaluate all the elements of $[A]$. The factorisation method is generally preferred over the Gaussian elimination method in computers having the facility of accumulating products in double length. The application of this method is illustrated by the following examples.

Example 1.9

Solve the following system of linear equations using factorisation method.

$$5x - 2y + z = 4 \tag{1}$$

$$7x + y - 5z = 8 \tag{2}$$

$$3x + 7y + 4z = 10 \tag{3}$$

Solution

The equation can be expressed in the matrix following form as,

$$\begin{bmatrix} 5 & -2 & 1 \\ 7 & 1 & -5 \\ 3 & 7 & 4 \end{bmatrix} \begin{Bmatrix} x_1 \\ x_2 \\ x_3 \end{Bmatrix} = \begin{Bmatrix} 4 \\ 8 \\ 10 \end{Bmatrix}$$

The coefficient matrix is written in the following form.

$$\begin{bmatrix} 1 & 0 & 0 \\ L_{21} & 1 & 0 \\ L_{31} & L_{32} & 1 \end{bmatrix} \begin{bmatrix} U_{11} & U_{12} & U_{13} \\ 0 & U_{22} & U_{23} \\ 0 & 0 & U_{33} \end{bmatrix} = \begin{bmatrix} 5 & -2 & 1 \\ 7 & 1 & -5 \\ 3 & 7 & 4 \end{bmatrix}$$

$$[L][U] = [A]$$

The elements of the triangular matrix are determined by multiplying $[L]$ and $[U]$ and equating to the corresponding elements in the coefficient matrix as outlined in the following steps.

$$1(U_{11}) + 0(0) + 0 = 5$$

$$\therefore U_{11} = 5 \tag{4}$$

$$1(U_{12}) + 0(U_{22}) + 0 = -2$$

$$\therefore U_{12} = -2 \tag{5}$$

$$1(U_{13}) + 0(U_{23}) + 0(U_{33}) = 1$$

$$\therefore U_{13} = 1 \tag{6}$$

$L_{21}(U_{11}) + 1(0) + 0(0) = 7$

$L_{21}(5) = 7$

$L_{21} = 1.4$ (7)

$L_{21}(U_{12}) + 1(U_{22}) + 0(0) = 1$

$1.4(-2) + U_{22} + 0 = 1$

$\therefore U_{22} = 3.8$ (8)

$L_{21}(U_{13}) + 1(U_{23}) + 0(U_{33}) = -5$

$1.4(1) + U_{23} + 0 = -5$

$\therefore U_{23} = -6.4$ (9)

$L_{31}(U_{11}) + U_{32}(0) + 0 = 3$

$L_{31}(5) + 0 + 0 = 3$

$\therefore L_{31} = 0.6$ (10)

$L_{31}(U_{12}) + L_{32}(U_{22}) + 0 = 7$

$0.6(-2) + L_{32}(3.8) + 0 = 7$

$\therefore L_{32} = 2.16$ (11)

$L_{31}(U_{13}) + L_{32}(U_{23}) + 1(U_{33}) = 4$

$0.6(1) + 2.16(-6.4) + U_{33} = 4$

$\therefore U_{33} = 17.22$ (12)

Substituting the element values obtained from Eqs. (4) to (12), the following matrix is formulated.

$$\begin{bmatrix} 1 & 0 & 0 \\ 1.4 & 1 & 0 \\ 0.6 & 2.16 & 1 \end{bmatrix} \begin{bmatrix} 5 & -2 & 1 \\ 0 & 3.8 & -6.4 \\ 0 & 0 & 17.22 \end{bmatrix} = \begin{bmatrix} 5 & -2 & 1 \\ 7 & 1 & -5 \\ 3 & 7 & 4 \end{bmatrix}$$

The set of equations can be written as

$$[L][U]\{x\} = \{C\}$$

$$\begin{bmatrix} 1 & 0 & 0 \\ 1.4 & 1 & 0 \\ 0.6 & 2.16 & 1 \end{bmatrix} \begin{bmatrix} 5 & -2 & 1 \\ 0 & 3.8 & -6.4 \\ 0 & 0 & 17.22 \end{bmatrix} \begin{Bmatrix} x \\ y \\ z \end{Bmatrix} = \begin{Bmatrix} 4 \\ 8 \\ 10 \end{Bmatrix}$$

Replacing $[U]\{x\} = \{y\}$

$$\begin{bmatrix} 1 & 0 & 0 \\ 1.4 & 1 & 0 \\ 0.6 & 2.16 & 1 \end{bmatrix} \begin{Bmatrix} y_1 \\ y_2 \\ y_3 \end{Bmatrix} = \begin{Bmatrix} 4 \\ 8 \\ 10 \end{Bmatrix}$$

Hence, we have $y_1 = 4$

$$1.4y_1 + y_2 = 8 \qquad\qquad \therefore y_2 = 2.4$$

$$0.6y_1 + 2.16y_2 + y_3 = 10$$

$$0.6(4) + 2.16(2.4) + y_3 = 10 \qquad\qquad \therefore y_3 = 2.416$$

$$\begin{bmatrix} 5 & -2 & 1 \\ 0 & 3.8 & -6.4 \\ 0 & 0 & 17.22 \end{bmatrix} \begin{Bmatrix} x \\ y \\ z \end{Bmatrix} = \begin{Bmatrix} y_1 \\ y_2 \\ y_3 \end{Bmatrix} = \begin{Bmatrix} 4 \\ 2.4 \\ 2.416 \end{Bmatrix}$$

$$17.22z = 2.416 \qquad\qquad \therefore z = 0.1403$$

$$3.8y - 6.4z = 2.4$$

$$3.8y - 6.4(0.1403) = 2.4 \qquad\qquad \therefore y = 0.8678$$

$$5x - 2y + z = 4$$

$$5x - 2(0.8678) + 0.1403 = 4 \qquad\qquad \therefore x = 1.119$$

$$\therefore x = 1.119, \quad y = 0.8678, \quad z = 0.1403$$

Check: Considering Eq. (3), we have

$$3x + 7y + 4z = 10$$

$$3(1.119) + 7(0.8678) + 4(0.1403) = 10$$

Example 1.10

Solve the following set of equations using factorization method.

$$8x_1 + 4x_2 + 2x_3 = 24 \qquad\qquad (1)$$

$$4x_1 + 10x_2 + 5x_3 + 4x_4 = 32 \qquad\qquad (2)$$

$$2x_1 + 5x_2 + 6.5x_3 + 4x_4 = 26 \qquad\qquad (3)$$

$$4x_2 + 4x_3 + 9x_4 = 21 \qquad\qquad (4)$$

Solution

The equation can be written in matrix form as

$$\begin{bmatrix} 8 & 4 & 2 & 0 \\ 4 & 10 & 5 & 4 \\ 2 & 5 & 6.5 & 4 \\ 0 & 4 & 4 & 9 \end{bmatrix} \begin{Bmatrix} x_1 \\ x_2 \\ x_3 \\ x_4 \end{Bmatrix} = \begin{Bmatrix} 24 \\ 32 \\ 26 \\ 21 \end{Bmatrix}$$

The coefficient matrix is written in the form

$$\begin{bmatrix} 1 & 0 & 0 & 0 \\ L_{21} & 1 & 0 & 0 \\ L_{31} & L_{32} & 1 & 0 \\ L_{41} & L_{42} & L_{43} & 0 \end{bmatrix} \begin{bmatrix} 2 & 2 & U_{13} & U_{14} \\ 0 & U_{22} & U_{23} & U_{24} \\ 0 & 0 & U_{33} & U_{34} \\ 0 & 0 & 0 & U_{44} \end{bmatrix} = \begin{bmatrix} 8 & 4 & 2 & 0 \\ 4 & 10 & 5 & 4 \\ 2 & 5 & 6.5 & 4 \\ 0 & 4 & 4 & 9 \end{bmatrix}$$

$$[L][U] = [A]$$

The elements of the triangular matrix are determined as follows:

$U_{11} = 8$ $\qquad\qquad$ $L_{21}U_{11} = 4$

$U_{12} = 4$ $\qquad\qquad$ $\therefore L_{21} = 0.5$

$L_{13} = 2$ $\qquad\qquad$ $L_{31}U_{11} = 2$

$U_{14} = 0$ $\qquad\qquad$ $\therefore L_{31} = 0.25$

$L_{41}U_{11} = 0$ $\qquad\qquad$ $\therefore L_{41} = 0$

$L_{21}U_{12} + U_{22} = 10$

$0.5(4) + U_{22} = 10$ $\qquad\qquad$ $\therefore U_{22} = 8$

$L_{31}U_{12} + L_{32}U_{22} = 5$

$0.25(4) + L_{32}(8) = 5$ $\qquad\qquad$ $\therefore U_{32} = 0.5$

$L_{41}U_{12} + L_{42}U_{22} = 4$

$0 + 8L_{42} = 4$ $\qquad\qquad$ $\therefore L_{42} = 0.5$

$L_{21}U_{13} + U_{23} = 5$

$0.5(2) + U_{23} = 5$ $\qquad\qquad$ $\therefore U_{23} = 4$

$L_{21}U_{14} + U_{24} = 4$

$0.5(0) + U_{24} = 4$ $\qquad\qquad$ $\therefore U_{24} = 4$

$L_{31}U_{13} + L_{32}U_{23} + U_{33} = 6.5$

$0.25(2) + 0.5(4) + U_{33} = 6.5$

$0.5 + 2 + U_{33} = 6.5$ $\qquad\qquad$ $\therefore U_{33} = 4$

$L_{31}U_{14} + L_{32}U_{24} + U_{31} = 4$

$0.25(0) + 0.5(4) + U_{31} = 4$ $\qquad\qquad$ $\therefore U_{34} = 2$

$L_{41}U_{13} + L_{42}U_{23} + L_{43}U_{33} = 4$

$0 + 0.5(4) + L_{43}(4) = 4$ $\qquad\qquad$ $\therefore L_{43} = 0.5$

$$L_{41}U_{14} + L_{42}U_{24} + L_{43}U_{34} + U_{44} = 9$$

$$0 + 0.5(4) + 0.5(2) + U_{44} = 9$$

$$2 + 1 + U_{44} = 9 \qquad\qquad \therefore U_{44} = 6$$

$$[L][U]\{x\} = \{C\}$$

$$
\begin{bmatrix}
1 & 0 & 0 & 0 \\
0.5 & 1 & 0 & 0 \\
0.25 & 0.5 & 1 & 0 \\
0 & 0.5 & 0.5 & 1
\end{bmatrix}
\begin{bmatrix}
8 & 4 & 2 & 0 \\
0 & 8 & 4 & 4 \\
0 & 0 & 4 & 2 \\
0 & 0 & 0 & 6
\end{bmatrix}
\begin{Bmatrix} x_1 \\ x_2 \\ x_3 \\ x_4 \end{Bmatrix}
=
\begin{Bmatrix} 24 \\ 32 \\ 26 \\ 21 \end{Bmatrix}
$$

Replacing $[U]\{x\} = \{y\}$

$$
\begin{bmatrix}
1 & 0 & 0 & 0 \\
0.5 & 1 & 0 & 0 \\
0.25 & 0.5 & 1 & 0 \\
0 & 0.5 & 0.5 & 1
\end{bmatrix}
\begin{Bmatrix} y_1 \\ y_2 \\ y_3 \\ y_4 \end{Bmatrix}
=
\begin{Bmatrix} 24 \\ 32 \\ 26 \\ 21 \end{Bmatrix}
$$

$$\therefore y_1 = 24$$

$$0.5y_1 + y_2 = 32 \qquad\qquad \therefore y_2 = 20$$

$$0.25y_1 + 0.5y_2 + y_3 = 26$$

$$0.25(24) + 0.5(20) + y_3 = 26 \qquad\qquad \therefore y_3 = 10$$

$$0(y_1) + 0.5(y_2) + 0.5y_3 + y_4 = 21$$

$$0 + 0.5(20) + 0.5(10) + y_4 = 21 \qquad\qquad \therefore y_4 = 6$$

Substituting the elements of y in equation $[U]\{x\} = \{y\}$, we have

$$
\begin{bmatrix}
8 & 4 & 2 & 0 \\
0 & 8 & 4 & 4 \\
0 & 0 & 4 & 2 \\
0 & 0 & 0 & 6
\end{bmatrix}
\begin{Bmatrix} x_1 \\ x_2 \\ x_3 \\ x_4 \end{Bmatrix}
=
\begin{Bmatrix} y_1 \\ y_2 \\ y_3 \\ y_4 \end{Bmatrix}
=
\begin{Bmatrix} 24 \\ 32 \\ 26 \\ 21 \end{Bmatrix}
$$

$$\therefore 6x_4 = 6 \qquad\qquad \therefore x_4 = 1$$

$$4x_3 + 2x_4 = 10 \qquad\qquad \therefore x_3 = 2$$

$$8x_2 + 4x_3 + 4x_4 = 20$$

$$8x_2 + 4(2) + 4(1) = 20 \qquad\qquad \therefore x_2 = 1$$

$$8x_1 + 4x_2 + 2x_3 + 0 = 24$$

$$8x_1 + 4(2) + 2(1) + 0 = 24 \qquad\qquad \therefore x_1 = 2$$

Hence, the solution is

$$x_1 = 2, \ x_2 = 1, \ x_3 = 2, \ x_4 = 1$$

Check: Considering Eq. (2), we have

$$4x_1 + 10x_2 + 5x_3 + 4x_4 = 32$$

$$4(2) + 10(1) + 5(2) + 4(1) = 32$$

1.6.2 Cholesky's Method

In the analysis of structural systems, the mathematical computations are often expressed in the form of real, symmetric, positive definite and banded matrices. Cholesky's method is advantageously used for inverting such matrices.

If a matrix $[A]$ is symmetric, positive, definite, and square matrix of order n, it may be decomposed uniquely into the form

$$[A] = [G][G]^T \tag{1}$$

where $[G]$ is a lower triangular matrix of order n with positive diagonal elements.

Hence the solution of a system of equations of this type, becomes

$$[A][X] = [C] \tag{2}$$

where $[X]$ and $[C]$ are the unknowns and constant matrices can be computed as

$$[G][G]^T [X] = [C] \tag{3}$$

Equation (3) can be solved as a pair of equations expressed as

$$[G][Y] = [C] \tag{4a}$$

and $\qquad [G]^T [X] = [Y] \tag{4b}$

As $[G]$ and $[G]^T$ are triangular matrices, considerable simplifications are possible in computations.

For a third order matrix $[A]$; the decomposition process is illustrated below:

$$[A] = \begin{bmatrix} a_{11} & a_{12} & a_{13} \\ a_{21} & a_{22} & a_{23} \\ a_{31} & a_{32} & a_{33} \end{bmatrix} \begin{bmatrix} g_{11} & 0 & 0 \\ g_{21} & g_{22} & 0 \\ g_{31} & g_{32} & g_{33} \end{bmatrix} \begin{bmatrix} g_{11} & g_{21} & g_{31} \\ 0 & g_{22} & g_{32} \\ 0 & 0 & g_{33} \end{bmatrix} \tag{5}$$

The six elements of matrix $[G]$ are obtained by the products of RHS and then equating to the corresponding elements on the LHS, we have the values of the elements as

$$g_{11}^2 = a_{11} \ \text{or} \ g_{11} = \sqrt{a_{11}}$$

$$g_{11}g_{21} = a_{12} \ \text{or} \ g_{21} = \left(\frac{a_{12}}{g_{11}} \right)$$

$$g_{11}g_{31} = a_{13} \text{ or } g_{31} = \left(\frac{a_{13}}{g_{11}}\right)$$

$$g_{21}^2 + g_{22}^2 = a_{22} \text{ or } g_{22} = \sqrt{a_{22} - g_{21}^2} \tag{6}$$

$$g_{21}g_{31} + g_{22}g_{32} \doteq a_{23} \text{ or } g_{32} = \left(\frac{a_{23} - g_{21}g_{31}}{g_{22}}\right)$$

$$g_{31}^2 + g_{32}^2 + g_{33}^2 = a_{33} \text{ or } g_{33} = \sqrt{a_{33} - g_{31}^2 - g_{32}^2}$$

Hence, $[G]$ matrix can be determined completely using Eq. (6). In general the following formula can be derived as

$$g_{ii} = \left[a_{ii} - \Sigma g_{ik}^2\right], \text{ where } i = 1, \dots, n \tag{7a}$$

$$g_{ij} = \left[a_{ji} - \Sigma g_{ik}g_{jk}\right] / g_{jj}, \text{ where } i = 2, \dots, n \text{ and } j < i \tag{7b}$$

$$g_{ij} = 0, \ i < j \tag{7c}$$

The application of Cholesky's method is illustrated by the following examples.

Example 1.11

Solve the given system of equations using Cholesky's method.

$$3x + 2y - z = 4 \tag{1}$$

$$2x + 4y + 2z = 8 \tag{2}$$

$$-x + 2y + 4z = 5 \tag{3}$$

Solution

Given equations can be written in the matrix form as

$$\begin{bmatrix} 3 & 2 & -1 \\ 2 & 4 & 2 \\ -1 & 2 & 4 \end{bmatrix} \begin{bmatrix} x \\ y \\ z \end{bmatrix} = \begin{bmatrix} 4 \\ 8 \\ 5 \end{bmatrix}$$

Hence $[A] = \begin{bmatrix} 3 & 2 & -1 \\ 2 & 4 & 2 \\ -1 & 2 & 4 \end{bmatrix}$

Step 1. Evaluation of $[G]$ matrix
Using Cholesky's algorithm, the elements of the matrix are computed as

$$g_{11} = \sqrt{a_{11}} = \sqrt{3} = 1.732$$

$$g_{21} = \left(\frac{a_{12}}{g_{11}}\right) = \left(\frac{2}{1.732}\right) = 1.155$$

$$g_{31} = \left(\frac{a_{13}}{g_{11}}\right) = \left(\frac{-1}{1.732}\right) = -0.577$$

$$g_{22} = \sqrt{a_{22} - g_{21}^2} = \sqrt{4 - (1.555)^2} = 1.633$$

$$g_{32} = \left(\frac{a_{23} - g_{21}g_{31}}{g_{22}}\right) = \left[\frac{2 - (1.155)(-0.577)}{1.633}\right] = 1.633$$

$$g_{33} = \sqrt{a_{33} - g_{31}^2 - g_{32}^2} = \sqrt{4 - [(-0.577)^2 + 1.633^2} = 1.0$$

The resulting matrix is

$$[G] = \begin{bmatrix} 1.732 & 0 & 0 \\ 1.155 & 1.633 & 0 \\ -0.577 & 1.633 & 1 \end{bmatrix}$$

Step 2. Forward solution

$$[G][Y] = [C]$$

$$\begin{bmatrix} 1.732 & 0 & 0 \\ 1.155 & 1.633 & 0 \\ -0.577 & 1.633 & 1 \end{bmatrix}\begin{bmatrix} y_1 \\ y_2 \\ y_3 \end{bmatrix} = \begin{bmatrix} 4 \\ 8 \\ 5 \end{bmatrix}$$

Solving the first equation for y_1 gives

$$1.732y_1 = 4$$
$$\therefore y_1 = 2.309$$

Solving the second equation for y_2 gives

$$1.155y_1 + 1.633y_2 = 8$$

$$1.155(2.309) + 1.633y_2 = 8 \qquad\qquad \therefore y_2 = 3.266$$

Solving the third equation for y_3 gives

$$-0.577y_1 + 1.633y_2 + y_3 = 5$$

$$-0.577(2.309) + 1.633(3.266) + y_3 = 5$$

Solving $y_3 = 1.000$

Step 3. Backward solution

Solve the equation

$$[G]^T [X] = [Y]$$

$$\begin{bmatrix} 1.732 & 1.155 & -0.577 \\ 0 & 1.633 & 1.633 \\ 0 & 0 & 1 \end{bmatrix}\begin{bmatrix} x \\ y \\ z \end{bmatrix} = \begin{bmatrix} 2.309 \\ 3.266 \\ 1.000 \end{bmatrix}$$

Solving the third equation for z, we get

$$z = 1.000$$

Solving the second equation for y, we get

$$1.633y + 1.633z = 3.266$$

$$1.633y + 1.633(1) = 3.266$$

$$\therefore y = 1.000$$

Solving the first equation for x, we get

$$1.732\,x + 1.155y - 0.577z = 2.309$$

$$1.732\,x + 1.155(1) - 0.577(1) = 2.309$$

$$\therefore x = 1.000$$

Thus, the result $x = y = z = 1.000$

Example 1.12

Solve the set of expressions $[A][X] = [B]$ using Cholesky's method.

Solution

The matrices A, X and B are defined as

$$[A] = \begin{bmatrix} 3 & -2 & 1 & 0 \\ -2 & 5 & -1 & 1 \\ 1 & -1 & 11 & -2 \\ 0 & 1 & -2 & 12 \end{bmatrix}$$

and

$$[X] = \begin{bmatrix} w \\ x \\ y \\ z \end{bmatrix} \text{ and } [B] = \begin{bmatrix} 7 \\ -11 \\ 28 \\ -29 \end{bmatrix}$$

Step 1. Evaluating [G] matrix

$$g_{11} = \sqrt{a_{11}} = \sqrt{3} = 1.732$$

$$g_{21} = \left(\frac{a_{21}}{g_{11}}\right) = \left(\frac{-2}{1.732}\right) = -1.155$$

$$g_{31} = \left(\frac{a_{31}}{g_{11}}\right) = \left(\frac{1}{1.732}\right) = 0.577$$

$$g_{41} = \left(\frac{a_{41}}{g_{11}}\right) = \left(\frac{0}{1.732}\right) = 0$$

$$g_{22} = \sqrt{a_{22} - g_{21}^2} = \sqrt{5 - (-1.555)^2} = 1.915$$

$$g_{32} = \left(\frac{a_{32} - g_{21}g_{31}}{g_{22}} \right) = \left[\frac{-1 - 0.577(-1.155)}{1.915} \right] = -0.174$$

$$g_{42} = \left(\frac{a_{42} - g_{41}g_{21}}{g_{22}} \right) = \left[\frac{1 - 0(-2)}{1.915} \right] = 0.522$$

$$g_{33} = \sqrt{a_{33} - g_{31}^2 - g_{32}^2} = \sqrt{11 - [(0.577)^2 + 0.174^2]} = 3.261$$

$$g_{43} = \left[\frac{a_{43} - g_{41}g_{31} - g_{42}g_{32}}{g_{33}} \right] = \left[\frac{-2 - 0(0.577) - 0.522(-0.174)}{3.261} \right] = -0.585$$

$$g_{44} = \sqrt{a_{44} - (g_{41}^2 + g_{42}^2 + g_{43}^2)}$$

$$= \sqrt{12 - [(0)^2 + 0.522^2 + (-0.585)^2]}$$

$$= 3.374$$

The resulting [G] matrix is compiled as

$$[G] = \begin{bmatrix} 1.732 & 0 & 0 & 0 \\ -1.155 & 1.915 & 0 & 0 \\ 0.577 & -0.174 & 3.261 & 0 \\ 0 & 0.522 & -0.585 & 3.374 \end{bmatrix}$$

Step 2. Forward solution

$$[G][Y] = [B]$$

$$\begin{bmatrix} 1.732 & 0 & 0 & 0 \\ -1.155 & 1.915 & 0 & 0 \\ 0.577 & -0.174 & 3.261 & 0 \\ 0 & 0.522 & -0.585 & 3.374 \end{bmatrix} \begin{bmatrix} y_1 \\ y_2 \\ y_3 \\ y_4 \end{bmatrix} = \begin{bmatrix} 7 \\ -11 \\ 28 \\ -29 \end{bmatrix}$$

Solving the first equation for y_1, gives

$$1.732 \, y_1 = 7 \qquad\qquad \therefore y_1 = 4.402$$

Solving the second equation for y_2, gives

$$-1.155 y_1 + 1.915 y_2 = -11$$

$$-1.155(4.402) + 1.915 y_2 = -11 \qquad \therefore y_2 = -3.306$$

Solving the third equation for y_3, gives

$$-0.577 y_1 - 0.174 y_2 + 3.261 y_3 = 28$$

$$-0.577(4.402) - 0.174(-3.306) + 3.261y_3 = 28$$

$$\therefore y_3 = 7.695$$

Solving the fourth equation for y_4, gives

$$0.522(-3.306) - 0.585(7.695) + 3.374y_4 = -29$$

$$\therefore y_4 = -6.749$$

Step 3. Backward solution

Solve the equation

$$[G]^T [X] = [Y]$$

$$\begin{bmatrix} 1.732 & -1.155 & 0.577 & 0 \\ 0 & 1.915 & -0.174 & 0.522 \\ 0 & 0 & 3.261 & -0.585 \\ 0 & 0 & 0 & 3.374 \end{bmatrix} \begin{bmatrix} w \\ x \\ y \\ z \end{bmatrix} = \begin{bmatrix} 4.402 \\ -3.306 \\ 7.695 \\ -6.749 \end{bmatrix}$$

Solving the fourth equation for z, we get

$$3.374z = -6.749 \qquad\qquad \therefore z = -2.000$$

Solving the third equation for y, we get

$$3.261y - 0.585z = 7.695$$

$$3.261y - 0.585(-2.0) = 7.695 \qquad\qquad \therefore y = 2.000$$

Solving the second equation for x, we get

$$1.915x - 0.174y = 0.522z = -3.306$$

$$1.915x - 0.174(2) = 0.522(-2) = -3.306 \therefore x = -1.000$$

Solving the first equation for w, we get

$$1.732w - 1.155x + 0.577y = 4.402$$

$$1.732w - 1.155(-1) + 0.577(2) = 4.402 \quad\therefore w = 1.000$$

Thus final solution is obtained as

$$w = 1, \qquad x = -1, \qquad y = 2, \qquad z = -2$$

1.6.3 Crout's Method

In the method developed by Crout, the given set of equations are expressed in the form

$$[A][X] = [C] \tag{1}$$

where $[A]$ = Coefficient matrix

$[X]$ = Variable matrix

$[C]$ = Constant matrix

The coefficient matrix is factorized into

$$[A] = [L][U] \qquad (2)$$

where $[L]$ = Lower triangular matrix

$[U]$ = Upper triangular matrix

After factorization, $[L^{-1}]$ and $[U^{-1}]$ are obtained separately as $[L]$ and $[U]$ are already obtained from Eq. (2), i.e.

$$[L][L^{-1}] = I \qquad (3a)$$
$$[U][U^{-1}] = I \qquad (3b)$$

where I is the indentity matrix.

The matrix $[X]$ can be evaluated as follows:

$$[A][X] = [C]$$
$$[L][U][X] = [C]$$
$$[X] = [U^{-1}] [L^{-1}][C] \qquad (4)$$

The lower and upper matrices are expressed as

$$L = \begin{bmatrix} l_{11} & 0 & 0 \\ l_{21} & l_{22} & 0 \\ l_{31} & l_{32} & l_{33} \end{bmatrix} \text{ and } U = \begin{bmatrix} u_{11} & u_{12} & u_{13} \\ 0 & u_{22} & u_{23} \\ 0 & 0 & u_{33} \end{bmatrix}$$

When we choose $l_{ii} = 1$, the method is called the Doolittle's method but if we choose $u_{ii} = 1$, then the method is called the Crout's method.

Example 1.13

Solve the following set of equations using Crout's technique.

$$3x_1 - x_2 + 2x_3 = 12 \qquad (1)$$
$$x_1 + 2x_2 + 3x_3 = 11 \qquad (2)$$
$$2x_1 - 2x_2 - x_3 = 12 \qquad (3)$$

Solution

The given equations can be represented in matrix form as

$$\begin{bmatrix} 3 & -1 & 2 \\ 1 & 2 & 3 \\ 2 & -2 & -1 \end{bmatrix} \begin{Bmatrix} x_1 \\ x_2 \\ x_3 \end{Bmatrix} = \begin{bmatrix} 12 \\ 11 \\ 2 \end{bmatrix}$$

$$[A][X] = [C]$$

The given matrix $[A]$ is factorized into a product of lower triangular matrix and unit upper triangular matrix.

$$\begin{bmatrix} L_{11} & 0 & 0 \\ L_{21} & L_{22} & 0 \\ L_{31} & L_{32} & L_{33} \end{bmatrix} \begin{bmatrix} 1 & U_{12} & U_{13} \\ 0 & 1 & U_{23} \\ 0 & 0 & 1 \end{bmatrix} = \begin{bmatrix} 3 & -1 & 2 \\ 1 & 2 & 3 \\ 2 & -2 & -1 \end{bmatrix}$$

$$[L][U] = [A]$$

$L_{11} = 3$ $\qquad\qquad\qquad\qquad$ $L_{21} = 1$

$L_{11}U_{12} = -1$ $\qquad\qquad\qquad\qquad\qquad\qquad$ $\therefore U_{12} = -\left(\dfrac{1}{3}\right) = -0.33$

$L_{11}U_{13} = 2$ $\qquad\qquad$ or $3U_{13} = 2$ $\qquad$ $\therefore U_{13} = 0.67$

$L_{21}U_{12} + L_{22} + 0 = 2$

$1(-0.33) + L_{22} + 0 = 2$ $\qquad\qquad\qquad\qquad$ $\therefore L_{22} = 2.33$

$L_{31} = 2$ $\qquad\qquad\qquad\qquad$ $U_{23} = 1$

$L_{31}U_{12} + L_{32}(1) + L_{33}(0) = 2$

$2(-0.33) + L_{32} = 2$ $\qquad\qquad\qquad\qquad$ $\therefore L_{32} = -1.34$

$L_{31}U_{13} + L_{32}U_{23} + L_{33} = -1$

$2(0.67) + (-1.34)1 + L_{33} = -1$ $\qquad\qquad\qquad$ $\therefore L_{33} = -1$

Hence the given matrix $[A]$ is factorized as

$$[A] = [L][U]$$

Therefore $\left[A^{-1}\right] = \left[L^{-1}\right]\left[U^{-1}\right]$

The inverse matrices $[U]$ and $[L]$ are determined separately.

$$[U] = \begin{bmatrix} 1 & -0.33 & 0.067 \\ 0 & 1 & 1 \\ 0 & 0 & 1 \end{bmatrix}$$

Since $[U][U^{(-1)}] = [I]$, we have

$$\begin{bmatrix} 1 & -0.33 & 0.67 \\ 0 & 1 & 1 \\ 0 & 0 & 1 \end{bmatrix} \begin{bmatrix} y_{11} & y_{12} & y_{13} \\ 0 & y_{22} & y_{23} \\ 0 & 0 & y_{33} \end{bmatrix} = \begin{bmatrix} 1 & 0 & 0 \\ 0 & 1 & 0 \\ 0 & 0 & 1 \end{bmatrix}$$

$y_{33} = 1$ $\qquad\qquad$ $y_{12} - 0.33y_{22} = 0$

$y_{22} = 1$ $\qquad\qquad$ $y_{12} = 0.33(1) = 0.33$

$y_{11} = 1$

$y_{13} - 0.33y_{23} + 0.67y_{33} = 0$

$y_{13} - 0.33y_{23} = -0.67(1)$

$y_{23} + y_{33} = 0$

$y_{23} = -y_{33} = -1$

$y_{13} - 0.33(-1) = -0.67$ $\qquad\qquad\qquad$ $\therefore y_{13} = -1$

Hence we have

$$[U^{-1}] = \begin{bmatrix} 1 & 0.33 & -1 \\ 0 & 1 & -1 \\ 0 & 0 & 1 \end{bmatrix}$$

$$[L] = \begin{bmatrix} 3 & 0 & 0 \\ 1 & 2.33 & 0 \\ 2 & -1.34 & -1 \end{bmatrix}$$

$$[L][L^{-1}] = [I]$$

$$\begin{bmatrix} 3 & 0 & 0 \\ 1 & 2.33 & 0 \\ 2 & -1.34 & -1 \end{bmatrix} \begin{bmatrix} z_{11} & 0 & 0 \\ z_{21} & z_{22} & 0 \\ z_{31} & z_{32} & z_{33} \end{bmatrix} = \begin{bmatrix} 1 & 0 & 0 \\ 0 & 1 & 0 \\ 0 & 0 & 1 \end{bmatrix}$$

$3z_{11} = 1$ \qquad\qquad $\therefore z_{11} = \left(\dfrac{1}{3}\right) = 0.33$

$z_{11} + 2.33 z_{21} = 0$

$0.33 + 2.33 z_{21} = 0$ \qquad\qquad $\therefore z_{21} = -0.1416$

$2.33 z_{22} = 1$ \qquad\qquad $\therefore z_{22} = 0.43$

$2z_{11} - 1.34 z_{21} - z_{31} = 0$

$2(0.33) - 1.34(-0.1416) - z_{31} = 0$ \qquad $\therefore z_{31} = 0.85$

$-1.34 z_{22} - z_{32} = 0$

$-1.34(0.43) - z_{32} = 0$ \qquad\qquad $\therefore z_{32} = -0.58$

$-1(z_{33}) = 1$ \qquad\qquad $\therefore z_{33} = -1$

Therefore $[L^{-1}] = \begin{bmatrix} 0.33 & 0 & 0 \\ -0.142 & 0.43 & 0 \\ 0.85 & -0.58 & -1 \end{bmatrix}$

$$[A^{-1}] = [U^{-1}][L^{-1}]$$

$$= \begin{bmatrix} 1 & 0.33 & -1 \\ 0 & 1 & -1 \\ 0 & 0 & 1 \end{bmatrix} \begin{bmatrix} 0.33 & 0 & 0 \\ -0.142 & 0.43 & 0 \\ 0.85 & -0.58 & -1 \end{bmatrix}$$

$$= \begin{bmatrix} -0.566 & 0.722 & 1 \\ -0.99 & 1.01 & 1 \\ 0.85 & -0.58 & -1 \end{bmatrix}$$

$$\begin{Bmatrix} x_1 \\ x_2 \\ x_3 \end{Bmatrix} = \begin{bmatrix} -0.566 & 0.722 & 1 \\ -0.99 & 1.01 & 1 \\ 0.85 & -0.58 & -1 \end{bmatrix} \begin{bmatrix} 12 \\ 11 \\ 2 \end{bmatrix} = \begin{Bmatrix} 3.15 \\ 1.23 \\ 1.82 \end{Bmatrix}$$

Check: Considering Eq. (1), we have

$$3x_1 - x_2 + 2x_3 = 12$$

$$3(3.15) - 1.23 + 2(1.82) = 11.86 \cong 12$$

1.7 MATRIX INVERSION METHOD

In matrix inversion method, the given set of equations are expressed in the matrix form and the solution is determined by finding the inverse of the coefficient matrix. The procedure involved is outlined as follows:

Given the set of simultaneous equations,

$$a_{11}x + a_{12}y + a_{13}z = k_1$$

$$a_{21}x + a_{22}y + a_{23}z = k_2$$

$$a_{31}x + a_{32}y + a_{33}z = k_3$$

These equations can be expressed in matrix from as

$$[A]\begin{Bmatrix} x \\ y \\ z \end{Bmatrix} = \begin{Bmatrix} k_1 \\ k_2 \\ k_3 \end{Bmatrix}$$

$$[A]\{X\} = \{K\}$$

Therefore $X = \left[A^{-1} \right]\{K\}$

where $[A^{(-1)}]$ is called the inverse of the matrix A.

Matrix inverse is defined so that,

$A^{-1} \cdot A = A \cdot A^{-1} = I = $ Identity matrix

The identity matrix is defined as

$$I = \begin{bmatrix} 1 & 0 & 0 \\ 0 & 1 & 0 \\ 0 & 0 & 1 \end{bmatrix}$$

The inverse of matrix is determined by finding the 'adjoint' and the determinant of the matrix.

The inverse of the matrix is defined as

$$A^{-1} = \left[\frac{\text{adj. } A}{|A|}\right] = \left[\frac{\text{Adjoint of matrix } A}{\text{Determinant of matrix } A}\right]$$

$$\text{adj. } A = \begin{bmatrix} A_{11} & A_{12} & A_{13} \\ A_{21} & A_{22} & A_{23} \\ A_{31} & A_{32} & A_{33} \end{bmatrix}^T = \text{Transpose of the cofactors of the elements of matrix } A$$

where $A_{11}, A_{12}, A_{13}, \ldots, A_{33}$ are called the cofactors of every element of matrix A. They can be evaluated by the determinants using the following procedure.

$$A_{11} = (-1)^2 \begin{vmatrix} a_{22} & a_{23} \\ a_{32} & a_{33} \end{vmatrix}$$

$$A_{12} = (-1)^3 \begin{vmatrix} a_{21} & a_{23} \\ a_{31} & a_{33} \end{vmatrix}$$

$$A_{13} = (-1)^4 \begin{vmatrix} a_{21} & a_{22} \\ a_{31} & a_{32} \end{vmatrix}$$

....
....

$$A_{ij} = (-1)^{i+j} \times \text{first minor of } a_{ij}$$

The determinant of A is expressed as $[A]$ and is evaluated as

$$|A| = a_{11}A_{11} + a_{21}A_{21} + a_{31}A_{31}$$

$$|A| = \Sigma\, a_{ia}A_{ia}$$

where i is selected as 1 if first row is used and 2 if second row is used and so on. Alternatively, we can use columns in which case

$$|A| = \Sigma\, a_{aj}A_{aj}$$

where $j = 1$ if expansion is carried out in first column and 2 if expansion is carried out on second column and so on.

The application of matrix inversion method is illustrated by the following examples.

Example 1.14

Solve the following simultaneous equations by matrix inversion method.

$$x + 2y - z = -3 \tag{1}$$

$$4x - 3y + 4z = 1 \tag{2}$$

$$2x - y + z = -2 \tag{3}$$

Solution

The equations are expressed in the matrix form

$$\begin{bmatrix} 1 & 2 & -1 \\ 4 & -3 & 4 \\ 2 & -1 & 1 \end{bmatrix} \begin{Bmatrix} x \\ y \\ z \end{Bmatrix} = \begin{Bmatrix} -3 \\ 1 \\ -2 \end{Bmatrix}$$

$$[A]\{X\} = \{K\}$$

Therefore $X = [A^{(-1)}]K$, where A^{-1} is the inverse of matrix A.

The cofactors of the matrix A are determined as follows:

$$A_{11} = (-1)^2 \begin{vmatrix} -3 & 4 \\ -1 & 1 \end{vmatrix} = -3 + 4 = 1$$

$$A_{12} = (-1)^3 \begin{vmatrix} 4 & 4 \\ 2 & 1 \end{vmatrix} = (-1)(4-8) = 4$$

$$A_{13} = (-1)^4 \begin{vmatrix} 4 & -3 \\ 2 & -1 \end{vmatrix} = -4 + 6 = 2$$

$$A_{21} = (-1)^3 \begin{vmatrix} 2 & -1 \\ -1 & 1 \end{vmatrix} = (-1)(2-1) = -1$$

$$A_{22} = (-1)^4 \begin{vmatrix} 1 & -1 \\ 2 & 1 \end{vmatrix} = 1 + 2 = 3$$

$$A_{23} = (-1)^5 \begin{vmatrix} 1 & 2 \\ 2 & -1 \end{vmatrix} = (-1)(-1-4) = 5$$

$$A_{31} = (-1)^4 \begin{vmatrix} 2 & -1 \\ -3 & 4 \end{vmatrix} = 8 - 3 = 5$$

$$A_{32} = (-1)^5 \begin{vmatrix} 1 & -1 \\ 4 & 4 \end{vmatrix} = (-1)(4+4) = -8$$

$$A_{33} = (-1)^6 \begin{vmatrix} 1 & -2 \\ 4 & -3 \end{vmatrix} = -3 - 8 = -11$$

Therefore adj. $A = \begin{bmatrix} A_{11} & A_{12} & A_{13} \\ A_{21} & A_{22} & A_{23} \\ A_{31} & A_{32} & A_{33} \end{bmatrix}^T$

$$= \begin{bmatrix} 1 & 4 & 2 \\ -1 & 3 & 5 \\ 5 & -8 & -11 \end{bmatrix}^T = \begin{bmatrix} 1 & -1 & 5 \\ 4 & 3 & -8 \\ 2 & 5 & -11 \end{bmatrix}$$

$$|A| = a_{11}A_{11} + a_{21}A_{21} + a_{31}A_{31}$$

$$= 1(1) + 4(-1) + 2(-5) = 7$$

Therefore $A^{-1} = \left[\dfrac{\text{adj. } A}{|A|} \right] = \dfrac{\begin{bmatrix} 1 & -1 & 5 \\ 4 & 3 & -8 \\ 2 & 5 & -11 \end{bmatrix}}{7}$

$$X = \left[A^{-1} \right]\{K\}$$

$$\begin{Bmatrix} x \\ y \\ z \end{Bmatrix} = (1/7) \begin{bmatrix} 1 & -1 & 5 \\ 4 & 3 & -8 \\ 2 & 5 & -11 \end{bmatrix} \begin{Bmatrix} -3 \\ 1 \\ -2 \end{Bmatrix}$$

Therefore $x = \left(\dfrac{1}{7} \right) \begin{bmatrix} 1 & -1 & 5 \end{bmatrix} \begin{Bmatrix} -3 \\ 1 \\ -2 \end{Bmatrix}$

$$= \left(\frac{1}{7} \right) \left[(1) \times (-3) + (-1 \times 1) + (5)(-2) \right] = (-2)$$

$$y = \left(\frac{1}{7} \right) \begin{bmatrix} 4 & 3 & -8 \end{bmatrix} \begin{Bmatrix} -3 \\ 1 \\ -2 \end{Bmatrix}$$

$$= \left(\frac{1}{7} \right) \left[-12 + 3 + 16 \right] = 1$$

$$z = \left(\frac{1}{7} \right) \begin{bmatrix} 2 & 5 & -11 \end{bmatrix} \begin{Bmatrix} -3 \\ 1 \\ -2 \end{Bmatrix}$$

$$= \left(\frac{1}{7} \right) \left[-6 + 5 + 22 \right] = 3$$

Therefore $x = -2, y = 1, z = 3$

Check: Considering Eq. (ii), we have

$$4x - 3y + 4z = 1$$

$$4(-2) - 3(1) + 4(3) = 1$$

Example 1.15

Solve the following set of simultaneous equations by matrix inversion method.

$$\begin{bmatrix} 3 & 1 & 1 \\ 1 & 4 & 1 \\ 2 & 1 & 2 \end{bmatrix} \begin{Bmatrix} x_1 \\ x_2 \\ x_3 \end{Bmatrix} = \begin{Bmatrix} 2 \\ 12 \\ 10 \end{Bmatrix}$$

Solution

$[A]\{X\} = \{K\}$ therefore $X = \left[A^{-1} \right]\{K\}$

Determination of A^{-1} by computing the cofactors of matrix A

$$A_{11} = (-1)^2 \begin{vmatrix} 4 & 1 \\ 1 & 2 \end{vmatrix} = (8-1) = 7$$

$$A_{12} = (-1)^3 \begin{vmatrix} 1 & 1 \\ 2 & 2 \end{vmatrix} = -(2-2) = 0$$

$$A_{13} = (-1)^4 \begin{vmatrix} 1 & 4 \\ 2 & 1 \end{vmatrix} = (1-8) = -7$$

$$A_{21} = (-1)^3 \begin{vmatrix} 1 & 1 \\ 1 & 2 \end{vmatrix} = -(2-1) = -1$$

$$A_{22} = (-1)^4 \begin{vmatrix} 3 & 1 \\ 2 & 2 \end{vmatrix} = (6-2) = 4$$

$$A_{23} = (-1)^5 \begin{vmatrix} 3 & 1 \\ 2 & 1 \end{vmatrix} = -(3-2) = -1$$

$$A_{31} = (-1)^4 \begin{vmatrix} 1 & 1 \\ 4 & 1 \end{vmatrix} = (1-4) = -3$$

$$A_{32} = (-1)^5 \begin{vmatrix} 3 & 1 \\ 1 & 1 \end{vmatrix} = -(3-1) = -2$$

$$A_{33} = (-1)^6 \begin{vmatrix} 3 & 1 \\ 1 & 4 \end{vmatrix} = (12-1) = 11$$

$$\text{adj. } A = \begin{bmatrix} 7 & 0 & -7 \\ -1 & 4 & -1 \\ -3 & -2 & 11 \end{bmatrix}^T = \begin{bmatrix} 7 & -1 & -3 \\ 0 & 4 & -2 \\ -7 & -1 & 11 \end{bmatrix}$$

$$|A| = a_{11}A_{11} + a_{21}A_{21} + a_{31}A_{31}$$

$$= 3(7) + 1(-1) + 2(-3) = 14$$

$$A^{-1} = \left[\frac{\text{adj. } A}{|A|}\right]$$

$$= \begin{bmatrix} 7/14 & -1/14 & -3/14 \\ 0 & 4/14 & -2/14 \\ -7/14 & -1/14 & 11/14 \end{bmatrix} = \begin{bmatrix} 0.5 & -0.07 & -0.21 \\ 0 & 0.285 & -0.143 \\ -0.5 & -0.07 & 0.785 \end{bmatrix}$$

$$X = \left[A^{-1}\right]\{K\}$$

$$= \begin{Bmatrix} x_1 \\ x_2 \\ x_3 \end{Bmatrix} \begin{bmatrix} 0.5 & -0.07 & -0.21 \\ 0 & 0.285 & -0.143 \\ -0.5 & -0.07 & 0.785 \end{bmatrix} \begin{Bmatrix} 2 \\ 12 \\ 10 \end{Bmatrix}$$

$$x_1 = [0.5 - 0.07 - 0.21] \begin{Bmatrix} 2 \\ 12 \\ 10 \end{Bmatrix}$$

$$= \left[(0.5 \times 2) - (0.07 \times 12) - (0.21 \times 10)\right] = -1.94 \cong -2.0$$

$$x_2 = [0 \quad 0.285 \quad -0.143] \begin{Bmatrix} 2 \\ 12 \\ 10 \end{Bmatrix}$$

$$= \left[(0 \times 2) - (0.285 \times 12) - (0.143 \times 10)\right] = 2.0$$

$$x_3 = [-0.5 \quad -0.07 \quad 0.785] \begin{Bmatrix} 2 \\ 12 \\ 10 \end{Bmatrix}$$

$$= \left[(-0.5 \times 2) - 0.07(12) - (0.785 \times 10)\right] = 6$$

Therefore $x_1 = 2$, $x_2 = 2$, $x_3 = 6$

Check: Considering Eq. (3), we have

$$2x_1 + x_2 + 2x_3 = 10$$

$$2(-2) + 2 + 2(6) = 10$$

Example 1.16

If C is a square matrix as given below

$$C = \begin{bmatrix} 2 & 1 & 1 \\ 1 & 2 & 1 \\ 1 & 1 & 2 \end{bmatrix}$$

show that $C \cdot C^{-1} = I$ where C^{-1} is the inverse of matrix C and I is the identity matrix.

Solution

The cofactors of the matrix C are evaluated as follows.

$$C_{11} = (-1)^2 \begin{vmatrix} 2 & 1 \\ 1 & 2 \end{vmatrix} = (4-1) = 3$$

$$C_{12} = (-1)^3 \begin{vmatrix} 1 & 1 \\ 1 & 2 \end{vmatrix} = -(2-1) = -1$$

$$C_{13} = (-1)^4 \begin{vmatrix} 1 & 2 \\ 1 & 1 \end{vmatrix} = (1-8) = -7$$

$$C_{21} = (-1)^3 \begin{vmatrix} 1 & 1 \\ 1 & 2 \end{vmatrix} = -(2-1) = -1$$

$$C_{22} = (-1)^4 \begin{vmatrix} 2 & 1 \\ 1 & 2 \end{vmatrix} = (4-1) = 3$$

$$C_{23} = (-1)^5 \begin{vmatrix} 3 & 1 \\ 2 & 1 \end{vmatrix} = -(2-1) = -1$$

$$C_{31} = (-1)^4 \begin{vmatrix} 1 & 1 \\ 2 & 1 \end{vmatrix} = (1-2) = -1.$$

$$C_{32} = (-1)^5 \begin{vmatrix} 2 & 1 \\ 1 & 1 \end{vmatrix} = -(2-1) = -1$$

$$C_{33} = (-1)^6 \begin{vmatrix} 2 & 1 \\ 1 & 2 \end{vmatrix} = (4-1) = 3$$

$$\text{adj. } C = \begin{bmatrix} 3 & -1 & -1 \\ -1 & 3 & -1 \\ -1 & -1 & 3 \end{bmatrix}^T = \begin{bmatrix} 3 & -1 & -1 \\ -1 & 3 & -1 \\ -1 & -1 & 3 \end{bmatrix}$$

$$|C| = c_{11}C_{11} + c_{21}C_{21} + c_{31}C_{31}$$

$$= 2(3) + 1(-1) + 1(-1) = 4$$

$$C^{-1} = \left[\frac{\text{adj. } C}{|C|}\right] = \begin{bmatrix} 0.75 & -0.25 & -0.25 \\ -0.25 & 0.75 & -0.25 \\ -0.25 & -0.25 & 0.75 \end{bmatrix}$$

$$C \cdot C^{-1} = \begin{bmatrix} 2 & 1 & 1 \\ 1 & 2 & 1 \\ 1 & 1 & 2 \end{bmatrix} \begin{bmatrix} 0.75 & -0.25 & -0.25 \\ -0.25 & 0.75 & -0.25 \\ -0.25 & -0.25 & 0.75 \end{bmatrix} = \begin{bmatrix} 1 & 0 & 0 \\ 0 & 1 & 0 \\ 0 & 0 & 1 \end{bmatrix}$$

Therefore $C \cdot C^{-1} = \begin{bmatrix} 2 & 1 & 1 \\ 1 & 2 & 1 \\ 1 & 1 & 2 \end{bmatrix} \begin{bmatrix} 0.75 & -0.25 & -0.25 \\ -0.25 & 0.75 & -0.25 \\ -0.25 & -0.25 & 0.75 \end{bmatrix} = \begin{bmatrix} 1 & 0 & 0 \\ 0 & 1 & 0 \\ 0 & 0 & 1 \end{bmatrix}$

Example 1.17

Using the augmented matrix method, determine the inverse of the matrix.

$$C = \begin{bmatrix} 2 & 1 & 1 \\ 1 & 2 & 1 \\ 1 & 1 & 2 \end{bmatrix}$$

Solution

Consider the given matrix and the unit matrix given below.

$$C = \begin{bmatrix} 2 & 1 & 1 \\ 1 & 2 & 1 \\ 1 & 1 & 2 \end{bmatrix} \text{ and } I = \begin{bmatrix} 1 & 0 & 0 \\ 0 & 1 & 0 \\ 0 & 0 & 1 \end{bmatrix}$$

Considering the given matrix and the first column of the unit matrix, we have

$$\begin{bmatrix} 2 & 1 & 1:1 \\ 1 & 2 & 1:0 \\ 1 & 1 & 2:0 \end{bmatrix} = \begin{bmatrix} 1 & 0.5 & 0.5:0.5 \\ 1 & 2 & 1:0 \\ 1 & 1 & 2:0 \end{bmatrix}$$

$$\begin{aligned} &:1: 0.5 \quad 0.5 \quad 0.5: \\ = &:0:1.5 \quad 0.5 \ -0.5: \text{........} R_2 - R_1 \\ &:0:0.5 \quad 1.5 \ -0.5: \text{........} R_3 - R_1 \end{aligned}$$

Now consider the modified matrix with the second column of the unit matrix, we have

$$\begin{aligned} &:0.5 \quad 0.5 \quad 0.5: 0: \quad :0.5 \quad 0.5 \quad 0.5 \qquad 0: \\ &:1.5 \quad 0.5 -0.5: 1: \ = \ :1 \quad 0.33 \ -0.33 \quad 0.67: \text{........} (R_2/1.5) \\ &:1.5 \quad 0.5 -0.5: 0: \quad :0.5 \quad 1.5 \ -1.5 \qquad 0: \end{aligned}$$

$$\begin{aligned} &:0:0.335 \qquad 0.665 \ -0.335: \text{.....} (-0.5R_2 - R_1) \\ &:0:0.33 \ -0.33 \qquad 0.67: \\ &:0:1.335 \ -0.335 \ -0.335: \text{.....} (-0.5R_2 - R_3) \end{aligned}$$

Now consider the modified matrix with the third column of the unit matrix, we have

$$
\begin{array}{lll}
\vdots 0.335 & 0.665 & -0.335 \vdots 0 \vdots \\
\vdots 0.33 & -0.33 & 0.67 \vdots 0 \vdots \\
\vdots 1.335 & -0.335 & -0.335 \vdots 1 \vdots
\end{array}
$$

$$
=
\begin{array}{lll}
\vdots 0.335 & 0.665 & -0.335 \vdots 0 \vdots \\
\vdots 0.33 & -0.33 & 0.67 \vdots 0 \vdots \\
\vdots 1 & -0.25 & -0.25 \vdots 0.75 \vdots ..... (R_3/1.335)
\end{array}
$$

$$
=
\begin{array}{lll}
\vdots 0 \vdots 0.75 & -0.25 & -0.25 \vdots .... (-0.335R_3 + R_1) \\
\vdots 0 \vdots -0.25 & -0.75 & -0.25 \vdots .... (-0.335R_3 + R_2) \\
\vdots 1 \vdots -0.25 & -0.25 & 0.75 \vdots
\end{array}
$$

The inverse of the matrix is given by

$$
C^{-1} = \begin{bmatrix} 0.75 & -0.25 & -0.25 \\ -0.25 & 0.75 & -0.25 \\ -0.25 & -0.25 & 0.75 \end{bmatrix}
$$

Example 1.18

Solve the following set of equations by matrix inversion using the augmented matrix method.

$$2x_1 - 2x_2 - x_4 = 1 \tag{1}$$

$$2x_2 - x_3 - 2x_4 = 2 \tag{2}$$

$$x_1 - 2x_2 + 3x_3 - 2x_4 = 3 \tag{3}$$

$$x_2 + 2x_3 + 2x_4 = 4 \tag{4}$$

Solution

The set of equations are expressed in the matrix form as

$$
\begin{bmatrix} 2 & -2 & 0 & -1 \\ 0 & 2 & 1 & 2 \\ 1 & -2 & 3 & -2 \\ 0 & 1 & 2 & 2 \end{bmatrix}
\begin{Bmatrix} x_1 \\ x_2 \\ x_3 \\ x_4 \end{Bmatrix} =
\begin{Bmatrix} 1 \\ 2 \\ 3 \\ 4 \end{Bmatrix}
$$

$$[A]\{X\} = \{C\}$$

To evaluate the inverse of the matrix, consider the matrix with the first column of the unit matrix.

$$
\begin{array}{llll}
\vdots 2 & -2 & 0 & -1 \vdots 1 \vdots \\
\vdots 0 & 2 & 1 & 2 \vdots 0 \vdots \\
\vdots 1 & -2 & 3 & -2 \vdots 0 \vdots \\
\vdots 0 & 2 & 1 & 2 \vdots 0 \vdots
\end{array}
=
\begin{array}{llll}
\vdots 1 & -1 & 0 & -0.5 \vdots 0.5 \vdots \\
\vdots 0 & 2 & 1 & 2 \vdots 0 \vdots \\
\vdots 1 & -2 & 3 & -2 \vdots 0 \vdots \\
\vdots 0 & 2 & 1 & 2 \vdots 0 \vdots
\end{array}
$$

$$\begin{bmatrix} 1 & -1 & 0 & -0.5 & 0.5 \\ 0 & 2 & 1 & 2 & 0 \\ 0 & -1 & 3 & -1.5 & -0.5 \\ 0 & 1 & 2 & 2 & 0 \end{bmatrix}$$

Considering the modified matrix and the second column of the identity matrix

$$\begin{bmatrix} -1 & 0 & -0.5 & 0.5 & 0 \\ 2 & 1 & 2 & 0 & 1 \\ 1 & -2 & 3 & -2 & 0 \\ 0 & 1 & 2 & 2 & 0 \end{bmatrix} = \begin{bmatrix} -1 & 0 & -0.5 & 0.5 & 0 \\ 1 & 0.5 & 1 & 0 & 0.5 \\ -1 & 3 & -1.5 & -0.5 & 0 \\ 0 & 2 & 2 & 2 & 0 \end{bmatrix}$$

$$= \begin{bmatrix} 0 & 0.5 & 0.5 & 0.5 & 0.5 \\ 1 & 0.5 & 1 & 0 & 0.5 \\ 0 & 3.5 & 0.5 & -1.5 & 0.5 \\ 0 & 5 & 0.5 & -1.5 & 0 \end{bmatrix}$$

Considering the modified matrix and the third column of the unit matrix

$$\begin{bmatrix} 0.5 & 0.5 & 0.5 & 0.5 & 0 \\ 0.5 & 1 & 0 & 0.5 & 1 \\ 3.5 & -0.5 & -0.5 & 0.5 & 0 \\ 5 & 0.5 & -0.5 & 0 & 0 \end{bmatrix}$$

$$= \begin{bmatrix} 0.5 & 0.5 & 0.5 & 0.5 & 0 \\ 0.5 & 1 & 0 & 0.5 & 0 \\ 1 & -0.143 & -0.143 & 0.143 & 0.286 \\ 5 & 0.5 & -0.5 & 0 & 0 \end{bmatrix}$$

$$= \begin{bmatrix} 0 & 0.5715 & 0.5715 & 0.4285 & -0143 \\ 0 & 1.0715 & 0.0715 & 0.4285 & -0143 \\ 1 & -0.143 & -0.143 & -0.143 & -0.286 \\ 0 & 1.215 & 1.215 & -1.715 & -1.43 \end{bmatrix} \begin{matrix} \dots -0.5R_1 + R_2 \\ \dots -0.5R_3 + R_2 \\ \\ \dots -5R_1 + R_2 \end{matrix}$$

Considering the modified matrix and the last column of the unit matrix

$$\begin{bmatrix} 0.5715 & 0.5715 & 0.4285 & -0143 & 0 \\ 1.0715 & 0.0715 & 0.4285 & -0.143 & 0 \\ -0.143 & -0.143 & 0.143 & -0.286 & 0 \\ 1.215 & 0.215 & -0.715 & -1.43 & 1 \end{bmatrix}$$

$$= \begin{bmatrix} \vdots & 0.5715 & 0.5715 & 0.4285 & -0143 & 0 & \vdots \\ \vdots & 1.0715 & 0.0715 & 0.4285 & -0143 & 0 & \vdots \\ \vdots & -0.143 & -0.143 & -0.143 & -0.286 & 0 & \vdots \\ \vdots & 1 & & 0.177 & -0.588 & -1.177 & 0.823 & \vdots \end{bmatrix}$$

$$= \begin{bmatrix} \vdots & 0 & \vdots & 0.4703 & 0.7645 & 0.5296 & -0.4703 & \vdots \\ \vdots & 0 & \vdots & 1.1181 & 1.0585 & 1.1181 & -0.8818 & \vdots \\ \vdots & 0 & \vdots & -0.1177 & -0.058 & -0.1177 & 0.1177 & \vdots \\ \vdots & 1 & \vdots & 0.1770 & 0.588 & -1.177 & 0.823 & \vdots \end{bmatrix}$$

Therefore

$$[X] = [A^{-1}][C]$$

$$= \begin{bmatrix} \vdots & 0 & \vdots & 0.4703 & 0.7645 & 0.5296 & -0.4703 & \vdots \{1\} \\ \vdots & 0 & \vdots & -0.1181 & 1.0585 & 1.1181 & -0.8818 & \vdots \{2\} \\ \vdots & 0 & \vdots & -0.1177 & 0.7645 & 0.5296 & -0.4703 & \vdots \{3\} \\ \vdots & 1 & \vdots & 0.1770 & -0.588 & -1.177 & 0.823 & \vdots \{4\} \end{bmatrix}$$

Hence we have the final solution as

$$\begin{Bmatrix} x_1 \\ x_2 \\ x_3 \\ x_4 \end{Bmatrix} = \begin{Bmatrix} 1.7069 \\ 1.8260 \\ 0.8220 \\ -1.238 \end{Bmatrix}$$

Check considering Eq. (3), we have applied as

$$x_1 - 2x_2 + 3x_3 - 2x_4 = 3$$

$$1.7069 - 2(1.8260) + 3(0.8220) - 2(-1.238) = 3.00$$

1.8 SOLUTION OF EIGEN PROBLEMS

In the analysis of problems dealing with structural stability and dynamics of structures, Eigen value problems are generally encountered and these can be solved using appropriate numerical techniques. In general, for any given matrix A, we have to find the column vector X and a constant λ such that

$$[A]\{X\} = \lambda\{X\}$$

or $\{[A] - \lambda\{I\}\}\{X\} = 0$

Consider the following set of equations:

$$a_{11}x_1 + a_{12}x_2 + a_{13}x_3 = \lambda x_1$$

$$a_{21}x_1 + a_{22}x_2 + a_{23}x_3 = \lambda x_2$$

$$a_{31}x_1 + a_{32}x_2 + a_{33}x_3 = \lambda x_3$$

We can express these equations in the form

$$(a_{11} - \lambda) x_1 + a_{12}x_2 + a_{13}x_3 = 0$$

$$a_{21}x_1 + (a_{22} - \lambda)x_2 + a_{23}x_3 = 0$$

$$a_{31}x_1 + a_{32}x_2 + (a_{33} - \lambda)x_3 = 0$$

The solution for these equations exist only when

$$\begin{vmatrix} (a_{11} - \lambda) & a_{12} & a_{13} \\ a_{21} & (a_{22} - \lambda) & a_{23} \\ a_{31} & a_{32} & (a_{33} - \lambda) \end{vmatrix} = 0$$

Expanding the determinant, we get a cubic equation in λ. The cubic equation is referred to as a *characteristic polynomial*. The roots of the equation, viz., $\lambda_1, \lambda_2, \lambda_3$ are called the *characteristic values* or *Eigen values*.

For λ_1, we get a set of $\begin{Bmatrix} x_1 \\ x_2 \\ x_3 \end{Bmatrix}$ Eigen vectors

For λ_2, we get a set of $\begin{Bmatrix} x_1 \\ x_2 \\ x_3 \end{Bmatrix}$ Eigen vectors

For λ_3, we get a set of $\begin{Bmatrix} x_1 \\ x_2 \\ x_3 \end{Bmatrix}$ Eigen vectors

The procedure based on the method of characteristic polynomial is used for the solution of the following Eigen value problems.

Example 1.19

Find the Eigen values and Eigen vector of the following matrix.

$$A = \begin{bmatrix} 5 & 0 & 1 \\ 0 & -2 & 0 \\ 1 & 0 & 5 \end{bmatrix}$$

Solution

Introducing λ, the determinant is written as

$$\begin{vmatrix} 5 - \lambda & 0 & 1 \\ 0 & -2 - \lambda & 0 \\ 0 & 0 & 5 - \lambda \end{vmatrix} = 0$$

Expanding the determinant

$$(5 - \lambda)\left[-(2 + \lambda)(5 - \lambda)\right] - 0 + (2 + \lambda) = 0$$

Therefore $-(5-\lambda)(5-\lambda)(2+\lambda)+(2+\lambda)=0$

$$(2+\lambda)\left[1-(5-\lambda)^2=0\right]$$

$$(2+\lambda)\left[1-25-\lambda^2+10\lambda\right]=0$$

$$(2+\lambda)\left[-\lambda^2+10\lambda-24\right]=0$$

$$-(2+\lambda)\left(\lambda^2-10\lambda+24\right)=0$$

Hence $\qquad (\lambda^2-10\lambda+24)=0$

$$(\lambda-6)(\lambda-4)=0$$

and $\qquad -(2+\lambda)=0$

Therefore $\qquad \lambda_1=-2 \qquad \lambda_2=4 \qquad \lambda_3=6$

For $\lambda_1=-2$, we have

$$[5-(-2)]x_1+(0)x_2+x_3=0$$

$$(7x_1+x_3)=0 \qquad\qquad\qquad (1)$$

$$(0)x_1+(0)x_2+(0)x_3=0 \qquad\qquad (2)$$

$$x_1+(0)x_2+7x_3=0 \qquad\qquad\qquad (3)$$

Assume $x_1=1$, then $(1+7x_3)=0 \therefore x_3=-\left(\dfrac{1}{7}\right)$

From Eq. (2), $x_2=0$

Therefore eigen vector $=\begin{Bmatrix} 1 \\ 0 \\ -1/7 \end{Bmatrix}$

For $\lambda_2=4$, we have

$$x_1+x_3=0 \qquad\qquad\qquad\qquad (4)$$

$$-6x_2=0 \qquad\qquad\qquad\qquad (5)$$

$$(x_1+x_3)=0 \qquad\qquad\qquad\qquad (6)$$

From Eq. (5), $x_2=5$

If $x_1=1, x_3=-1$

$\therefore$ The eigen vector $=\begin{Bmatrix} 1 \\ 0 \\ -1 \end{Bmatrix}$

For $\lambda_3 = .6$, we have

$$x_1 + x_3 = 0 \qquad (7)$$
$$-8x_2 = 0 \qquad (8)$$
$$x_1 - x_3 = 0 \qquad (9)$$

Therefore $x_2 = 0$

If $x_1 = 1, x_3 = 1$

Therefore the Eigen vector $= \begin{Bmatrix} 1 \\ 0 \\ 1 \end{Bmatrix}$

The application of iterative/power series method for dominant latent roots is illustrated by the following example.

Example 1.20

Find the dominant Eigen value and the corresponding Eigen vector of the following matrix.

$$A = \begin{bmatrix} 2 & 12 & 2 \\ 2 & 4 & 0 \\ 0 & 0 & 6 \end{bmatrix}$$

Solution

Let the initial Eigen vector be $Z_0 = \begin{bmatrix} 1 \\ 0 \\ 0 \end{bmatrix}$

Therefore, $Z_1 = AZ_0 = \begin{bmatrix} 2 & 12 & 2 \\ 2 & 4 & 0 \\ 0 & 0 & 6 \end{bmatrix}\begin{bmatrix} 1 \\ 0 \\ 0 \end{bmatrix} = \begin{bmatrix} 2 \\ 2 \\ 0 \end{bmatrix} = 2\begin{bmatrix} 1 \\ 1 \\ 0 \end{bmatrix}$

Therefore, $K_1 = 2$ and $Y_1 = \begin{bmatrix} 1 \\ 1 \\ 0 \end{bmatrix}$

Now

$$Z_2 = AY_1 = \begin{bmatrix} 2 & 12 & 2 \\ 2 & 4 & 0 \\ 0 & 0 & 6 \end{bmatrix}\begin{bmatrix} 1 \\ 1 \\ 0 \end{bmatrix} = \begin{bmatrix} 14 \\ 6 \\ 0 \end{bmatrix} = 14\begin{bmatrix} 1 \\ 0.43 \\ 0 \end{bmatrix}$$

Therefore, $K_2 = 14$ and $Y_2 = \begin{bmatrix} 1 \\ 0.43 \\ 0 \end{bmatrix}$

Now $\quad Z_3 = AY_2 = \begin{bmatrix} 2 & 12 & 2 \\ 2 & 4 & 0 \\ 0 & 0 & 6 \end{bmatrix} \begin{bmatrix} 1 \\ 0.43 \\ 0 \end{bmatrix} = \begin{bmatrix} 7.16 \\ 3.72 \\ 0 \end{bmatrix} = 7.16 \begin{bmatrix} 1 \\ 0.52 \\ 0 \end{bmatrix}$

Therefore, $K_3 = 7.16$ and $Y_3 = \begin{bmatrix} 1 \\ 0.52 \\ 0 \end{bmatrix}$

$Z_4 = AY_3 = \begin{bmatrix} 2 & 12 & 2 \\ 2 & 4 & 0 \\ 0 & 0 & 6 \end{bmatrix} \begin{bmatrix} 1 \\ 0.52 \\ 0 \end{bmatrix} = \begin{bmatrix} 8.24 \\ 4.08 \\ 0 \end{bmatrix} = 8.24 \begin{bmatrix} 1 \\ 0.5 \\ 0 \end{bmatrix}$

Therefore, $K_4 = 8.24$ and $Y_4 = \begin{bmatrix} 1 \\ 0.5 \\ 0 \end{bmatrix}$

$Z_5 = AY_4 = \begin{bmatrix} 2 & 12 & 2 \\ 2 & 4 & 0 \\ 0 & 0 & 6 \end{bmatrix} \begin{bmatrix} 1 \\ 0.5 \\ 0 \end{bmatrix} = \begin{bmatrix} 8 \\ 4 \\ 0 \end{bmatrix} = 8 \begin{bmatrix} 1 \\ 0.5 \\ 0 \end{bmatrix}$

Hence, the dominant latent root is 8 and the corresponding Eigen vector is $\begin{bmatrix} 1 \\ 0.5 \\ 0 \end{bmatrix}$

Using the above method, the other Eigen values and Eigen vectors can be determined by iteration.

The predominant latent root (λ) is 8. Hence, we form another matrix of the form

$B = (A - \lambda I) = \begin{bmatrix} 2 & 12 & 2 \\ 2 & 4 & 0 \\ 0 & 0 & 6 \end{bmatrix} - 8 \begin{bmatrix} 1 & 0 & 0 \\ 0 & 1 & 0 \\ 0 & 0 & 1 \end{bmatrix} = \begin{bmatrix} -6 & 12 & 2 \\ 2 & -4 & 0 \\ 0 & 0 & -2 \end{bmatrix}$

Now taking $Z_0 = \begin{bmatrix} 1 \\ 0 \\ 0 \end{bmatrix}$

$Z_1 = BZ_0 = \begin{bmatrix} -6 & 12 & 2 \\ 2 & -4 & 0 \\ 0 & 0 & -2 \end{bmatrix} \begin{bmatrix} 1 \\ 0 \\ 0 \end{bmatrix} = \begin{bmatrix} -6 \\ 2 \\ 2 \end{bmatrix} = -6 \begin{bmatrix} 1 \\ -0.33 \\ 0 \end{bmatrix}$ (1)

$Z_2 = BZ_1 = \begin{bmatrix} -6 & 12 & 2 \\ 2 & -4 & 0 \\ 0 & 0 & -2 \end{bmatrix} \begin{bmatrix} 1 \\ 0 \\ 0 \end{bmatrix} = \begin{bmatrix} 1 \\ -0.33 \\ 0 \end{bmatrix}$

$$= \begin{bmatrix} -9.96 \\ 3.32 \\ 0 \end{bmatrix} = -9.96 \begin{bmatrix} 1 \\ -0.33 \\ 0 \end{bmatrix} \tag{2}$$

Comparing Eqs (1) and (2), we find the largest latent root of B matrix is –9.96 and

the corresponding Eigen vector is given by $\begin{bmatrix} 1 \\ -0.33 \\ 0 \end{bmatrix}$

Hence, the latent root of matrix A is $(-9.96 + 8) = -1.96 \cong 2$

The last root can be determined by using the property that sum of Eigen values = sum of diagonal elements of matrix A

$$(8 - 1.96 + \lambda_3) = (2 + 4 + 6)$$

Therefore $\lambda_3 = 5.96 \cong 6.00$

Hence we have $\lambda_1 = 8, \lambda_2 = -1.96 \cong 2$, and $\lambda_3 = 6$

Alternatively, we can get λ_3 by using the property that the product of the eigen values is equal to the value of the determinant A. Hence, we have

$$(8)(1.96)(\lambda_3) = \begin{vmatrix} 2 & 12 & 2 \\ 2 & 4 & 0 \\ 0 & 0 & 6 \end{vmatrix} = -96$$

Therefore, $\lambda_3 = 6.1 \cong 6$

EXERCISES

1. Solve the following set of equations by Cramer's rule.
$$3x_1 + x_2 + x_3 = 4$$
$$x_1 + 4x_2 - x_3 = -5$$
$$x_1 + x_2 - 6x_3 = -12$$

2. Solve the following equations by the method of leading coefficients.
$$10x_1 + 2x_2 + x_3 = 59$$
$$x_1 + 8x_2 + 2x_3 = -4$$
$$2x_1 - x_2 + 20x_3 = 74$$

3. Solve the following equations using the method of determinants.
$$4x_1 + 10x_2 + 5x_3 + 4x_4 = 32$$
$$2x_1 + 5x_2 + 6.5x_3 + 4x_4 = 26$$
$$8x_1 + 4x_2 + 2x_3 = 24$$
$$4x_2 + 4x_3 + 9x_4 = 21$$

4. Using Gauss elimination method, solve the following set of equations.
$$3x_1 + x_2 - 2x_3 = -2$$
$$x_1 + 2x_2 + x_3 = 0$$
$$2x_1 - x_2 + x_3 = 7$$

5. Solve the following set of equations using the method of Gauss–Jordan.

$$8x_1 + 4x_2 + 2x_3 = 24$$
$$4x_2 + 4x_3 + 9x_4 = 21$$
$$4x_1 + 10x_2 + 5x_3 + 4x_4 = 32$$
$$2x_1 + 5x_2 + 6.5x_3 + 4x_4 = 26$$

6. Using Cholesky's method, solve the following set of equations.

$$x_1 + 4x_2 + x_3 = 12$$
$$2x_1 + x_2 + 2x_3 = 10$$
$$3x_1 + x_2 + x_3 = 2$$

7. Given the matrices A and b as defined below, solve the equation $[A]\{X\} = \{b\}$

$$[A] = \begin{bmatrix} 4 & 1 & 6 \\ 1 & 3 & 1 \\ 5 & 2 & 5 \end{bmatrix} \text{ and } \{b\} = \begin{Bmatrix} 20 \\ 10 \\ 24 \end{Bmatrix}$$

8. Find the inversion of the matrix M given below:

$$[M] = \begin{bmatrix} -2 & 1 & 0 \\ 1 & -2 & 1 \\ 0 & 1 & -2 \end{bmatrix}$$

9. Solve the following set of equations by the matrix inversion method.

$$\begin{bmatrix} 10 & 2 & 1 \\ 1 & 8 & 2 \\ 2 & -1 & 20 \end{bmatrix} \begin{Bmatrix} x_1 \\ x_2 \\ x_3 \end{Bmatrix} = \begin{Bmatrix} 50 \\ -4 \\ 74 \end{Bmatrix}$$

10. Given the matrix

$$[C] = \begin{bmatrix} 2 & 1 & 1 \\ 3 & 2 & 3 \\ 1 & 4 & 9 \end{bmatrix}$$

find the inverse $[C^{-1}]$ and show that $[C][C^{-1}]$ is an identity matrix.

11. For the following set of equations, determine the inverse of the coefficient matrix.

$$8x_1 + x_2 - x_3 = 8$$
$$2x_1 + x_2 + 9x_3 = 12$$
$$x_1 - 7x_2 + 3x_3 = -4$$

12. Generate the coefficient matrix $[A]$ for the following set of equations and determine its inverse also show that the product of the two matrices is an unit matrix.

$$9x_1 + 11x_2 + 2x_3$$
$$11x_1 + 16x_2 + 11x_3$$
$$7x_1 + 11x_2 + 9x_3$$

13. Determine the inverse of the matrix $A = \begin{bmatrix} 1 & 1 & 1 \\ 4 & 3 & -1 \\ 3 & 5 & 3 \end{bmatrix}$

14. Solve the system of equations $Ax = b$, where

$$A = \begin{bmatrix} 2 & 1 & 1 & -2 \\ 4 & 0 & 2 & 1 \\ 3 & 2 & 2 & 0 \\ 1 & 3 & 2 & -1 \end{bmatrix} \text{ and } b = \begin{bmatrix} -10 \\ 8 \\ 7 \\ -5 \end{bmatrix}$$

15. Solve the system of equation using Cholesky's method.

$$\begin{bmatrix} 1 & 1 & 1 \\ 4 & 3 & -1 \\ 3 & 5 & 3 \end{bmatrix} \begin{bmatrix} x_1 \\ x_2 \\ x_3 \end{bmatrix} = \begin{bmatrix} 1 \\ 0 \\ 0 \end{bmatrix}$$

16. Find the inverse of the matrix using Gauss–Jordan method

$$\begin{bmatrix} 1 & 2 & 3 \\ 2 & 4 & 1 \\ 2 & 3 & 1 \end{bmatrix}$$

17. Find the eigen value of the following matrix.

$$\begin{bmatrix} 3 & 1 & 1 \\ 1 & 4 & 2 \\ 1 & 2 & 5 \end{bmatrix}$$

18. Solve the following system of equations using the Crout's reduction technique.

$$x + 2y - z = -3$$
$$4x - 3y + 4z = 1$$
$$2x - y + z = -2$$

19. Find the eigen value and the eigen vector of the following matrix A.

$$[A] = \begin{bmatrix} 2 & 1 & 4 \\ 1 & -3 & -1 \\ 3 & -2 & 2 \end{bmatrix}$$

20. Find the dominant eigen value and the corresponding eigen vector of the matrix defined as

$$[A] = \begin{bmatrix} 3 & 1 & 1 \\ 1 & 4 & 1 \\ 2 & 1 & 2 \end{bmatrix}.$$

REFERENCES

1. Scarborough JB, *Numerical Mathematical Analysis*, 6th Edn, Oxford & IBH Publications, New Delhi, 1966.
2. Ferziger JH, *Numerical Methods for Engineering Application*, John Wiley & Sons, New York, 1981.
3. Alan Jeffry, *Mathematics for Engineers*, 2nd Edn, English Language Book Society, London, 1979.
4. Kunz KS, *Numerical Analysis*, McGraw Hill, New York, 1957.
5. Grinter LE, *Numerical Methods of Analysis in Engineering*, MacMillan Co, New York, 1949.
6. Jain MK, Iyengar SRK and Jain, RK, *Numerical Methods for Scientific and Engineering Computation*, 6th Edn, New Age International Publishers, New Delhi, 2012.
7. Rajasekaran S, *Numerical Methods in Science and Engineering – A Practical Approach*, AH Wheeler & Co. Delhi, 1986.
8. Atkinson K, *Elementary Numerical Analysis*, John Wiley & Sons, New York, 1985.
9. Sastry SS, *Introductory Methods of Numerical Analysis*, Prentice Hall India, New Delhi, 1979.
10. Wang PC, *Numerical and Matrix Methods in Structural Engineering*, McGraw Hill, New York, 1965.

REVIEW QUESTIONS

1. What are the various methods generally used for the solution of the linear system of equations?
2. Briefly outline the various steps involved in solving a set of equations using Cramer's rule or the method of determinants.
3. Narrate the method of solving simultaneous equations using the method of leading coefficients. Explain how this method is different from the method of determinants.
4. Specify the various steps involved in solving a set of equations using Gaussian elimination method.
5. What is the advantage of using Gauss–Jordan method in comparison to the Gaussian elimination method in solving a set of equations? List the various steps involved in a Gauss–Jordan method.
6. Briefly outline the concept of lower and upper triangular matrices in relation to the solution of a set of equations using factorization method.
7. Explain briefly the various steps involved in Cholesky's method of solving a set of equations.
8. Specify the various steps involved in the solution of a set of equations using Crout's method.
9. Explain the terms (a) Determinant of a matrix (b) Inverse of a matrix (c) Adjoint of a matrix and their mutual relation. How do you solve a given set of equations using matrix inversion method?

10. What are eigen value problems? Where do you encounter such problems? Explain the terms (a) Characteristic polynomial (b) Characteristic values (c) Eigen vector.

OBJECTIVE TYPE QUESTIONS

1. The solution of a linear set of simultaneous equations using Cramers' method involves
   a) the process of elimination
   b) evaluating the determinant of the coefficient matrix
   c) determining the transpose of the coefficient matrix

2. In the Gaussian elimination method of solving a set of equations
   a) the equations are expressed in the matrix form
   b) the coefficient matrix is factorized
   c) back substitution process is used

3. In solving a set of equations using the method of leading coefficients
   a) the coefficient matrix is determined
   b) the leading coefficients are reduced to unity
   c) the transpose of the coefficient matrix is determined

4. The use of Gauss–Jordan method in solving–set of simultaneous equations involves
   a) the elimination of unknowns in the equations
   b) diagonalisation of the coefficient matrix by successive row operations
   c) evaluating the determinant of the coefficient matrix

5. In using Cholesky's method for solving a set of equations
   a) the inverse of the coefficient matrix should be determined
   b) the transpose of the coefficient matrix is evaluated
   c) the coefficient matrix is expressed as a product of lower and upper triangular matrices

6. In solving a set of equations using Crout's method
   a) the leading coefficients are reduced to unit values
   b) the lower and upper triangular matrices have to be determined
   c) the coefficient matrix is to be inverted

7. Solving simultaneous equations using the matrix inversion method requires the
   a) determination of the ratio of the adjoint to the determinant of the coefficient matrix
   b) evaluation of the transpose of the coefficient matrix
   c) the coefficient matrix is factorized

8. In determining the solution of eigen value problems, we have to use the method of
   a) factorization
   b) matrix inversion
   c) characteristic polynomial

9. The eigen vectors resulting from a eigen value problem is generally represented by
   a) (3 × 3) matrix
   b) column matrix
   c) (4 × 4) matrix
10. The product of the eigen values of a given matrix is equal to the
    a) inverse of the matrix
    b) value of the determinant of the matrix
    c) transpose of the matrix

2 Solution of Linear System of Equations by Iterative Methods

2.1 GENERAL ASPECTS

Several iterative or indirect methods[1,2,3] have been developed over the years for the solution of a linear system of simultaneous equations. Generally for the system of equations with diagonally dominant mode, the iterative methods are used. For the iterative methods to accomplish rapid convergence, suitable initial values must be chosen. The most widely used iterative methods are

1. General Iteration methods
2. Jacobi Iteration or Gauss–Jacobi Iteration
3. Gauss–Seidal Iteration
4. Relaxation Method

2.2 GENERAL ITERATION METHODS

The general iterative method[4,5] for the solution of a system of linear simultaneous equations is outlined in the following steps:

$$x^{(k+1)} = Hx^k + c \quad \text{[for } k = 0, 1, 2, ...]} \tag{1}$$

where $x^{(k+1)}$ and x^k are the approximations for x at the $(k + 1)^{th}$ and k^{th} iteration respectively. H represents the iteration matrix depending on matrix A and c is a column vector. In the limiting case when $k \to \infty$, x^k converges to the exact solution.

$$x = A^{-1} b \tag{2}$$

and the iteration Eq. (1) can be represented after substitution from Eq. (2) as

$$A^{-1} b = HA^{-1} b + c \tag{3}$$

from Eq. (3), the column vector c can written as

$$c = (1 - H) A^{-1} b \tag{4}$$

The iteration process can proceed using the iteration matrix H and the column matrix c for the required number of iteration cycles.

2.3 JACOBI ITERATION OR GAUSS–JACOBI ITERATION

Consider the system of n linear algebraic equations represented as

$$a_{11}x_1 + a_{12}x_2 + ... + a_{1n}x_n = b_1$$
$$a_{21}x_1 + a_{22}x_2 + ... + a_{2n}x_n = b_2$$
$$\cdots\cdots\cdots\cdots\cdots\cdots\cdots\cdots$$
$$a_{n1}x_1 + a_{n2}x_2 + ... + a_{nn}x_n = b_n \tag{5}$$

Assuming the quantities a_{ii} in Eq. (1) are pivot elements, we can write this equation as

$$a_{11}x_1 = -a_{12}x_2 + a_{13}x_3 + \ldots + a_{1n}x_n) + b_1$$

$$a_{22}x_2 = -(a_{21}x_1 + a_{23}x_3 + \ldots + a_{2n}x_n) + b_2$$

$$\ldots\ldots\ldots\ldots\ldots\ldots\ldots\ldots\ldots\ldots\ldots$$

$$a_{nn}x_n = -(a_{n1}x_1 + a_{n2}x_2 + \ldots a_{n,n-1}x_{n-1}) + b_n \tag{6}$$

The Jacobi iteration method or Gauss–Jacobi iteration method[6,7,8] may now be defined as

$$x_1^{(k+1)} = -\frac{1}{a_{11}}\left(a_{12}x_2^{(k)} + a_{13}x_3^{(k)} + \ldots + a_{1n}x_n^{(k)} - b_1\right)$$

$$x_2^{(k+1)} = -\frac{1}{a_{22}}\left(a_{21}x_1^{(k)} + a_{23}x_3^{(k)} + \ldots + a_{2n}x_n^{(k)} - b_2\right)$$

$$\ldots\ldots\ldots\ldots\ldots\ldots\ldots\ldots\ldots\ldots\ldots\ldots\ldots\ldots\ldots\ldots$$

$$x_n^{(k+1)} = -\frac{1}{a_{nn}}\left(a_{n1}x_1^{(k)} + a_{n2}x_2^{(k)} + \ldots + a_{n,n-1}x_{n-1}^{(k)} - b_n\right)$$

where $k = 0, 1, 2, \ldots$ $\qquad\qquad$ (7)

In matrix form, the method can be expressed as

$$x^{(k+1)} = D^{-1}(L+U)x^k + D^{-1}b$$

$$= Hx^k + c, \text{ for } k = 0, 1, 2, \ldots \tag{8}$$

where $\quad H = -D^{-1}(L+U)$ and $c = D^{-1}b$

L and U are the lower and upper triangular matrices with zero diagonal entries and D is the diagonal matrix such that $A = (l + D + U)$

Equation (4) can also be expressed as

$$x^{(k+1)} = x^k - \left[I + D^{-1}(L+U)\right]x^k + D^{-1}b$$

$$= x^k - D^{-1}[D+L+U]x^k + D^{-1}b$$

$$= x^k - D^{-1}\left[b - Ax^k\right]$$

or $\qquad V^k = D^{-1}r^k$ $\qquad\qquad$ (9)

where $V^k = x^{(k+1)} - x^k$ is the error in the approximation and $r^k = \left[b - Ax^k\right]$ is the residual error vector.

Equation (5) can also be expressed as

$$DV^k = r^k$$

We can solve for V^k and find $x^{(k+1)} = x^k + V^k$

The equations mentioned above describe the Jacobi iteration procedure in an error format.

The use of Jacobi method is illustrated by the following example.

Example 2.1

Solve the following system of simultaneous equations using the Jacobi iteration method

$$4x_1 + x_2 + x_3 = 2$$
$$x_1 + 5x_2 + 2x_3 = -6$$
$$x_1 + 2x_2 + 3x_3 = -4$$

Solution

$$\begin{bmatrix} 4 & 1 & 1 \\ 1 & 5 & 2 \\ 1 & 2 & 3 \end{bmatrix} \begin{Bmatrix} x_1 \\ x_2 \\ x_3 \end{Bmatrix} = \begin{bmatrix} 2 \\ -6 \\ -4 \end{bmatrix}$$

Assuming the error format given in Eq. (9), with the initial approximation as

$x^{(0)} = [0.5, -0.5, -0.5]$ and perform the iterations in each case until convergence.

The exact solution is found to be $x_1 = 1, x_2 = -1$ and $x_3 = -1$.

Compute the lower and upper triangular matrices L and U with zero diagonals and the diagonal matrix D as shown below.

$$L = \begin{bmatrix} 0 & 0 & 0 \\ 1 & 0 & 0 \\ 1 & 2 & 0 \end{bmatrix} U = \begin{bmatrix} 0 & 1 & 1 \\ 0 & 0 & 2 \\ 0 & 0 & 0 \end{bmatrix} \text{ and } D = \begin{bmatrix} 4 & 0 & 0 \\ 0 & 5 & 0 \\ 0 & 0 & 3 \end{bmatrix}$$

$$H = -D^{-1}(L+U) = -\begin{bmatrix} 4 & 0 & 0 \\ 0 & 5 & 0 \\ 0 & 0 & 3 \end{bmatrix}^{-1} \begin{bmatrix} 0 & 1 & 1 \\ 1 & 0 & 2 \\ 1 & 2 & 0 \end{bmatrix}$$

$$= -\begin{bmatrix} 1/4 & 0 & 0 \\ 0 & 1/5 & 0 \\ 0 & 0 & 1/3 \end{bmatrix} \begin{bmatrix} 0 & 1 & 1 \\ 1 & 0 & 2 \\ 1 & 2 & 0 \end{bmatrix}$$

$$= \begin{bmatrix} 0 & -1/4 & -1/4 \\ -1/5 & 0 & -2/5 \\ -1/3 & -2/3 & 0 \end{bmatrix}$$

$$c = D^{-1}b = \begin{bmatrix} 1/4 & 0 & 0 \\ 0 & 1/5 & 0 \\ 0 & 0 & 1/3 \end{bmatrix} \begin{bmatrix} 2 \\ -6 \\ -4 \end{bmatrix} = \begin{bmatrix} 1/2 \\ -6/5 \\ -4/3 \end{bmatrix}$$

Therefore, Jacobi iteration process Eq. (1) becomes

$$x^{(k+1)} = \begin{bmatrix} 0 & -1/4 & -1/4 \\ -1/5 & 0 & -2/5 \\ -1/3 & -2/3 & 0 \end{bmatrix} x^k + \begin{bmatrix} 1/2 \\ -6/5 \\ -4/3 \end{bmatrix} \text{ for } k = 0, 1, 2, \ldots$$

Starting with $x^{(0)} = [0.5, -0.5, -0.5]^T$, we obtain

$$x^{(1)} = \begin{bmatrix} 0.75 \\ -1.1 \\ -1.1667 \end{bmatrix} \quad x^{(2)} = \begin{bmatrix} 1.0667 \\ -0.8833 \\ -0.8500 \end{bmatrix} \quad x^{(3)} = \begin{bmatrix} 0.9333 \\ -1.0733 \\ -1.1000 \end{bmatrix}$$

Alternately, we can write directly as

$$x_1^{(k+1)} = \frac{1}{4}\left[2 - x_2^{(k)} - x_3^{(k)}\right]$$

$$x_2^{(k+1)} = \frac{1}{5}\left[-6 - x_1^{(k)} - 2x_3^{(k)}\right]$$

$$x_3^{(k+1)} = \frac{1}{3}\left[-4 - x_1^{(k)} - 2x_2^{(k)}\right]$$

Starting with the initial approximation, $x_1^{(0)} = 0.5, x_2^{(0)} = -0.5, x_3^{(0)} = -0.5$, we get

$$x^{(1)} = [0.75, -1.1, -1.1667]^T$$

$$x^{(2)} = [1.0667, -0.8833, -0.8500]^T$$

$$x^{(3)} = [0.9333, -1.0733, -1.1000]^T$$

Using Eq. (9), we get for $x^{(0)} = [0.5, -0.5, -0.5]^T$

Considering

$$k = 0: \quad r^{(0)} = \left[b - Ax^{(0)}\right] = \begin{bmatrix} 2 \\ -6 \\ -4 \end{bmatrix} - \begin{bmatrix} 1 \\ -3 \\ -2 \end{bmatrix} = \begin{bmatrix} 1 \\ -3 \\ -2 \end{bmatrix}$$

$$V^{(0)} = D^{-1}r^{(0)} = \begin{bmatrix} 1/4 & 0 & 0 \\ 0 & 1/5 & 0 \\ 0 & 0 & 1/3 \end{bmatrix}\begin{bmatrix} 1 \\ -3 \\ -2 \end{bmatrix} = \begin{bmatrix} 0.25 \\ -0.6 \\ -0.6667 \end{bmatrix}$$

$$x^{(1)} = x^{(0)} + V^{(0)} = [0.75, -1.1, -1.1667]^T$$

$$k = 0: \quad r^{(1)} = \left[b - Ax^{(1)}\right] = \begin{bmatrix} 2 \\ -6 \\ -4 \end{bmatrix} - \begin{bmatrix} 0.7333 \\ -7.0834 \\ -4.9501 \end{bmatrix} = \begin{bmatrix} 1.2667 \\ 1.0834 \\ 0.9501 \end{bmatrix}$$

$$V^{(1)} = D^{-1}r^{(1)} = \begin{bmatrix} 1/4 & 0 & 0 \\ 0 & 1/5 & 0 \\ 0 & 0 & 1/3 \end{bmatrix}\begin{bmatrix} 1.2667 \\ 1.0834 \\ 0.9501 \end{bmatrix} = \begin{bmatrix} 0.3167 \\ 0.2167 \\ 0.3167 \end{bmatrix}$$

$$x^{(2)} = x^{(1)} + V^{(1)} = [1.0667, -0.8833, -0.8500]^T$$

$$k = 2: \quad r^{(2)} = \left[b - Ax^{(2)}\right] = \begin{bmatrix} 2 \\ -6 \\ -4 \end{bmatrix} - \begin{bmatrix} 2.5335 \\ -5.0498 \\ -3.2499 \end{bmatrix} = \begin{bmatrix} -0.5335 \\ -0.9502 \\ -0.7501 \end{bmatrix}$$

$$V^{(2)} = D^{-1}r^{(2)} = \begin{bmatrix} 1/4 & 0 & 0 \\ 0 & 1/5 & 0 \\ 0 & 0 & 1/3 \end{bmatrix} \begin{bmatrix} -0.5335 \\ -0.9502 \\ -0.7501 \end{bmatrix} = \begin{bmatrix} -0.1334 \\ -0.1900 \\ -0.2500 \end{bmatrix}$$

$$x^{(3)} = x^{(2)} + V^{(2)} = [0.9333, -1.0733, -1.1000]^T$$

Hence, both the techniques give the same results.

2.4 GAUSS–SEIDAL ITERATION

Gauss–Seidal iterative method[9] is an improvement over the Jacobi method in which the values of the variables are successively increased. In Gauss–Seidal method, the updated values of the variables are used instead of the values of the previous iteration. The limitation of this method is that it will converge to the correct solution only if the coefficient matrix has a strong leading diagonal. The given system of equations are rearranged for the diagonally dominant mode before starting the iteration process.

Example 2.2

Solve the following system of equations using the Gauss–Seidal iterative method.

$$5x_1 + x_2 - x_3 = 4$$
$$x_1 + 4x_2 + 2x_3 = 15$$
$$x_1 - 2x_2 + 5x_3 = 12$$

Solution

The equations are tested for the diagonally dominant mode by the following procedure.

$$|5| > |1| + |-1|$$
$$|4| > |1| + |2|$$
$$|5| > |1| + |-2|$$

Since the system is diagonally dominant, the iterative method can be used. The equations are rewritten in the following form:

$$x_1 = 0.8 - 0.2 x_2 + 0.2x_3 \qquad (1)$$
$$x_2 = 3.75 - 0.25 x_1 - 0.5x_3 \qquad (2)$$
$$x_3 = 2.4 - 0.2 x_1 + 0.4x_2 \qquad (3)$$

$x_i = 1$ for $i = 1, 2, 3$

From Eq. (1) $x_2 = 1$

$x_3 = 1$, therefore $x_1 = 0.8$

Eq. (2) $x_1 = 0.8$

$x_3 = 1.0$, therefore $x_2 = [3.75 - (0.25 \times 0.8) - (0.5 \times 1)] = 3.05$

Eq. (3) $x_1 = 0.8$

$x_2 = 3.05$, therefore $x_3 = [2.4 - (0.2 \times 0.8) + (0.4 \times 3.05)] = 3.46$

After the first iteration, the values of the variables:

$$x_1 = 0.8 \qquad x_2 = 3.05 \qquad x_3 = 3.46$$

In the second iteration, these values are used as initial values and a new set of values are obtained.

From Eq. (1) $x_2 = 3.05$

$x_3 = 3.46$, therefore $x_1 = [0.8 - (0.2 \times 3.05) + (0.2 \times 3.46)] = 0.882$

Eq. (2) $x_1 = 0.882$

$x_3 = 3.46$, therefore $x_2 = [3.75 - (0.25 \times 0.882) - (0.5 \times 3.46)] = 1.7995$

Eq. (3) $x_1 = 0.882$

$x_2 = 1.7995$, therefore $x_3 = [2.4 - (0.2 \times 0.882) + (0.4 \times 1.7995)] = 2.934$

The iterative procedure is repeated each time with updated values of the variables until the convergence is reached. Table 2.1 shows the number of iterations required for convergence and the final values.

Table 2.1: Gauss–Seidal iteration table

Iteration number	Values of variables		
	x_1	x_2	x_3
0	1.0	1.0	1.0
1	0.8	3.05	3.46
2	0.882	1.7995	2.934
3	1.0288	2.0211	3.0026
4	0.9963	1.9996	3.0005
5	1.0002	1.9997	2.9999
6	1.00	2.00	3.00

Example 2.3

Using Gauss–Seidal method, solve the following set of equations.

$$x_1 + 8x_2 + x_3 = 10$$
$$x_1 + x_2 + 7x_3 = 9$$
$$9x_1 + x_2 + x_3 = 11$$

Solution

The equations are arranged to exhibit the diagonally dominant mode for fast convergence. Hence, we have,

$$9x_1 + x_2 + x_3 = 11 \tag{1}$$
$$x_1 + 8x_2 + x_3 = 10 \tag{2}$$
$$x_1 + x_2 + 7x_3 = 9 \tag{3}$$

From Eq. (1)
$$9x_1 = 11 - x_2 - x_3$$
$$x_1 = 1.222 - 0.111x_2 - 0.111x_3 \tag{4}$$

Eq. (2)
$$8x_2 = 10 - x_1 - x_3$$
$$x_2 = 1.25 - 0.125x_1 - 0.125x_3 \tag{5}$$

Eq. (3)
$$7x_3 = 9 - x_1 - x_2$$
$$x_3 = 1.285 - 0.143x_1 - 0.143x_2 \tag{6}$$

The rearranged equations are

$$x_1 = 1.222 - 0.111x_2 - 0.111x_3$$
$$x_2 = 1.25 - 0.125x_1 - 0.125x_3$$
$$x_3 = 1.285 - 0.143x_1 - 0.143x_2$$

Iteration 1

$$x_2 = 0, x_3 = 0$$
$$x_1 = 1.222 - 0 - 0$$
$$x_2 = 1.25 - 0.125(1.222) - 0 = 1.097$$
$$x_3 = 1.285 - 0.143(1.222) - 0.143(1.097) = 0.953$$

Iteration 2

$$x_1 = 1.222, x_2 = 1.097, x_3 = 0.953$$
$$x_1 = 1.222 - 0.111(1.097) - 0.111(0.953) = 0.994$$
$$x_2 = 1.25 - 0.125(0.994) - 0.125(0.953) = 1.0066$$
$$x_3 = 1.285 - 0.143(0.994) - 0.143(1.0066) = 0.9998$$

Iteration 3

$$x_2 = 1.0066, x_3 = 0.9998$$
$$x_1 = 1.222 - 0.111(1.0066) - 0.111(0.9998) = 1$$
$$x_2 = 1.25 - 0.1259(1) - 0.125(0.9998) = 1$$
$$x_3 = 1.285 - 0.1439(1) - 0.143(0.9988) = 1$$

Hence we have the final values as $x_1 = x_2 = x_3 = 1$

Example 2.4

Solve the following set of equations using Gauss–Seidal method, using the first three iterations.

$$8x_1 + 2x_2 + 3x_3 = 30 \tag{1}$$
$$x_1 - 9x_2 + 2x_3 = 1 \tag{2}$$
$$2x_1 + 3x_2 + 6x_3 = 31 \tag{3}$$

Solution

The equations satisfy the criterion of diagonally dominant mode for faster convergence. The equations are rewritten in the form

$$x_1 = 3.75 - 0.25x_2 - 0.375x_3$$
$$x_2 = -0.11 + 0.11x_1 + 0.222x_3$$
$$x_3 = 5.16 - 0.33x_1 - 0.5x_2$$

Iteration 1

$$x_2 = 1, x_3 = 1$$
$$x_1 = 3.75 - 0.25(1) - 0.375(1) = 3.125$$
$$x_2 = -0.11 + 0.11(3.125) + 0.222(1) = 0.455$$
$$x_3 = 5.16 - 0.33(3.125) -) - 0.5(0.455) = 3.91$$

Iteration 2

$$x_2 = 0.455, x_3 = 3.91$$
$$x_1 = 3.75 - 0.25(0.455) - 0.375(3.91) = 2.171$$
$$x_2 = -0.11 + 0.11(2.171) + 0.222(3.91) = 0.988$$
$$x_3 = 5.16 - 0.33(2.171) - 0.5(0.988) = 3.95$$

Iteration 3

$$x_2 = 0.988, x_3 = 3.95$$
$$x_1 = 3.75 - 0.25(0.988) - 0.375(3.95) = 2.02$$
$$x_2 = -0.11 + 0.11(2.02) + 0.222(3.95) = 0.988$$
$$x_3 = 5.16 - 0.33(2.02) - 0.5(0.988) = 4.0$$

After three iterations, the values of the variables are

$$x_1 = 2.02$$

$$x_2 = 0.988$$

$$x_3 = 4.000$$

2.5 RELAXATION METHOD

This method was developed by Sir Richard Southwell, (1935) and was used for estimating the stresses and deflections of pin jointed framed structures by successive approximations. As the relaxation method developed, it was considered as a systematic procedure for solving a set of simultaneous linear equations. The relaxation method is also used in the solution of frames by moment distribution developed by Hardy Cross.[10]

Consider the following system of linear simultaneous equations:

$$a_{11}x_1 + a_{12}x_2 + a_{13}x_3 \div \ldots + a_{1n}x_n = b_1$$

$$a_{21}x_1 + a_{22}x_2 + a_{23}x_3 \div \ldots + a_{2n}x_n = b_2$$

$$a_{31}x_1 + a_{32}x_2 + a_{33}x_3 \div \ldots + a_{3n}x_n = b_3$$

$$\ldots\ldots\ldots\ldots\ldots\ldots\ldots\ldots\ldots\ldots\ldots\ldots\ldots\ldots\ldots\ldots$$

$$a_{n1}x_1 + a_{n2}x_2 + a_{n3}x_3 \div \ldots + a_{nn}x_n = b_n$$

In the first approximation, we consider only the diagonal terms and constants.

$$a_{11}x_1^1 = b_1, \text{ therefore } x_1^1 = \left(\frac{b_1}{a_{11}}\right)$$

$$a_{22}x_2^1 = b_2, \text{ therefore } x_2^1 = \left(\frac{b_2}{a_{22}}\right)$$

$$\ldots\ldots\ldots\ldots\ldots\ldots\ldots\ldots\ldots\ldots\ldots\ldots\ldots\ldots\ldots$$

$$a_{nn}x_3^1 = b_n, \text{ therefore } x_1^1 = \left(\frac{b_n}{a_{nn}}\right)$$

The values of $x_1, x_2, x_3, \ldots, x_n$ evaluated above are substituted in the given set of equations and the residuals are calculated from

$$R_i^1 = a_{i1}x_1^1 + a_{i2}x_2^1 + a_{i3}x_3^1 + \ldots + a_{in}x_n^1 - b_i$$

where $i = 1, 2, 3, \ldots\ldots, n$ represents the number of equations. These residuals are subtracted from RHS of equations yielding

$$a_{ii}x_i^2 = b_i - R_i^1$$

From this expression, the second approximation of x_i are obtained as

$$x_i^2 = \left(\frac{b_i - R_i^1}{a_{ii}}\right)$$

Using these values, new residuals are calculated from

$$R_i^2 = a_{i1}x_1^2 + a_{i2}x_2^2 + a_{i3}x_3^2 + \ldots + a_{in}x_n^2 - b_i$$

The third set of approximations are obtained as

$$x_i^3 = \left(\frac{b_i - R_i^2}{a_{ii}}\right)$$

The cycle of operations are repeated until the required convergence is reached. The application of the relaxation method for solving linear simultaneous equations is illustrated by the following examples.

Example 2.5

Solve the following system of equations by relaxation method.

$$50x_1 + 2x_2 - 3x_3 = 196 \tag{1}$$
$$3x_1 + 65x_2 + 2x_3 = 81 \tag{2}$$
$$-x_1 + x_2 + 33x_3 = 63 \tag{3}$$

Solution

Checking for the diagonally dominant mode, we have

$$|50| > |2| + |-3|$$
$$|65| > |3| + |2|$$
$$|33| > |-1| + |1|$$

Hence convergence is faster.
As a first approximation, we have

$$50x_1 = 196 \text{, therefore } x_1 = 3.92$$
$$65x_2 = 81 \qquad\qquad x_2 = 1.246$$
$$33x_3 = 63 \qquad\qquad x^3 = 1.909$$

Calculation of resultants

From Eq. (1)

$$R_i^1 = \left[(50 \times 3.92) + (2 \times 1.246) + (-3 \times 1.909) - 196\right] = -3.235$$

Eq. (2)

$$R_i^1 = \left[(3 \times 3.92) + (65 \times 1.246) + (2 \times 1.909) - 81\right] = 15.568$$

Eq. (3)

$$R_i^1 = \left[(-3.92) + (1.246) + (33 \times 1.909) - 63\right] = -2.667$$

Therefore, the second approximate values are

$$a_{ii}x_i^2 = b_i - R_i^1$$

or $\qquad 50x_1 = [196 - 3.235)$, hence $x_1 = 3.9847$

$$\text{Increment} = -\left(\frac{R_i^1}{a_{ii}}\right) = -\left(\frac{-3.235}{50}\right) = 0.0647$$

Also $65x_2 = (81 - 15.568)$, hence $x_2 = 1.006$

$\therefore$ increment $= -\left(\dfrac{15.568}{65}\right) = -0.2395$

$33 x_3 = [63 - 2.677)$, hence $x_3 = 1.990$

or increment $= -\left(\dfrac{-2.677}{33}\right) = 0.0811$

The process is repeated with new values of x_1, x_2 and x_3 and the revised residuals R_i^2 and so the corresponding increments determined.

The whole procedure is shown in Tables 2.2 and 2.3.

Table 2.2: Constants and residuals

a_{ii}	b_{ii}	R_i^1	R_i^2	R_i^3
50	196	−3.235	−0.7233	–
65	81	15.568	0.3243	–
33	63	−2.677	−0.3054	–

Table 2.3: Values of unknowns

x_1	x_2	x_3	Remarks
3.92	1.246	1.909	Basic values
0.0647	0.2395	0.0811	First increment $= -\left(\dfrac{R_i^1}{a_{ii}}\right)$
0.0144	0.005	0.0092	Second increment $= -\left(\dfrac{R_i^2}{a_{ii}}\right)$
4.000	1.000	2.000	Final values

Therefore $x_1 = 4.00$ $x_2 = 1.000$ $x_3 = 2.000$

Example 2.6

Using relaxation technique solve the following set of equations.

$$10x - 2y - 2z = -6$$
$$-x + 10y - z = -7$$
$$-x - y + 10z = -8$$

Solution

Checking for the diagonally dominant mode, we have

$$|10| > |-2| + |-2|$$
$$|10| > |-1| + |-1|$$
$$|10| > |-1| + |-1|$$

For the first approximation, we have

$$10x = -6 \text{ or } x = -0.6$$
$$10y = -7 \text{ or } y = -0.7$$
$$10z = -8 \text{ or } z = -0.8$$

The residuals are calculated using the first approximation values of x, y, and z in the three equations. Using the first residual, the second approximation values of the variables are computed. The procedure is repeated until a desirable convergence is achieved. The values obtained are compiled in Tables 2.4 and 2.5.

Table 2.4: Constants and residuals

a_{ii}	b_{ii}	R_i^1	R_i^2	R_i^3
10	− 6	3	0.54	0.174
10	− 7	1.4	0.43	0.098
10	− 8	1.3	0.44	0.097

Table 2.5: Values of unknowns

x	y	z	Remarks
− 0.6	− 0.7	− 0.8	Basic values
− 0.3	− 0.14	− 0.13	First increment
− 0.054	− 0.043	− 0.044	Second increment
− 0.0174	− 0.0098	− 0.0097	Third increment
− 0.9714	− 0.8928	− 0.9837	Final values

The final values of the variables are $x = -0.9714$ $y = -0.8928$ $z = -0.9837$

2.3.1 Over-relaxation and Under-relaxation

In relaxation method, the residuals are gradually reduced to zero in subsequent steps. In some cases, when the largest residual is reduced to zero, we may over relax it to less than zero so that when the other residuals are relaxed, the last reduced residual (which was made negative) will come back closer to zero. The process of relaxation will be shortened by the procedure of over-relaxation.

Alternatively, if by reducing one residual, the other residuals are also reduced, then under-relaxation may be used advantageously for faster convergence.

2.3.2 Block Relaxation

If the changes occured in all variables at a time, the operation is called *block relaxation*. In this process, the values of Δx_1, Δx_2, and Δx_3, ..., are all changed by the same amount and this will influence the values of the residuals ΔR_1, ΔR_2, and ΔR_3, etc.

2.3.3 Group Relaxation

In this technique, the unknowns are changed by different amounts at the same time to effect desirable changes in residuals.

2.3.4 Proportional Relaxation

After steps of relaxation, we may observe that the total change of each residual follows a certain pattern. If we proportion the total changes by a ratio and add on the previous changes, the residuals will be in favorable condition. This technique of applying a proportional amount of the total change in several relaxation steps is called *proportional relaxation*.

Example 2.7

Solve the following set of equations using the basic, block and group relaxation techniques.

$$2x_1 + y = -0.25$$
$$x_1 - 2y + z = -0.50$$
$$y - 2z = -0.75$$

Solution

The equations are written in the following form:

$$-2x_1 + y + 0.25 = R_1 = 0$$
$$x_1 - 2y + z + 0.50 = R_2 = 0$$
$$y - 2z + 0.75 = R_3 = 0$$

The operation tables with the values of the residuals, ΔR_1, ΔR_2, and ΔR_3 and values of variables Δx, Δy, and Δz are shown in Tables 2.6 and 2.7

Table 2.6: Operation table

Sl No	Values of variables	R_1	R_2	R_3
1.	Basic $\Delta x = 1$	-2	1	0
	$\Delta y = 1$	1	-2	1
	$\Delta z = 1$	0	1	-2
2.	Block relaxation			
	$\Delta x = \Delta y = \Delta z = 1$	-1	0	-1
3.	Group relaxation			
	$\Delta x = 1$			
	$\Delta y = 2$	0	0	-4
	$\Delta z = 3$			
4.	Block relaxation			
	$\Delta x = \Delta z = 1$	-2	2	-2

Table 2.7: Relaxation table

		x	y	z	R_1	R_2	R_3
	Initial	0	0	0	0.25	0.50	0.75
	Group (3) × 0.125	0.125	0.25	0.375	0.25	0.50	0.25
5.	Basic: (Δy × 0.25)	–	0.25	–	0.50	0	0.25
6.	Block (4) × 0.25	0.25	–	0.25	0	0.50	0
	Basic: (Δy × 0.25)	–	0.25	0	0.25	0	0.25
	Proportional						
	[(5) + (6)] × block						
	relaxation (2)	0.25	0.25	0.25	0	0	0
	Final values	0.625	1.00	0.875	0	0	
	Therefore	$x = 0.625,$	$y = 1.000,$	$z = 0.875$			

2.3.5 Analysis of Frameworks by Relaxation Method

Structural frameworks like continuous beams, portal frames, etc. can be easily solved by moment distribution procedure developed by Hardy Cross[10]. The moment distribution method may be considered as a variation of relaxation procedure by which the results are obtained by successive approximations. In solving the moments developed in frameworks subjected to external loads the following stepwise procedure based on the principle of relaxation can be adopted.

   i. The joints of the frame are assumed to be fixed.

   ii. Fixed end moments developed at the joints due to the type of loading are computed.

   iii. The stiffness factor and distribution factors are computed for each joint.

   iv. Unbalanced moments at the interior joints are distributed in proportion to the distribution factor at the joint.

   v. The distributed moments are carried over to the far ends according to the carryover factor.

   vi. The process of distribution and carryover are repeated until all the joints have zero or tolerably small residual moments.

   vii. The summation of all the moments at each joint gives the final moments.

The fixed end moments for four most common types of problems encountered in structural frameworks are compiled in Fig. 2.1.

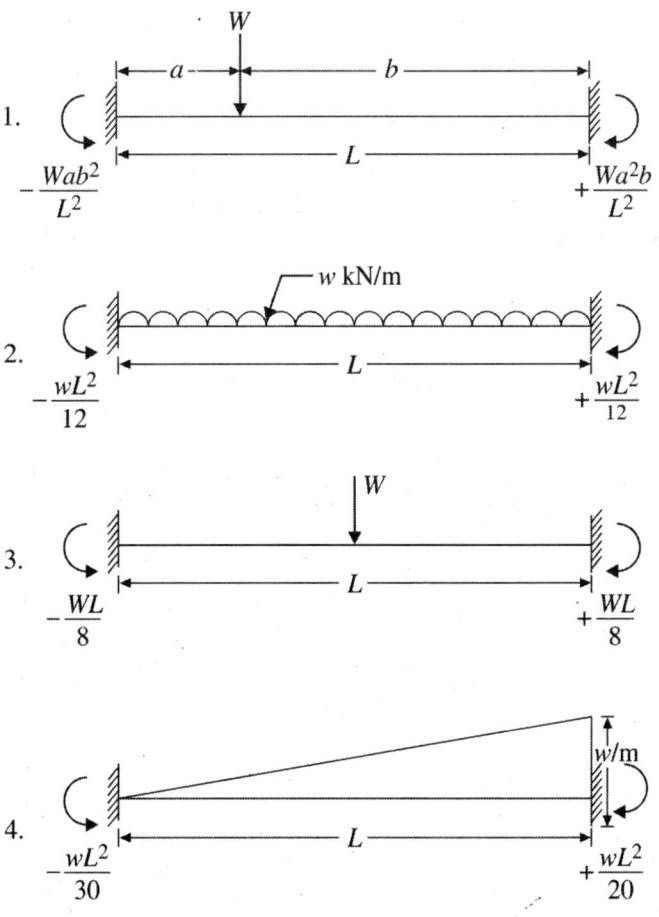

Fig. 2.1: Fixed beams with end moments

The application of modified relaxation method (moment distribution procedure) is illustrated by the following examples.

Example 2.8

Solve the given portal frame shown in Fig. 2.2 for fixed end moments using the moment distribution procedure.

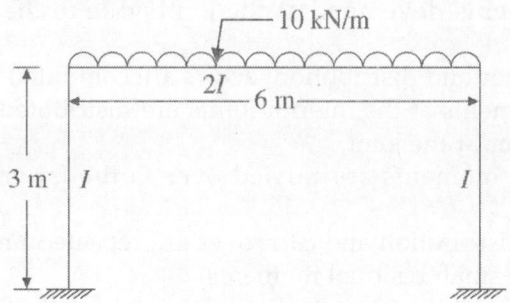

Fig. 2.2: Portal frame

Solution

The stiffness factors of the members AB, BC and CD are computed as

$$L_{AB} = L_{CD} = 3 \text{ m} \quad \text{and} \quad L_{BC} = 6 \text{ m}$$

$$k_{AB} = k_{CD} = \left[\frac{I}{L}\right] = \left[\frac{I}{3}\right] \quad \text{and} \quad k_{BC} = \left[\frac{I}{L}\right] = \left[\frac{2I}{6}\right] = \left[\frac{I}{3}\right]$$

The distribution factors are computed as

$$d_{BA} = d_{BC} = d_{CB} = d_{CD} = \frac{\dfrac{I}{3}}{\left[\left(\dfrac{I}{3}\right) + \left(\dfrac{I}{3}\right)\right]} = 0.5$$

Fixed end moment at B and C = $M_{FBC} = M_{FCB} = \left(\dfrac{wL^2}{12}\right) = \left(\dfrac{10 \times 6^2}{12}\right) = 30 \text{ kN} \cdot \text{m}$

The moment distribution is carried out as shown in Table 2.8.

Table 2.8: Moment distribution

A		B				C			D
		0.5	0.5			0.5	0.5		
			−30			+30			
	+7.5 ←	+15	+15			−15	−15 → −7.5		
			−7.5			+7.5			
	+1.875 ←	+3.75	+3.75 ←		→	−3.75	−3.75 → −1.875		
			−1.875			+1.875			
	+0.465 ←	+0.935	+0.935 ←		→	−0.935	−0.935 → −0.465		
	+9.845	−19.69	−19.69			+19.69	−19.69 → −9.845		

The resulting moments at A, B, C and D are

$$M_A = M_D = 9.845 \text{ kN} \cdot \text{m}$$
$$M_B = M_C = 19.69 \text{ kN} \cdot \text{m}$$

Example 2.9

Analyse the given continuous beam shown in Fig. 2.3 continuous beam for moments using the relaxation procedure.

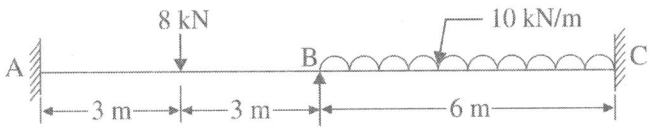

Fig. 2.3: Continuous beam

Solution

Stiffness factors:
$$k_{AB} = k_{BC} = \left[\frac{I}{L}\right] = \left[\frac{I}{6}\right]$$

Distribution factors:
$$d_{BA} = d_{BC} = \left[\frac{I/6}{\left[\left(\dfrac{I}{6}\right) + \left(\dfrac{I}{6}\right)\right]}\right] = 0.5$$

Fixed end moments:
$$M_{FAB} = \left(\frac{8 \times 6}{8}\right) = 6 \ \text{kN} \cdot \text{m}$$

$$M_{FBC} = \left(\frac{10 \times 6^2}{12}\right) = 30 \ \text{kN} \cdot \text{m}$$

The moment distribution is carried out as shown in Table 2.9.

Table 2.9: Moment distribution

A		B			C
		0.5	0.5		
− 6		+ 6	− 30		+ 30
+ 6 ◄		+ 12	+ 12		► + 6
0		+ 18	− 18		+ 36

The final moments at A, B and C are
$$M_A = 0 \ \text{kN} \cdot \text{m}$$
$$M_B = 18 \ \text{kN} \cdot \text{m}$$
$$M_C = 36 \ \text{kN} \cdot \text{m}$$

EXERCISES

1. Solve the following system of linear simultaneous equations using the Jacobi iteration method.

$$4x_1 + x_2 + x_3 = 2$$
$$x_1 + 5x_2 + 2x_3 = -6$$
$$x_1 + 2x_2 + 3x_3 = -4$$

2. Solve the following set of equations using Gauss–Seidal procedure.

$$4x_1 + 3x_2 + 6x_3 = 13$$
$$2x_1 - 4x_2 + x_3 = 8$$
$$3x_1 - 2x_2 + 6x_3 = 17$$

3. Carry out the three iterations of the Gauss–Seidal method for the following set of equations.

$$8x_1 + 2x_2 + 3x_3 = 30$$
$$x_1 - 9x_2 + 2x_3 = 1$$
$$2x_1 + 3x_2 + 6x_3 = 31$$

4. Using the Gauss–Seidal method, solve the following set of equations.

$$1x + 2y + 4z = 6$$
$$3x + y + 2z = 5$$
$$2x + 4y + z = 4$$

5. Solve the following set of equations using the Jacobi iteration procedure.

$$\begin{bmatrix} 4 & 1 & 0 & 1 \\ 1 & 4 & 1 & 0 \\ 0 & 1 & 4 & 1 \\ 1 & 0 & 1 & 4 \end{bmatrix} \begin{Bmatrix} x_1 \\ x_2 \\ x_3 \\ x_4 \end{Bmatrix} = \begin{Bmatrix} 2 \\ -2 \\ 2 \\ -2 \end{Bmatrix}$$

6. Solve the following set of equations using the Jacobi and Gauss–Seidal methods.

$$\begin{bmatrix} 4 & 0 & 2 \\ 0 & 5 & 2 \\ 5 & 4 & 10 \end{bmatrix} \begin{Bmatrix} x_1 \\ x_2 \\ x_3 \end{Bmatrix} = \begin{bmatrix} 4 \\ -3 \\ 2 \end{bmatrix}$$

7. Solve the following set of equations by the relaxation procedure.

$$3x + y + z = 13$$
$$x + 2y - z = 7$$
$$x + y + 4z = 18$$

8. Solve the following system of linear simultaneous equations by relaxation techniques.

$$4x_1 + 3x_2 + 6x_3 = 13$$
$$2x_1 - 4x_2 + x_3 = 8$$
$$3x_1 - 2x_2 + 6x_3 = 17$$

9. Analyze the continuous beam shown in Fig. 2.4 for moments using the relaxation moment distribution procedure.

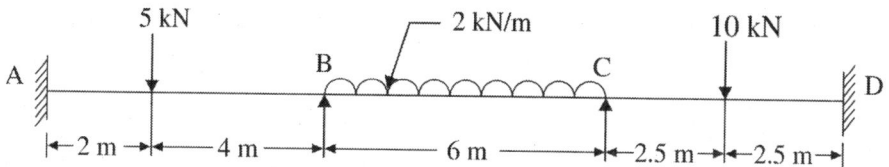

Fig. 2.4: Three span continuous beam

10. Find the moments at the joints of the rigid portal frame shown in Fig. 2.5 using the moment distribution procedure.

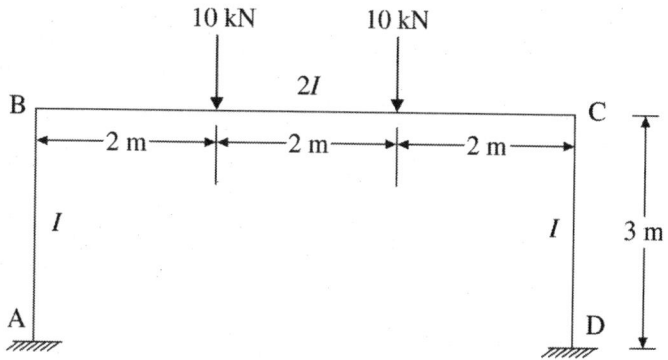

Fig. 2.5: Portal frame

REFERENCES

1. Dahlquist G and Bjorck A, *Numerical Methods*, Prentice Hall, Englewood Cliffs, New Jersey, 1974.

2. Grinter LE, *Numerical Methods of Analysis in Engineering*, McMillan Co, New York, 1949.

3. Atkinson K, *Elementary Numerical Analysis*, Wiley, New York, 1985.

4. Jain MK, Iyengar. SRK and Jain, RK, *Numerical Methods for Scientific and Engineering Computation*, 6th Edn, New Age International Publishers, New Delhi, 2012.

5. Gerald CF and Wheatley PO, *Applied Numerical Analysis*, 4th Edn, Addison Wesley, Reading, Mas, 1989.

6. Ralston A and Rabinowitz P, *A First Course in Numerical Analysis*, 2nd Edn, McGraw Hill, New York, 1978.

7. Sastry SS, *Introductory Methods of Numerical Analysis*, Prentice Hall, India, New Delhi, 1979.

8. Rajasekaran S, *Numerical Methods in Science and Engineering – A Practical Approach*, AH Wheeler and Co, New Delhi, 1986.

9. Yakowitz Sidney and Ference Szidarovszky, *An Introduction to Numerical Computations*, MacMillan Publishing Company, New York, 1986.

10. Reddy CS, *Basic Structural Analysis*, Tata McGraw Hill Publishing Co. Ltd, New Delhi, 1981.

REVIEW QUESTIONS

1. What are the various iterative methods of solving a system of linear simultaneous equations? List them in the order of their development.
2. Discuss briefly the principle of general iterative methods. What is iteration matrix?
3. Explain briefly Jacobi method of solving linear simultaneous equations.
4. Explain the terms
   a) upper and lower triangular matrices
   b) error format and
   c) zero diagonal matrix with reference to the Jacobi iteration procedure.
5. Explain the method of Gauss–Seidal iteration for solving the linear system of simultaneous equations.
6. In what way the Gauss–Seidal method is considered as an improvement over the Jacobi method in solving simultaneous equations?
7. Briefly explain the principle of relaxation methods and their application to the solution of linear simultaneous equations.
8. Explain the terms
   a) over and under-relaxation
   b) block relaxation
   c) group relaxation
   d) proportional relaxation.
9. Explain the terms
   a) constants
   b) residuals
   c) variables with reference to the relaxation methods.
10. Explain briefly the method of analyzing structural frameworks by relaxation method.

OBJECTIVE TYPE QUESTIONS

1. In solving equations using iterative methods
   a) iterative methods are faster
   b) direct methods are faster
   c) both consume the same time
2. Iterative methods are suitable for solving simultaneous equations
   a) of all types
   b) with a diagonally dominant mode
   c) with coefficient matrix without a strong leading diagonal
3. Jacobi iteration process involves the use of
   a) unit matrices
   b) symmetric matrices
   c) lower and upper triangular matrices with zero diagonal
4. In Jacobi iteration method of solving equations
   a) the values of the variables are successively increased
   b) updated values of the variables are used
   c) identity matrix is used

5. Gauss–Seidal method can be considered as
   a) an improvement over the Jacobi method
   b) an independent method
   c) a direct method
6. Relaxation methods converge faster for
   a) all types of equations
   b) equations with diagonally dominant mode
   c) analyzing structural frames
7. The process of relaxation is shortened by the procedure of
   a) back substitution
   b) over relaxation
   c) group relaxation
8. It all the variables are changed at a time, the relaxation procedure is termed as
   a) proportional relaxation
   b) group relaxation
   c) block relaxation
9. In analyzing frames by the relaxation method, the unbalanced moment at any joint is
   a) distributed equally between the adjacent members
   b) distributed in proportion to the distribution factor
   c) distributed to the member with the longer span length
10. The distributed moments are carried over to the far ends according to the
   a) distribution factor
   b) stiffness factor
   c) carry over factor

3

Solution of Nonlinear Equations

3.1 GENERAL ASPECTS

Many engineering problems involve the determination of the solution of nonlinear algebraic equations[1,2] of the polynomial form expressed as

$$f(x) = ax^n + bx^{n-1} + cx^{n-2} + d = 0$$

In problems involving the design of reinforced concrete sections,[3,4] it becomes necessary to solve quadratic equations of the type

$$ax^2 + bx + c = 0$$

Direct method gives the exact value of the roots expressed as

$$x = \frac{-b \pm \sqrt{b^2 - 4ac}}{2a}$$

Problems involving trigonometric functions are generally termed as *transcendental equations.*

Common examples of such equations are

$$x = \tan x$$
$$x \cdot \sin x = 1.0$$
$$x \log_{10} x = 1.2$$
$$a + \tan x = K$$
$$x^2 \cos x = K$$

Several methods have been developed to solve nonlinear algebraic and transcendental equations.[5,6] Some of the more prominent and widely used methods are outlined in the following sections.

3.2 GRAPHICAL METHOD

Consider the case of a function $f(x)$, defined between the intervals and and having opposite signs for $f(a)$ and $f(b)$. For such a function, there exists a real root between the two intervals. The function with the intervals and the root is graphically represented as shown in Fig. 3.1.

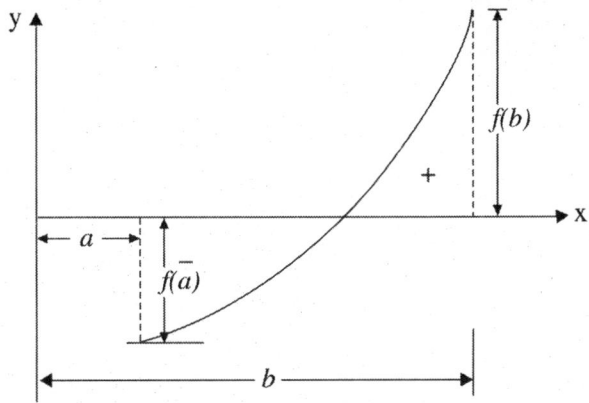

Fig. 3.1: Graphical determination of roots

Example 3.1

Find graphically the approximate value of a real root of the equation $2x - \log_{10} x = 7$

Solution

Rearranging the equation, we have

$$\log_{10} x = 2x - 7$$

The two functions $y_1 = \log_{10} x$ and $y_2 = 2x - 7$ are plotted on a graph sheet for different values of $x = 1, 2, 3, 4, \ldots$, as shown in Fig. 3.2. The intersections of the functions y_1 and y_2 will give the root of the equation. The values used to plot the two functions of y_1 and y_2 are listed in Table 3.1.

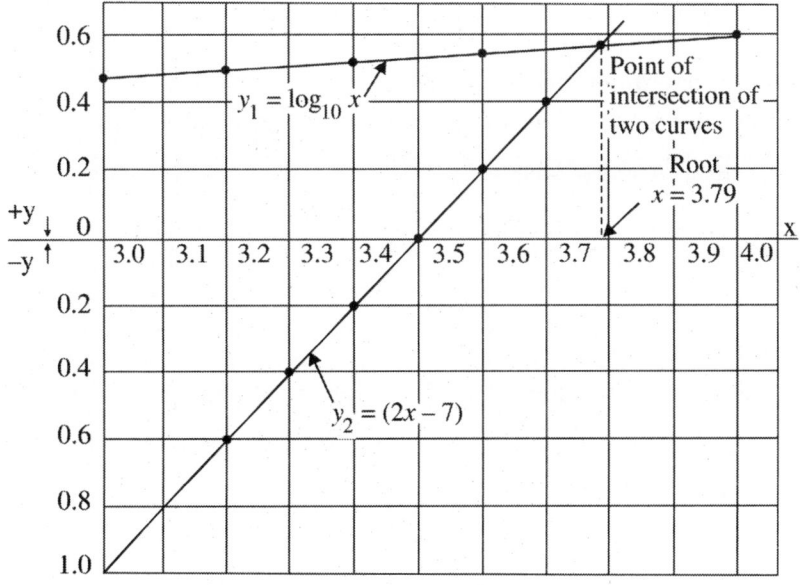

Fig. 3.2: Graphical method of finding roots

Table 3.1: Values of y_1 and y_2 for integral values of x

x	y_1	y_2
1	0	−5
2	0.301	−3
3	0.477	−1
4	0.602	+1

Table 3.1 indicates that the root must lie between 3 and 4. Table 3.2 gives the values of y_1 and y_2 for smaller intervals of x. Interpolating the approximate value of the root is 3.79.

Table 3.2: Values of y_1 and y_2 for specific integral values of x

x	y_1	y_2
3	0.477	−1
3.1	0.491	−0.8
3.2	0.505	−0.6
3.3	0.518	−0.4
3.5	0.544	0
3.6	0.556	0.2
3.7	0.568	0.4 ⎫ Root lies between
3.8	0.579	0.6 ⎭ these two values
3.9	0.591	0.8
4.0	0.602	1.0

Example 3.2

Evaluate the two smallest positive roots of the following equations to three significant figures.

(a) $e^x = 3x$ (b) $\sin x = \left(\dfrac{x}{2}\right)$

Solution

(a) For the exponential function, let and $y_1 = e^x$ and $y_2 = 3x$

Table 3.3 shows the values of y_1 and y_2 for integral values of x.

Table 3.3: Values of y_1 and y_2 for integral values of x

x	y_1	y_2
0	1.000	0
1	2.718	3
2	7.389	6

The root lies between 0 and 1

Table 3.4 shows the values of y_1 and y_2 for specific integral values of x.

Table 3.4: Values of y_1 and y_2 for specific integral values of x

x	y_1	y_2
0	1.000	0
0.1	1.105	0.3
0.2	1.221	0.6
0.3	1.350	0.9
0.4	1.492	1.2
0.5	1.648	1.5
0.6	1.822	1.8

Contd...

x	y_1	y_2
0.61	1.840	1.83
0.615	1.849	1.845
0.620	1.858	1.860

Interpolating, the real root of the equation $e^x = 3x$ is 0.618

(b) For the exponential function, $\sin x = \left(\dfrac{x}{2}\right)$ let $y_1 = \sin x$ and $y_2 = \left(\dfrac{x}{2}\right)$

Table 3.5 shows the values of y_1 and y_2 for integral values of x.

Table 3.5: Values of y_1 and y_2 for integral values of x

x	y_1	y_2
0	0	0
1	0.8414	0.5
2	0.9090	1.5

The root lies between 1 and 2

Table 3.6 shows the values of y_1 and y_2 for specific values of $\sin x$ and $(x/2)$.

Table 3.6: Values of $\sin x$ and $(x/2)$ for various values of x

x	$\sin x$	$(x/2)$
1.0	0.8414	0.5
1.2	0.9320	0.6
1.6	0.9995	0.8
1.8	0.9738	0.9
1.9	0.9463	0.95

The root lies between 1.8 and 1.9.

Table 3.7 shows the values of $\sin x$ and $(x/2)$ for various values of x between 1.8 and 1.9.

Table 3.7: Values of $\sin x$ and $(x/2)$ for various values of x

x	$\sin x$	$(x/2)$
1.85	0.9612	0.925
1.86	0.9580	0.930
1.87	0.9550	0.935
1.88	0.9525	0.940
1.889	0.9490	0.945

The real root of the equation $\text{six } n = \left(\dfrac{x}{2}\right)$ is 1.889.

Example 3.3

Find the approximate value of the smallest root of the following equations.

(a) $x \cdot \tan x = 1.0$ (b) $x - \tan x = 0$

Solution

(a) Considering the equation $(x \cdot \tan x) = 1.0$, therefore $x = (1/\tan x) = \cot x$

Table 3.8 lists the values of $(1/\tan x)$ for various values of x.

Table 3.8: Values of $(1/\tan x)$ for various values of x

x	$(1/\tan x)$	
0	∞	
1	0.642	The root lies between 0 and 1
2	0.45	

(b) Also $(x - \tan x) = 0$, therefore $x = \tan x$ (Table 3.9)

Table 3.9: Values of $(1/\tan x)$ and $\tan x$ for various values of x

x	$(1/\tan x)$	$\tan x$
0	∞	0
0.1	0.966	0.1
0.2	4.933	0.2027
0.3	3.232	0.3093
0.4	2.365	0.4220
0.5	1.830	0.5460
0.6	1.4616	0.6840
0.7	1.1872	0.8420
0.8	0.9712	1.0296
0.9	0.7935	1.2600
1.0	0.6420	1.5570

The values of the two equations are plotted in Fig. 3.3 alongwith the roots of the given equations.

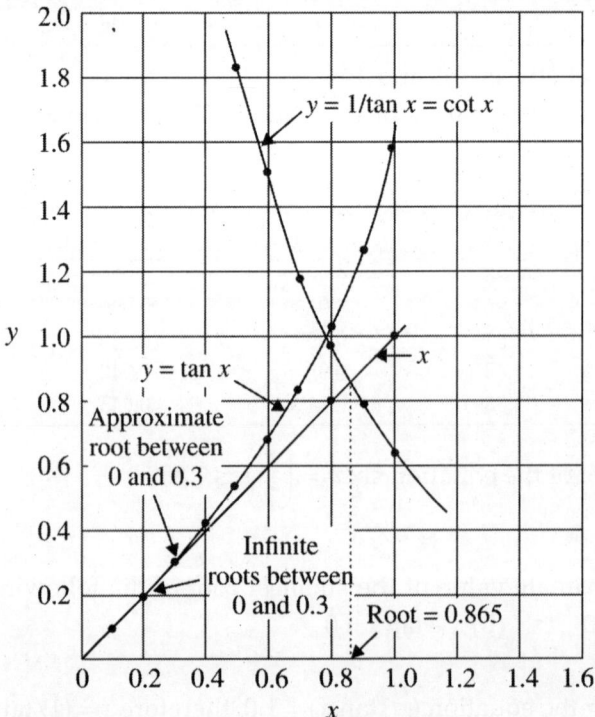

Fig. 3.3: Graphical determinaton of roots of equations

3.3 NEWTON–RAPHSON'S METHOD

It[7,8] is an excellent innovative procedure to determine the roots of an equation for which the approximate value of the root or the range of values within which the exact root lies. The equation proposed by Newton–Raphson to determine the root is expressed as follows.

$$x_{n+1} = \left[x_n - \frac{f(x)}{f'(x)} \right]$$

The graphical representation of the method is shown in Fig. 3.4.

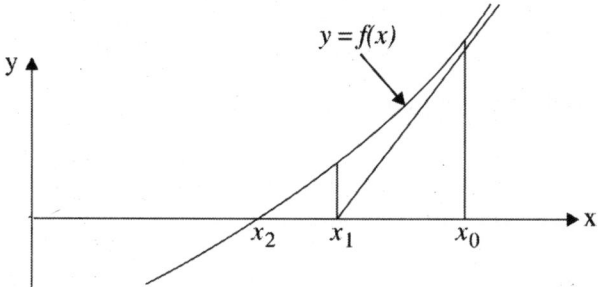

Fig. 3.4: Newton–Raphson's method

The application of this method is illustrated by the following examples.

Example 3.4

Determine the real root of the following equation correct to four decimal places using Newton–Raphson's method. Assume the approximate root obtained from graphical method as –1.9.

$$x^2 + 4 \sin x = 0$$

Solution

$$f(x) = x^2 + 4 \sin x$$
$$f'_x = 2x + 4 \cos x$$

$$x_n = -1.9 - \left[\frac{(-1.9)^2 + 4 \sin (-1.9)}{2(-1.9) + 4 \cos (-1.9)} \right] = -1.9344$$

$$x_{n+2} = -1.9344 - \left[\frac{(-1.9344)^2 + 4 \sin (-1.9344)}{2(-1.9344) + 4 \cos (-1.9344)} \right] = -1.9337$$

$$x_{n+3} = -1.9 - \left[\frac{(-1.9337)^2 + 4 \sin (-1.9337)}{2(-1.9337) + 4 \cos (-1.9337)} \right] = -1.9337$$

Therefore the exact root is –1.9337.

Example 3.5

Find the real root of the following equation using the Newton–Raphson's method assuming the approximate root as 0.61.

$$3x - \cos x - 1 = 0$$

Solution

$$f(x) = 3x - \cos x - 1 = 0$$
$$f'_x = 3 + \sin x$$

$$x_1 = 0.61 - \left[\frac{3(0.61) - \cos(0.61) - 1}{3 + \sin(0.61)}\right] = 0.6072$$

$$x_2 = 0.6072 - \left[\frac{3(0.6072) - \cos(0.6072) - 1}{3 + \sin(0.6072)}\right] = 0.6071$$

$$x_3 = 0.6071 - \left[\frac{3(0.6071) - \cos(0.6071) - 1}{3 + \sin(0.6071)}\right] = 0.6071$$

Hence the real root of the equation is 0.6071.

Example 3.6

Using the Newton–Raphson's method, find the root of the equation $2x - 3\sin x - 5 = 0$ given the approximate root as 2.6.

Solution

$$f(x) = 2x - 3 \sin x - 5$$
$$f'_x = 2 - 3 \cos x$$

$$x_1 = 2.6 - \left[\frac{2(2.6) - 3 \sin(2.6) - 5}{2 - 3 \cos(2.6)}\right] = 2.8945$$

$$x_2 = 2.8945 - \left[\frac{2(2.8945) - 3 \sin(2.8945) - 5}{2 - 3 \cos(2.8945)}\right] = 2.8832$$

$$x_3 = 2.8832 - \left[\frac{2(2.8832) - 3 \sin(2.8832) - 5}{2 - 3 \cos(2.8832)}\right] = 2.883209$$

Therefore the exact root of the equation is 2.8832.

Example 3.7

Find upto 4 decimal places the root of the equation $e^{-x} = \sin x$ assuming the approximate root as 0.6.

Solution

$$f(x) = e^{-x} - \sin x$$
$$f'_x = -e^{-x} - \cos x$$

$$x_1 = x_0 - \left[\frac{e^{-x} - \sin x}{-e^{-x} - \cos x}\right] = x_0 + \left[\frac{e^{-x} - \sin x}{e^{-x} + \cos x}\right]$$

$$= 0.6 + \left[\frac{e^{-0.6} - \sin(06)}{e^{-0.6} + (0.6)}\right] = 0.58848$$

$$x_2 = -0.58848 + \left[\frac{e^{-0.58848} - \sin(0.58848)}{e^{-0.58848} + \cos(0.58848)} \right] = 0.58853$$

The root of the equation is 0.5885.

Example 3.8

Find correct to four decimal places, the root of the trigonometric equation $f(x) =$ $\sin x - \left(\dfrac{x+1}{x-1} \right) = 0$ having the approximate root at $x = 0.4$

Solution

$$f'_x = \cos x - \left[\frac{(x-1)1 - (x+1)1}{(x-1)^2} \right]$$

$$= \cos x - \left[\frac{-2}{(x-1)^2} \right]$$

$$= \cos x + \left[\frac{2}{(x-1)^2} \right]$$

Therefore $x_1 = -0.4 - \left[\dfrac{\sin(-0.4) - \left(\dfrac{-0.4+1}{-0.4-1} \right)}{\cos(-0.4) + \left(\dfrac{2}{1.4^2} \right)} \right] = -0.4201$

$$x_2 = -0.4201 - \left[\frac{\sin(-0.4201) - \left(\dfrac{-0.4201+1}{-0.4201-1} \right)}{\cos(-0.4201) + \left(\dfrac{2}{1.4201^2} \right)} \right] = -0.42036$$

The exact root of the equation is -0.4203.

Example 3.9

Find the value of $\sqrt{12}$ by Newton–Raphson's method.

Solution

$$x^2 = \text{constant} = a = 12$$

or $\qquad x^2 - a = 0$

Therefore $\qquad f(x) = x^2 - a$

$$f'_x = 2x$$

$$x'_{n+1} = x_n + \left[\frac{x_n^2 - a}{2x_n} \right] = \frac{1}{2} \left[x_n + \frac{a}{x_n} \right]$$

Approximate root is assumed as $3.5 = x_n$

Therefore $x_1 = \dfrac{1}{2}\left[3.5 + \dfrac{12}{3.5}\right] = 3.464$

$$x_2 = \dfrac{1}{2}\left[3.464 + \dfrac{12}{3.464}\right] = 3.4641$$

$$x_3 = \dfrac{1}{2}\left[3.4641 + \dfrac{12}{3.4641}\right] = 3.4641$$

The exact value of $\sqrt{12}$ is 3.4641.

Example 3.10

Find the value of the exponential function e^{-1} using Newton–Raphson's method and assuming the approximate root $x_0 = 0.3$ and $e = 2.71$.

Solution

Let $e^{-1} = 1$ and $e = x^{-1} = \left(\dfrac{1}{x}\right)$

Therefore $\left(\dfrac{1}{x} - e\right) = 0$, hence $f(x_n) = \left(\dfrac{1}{x} - e\right)$ and $f'(x_n) = \left(-1/x_n^2\right)$

Using the expression

$$x_{n+1} = x_n - \left[\dfrac{f(x_n)}{f'(x_n)}\right] = x_n - \left[\dfrac{\left(\dfrac{1}{x_n} - e\right)}{\left(-\dfrac{1}{x_n^2}\right)}\right]$$

$$= x_n (2 - e \cdot x_n)$$

Therefore $x_1 = 0.3\,[2 - (2.71 \times 0.3)] = 0.3561$

$\qquad\qquad x_2 = 0.3561\,[2 - (2.71 \times 0.3561)] = 0.3685$

$\qquad\qquad x_3 = 0.3685\,[2 - (2.71 \times 0.3685)] = 0.36895$

$\qquad\qquad x_4 = 0.36895\,[2 - (2.71 \times 0.36895)] = 0.3690$

Hence the value of e^{-1} is 0.3690.

Example 3.11

Find the cube root of 10 using Newton–Raphson's method.

Solution

$$f(x) = x^p - a$$
$$f'_x = px^{p-1}$$

$$x_{n+1} = x_n - \left[\dfrac{f(x_n)}{f'(x_n)}\right] = x_n - \left[\dfrac{x_n^p - a}{px_n^{p-1}}\right] = \left[\dfrac{(p-1)x_n^p + a}{px_n^{p-1}}\right]$$

Hence, $a = 10$ and $p = 3$

$$x_{n+1} = \left[\frac{(3-1)x^3 + 10}{3x^{3-1}}\right] = \left[\frac{2x^3 + 10}{3x^2}\right]$$

Since $x^3 = 2^3 = 8$ and $3^3 = 27$, the value of the root lies between 2 and 3

Assuming $x_0 = 2$

$$x_1 = \left[\frac{2 \times 2^3 + 10}{3 \times 2^2}\right] = 2.167$$

$$x_2 = \left[\frac{2(2.167)^3 + 10}{3(2.167)^2}\right] = 2.1545$$

$$x_3 = \left[\frac{2(2.1545)^3 + 10}{3(2.1545)^2}\right] = 2.1544$$

$$x_4 = \left[\frac{2(2.1544)^3 + 10}{3(2.1544)^2}\right] = 2.1544$$

Hence the cube root of 10 is 2.1544.

Example 3.12

Calculate the value of $\sqrt[3]{\pi}$ to six decimal places using Newton–Raphson's method of iteration.

Solution

$$\pi = 3.1416$$

$$x_{n+1} = \left[\frac{(p-1)x_n^p + a}{px_n^{(p-1)}}\right]$$

In this case $a = 3.1416$ and $p = 3$.

Substituting the numerical values, we have

$$x_1 = \left[\frac{2x_0^3 + 3.1416}{3 \times 1.4^2}\right]$$

Assuming $x_0 = 1.4$

$$x_1 = \left[\frac{2(1.4)^3 + 3.1416}{3 \times 1.4^2}\right] = 1.467619$$

$$x_2 = \left[\frac{2(1.467619)^3 + 3.1416}{3 \times (1.467619)^2}\right] = 1.464599$$

$$x_3 = \left[\frac{2(1.464599)^3 + 3.1416}{3 \times (1.464599)^2}\right] = 1.4645936$$

$$x_4 = \left[\frac{2(1.4645936)^3 + 3.1416}{3 \times (1.4645936)^2} \right] = 1.464593$$

Hence the cube root of π is 1.464593.

Example 3.13

Calculate the value of $\sqrt{\pi}$ upto six decimal places using Newton–Raphson's method.

Solution

$$x_n = \frac{1}{2}[x_n + a/x_n]$$

Here $a = \pi = 3.1416$

Assuming $x_0 = 1.5$

$$x_1 = \frac{1}{2}\left[1.5 + \left(\frac{3.1416}{1.5} \right) \right] = 1.7972$$

$$x_2 = \frac{1}{2}\left[1.7972 + \left(\frac{3.1416}{1.7972} \right) \right] = 1.772626$$

$$x_3 = \frac{1}{2}\left[1.772626 + \left(\frac{3.1416}{1.772626} \right) \right] = 1.7724559$$

$$x_4 = \frac{1}{2}\left[1.7724559 + \left(\frac{3.1416}{1.7724559} \right) \right] = 1.772456$$

Hence the square root of π correct to six decimal places is 1.772456.

3.3.1 Double Roots

If $x = a$ is a multiple root of $f(x) = 0$ and it is also a root of $f'(x) = 0$. If $f''(a) = 0$, then $x = a$ is a double root of $f(x) = 0$. To get the double root, we have to solve $f'(x) = 0$ by using

$$x_{n+1} = x_n - \left[\frac{f'(x_n)}{f''(x_n)} \right]$$

By solving this relation, we get $x = b$ and if $f(b) = 0$, we say that $x = b$ is a double root of $f(x) = 0$.

If $f(b) \neq 0$, the value of x can be modified as

$$x = b \pm \sqrt{-2f(b)/f''(b)}$$

3.3.2 Newton's Modified Method

If $x = a$ is a double root of $f(x) = 0$ such that $f'(a) = 0$, using convergence criteria it can be proved that

$$E_{n+1} \cong E_n = \left(\frac{2-1}{2}\right) E_n$$

This shows that the rate of convergence is linear or geometric. The modified formula is given by the relations

$$x_{n+1} = x_n - \left[\frac{pf(x_n)}{f'(x_n)}\right]$$

This equation requires less computation than by Newton's method, if double root exists. Thus the following expressions can have the same value if there is a root with multiplicity p, if the initial approximation x_0 is chosen close to the exact value.

$$x_1 = x_0 - \left[\frac{pf(x_0)}{f'(x_0)}\right]$$

$$x_2 = x_0 - \left[\frac{(p-1)\, f'(x_0)}{f''(x_0)}\right]$$

$$x_3 = x_0 - \left[\frac{(p-2)\, f''(x_0)}{f'''(x_0)}\right]$$

Newton's modified method is illustrated by the following examples.

Example 3.14

Find the double root of the equation
$$f(x) = 2x^3 - 2x^2 - 2x + 2 = 0$$

Solution

$$f'(x) = 6x^2 - 4x - 2$$
$$f''(x) = 12x - 4$$

Choosing $x_0 = 0.9$, we obtain

$$x_1 = x_0 - \left[\frac{2f(x_0)}{f'(x_0)}\right]$$

$$f(0.9) = (2 \times 0.9^3) - (2 \times 0.9^2) - (2 \times 0.9) + 2 = 0.038$$
$$f'(0.9) = (6 \times 0.9^2) - (4 \times 0.9) - 2 = -0.74$$

$$x_1 = 0.9 - \left(\frac{2 \times 0.038}{-0.74}\right) = 1.0027$$

$$f''(0.9) = (12 \times 0.9) - 4 = 6.8$$

$$x_2 = 0.9 - \left[\frac{(-0.74)}{6.8}\right] = 1.088$$

The values of x_1 and x_2 show that this value is near unity. Hence an approximation is made as 1.001.

$f(1.001) = 2(1.001)^3 - 2(1.001)^2 - 2(1.001) + 2 = 4 \times 10^{-6}$

$f'(1.001) = 6(1.001)^2 - 4(1.001) - 2 = 8.006 \times 10^{-3}$

$f''(1.001) = (12 \times 1.001) - 4 = 8.012$

$$x_4 = x_3 = \left[\frac{2f(x_3)}{f'(x_3)}\right] = 1.001 - \left[\frac{2 \times 4 \times 10^{-6}}{8.006 \times 10^{-3}}\right] = 1.00000075$$

$$x_5 = x_3 = \left[\frac{2f'(x_3)}{f''(x_3)}\right] = 1.001 - \left[\frac{8.006 \times 10^{-3}}{8.012}\right] = 1.00000075$$

Hence the double root is 1.00.

For the same problem, if we apply Newton–Raphson's method, we have

$$x_1 = x_0 - \left[\frac{f(x_0)}{f'(x_0)}\right] = 0.9 - \left[\frac{0.038}{-0.74}\right] = 0.9513$$

$f(0.9513) = 2(0.9513)^3 - 2(0.9513)^2 - 2(0.9513) + 2 = 9.255 \times 10^{-3}$

$f'(0.9513) = 6(0.9513)^2 - 4(0.9513) - 2 = -0.3753$

$$x_2 = 0.9513 - \left[\frac{f(0.9513)}{f'(0.9513)}\right] = 0.9513 - \left[\frac{9.255 \times 10^{-3}}{-0.3753}\right] = 0.9759$$

$f(0.9759) = (2 \times 09759^3) - (2 \times 0.9759^2) - (2 \times 0.975^9) + 2 = 2.295 \times 10^{-3}$

$f'(0.9759) = (6 \times 0.9759^2) - (4 \times 0.9759) - 2 = -0.1893$

$$x_3 = 0.9759 - \left[\frac{f(0.9759)}{f'(0.9759)}\right] = 0.9759 - \left[\frac{2.295 \times 10^{-3}}{-0.1893}\right] = 0.9880$$

This shows that Newton–Raphson's method does not converge faster in cases where double root exists or with roots of multiplicity.

3.4 METHOD OF ITERATION

In this[8], the equations are solved by assuming a starting value of the variable x_0 and the iterations are continued with the updated values of the variable.

Given equation

$x_0 = \phi(x)$

$x_1 = \phi(x_0)$

$x_2 = \phi(x_1)$

$x_3 = \phi(x_2)$

....

....

$x_n = \phi(x_{n-1})$

The iterations are continued until the desired accuracy is achieved.

Example 3.15

Solve Kepler's equation iteratively for $m = 0.8$, $E = 0.2$, by writing in the form $x = m + E \sin x$ and starting with $x_0 = m$.

Solution

$$x_1 = 0.8 + 0.2 \sin (0.8) = 0.94347$$
$$x_2 = 0.8 + 0.2 \sin (0.\,0.94347) = 0.96192$$
$$x_3 = 0.8 + 0.2 \sin (0.96192) = 0.96405$$
$$x_4 = 0.8 + 0.2 \sin (0.96405) = 0.9643$$
$$x_5 = 0.8 + 0.2 \sin (0.9643) = 0.96433$$

Hence the root is 0.9643.

Example 3.16

Solve the equation $(2x - \log_{10} x) = 7$ by iteration method with $x_0 = 3.65$.

Solution

$$(2x - \log_{10} x) = 7$$

$$x = \frac{1}{2}[7 + \log_{10} x]$$

$$x_1 = \frac{1}{2}[7 + \log_{10} 3.65] = 3.7811$$

$$x_2 = \frac{1}{2}[7 + \log_{10} 3.7811] = 3.7888$$

$$x_3 = \frac{1}{2}[7 + \log_{10} 3.7888] = 3.7892$$

$$x_4 = \frac{1}{2}[7 + \log_{10} 3.7892] = 3.78927$$

Hence the root is 3.7892.

Example 3.17

Solve equation $x = 0.21 \sin (0.5 + x)$ by iteration method with the approximate root as 0.1.

Solution

$$x_1 = 0.21 \sin (0.5 + 0.1) = 0.1129$$
$$x_2 = 0.21 \sin (0.5 + 0.1129) = 0.1208$$
$$x_3 = 0.21 \sin (0.5 + 0.1208) = 0.1221$$
$$x_4 = 0.21 \sin (0.5 + 0.1221) = 0.12238$$
$$x_5 = 0.21 \sin (0.5 + 0.12238) = 0.12242$$
$$x_6 = 0.21 \sin (0.5 + 0.12242) = 0.12243$$

Hence the root is 0.12243.

Example 3.18

Find the only positive root of the equation $x^3 - x^2 - x - 1 = 0$ by iteration using the form $x = 1 + \dfrac{1}{x} + \dfrac{1}{x^2}$ beginning with $x_0 = 1$

Solution

$$x_1 = [1 + 1/1 + 1/1] = 3$$
$$x_2 = [1 + 1/3 + 1/32] = 1.444$$

$$x_3 = \left[1 + \frac{1}{1.444} + \frac{1}{1.444^2}\right] = 2.1720$$

....

....

$$x_{17} = 1.8396$$
$$x_{18} = 1.839$$

Hence the root is 1.8390.

Example 3.19

Find up to five decimal places a root of the equation $x \log_{10} x = -0.125$, assuming an initial value of 0.1536.

Solution

$$x = \left[\frac{-0.125}{\log_{10} x}\right]$$

$$x_1 = \left[\frac{-0.125}{\log_{10} 0.1536}\right] = 0.15363$$

$$x_2 = \left[\frac{-0.125}{\log_{10} 0.15363}\right] = 0.15365$$

$$x_3 = \left[\frac{-0.125}{\log_{10} 0.15365}\right] = 0.15366$$

$$x_4 = \left[\frac{-0.125}{\log_{10} 0.15366}\right] = 0.15367$$

$$x_5 = \left[\frac{-0.125}{\log_{10} 0.15367}\right] = 0.15367$$

Hence the root is 0.15367.

3.5 REGULA–FALSI OR INVERSE LINEAR INTERPOLATION METHOD

In this method[9], the fixed point is shifted to the left or right end such that
$$f(x_i) \cdot f(x_{i-1}) < 0 \text{ at each step.}$$

If x_i and x_{i-1} are two values between which the exact root lies, then the iterations are carried out using the relationship expressed as

$$x_{i+1} = \left[\frac{x_{i-1} f(x_i) - x_i f(x_{i-1})}{f(x_i) - f(x_{i-1})}\right]$$

Care being taken to ensure that $f(x_i) \cdot f(x_{i-1}) < 0$ at each step.

The application of this method is illustrated by the following numerical examples.

Example 3.20

Compute the real root of the equation

$x \log_{10} x - 1.2 = 0$ by the Regula–Falsi method.

Solution

$$f(x) = x \log_{10} x - 1.2$$

$x_1 = 1$	$f(x_1) = -1.2$
$x_2 = 2$	$f(x_2) = -0.5979$
$x_3 = 3$	$f(x_3) = +0.2313$

Therefore the root lies between 2 and 3

$$x_{i+1} = \left[\frac{x_{i-1} f(x_i) - x_i f(x_{i-1})}{f(x_i) - f(x_{i-1})} \right]$$

Choosing $x_i = 3$ and $x_{i-1} = 2$

$f(x_2) = -0.5979$ and $f(x_3) = +0.2313$

$$x_4 = \left[\frac{2(0.2313) - 3(-0.5979)}{0.2313 - (-0.5979)} \right] = 2.72$$

$f(x_4) = (2.72 \log_{10} 2.72 - 1.2) = -0.018$

Now $f(x_4) \cdot f(x_3) < 0$

Hence $[-0.018 \times 0.2313] = -0.0041634 < 0$

Choose $x_3 = 3$ and $x_4 = 2.72$

We have

$$x_5 = \left[\frac{2.72(0.2313) - 3(-0.018)}{0.2313 - (-0.018)} \right] = 2.74$$

Therefore the root $x_i = 2.74$.

Example 3.21

Solve the equation $x^2 - 9x + 1 = 0$ by Regula–Falsi method.

Solution

Assuming $x_1 = 2$ and $x_3 = 3$

$f(x_1) = -9$ and $f(x_2) = 1$

Hence the root lies between 2 and 3

$$x_3 = \left[\frac{(2 \times 1) - 3(-9)}{1 - (-9)} \right] = 2.9, \text{ therefore } f(x_3) = -0.711$$

Also $f(x_3) \cdot f(x_2) = (-0.711 \times 1) = -0.711 < 0$

Choosing x_2 and x_3;

$$x_4 = \left[\frac{(2.9 \times 1) - 3(-0.711)}{1 - (-0.711)} \right] = 2.9415$$

The procedure is continued until the value converges to 2.9428.

3.6 GRAEFFE'S METHOD

This method[10] is ideally suited for finding the roots of nth degree polynomial.

Consider the nth degree polynomial expressed as

$$x^n + a_1 x^{n-1} + a_2 x^{n-2} + a_3 x^{n-3} + \ldots + a_n = 0$$

In this method, known as the root squaring process, the coefficients are squared and the values of $(a_1^2 - 2a_2)$ and $(a_2^2 - 2a_1 a_3)$, etc. are determined. These are again squared and the process is repeated and finally the roots are evaluated. The method is illustrated by the following examples.

Example 3.22

Find the roots of the following equation using Graeffe's root squaring method.

$$x^3 - 12x^2 + 39.5x - 33 = 0$$

Solution

In this example $a_1 = -12 \quad a_2 = 39.5 \quad a_3 = -33$

The values of $(a_1^2 - 2a_2)$, $(a_2^2 - 2a_1 a_3)$ and a_3^2 and other values required for determining the roots are compiled in Table 3.10.

Table 3.10: Graeffe's root squaring table

Power $m*$	x^2	$(a_1^2 - 2a_2)$ $a_1 x^2$	$(a_2^2 - 2a_1 a_3)$ $a_2 x$	a_3^2 a_3
1	1	-12	39.5	-33
	1	144	1360.25	1089
		-79	-792	—
2	1	65	768.25	1089
		4225	5.9×10^5	1.186×10^6
		-1536.5	-1.41×10^5	—
4	1	2688.5	449000	1.186×10^6
		7.28×10^6	2.01×10^{11}	1.1406×10^{12}
		-0.898×10^6	-0.063×10^6	—
8	1	6.33×10^6	1.947×10^{11}	1.1406×10^{12} *

$m*$ is the power to which the accuracy of the root is required

Hence the roots are evaluated as

$$x_1 = \sqrt[8]{\frac{6.33 \times 10^6}{1}} = 7.082$$

$$x_2 = \sqrt[8]{\frac{1.947 \times 10^{11}}{6.33 \times 10^6}} = 3.6389$$

$$x_3 = \sqrt[8]{\frac{1.1406 \times 10^{12}}{1.947 \times 10^{11}}} = 1.2473$$

Example 3.23

Find the roots of the equation

$\lambda^3 - 18\lambda^2 + 74\lambda - 44 = 0$ by Graeffe's root squaring method

Solution

In this example $a_1 = -18$ $a_2 = 74$ $a_3 = -44$ (Table 3.11)

		$(a_1^2 - 2a_2)$	$(a_2^2 - 2a_1a_3)$	a_3^2
Power m	λ^3	$a_1\lambda^2$	a_2	a_3
1	1	-18	74	-44
		324	5476	1936
		-148	-1584	$-$
2	1	176	3892	1936
		30976	1.514×10^7	3.748×10^6
		-7784	-6.8147×10^5	$-$
4	1	23192	1.507×10^7	3.748×10^6
		5.378×10^8	2.27×10^{14}	1.4047×10^{13}
		-3.014×10^7	-1.7384×10^{11}	$-$
8	1	5.0766×10^8	2.268×10^{14}	1.4047×10^{13}

Table 3.11: Graeffe's root squaring table

Hence the roots are evaluated as

$$\lambda_1 = \sqrt[8]{\frac{5.0766 \times 10^8}{1}} = 12.2517$$

$$\lambda_2 = \sqrt[8]{\frac{2.268 \times 10^{14}}{5.0766 \times 10^8}} = 5.0846$$

$$\lambda_3 = \sqrt[8]{\frac{1.4047 \times 10^{13}}{2.268 \times 10^{14}}} = 0.7063$$

EXERCISES

1. Find graphically the approximate root of the equations:
   (a) $2x - \cos x - 1 = 0$
   (b) $x = e^{-x}$
   (c) $x = \sqrt[3]{(5-x)}$
   (d) $2 \tan x - x - 1 = 0$

2. Find to three decimal places, the roots of the equation

   $(0.1x - \log x) = 0$ between 1 and 2

3. Find the root of the equation $\log x = \cos x$ by Newton's method to five decimal places.

4. Find the roots of the equation $x^3 - 5x + 2 = 0$ to four decimal places.

5. Find $\sqrt{30}$ and $(1/3)^{1/4}$.

6. Find an approximate value of the roots of the equation $x = 0.21 \sin (0.5 + x)$.

7. Find the root of $x = e^{-x}$ with $x = 0.5$

8. Find the root of $x = \sin x + 0.5$ with $x = 1.5$.

9. In the solution of an eigen value problem, the characteristic equation is given by $\lambda^6 - 18\lambda^5 + 81\lambda^4 - 100\lambda^3 + 40\lambda^2 - 20\lambda + 4 = 0$ where λ is an eigen value.

   This equation has a root between 4 and 5. Determine the root to two decimal places by

   (a) Regula–Falsi method and (b) Newton's method.

10. Solve $f(x) = x^3 - 3.7x^2 + 6.25x - 4.609 = 0$ near $x = 1.5$

11. Using Graeffe's method, find the roots of the equation

   $$x^3 - 3.7x^2 + 6.25x - 4.609 = 0$$

12. Find the roots of the polynomial

   $$x^4 - 6x^3 + 8x^2 + 2x - 1 = 0$$

   using Graeffe's root squaring method.

REFERENCES

1. Dahlquist G and Bjorck A, *Numerical Methods*, Prentice Hall, Englewood Cliffs, NJ, 1974.

2. Ferziger JH, *Numerical Methods for Engineering Applications*, John Wiley, New York, 1981.

3. Krishna Raju N, *Reinforced Concrete Structural Concrete Elements*, New Age International, Publishers, New Delhi, 2016.

4. Krishna Raju N and Pranesh RN, *Reinforced Concrete Design*, New Age International, Publishers, New Delhi, 2003.

5. Atkinson K, *Elementary Numerical Analysis*, Wiley, New York, 1985.

6. Jain MK, Iyengar Jain, SRK and Jain RK, *Numerical Methods for Scientific and Engineering Computation*, 6th Edn, New Age International Publishers, New Delhi, 2012.

7. Ralph G Stanton, *Numerical Methods for Science and Engineering*, Prentice Hall of India, New Delhi, 1977.

8. Traub JF, *Iterative Methods for the Solution of Nonlinear Equations*, Prentice Hall, Engelwood Cliffs, 1964.

9. Johnson LW and RD Reiss, *Numerical Analysis*, 2nd Edn, Addison-Wesley, Reading, Mass, 1968.

10. Yakowitz Sidney and Ferenc Szidarovszky, *An Introduction to Numerical Computations* MacMillan Publishing Company, 1986.

REVIEW QUESTIONS

1. Specify the various methods generally used for solving the engineering problems involving nonlinear equations.

2. What are the advantages of the graphical method of finding the roots of nonlinear equations?

3. What is the preliminary requirement for solving the nonlinear equations using Newton–Raphson's method?

4. Briefly explain the steps involved in solving nonlinear equations using Newton–Raphson's method.

5. Explain the terms (a) double roots (b) convergence criteria with respect to the solution of nonlinear equations.

6. What is the specific advantage of using Newton's modified method in solving nonlinear equations with double roots?

7. Briefly explain the method iteration to solve nonlinear equations. What assumptions are made in using this method?

8. Outline the basic steps used in Regula–Falsi method in solving the nonlinear equations.

9. Briefly explain the Graeffe's method of solving n^{th} degree polynomial equation.

10. What are the various terms involving the coefficients used in the preparation of root squaring table using the Graeffe's method?

OBJECTIVE TYPE QUESTIONS

1. The roots of nonlinear algebraic equations can be determined by
   a) factorization method
   b) cholesky's method
   c) graphical method

2. Nonlinear algebraic equations involving trigonometric functions are termed as
   a) complex equations
   b) transcendental equations
   c) complimentary equations

3. Newton–Raphson's method can be used to determine the exact roots of equations when
   a) the approximate value of the root is known
   b) any value of the root is unknown
   c) the equations involve trigonometric functions

4. Newton–Raphson's method does not converge faster in cases where
   a) the equations are linear
   b) approximate root is not known
   c) double root exists

5. Newton's modified method converges faster in solving equations
   a) with roots of multiplicity
   b) of all types
   c) which are linear

6. In solving equations using the iterative method
   a) the starting value is not required
   b) convergence is faster
   c) starting value should be assumed

7. In using the Regula–Falsi method of solving the roots of a nonlinear equation, the fixed point is shifted to the left or right such that
   a) $f(x_i) \cdot f(x_{i-1}) > 0$
   b) $f(x_i) \cdot f(x_{i-1}) < 0$
   c) $f(x_i) \cdot f(x_{i-1}) = 0$

8. Solution of nonlinear equations using Graeffe's method involves the process of
   a) using the coefficients directly
   b) squaring the coefficients
   c) finding the differences between the coefficients

9. In using Graeffe's method for solving equations, the roots are obtained
   a) directly in one step
   b) after repeated root squaring process
   c) by substitution

10. The solution of nonlinear equations by Graeffe's method requires the
    a) process of elimination
    b) process of substitution
    c) preparation of root squaring table

Solution of Ordinary Differential Equations

4.1 EULER'S METHOD

Ordinary differential equations are often encountered in solving engineering problems of beams[1] and columns[2] which are loaded resulting in curved profiles. Euler[3] has formulated a simple procedure for the integration of ordinary differential equations. Consider the ordinary differential equation of the form,

$$\left(\frac{dp}{dl}\right) = f(p.l)$$

This method is a single step integration which depends on Taylor's expansion of the function $p(l)$ about some starting point say l_0 in the following way.

$$p(l) = p_0 + \frac{dp}{dl}(l - l_0) + \frac{1}{2}\cdot\frac{d^2p}{dl^2}(l - l_0)^2 + \cdots$$

If $(l - l_0)$ is defined to be equal to h and if h^2 is small compared with h, we can write

$$p(l_0 + h) = p_0 + \frac{dp}{dl}(l_0 + h - l_0) + \cdots = p_0 + h\left(\frac{dp}{dl}\right)$$

Therefore $p(l_0 + h) = p_0 + h \cdot f(p_0\ l_0)$

This equation can be used to compute the value of p at $l = (l_0 + h)$ knowing the value of $p = p_0$ at $l = l_0$, the process is repeated.

The geometric representation of the above equation is shown in Fig. 4.1

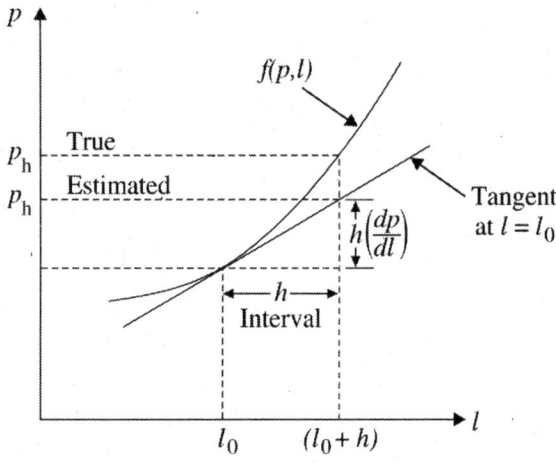

Fig. 4.1: Euler's method

In the Euler's method, a straight line approximation is used over the interval to replace the curving trajectory. To ensure reasonable accuracy, the interval must be kept very small. There can be substantial accumulation of errors over a given range. Because of its inherent inaccuracy, the Euler's method is seldom used in digital computations except as a starting routine or in the form of modified Euler's method referred to as Runge–Kutta[4] method. Due to its simplicity, this method is used for preliminary calculations.

The use of Euler's method is illustrated by the following examples.

Example 4.1

Solve the differential equation $\left(\dfrac{dp}{dl}\right) = p^2$ in the range $0 \le l \le 1$ for the initial condition $p = 0.5$ at $l = 0$, using Euler's method.

Solution

Given the initial value of $p = 0.5$ at $l = 0$

Let the interval be $h = 0.1$

$$p(l_0 + h) = p_0 + hf(p_0 l_0)$$

$$p_{0.1} = \left(p_0 + p_0^2 h\right) = 0.5 + (0.5)^2 (0.1) = 0.525$$

$$p_{0.2} = \left(p_{0.1} + p_{0.1}^2 h\right) = 0.525 + (0.525)^2 (0.1) = 0.5526$$

$$p_{0.3} = \left(p_{0.2} + p_{0.2}^2 h\right) = 0.5526 + (0.5526)^2 (0.1) = 0.5831$$

Similarly computing the other successive values, we have

$p_{0.4} = 0.6171$
$p_{0.5} = 0.6552$
$p_{0.6} = 0.6981$
$p_{0.7} = 0.7468$
$p_{0.8} = 0.8026$
$p_{0.9} = 0.8670$
$p_{1.0} = 0.9422$

Example 4.2

Given $\left(\dfrac{dy}{dx}\right) = \left(\dfrac{y-x}{y+x}\right)$

With $y = 1$ when $x_0 = 0$, find the value of y when $x = 0.1$ by Euler's method in five steps.

Solution

$x_0 = 0$ $y_0 = 0$;   interval $h = 0.02$

$$y_1 = y_0 + hf(x_0, y_0) = 1 + 0.02\left(\frac{y_0 - x_0}{y_0 + x_0}\right)$$

$$= 1 + 0.02 \left(\frac{1-0}{1+0} \right) = 1.02$$

$$y_2 = 1 + 0.02 \left(\frac{1.02 - 0.02}{1.02 + 0.02} \right) = 1.04$$

$$y_3 = 1 + 0.02 \left(\frac{1 - 0.04}{1 + 0.04} \right) = 1.0585$$

$$y_4 = 1 + 0.02 \left(\frac{1.0585 - 0.06}{1.0585 + 0.06} \right) = 1.07635$$

$$y_5 = 1 + 0.02 \left(\frac{1.07635 - 0.08}{1.07635 + 0.08} \right) = 1.0936$$

Example 4.3

Solve $\left(\frac{dy}{dt} \right) + y^2 = 0$ given the boundary condition that $y = 1$ and $t = 0$, find approximately the value of y for $t = 1$ by Euler's method in 5 steps.

Solution

$$\left(\frac{dy}{dt} \right) = -y^2; t_0 = 0, t_1 = 0.2, t_2 = 0.4, t_3 = 0.6, t_4 = 0.8, \text{ and } t_5 = 1.0$$

$$y_1 = y_0 + hf(x_0, y_0)$$
$$= 1 + 0.2(-1) = 0.8$$

$$y_2 = 0.8 + 0.2 \left[-(0.8)^2 \right] = 0.672$$

$$y_3 = 0.672 + 0.2 \left[-(0.672)^2 \right] = 0.5816$$

$$y_4 = 0.5816 + 0.2 \left[-(0.5816)^2 \right] = 0.5139$$

$$y_5 = 0.5139 + 0.2 \left[-(0.5139)^2 \right] = 0.4610$$

Hence, the value of $y_5 = 0.4610$ when $t_5 = 1.0$.

Example 4.4

Solve the initial value problem $y' = (x + y^2)$ given the boundary condition $y(0) = 0$ and $x_0 = 0$.

Find the value of y when $x = 0.8$ using 5 steps.

Solution

Given interval $h = 0.2$

$$x_0 = 0, \quad x_1 = 0.2, \quad x_2 = 0.4, \quad x_3 = 0.6, \quad x_4 = 0.8$$

$$y_1 = y_0 + hf(x_0, y_0)$$
$$= 0 + 0.2(0 + 0^2) = 0$$

$$y_2 = 0 + 0.2(0.2 + 0^2) = 0.04$$

$$y_3 = 0.04 + 0.2(0.4 + 0.04^2) = 0.12$$

$$y_4 = 0.12 + 0.2(0.6 + 0.12^2) = 0.242$$

$$y_5 = 0.242 + 0.2(0.8 + 0.242^2) = 0.4137$$

4.2 RUNGE–KUTTA METHOD

The method was first developed by C Runge and later modified and improved by W Kutta.[5] The method is a generalization of Simpson's rule. The method is simple to use and also allows adjustments of the length of the integration step from point to point without modification of the method. Let the differential equation be

$$\left(\frac{dy}{dx}\right) = f(x, y)$$

Let x and y assume values of x_n and y_n after the nth integration step. Using an integration step of interval h, we can compute the values as

$$K_1 = h \cdot f(x, y)$$

$$K_2 = h \cdot f\left(x + \frac{h}{2}, y + \frac{K_1}{2}\right)$$

$$K_3 = h \cdot f\left(x + \frac{h}{2}, y + \frac{K_2}{2}\right)$$

$$K_4 = h \cdot f(x + h, y + K_3)$$

Using these terms, Runge–Kutta[5] fourth order formula is expressed as

$$y(x + h) = y(x) + \frac{1}{6}(K_1 + 2K_2 + 2K_3 + K_4)$$

Example 4.5

Using Runge–Kutta fourth order formula, find $y(0.2)$, $y(0.4)$, and $y(0.6)$; given

$$\left(\frac{dy}{dx}\right) = (1 + y^2) \text{ with the initial condition } y = 0 \text{ when } x = 0.$$

Solution

$$x = 0$$
$$x_1 = 0.2; \quad \text{interval } h = 0.2$$
$$x_2 = 0.4$$

$x_3 = 0.6$

$$y_1 = y_0 + \frac{1}{6}\left(K_1 + 2K_2 + 2K_3 + K_4\right)$$

$$K_1 = h \cdot f\left(x_0, y_0\right) = 0.2\left(1 + 0^2\right) = 0.2$$

$$K_2 = h \cdot f\left(x_0 + \frac{h}{2}, y_0 + \frac{K_1}{2}\right) = 0.2f\left(0 + \frac{0.2}{2}, 0 + \frac{0.2}{2}\right)$$

$$= 0.2f\left(0.1, 0.1\right) = 0.2\left(1 + 0.1^2\right) = 0.202$$

$$y_1 = y_0 + \frac{1}{6}\left(K_1 + 2K_2 + 2K_3 + K_4\right)$$

$$K_3 = h \cdot f\left(x_0 + \frac{h}{2}, y_0 + \frac{K_2}{2}\right) = 0.2f\left(0 + \frac{0.2}{2}, 0 + \frac{0.202}{2}\right)$$

$$= 0.2f\left(0.1, 0.101\right) = 0.2\left(1 + 0.101^2\right) = 0.202$$

$$K_4 = h \cdot f\left(x_0 + h, y_0 + K_3\right) = 0.2f\left(0 + 0.2, 0 + 0.202\right)$$

$$= 0.2f\left(0.2, 0.202\right) = 0.2\left(1 + 0.202^2\right) = 0.2082$$

Therefore

$$y_1 = y_0 + \frac{1}{6}\left(K_1 + 2K_2 + 2K_3 + K_4\right)$$

$$= 0 + \frac{1}{6}\left[0.2 + \left(2 \times 0.202\right) + \left(2 \times 0.202\right) + 0.2082\right] = 0.203$$

$$y_2 = y_1 + \frac{1}{6}\left(K_1 + 2K_2 + 2K_3 + K_4\right)$$

$$K_1 = h \cdot f\left(x_1, y_1\right) = 0.2f\left(0.2, 0.203\right) = 0.2\left(1 + 0.203^2\right) = 0.2082$$

$$K_2 = h \cdot f\left(x_1 + \frac{h}{2}, y_1 + \frac{K_1}{2}\right) = 0.2f\left(0.2 + \frac{0.2}{2}, 0.203 + \frac{0.2082}{2}\right)$$

$$= 0.2f\left(0.3, 0.3071\right) = 0.2\left(1 + 0.3071^2\right) = 0.2188$$

$$K_3 = h \cdot f\left(x_1 + \frac{h}{2}, y_1 + \frac{K_2}{2}\right) = 0.2f\left(0.3, 0.203, 0 + \frac{0.2188}{2}\right)$$

$$= 0.2f\left(0.3, 0.3124\right) = 0.2\left(1 + 0.3124^2\right) = 0.2195$$

$$K_4 = h \cdot f\left(x_1 + h, y_1 + K_3\right) = 0.2f\left(0.2 + 0.2\right), \left(0.203 + 0.2195\right)$$

$$= 0.2f\,(0.4, 0.4225) = 0.2\left(1 + 0.4225^2\right) = 0.2357$$

Therefore

$$y_2 = 0.203 + 1/6\left[0.2082 + (2 \times 0.2188) + (2 \times 0.2196) + 0.2357\right]$$

$$= 0.4231$$

$$y_3 = y_2 + 1/6\left(K_1 + 2K_2 + 2K_3 + K_4\right)$$

$$K_1 = h \cdot f\,(x_2, y_2) = 0.2f\,(0.4, 0.4231) = 0.2\left(1 + 0.4231^2\right) = 0.2358$$

$$K_2 = h \cdot f\left(x_2 + \frac{h}{2}, y_2 + \frac{K_1}{2}\right) = 0.2f\left(0.4 + \frac{0.2}{2}, 0.4231 + \frac{0.2358}{2}\right)$$

$$= 0.2f\,(0.5, 0.541) = 0.2\left(1 + 0.541^2\right) = 0.2585$$

$$K_3 = h \cdot f\left(x_2 + \frac{h}{2}, y_2 + \frac{K_2}{2}\right) = 0.2f\left(0.5, \left[0.4231 + \frac{0.2585}{2}\right]\right)$$

$$= 0.2f\,(0.3, 0.5524) = 0.2\left(1 + 0.5524^2\right) = 0.261$$

$$K_4 = h \cdot f\left[(x_2 + h), (y_2 + K_3)\right] = 0.2f\,(0.4 + 0.2), (0.4231 + 0.261)$$

$$= 0.2f\,(0.6, 0.6841) = 0.2\left(1 + 0.6841^2\right) = 0.2936$$

$$y_3 = 0.4231 + 1/6\left[0.2358 + (2 \times 0.2585) + (2 \times 0.261) + 0.2936\right]$$

$$= 0.6845$$

Example 4.6

Using fourth order Runge–Kutta method,[6] solve the following equation taking each step of $t = 0.1$

$$\left(\frac{dy}{dx}\right) = \left[\frac{4t}{y} - t \cdot y\right]$$

Given $y(0) = 3$, show the details of computations.

Solution

For

$$t_0 = 0, \quad y_0 = 3$$
$$t_1 = 0.1, \text{ find } y_1$$
$$t_2 = 0.2, \text{ find } y_2; \qquad \text{interval } h = \Delta t = 0.1$$

$$y_1 = y_0 + \frac{1}{6}\left(K_1 + 2K_2 + 2K_3 + K_4\right)$$

$$K_1 = h \cdot f\,(t_0, y_0) = 0.1f\,(0, 3) = 0.1\left[\frac{4 \times 0}{3} - (0 \times 3)\right] = 0$$

$$K_2 = h \cdot f\left[\left(t_0 + \frac{h}{2}\right), \left(y_0 + \frac{K_1}{2}\right)\right] = 0.1f\left[\left(0 + \frac{0.1}{2}\right), \left(3 + \frac{0}{2}\right)\right]$$

$$= 0.1f\,(0.05, 3) = \left[\left(\frac{4 \times 0.05}{3}\right) - (0.05 \times 3)\right] = -0.00833$$

$$K_3 = h \cdot f\left[\left(t_0 + \frac{h}{2}\right), \left(y_0 + \frac{K_2}{2}\right)\right] = 0.1f\left[0.05, \left(3 + \frac{-0.0083}{2}\right)\right]$$

$$= 0.1f\,(0.05, 2.996) = 0.1\left[\left(\frac{4 \times 0.05}{2.996}\right) - (0.05 \times 2.996)\right] = -0.0083$$

$$K_4 = h \cdot f\left[(t_0 + h), (y_0 + K_3)\right] = 0.1f\left[(0 + 0.1), (3 - 0.0083)\right]$$

$$= 0.1f\,(0.1, 2.9917) = 0.1\left[\left(\frac{4 \times 0.1}{2.9917}\right) - (0.1 \times 2.9917)\right] = -0.0165$$

$$y_1 = 3 + \frac{1}{6}\left[0 + 2\,(-0.00833) + 2\,(-0.00833) - 0.0165\right] = 2.9917$$

$$y_2 = y_1 + \frac{1}{6}\left(K_1 + 2K_2 + 2K_3 + K_4\right)$$

$$K_1 = h \cdot f\,(t_1, y_1) = 0.1f\,(0.1, 2.9917)$$

$$= 0.1\left[\frac{4 \times 0.1}{2.9917} - (0.1 \times 2.9917)\right] = -0.0165$$

$$K_2 = h \cdot f\left[\left(t_1 + \frac{h}{2}\right), \left(y_1 + \frac{K_1}{2}\right)\right]$$

$$= 0.1f\left[\left(0.1 + \frac{0.1}{2}\right), \left(2.9917 - \frac{0.0165}{2}\right)\right] = 0.1f\,(0.15, 2.983)$$

$$= 0.1\left[\left(\frac{4 \times 0.15}{2.983}\right) - (2.983 \times 0.15)\right] = -0.0246$$

$$K_3 = h \cdot f\left[\left(t_1 + \frac{h}{2}\right), \left(y_1 + \frac{K_2}{2}\right)\right] = 0.1f\left[\left(0.1 + \frac{0.1}{2}\right), \left(2.9917 - \frac{0.0246}{2}\right)\right]$$

$$= 0.1f\,(0.15, 2.9794) = 0.1\left[\left(\frac{4 \times 0.15}{2.9794}\right) - (0.15 \times 2.9794)\right] = -0.0245$$

$$K_4 = h \cdot f\left[(t_1 + h), (y_1 + K_3)\right] = 0.1f\left[(0.1 + 0.1), (2.9917 - 0.0245)\right]$$

$$= 0.1f\,(0.2, 2.9672) = 0.1\left[\left(\frac{4 \times 0.2}{2.9672}\right) - (0.2 \times 2.9672)\right] = -\,0.03238$$

Therefore

$$y_2 = 2.9917 + \frac{1}{6}\left[-0.0165 + 2\left(-0.0246\right) + 2\left(-0.0246\right) - 0.03238\right]$$

$$= 2.9672$$

Example 4.7

Solve the following equation

$$\left(\frac{dy}{dx}\right) = (y - x)$$

by Runge–Kutta method given $y_0 = 1$. Find $y(0.1)$ and $y(0.2)$ correct to four decimal places.

Solution

At $\qquad x_0 = 0, \qquad y_0 = 1, \qquad h = 0.1$

$$y_1 = y_0 + \frac{1}{6}\left(K_1 + 2K_2 + 2K_3 + K_4\right)$$

$$K_1 = h \cdot f\,(x_0, y_0) = 0.1f\,(0, 1) = 0.1\,(1 - 0) = 0.1$$

$$K_2 = h \cdot f\left[\left(x_0 + \frac{h}{2}\right), \left(y_0 + \frac{K_1}{2}\right)\right] = 0.1f\left[\left(0 + \frac{0.1}{2}\right), \left(1 + \frac{0.1}{2}\right)\right]$$

$$= 0.1f\,(0.05, 1.05) = 0.1\,(1.05 - 0.05) = 0.1$$

$$K_3 = h \cdot f\left[\left(x_0 + \frac{h}{2}\right), \left(y_0 + \frac{K_2}{2}\right)\right] = 0.1f\left[\left(0 + \frac{0.1}{2}\right), \left(1 + \frac{0.1}{2}\right)\right]$$

$$= 0.1f\,(0.05, 1.05) = 0.1\,(1.05 - 0.05) = 0.1$$

$$K_4 = h \cdot f\left[(x_0 + h), (y_0 + K_3)\right] = 0.1f\left[(0 + 0.1), (1 + 0.1)\right]$$

$$= 0.1f\,(0.1, 1.1) = 0.1\,(1.1 - 0.1) = 0.1$$

$$y_1 = y\,(0.1) = 1.0 + \frac{1}{6}\left[0.1 + (2 \times 0.1) + (2 \times 0.1) + 0.1\right] = 1.1$$

$$y_2 = y_1 + \frac{1}{6}\left(K_1 + 2K_2 + 2K_3 + K_4\right)$$

$$K_1 = h \cdot f\,(x_1, y_1) = 0.1f\,(0, 1, 1.1) = 0.1\,(1.1 - 0.1) = 0.1$$

$$K_2 = h \cdot f\left[\left(x_1 + \frac{h}{2}\right), \left(y_1 + \frac{K_1}{2}\right)\right] = 0.1f\left[\left(0.1 + \frac{0.1}{2}\right), \left(1.1 + \frac{0.1}{2}\right)\right]$$

$$= 0.1f\,(0.15, 1.15) = 0.1\,(1.15 - 0.15) = 0.1$$

$$K_3 = h \cdot f\left[\left(x_1 + \frac{h}{2}\right), \left(y_1 + \frac{K_2}{2}\right)\right] = 0.1f\left[\left(0.1 + \frac{0.1}{2}\right), \left(1.1 + \frac{0.1}{2}\right)\right]$$

$$= 0.1f(0.15, 1.15) = 0.1(1.15 - 0.15) = 0.1$$

$$K_4 = h \cdot f\left[(x_1 + h), (y_1 + K_3)\right] = 0.1f\left[(0.1 + 0.1), (1.1 + 0.1)\right]$$

$$= 0.1f(0.2, 1.2) = 0.1(1.2 - 0.2) = 0.1$$

$$y_2 = y_1 + \frac{1}{6}\left(K_1 + 2K_2 + 2K_3 + K_4\right)$$

$$= 1.1 + \frac{1}{6}\left[0.1 + (2 \times 0.1) + (2 \times 0.1) + 0.1\right] = 1.2$$

Hence $y_2 = y(0.2) = 1.2$

4.3 TAYLOR'S SERIES

This[7,8] expansion can be used to solve the differential equations by a stepwise procedure. Starting from an initial value of the function, the first approximate value for a chosen step interval is computed. This value is used to estimate the second approximate value of the function from the next step interval. The procedure is repeated for the required number of intervals.

The Taylor's series expansion can be expressed as,

$$y_1 = y_0 + hy_0' + \frac{h^2}{2!}y_0'' + \frac{h^3}{3!}y_0''' + \frac{h^4}{4!}y_0'''' + \cdots$$

$$y_2 = y_1 + hy_1' + \frac{h^2}{2!}y_1'' + \frac{h^3}{3!}y_1''' + \frac{h^4}{4!}y_1'''' + \cdots$$

where h is the interval and $(dy/dx) = f(x)$.

For different values of x_0, x_1 and x_2 at intervals of h the values of the function y_1 and y_2 are determined. The application of this method is illustrated by the following examples.

Example 4.8

Solve numerically the differential equation $\left(\frac{dy}{dx}\right) = (x + y)$, when $y(1) = 0$ using Taylor's series up to $x = 1.2$ with the interval $h = 0.1$.

Solution

Given $x_0 = 1$ and $y_0 = 0$, we have to find y_1 when $x_1 = 1.1$ and y_2 when $x_2 = 1.2$.

$$y' = x + y; \qquad y_0' = (1 + 0) = 1$$

$$y'' = 1 + y'; \qquad y_0'' = (1 + 1) = 2$$

$$y''' = y''; \qquad y_0''' = 2$$

$$y'''' = y'''; \qquad y_0'''' = 2$$

$$y''''' = y''''; \qquad y_0''''' = 2$$

Therefore, using Taylor's series, we have the function,

$$y_1 = 0 + (0.1 \times 1) + \left(\frac{0.1^2}{2!} \times 2\right) + \left(\frac{0.1^3}{3!} \times 2\right) + \left(\frac{0.1^4}{4!} \times 2\right) + \left(\frac{0.1^5}{5!} \times 2\right) = 0.1103$$

Therefore $y_1 = 0.1103$

Now $\quad y_1' = (1.1 + 0.1103) = 1.2103$

$$y_1'' = (1 + 1.2103) = 2.2103$$

$$y_1''' = 2.2103$$

$$y_1'''' = 2.2103$$

Therefore, we have

$$y_2 = 0.1103 + (0.1 \times 1.2103) + \left(\frac{0.1^2}{2!} \times 2.2103\right) + \left(\frac{0.1^3}{3!} \times 2.2103\right) + \cdots = 0.243$$

4.4 MILNE'S PREDICTOR—CORRECTOR METHOD

This formula[9] can be used to solve differential equations. However, the method requires four values prior to the required value. These four values (x_0, y_0), (x_1, y_1), (x_2, y_2), and (x_3, y_3), are to be evaluated by using Taylor's series or Runge–Kutta[10] methods. The derivation of Milne's predictor and corrector formula is presented and its application is illustrated with the following numerical examples.

Derivation of Milne's Predictor—Corrector Formula

$$y(x_0 + nh) = y_0 + n\Delta y_0 + \frac{n(n-1)\Delta^2 y_0}{2!} + \frac{n(n-1)(n-2)\Delta^3 y_0}{3!}$$

$$+ \frac{n(n-1)(n-2)(n-3)\Delta^4 y_0}{4!} + \cdots \qquad (1)$$

Differentiating with respect to n we have

$$hy'(x_0 + nh) = \Delta y_0 + \frac{(2n-1)\Delta^2 y_0}{2} + \frac{(3n^2 - 6n + 2)\Delta^3 y_0}{6}$$

$$+ \frac{(2n^3 - 9n^2 + 11n - 3)\Delta^4 y_0}{12} + \cdots \qquad (2)$$

Substituting $n = 1, 2, 3$ and 4 in Eq. (2) we have

$$hy'(x_0 + h) = \Delta y_0 + \frac{\Delta^2 y_0}{2} - \frac{\Delta^3 y_0}{6} + \frac{\Delta^4 y_0}{12} \tag{3}$$

$$hy'(x_0 + 2h) = \Delta y_0 + \frac{3\Delta^2 y_0}{2} + \frac{\Delta^3 y_0}{3} - \frac{\Delta^4 y_0}{12} \tag{4}$$

$$hy'(x_0 + 3h) = \Delta y_0 + \frac{3\Delta^2 y_0}{2} + \frac{11\Delta^3 y_0}{6} + \frac{\Delta^4 y_0}{4} \tag{5}$$

$$hy'(x_0 + 4h) = \Delta y_0 + \frac{7\Delta^2 y_0}{2} + \frac{13\Delta^3 y_0}{3} - \frac{25\Delta^4 y_0}{12} \tag{6}$$

By definition,

$$y(x_0 + h) = y_1 > y'(x_0 + h) = y_1' \tag{7}$$

$$y(x_0 + 2h) = y_2 > y'(x_0 + 2h) = y_2' \tag{8}$$

$$y(x_0 + 3h) = y_3 > y'(x_0 + 3h) = y_3' \tag{9}$$

$$y(x_0 + 4h) = y_4 > y'(x_0 + 4h) = y_4' \tag{10}$$

Using Eqs (7) to (10) in Eqs (3) to (6), we have

$$y_1' = \frac{1}{h}\left[\Delta y_0 + \frac{\Delta^2 y_0}{2} - \frac{\Delta^3 y_0}{6} + \frac{\Delta^4 y_0}{12} + \cdots\right] \tag{11}$$

$$y_2' = \frac{1}{h}\left[\Delta y_0 + \frac{3\Delta^2 y_0}{2} - \frac{\Delta^3 y_0}{3} + \frac{\Delta^4 y_0}{12} + \cdots\right] \tag{12}$$

$$y_3' = \frac{1}{h}\left[\Delta y_0 + \frac{5\Delta^2 y_0}{2} - \frac{11\Delta^3 y_0}{6} + \frac{\Delta^4 y_0}{4} + \cdots\right] \tag{13}$$

$$y_4' = \frac{1}{h}\left[\Delta y_0 + \frac{7\Delta^2 y_0}{2} - \frac{13\Delta^3 y_0}{3} + \frac{25\Delta^4 y_0}{12} + \cdots\right] \tag{14}$$

Expressing finite difference operations in terms of ordinate,

$$\Delta y_0 = y_1 - y_0 \tag{15}$$
$$\Delta^2 y_0 = y_2 - 2y_1 + y_0 \tag{16}$$
$$\Delta^3 y_0 = y_3 - 3y_2 + 3y_1 - y_0 \tag{17}$$
$$\Delta^4 y_0 = y_4 - 4y_3 + 6y_2 - 4y_0 + y_0 \tag{18}$$

Substituting Eqs (15) to (18) in Eqs (11) to (14) and simplifying,

$$y_1' = \frac{1}{12h}\left[-3y_0 - 10y_1 + 18y_2 - 6y_3 + y_4\right] \tag{19}$$

$$y_2' = \frac{1}{12h}\left[y_0 - 8y_1 + 8y_3 - y_4\right] \tag{20}$$

$$y_3' = \frac{1}{12h}\left[-y_0 + 6y_1 - 18y_2 + 10y_3 + 3y_4\right] \tag{21}$$

$$y_4' = \frac{1}{12h}\left[3y_0 - 16y_1 + 36y_2 - 48y_3 + 25y_4\right] \tag{22}$$

Adding Eqs (19) and (21) and multiplying by 2,

$$2\left(y_1' + y_3'\right) = \frac{2}{12h}\left[-4y_0 - 4y_1 + 4y_3 + 4y_4\right] \tag{23}$$

From Eqs (19), (20) and (21), we have

$$\left(2y_1' + 2y_3' - y_2'\right) = \frac{1}{12h}\left[-9y_0 + 9y_4\right] = \frac{9}{12h}\left[y_4 - y_0\right] \tag{24}$$

Substituting Eq. (23) in Eq. (24),

$$y_4 = y_0 + \frac{4h}{3}\left(2y_1' - y_2' + 2y_3'\right) \tag{25}$$

Equation (25) can be written as

$$y_{n+1} = y_{n-3} + \frac{4h}{3}\left(2y_{n-2}' - y_{n-1}' + 2y_n'\right) \tag{26}$$

The above formula is known as Milne's predictor formula and can be expressed in the form

$$y_{n+1,p} = y_{n-3} + \frac{4h}{3}\left(2y_{n-2}' - y_{n-1}' + 2y_n'\right) \tag{27}$$

Milne's corrector formula can be obtained as follows:

$$y_2' + y_4' = \frac{1}{12h}\left[4y_0 - 24y_1 + 36y_2 - 40y_3 + 24y_4\right] \tag{28}$$

Using Eq. (28) and Eq. (21),

$$\left(y_2' + 4y_3' + y_4'\right) = \frac{3}{h}\left[y_4 - y_2\right] \tag{29}$$

Hence

$$y_4 = y_2 + \frac{h}{3}\left(y_2' + 4y_3' + y_4'\right) \tag{30}$$

Milne's corrector formula can be expressed in the form

$$y_{n+1,c} = y_{n-1} + \frac{h}{3}\left(y_{n-1}' + 4y_n' + y_{n+1}'\right) \tag{31}$$

Example 4.9

Given $\left(\dfrac{dy}{dx}\right) = 0.5\left(1 + x\right)^2 y^2$

$y(0) = 1$, $y(0.1) = 1.06$, $y(0.2) = 1.12$ and $y(0.3) = 1.21$

Find $y(0.4)$ using Milne's predictor—corrector formula.

Solution

n	x	y	$y' = 0.5\,(1+x)^2 y^2$
0	0	1	$y'_0 = 0.5\,(1+0)^2 1^2 = 0.5$
1	0.1	1.06	$y'_1 = 0.5\,(1+0.1)^2(1.06)^2 = 0.67978$
2	0.2	1.12	$y'_2 = 0.5\,(1+0.2)^2(1.12)^2 = 0.90317$
3	0.3	1.21	$y'_3 = 0.5\,(1+0.3)^2(1.21)^2 = 1.23716$

Using Milne's predictor formula, we have $h = 0.1$ and

$$y_{4,p} = y_0 + \frac{4h}{3}(2y'_1 - y'_2 + 2y'_3)$$

$$= 1 + \frac{4(0.1)}{3}\left[(2 \times 0.67978) - 0.90317 + (2 \times 1.23716)\right]$$

$$= 1.39076$$

$$y'_4 = \left[0.5\,(1+0.4)^2 \times 1.39076^2\right] = 1.8955$$

$$y_{4,c} = y_2 + \frac{h}{3}(y'_2 + 4y'_3 + y'_4)$$

$$= \left[1.8955 + \frac{0.1}{3}(0.90317 + 4\,(1.23716) + 1.8955\right]$$

$$= 2.15369$$

Example 4.10

Given $\left(\dfrac{dy}{dx}\right) = 2e^x - y$

$y(0) = 2$, $y(0.1) = 2.010$, $y(0.2) = 2.040$, find $y(0.4)$ and $y(0.5)$–correct to three decimal places applying Milne's predictor–corrector method.

Solution

n	x	y	$y' = 2e_x - y^2$
0	0	2	$y'_0 = (2e^0 - 2) = 0$
1	0.1	2.010	$y'_1 = (2e^{0.1} - 2.010) = 0.200$
2	0.2	2.040	$y'_2 = (2e^{0.2} - 2.040) = 0.403$
3	0.3	2.090	$y'_3 = (2e^{0.3} - 2.090) = 0.610$

Interval $h = 0.1$

$$y_{4,p} = y_0 + \frac{4h}{3}(2y'_1 - y'_2 + 2y'_3)$$

$$= 2 + \frac{4(0.1)}{3}\left[(2 \times 0.200) - 0.403 + (2 \times 0.610)\right]$$

$$= 2.162$$

$$y'_4 = \left[2e^{0.4} - 2.162\right]$$

$$= 0.822$$

$$y_{4,c} = y_2 + \frac{h}{3}(y_2' + 4y_3' + y_4')$$

$$= \left[2.040 + \frac{0.1}{3}(0.403 + 4(0.610) + 0.822)\right]$$

$$= 2.162$$

$$y_{5,p} = y_1 + \frac{4h}{3}(2y_2' - 4y_3' + 2y_4')$$

$$= 2.010 + \frac{4(0.1)}{3}\left[(2 \times 0.403) - 0.610 + (2 \times 0.822)\right]$$

$$= 2.225$$

$$y_5' = [2e^{0.5} - 2.255]$$

$$= 1.042$$

$$y_{5,c} = y_3 + \frac{h}{3}(y_3' - 4y_4' - y_3' + y_5')$$

$$= \left[2.090 + \frac{0.1}{3}(0.610 + 4(0.822) + 1.042)\right]$$

$$= 2.225$$

Example 4.11

Solve the following differential equation by Milne's method to obtain to the initial value problem $y' = x + y$; given $y(0) = 0$

Solution

Taylor series may be used to obtain $y(0.2)$, $y(0.4)$ and $y(0.6)$ correct to an accuracy of four decimal places.

$y' = x + y$	$y_0' = (x_0 + y_0) = 0$	$y_1' = (x_1 + y_1)$ $= (0.2 + 0.0214)$ $= 0.0414$	$y_2' = (0.4 + 0.052)$ $= 0.452$
$y'' = 1 + y'$	$y_0'' = (1 + y_0') = 1$	$y_1'' = 1 + y_1'$ $= 0.0414$	$y_2'' = (1 + 0.052)$ $= 1.452$
$y''' = y''$	$y_0''' = 1$	$y_1''' = 1.0414$	$y_2''' = 1.452$
$y^{iv} = y'''$	$y_0^{iv} = 1$	$y_1^{iv} = 0.0414$	$y_2^{iv} = 1.452$ $= 0.452$
$y^v = y^{iv}$	$y_0^v = 1$	$y_1^v = 0.0414$	$y_2^v = 1.452$

$$y_1 = y_0 + hy_0' + \frac{h^2}{2!}y_0'' + \frac{h^3}{3!}y_0''' + \frac{h^4}{4!}y_0^{iv} + \frac{h^5}{5!}y_0^v$$

$$= \left[0 + 0.2(0) + \frac{0.2^2}{2!} \times 1 + \frac{0.2^3}{3!} \times 1 + \frac{0.2^4}{4!} \times 1 + \frac{0.2^5}{5!} \times 1\right]$$

$$= 0.0214$$

$$y_2 = y_1 + hy_1' + \frac{h^2}{2!}y_1'' + \frac{h^3}{3!}y_1''' + \frac{h^4}{4!}y_1^{iv} + \frac{h^5}{5!}y_1^{v}$$

$$= \left[0.0214 + 0.2\,(0.0414) + \frac{0.2^2}{2!} \times 1.0414 + \frac{0.2^3}{3!} \times 1.0414 + \frac{0.2^4}{4!} \times 1.0414 + \frac{0.2^5}{5!} \times 1.0414 \right]$$

$$= 0.052$$

$$y_3 = y_2 + hy_2' + \frac{h^2}{2!}y_2'' + \frac{h^3}{3!}y_2''' + \frac{h^4}{4!}y_2^{iv} + \frac{h^5}{5!}y_2^{v}$$

$$= \left[0.052 + 0.2\,(0.452) + \frac{0.2^2}{2!} \times 0.452 + \frac{0.2^3}{3!} \times 1.452 + \frac{0.2^4}{4!} \times 1.452 + \frac{0.2^5}{5!} \times 1.452 \right]$$

$$= 0.1735$$

n	x	y	$y' = x + y$
0	0	0	0
1	0.2	0.0214	$y_1' = (0.2 + 0.0214) = 0.2214$
2	0.4	0.052	$y_2' = (0.4 + 0.052) = 0.452$
3	0.6	0.1735	$y_3' = (0.6 + 0.1735) = 0.7735$

$$y_{4,p} = y_0 + \frac{4h}{3}(2y_1' - y_2' + 2y_3')$$

$$= 0 + \frac{4(0.2)}{3}\left[(2 \times 0.2214) - 0.4520 + (2 \times 0.7735)\right]$$

$$= 0.4101$$

$$y_4' = x_4 + y_4$$

$$y_{4,c} = y_2 + \frac{h}{3}(y_2' + 4y_3' + y_4')$$

$$= 0.052 + \frac{0.2}{3}\left[0.4520 + (4 \times 0.7735) + 1.2101\right]$$

$$= 0.3691$$

Example 4.12

Solve the initial value problem

$$y' + 1 + y^2$$

Given $y(0) = 0$; choosing the interval $h = 0.1$. Compute five steps and compare the results using

a. Taylor's series
b. Euler–Cauchy's method
c. Runge–Kutta method
d. Exact method

Solution

a. Taylor's method

The values of y', y''... y^v, y'_0 ... to y^v_0, y'_1 ... to y^v_1, y'_2 ... to y^v_2, y'_3 ... to y^v_3 and y'_4 ... to y^v_4 are computed in the table shown below:

$y' = 1 + y^2$	$y'_0 = 1 + 0^{2=1}$	$y'_1 = 1 + 0.10531^2$	$y'_2 = 1 + 0.21252^2$
	$= 1$	$= 1.01110$	$= 1.04516$
$y'' = 2y$	$y''_0 = 1 + 2(0)$	$y''_1 = 1 + 2\,(0.10531)$	$y''_2 = 1 + 2\,(0.21252)$
	$= 1$	$= 1.21062$	$= 1.42504$
$y''' = 2y'$	$y'''_0 = 2(1)$	$y'''_1 = 2\,(1.01110)$	$y'''_2 = 2\,(1.04516)$
	$= 2$	$= 2.0222$	$= 2.09032$
$y^{iv} = 2y''$	$y^{iv}_0 = 2(1)$	$y^{iv}_1 = 2\,(1.21062)$	$y^{iv}_2 = 2\,(1.42504)$
	$= 2$	$= 2.42124$	$= 2.85008$
$y^v = 2y'''$	$y^v_0 = 2(1)$	$y^v_1 = 2\,(2.0222)$	$y^v_2 = 2\,(2.09032)$
	$= 2$	$= 4.0444$	$= 4.18064$
$y'_3 = 1 + 0.32482^2 = 1.10551$		$y'_4 = 1 + 0.44400^2 = 1.19714$	
$y''_3 = 1 + 2\,(0.32482) = 1.64964$		$y''_4 = 1 + 2\,(0.44400) = 1.88800$	
$y'''_3 = 1 + 2\,(1.10551) = 2.21102$		$y'''_4 = 2\,(1.119714) = 2.39428$	
$y^{iv}_3 = 1 + 2\,(1.64964) = 3.29928$		$y^{iv}_4 = 2\,(1.88800) = 3.776$	
$y^v_3 = 1 + 2\,(1.21102) = 4.42204$		$y^v_4 = 2\,(2.39428) = 4.78856$	

$$y_1 = y_0 + hy'_0 + \frac{h^2}{2!}y''_0 + \frac{h^3}{3!}y'''_0 + \frac{h^4}{4!}y^{iv}_0 + \frac{h^5}{5!}y^v_0$$

$$= \left[0 + 0.1(1) + \frac{0.1^2}{2!} \times 1 + \frac{0.1^3}{3!} \times 2 + \frac{0.1^4}{4!} \times 2 + \frac{0.1^5}{5!} \times 2\right]$$

$$= 0.10531$$

$$y_2 = y_1 + hy'_1 + \frac{h^2}{2!}y''_1 + \frac{h^3}{3!}y'''_1 + \frac{h^4}{4!}y^{iv}_1 + \frac{h^5}{5!}y^v_1$$

$$= 0.10531 + 0.1\,(1.01110) + \frac{0.1^2}{2!}(1.21062) + \frac{0.1^3}{3!}(2.0222) + \frac{0.1^4}{4!}(2.42124) + \frac{0.1^5}{5!}(4.0444)$$

$$= 0.21282$$

$$y_3 = y_2 + hy'_2 + \frac{h^2}{2!}y''_2 + \frac{h^3}{3!}y'''_2 + \frac{h^4}{4!}y^{iv}_2 + \frac{h^5}{5!}y^v_2$$

$$= 0.2182 + 0.1(1.04516) + \frac{0.1^2}{2!}(1.42504) + \frac{0.1^3}{3!}(2.09032) + \frac{0.1^4}{4!}$$

$$(2.85008) + \frac{0.1^5}{5!}(4.18064)$$

$$= 0.32482$$

$$y_4 = y_3 + hy_3' + \frac{h^2}{2!}y_3'' + \frac{h^3}{3!}y_3''' + \frac{h^4}{4!}y_3^{iv} + \frac{h^5}{5!}y_3^{v}$$

$$= 0.32482 + 0.1(1.10551) + \frac{0.1^2}{2!}(1.64964) + \frac{0.1^3}{3!}(2.21102) + \frac{0.1^4}{4!}$$

$$(3.29928) + \frac{0.1^5}{5!}(4.42204)$$

$$= 0.44400$$

$$y_5 = y_4 + hy_4' + \frac{h^2}{2!}y_4'' + \frac{h^3}{3!}y_4''' + \frac{h^4}{4!}y_4^{iv} + \frac{h^5}{5!}y_4^{v}$$

$$= 0.4440 + 0.1(1.19714) + \frac{0.1^2}{2!}(1.8880) + \frac{0.1^3}{3!}(2.39428) + \frac{0.1^4}{4!}(3.776) + \frac{0.1^5}{5!}(4.78856)$$

$$= 0.573569$$

b. Euler–Cauchy's Method

$$y_{n+1} = y_n + hf(x_n, y_n)$$

$$y_1 = y_0 + hf(x_0, y_0) = 0 + 0.1(1 + 0^2) = 0.10000$$

$$y_2 = y_1 + hf(x_1, y_1) = 0.1 + 0.1(1 + 0.1^2) = 0.20100$$

$$y_3 = y_2 + hf(x_2, y_2) = 0.201 + 0.1(1 + 0.201^2) = 0.30504$$

$$y_4 = y_3 + hf(x_3, y_3) = 0.30504 + 0.1(1 + 0.30504^2) = 0.41434$$

$$y_5 = y_4 + hf(x_4, y_4) = 0.41434 + 0.1(1 + 0.41434^2) = 0.53151$$

c. Runge–Kutta method

$$y_1 = y_0 + \frac{1}{6}(K_1 + 2K_2 + 2K_3 + K_4)$$

$$K_1 = hf(x_0, y_0) = 0.1(1 + y_0^2) = 0.1(1 + 0^2) = 0.1$$

$$K_2 = hf\left(x_0 + \frac{h}{2}, y_0 + \frac{K_1}{2}\right)$$

$$= 0.1f\left(0 + \frac{0.1}{2}, 0 + \frac{0.1}{2}\right)$$

$$= 0.1f(0.05, 0.05) = 0.1(1 + 0.05^2) = 0.10025$$

$$K_3 = hf\left(x_0 + \frac{h}{2}, y_0 + \frac{K_2}{2}\right)$$

$$= 0.1f\left(0 + \frac{0.1}{2}, 0 + \frac{0.10025}{2}\right)$$

$$= 0.1f\left(0.05, 0.05013\right) = 0.1\left(1 + 0.05013^2\right) = 0.10025$$

$$K_4 = hf\left(x_0 + h, y_0 + K_3\right)$$

$$= 0.1f\left(0.2 + 0.1, 0.20272 + 0.10655\right)$$

$$= 0.1\left(1 + 0.10025^2\right)$$

$$= 0.10101$$

$$y_1 = 0 + \frac{1}{6}\left[0.1 + 2\left(0.10025\right) + 2\left(0.10025\right) + 0.10101\right]$$

$$= 0.10034$$

$$y_2 = y_1 + \frac{1}{6}\left(K_1 + 2K_2 + 2K_3 + K_4\right)$$

$$K_1 = hf\left(x_1, y_1\right)$$

$$= 0.1f\left(0.1, 0.10034\right)$$

$$= 0.1\left(1 + 0.10034^2\right)$$

$$= 0.10101$$

$$K_2 = hf\left(x_1 + \frac{h}{2}, y_1 + \frac{K_1}{2}\right)$$

$$= 0.1f\left[0.1 + \frac{0.1}{2}, 0.10034 + \frac{0.10101}{2}\right]$$

$$= 0.1f\left(0.15, 0.15058\right)$$

$$= 0.1\left(1 + 0.15058^2\right)$$

$$= 0.10228$$

$$K_3 = hf\left(x_1 + \frac{h}{2}, y_1 + \frac{K_2}{2}\right)$$

$$= 0.1f\left[0.1 + \frac{0.1}{2}, 0.10034 + \frac{0.10228}{2}\right]$$

$$= 0.1f\left(0.15, 0.15148\right)$$

$$= 0.1\left(1 + 0.15148^2\right)$$

$$= 0.10230$$

$$K_4 = hf\left(x_1 + h, y_1 + K_3\right)$$

$$= 0.1f\left(0.1 + 0.1, 0.10034 + 0.10230\right)$$

$$= 0.1f\left(0.2 + 0.20264\right)$$

$$= 0.1\left(1 + 0.20264^2\right)$$

$$= 0.10411$$

$$y_2 = 0.10034 + \frac{1}{6}\left(0.10101 + 2\left(0.10228\right) + 2\left(0.10230\right) + 0.10411\right)$$

$$y_3 = y_2 + \frac{1}{6}\left(K_1 + 2K_2 + 2K_3 + K_4\right)$$

$$K_1 = hf\left(x_2, y_2\right)$$

$$= 0.1f\left(0.2, 0.20272\right)$$

$$= 0.1\left(1 + 0.20272^2\right)$$

$$= 0.10411$$

$$K_2 = hf\left(x_2 + \frac{h}{2}, y_2 + \frac{K_1}{2}\right)$$

$$= 0.1f\left[0.2 + \frac{0.1}{2}, 0.20272 + \frac{0.10411}{2}\right]$$

$$= 0.1f\left(0.25, 0.25478\right)$$

$$= 0.1\left(1 + 0.25478^2\right)$$

$$= 0.10649$$

$$K_3 = hf\left(x_1 + \frac{h}{2}, y_1 + \frac{K_2}{2}\right)$$

$$= 0.1f\left[0.2 + \frac{0.1}{2}, 0.20272 + \frac{0.10649}{2}\right]$$

$$= 0.1f\left(0.25, 0.25596\right)$$

$$= 0.1\left(1 + 0.25596^2\right)$$

$$= 0.10655$$

$$K_4 = hf\left(x_2 + h, y_2 + K_3\right)$$

$$= 0.1f\left(0.2 + 0.1, 0.20272 + 0.10655\right)$$

$$= 0.1f\left(0.3 + 0.30927\right)$$

$$= 0.1\left(1 + 0.30927^2\right)$$

$$= 0.10956$$

$$y_3 = y_2 + \frac{1}{6}(K_1 + 2K_2 + 2K_3 + K_4)$$

$$= 0.1(1 + 0.42274^2)$$

$$= 0.30395$$

$$y_4 = y_3 + \frac{1}{6}(K_1 + 2K_2 + 2K_3 + K_4)$$

$$K_1 = hf(x_3, y_3)$$

$$= 0.1f(0.3, 0.30395)$$

$$= 0.1(1 + 0.30395^2)$$

$$= 0.10957$$

$$K_2 = hf\left(x_3 + \frac{h}{2}, y_3 + \frac{K_1}{2}\right)$$

$$= 0.1f\left[0.3 + \frac{0.1}{2}, 0.30935 + \frac{0.10957}{2}\right]$$

$$= 0.1f(0.35, 0.364135)$$

$$= 0.1(1 + 0.364135^2)$$

$$= 0.113259$$

$$K_3 = hf\left(x_3 + \frac{h}{2}, y_3 + \frac{K_2}{2}\right)$$

$$= 0.1f\left[0.3 + \frac{0.1}{2}, 0.30935 + \frac{0.113259}{2}\right]$$

$$= 0.1f(0.35, 0.36598)$$

$$= 0.1(1 + 0.36598^2)$$

$$= 0.11339$$

$$K_4 = hf(x_3 + h, y_3 + K_3)$$

$$= 0.1f(0.3 + 0.1, 0.30935 + 0.11339)$$

$$= 0.1f(0.4 + 0.42274)$$

$$= 0.1(1 + 0.42274^2)$$

$$= 0.11787$$

$$y_4 = 0.30935 + \frac{1}{6}\left[0.10957 + 2(0.113259) + 2(0.11339) + 0.11787\right]$$

$$= 0.42281$$

$$y_5 = y_4 + \frac{1}{6}(K_1 + 2K_2 + 2K_3 + K_4)$$

$$K_1 = hf(x_4, y_4)$$

$$= 0.1f(0.4, 0.42281)$$

$$= 0.1(1 + 0.42281^2)$$

$$= 0.11788$$

$$K_2 = hf\left(x_4 + \frac{h}{2}, y_4 + \frac{K_1}{2}\right)$$

$$= 0.1f\left[0.3 + \frac{0.1}{2}, 0.42281 + \frac{0.11788}{2}\right]$$

$$= 0.1f(0.35, 0.48175)$$

$$= 0.1(1 + 0.48175^2)$$

$$= 0.12321$$

$$K_3 = hf\left(x_4 + \frac{h}{2}, y_4 + \frac{K_2}{2}\right)$$

$$= 0.1f\left[0.3 + \frac{0.1}{2}, 0.42281 + \frac{0.12321}{2}\right]$$

$$= 0.1f(0.35, 0.484415)$$

$$= 0.1(1 + 0.484415^2)$$

$$= 0.12347$$

$$K_4 = hf(x_4 + h, y_4 + K_3)$$

$$= 0.1f(0.3 + 0.1, 0.42221 + 0.12347)$$

$$= 0.1f(0.4 + 0.54628)$$

$$= 0.1(1 + 0.54628^2)$$

$$= 0.12984$$

$$y_5 = 0.42281 + \frac{1}{6}\left[0.11788 + 2(0.12321) + 2(0.12347) + 0.12984\right]$$

$$= 0.54632$$

d. Exact Method

$$y' = 1 + y^2$$

Solving this, we have $y = \tan x$

The values of tan x for various values of x and n are compiled in the following table.

n	x	$\tan x$
0	0	0
1	0.1	0.100033
2	0.2	0.202710
3	0.3	0.309340
4	0.4	0.422790
5	0.5	0.546300

The results of the solution of this equation using various methods are compiled in Table 4.1.

The comparative analysis indicates that Runge–Kutta method yields results nearest to the exact.

Table 4.1: Comparison of results using Taylor's series, Euler–Cauchy's, Runge–Kutta and exact methods

n	x	y_{Taylor}	$y_{Eul-Cauc}$	$y_{Rung-Kut}$	$Exact$
0	0	0	0	0	0
1	0.1	0.10531	0.10000	0.10034	0.10033
2	0.2	0.21282	0.20100	0.20272	0.20271
3	0.3	0.32482	0.30504	0.30935	0.30394
4	0.4	0.44400	0.41434	0.42281	0.42279
5	0.5	0.57389	0.53151	0.54632	0.54630

EXERCISES

1. Solve the following differential equation by Runge–Kutta method.

$$\left(\frac{dy}{dx}\right) = \left(4 + y^2\right), \text{ where } y(0) = 0$$

Find $y(0.2)$, $y(0.4)$ and $y(0.6)$ correct to four decimal places.

2. Solve the following differential equation using Runge-Kutta method

$$\left(\frac{dy}{dx}\right) = \left(e^x + 2y\right), \text{ given } y(0) = 2.0$$

Estimate $y(0.2)$, $y(0.4)$ and $y(0.6)$ the values of correct to four decimal places.

3. Using Euler's method, find the value of y when $x = 0.5$ for the differential equation

$$\left(\frac{dy}{dx}\right) = (y - x), \text{ given } y = 1 \text{ when } x = 0$$

4. Solve the differential equation

$$\left(\frac{dy}{dx}\right) = (2x + y^2) \text{ given the boundary condition } y(0) = 1.0$$

Find the value of y when $x = 0.4$ using Euler's method in four steps.

5. Solve the equation

$$\left(\frac{dy}{dx}\right) = (x + y)$$ by Runge-Kutta method from $x = 0$ to $x = 0.4$, with the initial condition $y(0) = 1.0$ and using the interval $h = 0.1$

6. Solve the following equation by Runge–Kutta method

$$\left(\frac{dy}{dx}\right) = (1 + t^2)$$ for the range $1 \geq t \geq 0$ with the initial condition $y(0) = 1.0$ for $t = 0$

Find $y(0.2)$ correct to four decimal places.

7. Solve the differential equation

$$\left(\frac{dy}{dt}\right) = 0.5 (1 + t^2)y^2$$ given $y(0) = 1.0$, $y(0.1) = 1.06$, $y(0.2) = 1.12$ and $y(0.3) = 1.21$

Find $y(0.4)$ using Milne predictor—corrector formula.

8. Solve the equation

$$\left(\frac{dy}{dt}\right) = (t + y)$$ when $y(1) = 0$, using Taylor's series method up to $t = 1.2$

Using an interval of $h = 0.1$

9. Solve the initial value problem

$$\left(\frac{dy}{dt}\right) = (y^2 + t)$$ given the boundary condition $y(0) = 0$ and $t(0) = 0$

Find the value of y when $t = 1.0$ using an interval $h = 0.2$

10. Solve the equation $\left(\frac{dy}{dt}\right) = (y - t)$ given $y(0) = 1$

Find $y(0.1)$ and $y(0.2)$ correct to four decimal places using the following methods:
   a) Runge–Kutta method
   b) Taylor's series method
   c) Euler's method

REFERENCES

1. Ferziger JH, *Numerical Methods for Engineering Applications*, John Wiley, New York, 1981.
2. Krishna Raju N, *Advanced Mechanics of Solids and Structures*, McGraw Hill Education (India) Pvt Ltd, Chennai, India, 2019.
3. Rajasekharan S, *Numerical Methods in Science and Engineering—A Practical Approach*, AH Wheeler and Co, New Delhi, 1986.
4. Sastry SS, *Introductory Methods of Numerical Analysis*, Prentice Hall, India, New Delhi, 1979.

5. Butcher JC, *The Numerical Analysis of Ordinary Differential Equations; Runge–Kutta and General Linear methods*, John Wiley, New York, 1987.

6. Aziz AK, *Numerical Solutions of Boundary Value Problems for Ordinary Differential Equations*, Academic Press, New York, 1974.

7. Atkinson K, *Elementary Numerical Analysis*, Wiley, New York, 1985.

8. Collatz L, *Numerical Treatment of Differential Equations*, Springer Verlag, Berlin, 1966.

9. Jain MK, Iyengar Jain SRK and RK, *Numerical Methods for Scientific and Engineering Computation*, 6th Edn, New Age International Publishers, New Delhi, 2012.

10. Gear CW, *Numerical Initial Value Problems in Ordinary Differential Equations*, Prentice Hall Englewood Cliffs, New Jersey, 1971.

REVIEW QUESTIONS

1. Explain briefly Euler's method of solving ordinary differential equations. Illustrate graphically Euler's solution indicating the true and estimated values of a given function over a defined interval.

2. What are the limitations of the Euler's method? Can you use this method for digital computations?

3. Briefly outline the basic principles of Runge–Kutta method of solving ordinary differential equations.

4. Illustrate the use of Runge–Kutta fourth order formula for finding the solution of ordinary differential equations.

5. Briefly outline Milne's predictor—corrector method of solving ordinary differential equations.

6. What are the prerequisites for the use of Milne's predictor—corrector method in solving ordinary differential equations?

7. Explain briefly Taylor's series expansion and its application in solving ordinary differential equations.

8. Explain the significance of finite difference operations in the derivation of Milne's corrector formula used to solve ordinary differential equations.

9. In solving an ordinary differential equation with a starting point and a given interval, which method do you consider as numerically simple and fast to obtain an approximate solution?

10. In a comparative analysis of the various methods of solving ordinary differential equations, specify the method which yields results nearest to the exact solution.

OBJECTIVE TYPE QUESTIONS

1. Euler's method of solving ordinary differential equations depends upon
    a) finite differences
    b) Taylor's expansion of the function
    c) simpson's rule

2. Euler's method can be successfully used for solving differential equations
   a) using initial value of the function
   b) assuming any arbitrary value of the function
   c) to compute exact value of the function

3. Runge–Kutta method of solving ordinary differential equations is a generalization of
   a) finite difference procedure
   b) simpson's rule
   c) integration procedure

4. The use of Runge–Kutta formula for solving differential equations involves the computation of
   a) two integration constants
   b) singe step integration constant
   c) four successive integration steps

5. The Taylor's method of solving differential equations requires
   a) an initial value of the function
   b) direct integration of the function
   c) stepwise integration process

6. Solving differential equations using Taylor's procedure involves the use of
   a) four integration steps
   b) Taylor's series expansion
   c) predictor—corrector formula

7. Milne's predictor—corrector method requires the use of
   a) Simpson's rule
   b) single step integration
   c) Taylor's series

8. Runge–Kutta method of solving differential equations involves the computation of
   a) two integration constants
   b) Taylor's series expansion
   c) four integration constants

9. Milne's predictor and corrector method for solving differential equations requires
   a) the previous value of the function
   b) four previous values of the function
   c) Taylor's series expansion

10. Among the numerical methods of solving differential equations, the method yielding solutions nearest to the exact method is
    a) Euler's method
    b) Taylors method
    c) Runge–Kutta method

Numerical Integration

5.1 GENERAL ASPECTS

Most of the engineering problems generally require the computation of areas, volumes of irregular figures such as bending moment diagrams, earthwork calculations in foundations and beams of variable depth forming the super structure of long span bridges. It is often necessary to differentiate or integrate functions which are defined in a tabular or graphical form rather than as explicit functions.

Structural engineers are confronted with the problem of computing the slopes and deflections of beams with different types of loading. There are several problems in the engineering domain which involve numerical integration.

Several techniques[1,2,3] and procedures have been developed by mathematicians and engineers over the last several decades to facilitate such computations. Some of the prominent and widely used methods ideally suited in engineering computations are presented in the following sections.

5.2 TRAPEZOIDAL AND SIMPSON'S RULES

5.2.1 Trapezoidal Rule for Areas

Trapezoidal rule[4,5] is a numerical method of evaluating the area A bounded between $x = a$ and $x = b$ under a curve defined by the function $y = f(x)$ as shown in Fig. 5.1.

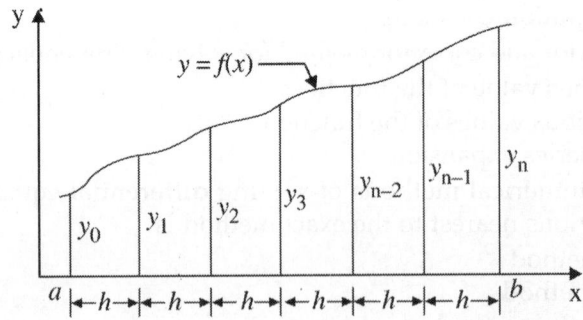

Fig. 5.1: Trapezoidal rule of numerical integration

The area bounded between the points a and b is computed as

$$A = \int_a^b y \cdot dx$$

where dA is the area between the two successive ordinates at an interval h

$$dA = \frac{h}{2}[y_{n-1} + y_n]$$

If ordinates are $y_0, y_1, y_2, \cdots, y_n$

$$dA_1 = \left(\frac{y_0 + y_1}{2}\right)h$$

$$dA_2 = \left(\frac{y_1 + y_2}{2}\right)h$$

....

$$dA_n = \left(\frac{y_{n-1} + y_n}{2}\right)h$$

Adding all the elemental areas, we have the total area as

$$A = \frac{h}{2}[y_0 + 2y_1 + 2y_2 + 2y_3 + \cdots + y_n]$$

$$A = h[y_0/2 + y_1 + y_2 + y_3 + \cdots + y_n/2]$$

Using this trapezoidal rule, we can integrate any given function between the prescribed limits choosing a suitable interval.

5.2.2 Trapezoidal Rule for Volumes

For the determination of volume under a surface defined by the function $Z = f(x, y)$ the horizontal projection of the surface is divided into grids as shown in Fig. 5.2.

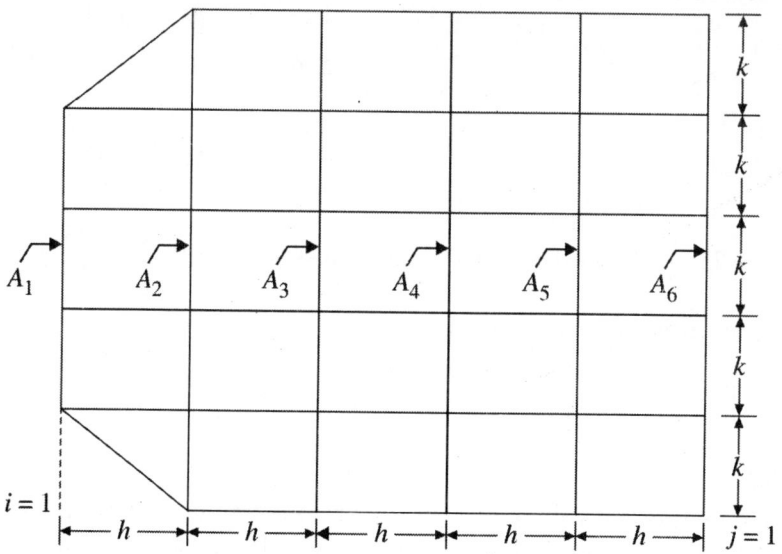

Fig. 5.2: Trapezoidal rule for volumes

The trapezoidal rule is first applied along one set of grid lines to get the areas. Then the rule is applied again in the other direction using areas as ordinates to get the volumes.

$$A_1 = k\left[\frac{1}{2}Z_{12} + Z_{13} + Z_{14} + Z_{15} + \frac{1}{2}Z_{16}\right]$$

$$A_2 = k\left[\frac{1}{2}Z_{21} + Z_{22} + Z_{23} + Z_{24+} + Z_{25+}\frac{1}{2}Z_{26}\right]$$

$$A_3 = -----------------$$

$$A_4 = -----------------$$

$$A_5 = -----------------$$

$$A_6 = -----------------$$

The volume is computed by the expression

$$V = h\left[\frac{1}{2}A_1 + A_2 + A_3 + A_4 + A_5 + \frac{1}{2}A_6\right]$$

Example 5.1

Evaluate the following integral numerically by using the trapezoidal rule.

$$I = \int_0^2 \frac{1}{(1+x)} \cdot dx \text{ with incremental value of } 0.25.$$

Solution

The value of the function is calculated at intervals of 0.25 as shown in Table 5.1.

Table 5.1: Values of $f(x)$ for different values of x									
x	0	0.25	0.50	0.75	1.00	1.25	1.50	1.75	2.00
$(1+x)$	1	1.25	1.50	1.75	2.00	2.25	2.50	2.75	3.00
$\frac{1}{(1+x)}$	1	0.80	0.67	0.57	0.50	0.44	0.40	0.36	0.33

$$I = 0.25\left[\frac{1}{2} + (0.8 + 0.67 + 0.57 + 0.50 + 0.44 + 0.40 + 0.36 + \frac{0.33}{2}\right] = 1.101$$

Checking by direct integration, we have

$$I = \int_0^2 \frac{1}{(1+x)} \cdot dx = \left[\log(1+x)\right]_0^2 = \log 3 = 1.098 \cong 1.101$$

Example 5.2

Table 5.2 contains the values of $f(x)$ for various values of x ranging from 0.2 to 0.8. Determine the area bounded by the curve between $x = 0.2$ and 0.8 by using trapezoidal rule.

Table 5.2: Given values of $f(x)$ for different values of x						
x	2.03	2.87	3.10	3.65	3.01	2.71	2.05
$f(x)$	2.03	2.87	3.10	3.65	3.01	2.71	2.05

Solution

$$A = 0.1\left[\frac{2.03}{2} + (2.87 + 3.10 + 3.65 + 3.01 + 2.71) + \frac{2.05}{2}\right] = 1.738$$

Example 5.3

A simply supported beam AB of span $L = 8$ m supports a load linearly varying from zero at A to 8 kN/m at B. Evaluate the area of the bending moment diagram due to the loading on the beam assuming an interval of 1 m.

Solution

The simply supported beam supporting the load is shown in Fig. 5.3.

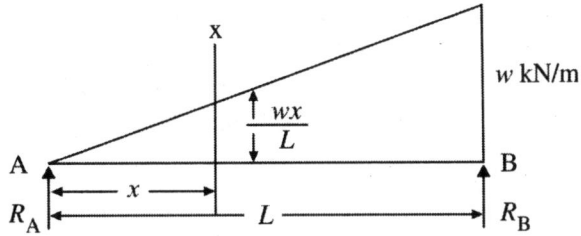

Fig. 5.3: Simply supported beam with triangular load

The reactions at A and B are obtained as

$$R_A = \left(\frac{wL}{2}\right)\left(\frac{L}{3}\right)\left(\frac{1}{L}\right) = \left(\frac{wL}{6}\right)$$

$$R_B = \left(\frac{wL}{2}\right)\left(\frac{2L}{3}\right)\left(\frac{1}{L}\right) = \left(\frac{wL}{3}\right)$$

$$M_{xx} = \left(\frac{wLx}{6}\right) - \left(\frac{wx^3}{6L}\right) = \frac{wL^2}{6}\left[\frac{x}{L} - \frac{x^3}{L^3}\right]$$

The ordinates of the bending moment diagram at 1 m intervals are obtained as follows:

$$M_A = M_0 = 0$$

$$M_1 = \frac{wL^2}{6}\left[\frac{1}{8} - \frac{1^3}{8^3}\right] = 0.0205wL^2 = \left(0.0205 \times 8 \times 8^2\right) = 10.496 \text{ kN·m}$$

$$M_2 = \frac{wL^2}{6}\left[\frac{2}{8} - \frac{2^3}{8^3}\right] = 0.039wL^2 = \left(0.039 \times 8 \times 8^2\right) = 19.968 \text{ kN·m}$$

$$M_3 = \frac{wL^2}{6}\left[\frac{3}{8} - \frac{3^3}{8^3}\right] = 0.0537wL^2 = \left(0.0537 \times 8 \times 8^2\right) = 27.494 \text{ kN·m}$$

$$M_4 = \frac{wL^2}{6}\left[\frac{4}{8} - \frac{4^3}{8^3}\right] = 0.0625wL^2 = \left(0.0625 \times 8 \times 8^2\right) = 32.00 \text{ kN} \cdot \text{m}$$

$$M_5 = \frac{wL^2}{6}\left[\frac{5}{8} - \frac{5^3}{8^3}\right] = 0.0635wL^2 = \left(0.0635 \times 8 \times 8^2\right) = 32.512 \text{ kN} \cdot \text{m}$$

$$M_6 = \frac{wL^2}{6}\left[\frac{6}{8} - \frac{6^3}{8^3}\right] = 0.0546wL^2 = \left(0.0546 \times 8 \times 8^2\right) = 27.996 \text{ kN} \cdot \text{m}$$

$$M_7 = \frac{wL^2}{6}\left[\frac{7}{8} - \frac{7^3}{8^3}\right] = 0.034wL^2 = \left(0.034 \times 8 \times 8^2\right) = 17.408 \text{ kN} \cdot \text{m}$$

$$M_8 = M_B = 0$$

Using trapezoidal rule, the area of the bending moment diagram is computed as

$$A = \frac{L}{8}\left[\frac{M_A}{2} + (M_1 + M_2 + M_3 + M_4 + M_5 + M_6 + M_7) + \frac{M_B}{2}\right]$$

$$= \frac{8}{8}\left[0 + (10.496 + 19.968 + 27.494 + 32.00 + 32.512 + 27.996 + 17.408) + 0\right]$$

$$= 167.874 \text{ kN} \cdot \text{m}^2$$

5.2.3 Simpson's Rule

In determining the areas by Simpson's rule[6], the given area is divided into equal intervals and the ordinates are numbered as shown in Fig. 5.4.

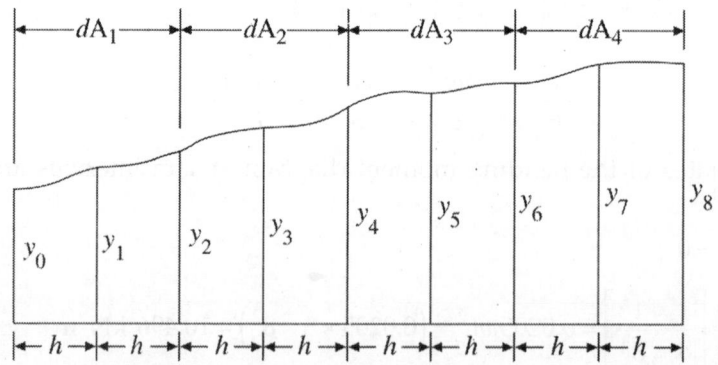

Fig. 5.4: Calculation of areas by Simpson's rule

Considering the ordinates y_0, y_1 and y_2 we have the bounded area

$$dA_1 = \frac{h}{3}(y_0 + 4y_1 + y_2)$$

Similarly considering y_2, y_3 and y_4, we have

$$dA_2 = \frac{h}{3}(y_2 + 4y_3 + y_4)$$

....

$$dA_n = \frac{h}{3}(y_{n-2} + 4y_{n-1} + y_n)$$

Adding the elemental areas, the total area obtained by the Simpson's rule as,

$$A = \frac{h}{3}[y_0 + 4y_1 + 2y_2 + 4y_3 + 2y_4 + 4y_5 + 2y_6 + \cdots + y_n]$$

The extension of Simpson's rule for finding the volume under a surface defined by the function $Z = f(x, y)$ is similar to the trapezoidal rule and is obtained by the following formula:

$$V = \frac{h}{3}[A_1 + 4A_2 + 2A_3 + 4A_4 + \cdots + A_n]$$

where $A_1, A_2, \cdots, A_n$ are the elemental areas and h is the interval between the areas.

Example 5.4

Evaluate the following integral numerically by using the trapezoidal rule.

$$I = \int_0^1 \frac{1}{(1+x)} \cdot dx \text{ assuming an interval of 0.2.}$$

Solution

The values are computed as shown in Table 5.3.

Table 5.3: Computation of values of $\left(\frac{1}{1+x}\right)$ for different values of x

x	0	0.2	0.40	0.6	0.8	1.00
$(1+x)$	1	1.2	1.4	1.6	1.8	2.0
$\left(\frac{1}{1+x}\right)$	1	0.833	0.714	0.625	0.555	0.50

Using Simpson's rule with an interval $h = 0.2$, the integral is computed as,

$$I = \frac{0.2}{3}[1 + 4(0.833 + 0.625) = 2(0.714 + 0.555) + 0.5] = 0.658$$

Checking by direct integration,

$$I = \int_0^1 \frac{1}{(1+x)} \cdot dx \left[\log(1+x)\right]_0^1 = \log 2 = 0.693 \cong 0.658$$

Example 5.5

Find the area of the bending moment diagram of the beam loaded as shown in Fig. 5.5 by Simpson's rule, assuming an interval of $(L/8)$.

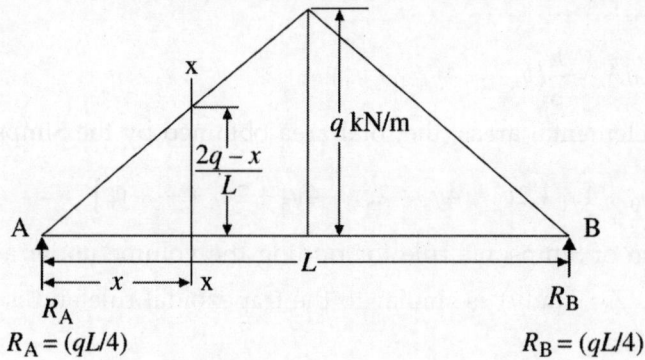

Fig. 5.5: Beam loaded with triangular load

Solution

$$M_{xx} = \frac{qLX}{4} - \frac{1}{2}\left(\frac{2qx}{L}\right)x\left(\frac{x}{3}\right) = \left[\frac{qLx}{4} - \frac{qx^3}{3L}\right] = qL^2\left[\frac{1}{4}\left(\frac{x}{L}\right) - \frac{1}{3}\left(\frac{x}{L}\right)^3\right]$$

$$M_0 = M_A = 0$$

$$M_1 = qL^2\left[\frac{1}{4}\left(\frac{1}{8}\right) - \frac{1}{3}\left(\frac{1}{8}\right)^3\right] = 0.03qL^2$$

$$M_2 = qL^2\left[\frac{1}{4}\left(\frac{2}{8}\right) - \frac{1}{3}\left(\frac{2}{8}\right)^3\right] = 0.057qL^2$$

$$M_3 = qL^2\left[\frac{1}{4}\left(\frac{3}{8}\right) - \frac{1}{3}\left(\frac{3}{8}\right)^3\right] = 0.076qL^2$$

$$M_4 = qL^2\left[\frac{1}{4}\left(\frac{4}{8}\right) - \frac{1}{3}\left(\frac{4}{8}\right)^3\right] = 0.083qL^2$$

$$M_5 = M_3$$

$$M_6 = M_4$$

$$M_7 = M_1$$

$$M_8 = M_B = 0$$

Using Simpson's rule

$$A = \frac{L}{(8 \times 3)}\left[0 + 4\left(0.03qL^2 + 0.076qL^2 + 0.03qL^2\right) + 2\left(0.057qL^2 + 0.083qL^2 + 0.057qL^2\right) + 0\right]$$

$$= 0.5025qL^3$$

Example 5.6

Using Simpson's rule with 5 ordinates, evaluate the integral

$$I = \int\limits_{0}^{\pi/2} \frac{d\theta}{\sqrt{1 - \left(\frac{1}{2}\right)\sin^2\theta}}$$

Solution

Range $(0$ to $\pi/2)$... four parts

Range interval $= h = \dfrac{\pi}{8}$

$$f(\theta) = \left(1 - \left(\frac{1}{2}\right)\sin^2\theta\right)^{-1/2}$$

Evaluate $f(\pi)$ at $(\pi/8)$ intervals as shown below:

θ	0	$(\pi/8)$	$(\pi/4)$	$(3\pi/8)$	$(\pi/2)$
$f(\theta)$	1.000	1.0387	1.1547	1.3206	1.4142

$$I = \frac{h}{3}[f_0 + 4f_1 + 2f_2 + 4f_3 + f_4]$$

$$= \frac{\pi}{8 \times 3}\Big[1.000 + (4 \times 1.0387) + (2 \times 1.1547) + (4 \times 1.3206) + 1.4142\Big]$$

$$= 1.854$$

5.2.4 Gaussian Quadrature Formula

The process of integrating a function of a single variable is known as *quadrature*. The expression for the integral so obtained is called a *quadrature formula*. The accuracy of quadrature formula depends on

a) Size of the interval

b) The range of integration

c) The degree of polynomial and

d) The point through which it passes

Hence the Gaussian quadrature can be expressed as

$$\int\limits_{-1}^{+1} f(x)\cdot dx = \Big[a_0 f(x_0) + a_1 f(x_1) + a_2 f(x_2)\Big]$$

The six unknowns namely a_0, a_1, a_2 and x_0, x_1, x_2 can be obtained using the 5th degree polynomial and the solution is

$$x_0 = \sqrt{(3 \times 5)}, \qquad x_1 = 0, \qquad x_2 = \sqrt{(3 \times 5)}$$

and $a_0 = (5/9)$ $\quad a_1 = (8/9)$ $\quad a_2 = (5/9)$

Hence the Gaussian quadrature formula[7] can be written as

$$\int_{-1}^{+1} f(x) \cdot dx = \frac{1}{9}\left[5f(-\sqrt{3/5}) + 8f(0) + 5f(\sqrt{3/5})\right]$$

The above formula is also referred to as *Gauss Legendre* three point formula.

Example 5.7

Evaluate the following integral using the Gaussian quadrature formula.

$$I = \int_0^2 \frac{dx}{(1+x)}$$

Solution

Transfer the interval (0, 2) to interval (–1, 1) as follows:

let $\qquad t = (ax + b)$

when $\qquad x = 0, t = -1$

therefore $-1 = 0 + b$ $\hspace{4cm}$ (1)

when $\qquad x = 2, t = 1$

therefore $\quad 1 = 2a + b$ $\hspace{4cm}$ (2)

Solving Eqs (1) and (2), we get

$$a = 1 \qquad \text{and} \qquad b = -1$$

Therefore $I = \int_0^2 \frac{dx}{(1+x)} = \int_{+1}^{+1} \frac{dt}{a(2+t)} = \int_{-1}^{+1} \frac{dt}{(2+t)}$

Using Gaussian quadrature formula

$$\int_{+1}^{+1} f(x) \cdot dx = \frac{1}{9}\left[5f(-\sqrt{3/5}) + 8f(0) + 5f(\sqrt{3/5})\right]$$

$$= \frac{1}{9}\left[5\left(\frac{1}{2-\sqrt{3/5}}\right) + 8\left(\frac{1}{2+0}\right) + 5\left(\frac{1}{2+\sqrt{3/5}}\right)\right]$$

$$= \frac{1}{9}[4.08 + 4.00 + 1.80] = 1.0977$$

The exact value obtained by integration of the function is

$$I = \int_0^2 \frac{dx}{(1+x)} = \left[\log(1+x)\right]_0^2 = (\log_e 3 - \log_e 1) = \log_e 2 = 1.098$$

5.3 NEWMARK'S METHOD

Newmark's method[8] is very useful in the computation of beam slopes and deflections for different types of loading. Newmark developed a numerical procedure in which the distributed load is replaced by equivalent concentrated loads at equally spaced pivotal points of the beam. The equivalent concentrated loads at pivotal points are equal and opposite to the reactions at the pivotal points when the segments of the beam between the pivotal points are treated as simply supported beams.

5.3.1 Equivalent Loads

The equivalent loads for different types of distributed loading are computed as follows. Referring to Fig. 5.6 in which the distributed load varies linearly between pivotal points, the equivalent loads are computed by the following procedure.

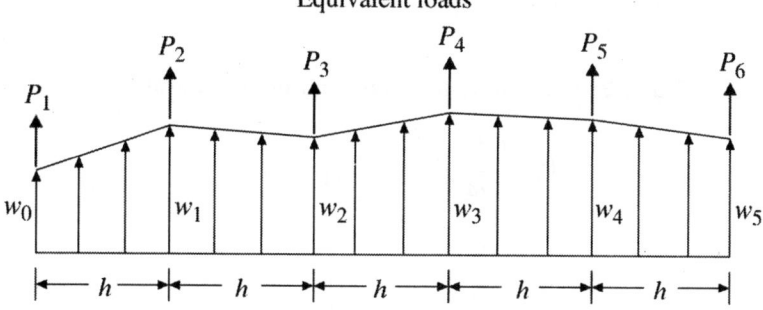

Fig. 5.6: Distributed load (linear between pivotal points)

The equivalent loads are computed by the following formulae

$$P_1 = \left(\frac{h}{6}\right)(2w_0 + w_1) \ldots \text{end load}$$

$$P_2 = \left(\frac{h}{6}\right)(w_0 + 4w_1 + w_2)$$

$$P_3 = \left(\frac{h}{6}\right)(w_1 + 4w_2 + w_3)$$

$$P_4 = \left(\frac{h}{6}\right)(w_2 + 4w_3 + w_4)$$

$$P_5 = \left(\frac{h}{6}\right)(w_3 + 4w_4 + w_5)$$

$$P_6 = \left(\frac{h}{6}\right)(2w_5 + w_4) \ldots \text{end load}$$

Similarly referring to Fig. 5.7 in which the distributed load varies parabolically between pivotal points, the equivalent loads are computed by the following formulae.

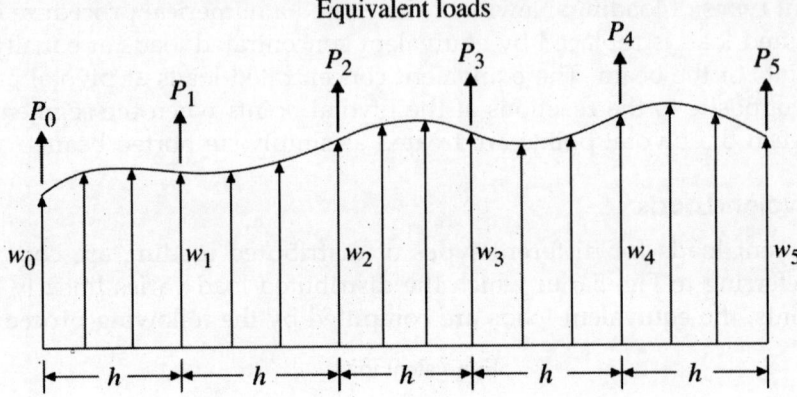

Fig. 5.7: Distributed load (second degree parabola)

$$P_0 = \left(\frac{h}{24}\right)(7w_0 + 6w_1 - w_2)$$

$$P_1 = \left(\frac{h}{12}\right)(w_0 + 10w_1 + w_2)$$

$$P_2 = \left(\frac{h}{12}\right)(w_1 + 10w_2 + w_3)$$

$$P_3 = \left(\frac{h}{12}\right)(w_2 + 10w_3 + w_4)$$

$$P_4 = \left(\frac{h}{12}\right)(w_3 + 10w_4 + w_5)$$

$$P_5 = \left(\frac{h}{24}\right)(7w_5 + 6w_4 - w_3)$$

5.3.2 Newmark's Procedure

This procedure can be conveniently used for the determination of moments, shears, slopes and deflections in a loaded beam.

The following notations are used:

w = Uniformly distributed load

M = Moment

V = Shear force

φ = Slope

y = Deflection

The inter-relations between these variables are expressed as

$$w = \left(\frac{dV}{dx}\right) or\ V = w \cdot dx$$

$$V = \left(\frac{dM}{dx}\right) M = V \cdot dx$$

$$\left(\frac{M}{EI}\right) = \left(\frac{d\varphi}{dx}\right) or\ \varphi = \left(\frac{M}{EI}\right) dx$$

$$\varphi = \left(\frac{dy}{dx}\right) or\ y = \varphi \cdot dx$$

The following stepwise procedure is adopted for the solution of a beam problem.

1. The beam is divided into suitable number of segments

2. The equivalent concentrated loads P at pivotal points are computed assuming the type of distribution of loads.

3. A trial shear force is assumed at left support and the shears in the succeeding segments are Equal to the preceding shear plus the equivalent concentrated load at the pivot point preceding the segment.

4. Using boundary conditions, the moment at the left support is assumed. The moments at the succeeding pivotal points are equal to

$$M_{n+1} = \left[M_n + \int_0^h V \cdot dx \right] = (M_n + V_n \cdot h)$$

The moments are obtained simply by successive addition of shears.

5. The moment at right support is evaluated and it should satisfy the boundary conditions. The error is distributed linearly at all pivotal points.

6. Corrections are applied for shears and moments.

7. Final moments and shears are obtained.

8. The beam is loaded with $\left(\frac{M}{EI}\right)$ diagram

9. Equivalent loads are obtained at pivotal points.

10. The determination of slope φ and deflection y is made in a manner similar to that of M and V.

The application of Newmark's method[9,10] for solving beam problems is illustrated by the following examples.

Example 5.8

Determine the maximum slope and deflection of the beam AB loaded as shown in Fig. 5.8.

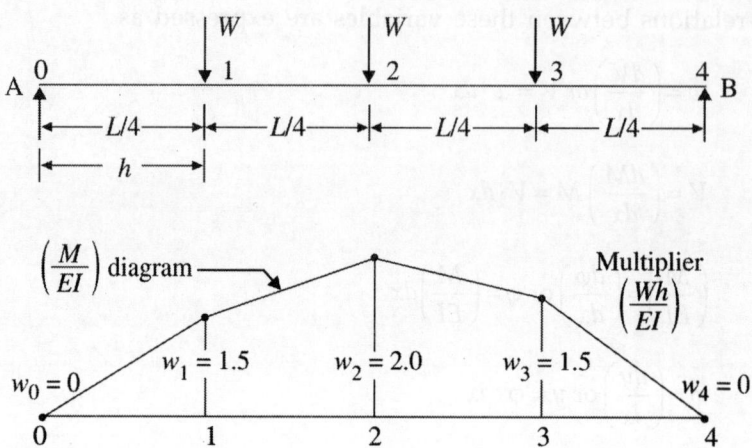

Fig. 5.8: Simply supported beam with concentrated loads

Solution

The numerical computation of moments, slopes and deflections are shown in Table 5.4.

The equivalent loads due to the $\left(\dfrac{M}{EI}\right)$ diagram loaded on the beam are computed as shown below:

$$P_0 = \left(\frac{h}{6}\right)(2w_0 + w_1) = \left(\frac{h}{6}\right)(0 + 1.5)\left(\frac{Wh}{EI}\right) = 0.25\left(\frac{Wh^2}{EI}\right)$$

$$P_1 = \left(\frac{h}{6}\right)(w_0 + 4w_1 + w_2) = \left(\frac{h}{6}\right)\left[0 + (4 \times 1.5) + 2\right]\left(\frac{Wh}{EI}\right) = 1.33\left(\frac{Wh^2}{EI}\right)$$

$$P_2 = \left(\frac{h}{6}\right)(w_1 + 4w_2 + w_3) = \left(\frac{h}{6}\right)\left[1.5 + (4 \times 2) + 1.5\right]\left(\frac{Wh}{EI}\right) = 1.833\left(\frac{Wh^2}{EI}\right)$$

$$P_3 = P_1 = 1.33\left(\frac{Wh^2}{EI}\right)$$

$$P_4 = P_0 = 0.25\left(\frac{Wh^2}{EI}\right)$$

Table 5.4: Computation of beam slopes and deflections

Nodal points	0	1	2	3	4	Multiplier
Equivalent load	P = -0.0	-1.0	-1.0	-1.0	0	W
Trial shear	V = 1.5	1.5	0.5	-0.5	-1.5	W
Trial moment	M = 0	1.5	2.0	1.5	0	Wh
Corrections to V and M are zero						
Equivalent load	P = 0.25	1.333	1.833	1.333	0.25	(Wh^2/EI)
Trial slope	ϕ = -2.5	-2.25	-0.92	0.92	2.25 → 2.50	(Wh^2/EI)
Trial deflection	y = 0	-2.25	-3.17	-2.25	0	(Wh^3/EI)

Maximum slope at support $= \phi_{max} = \dfrac{2.5\, Wh^2}{EI} = \dfrac{WL^2}{6.4\, EI}$

Maximum deflection at centre of span $= y_{max} = \dfrac{3.17\, Wh^3}{EI} = \dfrac{WL^3}{20.18\, EI}$

Example 5.9

A simply supported beam AB supports concentrated loads at one third span points as shown in Fig. 5.9. Calculate the deflections at the load points C and D and the maximum slope by Newmark's method.

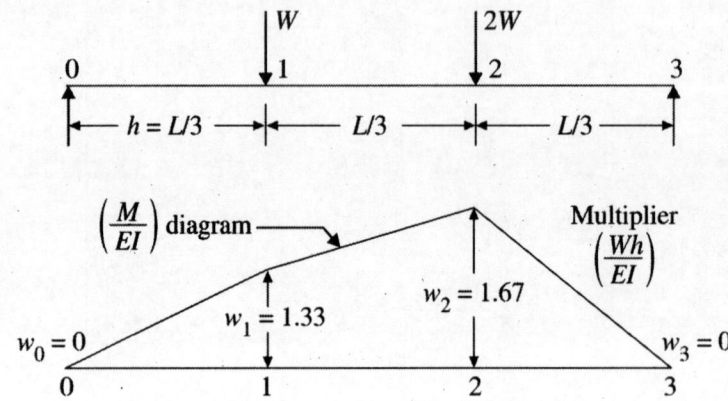

Fig. 5.9: Simply supported beam with loads at one-third span points

Solution

The numerical computation of moments, slopes and deflections at various nodal points in the beam is compiled in Table 5.5.

The equivalent loads (P) are computed by the following procedure. Referring to the $\left(\dfrac{M}{EI}\right)$ diagram shown in Fig. 5.9, we have

$$P_0 = \left(\frac{h}{6}\right)(2w_0 + w_1) = \left(\frac{h}{6}\right)(0 + 1.33)\left(\frac{Wh}{EI}\right) = 0.221\left(\frac{Wh^2}{EI}\right)$$

$$P_1 = \left(\frac{h}{6}\right)(w_0 + 4w_1 + w_2) = \left(\frac{h}{6}\right)[0 + (4 \times 1.33) + 1.67]\left(\frac{Wh}{EI}\right) = 1.165\left(\frac{Wh^2}{EI}\right)$$

$$P_2 = \left(\frac{h}{6}\right)(w_1 + 4w_2 + w_3) = \left(\frac{h}{6}\right)[1.33 + (4 \times 1.67) + 0]\left(\frac{Wh}{EI}\right) = 1.335\left(\frac{Wh^2}{EI}\right)$$

$$P_3 = \left(\frac{h}{6}\right)(2w_3 + w_2) = \left(\frac{h}{6}\right)(0 + 1.67)\left(\frac{Wh}{EI}\right) = 0.28\left(\frac{Wh^2}{EI}\right)$$

Table 5.5: Computation of beam slopes and deflections

Nodal points	0	1	2	3	Multiplier
Equivalent load	$P = 0$	-1.0	-2.0	0	W
Trial shear	$V = 1.33$ 1.33	0.33	-1.67 -1.67		W
Trial moment	$M = 0$	1.33	1.67	0	Wh

Corrections to V and M are zero

Load	$P = 0.221$	1.165	1.335	0.28	(Wh^2/EI)
Trial	$\phi = -1.386$ -1.165	0	1.335 6.615		(Wh^2/EI)
Trial	$y = 0$	-1.165	-1.165	0.17	(Wh^3/EI)

Corrections to $\phi = -(0.17/3) = -0.06$

Corrected

$$\phi = -1.446 \qquad -1.225 \qquad -0.06 \qquad 1.275 \quad 1.555 \; (Wh^2/EI)$$

$$y = 0 \qquad\qquad -1.225 \qquad -1.285 \qquad\qquad 0.01 \; (Wh^3/EI)$$

Maximum slope $= \phi_{max} = \phi_3 = \dfrac{1.555\,Wh^2}{EI} = \dfrac{0.1727\,WL^2}{EI}$

Maximum deflection $= y_{max} = y_2 = y_D = \dfrac{1.285\,Wh^3}{EI} = \dfrac{0.0475\,WL^3}{EI}$

Deflection at $= C = y_1 = y_c = \dfrac{1.225\,Wh^3}{EI} = \dfrac{0.0453\,WL^3}{EI}$

Example 5.10

A beam of length L and of uniform flexural rigidity EI is freely supported at the ends. The beam supports an uniformly distributed load of intensity w kN/m over the entire span length. Determine the deflection at the centre of span and the maximum slope adopting six segments and using Newmark's method. The loaded beam is shown in Fig. 5.10.

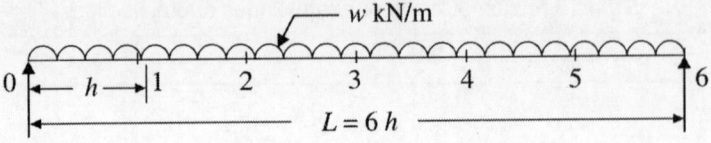

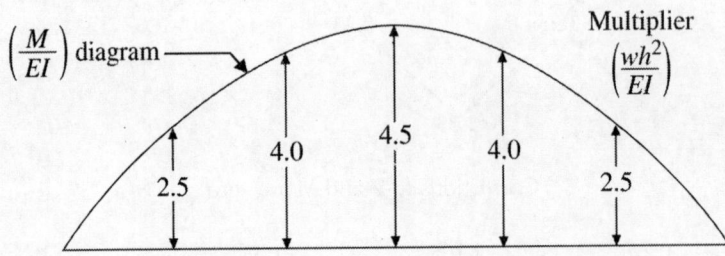

Fig. 5.10: Simply supported beam with uniformly distributed load

Solution

The numerical computation of beam slopes and deflections at various nodal points is compiled in Table 5.6.

The equivalent loads are calculated as shown below:

$$P_0 = \left(\frac{h}{24}\right)(7w_0 + 6w_1 - w_2)$$

$$= \left(\frac{h}{24}\right)(0 + 6 \times 2.5 - 4)\left(\frac{wh^2}{EI}\right) = 0.45\left(\frac{wh^3}{EI}\right)$$

$$P_1 = \left(\frac{h}{12}\right)(w_0 + 10w_1 + w_2)$$

$$= \left(\frac{h}{12}\right)(0 + 10 \times 2.5 + 4)\left(\frac{wh^2}{EI}\right) = 2.41\left(\frac{wh^3}{EI}\right)$$

$$P_2 = \left(\frac{h}{12}\right)(w_1 + 10w_2 + w_3)$$

$$= \left(\frac{h}{12}\right)(2.5 + 10 \times 4 + 4.5)\left(\frac{wh^2}{EI}\right) = 3.91\left(\frac{wh^3}{EI}\right)$$

$$P_3 = \left(\frac{h}{12}\right)(w_2 + 10w_3 + w_4)$$

$$= \left(\frac{h}{12}\right)(4 + 10 \times 4.5 + 4)\left(\frac{wh^2}{EI}\right) = 4.41\left(\frac{wh^3}{EI}\right)$$

Table 5.6: Computation of beam slopes and deflections

Nodal points	0	1	2	3	4	5	6	Multiplier
Load P =	−0.5	−1.0	−1.0	−1.0	−1.0	−1.0	−0.5	w
Trial V =	3.0	2.5	1.5	0.5	−0.5	−1.5	−2.5 → −3.0		wh
Trial M =	0	2.5	4.0	4.5	4.0	2.5	0	wh^2

Corrections to V and M are zero

Nodal points	0	1	2	3	4	5	6	Multiplier
Load P =	0.45	2.41	3.91	4.41	3.91	2.41	0.45	(wh^3/EI)
Trial ϕ =	−8.98	−8.53	−6.12	−2.21	2.20	6.11	8.52 → 8.97		(wh^3/EI)
Trial y =	0	−8.53	−14.65	−16.86	−14.66	−8.55	0	(wh^4/EI)

Maximum slope $= \phi_{max} = \dfrac{8.98\, wh^3}{EI} = \dfrac{0.041\, wL^3}{EI}$

Maximum deflection at centre of span $= y_{max} = \dfrac{16.86\, wh^4}{EI} = \dfrac{0.013\, wL^4}{EI}$

$$P_4 = P_2 = 3.91\left(\frac{wh^3}{EI}\right)$$

$$P_5 = P_1 = 2.41\left(\frac{wh^3}{EI}\right)$$

$$P_6 = P_0 = 0.45\left(\frac{wh^3}{EI}\right)$$

Example 5.11

A simply supported beam of variable moment of inertia is loaded partially with uniformly distributed load as shown in Fig. 5.11. Determine the maximum slope and deflection in the beam using six nodal points and Newmark's method.

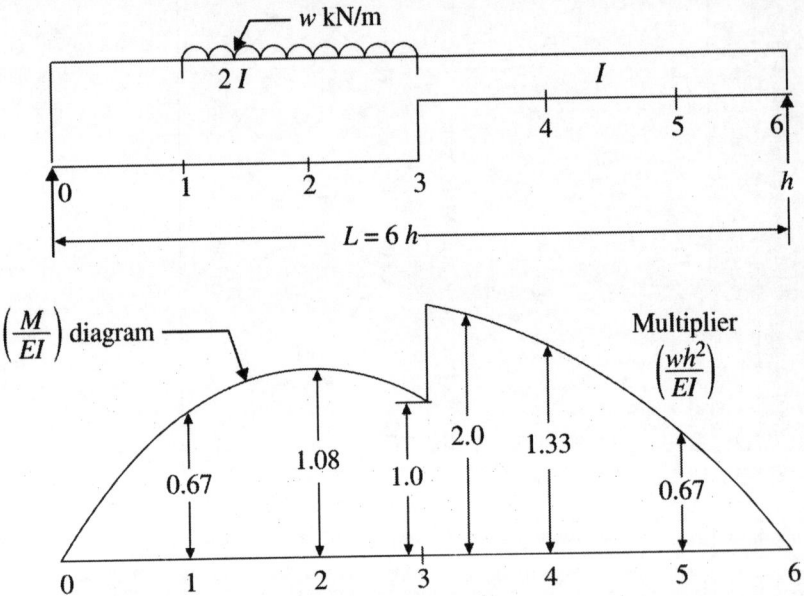

Fig. 5.11: Simply supported beam with variable moment of inertia

Solution

The numerical computation of beam slopes and deflections is compiled in Table 5.7. The equivalent loads are computed in the following steps:

$$P_0 = \left(\frac{h}{24}\right)(7w_0 + 6w_1 - w_2)$$

$$= \left(\frac{h}{24}\right)(0 + 6 \times 0.67 - 1.08)\left(\frac{wh^2}{EI}\right) = 0.11\left(\frac{wh^3}{EI}\right)$$

Table 5.7: Computation of beam slopes and deflections

Nodal points	0	1	2	3	4	5	6	Multiplier
Load $P =$	0	−0.5	−1.0	−0.5	0	0	0 / −0.5	w
Trial $V =$	1.5	1.0	0	−0.5	−0.5	−0.5		wh
Trial $M =$	0	1.0	2.5	2.5	2.0	1.5	1.0	wh^2
Correction to M	0	−0.17	−0.34	−0.50	−0.67	−0.83	−1.0	wh^2
Correct $M =$	0	1.33	2.16	2.0	1.33	0.67	0	wh^2
Load $P =$	0.11	0.65	1.04	1.43	1.33	0.67	0.11	(wh^3/EI)
Trial $\phi =$	−3.0 / −2.89	−2.24	−1.20	0.23	1.56	2.23	2.34	(wh^3/EI)
Trial $y =$	0	−2.89	−5.13	−6.33	−6.10	−4.54	−2.31	(wh^4/EI)
Correction to ϕ	0.39	0.39	0.39	0.39	0.39	0.39	0.39	
Correct $\phi =$	−2.61 / −2.50	−1.85	−0.81	0.62	1.95	2.62	2.73	(wh^3/EI)
Correct $y =$	0	−2.50	−4.35	−5.17	−4.55	−2.60	0	(wh^4/EI)

Corrections to $M = -(1/6) = -0.17$

Corrections to $\phi = (2.31/6) = 0.39$

$$\text{Maximum slope} = \phi_{max} = \phi_6 = \frac{2.73\ wh^3}{EI} = \frac{0.0126\ wL^3}{EI}$$

$$\text{Maximum deflection} = y_{max} = y_3 = \frac{5.17\ wh^4}{EI} = \frac{0.0039\ wL^4}{EI}$$

$$P_1 = \left(\frac{h}{12}\right)(w_0 + 10w_1 + w_2)$$

$$= \left(\frac{h}{12}\right)(0 + 10 \times 0.67 + 1.08)\left(\frac{wh^2}{EI}\right) = 0.65\left(\frac{wh^3}{EI}\right)$$

$$P_2 = \left(\frac{h}{12}\right)(w_1 + 10w_2 + w_3)$$

$$= \left(\frac{h}{12}\right)(0.67 + 10 \times 1.08 + 1.0)\left(\frac{wh^2}{EI}\right) = 1.04\left(\frac{wh^3}{EI}\right)$$

$$P_3 = \left(\frac{h}{24}\right)\left[(7w_3 + 6w_2 - w_1) + (7w_3 + 6w_4 - w_5)\right]$$

$$= \left(\frac{h}{24}\right)\left[(7 \times 1) + (6 \times 1.08) - 0.67\right] + \left[(7 \times 2) + (6 \times 1.33) - 0.67\right]\left(\frac{wh^2}{EI}\right)$$

$$= 1.43\left(\frac{wh^3}{EI}\right)$$

$$P_4 = \left(\frac{h}{12}\right)(w_3 + 10w_4 + w_5)$$

$$= \left(\frac{h}{12}\right)(2 + 10 \times 1.33 + 0.67)\left(\frac{wh^2}{EI}\right) = 1.33\left(\frac{wh^3}{EI}\right)$$

$$P_5 = \left(\frac{h}{12}\right)(w_4 + 10w_5 + w_6)$$

$$= \left(\frac{h}{12}\right)(1.33 + 10 \times 0.67 + 0)\left(\frac{wh^2}{EI}\right) = 0.67\left(\frac{wh^3}{EI}\right)$$

$$P_6 = \left(\frac{h}{24}\right)(7w_6 + 6w_5 - w_4)$$

$$= \left(\frac{h}{24}\right)(0 + 6 \times 0.67 - 1.33)\left(\frac{wh^2}{EI}\right) = 0.11\left(\frac{wh^3}{EI}\right)$$

Example 5.12

A simply supported beam is partially loaded with uniformly distributed load of w kN/m as shown in Fig. 5.12. Evaluate the deflection at the centre of span using Newmark's numerical technique. Assume the flexural rigidity EI is constant for the beam.

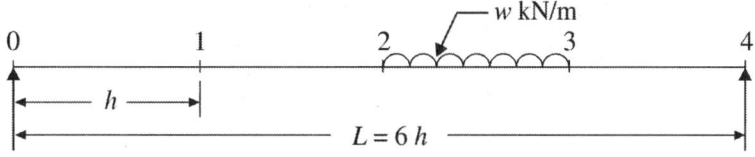

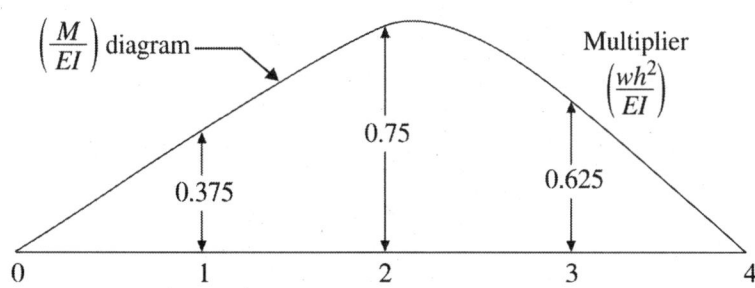

Fig. 5.12: Simply supported beam with partial uniformly distributed load

Solution

The numerical computation of beam slopes and deflections is compiled in Table 5.8, The equivalent loads are computed in the following steps:

$$P_0 = \left(\frac{h}{24}\right)(7w_0 + 6w_1 - w_2)$$

$$= \left(\frac{h}{24}\right)(0 + 6 \times 0.375 - 0.75)\left(\frac{wh^2}{EI}\right) = 0.0625\left(\frac{wh^3}{EI}\right)$$

$$P_1 = \left(\frac{h}{12}\right)(w_0 + 10w_1 + w_2)$$

$$= \left(\frac{h}{12}\right)(0 + 10 \times 0.375 + 0.75)\left(\frac{wh^2}{EI}\right) = 0.375\left(\frac{wh^3}{EI}\right)$$

$$P_2 = \left(\frac{h}{12}\right)(w_1 + 10w_2 + w_3)$$

$$= \left(\frac{h}{12}\right)(0.375 + 10 \times 0.75 + 0.625)\left(\frac{wh^2}{EI}\right) = 0.708\left(\frac{wh^3}{EI}\right)$$

$$P_3 = \left(\frac{h}{12}\right)(w_2 + 10w_3 + w_4)$$

$$= \left(\frac{h}{12}\right)\left[0.75 + (10 \times 0.625) + 0\right]\left(\frac{wh^2}{EI}\right)$$

Table 5.8: Computation of beam slopes and deflections

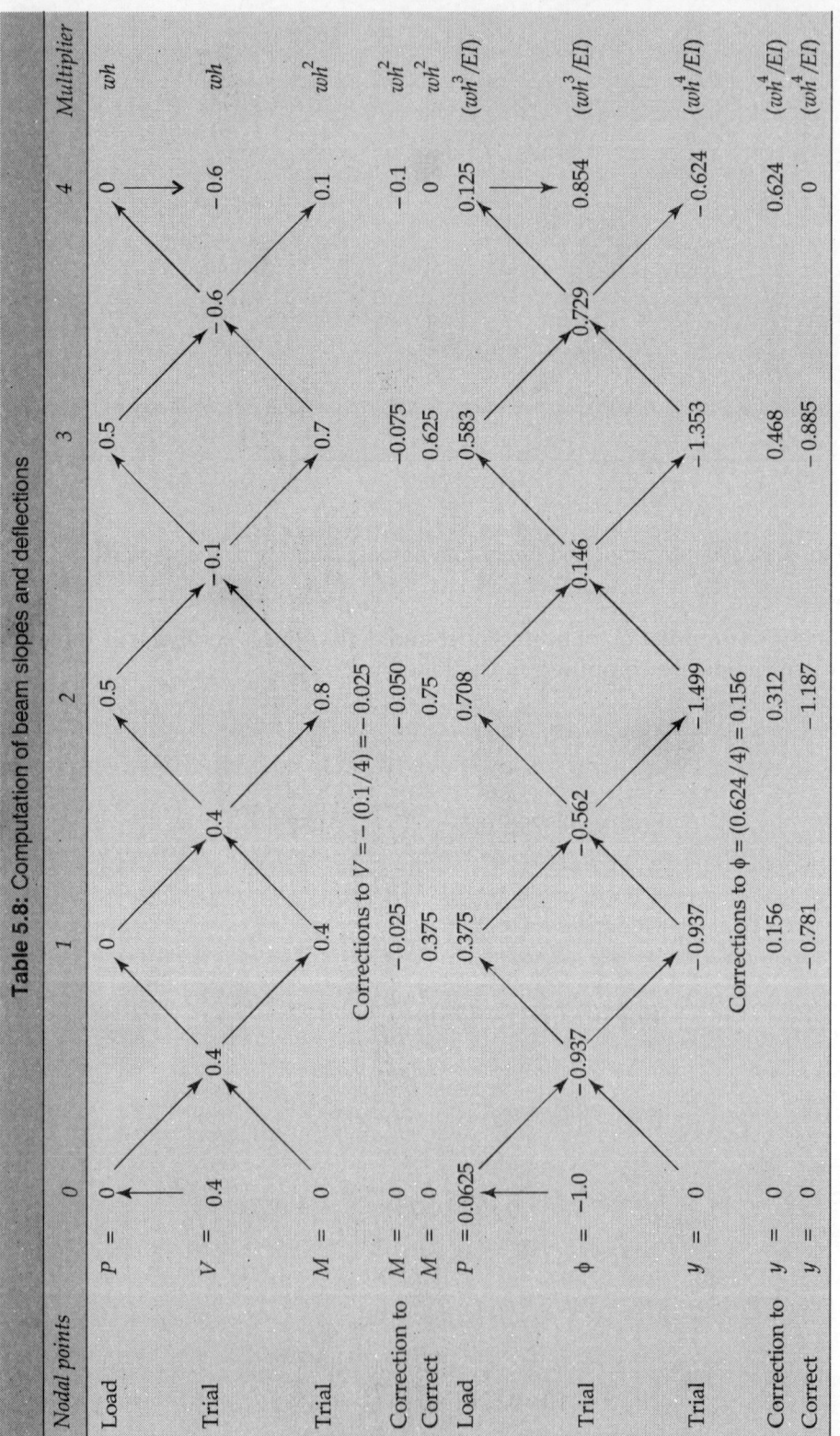

Maximum deflection $= y_{max} = y_3 = \dfrac{1.187}{EI} wh^4 = \dfrac{wL^4}{215.6\,EI}$

$$= 0.583 \left(\frac{wh^3}{EI} \right)$$

$$P_4 = \left(\frac{h}{24} \right) (7w_4 + 6w_3 - w_2)$$

$$= \left(\frac{h}{24} \right) (0 + 6 \times 0.625 - 0.75) \left(\frac{wh^2}{EI} \right)$$

$$= 0.125 \left(\frac{wh^3}{EI} \right)$$

Example 5.13

Find the maximum slope and deflection in a simply supported beam of span L supporting a triangular load as shown in Fig. 5.13. Consider 8 grid points and assume uniform flexural rigidity for the beam.

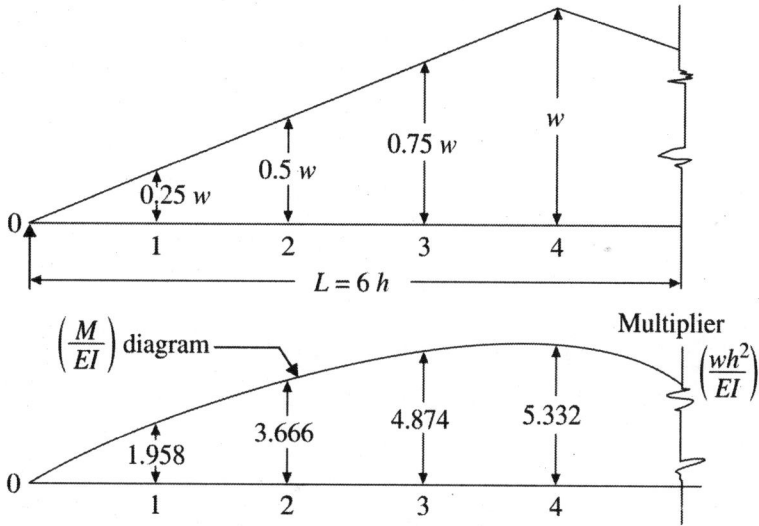

Fig. 5.13: Simply supported beam with triangular load

In view of the symmetry, only half the beam will be considered for analysis. The computation of beam slopes and deflections is shown in Table 5.9.

Solution

The calculation of equivalent loads is shown in the following steps.

$$P_0 = \left(\frac{h}{24} \right) (7w_0 + 6w_1 - w_2)$$

$$= \left(\frac{h}{24} \right) (0 + 6 \times 1.958 - 3.666) \left(\frac{wh^2}{EI} \right) = 0.335 \left(\frac{wh^3}{EI} \right)$$

Table 5.9: Computation of beam slopes and deflections

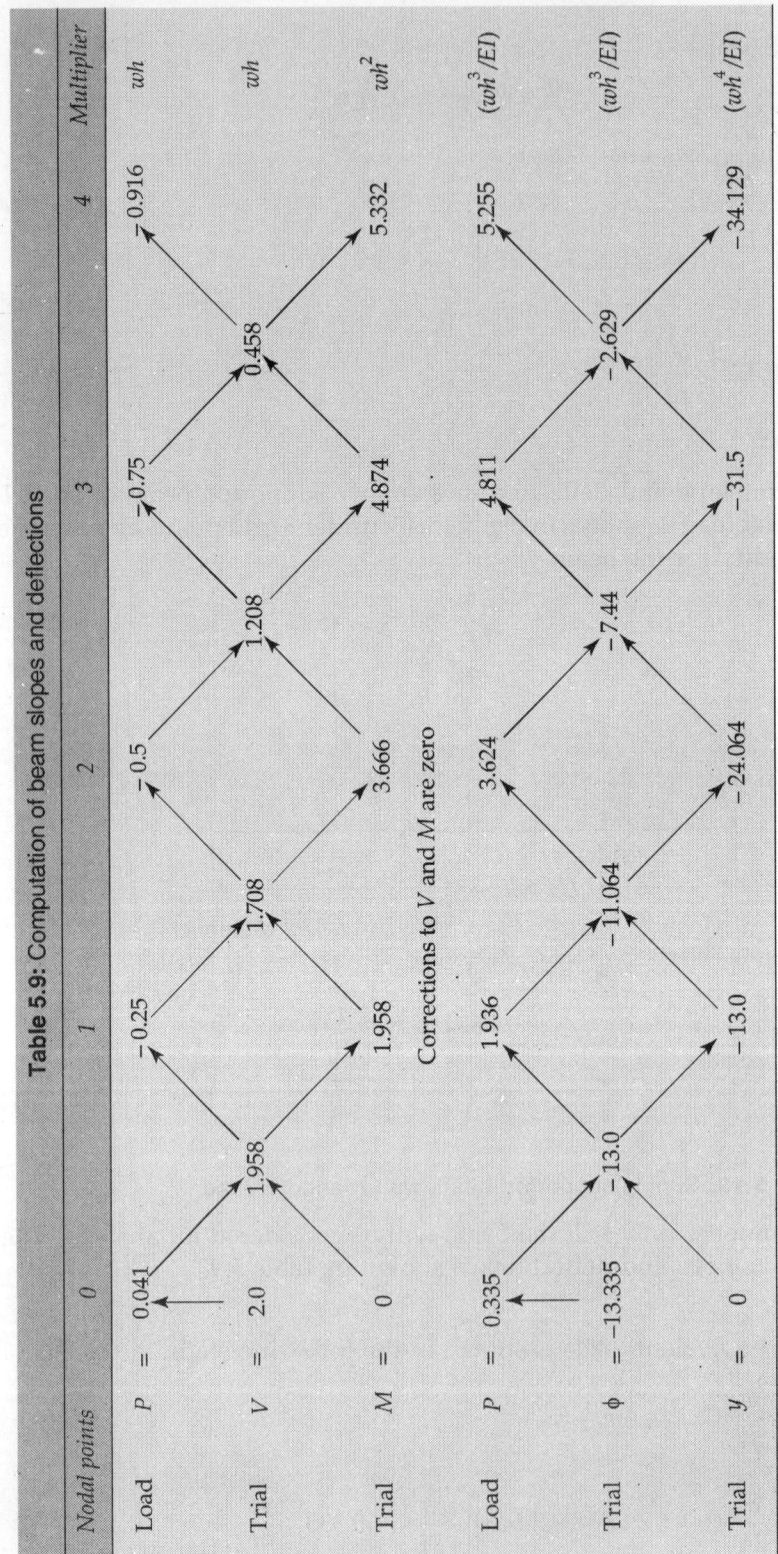

Nodal points	0	1	2	3	4	Multiplier
Load $P =$	0.041	−0.25	−0.5	−0.75	−0.916	wh
Trial $V =$	2.0	1.958	1.708	1.208	0.458	wh
Trial $M =$	0	1.958	3.666	4.874	5.332	wh^2
Load $P =$	0.335	1.936	3.624	4.811	5.255	(wh^3/EI)
Trial $\phi =$	−13.335	−13.0	−11.064	−7.44	−2.629	(wh^3/EI)
Trial $y =$	0	−13.0	−24.064	−31.5	−34.129	(wh^4/EI)

Corrections to V and M are zero

$$\text{Maximum slope} = \phi_{\max} = \phi_0 = \frac{13.335\,wh^3}{EI} = \frac{wL^3}{38.39\,EI}$$

$$\text{Maximum deflection} = y_{\max} = y_4 = \frac{34.129\,wh^4}{EI} = \frac{wL^4}{120\,EI}$$

$$P_1 = \left(\frac{h}{12}\right)(w_0 + 10w_1 + w_2)$$

$$= \left(\frac{h}{12}\right)(0 + 10 \times 1.958 + 3.666)\left(\frac{wh^2}{EI}\right) = 1.936\left(\frac{wh^3}{EI}\right)$$

$$P_2 = \left(\frac{h}{12}\right)(w_1 + 10w_2 + w_3)$$

$$= \left(\frac{h}{12}\right)(1.958 + 10 \times 3.666 + 4.874)\left(\frac{wh^2}{EI}\right) = 3.624\left(\frac{wh^3}{EI}\right)$$

$$P_3 = \left(\frac{h}{12}\right)(w_2 + 10w_3 + w_4)$$

$$= \left(\frac{h}{12}\right)\left[3.666 + (10 \times 4.874) + 5.332\right]\left(\frac{wh^2}{EI}\right) = 4.811\left(\frac{wh^3}{EI}\right)$$

$$P_4 = \left(\frac{h}{12}\right)(w_3 + 10w_4 + w_5)$$

$$= \left(\frac{h}{12}\right)\left[4.874 + (10 \times 5.332) + 4.874\right]\left(\frac{wh^2}{EI}\right) = 5.255\left(\frac{wh^3}{EI}\right)$$

Also $P_5 = P_3$ $P_6 = P_2$ $P_7 = P_1$

Example 5.14

A cantilever of length L, supports an uniformly distributed load of intensity w kN/m over its entire span length as shown in Fig. 5.14. Evaluate the maximum slope and deflection at the free end using Newmark's method.

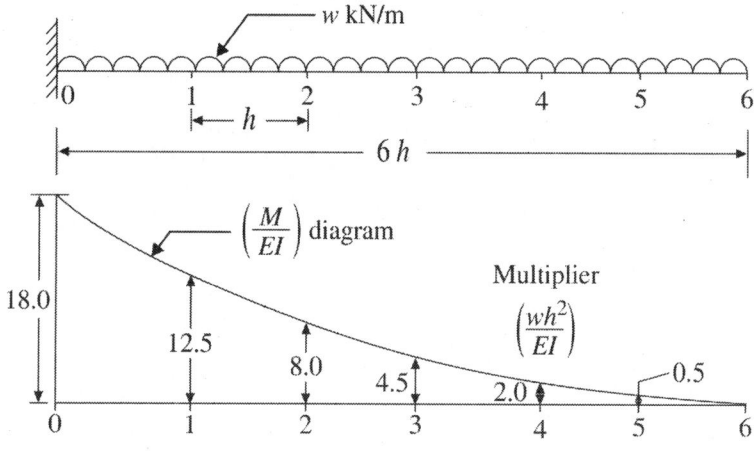

Fig. 5.14: Cantilever supporting uniformly distributed load (UDL)

Solution

The numerical computation of beam slopes and deflections is compiled in Table 5.10.

The equivalent loads are computed in the following steps:

$$P_0 = \left(\frac{h}{24}\right)(7w_0 + 6w_1 - w_2)$$

$$= \left(\frac{h}{24}\right)\left[(7 \times 18) + (6 \times 12.5) - 8\right]\left(\frac{wh^2}{EI}\right) = 8.04\left(\frac{wh^3}{EI}\right)$$

$$P_1 = \left(\frac{h}{12}\right)(w_0 + 10w_1 + w_2)$$

$$= \left(\frac{h}{12}\right)(18 + 10 \times 12.5 + 8)\left(\frac{wh^2}{EI}\right) = 12.58\left(\frac{wh^3}{EI}\right)$$

$$P_2 = \left(\frac{h}{12}\right)(w_1 + 10w_2 + w_3)$$

$$= \left(\frac{h}{12}\right)(12.5 + 10 \times 8 + 4.5)\left(\frac{wh^2}{EI}\right) = 8.08\left(\frac{wh^3}{EI}\right)$$

$$P_3 = \left(\frac{h}{12}\right)(w_2 + 10w_3 + w_4)$$

$$= \left(\frac{h}{12}\right)\left[8 + (10 \times 4.5) + 2\right]\left(\frac{wh^2}{EI}\right) = 4.58\left(\frac{wh^3}{EI}\right)$$

$$P_4 = \left(\frac{h}{12}\right)(w_3 + 10w_4 + w_5)$$

$$= \left(\frac{h}{12}\right)\left[4.5 + (10 \times 2) + 0.5\right]\left(\frac{wh^2}{EI}\right) = 2.08\left(\frac{wh^3}{EI}\right)$$

$$P_5 = \left(\frac{h}{12}\right)(w_4 + 10w_5 + w_6)$$

$$= \left(\frac{h}{12}\right)(2 + 10 \times 0.5 + 0)\left(\frac{wh^2}{EI}\right) = 0.58\left(\frac{wh^3}{EI}\right)$$

Table 5.10: Computation of beam slopes and deflections

Nodal points	0	1	2	3	4	5	6	Multiplier
Load	$P =$ -0.5	-1.0	-1.0	-1.0	-1.0	-1.0	-0.5	wh
Trial	$V =$ 6.0						0	wh
Trial	$M =$ -18.0	-12.5	-8.0	-4.5	-2.0	-0.5	0	wh^2

Intermediate V values (between nodes): 5.5, 4.5, 3.5, 2.5, 1.5, -0.5

Corrections to V and M are zero

Nodal points	0	1	2	3	4	5	6	Multiplier
Load	$P =$ -8.04	-12.58	-8.08	-4.58	-2.08	-0.58	-0.41	(wh^3/EI)
Trial	$\phi =$ 0						-35.98	(wh^3/EI)
Trial	$y =$ 0	-8.04	-28.66	-57.36	-90.64	-126	-161.94	(wh^4/EI)

Intermediate ϕ values (between nodes): -8.04, -20.62, -28.7, -33.28, -35.36, -35.94

$$\text{Maximum slope} = \phi_{max} = \phi_6 = \frac{35.98\, wh^3}{EI} = \frac{wL^3}{6.0003\, EI}$$

$$\text{Maximum deflection} = y_{max} = y_6 = \frac{161.94\, wh^4}{EI} = \frac{wL^4}{8\, EI}$$

$$P_6 = \left(\frac{h}{24}\right)(7w_6 + 6w_5 - w_4)$$

$$= \left(\frac{h}{24}\right)(0 + 6 \times 0.5 - 2)\left(\frac{wh^2}{EI}\right) = 0.041\left(\frac{wh^3}{EI}\right)$$

Example 5.15

A cantilever with varying moment of inertia and of span length L supports an uniformly distributed load of w kN/m as shown in Fig. 5.15. Assuming six grid points and using Newmark's method, estimate the maximum deflection and slope in the cantilever.

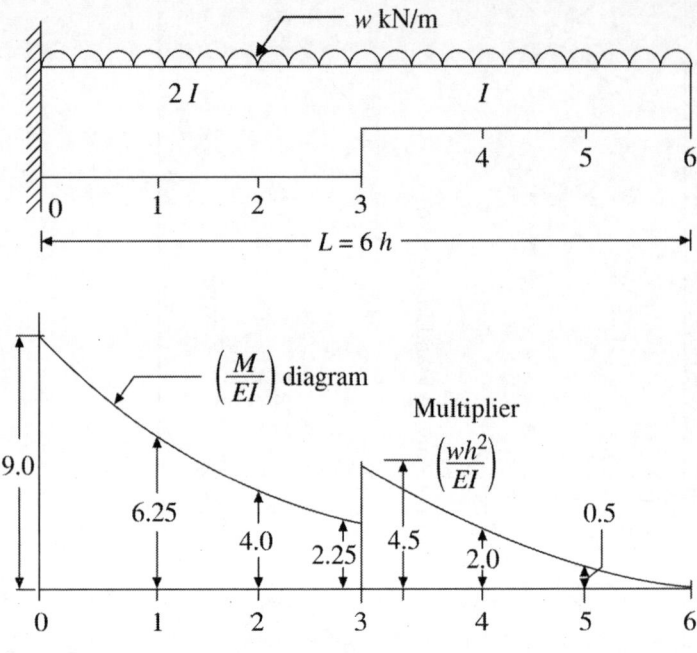

Fig. 5.15: Cantilever with variable moment of inertia supporting UDL

Solution

The numerical computation of beam slopes and deflections is compiled in Table 5.11.

The equivalent loads are computed in the following steps:

$$P_0 = \left(\frac{h}{24}\right)(7w_0 + 6w_1 - w_2)$$

$$= \left(\frac{h}{24}\right)\left[(7 \times 9) + (6 \times 6.25) - 4\right]\left(\frac{wh^2}{EI}\right) = 4.02\left(\frac{wh^3}{EI}\right)$$

Table 5.11: Computation of beam slopes and deflections

Nodal points	0	1	2	3	4	5	6	Multiplier
Load P =	-0.5	-1.0	-1.0	-1.0	-1.0	-1.0	-0.5 → 0	w
Trial V =	6.0	5.5	4.5	3.5	2.5	1.5	0.5 → 0	wh
Trial M =	-18.0	-12.5	-8.0	-4.5	-2.0	-0.5	0	wh^2
				Corrections to V and M are zero				
Load P =	-4.02	-6.29	-4.04	-3.18	-2.08	-0.58	-0.041 → 0	(wh^3/EI)
Trial ϕ =	0	-4.02	-10.31	-14.35	-17.53	-19.61	-20.19 → -20.23	(wh^3/EI)
Trial y =	-0	-4.02	-14.33	-28.68	-46.21	-65.82	-86.01	(wh^4/EI)

$$\text{Maximum slope} = \phi_{max} = \phi_6 = \frac{20.23\,wh^3}{EI} = \frac{wL^3}{10.6\,EI}$$

$$\text{Maximum deflection} = y_{max} = y_6 = \frac{86.01\,wh^4}{EI} = \frac{wL^4}{15.06\,EI}$$

$$P_1 = \left(\frac{h}{12}\right)(w_0 + 10w_1 + w_2)$$

$$= \left(\frac{h}{12}\right)(9 + 10 \times 6.25 + 4)\left(\frac{wh^2}{EI}\right) = 6.29\left(\frac{wh^3}{EI}\right)$$

$$P_2 = \left(\frac{h}{12}\right)(w_1 + 10w_2 + w_3)$$

$$= \left(\frac{h}{12}\right)(6.25 + 10 \times 4 + 2.25)\left(\frac{wh^2}{EI}\right) = 4.04\left(\frac{wh^3}{EI}\right)$$

$$P_3 = \left(\frac{h}{24}\right)\left[(7w_3 + 6w_2 - w_1) + (7w_3 + 6w_4 - w_5)\right]$$

$$= \left(\frac{h}{24}\right)\left[(7 \times 2.25) + (6 \times 4) - 6.25 + (7 \times 4.5) + (6 \times 2) - 0.5\right]\left(\frac{wh^2}{EI}\right)$$

$$= 3.18\left(\frac{wh^3}{EI}\right)$$

$$P_4 = \left(\frac{h}{12}\right)(w_3 + 10w_4 + w_5)$$

$$= \left(\frac{h}{12}\right)\left[4.5 + (10 \times 2) + 0.5\right]\left(\frac{wh^2}{EI}\right) = 2.08\left(\frac{wh^3}{EI}\right)$$

$$P_5 = \left(\frac{h}{12}\right)(w_4 + 10w_5 + w_6)$$

$$= \left(\frac{h}{12}\right)(2 + 10 \times 0.5 + 0)\left(\frac{wh^2}{EI}\right) = 0.58\left(\frac{wh^3}{EI}\right)$$

$$P_6 = \left(\frac{h}{24}\right)(7w_6 + 6w_5 - w_4)$$

$$= \left(\frac{h}{24}\right)(0 + 6 \times 0.5 - 2)\left(\frac{wh^2}{EI}\right) = 0.041\left(\frac{wh^3}{EI}\right)$$

Example 5.16

A cantilever of length L carries a load W at the free end and the second moment of area of the cantilever is I, $2I$ and $3I$ for each of the one third span lengths as shown in Fig. 5.16. Determine the deflection and slope at the free end using Newmark's method.

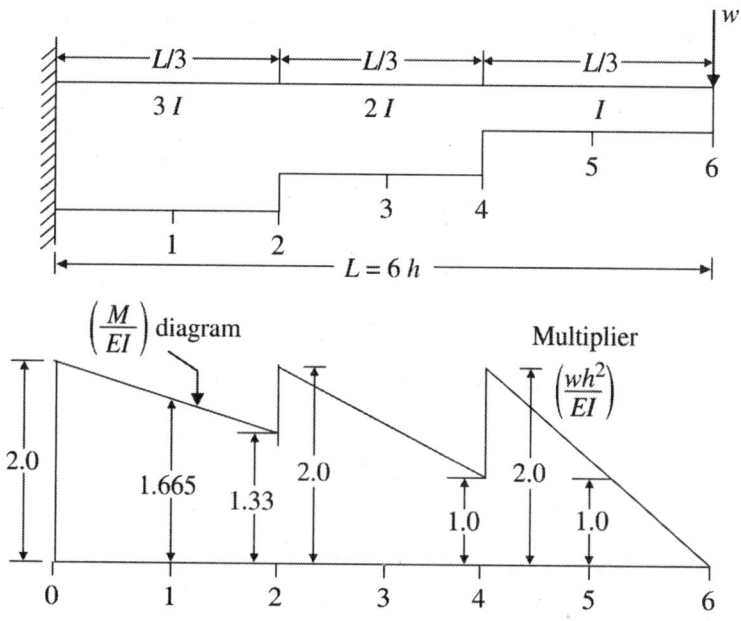

Fig. 5.16: Cantilever with variable moment of inertia supporting UDL

Solution

The numerical computation of beam slopes and deflections is compiled in Table 5.12.

The equivalent loads are computed in the following steps:

$$P_0 = \left(\frac{h}{6}\right)(2w_0 + w_1) = \left(\frac{h}{6}\right)(2 \times 2 + 1.665)\left(\frac{wh}{EI}\right) = 0.944\left(\frac{wh^2}{EI}\right)$$

$$P_1 = \left(\frac{h}{6}\right)(w_0 + 4w_1 + w_2) = \left(\frac{h}{6}\right)\left[2 + (4 \times 1.665) + 1.33\right]\left(\frac{wh}{EI}\right) = 1.665\left(\frac{wh^2}{EI}\right)$$

$$P_2 = \left(\frac{h}{6}\right)\left[(2w_2 + w_1) + (2w_2 + w_3)\right]$$

$$= \left(\frac{h}{6}\right)\left[(2 \times 1.33) + 1.665 + (2 \times 2) + 1.5\right]\left(\frac{wh}{EI}\right) = 1.6375\left(\frac{wh^2}{EI}\right)$$

$$P_3 = \left(\frac{h}{6}\right)(w_2 + 4w_3 + w_4) = \left(\frac{h}{6}\right)(2 + 4 \times 1.5 + 1)\left(\frac{wh}{EI}\right) = 1.50\left(\frac{wh^2}{EI}\right)$$

$$P_4 = \left(\frac{h}{6}\right)\left[(2w_4 + w_3) + (2w_4 + w_5)\right]$$

Table 5.12: Computation of beam slopes and deflections

Nodal points	0	1	2	3	4	5	6	Multiplier
Load P =	−0.944	−1.665	−1.6375	−1.50	−1.416	−1.0	−0.166	(wh^2/EI)
Trial ϕ =	0						−8.328	(wh^2/EI)
		−0.944	−2.609	−4.24	−5.74	−7.162	−8.162	
Trial y =	0	−0.944	−3.553	−7.703	−13.533	−20.695	−28.857	(wh^2/EI)

Corrections to $\overset{\circ}{\phi}$ is zero

Maximum slope $= \phi_{max} = \phi_6 = \dfrac{8.328\ wh^2}{EI} = \dfrac{0.231\ wL^2}{EI}$

Maximum deflection $= y_{max} = y_6 = \dfrac{28.857\ wh^3}{EI} = \dfrac{0.133\ wL^3}{EI}$

$$= \left(\frac{h}{6}\right)\left[(2\times 1)+1.5+(2\times 2)+1\right]\left(\frac{wh}{EI}\right)=1.416\left(\frac{wh^2}{EI}\right)$$

$$P_5 = \left(\frac{h}{6}\right)(w_4+4w_5+w_6)=\left(\frac{h}{6}\right)\left[2+(4\times 1)+0\right]\left(\frac{wh}{EI}\right)=1.0\left(\frac{wh^2}{EI}\right)$$

$$P_6 = \left(\frac{h}{6}\right)(2w_6+w_5)=\left(\frac{h}{6}\right)(0+1)\left(\frac{wh}{EI}\right)=0.166\left(\frac{wh^2}{EI}\right)$$

Example 5.17

A beam of length L, with variable moment of inertia is subjected to a moment M at the left hand support as shown in Fig. 5.17. Calculate the deflection at the panel points. Also evaluate the maximum deflection in the beam.

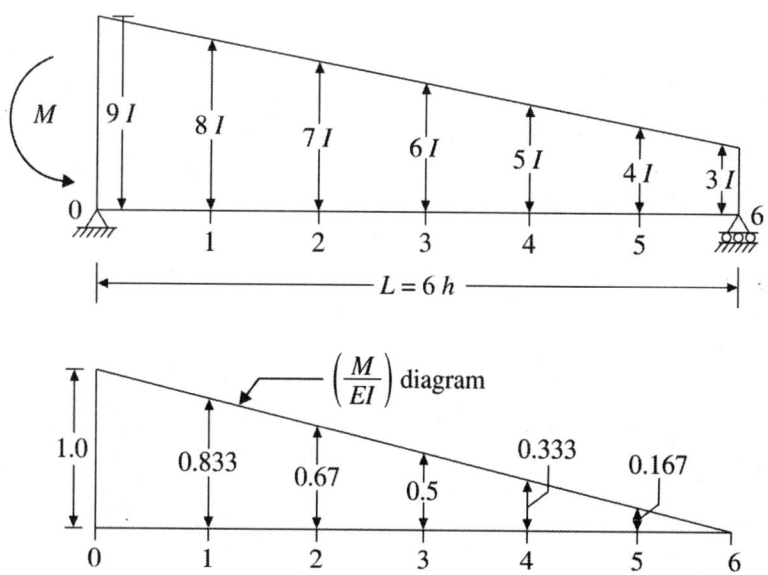

Fig. 5.17: Simply supported beam subjected to moment

Solution

The numerical computation of beam slopes and deflections is compiled in Table 5.13.

The equivalent loads are computed in the following steps:

Referring to Fig. 5.17, the ordinates of (M/EI) diagram at various panel points are obtained as follows:

$$w_0 = \left(\frac{1}{9EI}\right)=\left(\frac{0.111}{EI}\right)$$

$$w_1 = \left(\frac{0.833}{8EI}\right)=\left(\frac{0.104}{EI}\right)$$

Table 5.13: Computation of beam slopes and deflections

Nodal points	0	1	2	3	4	5	6	Multiplier
Load, P =	5.43	10.378	9.5	8.26	6.52	3.89	0.7	$(h/100\,EI)$
Trial, φ = −29.43	−2.4	−13.63	−4.13	4.13	10.65	14.54	15.24	$(h/100\,EI)$
Trial, y =	0	−24	−37.63	−41.76	−37.63	−26.98	−12.44	$(h^2/100\,EI)$
Correction to slope, φ =		2.073	2.073	2.073	2.073	2.073	2.073	$(h/100\,EI)$
Correct, φ = −27.36	−21.92	−11.55	−2.05	6.20	12.72	16.60	17.31	$(h/100\,EI)$
Correct, y =	−0	−21.92	−33.47	−35.52	−29.32	−16.60	0	$(h^2/100\,EI)$

Corrections to φ = (12.44/6) = 2.073

Maximum deflection for unit moment $= y_{max} = y_3 = \dfrac{35.52\,h^2}{100\,EI} = \dfrac{0.355\,L^2}{EI}$

Maximum deflection for moment $M = y_{max} = y_3 = \dfrac{0.355\,Mh^2}{EI} = \dfrac{0.09896\,ML^2}{EI}$

$$w_2 = \left(\frac{0.67}{7EI}\right) = \left(\frac{0.0957}{EI}\right)$$

$$w_3 = \left(\frac{0.5}{6EI}\right) = \left(\frac{0.0833}{EI}\right)$$

$$w_4 = \left(\frac{0.333}{5EI}\right) = \left(\frac{0.066}{EI}\right)$$

$$w_5 = \left(\frac{0.167}{4EI}\right) = \left(\frac{0.04175}{EI}\right)$$

Equivalent loads are computed using Newmark's formula at the various panel points according to the stepwise procedure given below.

$$P_0 = \left(\frac{h}{6}\right)(2w_0 + w_1) = \left(\frac{h}{6}\right)(2 \times 0.111 + 0.104)(EI) = 0.0543\left(\frac{h}{EI}\right)$$

$$P_1 = \left(\frac{h}{6}\right)(w_0 + 4w_1 + w_2) = \left(\frac{h}{6}\right)[0.111 + (4 \times 0.104) + 0.0957](EI) = 0.10378\left(\frac{h}{EI}\right)$$

$$P_2 = \left(\frac{h}{6}\right)(w_1 + 4w_2 + w_3) = \left(\frac{h}{6}\right)[0.104 + (4 \times 0.0957) + 0.0833](EI) = 0.095\left(\frac{h}{EI}\right)$$

$$P_3 = \left(\frac{h}{6}\right)(w_2 + 4w_3 + w_4) = \left(\frac{h}{6}\right)[0.0957 + (4 \times 0.0833) + 0.0666](EI) = 0.0826\left(\frac{h}{EI}\right)$$

$$P_4 = \left(\frac{h}{6}\right)(w_3 + 4w_4 + w_5) = \left(\frac{h}{6}\right)[0.0833 + (4 \times 0.0666) + 0.04175](EI) = 0.0652\left(\frac{h}{EI}\right)$$

$$P_5 = \left(\frac{h}{6}\right)(w_4 + 4w_5 + w_6) = \left(\frac{h}{6}\right)[0.0666 + (4 \times 0.04175) + 0](EI) = 0.0389\left(\frac{h}{EI}\right)$$

$$P_6 = \left(\frac{h}{6}\right)(2w_6 + w_5) = \left(\frac{h}{6}\right)(0 + 0.04175)(EI) = 0.006958\left(\frac{h}{EI}\right)$$

Example 5.18

A propped cantilever of length L supports a uniformly distributed load of w kN/m over the entire Length. Calculate the maximum slope and deflection in the cantilever, assuming six nodal points. Assume EI is constant. The loaded propped cantilever is shown in Fig. 5.18.

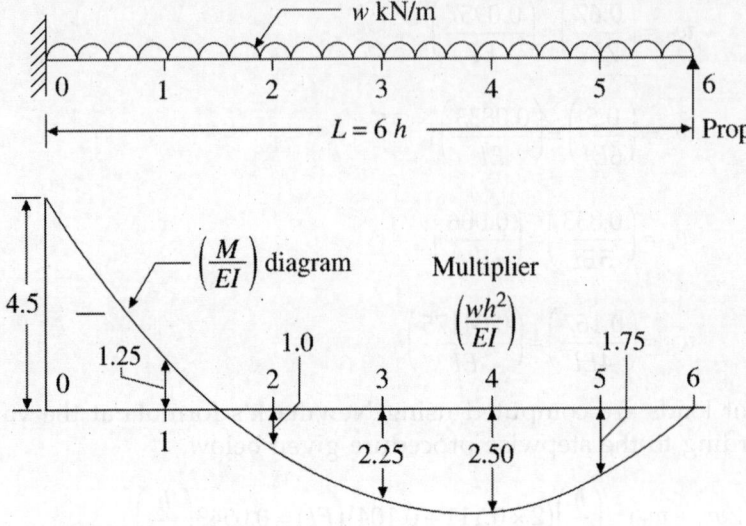

Fig. 5.18: Propped cantilever supporting uniformly distributed load

Solution

The bending moment diagram is first determined and then Newmark's method is applied to evaluate the slope and deflection.

Since the deflection at the nodal point 6 (prop) is zero, the reaction R at the prop is determined by equating the deflection at the free end of the cantilever supporting uniformly distributed load w.

$$\frac{R(6h)^3}{3EI} = \frac{w(6h)^4}{8EI}$$

Solving, $\qquad R = \left(\frac{9}{4}\right)wh$

The ordinates of the bending moment diagram are calculated in the following steps.

$$w_0 = \left(\frac{9}{4}\right)wh(6h) - 0.5w(6h)^2 = -4.5wh^2$$

$$w_1 = \left(\frac{9}{4}\right)wh(5h) - 0.5w(5h)^2 = -1.25wh^2$$

$$w_2 = \left(\frac{9}{4}\right)wh(4h) - 0.5w(4h)^2 = -1.0wh^2$$

$$w_3 = \left(\frac{9}{4}\right)wh(3h) - 0.5w(3h)^2 = 2.25wh^2$$

$$w_4 = \left(\frac{9}{4}\right)wh(2h) - 0.5w(2h)^2 = 2.5wh^2$$

$$w_5 = \left(\frac{9}{4}\right)wh(h) - 0.5w(h)^2 = 1.75wh^2$$

The equivalent loads are calculated as follows:

$$P_0 = \left(\frac{h}{24}\right)(7w_0 + 6w_1 - w_2)$$

$$= \left(\frac{h}{24}\right)\left[(7)\times(-4.5) + (6)\times(-1.25) - 1.0\right]\left(\frac{wh^2}{EI}\right) = -1.663\left(\frac{wh^3}{EI}\right)$$

$$P_1 = \left(\frac{h}{12}\right)(w_0 + 10w_1 + w_2)$$

$$= \left(\frac{h}{12}\right)\left[(-4.5) + (10)(-1.25) + 1.0\right]\left(\frac{wh^2}{EI}\right) = -1.33\left(\frac{wh^3}{EI}\right)$$

$$P_2 = \left(\frac{h}{12}\right)(w_1 + 10w_2 + w_3)$$

$$= \left(\frac{h}{12}\right)\left[(-1.25) + (10\times1) + 2.25\right]\left(\frac{wh^2}{EI}\right) = 0.916\left(\frac{wh^3}{EI}\right)$$

$$P_3 = \left(\frac{h}{12}\right)(w_2 + 10w_3 + w_4)$$

$$= \left(\frac{h}{12}\right)(1 + 10\times2.25 + 2.5)\left(\frac{wh^2}{EI}\right) = 2.166\left(\frac{wh^3}{EI}\right)$$

$$P_4 = \left(\frac{h}{12}\right)(w_3 + 10w_4 + w_5)$$

$$= \left(\frac{h}{12}\right)\left[(2.25) + (10)(2.5) + 1.75\right]\left(\frac{wh^2}{EI}\right) = 2.416\left(\frac{wh^3}{EI}\right)$$

$$P_5 = \left(\frac{h}{12}\right)(w_4 + 10w_5 + w_6)$$

$$= \left(\frac{h}{12}\right)\left[(2.5) + (10)(1.75) + 0\right]\left(\frac{wh^2}{EI}\right) = 1.666\left(\frac{wh^3}{EI}\right)$$

$$P_6 = \left(\frac{h}{24}\right)(w_6 + 10w_5 + w_4)$$

$$= \left(\frac{h}{24}\right)\left[(0 + (6)(1.75) - 2.5]\left(\frac{wh^2}{EI}\right) = 0.333\left(\frac{wh^3}{EI}\right)\right]$$

The equivalent loads calculated are used for the numerical computation of slopes and deflections as per Newmark's numerical integration procedure.

The numerical computation of slopes and deflections in the propped cantilever is compiled in Table 5.14.

Example 5.19

A beam fixed at both ends with a span length of L supports a uniformly distributed load of intensity w kN/m over the entire span length. Estimate the maximum deflection in the beam by Newmark's method. The loaded beam together with the bending moment diagram is shown in Fig. 5.19.

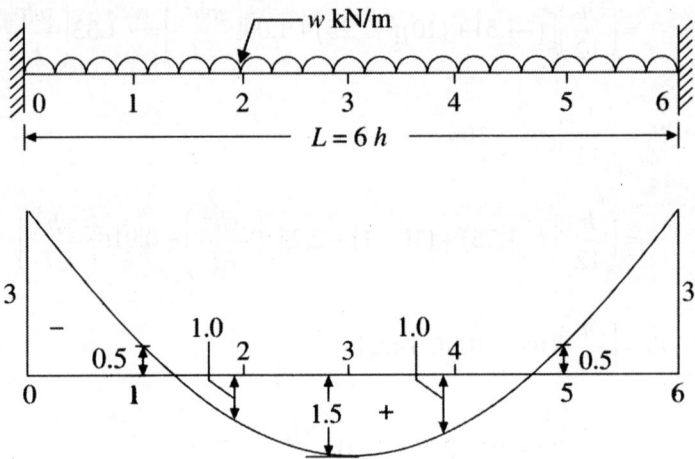

Fig. 5.19: Fixed beam supporting uniformly distributed load

Solution

The ordinates of the bending moment diagram are as follows:

$$w_0 = -3wh^2$$

$$w_1 = -0.5wh^2$$

$$w_2 = 1.0wh^2$$

$$w_3 = 1.5wh^2$$

$$w_4 = w_2 \qquad\qquad w_5 = w_1 \qquad\qquad w_6 = w_0$$

Table 5.14: Computation of beam slopes and deflections

Nodal points	0	1	2	3	4	5	6	Multiplier
Load P =	−1.663	−1.33	0.916	2.166	2.416	1.666	0.333	(wh^3/EI)
Trial ϕ =	0	−1.663	−2.993	−2.077	0.089	2.505	4.171 → 4.504	(wh^3/EI)
Trial y =	0	−1.663	−4.656	−6.733	−6.644	−4.139	0.032	(wh^4/EI)

Corrections to ϕ = − (0.032/6) = −0.005

	0	1	2	3	4	5	6	
Correction to ϕ =		−0.005	−0.005	−0.005	−0.005	−0.005	−0.005	(wh^3/EI)
Correct ϕ =		−1.668	−2.998	−2.082	0.084	2.500	4.166	(wh^3/EI)
Correct y =	0	−1.668	−4.666	−6.748	−6.664	−4.164	0	(wh^4/EI)

$$\text{Maximum slope} = \phi_{max} = \phi_6 = \frac{4.166\ wh^3}{EI} = \frac{0.0192\ wL^3}{EI}$$

$$\text{Maximum deflection} = y_{max} = y_3 = \frac{6.748\ wh^4}{EI} = \frac{0.0052\ wL^4}{EI}$$

The equivalent loads are computed as shown below:

$$P_0 = \left(\frac{h}{24}\right)(7w_0 + 6w_1 - w_2)$$

$$= \left(\frac{h}{24}\right)\left[(-3 \times 7) + (6) \times (-0.5) - 1.0\right]\left(\frac{wh^2}{EI}\right) = -1.04\left(\frac{wh^3}{EI}\right)$$

$$P_1 = \left(\frac{h}{12}\right)(w_0 + 10w_1 + w_2)$$

$$= \left(\frac{h}{12}\right)\left[(-3) + (10)(-0.5) + 1.0\right]\left(\frac{wh^2}{EI}\right) = -0.583\left(\frac{wh^3}{EI}\right)$$

$$P_2 = \left(\frac{h}{12}\right)(w_1 + 10w_2 + w_3)$$

$$= \left(\frac{h}{12}\right)\left[(-0.5) + (10 \times 1) + 1.5\right]\left(\frac{wh^2}{EI}\right) = 0.916\left(\frac{wh^3}{EI}\right)$$

$$P_3 = \left(\frac{h}{12}\right)(w_2 + 10w_3 + w_4)$$

$$= \left(\frac{h}{12}\right)\left[1 + (10 \times 1.5) + 1.0\right]\left(\frac{wh^2}{EI}\right) = 1.416\left(\frac{wh^3}{EI}\right)$$

$$P_4 = P_2$$
$$P_5 = P_1$$
$$P_6 = P_0$$

The numerical computation of beam slopes and deflections is compiled in Table 5.15.

Example 5.20

Find the deflection at the free end and at the centre of the double overhang beam shown in Fig. 5.20 using Newmark's method.

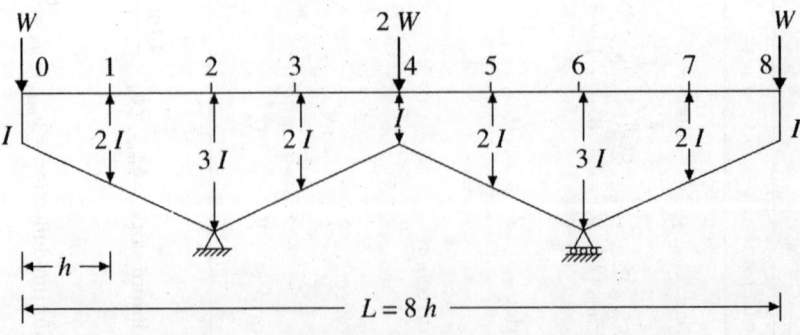

Fig. 5.20: Double cantilever beam supporting concentrated loads

Table 5.15: Computation of maximum deflection

Nodal points	0	1	2	3	4	5	6	Multiplier
Load P =	−1.04	−0.583	0.916	1.416	0.916	−0.583	−1.04	(wh^3/EI)
Trial ϕ =	0	−1.623	−0.707	0.709	1.625	1.04	0	(wh^3/EI)
Trial y =	0	−1.04	−2.663	−3.37	−2.663	−1.04	0	(wh^4/EI)

(Intermediate ϕ slope values between nodes: −1.04, −1.623, −0.707, 0.709, 1.625, 1.04)

$$\text{Maximum deflection at centre of span} = y_{max} = y_3 = \frac{3.37\, wh^4}{EI} = \frac{0.0026\, wL^4}{EI}$$

Solution

Bending moments at various sections of the beam are obtained as,

$$M_0 = 0 \quad M_1 = -wh \quad M_2 = -2wh$$

$$M_3 = (-w \times 3h + 2wh) = -wh$$

$$M_4 = (-w \times 4h + 2w \times 2h) = 0$$

The ordinates of the (M/EI) diagram at various nodal points are computed as follows:

$$w_0 = 0 \quad w_1 = -0.5\left(\frac{wh}{EI}\right) \quad w_2 = -0.67\left(\frac{wh}{EI}\right)$$

$$w_3 = -0.5\left(\frac{wh}{EI}\right) \qquad w_4 = 0$$

The equivalent loads are calculated using Newmark's formula.

$$P_0 = \left(\frac{h}{6}\right)(2w_0 + w_1) = \left(\frac{h}{6}\right)(0 - 0.5)\left(\frac{wh}{EI}\right) = -0.0833\left(\frac{wh^2}{EI}\right)$$

$$P_1 = \left(\frac{h}{6}\right)(w_0 + 4w_1 + w_2) = \left(\frac{h}{6}\right)\left[0 + 4(-0.5) - 0.67\right](wh/EI) = -0.4445\left(\frac{wh^2}{EI}\right)$$

$$P_2 = \left(\frac{h}{6}\right)(w_1 + 4w_2 + w_3) = \left(\frac{h}{6}\right)\left[-0.5 - 4 \times (0.67) - 0.5\right](wh/EI) = -0.6133\left(\frac{wh^2}{EI}\right)$$

$$P_3 = \left(\frac{h}{6}\right)(w_2 + 4w_3 + w_4) = \left(\frac{h}{6}\right)\left[-0.67 - 4 \times 0.5 + 0\right](wh/EI) = -0.446\left(\frac{wh^2}{EI}\right)$$

$$P_4 = \left(\frac{h}{6}\right)(w_3 + 4w_4 + w_5) = \left(\frac{h}{6}\right)\left[-0.5 - 4 \times 0 - 0.5\right](wh/EI) = -0.167\left(\frac{wh^2}{EI}\right)$$

The equivalent loads are used for the computation of slopes and deflections at various nodal points by the numerical summation technique shown in Table 5.16.

5.4 BUCKLING OF SIMPLY SUPPORTED STRAIGHT COLUMNS

The elastic buckling load of columns under axial loads can be determined by Newmark's numerical integration procedure. The deflection pattern under buckling loads for the lowest mode of buckling will be generally a curve without any reversal of curvature and hence it can easily be assumed. The following procedure is adopted to compute the elastic buckling load of axially loaded columns (Table 5.17).

1. Divide the beam into an equal number of panels and assume some arbitrary deflection (y_a) at nodal points.
2. The moment at each pivotal point is equal to the product of the axial force P and the Deflection y_a.

Table 5.16: Computation of beam slopes and deflections

Nodal points	0	1	2	3	4	Multiplier
Load P =	−0.0833	−0.4445	−0.6133	−0.446	−0.167	(wh^2/EI)
Trial ϕ =	1.7531	1.6698	1.2253	0.612	0.166	0	(wh^2/EI)
Trial y =	2.8951	1.2253	0	0.612	0.779	(wh^3/EI)

Deflection at free end $= \dfrac{2.8951\ wh^3}{EI} = \dfrac{0.00565\ wL^3}{EI}$

Deflection at the centre $= \dfrac{0.779\ wh^3}{EI} = \dfrac{0.00152\ wL^3}{EI}$

Table 5.17: Computation of column slopes and deflections

Nodal points	0	1	2	3	4	5	6	Multiplier
Assumed deflection y_a =	0	-4	-7	-10	-7	-4	-0	
$\dfrac{-Py_a}{EI} = \dfrac{M}{EI}$ =	0	4	7	10	7	4	0	(P/EI)
Load P =	0.708	3.916	7.0	9.5	7.0	3.916	-0.708	(Ph/EI)
Trial ϕ =	-16.374	-15.166 -11.75	7.0 -4.75	9.5 4.75	7.0 11.75	3.916 15.666	16.374	(Ph/EI)
Deflection y =	0	-15.166	-27.416	-32.166	-27.416	-15.666	0	(Ph^2/EI)
Ratio (y_a/y) =	0	0.255	0.255	0.31	0.255	0.255	0	(EI/h^2)

Maximum slope $= \phi_{max} = \phi_0 = \dfrac{16.374\ Ph}{EI}$

Maximum deflection $= y_{max} = y_3 = \dfrac{32.166\ Ph^2}{EI}$

3. The (M/EI) diagram being known, compute the equivalent loads P_0, P_1, P_2, ..., P_n.
4. Numerical Integration is carried out with these load values at the nodal points and a new Set of deflections y are obtained.
5. Calculate the ratio of (y_a/y) at the nodal points. For the first few trials, the values of the Critical load computed for the pivotal points will not be the same. Then a closer approximation of the critical load is obtained by the equation,

$$P_{cr} = \left[\frac{\sum y_a \cdot y}{\sum y^2}\right]$$

6. Alternatively, the procedure is repeated with the new set of assumed deflections as y_a and The numerical integration is carried out until the critical loads computed for each nodal point differ within an allowable limit.

The procedure is illustrated by the following examples.

Example 5.21

Calculate the buckling load of a column of length L, having a uniform flexural rigidity EI and subjected to an axial load P. Assume six intervals and adopt the numerical integration technique. The given column with the (M/EI) is shown in Fig. 5.21.

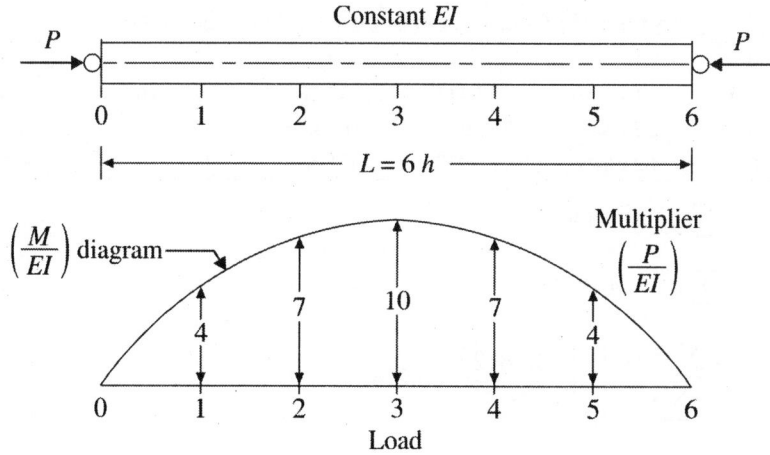

Fig. 5.21: Buckling load of pin-ended column

Solution

The equivalent loads are computed as follows:

$$P_0 = \left(\frac{h}{24}\right)(7w_0 + 6w_1 - w_2)$$

$$= \left(\frac{h}{24}\right)\left[0 + (6 \times 4) - 7\right]\left(\frac{P}{EI}\right) = 0.708\left(\frac{Ph}{EI}\right)$$

$$P_1 = \left(\frac{h}{12}\right)(w_0 + 10w_1 + w_2)$$

$$= \left(\frac{h}{12}\right)\left[0 + (10 \times 4) + 7\right]\left(\frac{P}{EI}\right) = 3.916\left(\frac{Ph}{EI}\right)$$

$$P_2 = \left(\frac{h}{12}\right)(w_1 + 10w_2 + w_3)$$

$$= \left(\frac{h}{12}\right)\left[4 + (10 \times 7) + 10\right]\left(\frac{P}{EI}\right) = 7\left(\frac{Ph}{EI}\right)$$

$$P_3 = \left(\frac{h}{12}\right)(w_2 + 10w_3 + w_4)$$

$$= \left(\frac{h}{12}\right)\left[7 + (10 \times 10) + 7\right]\left(\frac{P}{EI}\right) = 9.5\left(\frac{Ph}{EI}\right)$$

$$P_4 = P_2 \qquad\qquad P_5 = P_1 \qquad\qquad P_6 = P_0$$

The equivalent loads are used for the computation of slope and deflection in Table 5.18.

Table 5.18: Computation of buckling load parameters							
y_a	0	-4	-7	-10	-7	-4	0
y	0	-15.666	-27.416	-32.166	-27.416	-15.666	0
y^2	0	245.42	751.63	1034.65	751.63	245.42	0
$y_a \cdot y$	0	62.664	191.912	321.66	191.912	62.664	0

$$\sum y_a \cdot y = 830.812$$

$$\sum y^2 = 3028.75$$

$$\left[\frac{\sum y_a \cdot y}{\sum y^2}\right] = \left[\frac{830.812}{3028.75}\right] = 0.2743$$

$$\left(\frac{P_{cr} \cdot h^2}{EI}\right) = 0.2743$$

$$P_{cr} = \left[\frac{0.2743EI}{h^2}\right] = \left[\frac{0.2743EI}{\left(\frac{L}{6}\right)^2}\right] = 9.875\left(\frac{EI}{L^2}\right)$$

Exact value $= P_{cr} = \left(\dfrac{\pi^2 EI}{L^2}\right) = 9.869\left(\dfrac{EI}{L^2}\right)$

Example 5.22

Calculate the buckling load of a hinged column with variable moment of inertia as shown in Fig. 5.22, using Newmark's numerical integration procedure.

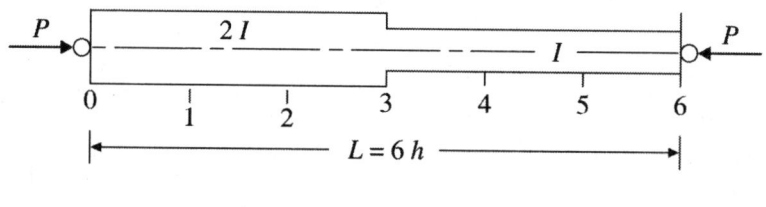

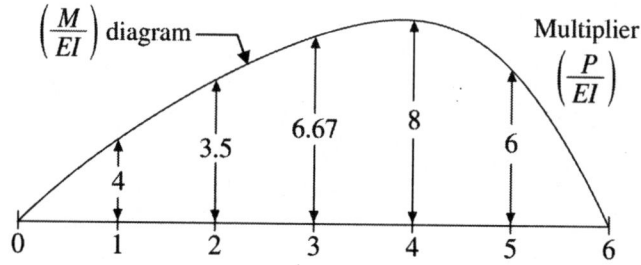

Fig. 5.22: Hinged column with variable moment of inertia

Solution

The equivalent loads are calculated as follows:

$$P_0 = \left(\frac{h}{24}\right)(7w_0 + 6w_1 - w_2)$$

$$= \left(\frac{h}{24}\right)[0 + (6 \times 2) - 3.5]\left(\frac{P}{EI}\right) = 0.354\left(\frac{Ph}{EI}\right)$$

$$P_1 = \left(\frac{h}{12}\right)(w_0 + 10w_1 + w_2)$$

$$= \left(\frac{h}{12}\right)[0 + (10 \times 2) + 3.5]\left(\frac{P}{EI}\right) = 1.958\left(\frac{Ph}{EI}\right)$$

$$P_2 = \left(\frac{h}{12}\right)(w_1 + 10w_2 + w_3)$$

$$= \left(\frac{h}{12}\right)[2 + (10 \times 3.5) + 6.67]\left(\frac{P}{EI}\right) = 3.64\left(\frac{Ph}{EI}\right)$$

Table 5.19: Computation of slopes and deflections

Nodal points	0	1	2	3	4	5	6	Multiplier
Assumed deflection y_a =	0	–4	–7	–10	–8	–6	0	0
$\dfrac{-Py_a}{EI} = \dfrac{M'}{EI}$ =	0	2	3.5	6.67	8	6	0	(P/EI)
Load P = 0.354		1.958	3.64	6.516	7.722	5.67	1.166	(Ph/EI)
Trial φ = –10.0		–9.646	–7.688	–4.048	2.468	10.19	15.86 → 17.026	(Ph/EI)
Trial y = 0		–9.646	–17.334	–21.382	–18.914	–8.124	7.136	(Ph^2/EI)

Correction to $y = -(7.136/6) = -1.189$

Nodal points	0	1	2	3	4	5	6	Multiplier
Correction to y = 0		–1.189	–2.378	–3.567	–4.756	–5.945	–7.136	(Ph^2/EI)
Correct y = 0		–10.835	–19.712	–24.949	–23.67	–14.669	0	(Ph^2/EI)
Ratio (y_a/y) = 0		0.369	0.355	0.400	0.338	0.409	0	(EI/h^2)

$$P_3 = \left(\frac{h}{12}\right)(w_2 + 10w_3 + w_4)$$

$$= \left(\frac{h}{12}\right)\left[3.5 + (10 \times 6.67) + 8\right]\left(\frac{P}{EI}\right) = 6.516\left(\frac{Ph}{EI}\right)$$

$$P_4 = \left(\frac{h}{12}\right)(w_3 + 10w_4 + w_5)$$

$$= \left(\frac{h}{12}\right)\left[6.67 + (10 \times 8) + 6\right]\left(\frac{P}{EI}\right) = 7.722\left(\frac{Ph}{EI}\right)$$

$$P_5 = \left(\frac{h}{12}\right)(w_4 + 10w_5 + w_6)$$

$$= \left(\frac{h}{12}\right)\left[8 + (10 \times 6) + 0\right]\left(\frac{P}{EI}\right) = 5.67\left(\frac{Ph}{EI}\right)$$

$$P_0 = \left(\frac{h}{24}\right)(7w_6 + 6w_5 - w_4)$$

$$= \left(\frac{h}{24}\right)\left[0 + (6 \times 6) - 8\right]\left(\frac{P}{EI}\right) = 1.166\left(\frac{Ph}{EI}\right)$$

These equivalent loads are used for the computation of slopes and deflections by the numerical integration procedure is outlined in Table 5.19.

The buckling load parameters are computed as shown in Table 5.20.

Table 5.20: Computation of buckling load parameters							
y_a	0	-4	-7	-10	-8	-6	0
y	0	-10.836	-19.714	-24.952	-23.67	-14.668	0
y^2	0	117.4	388.64	622.50	560.27	215.15	0
$y_a \cdot y$	0	43.344	138	240.5	189.36	88	0

$$\sum y_a \cdot y = 708.204$$

$$\sum y^2 = 1904$$

$$\left[\frac{\sum y_a \cdot \leq y}{\sum y^2}\right] = \left[\frac{708.204}{1904}\right] = 0.372$$

$$\left(\frac{P_{cr} \cdot h^2}{EI}\right) = 0.372$$

$$P_{cr} = \left[\frac{0.372EI}{h^2} \right] = \left[\frac{0.372EI}{\left(\dfrac{L}{6}\right)^2} \right] = 13.4 \left(\frac{EI}{L^2} \right)$$

The accuracy of the load can be improved by repeating the procedure assuming the final values of deflection (y) obtained as initial values.

Example 5.23

Calculate the buckling load of a column fixed at one end and pinned at the other end. The column has a variable moment of inertia as shown in Fig. 5.23. Adopt numerical integration technique of Newmark with six panels.

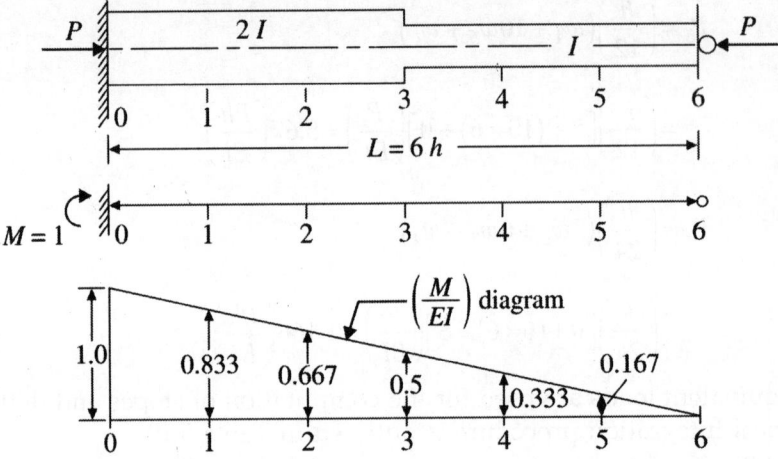

Fig. 5.23: Buckling load of column fixed at one end and pinned at other end

Solution

The column is assumed to be pinned at both ends and the analysis is carried out for deflections, as shown in Table 5.21.

A separate analysis is made for deflections when a moment M is applied at the left end fixed support as shown in Table 5.22.

EXERCISES

1. Evaluate the following integral numerically using Simpson's rule.

$$I = \int_0^1 \left[\frac{1}{\left(1+x^2\right)} \right] \cdot dx$$

Assume five intervals for computation.

2. The values of a function $f(x)$ are given in the following table for various values of x from 0.5 to 1.0

x	0.5	0.6	0.7	0.8	0.9	1.0
$f(x)$	1.25	1.36	1.49	1.64	1.81	2.0

Table 5.21: Computation of column slopes and deflections

Case 1. Both ends are pinned

Nodal points		0	1	2	3	4	5	6	Multiplier
Assumed deflection	$y =$	0	−4	−15	−28	−32	−22	0	
$-\dfrac{Py_a}{EI} = \dfrac{M}{EI} =$		0	2	7.5	14.28	32	22	0	(P/EI)
Load	$P =$	0.19	2.29	7.58	21.1	30.8	21.0	4.17	(Ph/EI)
Trial	$\phi =$	−30	−29.81	−27.52	−19.94	1.16	31.96	52.96 / 57.13	(Ph/EI)
Trial	$y =$	0	−29.81	−57.33	−77.27	−76.11	−44.15	8.81	(Ph^2/EI)

Correction to $\phi = -(8.81/6) = -1.47$

		0	1	2	3	4	5	6	Multiplier
Correction to	$y =$	0	−1.47	−2.94	−4.41	−5.88	−7.35	0	(Ph^2/EI)
Correct	$\phi =$	−31.47							
Correct	$y =$	0	−31.28	−60.27	−81.68	−81.99	−51.50	0	(Ph^2/EI)

A separate analysis is made for deflections when a moment M is applied at the left hand support as shown in Table 5.22.

Table 5.22: Computation of column slopes, deflections and buckling load parameters

Case 2. Column with applied moment M [Refer to Fig. 5.23 for (M/EI) values]

Nodal points	0	1	2	3	4	5	6	Multiplier
(M/EI) =	0.50	0.417	0.333	0.50	0.333	0.167	0	$(1/EI)$
Load P =	0.236	0.417	0.333	0.362	0.333	0.167	0.028	(h/EI)
Trial ϕ =	−1.20	−0.547	−0.214	0.148	0.481	0.648	0.676	(h/EI)
Trial y =	0	−0.964	−1.511	−1.725	−1.577	−1.096	−0.448	(h^2/EI)

Correction to ϕ = (0.448/6) = 0.075

Nodal points	0	1	2	3	4	5	6	Multiplier
Correct ϕ =	−1.125							
Correction to y =	0	0.075	0.15	0.225	0.30	0.375	0.450	(h^2/EI)
Final y =	0	0.889	−1.361	−1.501	−1.278	0.722	0	(h^2/EI)

Since the left end is fixed for the column, the rotation ϕ = 0, applying correction for ϕ = 0, for values in case 2, we have following computations:

Correction $M_L = (-31.47/-1.125) = -28P$ applying correction of $-28P$ to values of y in case 2

Nodal points	0	1	2	3	4	5	6	Multiplier
Correction to y =	0	24.9	38.1	42.1	35.8	20.3	0	(Ph^2/EI)
y from case-1 =	0	−31.28	−60.27	−81.68	−81.99	−51.50	−31.30	(Ph^2/EI)
Final y =	0	−6.39	−22.17	−39.58	−46.19	−31.30		(Ph^2/EI)
Ratio (y_a/y) =	0	0.627	0.671	0.708	0.693	0.703		(EI/h^2)

Repeated computations by taking the last y as y_a will give more accurate results.

Buckling load $P_{cr} = \dfrac{\sum y \cdot y_a}{\sum y^2} = 0.697\left(\dfrac{EI}{h^2}\right) = 25.1\left(\dfrac{EI}{L^2}\right)$

Determine the area bounded by the curve between $x = 0.5$ and 1.0 using the trapezoidal rule.

3. The following table gives the areas of cross-sections measured in a road project for earth work computation at intervals of 10 m.

Areas	A_1	A_2	A_3	A_4	A_5	A_6	A_7	A_8
m^2	126	248	118	90	320	120	75	180

Calculate the volume of earth work involved using the trapezoidal rule.

4. A simply supported beam of span 6 m supports a uniformly distributed load of intensity 2 kN/m over the entire span. Estimate the area of the bending moment diagram Considering 1 m intervals using a) trapezoidal rule and b) Simpson's rule.

5. A cantilever of span 5 m supports a uniformly distributed load of 4 kN/m over the entire span. Considering 1 m intervals, compute the area of the bending moment diagram using Simpson's rule.

6. In calculating the capacity of a reservoir, a contour interval of 1 m was used. The area measured Over six contour intervals are as follows:

Areas	A_1	A_2	A_3	A_4	A_5	A_6
m^2	4200	5800	6950	8748	10560	14670

7. Estimate the volume capacity of the reservoir using a) Simpson's rule and b) trapezoidal rule.

Determine the maximum slope and deflection of the beam AB loaded as shown in Fig. 5.24 using Newmark's method. Assume constant flexural rigidity for the beam.

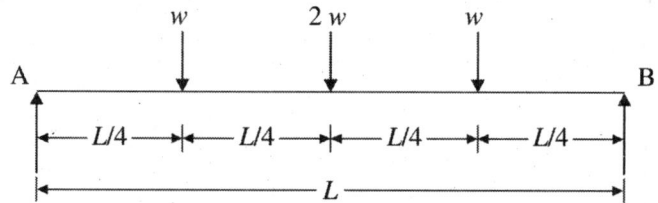

Fig. 5.24: Simply supported beam carrying point loads

8. A simply supported beam AB of variable moment of inertia supports a concentrated load of intensity 10 kN at the centre of span as shown in Fig. 5.25. Estimate the deflection at the centre of span. Assume $EI = (11.57 \times 10^{12})$ N/mm^2 and nodal points at (1/8) span intervals.

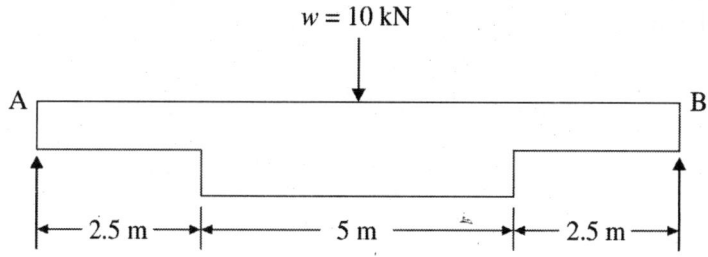

Fig. 5.25: Simply supported beam of variable moment of inertia (point loads)

9. A simply supported beam of span 12 m with variable moment of inertia supports a uniformly distributed load of intensity 5 kN/m as shown in Fig. 5.26. Assuming nodal points at (1/12) span intervals and $EI = (7.5 \times 10^{16})$ N/mm^2, estimate the maximum deflection in the beam.

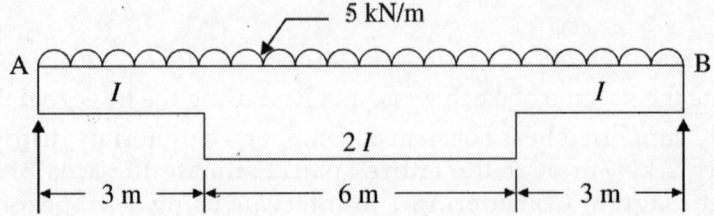

Fig. 5.26: Simply supported beam of variable moment of inertia (UDL)

10. A cantilever of L is loaded as shown in Fig. 5.27. Calculate the deflection and slope at the free end. Assume constant flexural rigidity for the cantilever.

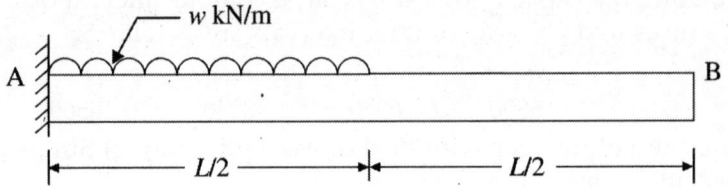

Fig. 5.27: Cantilever on supporting partial load (UDL)

11. A cantilever AB of length L supports uniformly distributed load of intensity w kN/m as shown in Fig. 5.28. Estimate the deflection and slope at the free end of the cantilever.

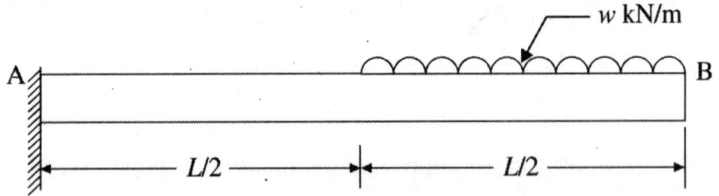

Fig. 5.28: Cantilever supporting partial load (UDL)

12. A propped cantilever of length L supports a concentrated load of w kN at the centre of span as shown in Fig. 5.29. Calculate the maximum deflection in the propped cantilever using numerical integration.

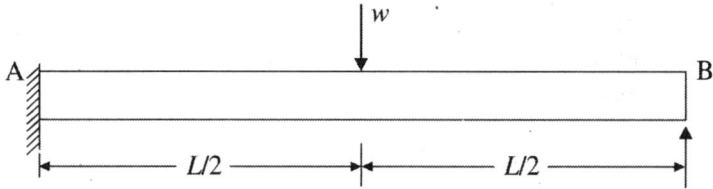

Fig. 5.29: Propped cantilever supporting central point load

13. A simply supported beam of span L carries a concentrated load W kN at the centre of span. The beam has a variable moment of inertia as shown in Fig. 5.30. Calculate the central deflection, dividing the beam into six equal panels and using Newmark's method.

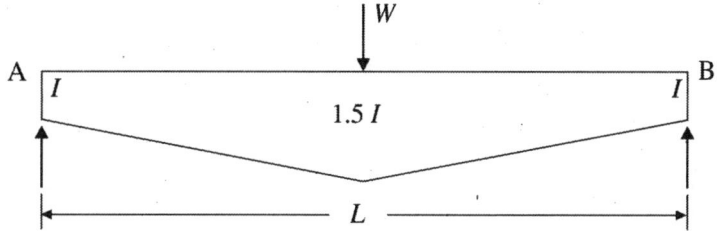

Fig. 5.30: Simply supported beam of variable moment of inertia (point load)

14. Find the maximum deflection of a tapered cantilever beam of rectangular cross section tapering in plan and supporting a concentrated load w as shown in Fig. 5.31 using Newmark's method.

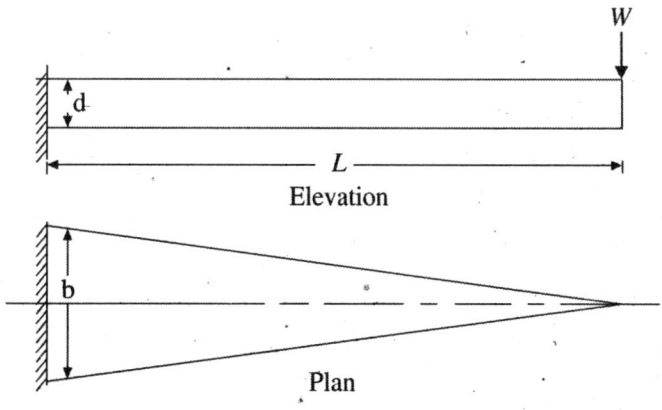

Fig. 5.31: Cantilever of variable cross-section (point load)

15. A simply supported beam of span length L supports a uniformly distributed load as shown in Fig. 5.32. The beam has a variable moment of inertia. Calculate the maximum deflection in the beam by numerical integration method.

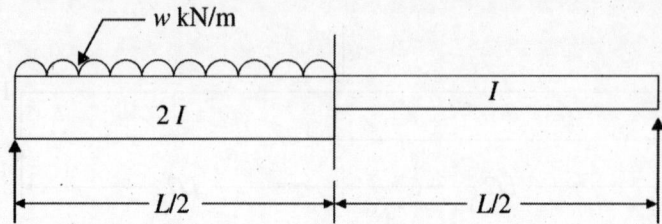

Fig. 5.32: Simply supported beam of variable moment of inertia (partial UDL)

16. A simply supported beam of span length L and having variable moment of inertia supports a concentrated load P at the centre of span as shown in Fig. 5.33. Compute the deflection at the centre of span dividing the beam into eight equal panels.

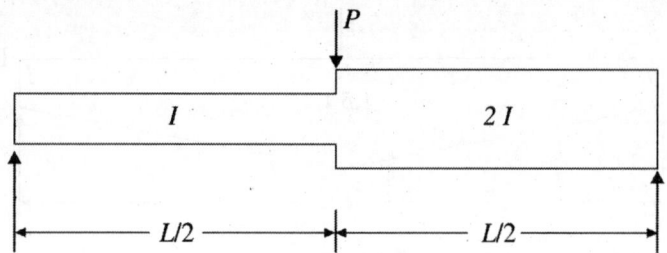

Fig. 5.33: Simply supported beam of variable moment of inertia (point load)

17. Evaluate the maximum slope and deflection of the beam shown in Fig. 5.34 by numerical integration taking 10 subintervals. Assume $I = 10^{10}$ mm^4 and $E = (2 \times 10^5)$ N/mm^2

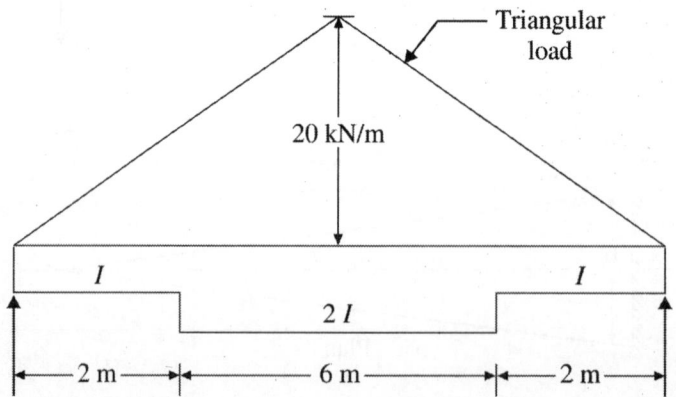

Fig. 5.34: Simply supported beam of variable moment of inertia (triangular load)

18. A cantilever is loaded as shown in Fig. 5.35. Evaluate the deflection and slope using numerical integration procedure. Assume $I = 10^{12}$ mm^4 and $E = (2 \times 10^5)$ N/mm^2. Adopt four subintervals.

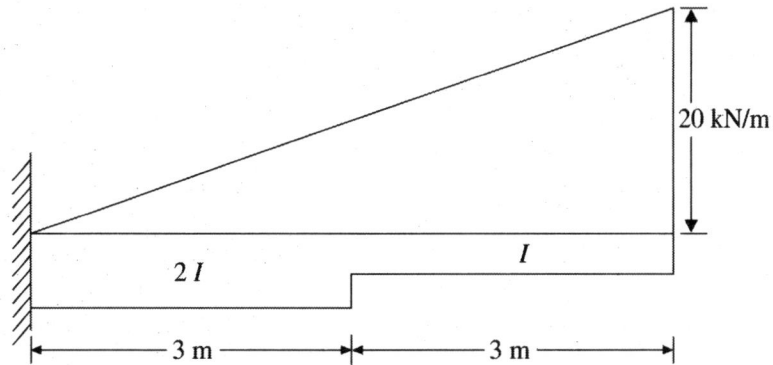

Fig. 5.35: Cantilever of variable moment of inertia (triangular load)

19. A pin ended column of length L has a variable moment of inertia, I, $2I$ and $3I$ for the successive one-third span intervals. Using the numerical integration procedure, estimate the buckling load of the column.

20. A column of length 4 m is of uniform flexural rigidity. The column is fixed at one end and pinned at the other end. Estimate the buckling load of the column using the numerical integration procedure. Assume $EI = 320$ kN·m^2.

REFERENCES

1. Davis, PJ and P Rabinowitz, *Methods of Numerical Integration*, 2nd Edn, Academic Press, New York, 1984.

2. Ferziger JH, *Numerical Methods for Engineering Applications*, John Wiley & Sons, New York, 1981.

3. Gooden WG, *Numerical Analysis of Beam and Column Structures*, Prentice Hall, New Jersey, 1965.

4. Jain MK, Iyengar SRK and Jain RK, *Numerical Methods for Scientific and Engineering Computation*, 6th Edn, New Age International Publishers, New Delhi, 2012.

5. Bakhvalov NS, *Numerical Methods*, Mir Publishers, Moscow, 1975.

6. Rajasekharan S, *Numerical Methods in Science and Engineering-A Practical Approach*, A.H. Wheeler & Co. New Delhi, 1986.

7. Stroud AH and Secrist D, *Gaussian Quadrature Formulas*, Prentice-Hall, Englewood Cliffs, New Jersey, 1966.

8. Newmark NM, *Numerical Procedure for Computing, Deflections, Moments and Buckling Loads*, Transactions of the American Society of Civil Engineers, 108, 1943.

9. Grinter LE, *Numerical Methods of Analysis in Engineering*, McMillan Co, New York, 1949.

10. Dahlquist G and Bjorck A, *Numerical Methods*, Prentice-Hall, Englewood Cliffs, New Jersey, 1974.

REVIEW QUESTIONS

1. List the various engineering problems in which numerical integration techniques can be advantageously used for solving them.

2. What is trapezoidal rule? In what way this method is useful to solve engineering problems?

3. Discuss briefly the final equations used in the trapezoidal rule for computing the areas and volumes in engineering problems.

4. Explain the method of Simpson's rule in solving integration problems of various functions. Specify the equations used for computing the areas and volumes using this method.

5. Between the trapezoidal rule and Simpson's method, which of these yield results nearer to the exact value?

6. Discuss briefly the basis of Gaussian quadrature formula. What are the factors influencing the accuracy of this method?

7. Explain briefly Newmark's numerical integration method of determining the slopes and deflections in loaded beams.

8. Explain the terms a) Equivalent loads b) (M/EI) diagram with reference to Newmark's method.

9. Briefly discuss the application of Newmark's method for solving the buckling load of straight columns with hinged ends.

10. Explain the numerical integration method of determining the buckling load of a column pinned at one end and fixed at the other end with variable moment of inertia.

OBJECTIVE TYPE QUESTIONS

1. In the solution of structural problems, numerical methods can be conveniently used to get
   a) exact solutions
   b) approximate solutions
   c) variable solutions

2. Trapezoidal rule can be used to compute the
   a) deflections of loaded beams
   b) slopes of loaded beams
   c) areas of the bending moment diagrams

3. In computing the elemental areas using Simpson's rule, the number of successive ordinates to be considered are
   a) two
   b) three
   c) four

4. The accuracy of Trapezoidal and Simpson's rules in determining the areas and volumes of figures increases with
   a) longer interval length
   b) shorter interval length
   c) variable interval length

5. The derivation of Gaussian quadrature formula used in the integration of functions involves
   a) four unknowns
   b) five unknowns
   c) six unknowns

6. The accuracy of the Gaussian quadrature formula depends upon
   a) type of integral function
   b) degree of polynomial used
   c) type of structural problem

7. Newmark's method of numerical integration can be used only in cases where the bending moment diagram of the loaded beam is
   a) unknown
   b) known
   c) not required

8. Newmark's method involves the computation of equivalent loads at the nodal points by Considering
   a) two successive ordinates of the (M/EI) diagram
   b) four successive ordinates of the (M/EI) diagram
   c) three successive ordinates of the (M/EI) diagram

9. Newmark's numerical integration method can be used only in beams having
   a) variable flexural rigidity
   b) uniform flexural rigidity
   c) uniform section

10. Newmark's method can be used for the determination of buckling loads of columns with
    a) both ends fixed
    b) one end fixed and the other end hinged
    c) both ends hinged

6

Finite Difference Methods

6.1 GENERAL FEATURES

Most of the problems in the domain of structural engineering involve ordinary differential equations[1] to determine moments, shear forces and deflections in beams and buckling in columns with different end conditions. Partial differential equations[2] are invariably required in solving problems of two dimensional structural elements like bending of plates and the solution of vibration problems in beams. Direct solutions are possible in cases where the load distribution, sectional properties and boundary configurations are easily represented by mathematical expressions. For complex loading and boundary conditions and variable section properties, exact solutions are not available and numerical techniques such as finite difference methods[3,4] can be advantageously employed for the solution of such problems.

In the finite difference method, at each of the pivotal point of the intervals, an equation expressing the differential equation by the finite differences can be established. A set of simultaneous equations[5] are developed and they are solved using the boundary conditions at the pivotal points. The computation can be easily handled mechanically on calculators or digital computers[6].

6.2 EXPRESSION OF DERIVATIVES BY FINITE DIFFERENCES

The derivatives of a function expressed as

$$y = f(x) \text{ are } \left(\frac{dy}{dx}\right), \left(\frac{d^2y}{dx^2}\right), \dots$$

Referring to Fig. 6.1, the rate of change of y with respect to x at any point is written as below.

$$\left(\frac{\Delta y}{\Delta x}\right)_n = \left[\frac{y_{n+1} - y_n}{h}\right] \text{ or } \left[\frac{y_n - y_{n-1}}{h}\right]$$

$$\left(\frac{\Delta^2 y}{\Delta x^2}\right)_n = \left[\frac{y_{n+1} - y_n}{h^2} - \frac{y_n - y_{n-1}}{h^2}\right] = \left[\frac{y_{n+1} - 2y_n + y_{n-1}}{h^2}\right]$$

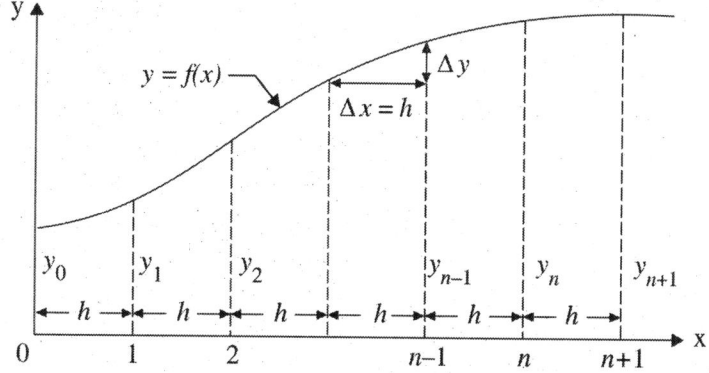

Fig. 6.1: Derivatives of a function

By using different sets of points, the finite differences[7,8] at a point can be expressed in three different ways such as,

1. Backward differences
2. Forward differences
3. Central differences

1. Backward Differences

The points used are all in the descending order with respect to the point under consideration.

For example:

$$\Delta y_n = (y_n - y_{n-1})$$

$$\Delta y_{n-1} = (y_{n-1} - y_{n-2})$$

$$\Delta^2 y_n = [\Delta y_n - \Delta y_{n-1}] = [(y_n - y_{n-1}) - (y_{n-1} - y_{n-2})]$$

$$= [y_n - 2y_{n-1} + y_{n-2}]$$

$$\Delta^3 y_n = [\Delta^2 y_n - \Delta^2 y_{n-1}] = [(y_n - 2y_{n-1} + y_{n-2}) - (y_{n-1} - 2y_{n-2} + y_{n-3})]$$

$$= [y_n - 3y_{n-1} + 3y_{n-2} - y_{n-3}]$$

$$\Delta^4 y_n = [\Delta^3 y_n - \Delta^3 y_{n-1}]$$

$$= [(y_n - 3y_{n-1} + 3y_{n-2} - y_{n-3}) - (y_{n-1} - 3y_{n-2} + 3y_{n-3} - y_{n-4})]$$

$$= [y_n - 4y_{n-1} + 6y_{n-2} - 4y_{n-3} + y_{n-4}]$$

The backward differences can be shown on a schematic diagram with the coefficients of different operators as shown in Fig. 6.2.

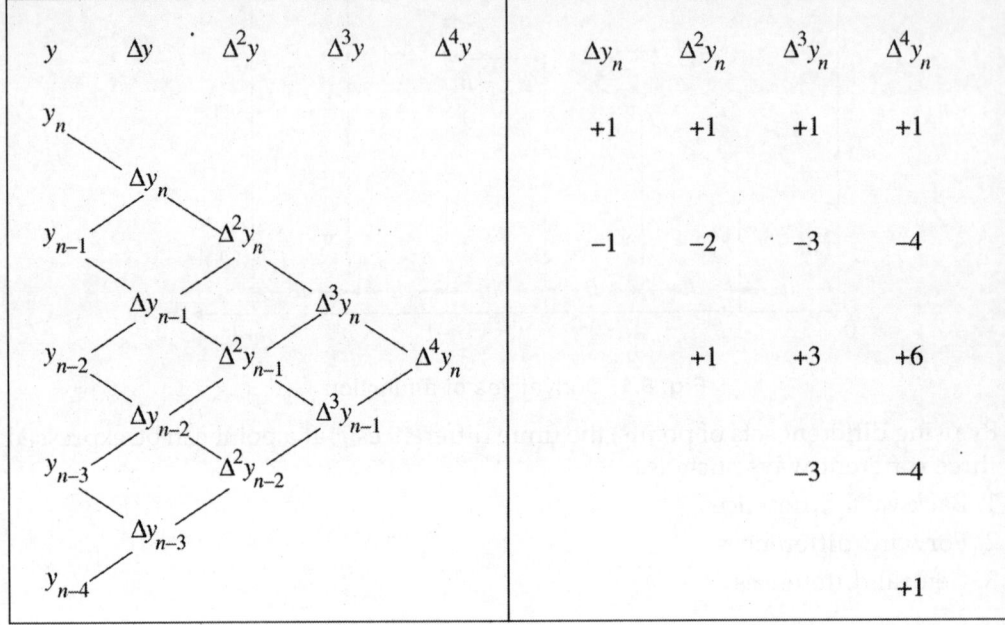

y	Δy	$\Delta^2 y$	$\Delta^3 y$	$\Delta^4 y$	Δy_n	$\Delta^2 y_n$	$\Delta^3 y_n$	$\Delta^4 y_n$
y_n					+1	+1	+1	+1
y_{n-1}					−1	−2	−3	−4
y_{n-2}					+1	+3	+6	
y_{n-3}							−3	−4
y_{n-4}								+1

Fig. 6.2: Backward differences

2. Forward Differences

The points used are in the ascending order with respect to the point under consideration.

$$\Delta y_n = (y_{n+1} - y_n)$$

$$\Delta^2 y_n = [\Delta y_{n+1} - \Delta y_n] = [(y_{n+2} - y_{n+1}) - (y_{n+1} - y_n)]$$

$$= [y_n - 2y_{n+1} + y_{n+2}]$$

Similarly

$$\Delta^3 y_n = [\Delta^2 y_{n+1} - \Delta^2 y_n] = [(y_{n+1} - 2y_{n+2} + y_{n+3}) - (y_n - 2y_{n+1} + y_{n+2})]$$

$$= [-y_n + 3y_{n+1} - 3y_{n+2} + y_{n+3}]$$

$$\Delta y_n = [\Delta^3 y_{n+1} - \Delta^3 y_n]$$

$$= [(-y_{n+1} + 3y_{n+2} - 3y_{n+3} + y_{n+4}) - (-y_n + 3y_{n+1} - 3y_{n+2} + y_{n+3})]$$

$$= [y_n - 4y_{n+1} + 6y_{n+2} - 4y_{n+3} + y_{n+4}]$$

The forward differences can be represented in a schematic diagram as shown in Fig. 6.3.

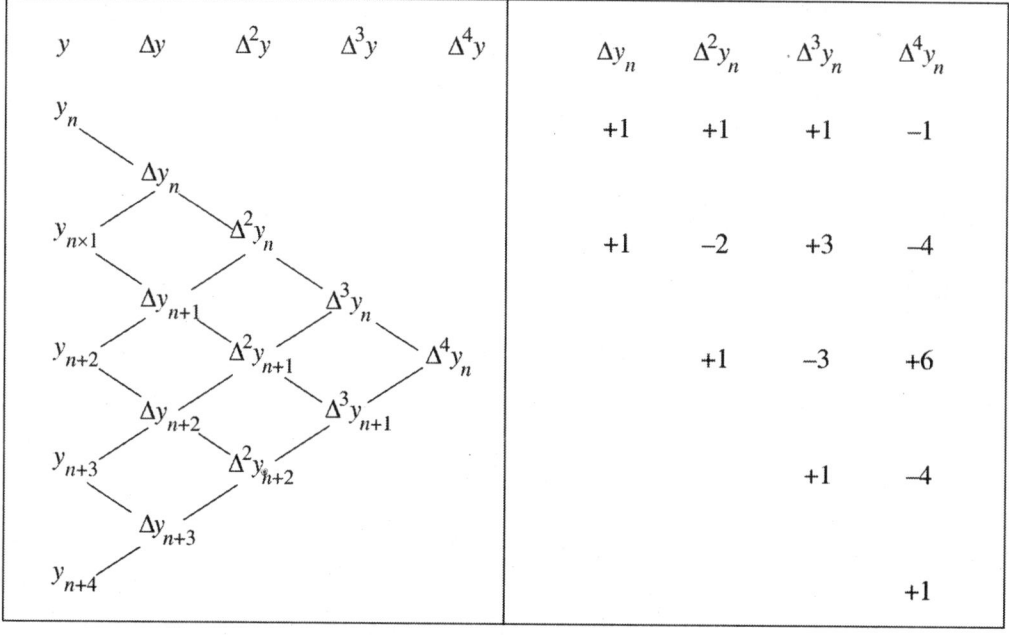

y	Δy	$\Delta^2 y$	$\Delta^3 y$	$\Delta^4 y$		Δy_n	$\Delta^2 y_n$	$\Delta^3 y_n$	$\Delta^4 y_n$
						+1	+1	+1	−1
						+1	−2	+3	−4
						+1	−3	+6	
							+1	−4	
								+1	

Fig. 6.3: Forward differences

3. Central Differences

In this case, the points are located symmetrically with respect to the point under consideration. The expression $\Delta y_{n+\frac{3}{2}}$ denotes the finite difference taken at the point mid way between $x = x_{n+1}$ and $x = x_{n+2}$. The even order differences are taken over the interval h. The odd order differences are derived from the difference with interval equal to $2h$.

Referring to Fig. 6.4, we have

$$\Delta y_n = \left[\frac{y_{n+1} - y_{n-1}}{2}\right]$$

Therefore, $2\Delta y_n = (y_{n+1} - y_{n-1})$

$$\Delta y_n = \left[y_{n+\left(\frac{1}{2}\right)} - y_{n-\left(\frac{1}{2}\right)}\right]$$

$$\Delta^2 y_n = \left[\Delta y_{n+\left(\frac{1}{2}\right)} - \Delta y_{n-\left(\frac{1}{2}\right)}\right] = \left[(y_{n+1} - y_n) - (y_n - y_{n-1})\right]$$

$$= \left[-2y_n + y_{n+1} + y_{n-1}\right]$$

$$\Delta^3 y_n = \left[\frac{\Delta^2 y_{n+1} - \Delta^2 y_{n-1}}{2}\right]$$

$$2\Delta^3 y_n = \left(-2y_{n+1} + y_{n+2} + y_n\right) - \left(-2y_{n-1} + y_n + y_{n-2}\right)$$
$$= \left[0.y_n - 2y_{n+1} + 2y_{n-1} + y_{n+2} - y_{n-2}\right]$$

In a similar manner, we can obtain the value of

$$\Delta^4 y_n = \left[\Delta^3 y_{n+1} - \Delta^3 y_n\right]$$
$$= \left[y_n - 4y_{n+1} + 6y_{n+2} - 4y_{n+3} + y_{n+4}\right]$$

The schematic diagram for the fourth order differences is shown in Fig. 6.5.

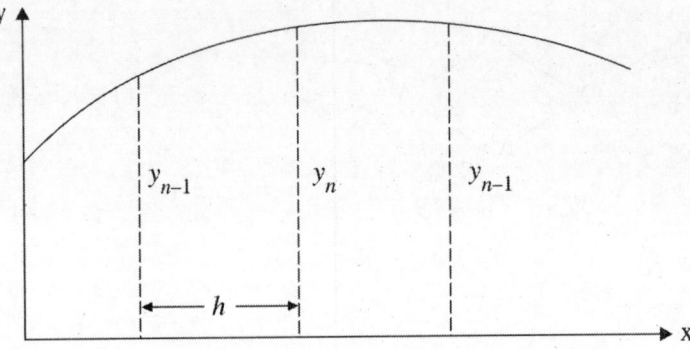

Fig. 6.4: Central differences

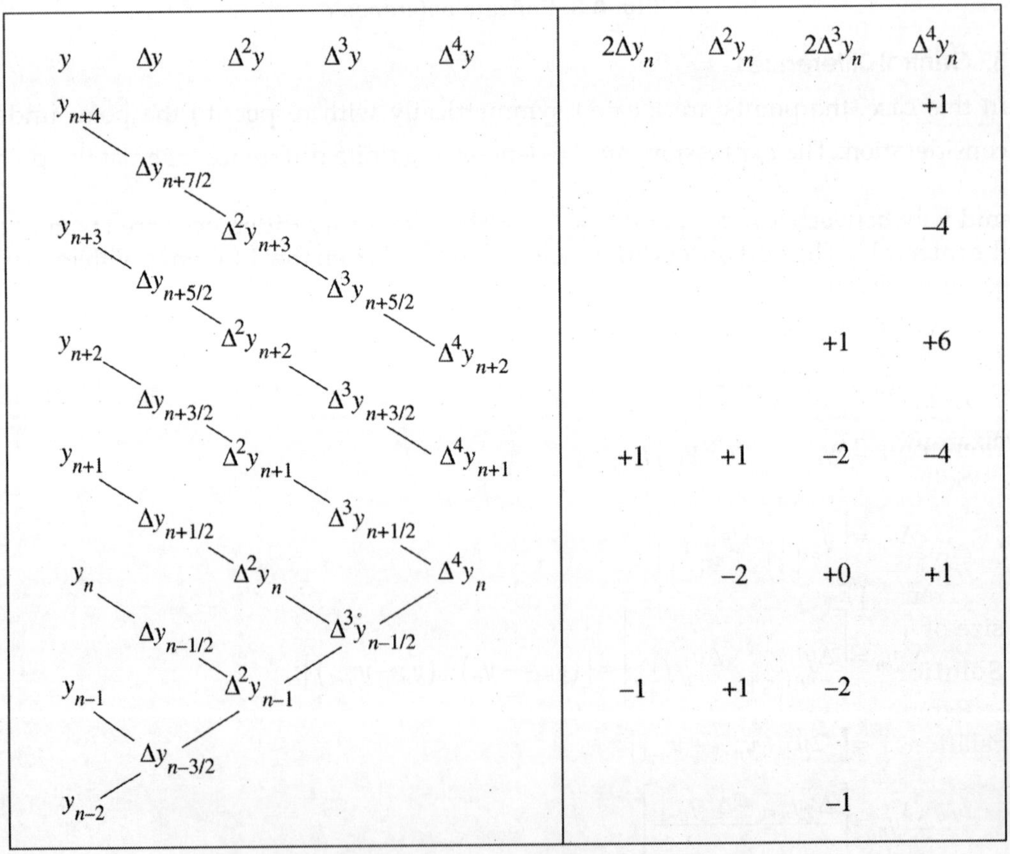

y	Δy	$\Delta^2 y$	$\Delta^3 y$	$\Delta^4 y$	$2\Delta y_n$	$\Delta^2 y_n$	$2\Delta^3 y_n$	$\Delta^4 y_n$
y_{n+4}								+1
	$\Delta y_{n+7/2}$							
y_{n+3}		$\Delta^2 y_{n+3}$						−4
	$\Delta y_{n+5/2}$		$\Delta^3 y_{n+5/2}$					
y_{n+2}		$\Delta^2 y_{n+2}$		$\Delta^4 y_{n+2}$			+1	+6
	$\Delta y_{n+3/2}$		$\Delta^3 y_{n+3/2}$					
y_{n+1}		$\Delta^2 y_{n+1}$		$\Delta^4 y_{n+1}$	+1	+1	−2	−4
	$\Delta y_{n+1/2}$		$\Delta^3 y_{n+1/2}$					
y_n		$\Delta^2 y_n$		$\Delta^4 y_n$	−2	+0	+1
	$\Delta y_{n-1/2}$		$\Delta^3 y_{n-1/2}$					
y_{n-1}		$\Delta^2 y_{n-1}$			−1	+1	−2
	$\Delta y_{n-3/2}$							
y_{n-2}								−1

Fig. 6.5: Schematic shown the 4th order differences

Example 6.1

Solve the following initial value problem

$$y'' - y' - 2y = 3e^{2x}$$

Solution

Given $y(0) = 0$ and $y'(0) = -2$

Transform the given equation into finite difference form and solve it by taking step size of

$$y'(0) = -2$$

Solution

$$\left[\frac{y_{n+1} - y_{n-1}}{2}\right] = -2$$

Hence $(y_{n+1} - y_{n-1}) = -4h = (-4 \times 0.25) = -1$

If $n = 0$, we have $(y_1 - y_{-1}) = -1$

Therefore $y_{-1} = (y_1 + 1)$

The corresponding finite difference equation is

$$\left[\frac{y_{n+1} - 2y_n + y_{n-1}}{h^2}\right] - \left[\frac{y_{n+1} - y_{n-1}}{2h}\right] - 2y_n = 3e^{2x_n}$$

If $n = 0$, $y_0 = 0$

$$\left[\frac{y_1 - 0 + y_{-1}}{h^2}\right] - \left[\frac{y_1 - y_{-1}}{2h}\right] - 2(0) = 3e^0 = 3$$

$$\left[\frac{y_1 + 1 + y_1}{h^2}\right] - \left[\frac{y_1 - (y_1 + 1)}{2h}\right] = 3$$

$$\left[\frac{2y_1 + 1}{(0.25)^2}\right] - \left[\frac{1}{2(0.25)}\right] = 3$$

or $y_1 = -0.34375$

Example 6.2

Solve the following boundary value problem

$$y'' - 3y' - 10y = 10x$$

Given $y(0) = 0$ and $y(1) = 100$

Transform the given problem into a finite difference equation by taking a step size of $h = 0.25$.

Solution

Expressing the given equation in the finite difference form, we have the following relations.

$$\left[\frac{y_{n+1} - 2y_n + y_{n-1}}{h^2}\right] - \left[\frac{3(y_{n+1} - y_{n-1})}{2h}\right] - 10y_n = 10x_n$$

For $n = 1$, we have

$$\left[\frac{y_2 - 2y_1 + 0}{h^2}\right] - \left[\frac{3(y_2 - 0)}{2h}\right] - 10y_1 = 10(0.25) = 2.5$$

$$\left[\frac{y_2 - 2y_1}{(0.25)^2}\right] - \left[\frac{3(y_2 - 0)}{2(0.25)}\right] - 10y_1 = 2.5$$

$$16y_2 - 32y_1 - 6y_2 - 10y_1 = 2.5$$

$$-42y_1 + 10y_2 = 2.5 \tag{1}$$

For $n = 2$, we have

$$\left[\frac{y_3 - 2y_2 + y_1}{(0.25)^2}\right] - \left[\frac{3(y_3 - y_1)}{2(0.25)}\right] - 10y_2 = 10(0.5) = 5$$

Simplifying,
$$10y_1 - 42y_2 + 10y_3 = 5 \tag{2}$$

For $n = 3$, we have

$$\left[\frac{y_4 - 2y_3 + y_2}{(0.25)^2}\right] - \left[\frac{3(y_4 - y_2)}{2(0.25)}\right] - 10y_3 = 10(0.75) = 7.5$$

$$\left[\frac{100 - 2y_3 + y_2}{(0.25)^2}\right] - \left[\frac{3(100 - y_2)}{2(0.25)}\right] - 10y_3 = 7.5$$

Simplifying, $y_3 = 0.5238y_2 + 23.63 \tag{3}$

Substituting the value of y_3 from Eq. (3) in Eq. (2)

$$10y_1 - 42y_2 + 10(0.5238y_2 + 23.63) = 5$$

$$10y_1 - 36.762y_2 = -231.3$$

$$y_1 = -23.13 + 3.6762y_2 \tag{4}$$

Substituting Eq. (4) in Eq. (1), we have

$$-42(-23.13 + 3.6762y_2) + 10y_2 = 2.5$$

Simplifying, $y_2 = 6.710$
Substituting the value of y_2 in Eq. (4)

$y_1 = -23.13 + 3.6762(6.71)$

$y_1 = 1.536$
From Eq. (3), we have
$y_3 = 0.5238(6.71) + 23.63$
$y_3 = 27.145$
Hence the final values are
$y_1 = 1.536$
$y_2 = 6.710$
$y_3 = 27.145$

6.3 STATICALLY DETERMINATE BEAM PROBLEMS

6.3.1 General Procedure

Consider a simply supported beam of span length L, supporting a uniformly distributed load of intensity w kN/m as shown in Fig. 6.6. The differential equation relating the load w and the moment at a distance x from the support is expressed as,

$$\left(\frac{d^2M}{dx^2}\right) = w$$

Also $\left(\frac{d^2y}{dx^2}\right) = \left(\frac{M}{EI}\right)$

and $\left(\frac{d^4y}{dx^4}\right) = \left(\frac{w}{EI}\right)$

where

w = Intensity of load (+ve upward)

M = Bending moment at any section

h = Distance interval between the points

y = Deflection (+ve upward)

L = Span of the beam

E = Modulus of elasticity

I = Second moment of area of the section

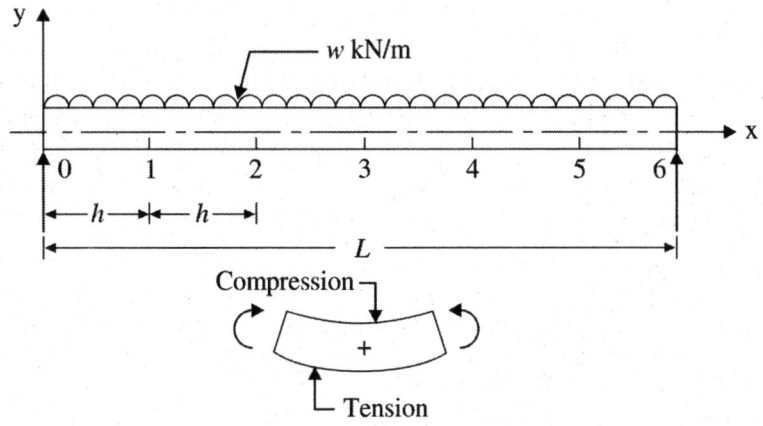

Fig. 6.6: Flexure of beams

The equations for M and y are second order differential equations[9]. Using central differences, the moments and deflections at a typical pivotal point n can be expressed as,

$$M_{n-1} = (2M_n + M_{n+1}) = -h^2 w_n \qquad (1)$$

$$y_{n-1} - 2y_n + y_{n+1} = \left(\frac{h^2 M_n}{EI_n} \right) \tag{2}$$

Using the fourth order central differences, we can write the relation between the deflection at any point and the load as,

$$[y_{n+2} - 4y_{n+1} + 6y_n - 4y_{n-1} + y_{n-2}] = \left(\frac{w_n h^4}{EI_n} \right) \tag{3}$$

Using the boundary conditions, a set of linear simultaneous equations, equal to the number of unknown variables are established and they are solved to get themoments and deflections. The application of the finite difference technique to beam problems is illustrated by the following examples.

Example 6.3

A beam of length L supports a uniformly distributed load of intensity w kN/m. Calculate the maximum moment and deflections in the beam. Assume as constant.

Referring to Fig. 6.7, divide the beam into 4 equal parts with nodal points 0, 1, 2, 3 and 4.

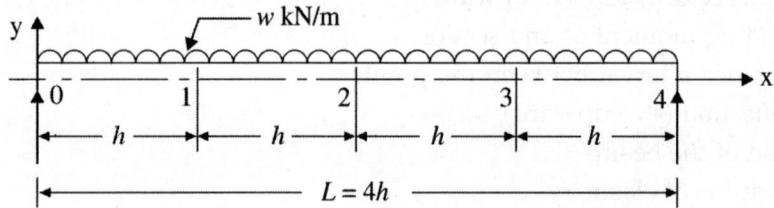

Fig. 6.7: Simply supported beam with UDL

Solution

Applying the central differences to moments at various nodal points, we have the relation,

$$M_{n-1} - 2M_n + M_{n+1} = -h^2 w_n$$

Applying this equation to points 1, 2 and 3, we get

$$M_0 - 2M_1 + M_2 = -h^2 w \tag{1}$$

$$M_1 - 2M_2 + M_3 = -h^2 w \tag{2}$$

$$M_2 - 2M_3 + M_4 = -h^2 w \tag{3}$$

Since $M_0 = M_4 = 0$ and $M_1 = M_3$ by symmetry from Eqs (1) and (2), we have

$$-2M_1 + M_2 = -wh^2$$

$$\underline{M_1 - 2M_2 = -wh^2}$$

Adding $\qquad -M_2 = -2wh^2$

or $\qquad M_2 = 2wh^2 = 2w(L/4)^2 = \left(\dfrac{wL^2}{8}\right)$

Also $\quad -2M_1 = \left(-wh^2 - M_2\right) = \left(-wh^2 - 2wh^2\right) = -3wh^2$

Hence $\quad M_1 = M_3 = \left(\dfrac{3}{2}\right)(wh^2) = \left(\dfrac{3}{2}\right)\left[w\left(\dfrac{L}{4}\right)^2\right] = \left(\dfrac{3}{32}\right)wL^2$

Applying the equation for deflections,

$$y_{n-1} - 2y_n + y_{n+1} = \left(\dfrac{h^2 M_n}{EI_n}\right)$$

$$y_0 - 2y_1 + y_2 = \left(\dfrac{h^2}{EI}\right)\left(\dfrac{3}{32}\right)wL^2 \qquad (1)$$

$$y_1 - 2y_2 + y_3 = \left(\dfrac{h^2}{EI}\right)\left(\dfrac{wL^2}{8}\right) \qquad (2)$$

$$y_2 - 2y_3 + y_4 = \left(\dfrac{h^2}{EI}\right)\left(\dfrac{3}{32}\right)wL^2 \qquad (3)$$

Boundary conditions are

$$y_0 = y_4 = 0$$

$$y_1 = y_3$$

From Eqs (1) and (2)

$$-2y_1 + y_2 = \left(\dfrac{h^2}{EI}\right)\left(\dfrac{3}{32}\right)wL^2$$

$$2y_1 - 2y_2 = \left(\dfrac{h^2}{EI}\right)\left(\dfrac{wL^2}{8}\right)$$

Adding the two equations, we have

$$-y_2 = \left(\dfrac{h^2}{EI}\right)\left[\left(\dfrac{3}{32}\right) + \left(\dfrac{1}{8}\right)\right]$$

Hence $y_2 = -\left(\dfrac{7}{32}\right)\left(\dfrac{h^2 wL^2}{EI}\right) = -\left(\dfrac{7}{32}\right)\left(\dfrac{L^2 wL^2}{16EI}\right) = -\left(\dfrac{7}{512}\right)\left(\dfrac{wL^4}{EI}\right)$

$$2y_3 - 2y_2 = \left(\dfrac{h^2}{EI}\right)\left(\dfrac{wL^2}{8}\right)$$

$$2y_3 = \left(\frac{h^2}{EI}\right)\left(\frac{wL^2}{8}\right) - 2\left(\frac{7}{512}\right)\left(\frac{wL^4}{EI}\right)$$

Hence $y_3 = -\left(\frac{5}{512}\right)\left(\frac{wL^4}{EI}\right)$

The accuracy of the results will improve if the nodal points are increased.

Example 6.4

A simply supported beam of span L and constant flexural rigidity EI supports a concentrated load P at the centre of span. Estimate the maximum deflection in the beam.

Referring to Fig. 6.8 and applying the finite difference equation to points 1, 2 and 3 respectively, we have the following equations:

$$y_{n-1} - 2y_n + y_{n+1} = \left(\frac{h^2 M_n}{EI_n}\right)$$

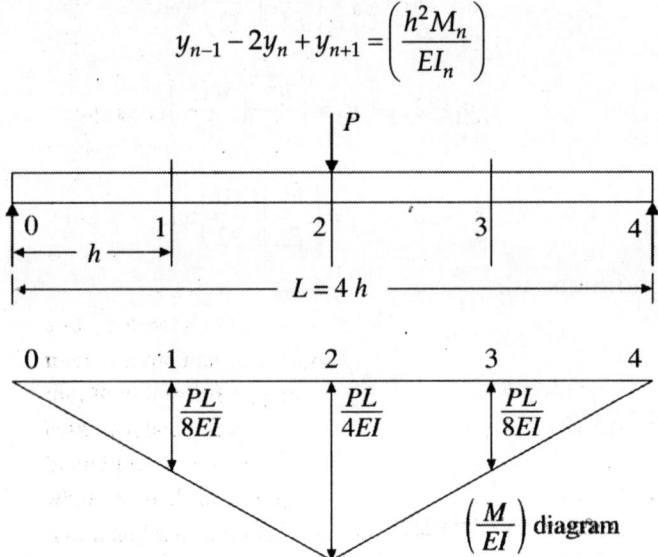

Fig. 6.8: Beam with concentrated load

Solution

Considering the nodal points 1, 2 and 3

$$y_0 - 2y_1 + y_2 = \left(\frac{PL}{8EI}\right)(L/4)^2 \tag{1}$$

$$y_1 - 2y_2 + y_3 = \left(\frac{PL}{4EI}\right)(L/4)^2 \tag{2}$$

$$y_2 - 2y_3 + y_4 = \left(\frac{PL}{8EI}\right)(L/4)^2 \tag{3}$$

Boundary conditions are:

$$y_0 = y_4 = 0$$
$$y_1 = y_3$$

From Eqs (1) and (2)

$$-2y_1 + y_2 = \left(\frac{PL}{8EI}\right)(L/4)^2$$

$$2y_1 - 2y_2 = \left(\frac{PL}{4EI}\right)(L/4)^2$$

Adding the two equations, we have

$$-y_2 = \left(\frac{L}{4}\right)^2\left[\frac{1}{8} + \frac{1}{4}\right]\left(\frac{PL}{EI}\right) = \frac{3PL^3}{128EI}$$

Hence
$$y_2 = -\frac{PL^3}{42.66EI}$$

From Eq. (2), we have

$$2y_1 - 2y_2 = \frac{PL^3}{64EI}$$

or
$$2y_1 = \frac{PL^3}{64EI} + 2\left(-\frac{3PL^3}{128EI}\right)$$

Hence $y_1 = y_3 = -\dfrac{PL^3}{32EI}$

The accuracy of the results will improve if the nodal points are increased.

Example 6.5

A simply supported beam of span L supports a triangular load of intensity w kN/m at the centre of the span and zero at supports as shown in Fig. 6.9. Estimate the moments and the maximum deflection at the centre of span.

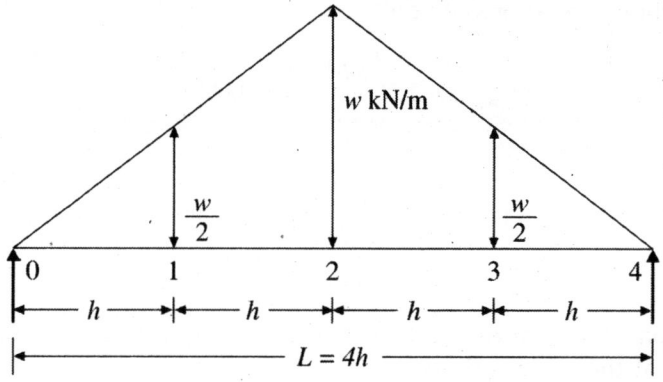

Fig. 6.9: Beam with triangular load

Solution

Applying the finite difference equation to points 1, 2 and 3 respectively, we have the following equations:

$$M_0 - 2M_1 + M_2 = -\left(\frac{wh^2}{2}\right) \tag{1}$$

$$M_1 - 2M_2 + M_3 = -wh^2 \tag{2}$$

$$M_2 - 2M_3 + M_4 = -\left(\frac{wh^2}{2}\right) \tag{3}$$

The boundary conditions are

$$M_0 = M_4 = 0 \text{ and } M_1 = M_3$$

From Eqs (1) and (2)

$$M_2 = 1.5 \, wh^2$$

Also $M_1 = M_3 = wh^2$

Applying the finite difference equation of deflections to points 1, 2 and 3 respectively, we have the following equations:

$$y_0 - 2y_1 + y_2 = \left(\frac{h^2}{EI}\right)(wh)^2 \tag{4}$$

$$y_1 - 2y_2 + y_3 = \left(\frac{h^2}{EI}\right)(1.5wh)^2 \tag{5}$$

$$y_2 - 2y_3 + y_4 = \left(\frac{h^2}{EI}\right)(wh)^2 \tag{6}$$

The boundary conditions are

$$y_0 = y_4 = 0$$

$$y_1 = y_3$$

Solving the above equations we get

$$y_2 = y_{max} = -2.5\left(\frac{wh^4}{EI}\right) = -0.0097\left(\frac{wL^4}{EI}\right)$$

$$y_1 = y_3 = -1.75\left(\frac{wh^4}{EI}\right) = -0.0068\left(\frac{wL^4}{EI}\right)$$

Example 6.6

A beam of span L, supports loads as shown in Fig. 6.10. Estimate the moments and deflections at the nodal points.

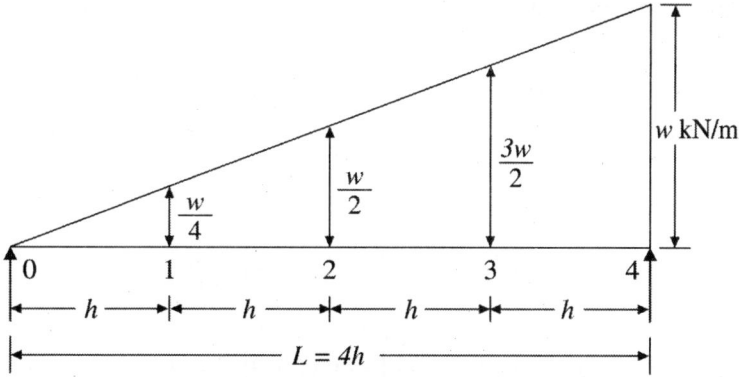

Fig. 6.10: Beam with triangular load

Applying the finite difference equation of moments for points 1, 2 and 3 respectively, we have the following equations.

$$M_0 - 2M_1 + M_2 = -\left(\frac{wh^2}{4}\right)$$ (1)

$$M_1 - 2M_2 + M_3 = -\left(\frac{wh^2}{2}\right)$$ (2)

$$M_2 - 2M_3 + M_4 = -\left(\frac{3wh^2}{4}\right)$$ (3)

The boundary conditions are

$$M_0 = M_4 = 0$$

Solving the equations, we get the moments as,

$$M_1 = 0.625wh^2 = 0.0391wL^2$$

$$M_2 = wh^2 = 0.0625wL^2$$

$$M_3 = 0.875wh^2 = 0.0547wL^2$$

Applying the finite difference equation for deflections at points 1, 2 and 3, we have

$$y_0 - 2y_1 + y_2 = \left(\frac{h^2}{EI}\right)\left(0.0625wh^2\right)$$

$$y_1 - 2y_2 + y_3 = \left(\frac{h^2}{EI}\right)\left(wh^2\right)$$

$$y_2 - 2y_3 + y_4 = \left(\frac{h^2}{EI}\right)\left(0.875wh^2\right)$$

The boundary conditions are

$$y_0 = y_4 = 0$$

Solving the set of equations, we get

$$y_1 = -1.187 \left(\frac{wh^4}{EI} \right) = -0.00463 \left(\frac{wL^4}{EI} \right)$$

$$y_2 = -1.749 \left(\frac{wh^4}{EI} \right) = -0.00682 \left(\frac{wL^4}{EI} \right)$$

$$y_3 = -1.311 \left(\frac{wh^4}{EI} \right) = -0.00513 \left(\frac{wL^4}{EI} \right)$$

Example 6.7

A simply supported beam with variable moment of inertia, supports a uniformly distributed load of intensity w kN/m as shown in Fig. 6.11. Estimate the maximum deflection in the beam.

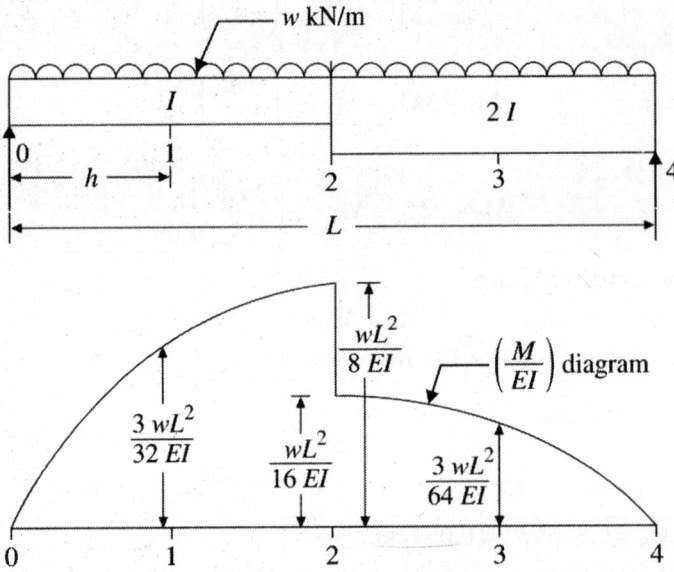

Fig. 6.11: Beam with variable moment of inertia (UDL)

Solution

Referring to Fig. 6.11 and applying the finite difference equation for deflections at points 1, 2 and 3, respectively, we have,

$$y_0 - 2y_1 + y_2 = \frac{3}{32} \left(\frac{wL^2}{EI} \right) \left(\frac{L^2}{16} \right)$$

$$y_1 - 2y_2 + y_3 = \left[\frac{\left(\frac{wL^2}{8EI} \right) + \left(\frac{wL^2}{16EI} \right)}{2} \right] \left(\frac{L^2}{16} \right)$$

$$y_2 - 2y_3 + y_4 = \frac{3}{64}\left(\frac{wL^2}{EI}\right)\left(\frac{L^2}{16}\right)$$

Solving the three equations using the boundary conditions, $y_0 = y_4 = 0$, we get the final deflections as,

$$y_1 = -\left(\frac{wL^4}{124.12EI}\right)$$

$$y_2 = y_{max} = -\left(\frac{wL^4}{97.5EI}\right)$$

$$y_3 = -\left(\frac{wL^4}{151.6EI}\right)$$

Example 6.8

A simply supported beam of length L, supports a uniformly distributed load of intensity w kN/m over the middle half span. Estimate the maximum deflection in the beam.

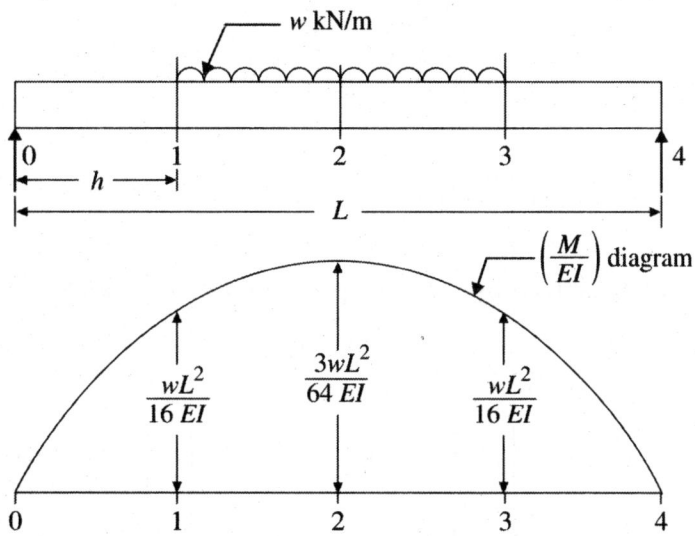

Fig. 6.12: Beam with partial loading (UDL)

Solution

Referring to Fig. 6.12 and applying the finite difference equation for deflections at points 1, 2 and 3, respectively, we have

$$y_0 - 2y_1 + y_2 = \left(\frac{wL^2}{16EI}\right)\left(\frac{L}{4}\right)^2$$

$$y_1 - 2y_2 + y_3 = \left(\frac{3wL^2}{32EI}\right)\left(\frac{L}{4}\right)^2$$

$$y_2 - 2y_3 + y_4 = \left(\frac{wL^2}{16EI}\right)\left(\frac{L}{4}\right)^2$$

The boundary conditions are

$$y_0 = y_4 = 0 \text{ and } y_1 = y_3$$

Solving the equations, the deflections at the nodal points are obtained as,

$$y_1 = y_3 = -\left(\frac{wL^4}{146.28EI}\right)$$

$$y_2 = y_{max} = -\left(\frac{wL^4}{102.4EI}\right)$$

Example 6.9

A simply supported beam supports a symmetrically varying load as shown in Fig. 6.13. Calculate the maximum deflection in the beam.

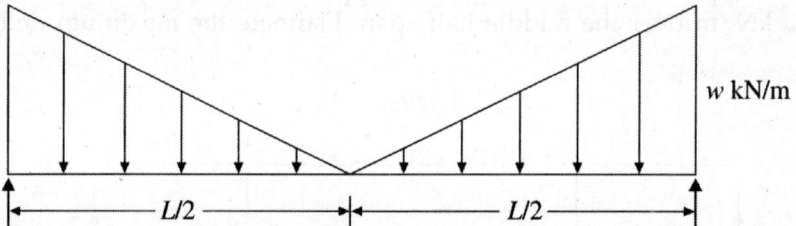

Fig. 6.13: Beam with triangular load

Solution

The problem can be solved by the superposition of two separate loading cases as shown in Fig. 6.14.

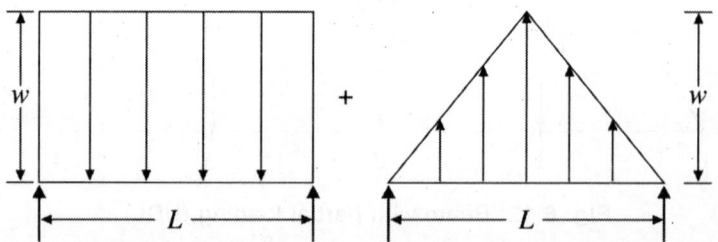

Fig. 6.14: Combination of loads on beam (Fig. 6.13)

The maximum deflection occurs at the centre of the span. The deflection at centre of span due to uniformly distributed load of w acting downwards (Example 3) is superposed with the upward deflection due to triangular load (Example 5). The resulting deflection is computed as

$$y_r = -\left(\frac{5}{512}\right)\left(\frac{wL^4}{EI}\right) + 0.0097\left(\frac{wL^4}{EI}\right)$$

$$y_r = -0.00397 \left(\frac{wL^4}{EI} \right)$$

Example 6.10

A simply supported beam supports a parabolic loading as shown in Fig. 6.15. Estimate the moments and deflections at the nodal points.

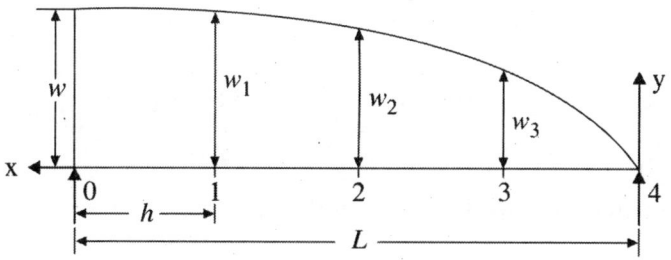

Fig. 6.15: Beam with parabolic loading

Solution

The equation of the parabolic loading is

$$w_x = \left[\frac{w \cdot x(2L - x)}{L^2} \right] = w \left(\frac{x}{L} \right) \left(2 - \frac{x}{L} \right)$$

At $\left(\dfrac{x}{L} \right) = 0.75$, $w_1 = w(0.75)(2 - 0.75) = 0.9375w$

$\left(\dfrac{x}{L} \right) = 0.50$, $w_1 = w(0.50)(2 - 0.50) = 0.75w$

$\left(\dfrac{x}{L} \right) = 0.25$, $w_1 = w(0.25)(2 - 0.25) = 0.4375w$

Applying the finite difference equation of moments for points 1, 2 and 3 respectively, we have the following equations.

$$M_0 - 2M_1 + M_2 = -w_1 h^2 = -0.9375wh^2 \tag{1}$$

$$M_1 - 2M_2 + M_3 = -w_2 h^2 = -0.75wh^2 \tag{2}$$

$$M_2 - 2M_3 + M_4 = -w_3 h^2 = -0.4375wh^2 \tag{3}$$

Boundary conditions are $M_0 = M_4 = 0$
Solving the above equations, we get

$$M_1 = 1.187wh^2 = 0.074wL^2$$

$$M_2 = 1.4368wh^2 = 0.0898wL^2$$

$$M_3 = 0.9375wh^2 = 0.0585wL^2$$

Applying the finite difference equation for deflections at points 1, 2 and 3, respectively, we have

$$y_0 - 2y_1 + y_2 = 0.074wL^2\left(\frac{L^2}{16EI}\right) = 4.625 \times 10^{-3}\left(\frac{wL^4}{EI}\right)$$

$$y_1 - 2y_2 + y_3 = 0.0898wL^2\left(\frac{L^2}{16EI}\right) = 5.612 \times 10^{-3}\left(\frac{wL^4}{EI}\right)$$

$$y_2 - 2y_3 + y_4 = 0.0585wL^2\left(\frac{L^2}{16EI}\right) = 3.656 \times 10^{-3}\left(\frac{wL^4}{EI}\right)$$

Also $y_0 = y_4 = 0$

Solving these equations, we have the deflections as,

$$y_1 = -7.2 \times 10^{-3}\left(\frac{wL^4}{EI}\right)$$

$$y_2 = -9.7 \times 10^{-3}\left(\frac{wL^4}{EI}\right)$$

$$y_3 = -6.7 \times 10^{-3}\left(\frac{wL^4}{EI}\right)$$

Example 6.11

A simply supported beam supports a sinusoidal loading given by the relation $w_x = w\sin\left(\frac{\pi}{2}\right)\left(\frac{x}{L}\right)$. Evaluate the deflections at the nodal points.

Solution

Referring to Fig. 6.16, the intensity of loading at the various nodal points are computed as follows:

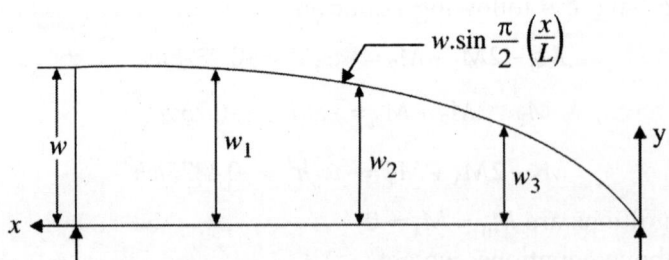

Fig. 6.16: Beam with sinusoidal loading

$$w_1 = w\sin\left(\frac{\pi}{2}\right)\left(\frac{3L}{4L}\right) = 0.924w$$

$$w_2 = w\sin\left(\frac{\pi}{2}\right)\left(\frac{L}{2L}\right) = 0.707w$$

$$w_3 = w \sin\left(\frac{\pi}{2}\right)\left(\frac{L}{4L}\right) = 0.383w$$

Applying the finite difference equation of moments for points 1, 2 and 3 respectively, we have the following equations.

$$M_0 - 2M_1 + M_2 = -w_1 h^2 = -0.924w(L/4)^2$$

$$M_1 - 2M_2 + M_3 = -w_2 h^2 = -0.707w(L/4)^2$$

$$M_2 - 2M_3 + M_4 = -w_3 h^2 = -0.383w(L/4)^2$$

Boundary conditions are $M_0 = M_4 = 0$

Solving the above equations, we get

$$M_1 = 0.0713wL^2$$

$$M_2 = 0.0849wL^2$$

$$M_3 = 0.0544wL^2$$

Applying the finite difference equation for deflections at points 1, 2 and 3, respectively, we have

$$y_0 - 2y_1 + y_2 = 0.0713wL^2\left(\frac{L^2}{16EI}\right)$$

$$y_1 - 2y_2 + y_3 = 0.0849wL^2\left(\frac{L^2}{16EI}\right)$$

$$y_2 - 2y_3 + y_4 = 0.0544\left(\frac{L^2}{16EI}\right).$$

The boundary conditions are

$$y_0 = y_4 = 0$$

Solving the equations, the deflections at the nodal points are obtained as,

$$y_1 = -6.9249 \times 10^{-3}\left(\frac{wL^4}{EI}\right)$$

$$y_2 = -9.2873 \times 10^{-3}\left(\frac{wL^4}{EI}\right)$$

$$y_3 = -6.310 \times 10^{-3}\left(\frac{wL^4}{EI}\right)$$

Example 6.12

A cantilever of length L supports a concentrated load W at the free end as shown in Fig. 6.17. Estimate the deflection at the nodal points at quarter span intervals.

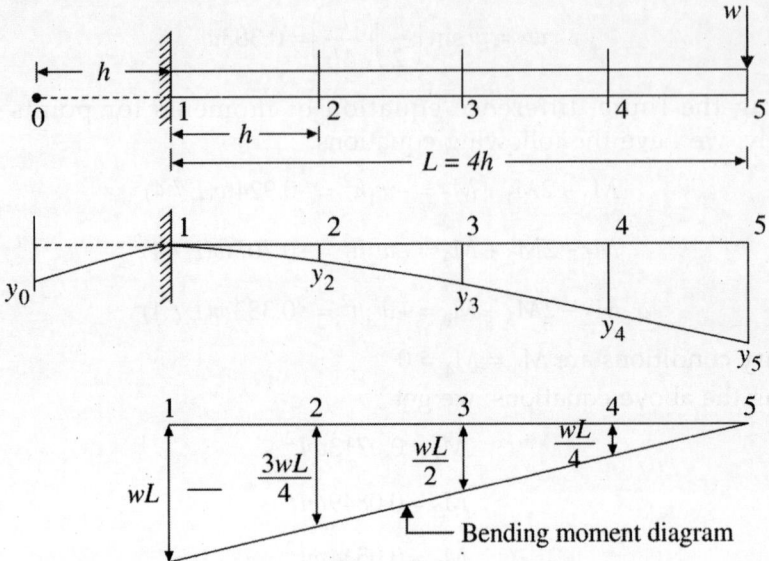

Fig. 6.17: Cantilever with a concentrated load at the free end

Solution

Assuming an imaginary span of length equal to the nodal interval, as shown in Fig. 6.17, we can apply the finite difference equation of deflections as follows:

$$y_0 - 2y_1 + y_2 = -\left(\frac{WL}{EI}\right)(L/4)^2 \tag{1}$$

$$y_1 - 2y_2 + y_3 = -\left(\frac{3L}{4EI}\right)(L/4)^2 \tag{2}$$

$$y_2 - 2y_3 + y_4 = -\left(\frac{WL}{2EI}\right)(L/4)^2 \tag{3}$$

$$y_3 - 2y_4 + y_5 = -\left(\frac{WL}{4EI}\right)(L/4)^2 \tag{4}$$

The boundary conditions are $y_1 = 0$ and $y_0 = y_2$

Solving the above Eqs (1) to (4), the deflections are obtained as:

$$y_2 = -\left(\frac{WL^3}{32EI}\right) = -0.0312\left(\frac{WL^3}{EI}\right)$$

$$y_3 = -\left(\frac{7WL^3}{64EI}\right) = -0.1093\left(\frac{WL^3}{EI}\right)$$

$$y_4 = -\left(\frac{14WL^3}{64EI}\right) = -0.2187\left(\frac{WL^3}{EI}\right)$$

$$y_5 = -\left(\frac{22WL^3}{64EI}\right) = -0.3437\left(\frac{WL^3}{EI}\right)$$

The exact value obtained from double integration or moment area method is

$$y_{max} = y_5 = -\left(\frac{WL^3}{3EI}\right) = -0.333\left(\frac{WL^3}{EI}\right)$$

Example 6.13

A cantilever of length L supports a uniformly distributed load of intensity w kN/m over the complete. Span length as shown in Fig. 6.18. Estimate the deflections at quarter span points.

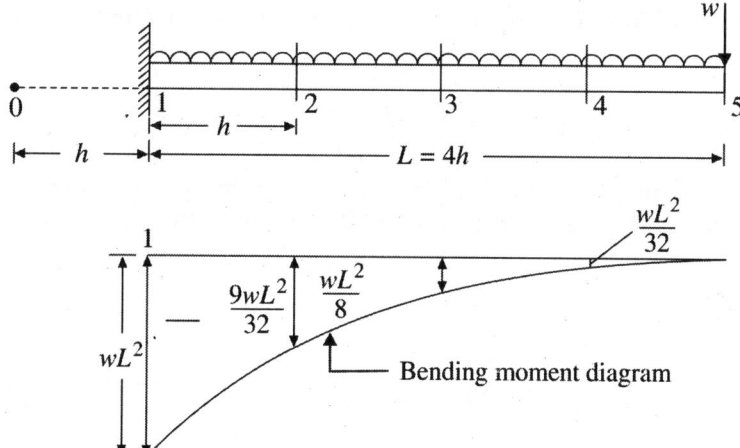

Fig. 6.18: Cantilever with uniformly distributed load

Solution

Applying the finite difference equation for deflections at points 1, 2, 3 and 4 respectively, we have

$$y_0 - 2y_1 + y_2 = -\left(\frac{wL^2}{2EI}\right)(L/4)^2 \tag{1}$$

$$y_1 - 2y_2 + y_3 = -\left(\frac{9wL^2}{32EI}\right)(L/4)^2 \tag{2}$$

$$y_2 - 2y_3 + y_4 = -\left(\frac{wL^2}{8EI}\right)(L/4)^2 \tag{3}$$

$$y_3 - 2y_4 + y_5 = -\left(\frac{wL^2}{32EI}\right)(L/4)^2 \tag{4}$$

The boundary conditions are $y_1 = 0$ and $y_0 = y_2$

Solving Eqs (1) to (4), the deflections are obtained as:

$$y_2 = -\left(\frac{wL^4}{64EI}\right) = -0.00156\left(\frac{wL^4}{EI}\right)$$

$$y_3 = -\left(\frac{25WL^4}{512EI}\right) = -0.0488\left(\frac{wL^4}{EI}\right)$$

$$y_4 = -\left(\frac{46WL^4}{512EI}\right) = -0.0898\left(\frac{wL^4}{EI}\right)$$

$$y_5 = -\left(\frac{68WL^4}{512EI}\right) = -0.13428\left(\frac{wL^4}{EI}\right)$$

The exact solution obtained from double integration or moment area method is

$$y_{max} = y_5 = -\left(\frac{wL^4}{8EI}\right) = -0.125\left(\frac{wL^4}{EI}\right)$$

Example 6.14

A cantilever of length L with varying moment of inertia, supports a concentrated load at the free end As shown in Fig. 6.19. Calculate the deflections at the nodal points.

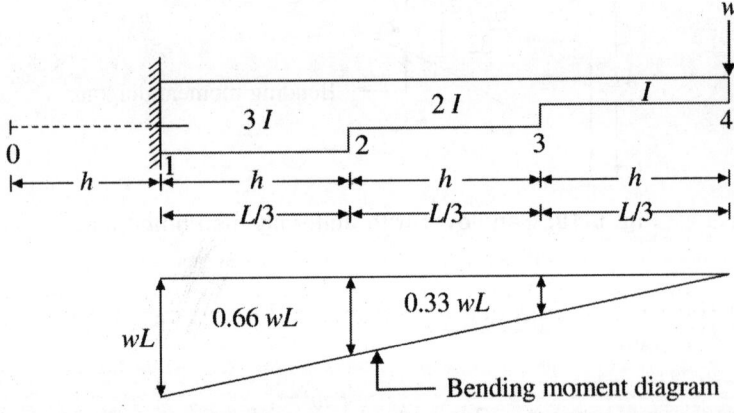

Fig. 6.19: Cantilever of variable moment of inertia supporting concentrated load

Assuming an imaginary span of length equal to nodal interval ($L/3$) and applying the finite difference equation for deflections at points 1, 2 and 3 respectively, we have the following equations.

$$y_0 - 2y_1 + y_2 = -\left(\frac{wL \cdot h^2}{3EI}\right) \tag{1}$$

$$y_1 - 2y_2 + y_3 = -\left(\frac{0.67wL \cdot h^2}{2.5EI}\right) \tag{2}$$

$$y_2 - 2y_3 + y_4 = -\left(\frac{0.33wL \cdot h^2}{1.5EI}\right) \tag{3}$$

The boundary conditions are $y_1 = 0$ and $y_0 = y_2$

Solving the equations, the deflections at the nodal points are obtained as,

$$y_2 = -0.165 \left(\frac{WL \cdot h^2}{EI} \right) = -0.0183 \left(\frac{WL^3}{EI} \right)$$

$$y_3 = -0.598 \left(\frac{WL \cdot h^2}{EI} \right) = -0.066 \left(\frac{WL^3}{EI} \right)$$

$$y_4 = -1.251 \left(\frac{WL \cdot h^2}{EI} \right) = -0.139 \left(\frac{WL^3}{EI} \right)$$

Example 6.15

Evaluate the deflections at the pivotal points of a uniformly loaded, simply supported beam whose moment of inertia varies linearly from I at its left end to $5I$ at its right end, as shown in Fig. 6.20. Use central difference expressions with errors of order and four subintervals.

Solution

Referring to Fig. 6.20 (b) showing the $\left(\dfrac{M}{EI} \right)$ diagram and applying central difference equations for nodal points 1, 2 and 3, we have the following deflection relation equations.

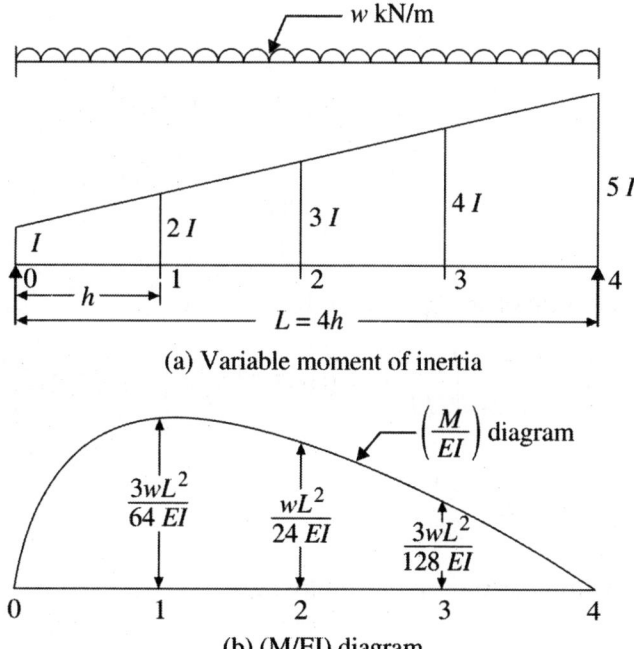

(a) Variable moment of inertia

(b) (M/EI) diagram

Fig. 6.20: Simply supported beam of variable moment of inertia

$$y_0 - 2y_1 + y_2 = \left(\frac{3wL^2}{64EI}\right)(L/4)^2 \tag{1}$$

$$y_1 - 2y_2 + y_3 = \left(\frac{wL^2}{24EI}\right)(L/4)^2 \tag{2}$$

$$y_2 - 2y_3 + y_4 = \left(\frac{3wL^2}{128EI}\right)(L/4)^2 \tag{3}$$

The boundary conditions are $y_0 = y_4 = 0$ and eliminating y_0 from Eqs (1) and (3), we have the relation

$$-2y_1 + 2y_2 = \frac{3}{2048}\left(\frac{wL^4}{EI}\right) \tag{4}$$

Similarly eliminating y_2 from Eqs (2) and (3), we have the relation

$$y_1 - 3y_3 = \frac{17}{3072}\left(\frac{wL^4}{EI}\right) \tag{5}$$

Solving Eqs (4) and (5) we get

$$y_3 = -0.00313\left(\frac{wL^4}{EI}\right)$$

Also

$$y_1 = -0.00939\left(\frac{wL^4}{EI}\right) + 0.00553\left(\frac{wL^4}{EI}\right)$$

$$= -0.00386\left(\frac{wL^4}{EI}\right)$$

Substituting the value of in Eq. (1), we have

$$y_2 = 2y_1 + \left(\frac{3}{1024}\right)\left(\frac{wL^4}{EI}\right) = -0.00772\left(\frac{wL^4}{EI}\right) + 0.00292\left(\frac{wL^4}{EI}\right)$$

$$= -0.004797\left(\frac{wL^4}{EI}\right)$$

Hence the deflections at the pivotal points are

$$y_1 = -0.00386\left(\frac{wL^4}{EI}\right)$$

$$y_2 = -0.004797\left(\frac{wL^4}{EI}\right)$$

$$y_3 = -0.00313\left(\frac{wL^4}{EI}\right)$$

Example 6.16

A timber beam has a linear taper in depth from the ends to the centre of the span is loaded as shown in Fig. 6.21. The width of the beam is 200 mm. Evaluate the deflection at the centre of the beam using four subintervals. Assume $E = 13$ kN/mm².

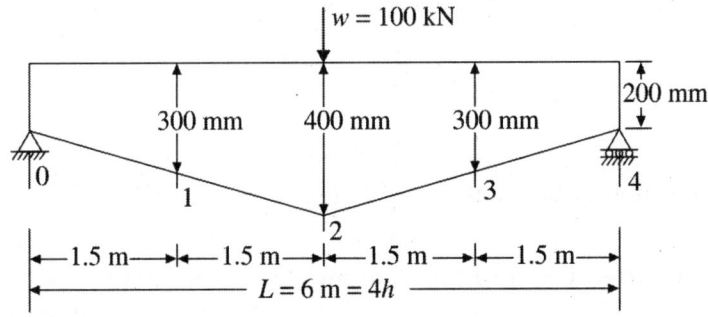

Fig. 6.21: Beam of variable moment of inertia with point load

Solution

$$I_0 = \left[\frac{200 \times 200^3}{12}\right] = 1.33 \times 10^8 \, mm^4$$

$$I_1 = I_3 = \left[\frac{200 \times 300^3}{12}\right] = 4.50 \times 10^8 \, mm^4$$

$$I_2 = \left[\frac{200 \times 400^3}{12}\right] = 10.67 \times 10^8 \, mm^4$$

Applying the finite difference equation for deflections at pivotal points, we have

$$y_0 - 2y_1 + y_2 = \left(\frac{wL}{8EI_1}\right)h^2 = \left(\frac{wL}{8EI_1}\right)\left(\frac{L^2}{16}\right) \tag{1}$$

$$y_1 - 2y_2 + y_3 = \left(\frac{wL}{4EI_2}\right)h^2 = \left(\frac{wL}{4EI_2}\right)\left(\frac{L^2}{16}\right) \tag{2}$$

$$y_2 - 2y_3 + y_4 = \left(\frac{wL}{8EI_3}\right)h^2 = \left(\frac{wL}{8EI_3}\right)\left(\frac{L^2}{16}\right) \tag{3}$$

The boundary conditions are

$$y_0 = y_4 = 0 \text{ and } y_1 = y_2$$

From Eqs. (1) and (2) we have

$$(2y_1 - 2y_2) = \left(\frac{WL^3}{64EI_2}\right) = \left(\frac{2WL^3}{128EI_2}\right)$$

Also

$$(-2y_1 + y_2) = \left(\frac{WL^3}{128EI_1}\right)$$

Hence

$$-y_2 = \left(\frac{WL^3}{128EI_2}\right)\left[\frac{2}{I_2} + \frac{1}{I_1}\right]$$

$$= \left(\frac{100 \times 6000^3}{128 \times 13 \times 10^8}\right)\left[\frac{2}{10.67} + \frac{1}{4.5}\right]$$

$$= 53.09 \text{ mm}$$

Thus the deflection of beam at centre of span $= y_2 = -53.09$ mm

Example 6.17

A simply supported beam of variable moment of inertia supports a uniformly distributed load of w kN/m over the entire span length as shown in Fig. 6.22. Using fourth order central differences. Evaluate the deflections at quarter and mid span points. Adopt four subintervals.

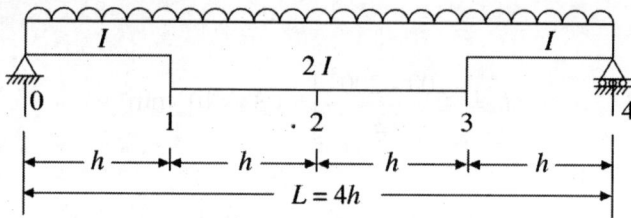

Fig. 6.22: Beam of variable moment of inertia with UDL

Solution

The deflections can be directly computed by applying the fourth order central differences and applying the finite difference equation at points 1, 2 and 3.

$$y_{n+2} - 4y_{n+1} + 6y_n - 4y_{n-1} + y_{n-2} = -\left(\frac{w_n h^4}{EI_n}\right)$$

For $n = 1$, we have

$$y_3 - 4y_2 + 6y_1 - 4y_2 + y_{-1} = -\left(\frac{wh^4}{1.5EI}\right)$$

For $n = 2$, we have

$$y_4 - 4y_3 + 6y_2 - 4y_1 + y_0 = -\left(\frac{wh^4}{2EI}\right)$$

The boundary conditions are

$$y_0 = y_4 = 0 \quad y_1 = y_3 \quad y_{-1} = -y_3 = -y_1$$

Therefore
$$6y_1 - 4y_2 = -0.67\left(\frac{wh^4}{EI}\right) \qquad (1)$$

$$-8y_1 + 6y_2 = -0.5\left(\frac{wh^4}{EI}\right) \qquad (2)$$

From Eqs (1) and (2), we have final deflections at nodal points 1 and 2 as

$$y_1 = y_3 = -0.00586\left(\frac{wh^4}{EI}\right)$$

$$y_2 = -0.00813\left(\frac{wh^4}{EI}\right)$$

Example 6.18

A simply supported beam of variable moment of inertia supports a concentrated load as shown in Fig. 6.23. Estimate the deflections at the nodal points using fourth order central differences.

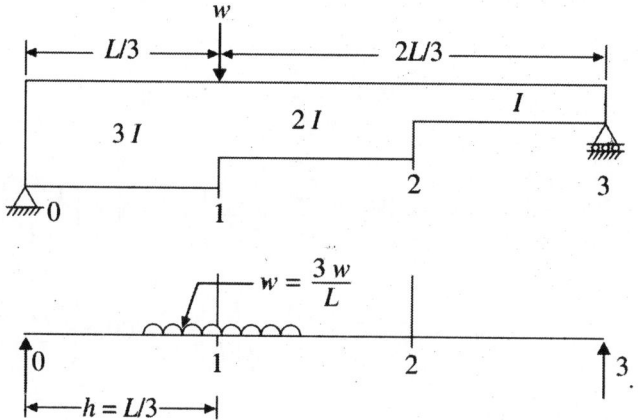

Fig. 6.23: Beam of variable moment of inertia with concentrated load

Solution

Using the finite difference equations,

$$y_{n-2} - 4y_{n-1} + 6y_n - 4y_{n+1} + y_{n+2} = -\left(\frac{w_n h^4}{EI_n}\right)$$

For $n = 1$, we have

$$y_{-1} - 4y_0 + 6y_1 - 4y_2 + y_3 = -\left(\frac{wh^4}{E(2.5I)}\right)$$

For $n = 2$, we have

$$y_0 - 4y_1 + 6y_2 - 4y_3 + y_4 = 0$$

The boundary conditions are

$$y_{-1} = -y_1 \quad y_0 = y_3 = 0 \quad y_4 = -y_2$$

$$5y_1 - 4y_2 = -0.4\left(\frac{wh^4}{EI}\right)$$

$$-4y_1 + 5y_2 = 0$$

Therefore $4y_1 = 5y_2$ and $y_1 = 1.25y_2$

Substituting for y_1 in terms of y_2

$$5(1.25y_2) - 4y_2 = -0.4\left(\frac{wh^4}{EI}\right)$$

Hence

$$y_2 = -0.177\left(\frac{wh^4}{EI}\right) = -0.0022\left(\frac{wL^4}{EI}\right)$$

And

$$y_1 = 1.25y_2 = 1.25\left[-0.0022\left(\frac{wL^4}{EI}\right)\right]$$

$$y_1 = -0.0027\left(\frac{wL^4}{EI}\right) \quad \text{But } w = \left(\frac{3W}{L}\right)$$

Hence

$$y_1 = -0.0027\left(\frac{3W}{L}\right)\left(\frac{L^4}{EI}\right) = -0.0081\left(\frac{WL^3}{EI}\right)$$

$$y_2 = -0.0022\left(\frac{3W}{L}\right)\left(\frac{L^4}{EI}\right) = -0.0066\left(\frac{WL^3}{EI}\right)$$

6.4 STATICALLY INDETERMINATE BEAM PROBLEMS

Example 6.19

A beam of span is fixed at both ends A and B and supports a uniformly distributed load of intensity w kN/m as shown in Fig. 6.24. Estimate the deflections at quarter span intervals using second order central differences[10].

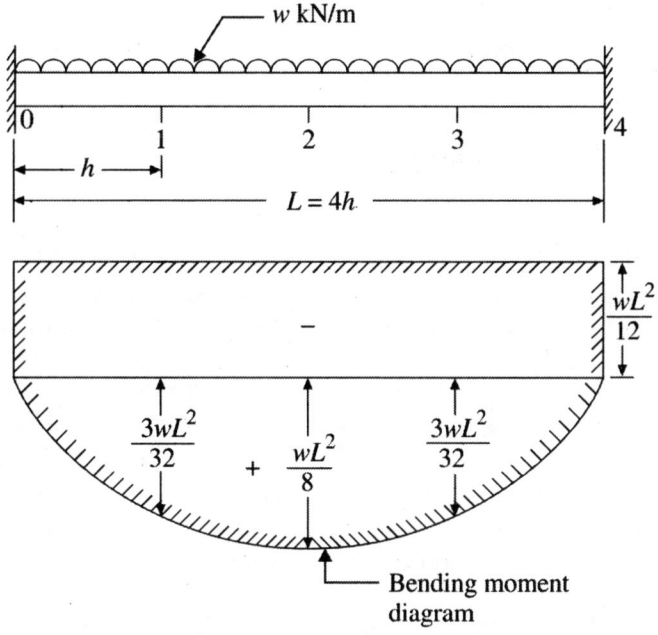

Fig. 6.24: Fixed beam deflections

Solution

Applying second order central differences, the general equation of deflection is expressed as,

$$y_{n-1} - 2y_n + y_{n+1} = \left(\frac{h^2 M_n}{EI_n}\right)$$

Applying the above equation successively to points 1, 2 and 3, we have

$$y_0 - 2y_1 + y_2 = \left(\frac{L}{4}\right)^2 \left[\left(\frac{3}{32}\frac{wL^2}{EI}\right) - \left(\frac{wL^2}{12EI}\right)\right] \qquad (1)$$

$$y_1 - 2y_2 + y_3 = \left(\frac{L}{4}\right)^2 \left[\left(\frac{wL^2}{8EI}\right) - \left(\frac{wL^2}{12EI}\right)\right] \qquad (2)$$

$$y_2 - 2y_3 + y_4 = \left(\frac{L}{4}\right)^2 \left[\left(\frac{3}{32}\frac{wL^2}{EI}\right) - \left(\frac{wL^2}{12EI}\right)\right] \qquad (3)$$

The boundary conditions are given by

$$y_1 = y_3 \quad y_0 = y_4 = 0 \quad y_2 = y_{max}$$

Solving Eqs (1) and (2)

$$y_2 = y_{max} = -\left(\frac{wL^4}{307.2EI}\right)$$

Exact value of $y_{max} = -\left(\dfrac{wL^4}{384EI}\right)$

$$y_1 = y_3 = -\left(\dfrac{wL^4}{512EI}\right)$$

Example 6.20

A two span continuous beam ABC has equal spans $AB = BC = L$. The beam supports concentrated load of W kN at each mid span points as shown in Fig. 6.25. Estimate the deflection under the load points using finite difference technique.

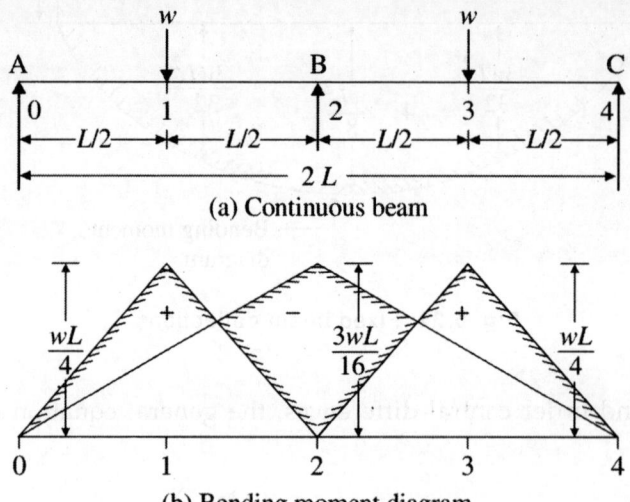

(a) Continuous beam

(b) Bending moment diagram

Fig. 6.25: Continuous beam with point loads

Solution

Referring to Fig. 6.25 and applying the finite difference equation successively to points 1, 2 and 3, we have the following relations:

$$y_0 - 2y_1 + y_2 = \left(\frac{L}{2}\right)^2\left(\frac{wL}{4} - \frac{3wL}{32}\right)\frac{1}{EI}$$

$$y_1 - 2y_2 + y_3 = \left(\frac{L}{2}\right)^2\left(-\frac{3wL}{16}\right)\frac{1}{EI}$$

$$y_2 - 2y_3 + y_4 = \left(\frac{L}{2}\right)^2\left(\frac{wL}{4} - \frac{3wL}{32}\right)\frac{1}{EI}$$

The boundary conditions are

$$y_1 = y_3 \qquad y_0 = y_2 = y_4 = 0$$

Solving the above equations, we have

$$-2y_1 = \left(\frac{L^2}{4}\right)\left(\frac{5wL}{32EI}\right)$$

Therefore
$$y_1 = y_3 = -\left(\frac{5WL^3}{256EI}\right)$$

Example 6.21

A propped cantilever AB fixed at A and propped at B is of length L and has constant flexural rigidity. The cantilever supports a concentrated load of W at the centre of span as shown in Fig. 6.26. Assuming four subintervals, estimate the deflection under the load.

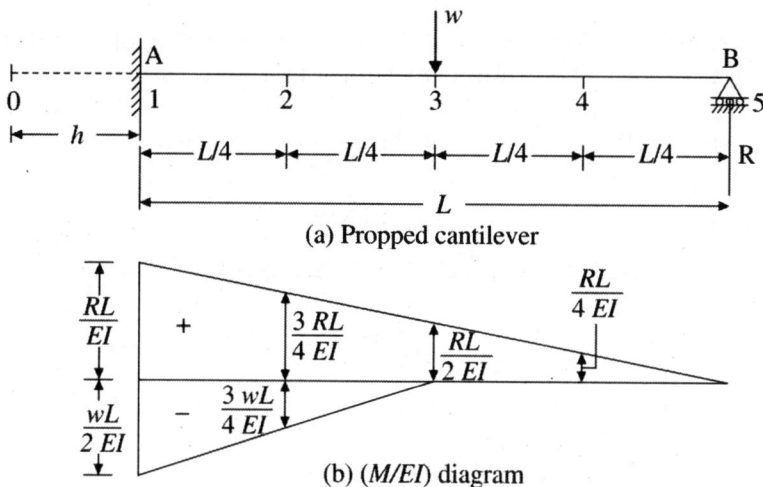

(a) Propped cantilever

(b) (M/EI) diagram

Fig. 6.26: Propped cantilever with point load

Solution

Referring to Fig. 6.26 and applying finite difference equations to the panel points, we have the following relations:

$$y_0 - 2y_1 + y_2 = \left(RL - \frac{WL}{2}\right)\left(\frac{L^2}{16EI}\right) \tag{1}$$

$$y_1 - 2y_2 + y_3 = \left(\frac{3RL}{4} - \frac{WL}{4}\right)\left(\frac{L^2}{16EI}\right) \tag{2}$$

$$y_2 - 2y_3 + y_4 = \left(\frac{RL}{2}\right)\left(\frac{L^2}{16EI}\right) \tag{3}$$

$$y_3 - 2y_4 + y_5 = \left(\frac{RL}{4}\right)\left(\frac{L^2}{16EI}\right) \tag{4}$$

The boundary conditions are
$$y_0 = y_2 \qquad y_1 = y_5 = 0$$

By solving the, the redundant reaction R is obtained as $R = \left(\dfrac{7w}{22}\right)$ substituting this value in Eqs (1) to (4) and solving, the deflections at the panel points are as follows:

$$y_3 = y_{max} = -0.0106\left(\frac{wL^3}{EI}\right)$$

$$y_2 = y_4 = -0.00568\left(\frac{wL^3}{EI}\right)$$

Example 6.22

A propped cantilever AB fixed at A and propped at B is of length L and has constant flexural rigidity. The cantilever supports a uniformly distributed load of intensity w kN/m over the whole length as shown in Fig. 6.27. Considering four subintervals, estimate the deflections at the panel points using the finite difference method.

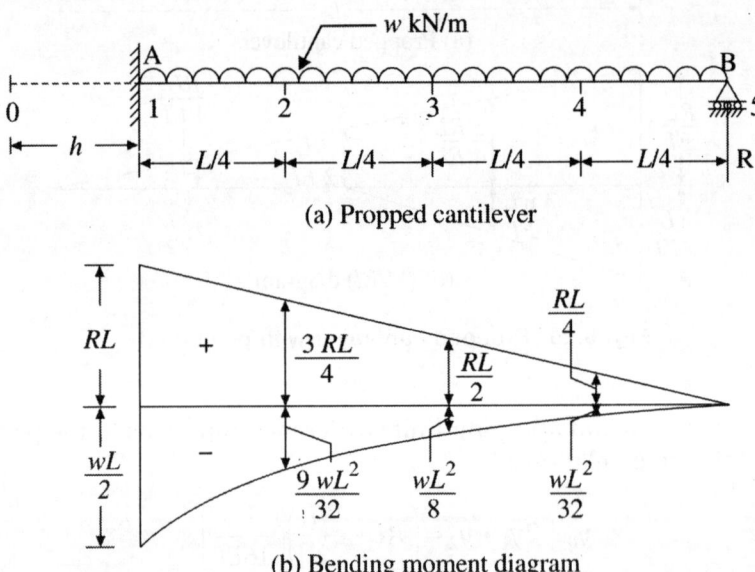

(a) Propped cantilever

(b) Bending moment diagram

Fig. 6.27: Propped cantilever supporting UDL

Solution

Referring to Fig. 6.27 and applying the second order finite differences, we have the following relations:

$$y_0 - 2y_1 + y_2 = \left(RL - \frac{wL^2}{2}\right)\left(\frac{L^2}{16EI}\right) \tag{1}$$

$$y_1 - 2y_2 + y_3 = \left(\frac{3RL}{4} - \frac{9wL^2}{32}\right)\left(\frac{L^2}{16EI}\right) \tag{2}$$

$$Y_2 - 2y_3 + y_4 = \left(\frac{RL}{2} - \frac{wL^2}{8}\right)\left(\frac{L^2}{16EI}\right) \tag{3}$$

$$Y_3 - 2y_4 + y_5 = \left(\frac{RL}{4} - \frac{wL^2}{32}\right)\left(\frac{L^2}{16EI}\right) \tag{4}$$

The boundary conditions are

$$y_0 = y_2 \quad y_1 = y_5 = 0$$

By solving we have the redundant reaction $R = 0.386wL$ substituting this value in Eqs (1) to (4) and solving, the deflections at the panel points are as follows:

$$y_2 = -0.0035\left(\frac{wL^4}{EI}\right)$$

$$y_3 = -0.0065\left(\frac{wL^4}{EI}\right)$$

$$y_4 = -0.0053\left(\frac{wL^4}{EI}\right)$$

Example 6.23

A fixed beam of variable flexural rigidity supports a concentrated load W as shown in Fig. 6.28. Estimate the deflection under the load considering three subintervals of the beam.

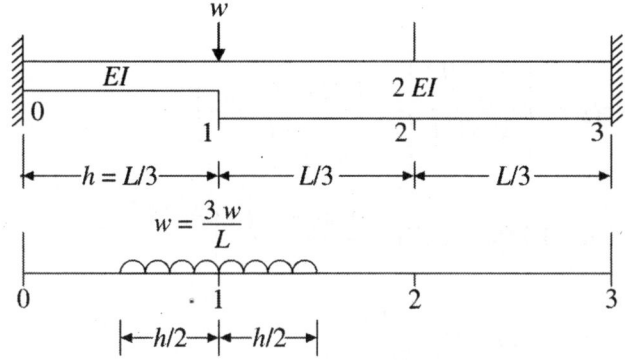

Fig. 6.28: Fixed beam with variable flexural rigidity

Solution

Applying fourth order finite difference expression, we have the following relations:

$$y_{n-2} - 4y_{n-1} + 6y_n - 4y_{n+1} + y_{n+2} = -\left(\frac{w_n h^4}{EI_n}\right)$$

For $n = 1$, we have

$$y_{-1} - 4y_0 + 6y_1 - 4y_2 + y_3 = -\left(\frac{wh^4}{1.5EI}\right)$$

For $n = 2$, we have

$$y_0 - 4y_1 + 6y_2 - 4y_3 + y_4 = 0$$

The boundary conditions are

$$y_{-1} = y_1 \quad y_0 = y_3 = 0 \quad y_4 = y_2$$

Hence $\quad 7y_1 - 4y_2 = -\left(\dfrac{wh^4}{1.5EI}\right)$

$$-4y_1 + 7y_2 = 0$$

Therefore $\qquad y_1 = 1.75y_2$

Substituting for y_2

$$7(1.75y_2) - 4y_2 = -\left(\dfrac{wh^4}{1.5EI}\right)$$

$$8.25\,y_2 = -\left(\dfrac{wh^4}{1.5EI}\right) = -\left(\dfrac{w\left(\dfrac{L}{3}\right)^4}{1.5EI}\right)$$

Therefore $\qquad y_2 = -\left(\dfrac{wL^4}{1063EI}\right)$

But $\qquad\qquad w = \left(\dfrac{3w}{L}\right)$

hence we have $\quad y_2 = -\left[\dfrac{\left(\dfrac{3w}{L}\right)L^4}{1063EI}\right] = -\left(\dfrac{0.00282wL^3}{EI}\right)$

$$y_1 = 1.75y_2 = 1.75\left(-\dfrac{0.00282wL^3}{EI}\right)$$

$$y_1 = -0.00493\left(\dfrac{wL^3}{EI}\right)$$

6.5 BUCKLING OF COLUMNS

6.5.1 General Aspects

The finite difference method is ideally suited to evaluate approximate solutions of the buckling loads of columns. The method is particularly suitable for columns of variable cross-section since the method involves the division of the column into finite number of subintervals. While the finite difference method yields approximate solutions for complicated cases of columns, rigorous methods resulting in exact solutions involve laborious computations and they are not universally applicable for all problems.

Consider a long column of length pinned at both ends as shown in Fig. 6.29.

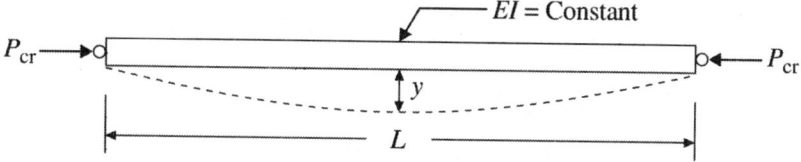

Fig. 6.29: Long column pinned at both ends

Solution

The critical load can be determined by using the equation,

$$\left(\frac{d^2y}{dx^2}\right) = \left(\frac{M}{EI}\right) = -\left(\frac{P_{cr}\cdot y}{EI}\right)$$

where

y = Central deflection of the column

EI = Flexural rigidity

P_{cr} = Critical or buckling load

Differentiating the expression twice, we have the fourth order equation,

$$\left(\frac{d^4y}{dx^4}\right) = -\left(\frac{P_{cr}\cdot y}{EI}\right)\left(\frac{d^2y}{dx^2}\right)$$

Expressing this equation in finite difference form, we have

$$\left[\frac{y_{n+2}-4y_{n+1}+6y_n-4y_{n-1}+y_{n-2}}{h^4}\right] = -\left(\frac{P_{cr}}{EI}\right)\left[\frac{y_{n+1}-2y_n+y_{n-1}}{h^2}\right]$$

Hence, the general finite difference equation is expressed as

$$\left(y_{n+2}-4y_{n+1}+6y_n-4y_{n-1}+y_{n-2}\right) = -\left(\frac{P_{cr}\cdot h^2}{EI}\right)\left(y_{n+1}-2y_n+y_{n-1}\right)$$

Using this general equation, the critical loads are obtained for columns with different boundary conditions.

Example 6.24

Estimate the lowest buckling load of a uniform pin ended column of length L and flexural rigidity EI using three subintervals (Fig. 6.30).

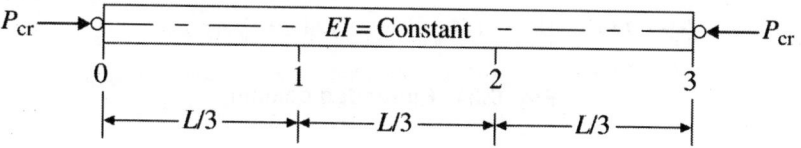

Fig. 6.30: Long column with hinged ends

Solution

Referring to Fig. 6.30 the governing equation in the finite difference form is written as

$$\left(y_{n+2}-4y_{n+1}+6y_n-4y_{n-1}+y_{n-2}\right) = -\left(\frac{P_{cr}\cdot h^2}{EI}\right)\left(y_{n+1}-2y_n+y_{n-1}\right)$$

Due to symmetry, $y_1 = y_2$ and if $n = 1$

$$(y_3 - 4y_2 + 6y_1 - 4y_0 + y_{-1}) = -\left(\frac{P_{cr} \cdot h^2}{EI}\right)(y_2 - 2y_1 + y_0)$$

The boundary conditions are

$$y_1 = y_2, \quad y_0 = y_3 = 0, \quad y_{-1} = -y_1$$

Substituting these values, we get

$$(-4y_1 + 6y_1 - y_1) = -\left(\frac{P_{cr} \cdot h^2}{EI}\right)(y_1 - 2y_1)$$

$$y_1 = -\left(\frac{P_{cr} \cdot h^2}{EI}\right)(-y_1)$$

Therefore $\left(\dfrac{P_{cr} \cdot h^2}{EI}\right) = 1$

Hence $$P_{cr} = \left(\frac{EI}{h^2}\right) = \left(\frac{EI}{(L/3)^2}\right) = \left(\frac{9EI}{L^2}\right)$$

The exact solution of the Euler's buckling load is given by the expression,

$$P_{cr} = \left(\frac{\pi^2 EI}{L^2}\right) = \left(\frac{9.87 EI}{L^2}\right)$$

However, the accuracy of the solution can be improved by considering four subintervals as illustrated in the following example.

Example 6.25

Estimate the buckling load of a pin ended column of length L and uniform section considering four subintervals and compare the approximate value with the exact Euler critical load.

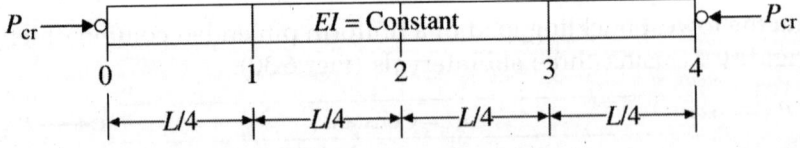

Fig. 6.31: Pin-ended column

Solution

Referring to Fig. 6.31 and considering four subintervals, the governing finite difference equation is expressed as,

$$(y_{n+2} - 4y_{n+1} + 6y_n - 4y_{n-1} + y_{n-2}) = -\left(\frac{P_{cr} \cdot h^2}{EI}\right)(y_{n+1} - 2y_n + y_{n-1})$$

If $n = 1$

$$\left(y_3 - 4y_2 + 6y_1 - 4y_0 + y_{-1}\right) = -\left(\frac{P_{cr} \cdot h^2}{EI}\right)\left(y_2 - 2y_1 + y_0\right)$$

If $n = 2$

$$\left(y_4 - 4y_3 + 6y_2 - 4y_1 + y_0\right) = -\left(\frac{P_{cr} \cdot h^2}{EI}\right)\left(y_3 - 2y_2 + y_1\right)$$

The boundary conditions are

$$y_0 = y_4 = 0 \quad y_1 = y_3 \quad y_{-1} = -y_1$$

Using the boundary conditions, we have the relations

$$\left(6y_1 - 4y_2\right) = -\left(\frac{P_{cr} \cdot h^2}{EI}\right)\left(y_2 - 2y_1\right)$$

$$\left(-8y_1 - 6y_2\right) = -\left(\frac{P_{cr} \cdot h^2}{EI}\right)\left(2y_1 - y_2\right)$$

Put $-\left(\dfrac{P_{cr} \cdot h^2}{EI}\right) = C$ then we have

$$\left(6 + 2C\right)y_1 - \left(4 + C\right)y_2 = 0$$
$$-\left(8 + 2C\right)y_1 + \left(6 + 2C\right)y_2 = 0$$

Solution exists only when

$$\begin{vmatrix} (6+2C) & -(4+C) \\ -(8+2C) & (6+2C) \end{vmatrix} = 0$$

Expanding and multiplying, we get

$$\left(6 + 2C\right)^2 - \left(4 + C\right)\left(8 + 2C\right) = 0$$

Solving, $C = 3.414$ or -0.5858

That is $-\left(\dfrac{P_{cr} \cdot h^2}{EI}\right) = -0.5858$

or

$$P_{cr} = 0.5858\left(\frac{EI}{h^2}\right) = \left[\frac{0.5858EI}{(L/4)^2}\right]$$

$$P_{cr} = \left(\frac{9.37EI}{L^2}\right)$$

The exact solution of the Euler's buckling load is given by the expression,

$$P_{cr} = \left(\frac{\pi^2 EI}{L^2}\right) = \left(\frac{9.87 EI}{L^2}\right)$$

The error in the approximate solution is of the order of 5.06%.

Example 6.26

Determine the critical load for the pin ended column with variable moment of inertiaas shown in Fig. 6.32.

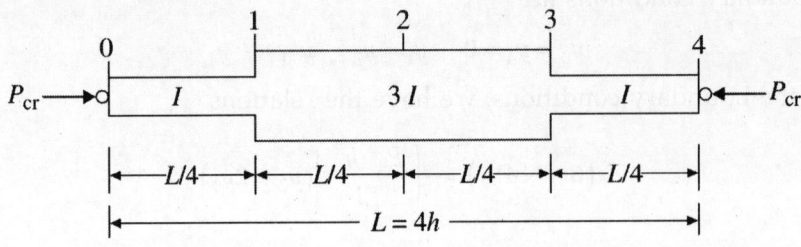

Fig. 6.32: Pin-ended column of variable moment of inertia

Solution

In view of the symmetry, only half the column is analysed using the governing finite difference equation.

$$(y_{n+2} - 4y_{n+1} + 6y_n - 4y_{n-1} + y_{n-2}) = -\left(\frac{P_{cr} \cdot h^2}{EI}\right)(y_{n+1} - 2y_n + y_{n-1})$$

If $n = 1$

$$(y_3 - 4y_2 + 6y_1 - 4y_0 + y_{-1}) = -\left(\frac{P_{cr} \cdot h^2}{EI}\right)(y_2 - 2y_1 + y_0)$$

If $n = 2$

$$(y_4 - 4y_3 + 6y_2 - 4y_1 + y_0) = -\left(\frac{P_{cr} \cdot h^2}{EI}\right)(y_3 - 2y_2 + y_1)$$

The boundary conditions are

$$y_0 = y_4 = 0 \quad y_1 = y_3 \quad y_{-1} = -y_1$$

Substituting the boundary conditions, we have the following relations

$$(6y_1 - 4y_2) = -0.5\left(\frac{P_{cr} \cdot h^2}{EI}\right)(y_2 - 2y_1)$$

$$(-8y_1 - 6y_2) = -0.33\left(\frac{P_{cr} \cdot h^2}{EI}\right)(2y_1 - y_2)$$

Put $-\left(\dfrac{P_{cr} \cdot h^2}{EI}\right) = C$ then we have

$$(6+C)y_1 - (4+0.5C)y_2 = 0$$

$$-(8+0.66C)y_1 + (6+0.66C)y_2 = 0$$

Solution exists only when

$$\begin{vmatrix} (6+2C) & -(4+0.5C) \\ -(8+0.66C) & (6+0.66C) \end{vmatrix} = 0$$

That is, when

$$(6+C)(6+0.66C) - (8+0.66C)(4+0.5C) = 0$$

$$0.33C^2 + 3.32C + 4 = 0$$

Solving, C = – 1.4 and – 8.65, thus we have

$$-\left(\frac{P_{cr} \cdot h^2}{EI}\right) = -1.4$$

$$P_{cr} = \left(\frac{1.4EI}{h^2}\right) = \left[\frac{1.4EI}{(L/4)^2}\right]$$

or $P_{cr} = \left(\dfrac{22.4EI}{L^2}\right)$

Example 6.27

Estimate the critical load for the stepped column shown in Fig. 6.33, which is pinned one end and fixed at the other end.

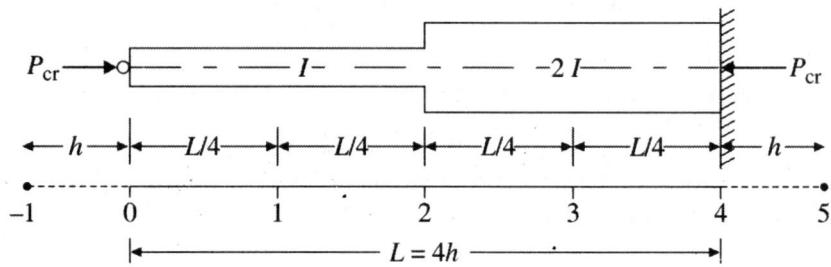

Fig. 6.33: Column fixed at one end and pinned at the other end

Solution

Four segments are considered and the governing finite difference equation

$$(y_{n+2} - 4y_{n+1} + 6y_n - 4y_{n-1} + y_{n-2}) = -\left(\frac{P_{cr} \cdot h^2}{I}\right)(y_{n+1} - 2y_n + y_{n-1})$$

At point 1, $n = 1$

$$(y_3 - 4y_2 + 6y_1 - 4y_0 + y_{-1}) = -\left(\frac{P_{cr} \cdot h^2}{EI}\right)(y_2 - 2y_1 + y_0)$$

At point 2, $n = 2$

$$\left(y_4 - 4y_3 + 6y_2 - 4y_1 + y_0\right) = -\left(\frac{P_{cr} \cdot h^2}{EI}\right)\left(y_3 - 2y_2 + y_1\right)$$

At point 3, $n = 3$

$$\left(y_5 - 4y_4 + 6y_3 - 4y_2 + y_1\right) = -\left(\frac{P_{cr} \cdot h^2}{EI}\right)\left(y_4 - 2y_3 + y_2\right)$$

The boundary conditions are

$$y_0 = y_4 = 0 \qquad y_{-1} = -y_1$$

Slope at fixed end $4 = \left(\dfrac{dy}{dx}\right)_4 = 0$ or $y_5 = y_3$

Applying the boundary conditions and putting $\left(\dfrac{P_{cr} \cdot h^2}{EI}\right) = C$

The above equations reduce to

$$y_3 - (4 - C)y_2 + (5 - 2C)y_1 = 0$$

$$-(4 - 0.667C)y_3 + (6 - 1.333C)y_2 - (4 - 0.667C)y_1 = 0$$

$$(7 - C)y_3 - (4 - 0.5C)y_2 + y_1 = 0$$

For this set of homogeneous linear equations, besides the trivial solution of the other possible solutions exist only when determinant of the coefficients is zero, or

$$\begin{vmatrix} 1 & -(4 - C) & (5 - 2C) \\ -(4 - 0.667C) & (6 - 1.333C) & -(4 - 0.667C) \\ (7 - C) & -(4 - 0.5C) & 1 \end{vmatrix} = 0$$

Expanding the determinant, the following cubic equation is obtained:

$$C^3 - 12C^2 + 39.5C - 33 = 0$$

Solving this equation by Graeffe's root squaring method discussed in Section 3.6, we have the following solutions.

$$C = 1.29, \qquad P_{cr} = \left(\frac{1.29EI}{h^2}\right) = \left(\frac{20.7EI}{L^2}\right)$$

$$C = 3.64, \qquad P_{cr} = \left(\frac{3.64EI}{h^2}\right) = \left(\frac{58.3EI}{L^2}\right)$$

$$C = 7.17, \qquad P_{cr} = \left(\frac{7.17EI}{h^2}\right) = \left(\frac{115EI}{L^2}\right)$$

The lowest buckling load is

$$P_{cr} = \left(\frac{20.7EI}{L^2}\right)$$

Example 6.28

Estimate the critical load of the column shown in Fig. 6.34, using the method of finite defferenecs. Use a grid spacing of quarter length intervals.

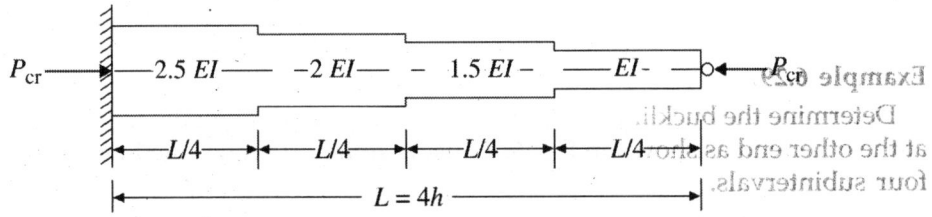

Fig. 6.34: Column with fixed and pinned ends with variable flexural rigidity

Solution

The governing differential equation of finite difference form is expressed as,

$$y_{n-2} - 4y_{n-1} + 6y_n - 4y_{n+1} + y_{n+2} = -\left(\frac{P_{cr} \cdot h^2}{EI}\right)(y_{n+1} - 2y_n + y_{n-1})$$

Applying the above equations to the nodal points 1, 2 and 3 respectively, we get the following equations.

$$y_{-1} - 4y_0 + 6y_1 - 4y_2 + y_3 = -\left(\frac{P_{cr} \cdot h^2}{2.25EI}\right)(y_2 - 2y_1 + y_0)$$

$$y_0 - 4y_1 + 6y_2 - 4y_3 + y_4 = -\left(\frac{P_{cr} \cdot h^2}{1.75EI}\right)(y_3 - 2y_2 + y_1)$$

$$y_1 - 4y_2 + 6y_3 - 4y_4 + y_5 = -\left(\frac{P_{cr} \cdot h^2}{1.25EI}\right)(y_4 - 2y_3 + y_2)$$

The boundary conditions are

$$y_0 = y_4 = 0 \qquad y_{-1} = -y_1 \qquad y_3 = y_5$$

Put $\left(\dfrac{P_{cr} \cdot h^2}{EI}\right) = C$, then we have

$$(5y_1 - 4y_2 + y_3) = -\frac{C}{2.25}(y_2 - 2y_1)$$

$$(-4y_1 + 6y_2 - 4y_3) = -\frac{C}{1.75}(y_3 - 2y_2 + y_1)$$

$$(y_1 - 4y_2 - 7y_3) = -\frac{C}{1.25}(y_2 - 2y_3)$$

Rearranging the terms, the solution exists only when,

$$\begin{vmatrix} (5 - 0.88C) & (0.44C - 4) & 1 \\ (0.57C - 4) & (6 - 1.14C) & (0.57C - 4) \\ (0) & (0.8C - 4) & (7 - 1.6C) \end{vmatrix} = 0$$

Expanding the determinant and solving the cubic equation yields the lowest critical load as

$$P_{cr} = \left(\frac{14.14EI}{L^2}\right)$$

Example 6.29

Determine the buckling load for the tapering column pinned at one end and fixed at the other end as shown in Fig. 6.35, using finite difference method and employing four subintervals.

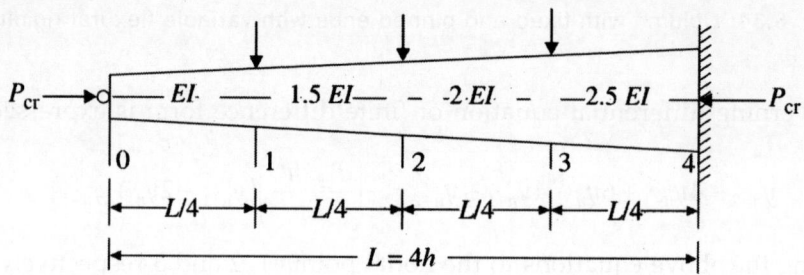

Fig. 6.35: Tapering column with pinned and fixed ends

Solution

Applying the finite difference scheme in terms of deflections, we have

$$y_{n-2} - 4y_{n-1} + 6y_n - 4y_{n+1} + y_{n+2} = -\left(\frac{P_{cr} \cdot h^2}{EI}\right)(y_{n+1} - 2y_n + y_{n-1})$$

Considering the nodal points 1, 2 and 3 respectively, we get the following equations:

$$y_{-1} - 4y_0 + 6y_1 - 4y_2 + y_3 = -\left(\frac{P_{cr} \cdot h^2}{1.25EI}\right)(y_2 - 2y_1 + y_0)$$

$$y_0 - 4y_1 + 6y_2 - 4y_3 + y_4 = -\left(\frac{P_{cr} \cdot h^2}{1.5EI}\right)(y_3 - 2y_2 + y_1)$$

$$y_1 - 4y_2 + 6y_3 - 4y_4 + y_5 = -\left(\frac{P_{cr} \cdot h^2}{1.75EI}\right)(y_4 - 2y_3 + y_2)$$

The boundary conditions are

$$y_0 = y_4 = 0 \qquad y_{-1} = -y_1 \qquad y_3 = y_5$$

Using the boundary conditions and substituting the value of $\left(\dfrac{P_{cr} \cdot h^2}{EI}\right) = C$, the solution exists only when the determinant shown below is zero.

$$\begin{vmatrix} (5-1.6C) & (-4+0.8C) & 1 \\ (-4+0.67C) & (6-1.33C) & -(4-0.67C) \\ 1 & (-4-0.57C) & (7-1.14C) \end{vmatrix} = 0$$

Expanding the above determinant and equating to zero, we obtain a cubic equation which in turn is solved by Graeefe's root squaring method. The least value of is obtained as,

$$\left(\frac{P_{cr} \cdot h^2}{EI} \right) = C = 1.609$$

or
$$P_{cr} = \left(\frac{1.609EI}{h^2} \right) = \left(\frac{1.609EI}{(L/4)^2} \right)$$

$$= \left(\frac{25.746EI}{L^2} \right)$$

6.6 VIBRATIONS OF BEAMS

6.6.1 General Aspects

The finite difference method can be advantageously employed for solving vibration problems of statically determinate and indeterminate beams with constant and variable moment of inertia.

In a normal mode of vibration the deflection of a beam can be expressed by the expression,

$$y = y_{max} \sin \omega t$$

$$\left(\frac{dy}{dx} \right) = y_{max} \omega \cos \omega t$$

$$\left(\frac{d^2 y}{dx^2} \right) = -\omega^2 y_{max} \cdot \sin \omega t$$

Where y_{max} = maximum deflection

ω = circular frequency of vibration in rad/sec

t = time in seconds

. If m is the mass of the beam per unit length and a = acceleration due to gravity, the distributed inertia force is given by $- ma$.

The acceleration of the motion is

$$a = \left(\frac{d^2 y}{dt^2} \right) = -\omega^2 y$$

Hence, the differential equation of deflection of a beam reduces to

$$\frac{d^2}{dx^2} \left(EI \frac{d^2 y}{dx^2} \right) = \omega^2 \cdot my$$

For a prismatic beam, the equation reduces to

$$\left(EI\frac{d^4y}{dx^4}\right) = \omega^2 \cdot my$$

Expressing in the finite difference form, the fourth order equation is given by

$$EI\left[\frac{y_{n+2} - 4y_{n+1} + 6y_n - 4y_{n-1} + y_{n-2}}{h^4}\right] = \omega^2 \cdot my$$

and hence

$$\left(y_{n+2} - 4y_{n+1} + 6y_n - 4y_{n-1} + y_{n-2}\right) = \left(\frac{\omega^2 mh^4}{EI}\right)y$$

If we put $\lambda = \left(\dfrac{\omega^2 mh^4}{EI}\right)$, the typical finite difference equation at point n becomes,

$$\left(y_{n+2} - 4y_{n+1} + (6 - \lambda)y_n - 4y_{n-1} + y_{n-2}\right) = 0$$

Using the above governing equation, the natural frequency of the beam can be determined. The application of this principle is illustrated by the following examples.

Example 6.30

Find the natural frequency of vibration of a simply supported beam with a self weight of m per unit length as shown in Fig. 6.36 using finite difference method and adopting four subintervals.

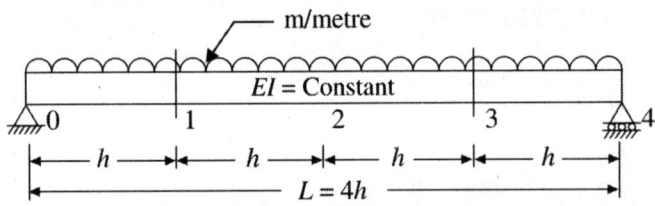

Fig. 6.36: Simply supported beam with UDL

Solution

Referring to Fig. 6.36 and applying the governing finite difference equation, we have

$$y_{n+2} - 4y_{n+1} + 6y_n - 4y_{n-1} + y_{n-2} = 0$$

For $n = 1$, we have

$$y_3 - 4y_2 + 6y_1 - 4y_2 + y_{-1} = 0$$

For $n = 2$, we have

$$y_4 - 4y_3 + 6y_2 - 4y_1 + y_0 = 0$$

The boundary conditions are

$$y_0 = y_4 = 0 \qquad y_1 = y_3 \qquad y_{-1} = -y_3 = -y_1$$

Applying the boundary conditions, the resulting equations are,

$$(6-\lambda)y_1 - 4y_2 = 0$$

$$-8y_1 - (6-\lambda)y_2 = 0$$

The solution for these equations is possible only when the determinant

$$\begin{vmatrix} (6-\lambda) & -4 \\ -8 & (6-\lambda) \end{vmatrix} = 0$$

$$(6-\lambda)^2 - 32 = 0$$

$$(\lambda^2 - 12\lambda + 4) = 0$$

Solving the quadratic equation, $\lambda = 11.656$ and 0.343. Taking the least value

$$\left(\frac{\omega^2 mh^4}{EI}\right) = \lambda = 0.343$$

or $$\omega = 9.37\sqrt{\frac{EI}{mL^4}}$$

The natural frequency is $f = \left(\dfrac{\omega}{2\pi}\right) = \dfrac{1.5}{L^2}\sqrt{\dfrac{EI}{m}}$

Example 6.31

A simply supported beam of negligible weight, supports a concentrated load W at the centre of span as shown in Fig. 6.37. Find the natural frequency of vibration of the beam, assuming four divisions. If $W = $ kN, $L = $ kN·m^2 and $EI = 20,000$ kN·m^2 and $g = $ m/s^2, calculate the natural frequency of the beam.

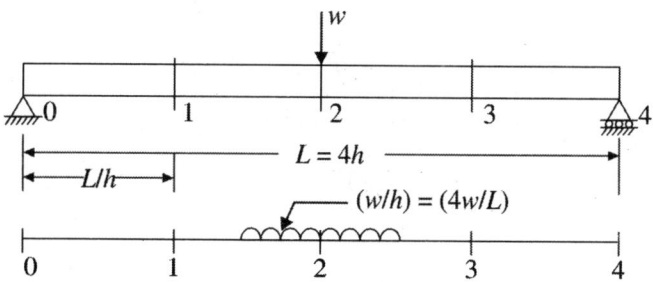

Fig. 6.37: Beam with concentrated load

Solution

The concentrated load W is assumed to act over a length $h = \left(\dfrac{L}{4}\right)$

$$\text{Weight/metre} = \left(\frac{4W}{L}\right)$$

$$\text{Mass/metre} = \left(\frac{4W}{Lg}\right)$$

Only half the beam is analyzed in view of symmetry. Applying the governing finite difference equations, we have the following relations:

$$y_{n+2} - 4y_{n+1} + 6y_n - 4y_{n-1} + y_{n-2} = 0$$

For $n = 1$, we have

$$y_3 - 4y_2 + 6y_1 - 4y_2 + y_{-1} = 0$$

For $n = 2$, we have

$$y_4 - 4y_3 + 6y_2 - 4y_1 + y_0 = 0$$

The boundary conditions are

$$y_0 = y_4 = 0 \qquad y_1 = y_3 \qquad y_{-1} = -y_3 = -y_1$$

Substituting the boundary conditions, the resulting equations are,

$$6y_1 - 4y_2 = 0$$

$$-8y_1 - (6 - \lambda)y_2 = 0$$

The solution for these equations is possible only when the determinant

$$\begin{vmatrix} 6 & -4 \\ -8 & (6-\lambda) \end{vmatrix} = 0$$

$$36 - 6\lambda - 32 = 0$$

$$\lambda = 0.67 = \left(\frac{\omega^2 m h^4}{EI} \right)$$

$$\omega^2 = \left(\frac{0.67 EI}{m h^4} \right) \quad \text{or} \quad \omega = 0.818 \sqrt{\frac{EI}{m h^4}}$$

$$\omega = 0.818 \sqrt{\frac{EI(Lg)}{4W(L/4)^4}}$$

$$= 0.818 \sqrt{\frac{64 EIg}{WL^3}}$$

$$= 6.55 \sqrt{\frac{EIg}{WL^3}}$$

Hence the natural frequency is given by

$$f = \frac{\omega}{2\pi} = 1.04 \sqrt{\frac{EIg}{WL^3}} = 1.04 \sqrt{\frac{20,000 \times 9.81}{200 \times 6^3}} = 2.2 \text{ cycles/sec}$$

Example 6.32

A simply supported beam of length L supports a concentrated load W at the centre of span. The total self weight t of the beam is $W/2$. Find the natural frequency of vibration of the beam shown in Fig. 6.38.

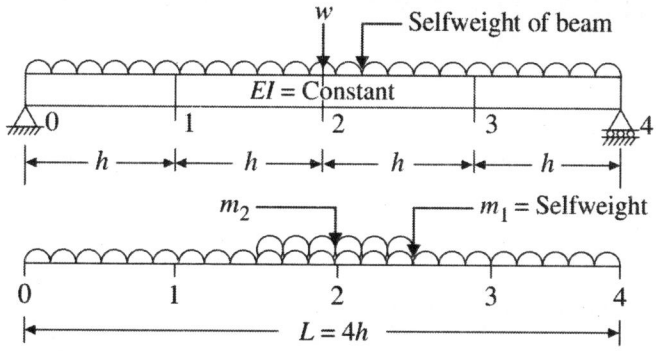

Fig. 6.38: Beam with selfweight and concentrated load

Solution

Concentrated load = W

Equivalent uniformly distributed load = $\left(\dfrac{W}{h}\right) = \dfrac{W}{(L/4)} = \left(\dfrac{4W}{L}\right)$

$$\text{Mass} = m_2 = \left(\dfrac{4W}{Lg}\right)$$

$$\text{Selfweight of the beam} = \left(\dfrac{W}{2}\right)$$

$$\text{Selfweight/metre} = \left(\dfrac{W}{2L}\right)$$

$$\text{Self mass/metre} = m_1 = \left(\dfrac{W}{2Lg}\right)$$

From symmetry considerations, only half the beam will be analyzed.

At nodal point 1, the mass acting is and let it corresponds to $\lambda = \left(\dfrac{Wm_1h^4}{EI}\right)$

At nodal point 2, the mass acting is $(m_1 + m_2)$ and is expressed as

$$(m_1 + m_2) = \left[\dfrac{W}{2Lg} + \dfrac{4W}{Lg}\right] = \dfrac{W}{2Lg}(1+8) = 9\left(\dfrac{W}{2Lg}\right) = 9m_1 = 9\lambda$$

Applying the governing finite difference equation

$$y_{n+2} - 4y_{n+1} + 6y_n - 4y_{n-1} + y_{n-2} = 0$$

For $n = 1$, we have

$$y_3 - 4y_2 + 6y_1 - 4y_2 + y_{-1} = 0$$

For $n = 2$, we have

$$y_4 - 4y_3 + 6y_2 - 4y_1 + y_0 = 0$$

The boundary conditions are

$$y_0 = y_4 = 0 \qquad y_1 = y_3 \qquad y_{-1} = -y_3 = -y_1$$

Hence we have

$$(6-\lambda)y_1 - 4y_2 = 0$$

$$-8y_1 - (6-9\lambda)y_2 = 0$$

The solution for these equations is possible only when the determinant

$$\begin{vmatrix} (6-\lambda) & -4 \\ -8 & (6-9\lambda) \end{vmatrix} = 0$$

$$(6-\lambda)(6-9\lambda) - 32 = 0$$

$$9\lambda^2 - 60\lambda + 4 = 0$$

Hence $\lambda = 0.067$ and 6.6

Selecting the least value of λ, we have

$$\lambda = 0.067 = \left(\frac{\omega^2 m h^4}{EI}\right)$$

or

$$\omega^2 = \left(\frac{0.067EI}{mh^4}\right) = \left[\frac{0.067EI(2Lg)}{W(L/4)^4}\right]$$

$$\omega^2 = \left(\frac{34.304EIg}{WL^3}\right)$$

Thus

$$\omega = 5.856\sqrt{\frac{EIg}{WL^3}}$$

The natural frequency of vibration of the beam is $f = \dfrac{\omega}{2\pi} = 0.932\sqrt{\dfrac{EIg}{WL^3}}$

Example 6.33

A beam of uniform section with a mass of 5000 kg/m is simply supported at one end and fixed at the other end as shown in Fig. 6.39. If the flexural rigidity of the beam is $EI = 50{,}000$ kg.m^2 and the span of the beam $L = 4$ m, estimate the natural frequency of vibration of the beam.

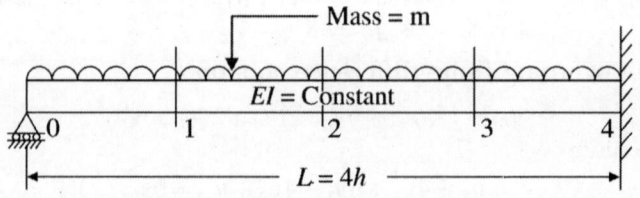

Fig. 6.39: Beam fixed at one end and simply supported at other end

The governing finite difference equation is expressed as

$$(y_{n+2} - 4y_{n+1} + (6-\lambda)y_n - 4y_{n-1} + y_{n-2}) = 0$$

At point 1, $n = 1$

$$\left(y_3 - 4y_2 + (6 - \lambda)y_1 - 4y_0 + y_{-1}\right) = 0$$

At point 2, $n = 2$

$$\left(y_4 - 4y_3 + (6 - \lambda)y_2 - 4y_1 + y_0\right) = 0$$

At point 3, $n = 3$

$$\left(y_5 - 4y_4 + (6 - \lambda)y_3 - 4y_2 + y_1\right) = 0$$

The boundary conditions are

$$y_0 = y_4 = 0 \qquad y_{-1} = -y_1 \qquad y_5 = y_3$$

Substituting the boundary conditions, the resulting equations are,

$$(5 - \lambda)y_1 - 4y_2 + y_3 = 0$$

$$-4y_1 - (6 - \lambda)y_2 - 4y_3 = 0$$

$$y_1 - 4y_2 + (7 - \lambda)y_3 = 0$$

Solution is possible if the determinant is zero

$$\begin{vmatrix} (5 - \lambda) & -4 & 1 \\ -4 & (6 - \lambda) & -4 \\ 1 & -4 & (7 - \lambda) \end{vmatrix} = 0.$$

Expanding and simplifying, we get

$$\lambda^3 - 18\lambda^2 + 74\lambda - 44 = 0$$

Solving by Graeffe's root squaring method, the values of obtained are

$$\lambda = 12.34, \quad 5.00, \quad 0.713$$

Selecting the least value of λ,

$$0.713 = \lambda = \left(\frac{\omega^2 m h^4}{EI}\right)$$

$$\omega^2 = \left(\frac{0.713 EI}{m h^4}\right) = \left(\frac{182.528 EI}{m L^4}\right)$$

Thus

$$\omega = 13.51 \sqrt{\frac{EI}{m L^4}}$$

The natural frequency of vibration of the beam is

$$f = \frac{\omega}{2\pi} = 2.15 \sqrt{\frac{EI}{m L^4}}$$

$$f = 2.15 \sqrt{\frac{50,000}{5000 \times 256}}$$

$$f = 0.42 \text{ cycles/second}$$

Example 6.34

A steel beam of uniform section is simply supported and carries loads as shown in Fig. 6.40 at quarter span points from either supports. Determine the lowest natural frequency of vibration of the beam neglecting the mass of the beam.

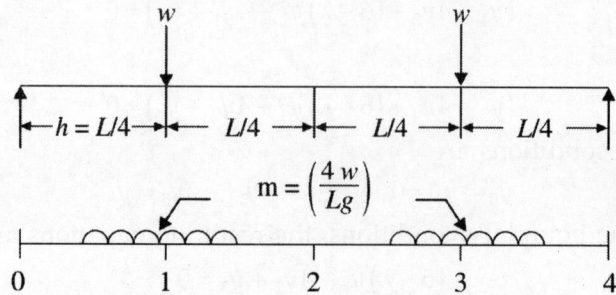

Fig. 6.40: Beam with two concentrated loads

Applying the finite difference equation, we have

$$y_{n-2} - 4y_{n-1} + (6 - \lambda)y_n - 4y_{n+1} + y_{n+2} = 0$$

For $n = 1$, we have

$$y_{-1} - 4y_0 + (6 - \lambda)y_1 - 4y_2 + y_3 = 0$$

For $n = 2$, we have

$$y_0 - 4y_1 + 6y_2 - 4y_3 + y_4 = 0$$

The boundary conditions are

$$y_{-1} = -y_1 \qquad y_0 = y_4 = 0 \qquad y_1 = y_3$$

Substituting the boundary conditions, we have the following relations:

$$(6 - \lambda)y_1 - 4y_2 = 0$$

$$-8y_1 + 6y_2 = 0$$

Solution is possible if the determinant is zero

$$\begin{vmatrix} (6 - \lambda) & -4 \\ -8 & 6 \end{vmatrix} = 0$$

Solving
$$\lambda = 0.67$$

$$0.67 = \lambda = \left(\frac{\omega^2 m h^4}{EI} \right)$$

Therefore
$$\omega = 13.088 \sqrt{\frac{EI}{mL^4}}$$

$$2\pi f = 13.088 \sqrt{\frac{EI}{\left(\frac{4W}{Lg} \right) L^4}}$$

$$f = 1.04 \sqrt{\frac{EIg}{WL^3}}$$

Example 6.35

A beam of length L is fixed at both ends and supports a concentrated load of W at the centre of span as shown in Fig. 6.41. Obtain an expression for the natural frequency of vibration of the beam neglecting the mass of the beam.

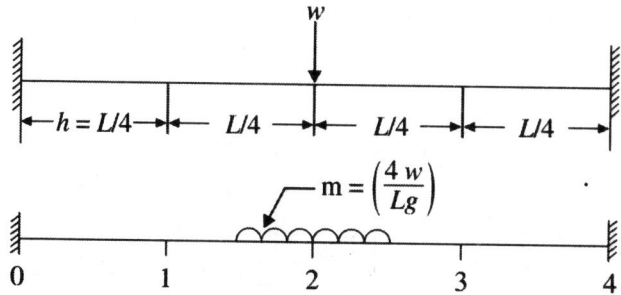

Fig. 6.41: Fixed beam with concentrated load

Solution

The governing finite difference equation is

$$y_{n-2} - 4y_{n-1} + (6-\lambda)y_n - 4y_{n+1} + y_{n+2} = 0$$

For $n = 1$, we have

$$y_{-1} - 4y_0 + (6-\lambda)y_1 - 4y_2 + y_3 = 0$$

For $n = 2$, we have

$$y_0 - 4y_1 + 6y_2 - 4y_3 + y_4 = 0$$

The boundary conditions are

$$y_{-1} = y_1 \qquad y_0 = y_4 = 0 \qquad y_1 = y_3$$

Substituting the boundary conditions, we have the following relations:

$$8y_1 - 4y_2 = 0$$

$$-8y_1 + (6-\lambda)y_2 = 0$$

Solving $\lambda = 2$

$$\lambda = \left(\frac{\omega^2 m h^4}{EI}\right) = 2$$

or

$$\omega = \sqrt{\left(\frac{2EI}{mh^4}\right)} = \sqrt{\frac{2EI}{\left(\frac{4W}{Lg}\right)h^4}}$$

$$\omega = 11.313\sqrt{\frac{EIg}{WL^3}}$$

$$2\pi f = 11.313\sqrt{\frac{EIg}{WL^3}}$$

$$f = 1.80\sqrt{\frac{EIg}{WL^3}}$$

6.7 BEAMS ON ELASTIC FOUNDATIONS

6.7.1 General Equations

In the case of beams resting on elastic foundations, the deflections are proportional to the spring constant of the elastic medium of the foundation. Consider a beam resting on elastic foundation as shown in Fig. 6.42.

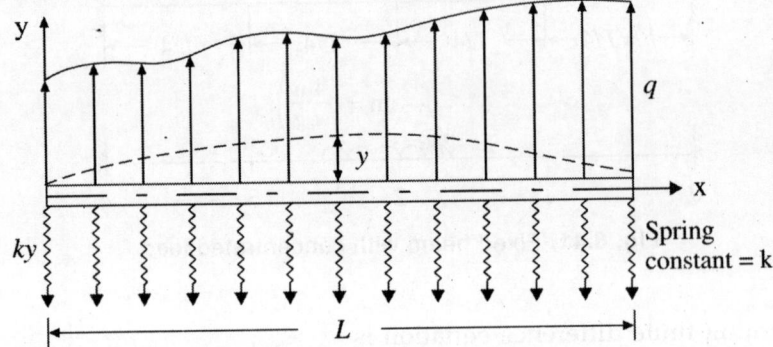

Fig. 6.42: Beam on elastic foundation

The governing differential equation is

$$EI\left(\frac{d^4y}{dx^4}\right) = -ky + q$$

where q = load on the beam

k = spring constant

Therefore $\left(\dfrac{d^4y}{dx^4}\right) = -\left(\dfrac{ky}{EI}\right) + \left(\dfrac{q}{EI}\right)$

The finite difference equation can be written as

$$\left[\frac{y_{n+2} - 4y_{n+1} + 6y_n - 4y_{n-1} + y_{n-2}}{h^4}\right] = -\left(\frac{ky_n}{EI}\right)$$

$$y_{n+2} - 4y_{n+1} + \left(6 + \frac{kh^4}{EI_n}\right)y_n - 4y_{n-1} + y_{n-2} = \left(\frac{q_n h^4}{EI_n}\right)$$

Introducing the nondimensional parameter

$$\beta = L \cdot \sqrt[4]{(k/EI_n)}$$

We have the finite difference equation as

$$y_{n+2} - 4y_{n+1} + \left(6 + \frac{\beta^4}{(L/h)^4}\right)y_n - 4y_{n-1} + y_{n-2} = \left(\frac{q_n h^4}{EI_n}\right)$$

If Z = number of divisions = (L/h), the equation can be written as

$$y_{n+2} - 4y_{n+1} + \left(6 + (\beta/Z)^4\right)y_n - 4y_{n-1} + y_{n-2} = \left(\frac{q_n h^4}{EI_n}\right)$$

Where q_n is positive when acting upward. The application of this equation to practical foundation problems is illustrated by the following examples.

Example 6.36

A concrete foundation strip 40 m long and having a cross section of 1 m by 1 m is resting on soil and supports concentrated loads of 1000 kN each at 10 m intervals as shown in Fig. 6.43.

If $E = 2 \times 10^7$ kN/m² and $k = 10^5$ kN/m², calculate the deflection and bending moments under the load points.

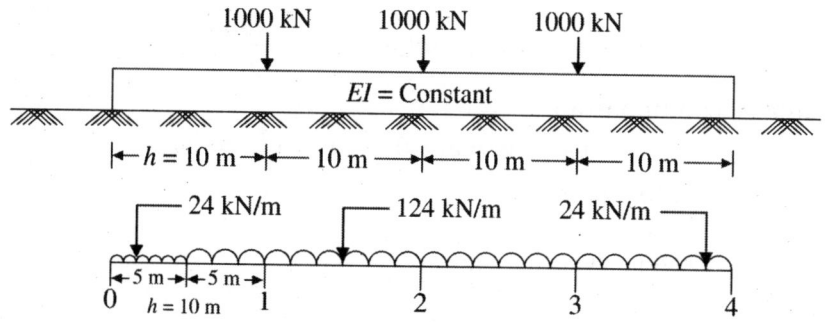

Fig. 6.43: Concrete strip footing foundation

Solution

Referring to Fig. 6.43, for the given concrete beam on elastic foundation, we have the following data:

$$k = 10^5 \, \text{kN/m}^2$$

$$I = \left(\frac{bd^3}{12}\right) = \left(\frac{1 \times 1^3}{12}\right) = \left(\frac{1}{12}\right) \, \text{kN/m}^2$$

$$E = 2 \times 10^7 \, \text{kN·m}^2$$

$$EI = \left(\frac{2 \times 10^7 \times 1}{12}\right) = 1.666 \times 10^6$$

The nondimensional parameter β is given by

$$\beta = L \cdot \sqrt[4]{\left(\frac{k}{EI_n}\right)} = 40 \times \sqrt[4]{\left(\frac{10^5}{1.666 \times 10^6}\right)} = 19.80$$

Number of divisions $= Z = (L/h) = \left(\frac{40}{10}\right) = 4$

Therefore $\left(\dfrac{\beta}{Z}\right)^4 = \left(\dfrac{19.80}{4}\right)^4 = 600$

The finite difference equation is written as

$$y_{n-2} - 4y_{n-1} + \left(6 + \left(\frac{\beta}{Z}\right)^4\right) y_n - 4y_{n+1} + y_{n+2} = \left(\frac{q_n h^4}{EI_n}\right)$$

For $n = 1$, we have

$$y_{-1} - 4y_0 + 606y_1 - 4y_2 + y_3 = -\left(\frac{124h^4}{EI}\right) \qquad (1)$$

For $n = 2$, we have

$$y_0 - 4y_1 + 606y_2 - 4y_3 + y_4 = -\left(\frac{124h^4}{EI}\right) \qquad (2)$$

For $n = 3$, we have

$$y_1 - 4y_2 + 606y_3 - 4y_4 + y_5 = -\left(\frac{124h^4}{EI}\right) \qquad (3)$$

The boundary conditions are

$$y_{-1} = -y_1 \qquad y_0 = y_4 = 0 \qquad y_1 = y_3 y_5 = -y_1$$

From Eqs (1) and (2), we have

$$600y_1 - 4y_2 = -\left(\frac{124h^4}{EI}\right) \qquad (4)$$

$$-8y_1 + 606y_2 = -\left(\frac{124h^4}{EI}\right) \qquad (5)$$

Substituting the values of $h = 10$ m and $EI = 1.666 \times 10^6 \, \text{kN} \cdot \text{m}^2$
and solving Eqs (4) and (5) we get

$$y_1 = -0.001227 \text{ m}$$
$$y_2 = -0.00129 \text{ m}$$

The moments at the points 1 and 2 are given by

$$M_1 = \frac{EI}{h^2}(y_2 - 2y_1 + y_0)$$

$$= \left(\frac{1.666 \times 10^6}{10^2}\right)\left[-0.00129 - 2(-0.001227)\right]$$

$$= 19.32 \text{ kN} \cdot \text{m}$$

$$M_2 = \frac{EI}{h^2}(y_3 - 2y_2 + y_1) = \frac{EI}{h^2}(2y_1 - 2y_2)$$

$$= \left(\frac{1.666 \times 10^6}{10^2}\right)\left[2(-0.001227 + 0.00129)\right]$$

$$= 1.0495 \text{ kN} \cdot \text{m}$$

Example 6.37

A beam supports a triangular load varying from zero at A to 100 kN/m at B as shown in Fig. 6.44. The length of the beam $L = 4$ m. Given the spring constant of the foundation $k = 10^5$ kN/m² and flexural rigidity of the beam $EI = 10^5 \, \text{kN} \cdot \text{m}^2$, calculate the deflections at the nodal points assuming four subintervals.

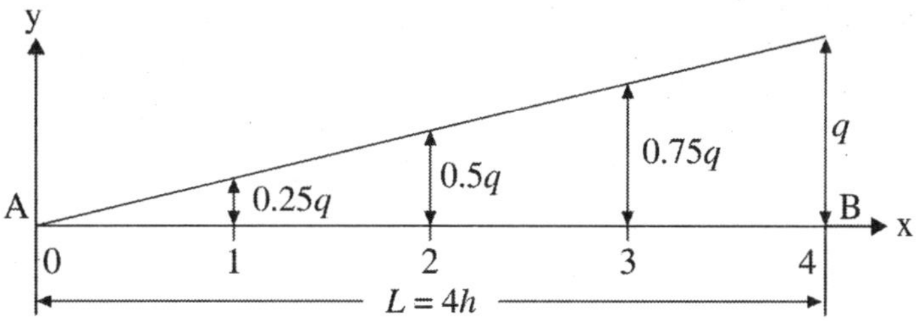

Fig. 6.44: Beam supporting triangular load

Solution

Referring to Fig. 6.44, we have the following parameters:

$$L = 4 \text{ m}$$
$$k = 10^5 \text{ kN/m}^2$$
$$EI = \text{kN·m}^2$$
$$q = 100 \text{ kN/m}$$
$$h = 1 \text{ m}$$

Therefore $\beta = L \cdot \sqrt[4]{\left(\dfrac{k}{EI_n}\right)} = 4 \times \sqrt[4]{\left(\dfrac{10^5}{10^5}\right)} = 4.0$

Number of divisions = $Z = (L/h) = 4$

$$\left(\frac{qh^4}{EI}\right) = \left(\frac{100 \times 1^4}{10^5}\right) \text{m} = \left(\frac{1}{10^3}\right) \text{m} = 1 \text{ mm}$$

The finite difference expression in terms of the relative rigidity of the foundation is given by

$$y_{n-2} - 4y_{n-1} + \left(6 + \left(\frac{\beta}{Z}\right)^4\right) y_n - 4y_{n+1} + y_{n+2} = \left(\frac{q_n h^4}{EI_n}\right)$$

Applying this equation to points 0, 1,2, 3 and 4 respectively, we have

$$y_{-2} - 4y_{-1} + 7y_0 - 4y_1 + y_2 = 0$$

$$y_{-1} - 4y_0 + 7y_1 - 4y_2 + y_3 = -\left(\frac{0.25qh^4}{EI}\right)$$

$$y_0 - 4y_1 + 7y_2 - 4y_3 + y_4 = -\left(\frac{0.5qh^4}{EI}\right)$$

$$y_1 - 4y_2 + 7y_3 - 4y_4 + y_5 = -\left(\frac{0.75qh^4}{EI}\right)$$

$$y_2 - 4y_3 + 7y_4 - 4y_5 + y_6 = -\left(\frac{qh^4}{EI}\right)$$

The boundary conditions are that the moments and shears at each end are zero.

$$M = EI\left(\frac{d^2 y}{dx^2}\right) \text{ and } V = \left(\frac{dM}{dx}\right)$$

For the point 0, we have

$$y_{n+1} - 2y_n + y_{n-1} = 0 \text{ and putting } n = 0 \text{ we have}$$

$$y_1 - 2y_0 + y_{-1} = 0 \text{ or } y_{-1} = (2y_0 - y_1)$$

Also $-y_{-2} + 2y_{-1} - 2y_1 + y_2 = 0$

Substituting for y_1

$$y_{-2} = (2y_{-1} - 2y_1 + y_2) = \left[2(2y_0 - y_1) - 2y_1 + y_2\right] = (4y_0 - 4y_1 + y_2)$$

The boundary conditions at the last pivotal point are given by

$$y_{n+1} = (2y_n - y_{n-1}) \text{ and } y_{n+2} = (4y_n - 4y_{n-1} + y_{n-2})$$

Substituting these boundary conditions, we get the following equations:

$$(3y_0 - 4y_1 + 2y_2) = 0$$

$$(-2y_0 + 6y_1 - 4y_2 + y_3) = -\left(\frac{0.25qh^4}{EI}\right)$$

$$(y_0 - 4y_1 + 7y_2 - 4y_3 + y_4) = -\left(\frac{0.5qh^4}{EI}\right)$$

$$(y_1 - 4y_2 + 6y_3 - 2y_4) = -\left(\frac{0.75qh^4}{EI}\right)$$

$$(2y_2 - 4y_3 + 3y_4) = -\left(\frac{qh^4}{EI}\right)$$

Solving these equations, we get the deflections as

$$y_0 = -0.007\left(\frac{qh^4}{EI}\right) = -0.007 \text{ mm}$$

$$y_1 = -0.245\left(\frac{qh^4}{EI}\right) = -0.245 \text{ mm}$$

$$y_2 = -0.493\left(\frac{qh^4}{EI}\right) = -0.493 \text{ mm}$$

$$y_3 = -0.751\left(\frac{qh^4}{EI}\right) = -0.751 \text{ mm}$$

$$y_4 = -1.000\left(\frac{qh^4}{EI}\right) = -1.000 \text{ mm}$$

Example 6.38

Evaluate the deflections at all pivotal points of a beam resting on elastic foundation shown in Fig. 6.45. Hence evaluate the bending moments at the pivotal points assuming the following data:

$$E = 10^7 \text{ kN/m}^2, \quad I = 1 \text{ m}^4, \quad k = 15 \times 10^4 \text{ kN/m}^2$$

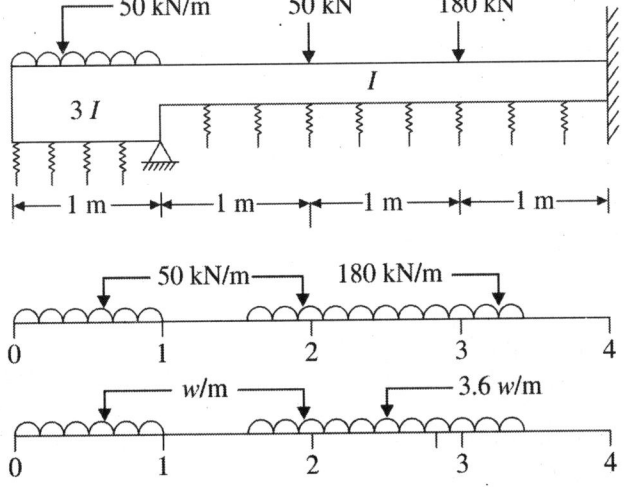

Fig. 6.45: Propped beam on elastic foundation

The finite difference equation can be written in the form

$$y_{n-2} - 4y_{n-1} + \left(6 + \frac{\beta^4}{Z^4}\right)y_n - 4y_{n+1} + y_{n+2} = \left(\frac{q_n h^4}{EI_n}\right)$$

where $\beta = L \cdot \sqrt[4]{\left(\frac{k}{EI}\right)}$

If Z = number of divisions = 4

$$\beta = L \cdot \sqrt[4]{\left(\frac{k}{EI}\right)} = 4. \sqrt[4]{\left(\frac{15 \times 10^4}{10^7 \times 1}\right)} = 1.4$$

Thus

$$\left(\frac{\beta}{Z}\right)^4 = \left(\frac{1.4}{4}\right)^4 = 0.015$$

Applying the finite difference equation to nodal points, 0, 2 and 3, we have

$$y_{-2} - 4y_{-1} + 6.015y_0 - 4y_1 + y_2 = -\left(\frac{0.5wh^4}{3EI}\right) \qquad (1)$$

$$- 4y_1 + 6.015y_2 - 4y_3 + y_4 = -\left(\frac{wh^4}{EI}\right) \qquad (2)$$

$$y_1 - 4y_2 + 6.015y_3 - 4y_4 + y_5 = -\left(\frac{3.6wh^4}{EI}\right) \qquad (3)$$

The boundary conditions are $y_1 = y_4 = 0$ and at $n = 0$, bending moment and shear force $= 0$.

Using the condition of SF $= 0$, we get

$$y_{n+2} - 2y_{n+1} + 2y_{n-1} - y_{n-2} = 0$$

$$y_2 - 2y_1 + 2y_{-1} - y_{-2} = 0$$

$$y_{-2} = 2y_{-1} - 2y_1 + y_2 \tag{4}$$

Using the condition BM $= 0$, we get

$$y_{n-1} - 2y_n + y_{n+1} = 0$$

$$y_{-1} - 2y_0 + y_1 = 0$$

$$y_{-1} = 2y_0 - y_1 \tag{5}$$

From Eqs (4) and (5), we have

$$y_{-2} = 2(2y_0 - y_1) - 2y_1 + y_2$$

$$y_{-2} = 4y_0 - 4y_1 + y_2 \tag{6}$$

Substituting from Eqs (5) and (6) in Eq. (1), we have

$$-4y_{-1} + 6.015y_0 - 4y_1 + y_2 = -\left(\frac{0.5wh^4}{3EI}\right)$$

$$4y_0 - 4y_1 + y_2 - 4(2y_0 - y_1) + 6.015y_0 - 4y_1 + y_2 = -0.167\left(\frac{wh^4}{EI}\right)$$

$$2.015y_0 + 2y_2 = -0.167\left(\frac{wh^4}{EI}\right) \tag{7}$$

$$y_0 + 6.015y_2 - 4y_3 = -\left(\frac{wh^4}{EI}\right) \tag{8}$$

$$-4y_2 + 7.015y_3 = -\left(\frac{3.6wh^4}{EI}\right) \tag{9}$$

From Eqs (7) and (9), we have

$$4.03y_0 + 4y_2 = -0.334\left(\frac{wh^4}{EI}\right)$$

$$7.015y_3 - 4y_2 = -3.6\left(\frac{wh^4}{EI}\right)$$

Therefore $$4.03y_0 + 7.015y_3 = -3.934\left(\frac{wh^4}{EI}\right) \tag{10}$$

From Eqs (8) and (9), we have

$$-6.015y_2 + 10.548y_3 = -5.4135\left(\frac{wh^4}{EI}\right)$$

$$y_0 + 6.015y_2 - 4y_3 = -\left(\frac{wh^4}{EI}\right)$$

Therefore $\qquad y_0 + 6.548y_3 = -6.4135\left(\frac{wh^4}{EI}\right)$ $\qquad$ (11)

Solving Eqs (10) and (11), we have

$$y_0 = \left(\frac{wh^4}{EI}\right)$$

$$y_2 = -\left(\frac{wh^4}{EI}\right)$$

$$y_3 = -1.13\left(\frac{wh^4}{EI}\right)$$

Hence the deflections are obtained as

$$y_0 = \left(\frac{50 \times 1^4}{10^7}\right) = \left(5 \times 10^{-6}\right) \text{ m}$$

$$y_2 = -\left(\frac{50 \times 1^4}{10^7}\right) = -\left(5 \times 10^{-6}\right) \text{ m}$$

$$= 0.87wh^2 = \left(0.87 \times 50 \times 1^2\right) \text{ m}$$

The bending moments at nodal point 1 is expressed as

$$M_1 = EI\left(\frac{d^2y}{dx^2}\right) = EI\left[\frac{y_{n+1} - 2y_n + y_{n-1}}{h^2}\right] = EI\left[\frac{y_2 - 2y_1 + y_0}{h^2}\right] = 0$$

Bending moment at nodal point 2 is evaluated as

$$M_2 = EI\left[\frac{y_3 - 2y_2 + y_1}{h^2}\right] = EI\left[\frac{-1.13 - 2(-1) + 0}{h^2}\right]\left(\frac{wh^4}{EI}\right) \text{kN} \cdot \text{m}$$

$$= 0.87wh^2 = \left(0.87 \times 50 \times 1^2\right)$$

$$= 43.5 \text{ kN} \cdot \text{m}$$

Bending moment at point 3 is computed as

$$M_3 = EI\left[\frac{y_4 - 2y_3 + y_2}{h^2}\right] = EI\left[\frac{-2(-1.13) - 1}{h^2}\right]\left(\frac{wh^4}{EI}\right)$$

$$= 1.26wh^2 = \left(1.26 \times 50 \times 1^2\right)$$

$$= 63 \text{ kN} \cdot \text{m}$$

Bending moment at point 4 is given by

$$M_4 = EI\left[\frac{y_5 - 2y_4 + y_3}{h^2}\right] \quad \text{Since } y_5 = y_3$$

$$= EI\left[\frac{2y_3}{h^2}\right] = EI\left[\frac{2(-1.13)}{h^2}\right]\left(\frac{wh^4}{EI}\right) = -113 \text{ kN·m}$$

Example 6.39

A beam of constant flexural rigidity rests on an elastic foundation whose spring constant varies from k to 0 linearly from A to B. The beam supports a triangular load of intensity q at the centre of the span, linearly reducing to zero at the supports as shown in Fig. 6.46. Estimate the deflections at the nodal points, considering eight divisions of the beam.

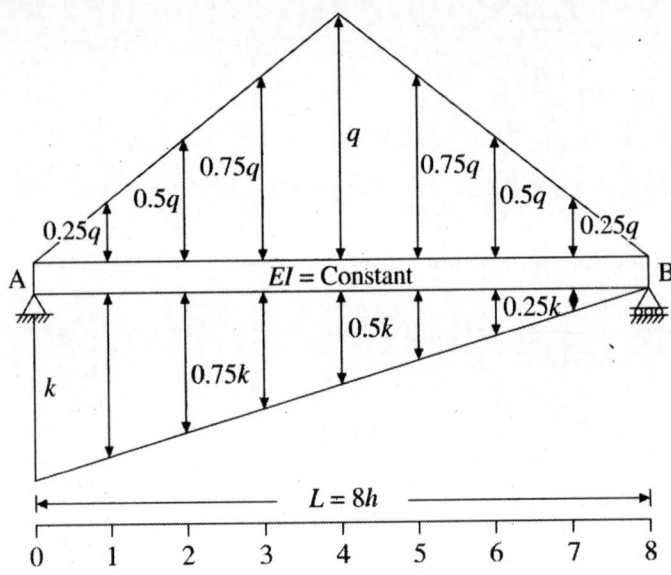

Fig. 6.46: Beam on elastic foundation with variable loading

Solution

Referring to Fig. 6.46

The governing differential equation is written as,

The governing finite difference equation is expressed as

$$\left(y_{n+2} - 4y_{n+1} + 6y_n - 4y_{n-1} + y_{n-2}\right) = \left(\frac{-ky}{EI} + \frac{q}{EI}\right)h^4$$

At point 1, $n = 1$

$$\left(y_3 - 4y_2 + 6y_1 - 4y_0 + y_{-1}\right) = -\left(\frac{0.875ky_1h^4}{EI}\right) + \left(\frac{0.25qh^4}{EI}\right) \tag{1}$$

At point 2, $n = 2$

$$\left(y_4 - 4y_3 + 6y_2 - 4y_1 + y_0\right) = -\left(\frac{0.75ky_2h^4}{EI}\right) + \left(\frac{0.5qh^4}{EI}\right) \tag{2}$$

At point 3, $n = 3$

$$\left(y_5 - 4y_4 + 6y_3 - 4y_2 + y_1\right) = -\left(\frac{0.025ky_3h^4}{EI}\right) + \left(\frac{0.75qh^4}{EI}\right) \tag{3}$$

At point 4, $n = 4$

$$\left(y_6 - 4y_5 + 6y_4 - 4y_3 + y_2\right) = -\left(\frac{0.5ky_4h^4}{EI}\right) + \left(\frac{qh^4}{EI}\right) \tag{4}$$

At point 5, $n = 5$

$$\left(y_7 - 4y_6 + 6y_5 - 4y_4 + y_3\right) = -\left(\frac{0.375ky_5h^4}{EI}\right) + \left(\frac{0.75qh^4}{EI}\right) \tag{5}$$

At point 6, $n = 6$

$$\left(y_8 - 4y_7 + 6y_6 - 4y_5 + y_4\right) = -\left(\frac{0.25ky_6h^4}{EI}\right) + \left(\frac{0.5qh^4}{EI}\right) \tag{6}$$

At point 7, $n = 7$

$$\left(y_9 - 4y_8 + 6y_7 - 4y_6 + y_5\right) = -\left(\frac{0.125ky_7h^4}{EI}\right) + \left(\frac{0.25qh^4}{EI}\right) \tag{7}$$

The boundary conditions are as follows:

At nodal point $n = 0$, the bending moment $M = 0$

Hence $\quad y_{n+1} - 2_n + y_{n-1} = 0$

$$y_1 - 2y_0 + y_{-1} = 0$$

Since $y_{-1} = -y_n$ and $y_0 = 0$

At nodal point $n = 8$, the bending moment $M = 0$

Hence $y_{n+1} - 2y_n + y_{n-1} = 0$

$$y_0 - 2y_8 + y_7 = 0$$

Since $\quad y_9 = -y_7$ and $y_8 = 0$

Rearranging the equations using the boundary conditions, we have the following relations:

$$5y_1 - 4y_2 + y_3 = -\left(\frac{0.875ky_1h^4}{EI}\right) + \left(\frac{0.25q_{h^4}}{EI}\right) \tag{8}$$

$$-4y_1 + 6y_2 - 4y_3 + y_4 = -\left(\frac{0.75ky_2h^4}{EI}\right) + \left(\frac{0.5qh^4}{EI}\right) \tag{9}$$

$$y_1 - 4y_2 + 6y_3 - 4y_4 + y_5 = -\left(\frac{0.625ky_3h^4}{EI}\right) + \left(\frac{0.75qh^4}{EI}\right) \tag{10}$$

$$y_2 - 4y_3 + 6y_4 - 4y_5 + y_6 = -\left(\frac{0.5ky_4h^4}{EI}\right) + \left(\frac{qh^4}{EI}\right) \tag{11}$$

$$y_3 - 4y_4 + 6y_5 - 4y_6 + y_7 = -\left(\frac{0.375ky_5h^4}{EI}\right) + \left(\frac{0.75qh^4}{EI}\right) \qquad (12)$$

$$y_4 - 4y_5 + 6y_6 - 4y_7 = -\left(\frac{0.25ky_6h^4}{EI}\right) + \left(\frac{0.5qh^4}{EI}\right) \qquad (13)$$

$$y_5 - 4y_6 + 5y_7 = -\left(\frac{0.125ky_7h^4}{EI}\right) + \left(\frac{0.25qh^4}{EI}\right) \qquad (14)$$

By solving Eqs (8) to (14), we can evaluate the deflections y_1 to y_7 at various nodal points.

6.8 MEMBRANE PROBLEMS

6.8.1 General Equations

A thin membrane is the space counterpart of the plane cable and the load is supported by the development of tensile stresses in the membrane acting at each point of the slope of the membrane. Consider a thin membrane stretched at edges by a tensile force 's' per unit length as shown in Fig. 6.47. The membrane is subjected to a lateral load of intensity 'w' per unit area. This causes the membrane to deflect slightly in the 'z' direction.

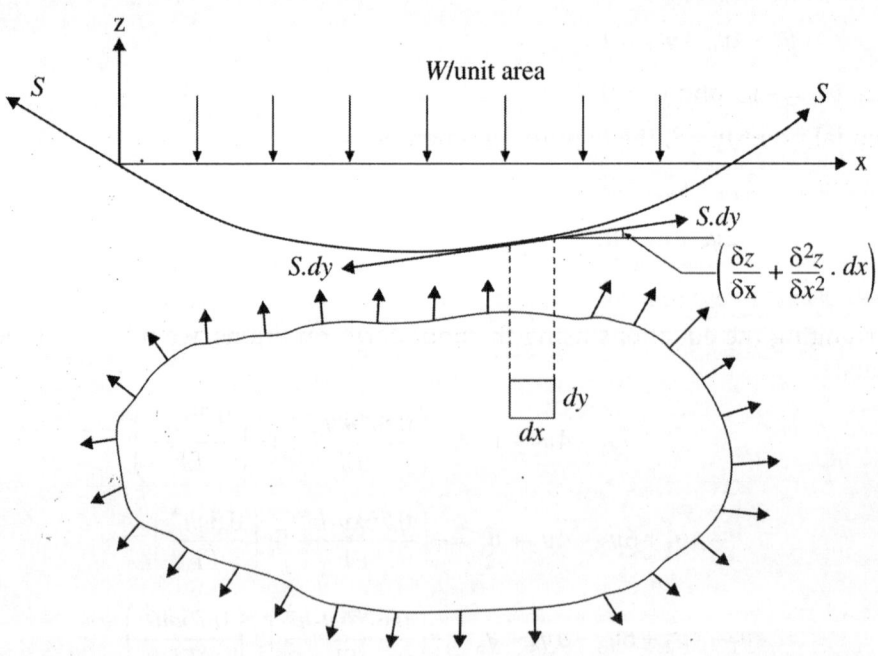

Fig.6.47: Lateral deflections of a thin membrane

Assuming the weight of the membrane is negligible, and resolving the forces in the 'z' direction, the equilibrium equation can be written as,

$$s \cdot \left(\frac{\partial^2 z}{\partial x^2} \right) \cdot dx + s \cdot \left(\frac{\partial^2 y}{\partial y^2} \right) \cdot dx \cdot dy - w \cdot dx \cdot dy = 0$$

or

$$\left[\frac{\partial^2 z}{\partial x^2} + \frac{\partial^2 y}{\partial y^2} \right] = \left(\frac{w}{s} \right); \text{ the deflection at the boundaries, } z = 0$$

The above equation is referred to as Poisson's equation, written in the form

$$\nabla^2 z = \left(\frac{w}{s} \right) \text{ where } \nabla^2 = \left[\frac{\partial^2}{\partial x^2} + \frac{\partial^2}{\partial y^2} \right] = \text{operator and } \left(\frac{w}{s} \right) \text{ is a constant.}$$

The typical finite difference equation with equal spacing's of interval h is written as

$$(z_{i,\,j+1} + z_{i,\,j-1} + z_{i,\,j+1} + z_{i,\,j-1} - 4z_{i,\,j}) = \left(\frac{h^2 \cdot w}{s} \right)$$

The sign convention being that the downward deflections are negative.

The finite difference equation can easily be written by referring to the coefficients of the equation shown in Fig. 6.48. The use of this equation is illustrated by the following examples.

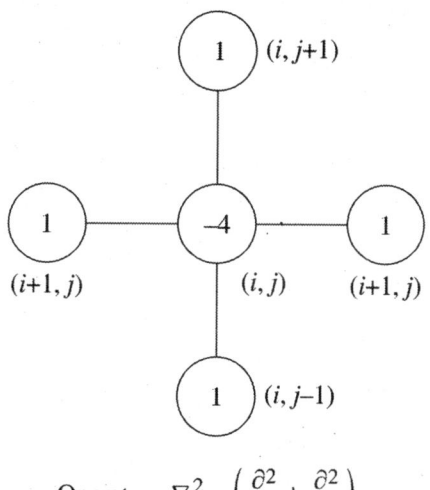

$$\text{Operator} : \nabla^2 = \left(\frac{\partial^2}{\partial x^2} + \frac{\partial^2}{\partial y^2} \right)$$

Fig. 6.48: Coefficients of Poisson's equation

Example 6.40

A thin membrane is stretched with a constant tensile force of 100 N/cm across a square frame, the length of the sides being 600 mm. The uniform lateral load on the membrane is 1 N/cm². Find the deflections at the various grid points at 10 cm intervals. Also find the maximum slope of the membrane.

Solution

Consider the membrane shown in Fig. 6.49 and using symmetry considerations, only six pivotal points (1 to 6) are to be considered.

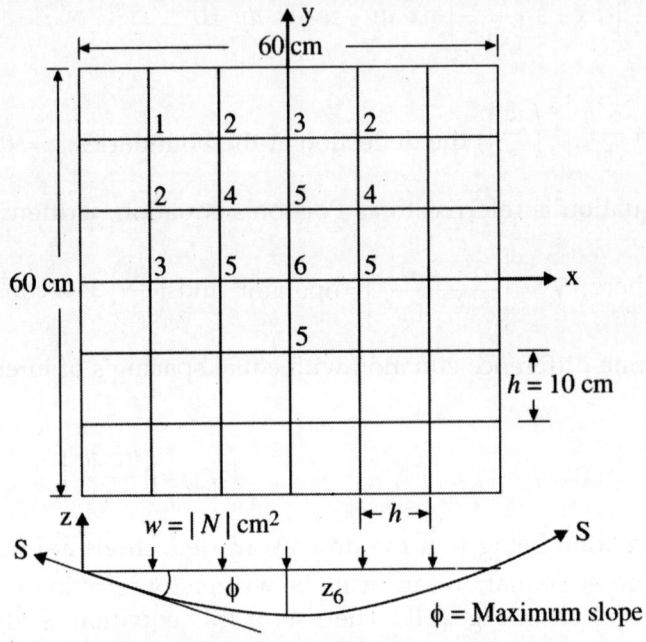

Fig. 6.49: Laterally loaded membrane

The deflections at the boundaries are zero. Applying the finite difference equation to each of these pivotal points 1, 2, 3, 4, 5 and 6 respectively, we have the following equations.

$$-4z_1 + 2z_2 \dots\dots\dots\dots\dots\dots\dots\dots = \left(\frac{h^2 \cdot w}{s}\right)$$

$$z_1 - 4z_2 + z_3 + z_4 \dots\dots\dots\dots\dots\dots = \left(\frac{h^2 \cdot w}{s}\right)$$

$$2z_2 - 4z_3 + z_5 \dots\dots\dots\dots\dots\dots = \left(\frac{h^2 \cdot w}{s}\right)$$

$$2z_2 - 4z_4 + 2z_5 \dots\dots\dots\dots\dots\dots = \left(\frac{h^2 \cdot w}{s}\right)$$

$$z_3 + 2z_4 - 4z_5 + z_6 \dots\dots\dots\dots\dots = \left(\frac{h^2 \cdot w}{s}\right)$$

$$4z_5 - 4z_6 \dots\dots\dots\dots\dots\dots\dots = \left(\frac{h^2 \cdot w}{s}\right)$$

Solving these equations and substituting the values,

$$h = 10 \text{ cm} \qquad w = 1 \text{ N/cm}^2 \qquad s = 100 \text{ N/cm} \quad \text{and} \quad \left(\frac{h^2 \cdot w}{s}\right) = 1$$

we get the deflections at the nodal points as,

$$z_1 = -0.95\left(\frac{h^2 \cdot w}{s}\right) = -0.95 \text{ cm}$$

$$z_2 = -1.45\left(\frac{h^2 \cdot w}{s}\right) = -1.45 \text{ cm}$$

$$z_3 = -1.54\left(\frac{h^2 \cdot w}{s}\right) = -1.54 \text{ cm}$$

$$z_4 = -2.12\left(\frac{h^2 \cdot w}{s}\right) = -2.12 \text{ cm}$$

$$z_5 = -2.34\left(\frac{h^2 \cdot w}{s}\right) = -2.34 \text{ cm}$$

$$z_6 = -2.59\left(\frac{h^2 \cdot w}{s}\right) = -2.59 \text{ cm}$$

The maximum slope occurs at point 3 and is evaluated as

$$\phi_{max} = \left(\frac{z_3 - 0}{h}\right) = \left(\frac{1.54}{10}\right) = 0.154 \text{ radians}$$

Example 6.41

A thin membrane is stretched with a constant tensile force of 2 N/mm at the boundary as shown in Fig. 6.50. The membrane is laterally loaded with a pressure of 0.001 N/mm². Determine the deflection of the membrane at the pivotal points and the maximum slope of the membrane. Adopt nodal points at 100 mm intervals.

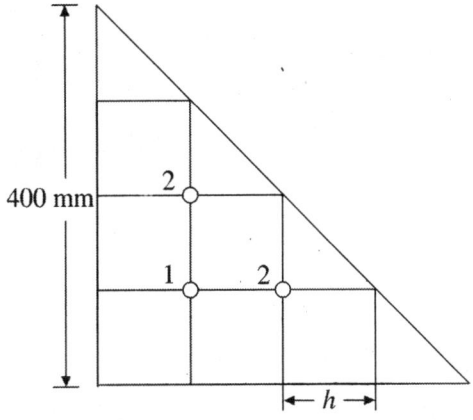

Fig. 6.50: Laterally loaded triangular shaped membrane

Solution

Referring to Fig. 6.50, the finite difference equation applied to points 1 and 2 are as follows:

$$2z_2 - 4z_1 = \left(\frac{h^2 \cdot w}{s}\right)$$

$$z_1 - 4z_2 = \left(\frac{h^2 \cdot w}{s}\right)$$

Solving these two equations, we get the values of

$$z_1 = -0.4285\left(\frac{h^2 \cdot w}{s}\right)$$

$$z_2 = -0.3570\left(\frac{h^2 \cdot w}{s}\right)$$

Substituting the values of $h = 100$ mm, $w = 0.001$ N/mm^2 and $s = 2$ N/mm

$$\left(\frac{h^2 \cdot w}{s}\right) = \left(\frac{100^2 \times 0.001}{2}\right) = 5 \text{ mm}$$

Therefore
$$z_1 = (-0.4285 \times 5) = -2.14 \text{ mm}$$
$$z_2 = (-0.3570 \times 5) = -1.785 \text{ mm}$$

The maximum slope occurs at point 1 and is obtained as

$$\phi_{max} = \left(\frac{z_1 - 0}{h}\right) = \left(\frac{2.14}{100}\right) = 0.0214 \text{ radians}$$

Example 6.42

Determine the lateral deflections of a membrane with boundaries of the frame shown in Fig. 6.51 subjected toa lateral load intensity of 0.05 N/mm^2. The boundary force is 1 N/mm^2. Adopt 100 mm grids.

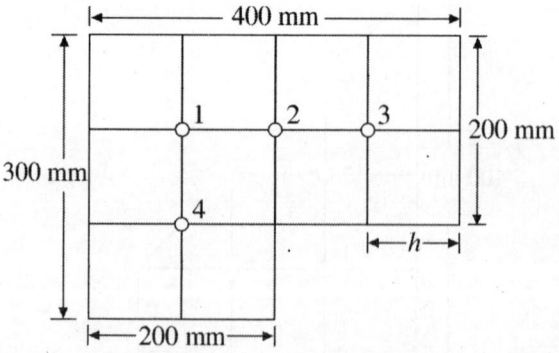

Fig. 6.51: Laterally loaded membrane

Solution

Referring to Fig. 6.51 and applying the finite difference equation to nodal points 1, 2, 3 and 4, we have the following equations:

For point 1,

$$z_2 + z_4 - 4z_1 = \left(h^2 \cdot \frac{w}{s}\right)$$

For point 2,

$$z_3 + z_1 - 4z_2 = \left(h^2 \cdot \frac{w}{s}\right)$$

For point 3,

$$z_2 - 4z_3 = \left(h^2 \cdot \frac{w}{s}\right)$$

For point 4,

$$z_1 - 4z_4 = \left(h^2 \cdot \frac{w}{s}\right)$$

Solving the four equations and substituting the values of

$$h = 100 \text{ mm}, \qquad w = 0.05 \text{ N/mm}^2, \qquad s = 1 \text{ N/mm}$$

The deflections at the nodal points are obtained as

$z_1 = -22.68 \text{ mm}$
$z_2 = -22.58 \text{ mm}$
$z_3 = -18.13 \text{ mm}$
$z_4 = -18.17 \text{ mm}$

The maximum slope develops at the nodal point 1 and is evaluated as

$$\phi_{max} = \phi_1 = \left(\frac{z_1 - 0}{h}\right) = \left(\frac{22.68 - 0}{100}\right) = 0.2268 \text{ radians}$$

Example 6.43

Determine the nodal deflections and the maximum slope in the membrane shown in Fig. 6.52, when it is laterally loaded with a pressure intensity of 0.03 N/mm². The boundary force is 1.5 N/mm². Adopt 20 mm grids.

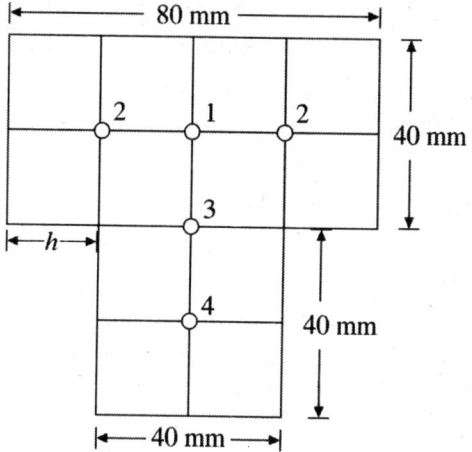

Fig. 6.52: Laterally loaded membrane

Referring to Fig. 6.52 and applying the finite difference equation to nodal points 1, 2, 3 and 4, we have the following equations:

$$2z_2 + z_3 - 4z_1 = \left(h^2 \cdot \frac{w}{s} \right)$$

$$z_1 - 4z_2 = \left(h^2 \cdot \frac{w}{s} \right)$$

$$z_1 - 4z_3 + z_4 = \left(h^2 \cdot \frac{w}{s} \right)$$

$$z_3 - 4z_4 = \left(h^2 \cdot \frac{w}{s} \right)$$

Solving the equations, we get the deflections as

$$z_1 = -0.3479 \left(h^2 \cdot \frac{w}{s} \right)$$

$$z_2 = -0.3916 \left(h^2 \cdot \frac{w}{s} \right)$$

$$z_3 = -0.4255 \left(h^2 \cdot \frac{w}{s} \right)$$

$$z_4 = -0.3563 \left(h^2 \cdot \frac{w}{s} \right)$$

Substituting the values of $h = 20$ mm $w = 0.03$ N/mm^2 $s = 1.5$ N/mm

$$\left(h^2 \cdot \frac{w}{s} \right) = \left(20^2 \times \frac{0.03}{1.5} \right) = 8$$

The deflections at the nodal points are obtained as

$$z_1 = (-0.3479 \times 8) = -2.7832 \text{ mm}$$
$$z_2 = (-0.3916 \times 8) = -3.1328 \text{ mm}$$
$$z_3 = (-0.4255 \times 8) = -3.4040 \text{ mm}$$
$$z_4 = (-0.3563 \times 8) = -2.8504 \text{ mm}$$

The maximum slope develops at the nodal point 3 and is evaluated as,

$$\phi_{max} = \phi_3 = \left(\frac{z_3 - 0}{h} \right) = \left(\frac{3.4040}{20} \right) = 0.1702 \text{ radians}$$

6.9 TORSION PROBLEMS

6.9.1 Membrane Analogy

Torsion of prismatic bars having different types of cross sections can be solved by membrane analogy proposed by Prandtl in 1903. The problem of elastic torsion of a prismatic bar is analogous to the problem of a laterally loaded membrane.

Consider the relation,

$$(w/s) = 2 \, G\theta$$

where w = Lateral load on membrane per unit area

   s = Tensile stretching force at the periphery of the membrane per unit length

   G = Rigidity or shear modulus of the material of the bar

   θ = Angle of twist per unit length of the bar

  Let M_t = Torque applied on the bar

   τ = Shear stress developed in the bar

   A membrane is stretched over the cross-section of the prismatic bar as shown in Fig. 6.53.

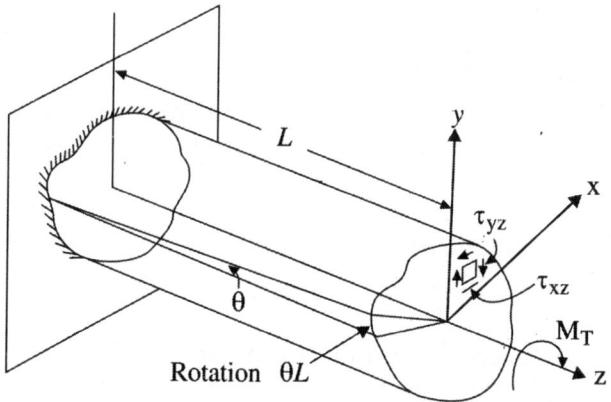

(a) Shaft subjected to torque M_T

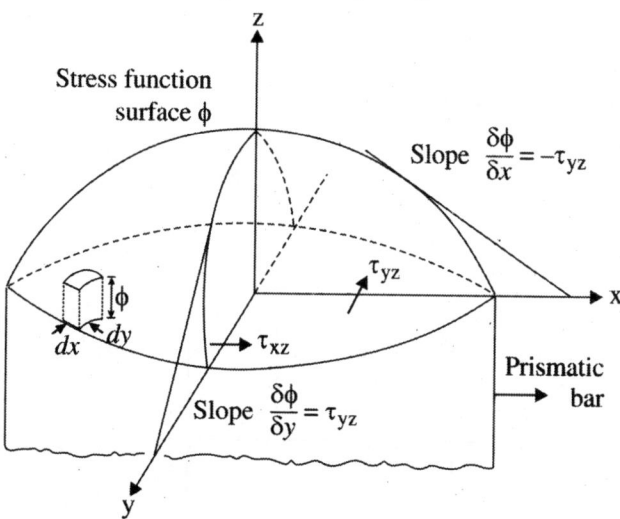

(b) Membrane stretched on cross-section

Fig. 6.53: Torsion of prismatic bars

The important observations made by Prandtl are as follows:

1. The deflection contour lines of the membrane correspond to the lines of shear stress in the bar.

2. The maximum slope at any point of the deflected surface is equal to the magnitude of the shear stress at the corresponding point of the twisted bar.

3. The torque applied on the twisted bar is given by twice the volume included between the surface of the deflected membrane and its plane before deflection.

The propositions listed above are expressed mathematically as follows:

$$\nabla^2 \phi = -2G\theta$$

where ϕ = torsion function

$$\left(\frac{\partial \phi}{\partial y}\right) = \tau_{xz} \text{ and } \left(\frac{\partial \phi}{\partial x}\right) = \tau_{yz}$$

$$M_T = 2\iint \phi \cdot dx \cdot dy = 2V$$

where V = volume included between the surface of the deflected membrane and its plane before deflection.

Using these propositions, we can calculate the shear stresses and the angle of twist in prismatic bars having square, triangular ELL and Tee sections, utilizing finite difference technique.

The application of membrane analogy along with finite difference method to torsional problems of prismatic bars of different types of cross-section is illustrated by the following numerical problems.

Example 6.44

A shaft of square cross-section 400 mm is subjected to a torque of 25 kN·m. Using finite difference analogy, determine the following (Fig. 6.54):

1. The angle of twist of the shaft per unit length
2. The torsional shear stress at all pivotal points at intervals of 100 mm
3. The maximum shear stress

Solution

Assume the value of G = 12000 N/mm²

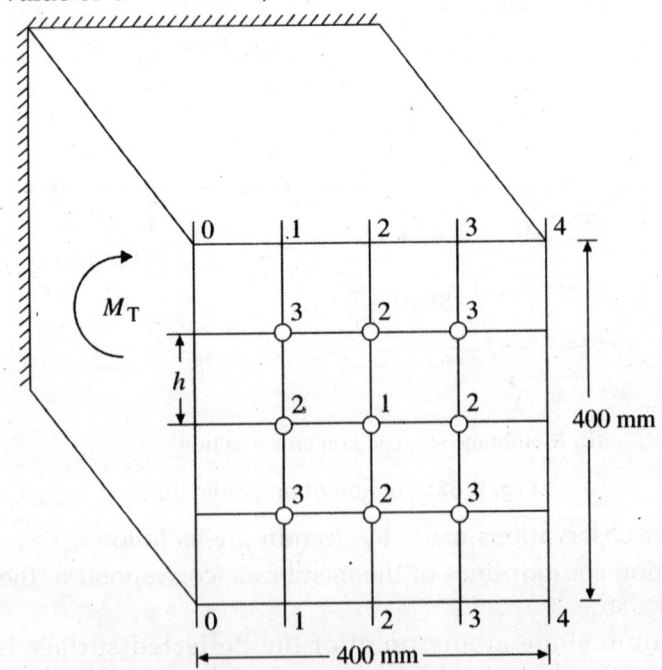

Fig. 6.54: Square shaft subjected to torsion

Referring to Fig. 6.54 and applying finite difference equations to nodal points 1, 2 and 3, we have the following equations:

$$-4z_1 + 4z_2 = \left(h^2 \cdot \frac{w}{s}\right)$$

$$z_1 - 4z_2 + 2z_3 = \left(h^2 \cdot \frac{w}{s}\right)$$

$$2z_2 - 4z_3 = \left(h^2 \cdot \frac{w}{s}\right)$$

Solving these equations the lateral deflections at the nodal points are obtained as

$$z_1 = -1.125\left(h^2 \cdot \frac{w}{s}\right)$$

$$z_2 = -0.875\left(h^2 \cdot \frac{w}{s}\right)$$

$$z_3 = -0.688\left(h^2 \cdot \frac{w}{s}\right)$$

Considering the sections, 0–0, 1–1, 2–2, 3–3, and 4–4 shown in Fig. 6.54, the area between the deflected membrane and the plane of the shaft along these sections are obtained by Simpson rule.

$$A_{00} = 0$$

$$A_{11} = (h/3)[0 + 4z_1 + 2z_2 + 4z_3 + 0] = 2.416\left(h^3 \cdot \frac{w}{s}\right)$$

$$A_{22} = (h/3)[0 + 4z_2 + 2z_1 + 4z_2 + 0] = 3.083\left(h^3 \cdot \frac{w}{s}\right)$$

Hence the volume V is computed as

$$V = (h/3)[A_{00} + 4A_{11} + 2A_{22} + 4A_{11} + A_{00}] = 8.5\left(h^4 \cdot \frac{w}{s}\right)$$

$$M_T = M_T = 2V = 17\left(h^4 \cdot \frac{w}{s}\right)$$

Since $\left(\dfrac{w}{s}\right) = 2G\theta$

$$M_T = (17 \times 2G\theta \times h^4) = 34G\theta h^4$$

The side length of the square section = a = 400 mm

Nodal interval = h = 100 mm, Hence $h = (a/4)$

Therefore $M_T = 34G\theta h^4 = 0.1328\ G\theta a^4$

This result compares favorably with the classical solution of

$$M_T = 0.1406\ G\theta a^4$$

Substituting the value of torque, we have

$$(25 \times 10^6) = (34 \times 12000 \times \theta \times 100^4)$$

Hence $\theta = (0.612 \times 10^{-6})$ radians.

The maximum slope which is equal to the shear stress, occurs at point 2 and computed as,

$$\phi_{max} = \tau_{max} = \tau_2 = \left(\frac{z_2 - 0}{h}\right)\left(\frac{wh^2}{s}\right) = \left(\frac{0.875wh^2}{h \cdot s}\right) = 0.875(wh/s)$$

$$\tau_2 = (0.875 \times 2G\theta \times h)$$
$$= (0.875 \times 2 \times 12000 \times 0.612 \times 10^{-6} \times 100)$$
$$= 1.2852 \ N/mm^2$$

$$\tau_1 = \left(\frac{z_1 - z_2}{h}\right) = \left(\frac{1.125 - 0.875}{h}\right)\left(\frac{wh^2}{s}\right)$$

$$= 0.25 \ (wh/s)$$
$$= (0.25 \times G\theta \times h)$$
$$= (0.25 \times 2 \times 12000 \times 0.612 \times 10^{-6} \times 100)$$
$$= 0.3672 \ N/mm^2$$

$$\tau_3 = \tau_3 = \left(\frac{z_3 - 0}{h}\right) = 0.688(wh/s)$$

$$= (0.688 \times 2G\theta \times h)$$
$$= (0.688 \times 2 \times 12000 \times 0.612 \times 10^{-6} \times 100)$$
$$= 1.01 \ N/mm^2$$

Example 6.45

A bar of triangular section shown in Fig. 6.55 is subjected to a twisting moment of 30 kN·m. Using f membrane analogy, determine the shear stress at the nodal points and the angle of twist per unit length of the shaft, assuming the nodal interval as 100 mm. Adopt $G = 10000 \ N/mm^2$.

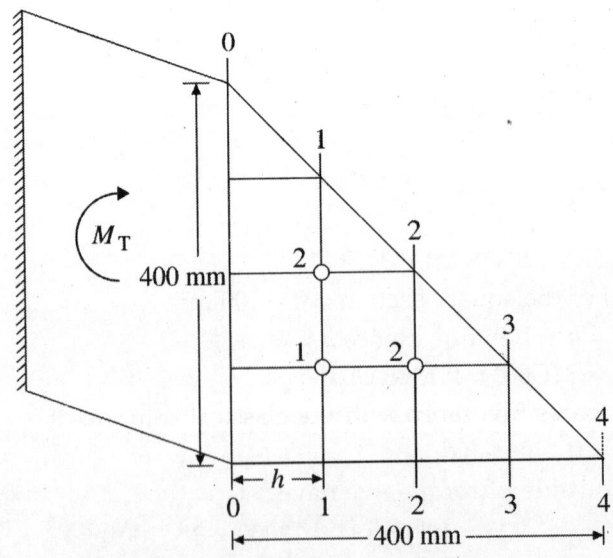

Fig. 6.55: Triangular shaft subjected to torque

Referring to the procedure adopted in Example 6.41, the deflection of the membrane at nodal points 1 and 2 are obtained as,

$$z_1 = -0.4285 \ (h^2 \cdot w/s)$$
$$z_2 = -0.3570 \ (h^2 \cdot w/s)$$

From Fig. 6.55, the areas under section 1–1 and 2–2 are computed as:

$$A_{11} = (h/3) \ [4z_1 + 2z_2] = 0.81 \ (wh^3/s)$$
$$A_{22} = (h/3) \ [4z_2] = 0.48 \ (wh^3/s)$$
$$A_{00} = A_{33} = A_{44} = 0$$

Hence the volume under the membrane is given by

$$V = (h/3) \ [4A_{11} + A_{22}] = 1.4044 \ (wh^4/s)$$

$$M_T = 2V = \left[2 \times 1.4044 \left(\frac{wh^4}{s}\right)\right] = 2.8088 \left(\frac{wh^4}{s}\right)$$

Since $\left(\dfrac{w}{s}\right) = 2G\theta$

$$M_T = [2.8088 \times 2 \times 10000 \times \theta \times 100^4] = (30 \times 10^6)$$

Therefore $\quad \theta = (5.34 \times 10^{-6})$ radians

Shear stress = slope at that point

$$\phi_1 = \left(\frac{z_1 - 0}{h}\right) = 0.4285 \ (wh/s)$$

$$\phi_2 = \left(\frac{z_2 - 0}{h}\right) = 0.3570 \ (wh/s)$$

$$\tau_1 = (0.4285 \times 2G\theta \times h)$$
$$= (0.4285 \times 2 \times 10000 \times 5.34 \times 10^{-6} \times 100)$$
$$= 4.576 \ \text{N/mm}^2$$
$$\tau_2 = (0.3570 \times 2G\theta \times h)$$
$$= (0.3570 \times 2 \times 10000 \times 5.34 \times 10^{-6} \times 100)$$
$$= 3.812 \ \text{N/mm}^2$$

Example 6.46

Estimate the maximum shear stress intensity in a prismatic bar of cross-section as shown in Fig. 6.56, by using membrane analogy and finite differences. The bar is subjected to a torsional moment of 20 kN·m. Assume the modulus of rigidity of the material as 12000 N/mm². Adopt a grid spacing of 20 mm equal in both directions. Also evaluate the angle of twist per unit length of the shaft.

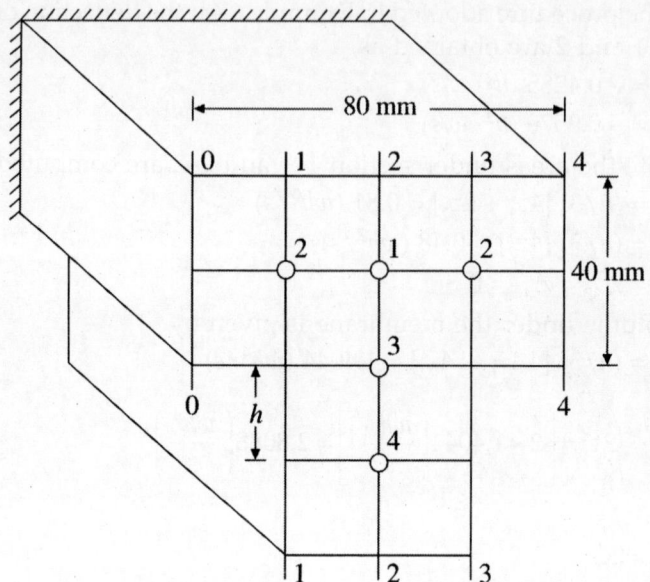

Fig. 6.56: Prismatic bar subjected to torque

Solution

Referring to Example 6.43, the deflections under the membrane at nodal points 1, 2, 3 and 4 are given by

$$z_1 = -0.3479 \; (wh^2/s)$$
$$z_2 = -0.3917 \; (wh^2/s)$$
$$z_3 = -0.4255 \; (wh^2/s)$$
$$z_4 = -0.3563 \; (wh^2/s)$$

Applying Simpson's rule to determine the areas under the membrane at sections 1–1, 2–2 and 3–3,

we have

$$A_{11} = (h/3) \, [0 + 4(0) + 2(0) + 4z_2 + 0] = 0.5220 \; (wh^3/s)$$
$$A_{22} = (h/3) \, [0 + 4z_4 + 2z_3 + 4z_1 + 0] = 1.2226 \; (wh^3/s)$$

Hence the volume under the membrane is

$$V = \left(\frac{h}{3}\right) \! \left[A_{00} + 4A_{11} + 2A_{22} + 4A_{33} + A_{44}\right]$$

Since $\quad A_{00} = A_{44} = 0$ and $A_{11} = A_{33}$

$$V = \left(\frac{h}{3}\right) \! \left[(4 \times 0.5220) + 2(1.2226) + (4 \times 0.5220)\right](wh^3/s)$$

$$= 2.207 \; (wh^4/s)$$

Since $\quad (w/s) = 2G\theta$

$$M_T = 2V = (2 \times 2.207 \times 2G\theta \times h^4) = 8.828G\theta h^4$$

Hence $\;(20 \times 10^6) = 8.828 \; G\theta h^4 = [8.828 \times 12000 \times \theta \times 20^4]$

Solving $\qquad \theta = (1.1799 \times 10^{-3})$ radians

$$\text{Maximum slope} = \phi_4 = \left(\frac{z_4 - 0}{h}\right) = 0.3563 \ (wh/s)$$

$$\begin{aligned}
\tau_{max} = \tau_4 &= (0.3563 \times 2G\theta \times h) \\
&= (0.3563 \times 2 \times 12000 \times 1.1799 \times 10^{-3} \times 20) \\
&= 201.79 \ \text{N/mm}^2
\end{aligned}$$

6.10 BENDING OF LATERALLY LOADED THIN PLATES

6.10.1 General Equations

The governing differential equation of a thin plate supporting lateral load of intensity 'w' per unit area is given by

$$\nabla^4 Z = (w/D)$$

Where the operator

$$\nabla^4 = \left[\frac{\partial^4}{\partial x^4} + \frac{2\partial^4}{\partial x^2 \cdot \partial y^2} + \frac{\partial^4}{\partial y^4}\right]$$

z = Upward deflection (+ ve)

w = Intensity of uniformly distributed load per unit area of the plate

D = Stiffness of the plate = $[Et^3/12(1 - \mu^2)]$

t = Thickness of the plate

E = Modulus of elasticity

μ = Poisson's ratio

The bending moments M_x, M_y and torsional moments M_{xy}, M_{yx} and shear forces V_x, V_y per unit length are related to deflections and expressed as detailed below:

$$M_x = D\left[\frac{\partial^2 z}{\partial x^2} + \mu \cdot \frac{\partial^2 z}{\partial y^2}\right]$$

$$M_y = D\left[\frac{\partial^2 z}{\partial y^2} + \mu \cdot \frac{\partial^2 z}{\partial x^2}\right]$$

$$M_{xy} = M_{yx} = D(1-\mu)\left[\frac{\partial^2 z}{\partial x \cdot \partial y}\right]$$

$$V_x = D \cdot \frac{\partial}{\partial x}\left[\frac{\partial^2 z}{\partial x^2} + \frac{\partial^2 z}{\partial y^2}\right] = D \cdot \frac{\partial}{\partial x}[\nabla^2 z]$$

$$V_y = D \cdot \frac{\partial}{\partial y}\left[\frac{\partial^2 z}{\partial x^2} + \frac{\partial^2 z}{\partial y^2}\right] = D \cdot \frac{\partial}{\partial y}[\nabla^2 z]$$

The notations and their positive directions are as shown in Fig. 6.57.

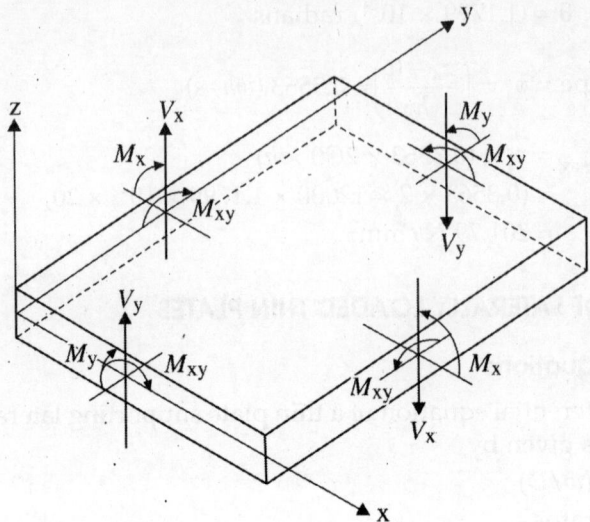

Fig. 6.57: Moments and forces in laterally loaded plate

The finite difference equation in Cartesian coordinates for a plate with nodal points shown in Fig. 6.58 is expressed as

$$\nabla^4 z = \left(\frac{h^4 w}{D}\right)$$

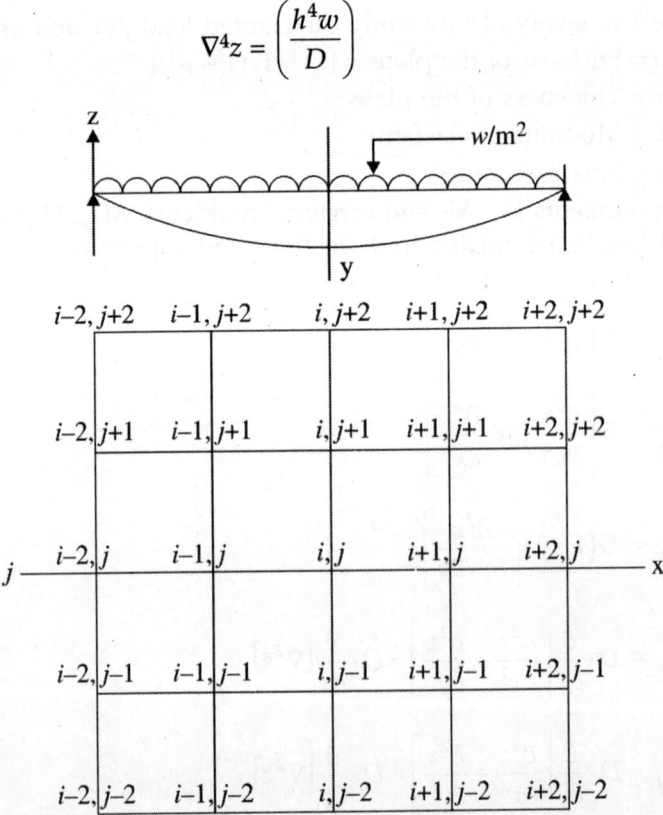

Fig. 6.58: Cartesian coordinates at various nodal points in a laterally loaded plate

where the operator ∇^4 can be expressed in terms of the deflections at the various nodes (i, j) as

$$\nabla^4 = 20z_{ij} - 8\left[z_{i,\,j+1} + z_{i,\,j-1} + z_{i+1,\,j} + z_{i-1,\,j}\right]$$

$$+ 2\left[z_{i+1,\,j+1} + z_{i+1,\,j-1} + z_{i-1+1,\,j+1} + z_{i-1,\,j-1}\right]$$

$$+ 1\left[z_{i,\,j+2} + z_{i+2,\,j} + z_{i-2,\,j} + z_{i,\,j-2}\right]$$

The coefficients of the typical finite difference equation can be schematically represented by a typical net work shown in Fig. 6.59.

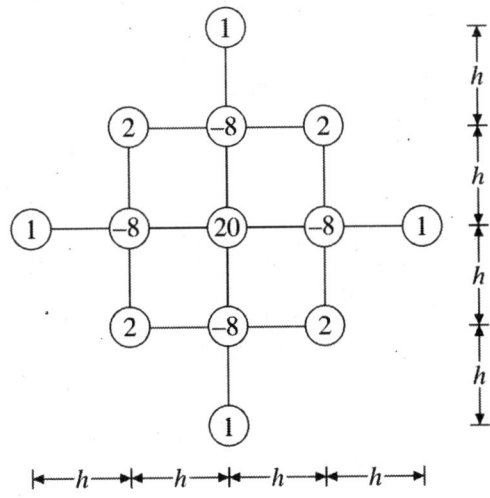

Fig. 6.59: Coefficients of finite difference equation

The application of this finite difference equation to different types of plate problemsis illustrated by the following examples.

Example 6.47

Determine the deflections at the pivotal points of a simply supported square plate of side length 'a' supporting a uniformly distributed load of 'w' kN/m². Also evaluate the maximum bending moment in each direction. Adopt four grids in each direction.

Solution

The square plate of side length 'a' shown in Fig. 6.60 is divided into four grids in both directions. The plate is extended in all directions by an additional interval 'h' to facilitate the formation of finite difference equations and the nodal points are numbered with due regard to symmetry.

Applying the finite difference equation successively to the nodal ponts 1, 2 and 3, we have the following equations:

$$20z_1 - 32z_2 + 8z_3 = -(wh^4 / D)$$

$$-8z_1 + 24z_2 - 16z_3 = -(wh^4 / D)$$

$$2z_1 - 16z_2 + 20z_3 = -(wh^4 / D)$$

Expressing these equations in the matrix form, we have

$$
\begin{bmatrix} 20 & -32 & 8 \\ -8 & 24 & -16 \\ 2 & -16 & 20 \end{bmatrix} \begin{Bmatrix} z_1 \\ z_2 \\ z_3 \end{Bmatrix} = \begin{Bmatrix} 1 \\ 1 \\ 1 \end{Bmatrix} \left(-\frac{wh^4}{D} \right)
$$

$$[A]\{z\} = \{K\}$$

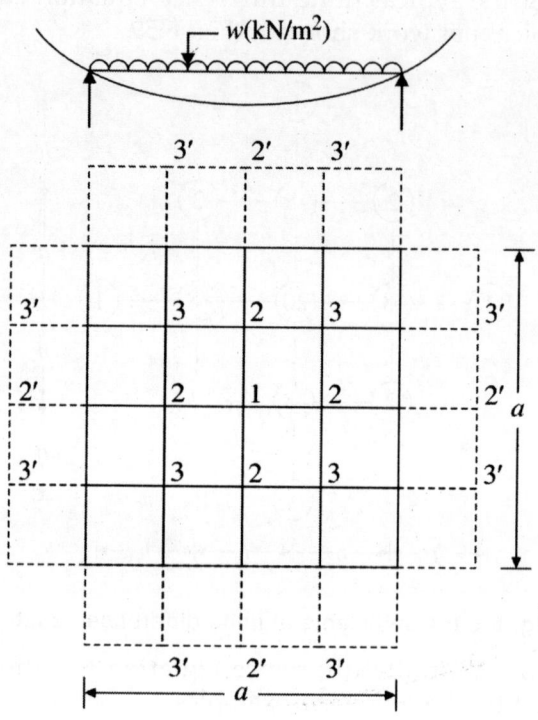

Fig. 6.60: Simply supported square plate with UDL

The inverse of matrix $[A]$ is obtained by the cofactor method as follows:

$$A_{11} = \begin{bmatrix} 24 & -16 \\ -16 & 20 \end{bmatrix} = (480 - 256) = 224$$

$$A_{12} = -\begin{bmatrix} -8 & -16 \\ 2 & 20 \end{bmatrix} = -(-160 + 32) = 128$$

$$A_{13} = \begin{bmatrix} -8 & 24 \\ 2 & -16 \end{bmatrix} = (128 - 48) = 80$$

$$A_{21} = -\begin{bmatrix} -32 & 8 \\ -16 & 20 \end{bmatrix} = -(640 + 128) = 512$$

$$A_{22} = \begin{bmatrix} 20 & 8 \\ 2 & 20 \end{bmatrix} = (400 - 16) = 384$$

$$A_{23} = -\begin{bmatrix} 20 & -32 \\ 2 & -16 \end{bmatrix} = -(-320 + 64) = 256$$

$$A_{31} = \begin{bmatrix} -32 & 8 \\ 24 & -16 \end{bmatrix} = -(512 - 192) = 320$$

$$A_{32} = -\begin{bmatrix} 20 & 8 \\ -8 & 24 \end{bmatrix} = -(-320 + 64) = 256$$

$$A_{33} = \begin{bmatrix} 20 & -32 \\ -8 & 24 \end{bmatrix} = (480 - 256) = 224$$

$$[M] = \begin{bmatrix} 224 & 128 & 80 \\ 512 & 384 & 256 \\ 320 & 256 & 224 \end{bmatrix}$$

$$[M]^T = \begin{bmatrix} 224 & 512 & 320 \\ 128 & 384 & 256 \\ 80 & 256 & 224 \end{bmatrix}$$

$$[A] = 20(480 - 256) + 32(-160 + 32) + 8(128 - 48) = 1024$$

$$[A^{-1}] = \frac{[M]^T}{[A]} = \begin{bmatrix} 0.2128 & 0.500 & 0.3125 \\ 0.1250 & 0.375 & 0.2500 \\ 0.0780 & 0.250 & 0.2180 \end{bmatrix}$$

$$[z] = [A^{-1}][K] = \begin{bmatrix} 0.2128 & 0.500 & 0.3125 \\ 0.1250 & 0.375 & 0.2500 \\ 0.0780 & 0.250 & 0.2180 \end{bmatrix} \begin{Bmatrix} 1 \\ 1 \\ 1 \end{Bmatrix} \left(-\frac{wh^4}{D} \right)$$

Therefore $z_1 = -1.0313\ (wh^4/D) = -0.004\ (wa^4/D)$
$z_2 = -0.75\ (wh^4/D) = -0.003\ (wa^4/D)$
$z_3 = -0.546\ (wh^4/D) = -0.00213\ (wa^4/D)$

The bending moment at the centre is maximum since the plate is simply supported and subjected to uniformly distributed load.

$$\frac{\partial^2 z}{\partial x^2} = \left[\frac{z_2 - 2z_1 + z_2}{h^2} \right] = \frac{2(z_2 - z_1)}{h^2} = 0.5626 \left(\frac{wh^2}{D} \right)$$

$$\frac{\partial^2 z}{\partial y^2} = \left[\frac{z_2 - 2z_1 + z_2}{h^2} \right] = \frac{2(z_2 - z_1)}{h^2} = 0.5626 \left(\frac{wh^2}{D} \right)$$

$$M_x = D \left[\frac{\partial^2 z}{\partial x^2} + \mu \frac{\partial^2 z}{\partial y^2} \right]$$

$$= D\left[0.5626\left(\frac{wh^2}{D}\right) + 0.3 \times 0.5626\left(\frac{wh^2}{D}\right)\right] \text{ since } \mu = 0.3$$

$$= 0.7314wh^2 = 0.7314w(a/4)^2$$

$$= 0.0457wa^2$$

The bending moment $M_x = 0.0457wa^2$, compares favorably with the classical solution of $M_x = 0.0479wa^2$.

Example 6.48

Determine the maximum deflection of a uniformly loaded square plate of side length 'a' having clamped supports as shown in Fig. 6.61. Adopt a grid spacing of $h = (a/4)$. The intensity of loading is 'w' per unit area.

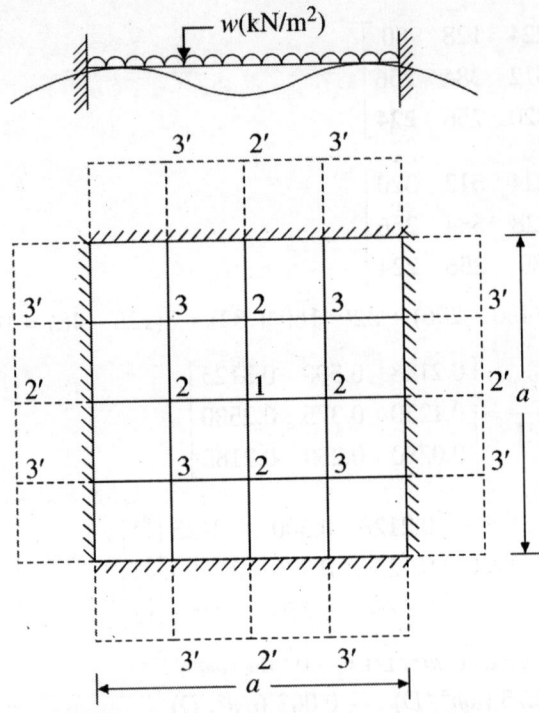

Fig. 6.61: Square plate fixed at supports with UDL

Applying the finite difference equation successively to the nodal points 1, 2 and 3, we have the following equations.

$$20z_1 - 32z_2 + 8z_3 = -(wh^4/D) \tag{1}$$

$$20z_2 - 8z_1 - 16z_3 + 4z_2 + z_2 + z_2 = -(wh^4/D)$$

$$-8z_1 + 26z_2 - 16z_3 = -\left(\frac{wh^4}{D}\right) \tag{2}$$

$$20z_3 - 16z_2 + 2z_1 + z_3 + z_3 + z_3 + z_3 = -(wh^4/D)$$

$$2z_1 + 16z_2 + 24z_3 = -\left(\frac{wh^4}{D}\right) \tag{3}$$

Expressing the equations 1, 2 and 3 in the matrix form, we have

$$\begin{bmatrix} 20 & -32 & 8 \\ -8 & 26 & -16 \\ 2 & -16 & 24 \end{bmatrix} \begin{Bmatrix} z_1 \\ z_2 \\ z_3 \end{Bmatrix} = \begin{Bmatrix} 1 \\ 1 \\ 1 \end{Bmatrix} \left(-\frac{wh^4}{D} \right)$$

$$[A]\{z\} = \{K\}$$

The inverse of matrix $[A]$ is obtained by the cofactor method as follows:

$$A_{11} = \begin{bmatrix} 26 & -16 \\ -16 & 24 \end{bmatrix} = 368$$

$$A_{12} = -\begin{bmatrix} -8 & -16 \\ 2 & 24 \end{bmatrix} = 160$$

$$A_{13} = \begin{bmatrix} -8 & 26 \\ 2 & -16 \end{bmatrix} = 76$$

$$A_{21} = -\begin{bmatrix} -32 & 8 \\ -16 & 24 \end{bmatrix} = 640$$

$$A_{22} = \begin{bmatrix} 20 & 8 \\ 2 & 24 \end{bmatrix} = 464$$

$$A_{23} = -\begin{bmatrix} 20 & -32 \\ 2 & -16 \end{bmatrix} = 256$$

$$A_{31} = \begin{bmatrix} -32 & 8 \\ 26 & -16 \end{bmatrix} = 304$$

$$A_{32} = -\begin{bmatrix} 20 & 8 \\ -8 & -16 \end{bmatrix} = 256$$

$$A_{33} = \begin{bmatrix} 20 & -32 \\ -8 & 26 \end{bmatrix} = 264$$

Therefore $[M] = \begin{bmatrix} 368 & 160 & 76 \\ 640 & 464 & 256 \\ 304 & 256 & 264 \end{bmatrix}$

$$[M]^T = \begin{bmatrix} 368 & 640 & 304 \\ 160 & 464 & 256 \\ 76 & 256 & 264 \end{bmatrix}$$

$$[A] = 20(368) + 32(-160) + 8(76) = 2848$$

$$[A^{-1}] = \frac{[M]^T}{[A]} = \begin{bmatrix} 0.1290 & 0.2247 & 0.1067 \\ 0.0560 & 0.1630 & 0.0898 \\ 0.0279 & 0.0898 & 0.0930 \end{bmatrix}$$

$$\begin{bmatrix} z_1 \\ z_2 \\ z_3 \end{bmatrix} = \begin{bmatrix} 0.1290 & 0.2247 & 0.1067 \\ 0.0560 & 0.1630 & 0.0898 \\ 0.0279 & 0.0898 & 0.0930 \end{bmatrix} \begin{Bmatrix} 1 \\ 1 \\ 1 \end{Bmatrix} \left(-\frac{wh^4}{D} \right)$$

Therefore $z_1 = -0.4604\ (wh^4/D) = -0.00179\ (wa^4/D)$

$z_2 = -0.3088\ (wh^4/D) = -0.0012\ (wa^4/D)$

$z_3 = -0.2098\ (wh^4/D) = -0.0008\ (wa^4/D)$

The maximum deflection at the centre of the plate is obtained as,

$$z_1 = z_{max} = -0.00179\ (wa^4/D)$$

Example 6.49

A simply supported rectangular plate of sides '2a' and 'a' supports a uniformly distributed load of intensity 'w' per unit area. By finite difference method determine the approximate deflections at the nodal points using a grid spacing of $h = (a/2)$.

The governing differential equation for deflection of the plate is

$$\nabla^4 z = \left(\frac{w}{D} \right) \text{ with the usual notations}$$

Solution

Referring to Fig. 6.62 and applying finite difference equation to the nodal points 1, 2 respectively, we have the following equations:

$$20z_1 - 16z_2 - z_1 - z_1 = -(wh^4/D)$$

$$18z_1 - 16z_2 = -\left(\frac{wh^4}{D} \right) \tag{1}$$

$$20z_2 - 8z_1 - z_2 - z_2 - z_2 + z_2 = -0.5(wh^4/D)$$

$$-8z_1 + 16z_2 = -0.5\left(\frac{wh^4}{D} \right) \tag{2}$$

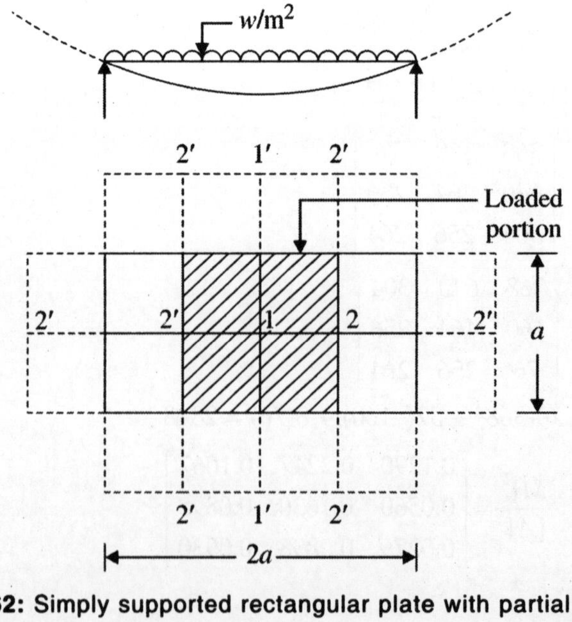

Fig. 6.62: Simply supported rectangular plate with partial loading

Solving Eqs 1 and 2, we have the solution as

$$z_1 = -0.1316\left(\frac{wh^4}{D}\right)$$

$$z_2 = -0.0863\left(\frac{wh^4}{D}\right)$$

Substituting, $h = (a/2)$, the deflections at the nodal points are obtained as

$$z_1 = -0.0082\left(\frac{wa^4}{D}\right)$$

$$z_2 = -0.0054\left(\frac{wa^4}{D}\right)$$

Example 6.50

A rectangular plate of size 3 m by 6 m is simply supported on all the four sides and supports a uniformly distributed load of intensity 500 kN/m² over one half of the plate as shown in Fig. 6.63. Estimate the deflections at the pivotal points of the plate assuming the thickness of the plate $t = 50$ mm. Poisson's ratio $\mu = 0.25$ and the modulus of elasticity $E = 2 \times 10^5$ N/mm².

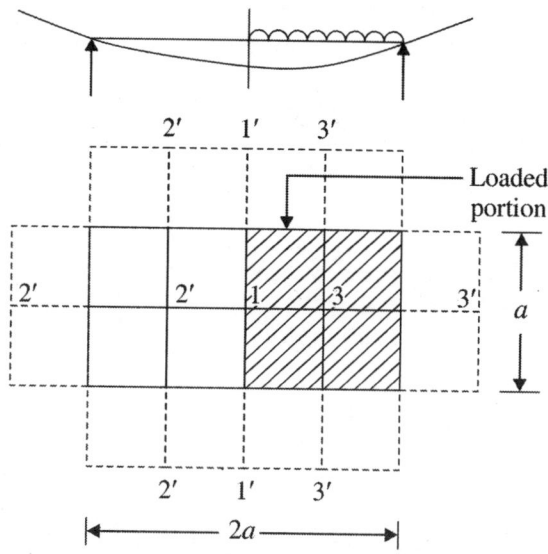

Fig. 6.63: Simply supported rectangular plate with partial loading

Solution

Referring to Fig. 6.63 and applying finite difference equation to the nodal points 1, 2 and 3 respectively, we have the following equations:

$$20z_1 - 8z_2 - 8z_3 - z_1 - z_1 = -0.5\,(wh^4/D)$$

$$18z_1 - 8z_2 - 8z_3 = -0.5\,(wh^4/D) \tag{1}$$

$$20z_2 - 8z_1 - z_2 - z_2 - z_2 + z_3 = 0$$

$$-8z_1 + 17z_2 + z_3 = 0 \tag{2}$$

$$20z_3 - 8z_1 - z_3 - z_3 - z_3 + z_2 = -(wh^4/D)$$
$$-8z_1 + z_2 + 17z_3 = -(wh^4/D) \qquad (3)$$

Solving Eqs (1), (2) and (3), we get the deflections at the nodal points, as follows:

$$z_1 = -0.0865 \, (wh^4/D) = -0.0054 \, (wh^4/D)$$
$$z_1 = -0.035 \, (wh^4/D) = -0.00218 \, (wh^4/D)$$
$$z_1 = -0.0975 \, (wh^4/D) = -0.00609 \, (wh^4/D)$$

D = Flexural rigidity of the plate

$$= \left[\frac{Et^3}{12(1-\mu^2)}\right] = \left[\frac{2 \times 10^5 \times 50^3}{(121 - 0.25^2)}\right] = (2.22 \times 10^9) \, \text{N} \cdot \text{mm}$$

$$\left(\frac{wa^4}{D}\right) = \left[\frac{500 \times 10^3 \times 3000^4}{10^6 \times 2.22 \times 10^9}\right] 18240 \, \text{mm}$$

Substituting these values, the deflections are obtained as,

$$z_1 = -0.0054(18240) = -98.5 \, \text{mm}$$
$$z_2 = -0.00218(18240) = -39.7 \, \text{mm}$$
$$z_3 = -0.00609(18240) = -111.1 \, \text{mm}$$

Example 6.51

A rectangular plate of side lengths and is simply supported at the two adjacent edges and fixed at the other two edges as shown in Fig. 6.64. The plate supports a UDL of intensity w kN/m², over the entire plate area. Using a grid spacing of $h = (a/2)$, compute the deflections at the nodal points using the finite difference method.

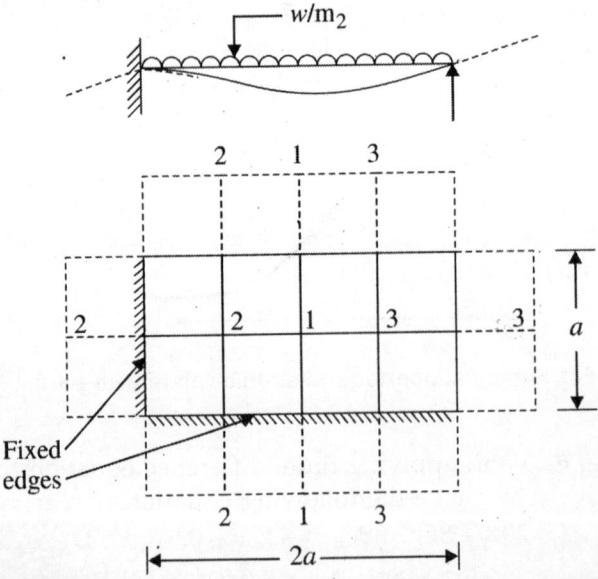

Fig. 6.64: Rectangular plate with adjacent edges fixed at supports with UDL

Solution

Referring to Fig. 6.64 and applying the finite difference equations to the nodal points 1, 2 and 3 respectively, we have the following equations:

$$20z_1 - 8z_2 - 8z_3 - z_1 + z_1 = -(wh^4/D)$$

$$20z_1 - 8z_2 - 8z_3 = -(wh^4/D) \qquad (1)$$

$$20z_2 - 8z_1 - z_2 + z_3 + z_2 + z_2 = -(wh^4/D)$$

$$-8z_2 + 21z_2 + z_3 = -(wh^4/D) \qquad (2)$$

$$20z_3 - 8z_1 - z_3 - z_3 + z_3 + z_2 = -(wh^4/D)$$

$$-8z_1 + z_2 + 19z_3 = -(wh^4/D) \qquad (3)$$

The above three equations can be written in the matrix form as

$$\begin{bmatrix} 20 & -8 & -8 \\ -8 & 21 & 1 \\ -8 & 1 & 19 \end{bmatrix} \begin{Bmatrix} z_1 \\ z_2 \\ z_3 \end{Bmatrix} = \begin{Bmatrix} 1 \\ 1 \\ 1 \end{Bmatrix} \left(-\frac{wh^4}{D} \right)$$

The deflections are expressed as

$$\{z\} = [A^{-1}] (K)$$

$$\begin{bmatrix} z_1 \\ z_2 \\ z_3 \end{bmatrix} = \begin{bmatrix} 0.0072 & 0.026 & 0.029 \\ 0.026 & 0.057 & 0.008 \\ 0.029 & 0.008 & 0.064 \end{bmatrix} \begin{Bmatrix} 1 \\ 1 \\ 1 \end{Bmatrix} \left(-\frac{wh^4}{D} \right)$$

Therefore $z_1 = -0.127(wh^4/D) = -0.00793(wh^4/D)$

$z_2 = -0.091(wh^4/D) = -0.00568(wh^4/D)$

$z_3 = -0.1014(wh^4/D) = -0.00633(wh^4/D)$

Example 6.52

A square plate of size 4 m by 4 m is clamped along the opposite edges and simply supported at the other edges as shown in Fig. 6.65. The plate supports a UDL of 50 kN/m². Thickness of the plate is 50 mm, Poisson's ratio is 0.25 and the modulus of elasticity is 2×10^5 N/mm². Using a grid interval of 1 m, estimate the maximum deflection in the plate.

Solution

Referring to Fig. 6.65, and applying finite difference equation to the nodal points 1, 2, 3 and 4 respectively, we have the following equations.

$$20z_1 - 16z_2 - 16z_4 + 8z_3 = -(wh^4/D)$$

$$20z_1 - 16z_2 + 8z_3 - 16z_4 = -(wh^4/D) \qquad (1)$$

$$20z_2 - 16z_3 - 8z_1 + 4z_4 - z_2 + z_2 = -(wh^4/D)$$

$$-8z_1 + 20z_2 - 16z_3 + 4z_4 = -(wh^4/D) \qquad (2)$$

$$20z_3 - 8z_2 - 8z_4 + 2z_1 + z_3 - z_3 + z_3 + z_3 = -(wh^4/D)$$

$$2z_1 - 8z_2 + 22z_3 - 8z_4 = -(wh^4/D) \qquad (3)$$

$$20z_4 - 16z_3 - 8z_1 + 4z_2 + z_4 + z_4 = -(wh^4/D)$$

$$-8z_1 + 4z_2 - 16z_3 - 22z_4 = -(wh^4/D) \qquad (4)$$

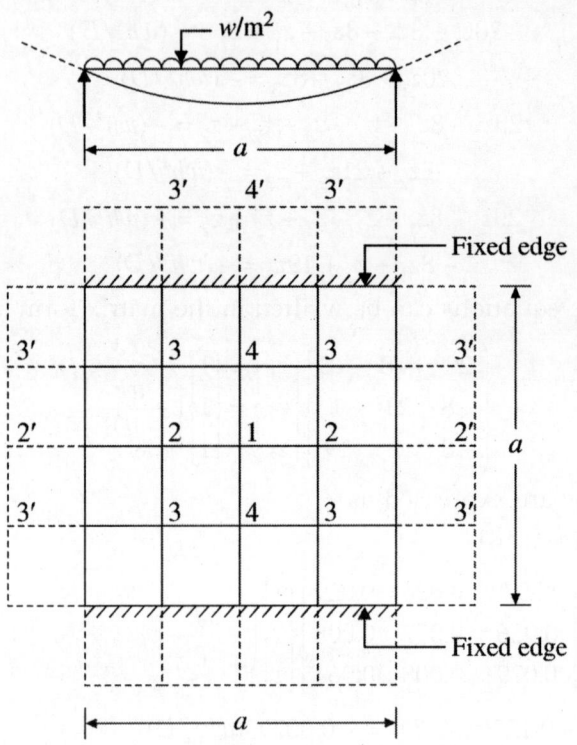

Fig. 6.65: Square plate fixed at opposite edges with UDL

Solving Eqs (1)–(4), we get the maximum deflection at the nodal point 1 given by

$$z_1 = -0.00225 \ (wa^4/D)$$

$$D = \frac{Et^3}{12} = \left[\frac{2 \times 10^5 \times 50^3}{12(1 - 0.25^2)} \right] = (2.22 \times 10^9) \ \text{N·mm}$$

$$\left(\frac{wa^4}{D} \right) = \left[\frac{50 \times 10^5 \times 4000^4}{10^6 \times 2.22 \times 10^9} \right] = 5765 \ \text{mm}$$

Hence, the maximum deflection at the centre of the plate is

$$z_1 = -0.00225(5765) = -12.97 \ \text{mm}$$

Example 6.53

Determine the maximum deflection of a simply supported square plate of reinforced cement concrete subjected to a distributed load in the form of a triangular prism, as shown in Fig. 6.66. The side length of the plate is 4 m. Assume the value of $w = 4 \ \text{kN/m}^2$. The thickness of the slab $t = 00$ mm. $\mu = 0.15$ and $E = 28000 \ \text{N/mm}^2$. Adopt 4 grid intervals.

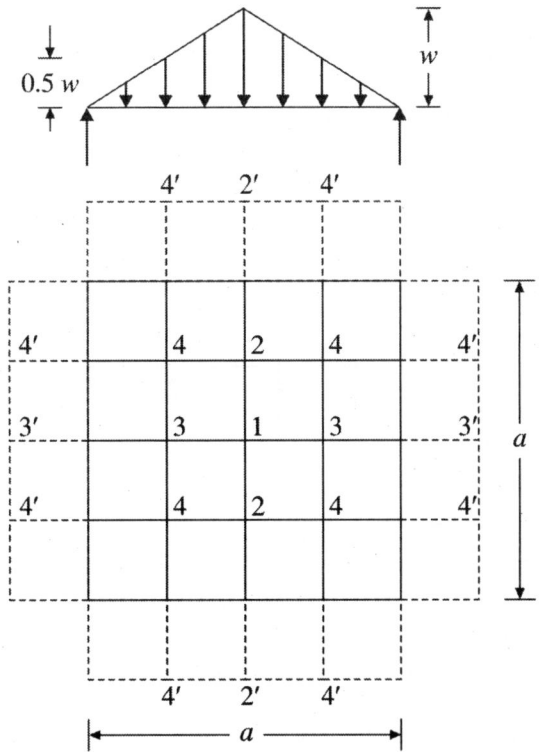

Fig. 6.66: Simply supported square plate supporting triangular load

Solution

Referring to Fig. 6.66, and applying finite difference equation to the nodal points 1, 2, 3 and 4 respectively, we have the following equations.

$$20z_1 - 16z_2 - 16z_3 + z_4 = -(wh^4/D) \tag{1}$$

$$20z_2 - 8z_1 - 16z_4 + 4z_3 = -(wh^4/D) \tag{2}$$

$$20z_3 - 16z_4 - 8z_1 + 4z_2 = -0.5 = -(wh^4/D) \tag{3}$$

$$20z_4 - 8z_2 - 8z_3 + 2z_1 = -0.5 = -(wh^4/D) \tag{4}$$

Solving these equations, the deflections at the nodal points are obtained as

$$z_1 = -0.00293 \, (wa^4/D)$$
$$z_2 = -0.00204 \, (wa^4/D)$$
$$z_3 = -0.00148 \, (wa^4/D)$$

Hence the maximum deflection at the centre of the plate is

$$z_1 = -0.00293 \, (wa^4/D) = -0.00293(429) = -1.256 \text{ mm}$$

Example 6.54

A rectangular plate of side length a and $2a$ is simply supported on all sides and also in the middle in the shorter direction of the span as shown in Fig. 6.67. One half of the plate is loaded with a UDL of intensity w kN/m². Dividing the plate into eighteen equal segments, calculate the deflection at the nodal points of the plate.

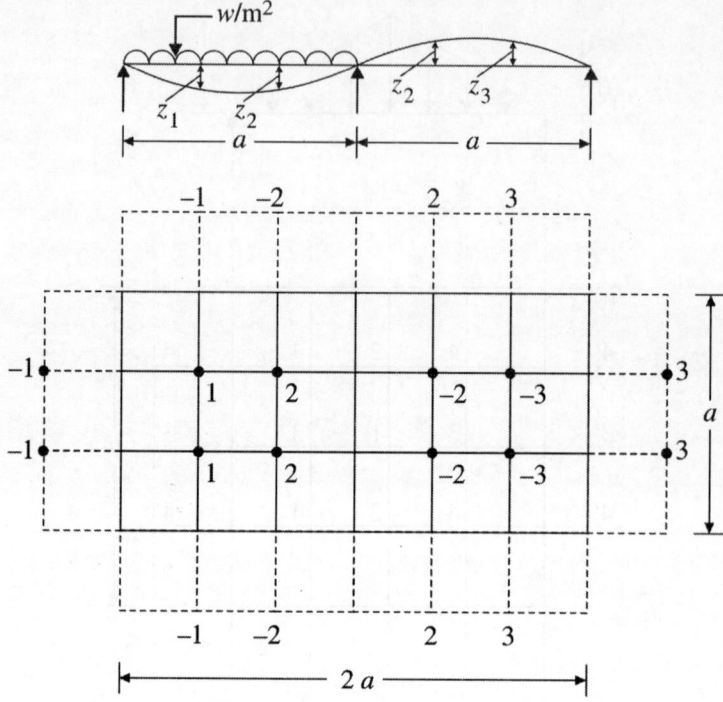

Fig. 6.67: Continuous plate with partial loading

Applying the finite difference equation to the nodal points 1, 2, and 3 we have the following equations.

$$20z_1 - 8z_2 - 8z_1 + 2z_2 - z_1 - z_1 = -(wh^4/D)$$

$$10z_1 - 6z_2 = -(wh^4/D) \tag{1}$$

$$20z_2 - 8z_1 - 8z_2 + 2z_1 - z_2 - z_2 = -(wh^4/D)$$

$$-6z_1 + 10z_2 = -(wh^4/D) \tag{2}$$

$$-20z_3 + 8z_2 + 8z_3 - 2z_2 + z_3 + z_3 = 0$$

$$-6z_2 - 10z_3 = -(wh^4/D) \tag{3}$$

Solving Eqs (1), (2) and (3), the deflections are obtained as

$$z_1 = -0.25 \, (wh^4/D) = -0.00308 \, (wa^4/D)$$
$$z_2 = -0.25 \, (wh^4/D) = -0.00308 \, (wa^4/D)$$
$$z_3 = -0.15 \, (wh^4/D) = -0.0018 \, (wa^4/D)$$

Example 6.55

A simply supported RCC square slab of 3 m side length, supports a load of intensity zero at one edge, varying linearly to a value of 8 kN/m² at the opposite edge as shown in Fig. 6.68. If the thickness of the slab is 120 mm and the Poisson's ratio is 0.15, modulus of elasticity is 30,000 N/mm², estimate the maximum deflection n he slab. Adopt 4 grids in each direction.

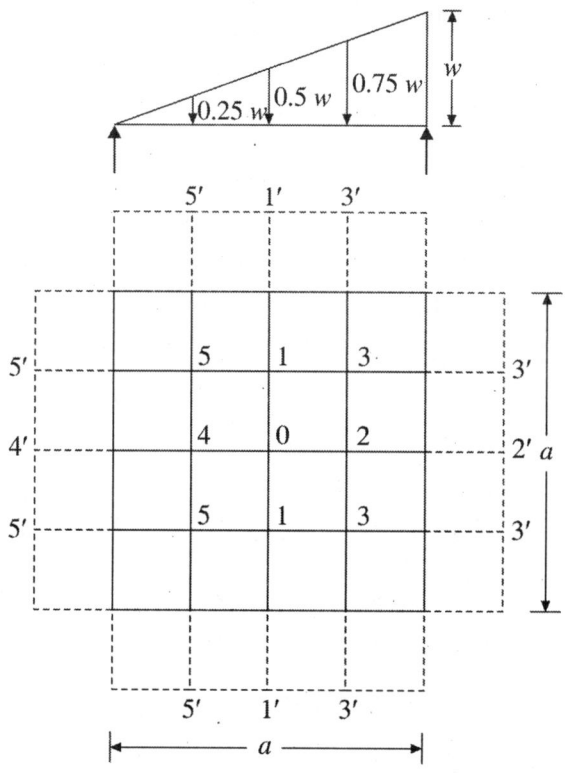

Fig. 6.68: Simply supported plate with triangular loading

Solution

Referring to Fig. 6.68, and applying finite difference equation to the nodal points 1, 2, 3, 4 and 5 respectively, we have the following equations.

$$20z_0 - 16z_1 - 8z_2 - 8z_4 + 4z_5 + 4z_3 = -0.5 \ (wh^4/D) \tag{1}$$

$$20z_1 - 8z_0 - 8z_5 - 8z_3 + 2z_2 + 2z_4 = -0.5 \ (wh^4/D) \tag{2}$$

$$20z_2 - 16z_3 - 8z_0 + 4z_1 - z_2 + z_4 = -0.75 \ (wh^4/D) \tag{3}$$

$$20z_3 - 8z_1 - 8z_2 + 2z_0 + z_3 - z_3 - z_3 + z_5 = -0.75 \ (wh^4/D) \tag{4}$$

$$20z_4 - 16z_5 - 8z_0 + 4z_1 - z_4 + z_2 = -0.25 \ (wh^4/D) \tag{5}$$

$$20z_5 - 8z_1 - 8z_4 + 2z_0 + z_5 + z_3 - z_5 - z_5 = -0.25 \ (wh^4/D) \tag{6}$$

Solving these equations, the deflections at the nodal points are obtained as

$$z_0 = -0.002015 \ (wa^4/D)$$
$$z_1 = -00147 \ (wa^4/D)$$
$$z_2 = -0.00163 \ (wa^4/D)$$
$$z_3 = -0.0012 \ (wa^4/D)$$
$$z_4 = -0.0013 \ (wa^4/D)$$
$$z_5 = -0.00093 \ (wa^4/D)$$

$$D = \frac{Et^3}{12(1-\mu^2)} = \left[\frac{30000 \times 120^3}{12(1-0.15^2)}\right] = (4.419 \times 10^9) \ \text{N·mm}$$

$$\left(\frac{wa^4}{D}\right) = \left[\frac{8 \times 10^3 \times 3000^4}{10^6 \times 4.419 \times 10^9}\right] = 146.6 \text{ mm}$$

The maximum deflection in the plate occurs at the centre of the plate and its value is given by

$$z_0 = -0.002015\ 9\ (wa^4/D) = -0.002015(146.6) = 0.295 \text{ mm (downwards)}$$

Example 6.56

A simply supported square plate of side length 'a' supports a trapezoidal load varying from $0.5w$ at one edge to w at the opposite edge as shown in Fig. 6.69. Estimate the deflection at the various nodal points using a grid interval of $h = (a/4)$.

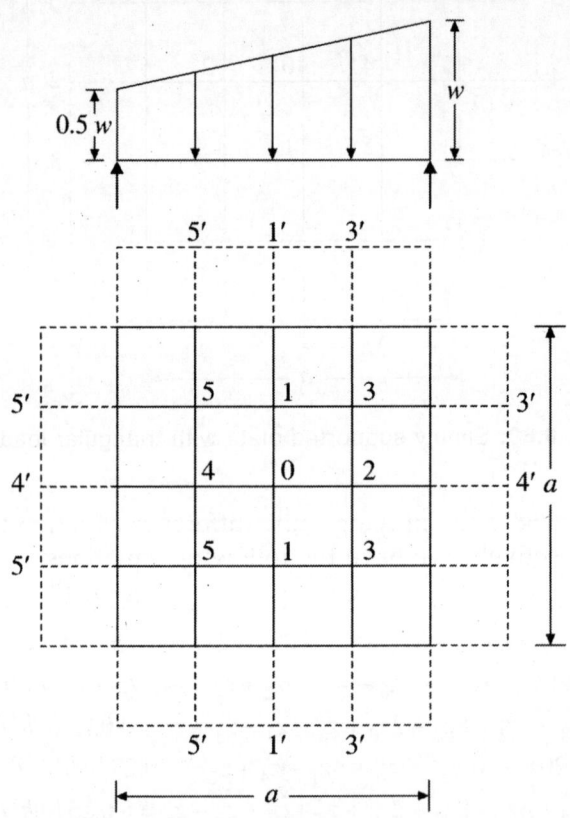

Fig. 6.69: Simply supported square plate with trapezoidal loading

Solution

Applying the finite difference equation to the nodal points 1, 2, 3, 4 and 5 the following equations are obtained.

$$20z_0 - 16z_1 - 8z_2 + 2z_3 - 8z_4 + 4z_5 = -0.75\ (wh^4/D) \tag{1}$$

$$20z_1 - 8z_0 - 8z_3 - 8z_5 + 2z_2 + 2z_4 = -0.75\ (wh^4/D) \tag{2}$$

$$20z_2 - 8z_0 - 16z_3 + 4z_1 - z_2 + z_4 = -0.875\ (wh^4/D) \tag{3}$$

$$20z_3 - 8z_1 - 8z_2 + 2z_0 + z_3 - z_3 - z_3 + z_5 = -0.875\ (wh^4/D) \tag{4}$$

$$20z_4 - 16z_5 - 8z_0 + 4z_1 + z_2 - z_4 = -0.625\,(wh^4/D) \tag{5}$$

$$20z_5 - 8z_4 - 8z_1 + 2z_0 + z_5 + z_3 - z_5 - z_5 = -0.625\,(wh^4/D) \tag{6}$$

Solving these equations, the deflections at the nodal points are obtained as

$$z_0 = -0.773\,(wh^4/D) = -0.0030\,(wh^4/D)$$
$$z_1 = -0.563(wh^4/D) = -0.0022(wh^4/D)$$
$$z_2 = -0.584(wh^4/D) = -0.00228(wh^4/D)$$
$$z_3 = -0.427(wh^4/D) = -0.00167(wh^4/D)$$
$$z_4 = -0.541(wh^4/D) = -0.00211(wh^4/D)$$
$$z_5 = -0.394(wh^4/D) = -0.00154(wh^4/D)$$

EXERCISES

1. A simply supported beam of span length L supports concentrated loads of magnitude W kN at quarter span Intervals, Assuming constant flexural rigidity of the beam, estimate the deflection of the beam at mid span using finite diffence method.

2. A simply supported beam of span 4 m, supports a uniformly distributed load of 10 kN/m. If the flexural rigidity of end quarter spans is half that of the middle half span, estimate the maximum deflection of the beam. Assume the flexural rigidity of the beam $EI = (3468 \times 10^9)$ N/mm^2.

3. A cantilever of length L supports a uniformly distributed load of w kN/m. If the flexural rigidity for a length of $(L/3)$ from free end is EI and for the middle third length is $2EI$ and for the remaining length is $3EI$, estimate the deflection at the free end of the cantilever.

4. A beam ABCD with $AB = BC = CD = (L/3)$ is fixed at A and D. The beam supports concentrated loads of magnitude W at B and C. If the flexural rigidity of $AB = CD = EI$ and $BC = 1.5\ EI$, estimate the maximum deflection in the beam using finite difference method.

5. A propped cantilever of length 4 m supports a uniformly distributed load of 8 kN/m over the whole span length. Assuming $EI = 30 \times 10^8$ N·mm^2 and adopting a grid interval of $h = L/4$, estimate the deflection at the centre of the span.

6. Estimate the lowest buckling load of pin ended column with varying flexural rigidity as shown in Fig. 6.70.

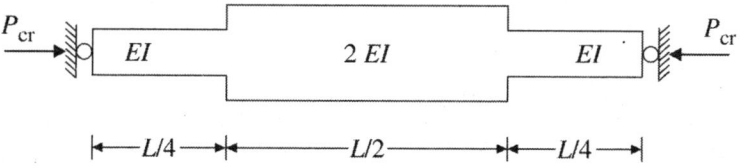

Fig. 6.70: Column with pinned ends

7. Calculate the buckling load of the column with pinned ends shown in Fig. 6.71. Assume the flexural rigidity $EI = 30 \times 10^8$ N·mm^2.

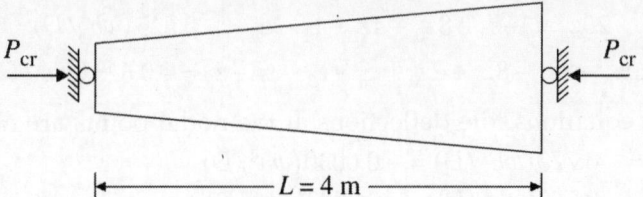

Fig. 6.71: Column with variable moment of inertia

8. A simply supported beam of span length 4 m carries a concentrated load of 50 kN at the centre of span. The total selfweight of the beam is 25 kN. If $EI = 5 \times 10^{10}$ N·mm^2, fine the natural frequency of vibration of the beam.

9. A propped cantilever beam of 3 m length supports a uniformly distributed load of 10 kN/m which includes the selfweight of the beam. If $EI = 9 \times 10^{16}$ N·mm^2, estimate the natural frequency of the cantilever beam using finite difference technique and dividing the beam into four grids.

10. A uniform steel beam of length L is simply supported and carries concentrated loads of magnitude W at quarter span intervals. Determine the lowest natural frequency of the system neglecting the mass of the beam.

11. A thin membrane is attached with a constant tensile force of 2 N/mm of its boundary across a rectangular frame of length 4 cm and breadth 3 cm. A uniform lateral pressure of 0.05 N/mm^2 is applied on the membrane. Using a grid spacing of 10 mm, determine the deflections at the nodal points and the maximum slope.

12. Determine the lateral deflection of a membrane with boundaries of a frame shown in Fig. 6.72 due to a uniform lateral pressure of intensity 0.05 N/mm^2. The boundary force is 5 N/mm. Adopt a grid spacing of 100 mm.

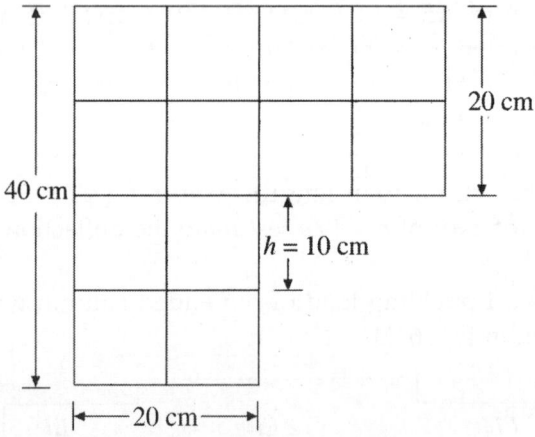

Fig. 6.72: Lateral deflection of membrane

13. A bar of rectangular cross-section 30 cm by 40 cm is subjected to a torsional moment of 30 kN·m. Using finite differences and membrane analogy, determine the maximum torsional shear stress and the angle twist per unit length of the bar. Assume modulus of rigidity $G = 12000$ N/mm^2 and a grid spacing of 100 mm.

14. A bar having the cross-section of a right angled triangle of side length 80 cm is subjected to a torque of 60 kN·m. Determine the angle of twist per unit length and the maximum shear stress in the bar assuming 200 mm length grids. Adopt $G = 12000 \, \text{N/mm}^2$.

15. A thin rectangular plate of length $4h$ and width $3h$ is simply supported at all the edges and supports a lateral load of $w \, \text{kN/m}^2$. If the stiffness of the plate is D, estimate the maximum deflection of the plate using a grid spacing of h.

16. A simply supported square plate of side length a supports a lateral load in the form of a pyramid symmetrically located on the plate with the intensity of load at the centre of plate being w and linearly reducing to zero at the supports. If D is the stiffness of the plate, determine the deflection at the various nodal points assuming a grid spacing of $h = (a/4)$.

17. A propped cantilever AB is fixed at A and propped at B. The length of the cantilever is 4 m. It supports a uniformly distributed load of 2 kN/m over the whole span length. Using finite difference method, estimate the maximum deflection in the propped cantilever assuming the flexural rigidity $EI = (33.28 \times 10^4) \, \text{kN·m}^2$.

18. A two span continuous beam ABC has equal spans $AB = BC = 4$ m. The beam supports concentrated loads of 2 kN at each mid span points. Using finite difference method, estimate the deflection under the load points assuming the flexural rigidity of the beam as $10^4 \, \text{kN·m}^2$.

19. Determine the critical load for a pin ended column with variable moment of inertia of I for the quarter span lengths from the ends and $3I$ for the central half of the column using finite difference technique. Assume the length of the column as 5 m and the flexural rigidity as $EI = 10^4 \, \text{kN·m}^2$.

20. A thin square plate of side length 4 m is simply supported at the edges and supports a UDL of 8 kN/m^2. If the stiffness of the plate is $(8 \times 10^{15}) \, \text{kN·m}^2$, using finite difference method evaluate the maximum deflection of the plate.

REFERENCES

1. Ferzieger JH, *Numerical Methods for Engineering Applications*, 2nd Edn, John Wiley & Sons, New York, 1981.

2. Davies PJ and Rabinowitz, *Methods of Numerical Integration*, 2nd Edn, Academic Press, New York, 1984.

3. Jain MK, Iyengar SRK and Jain RK, *Numerical Methods for Scientific and Engineering Computation*, 6th Edn, New Age International Publishers, New Delhi, 2012.

4. Ralph G Stanton, *Numerical Method for Science and Engineering*, Prentice Hall of India, New Delhi, 1977.

6. Rajasekharan S, *Numerical Methods in Science and Engineering–A Practical Approach*, A.H. Wheeler & Co. New Delhi, 1986.

7. Ralph G Stanton, *Numerical Method for Science and Engineering*, Prentice Hall of India, New Delhi, 1977.

8. Traub JF, *Iterative Methods for the Solution of Nonlinear Equations*, Prentice Hall, Engelwood Cliffs, 1964.
9. Johnson LW and Reiss RD *Numerical Analysis*, 2nd Edn, Addison-Wesley, Reading, Mass, 1968.
10. Yakowitz Sidney and Ferenc Szidarovszky, *An Introduction to Numerical Computations*. McMillan Publishing Company, 1986.

REVIEW QUESTIONS

1. Briefly explain the necessity of using finite difference methods for solving structural engineering problems of bending of beams, buckling of columns.
2. Specify the various types of differences used in solving structural problems and their suitability for a given structural problem.
3. Mention the basic finite difference equations used in solving structural problems using the backward, forward and central differences.
4. Briefly explain the application of fourth order central difference equation for solving a simply supported beam supporting uniformly distributed load.
5. What is the specific advantage of using finite difference techniques in determining deflections of beams with variable moment of ineria?
6. Explain with a typical example the method of solving the deflections of statically indeterminate structures like propped cantilever, fixed and continuous beams.
7. Discuss briefly the advantages of using the finite difference techniques for solving buckling problems of columns with variable moment of inertia.
8. Derive the finite difference governing equation used for determining the natural frequency of a beam.
9. Specify the governing finite difference equation used for solving problems of beams on on elastic foundations.
10. Briefly explain the method of using the finite difference methods for solving
    a) Torsion problems b) Deflections of laterally loaded plates.

OBJECTIVE TYPE QUESTIONS

1. The application of the finite difference method for the solution of beam problems results in
   a) quadratic equations
   b) simultaneous equations
   c) transcendental equations
2. In solving the problem of deflections in loaded beams using finite difference technique, normally the equations are formed using
   a) forward differences
   b) backward differences
   c) central differences

3. In determining deflections of a loaded statically indeterminate structure like a propped cantilever using the finite difference method, the second order finite difference equations are formed considering
    a) successive nodal points
    b) an imaginary span behind the fixed support
    c) an imaginary span beyond the prop
4. The problem of determining the deflections at the nodal points of a fixed beam by using the finite difference technique, involves the application of
    a) second order finite difference expression
    b) backward differences
    c) fourth order finite difference expression
5. The finite difference method is ideally suited for determining the buckling loads of columns with
    a) uniform flexural rigidity
    b) hinged supports
    c) variable flexural rigidity
6. The finite difference method can be advantageously used for solving the vibration problems of
    a) statically determinate beams
    b) statically indeterminate beams
    c) statically determinate and indeterminate beams
7. In solving problems of beams on elastic foundations using the finite difference method, the equations are formed by considering the
    a) the nodal points within the length of the beam
    b) imaginary span beyond one end of the beam
    c) imaginary span beyond both ends of the beam
8. In applying the finite difference method to solve the problem of a laterally loaded membrane the maximum deflection occurs at the nodal point
    a) coinciding with the edges of the membrane
    b) corresponding to the centre of the membrane
    c) where the slope of the membrane is maximum
9. In determining the maximum shear stress intensity in prismatic bars of different cross sections subjected to torsion by using the membrane analogy and finite difference method, the shear stress can be obtained
    a) directly by solving the finite difference equations
    b) by determining the volume under the membrane
    c) by determining the maximum slope of the emembrane
10. In solving laterally loaded thin plates using the finite difference equations, the coefficient corresponding to the central grid point of the plate is
    a) -8
    b) 20
    c) 2

7   Optimization

7.1 PRINCIPLES OF OPTIMIZATION

According to Gallaghar and Zienkiewicz[1], the primary aim of optimization in engineering problems is to determine the most suitable combination of the significant design variables, so as to achieve a satisfactory design solution subject to the behavioral and geometric constraints imposed, with the goal of optimality being defined by the objective function for specified loading or environmental conditions.

Almost all problems in design, operation and analysis of manufacturing plants and industrial processes require the most economical or optimal solution so that the available resources can be utilized to achieve the maximum production resulting in maximum profits.

The *salient features* of optimization are as follows:

1. The main objective of optimization is the improvement of the system.
2. No single answer is normally found to any problem and it is necessary to choose the best solution for a given problem from the multitude of possible solutions.
3. It is always necessary to define the objective of the study.
4. Optimization is necessary to maximize profits or minimize costs.
5. The problem must be formulated so as to present the information in a quantitative form.
6. The system should be formulated so that there are an infinite number of solutions. This is a necessary condition for optimization.

The three basic features of the optimization problem are listed below:

  (i) The design variables
 (ii) The objective function
(iii) The constraints

A typical example of an optimization problem in structural engineering is the design of a hollow circular strut subjected to an axial load. The aim or objective of design is to reduce the weight such that the cost is minimum, subject to the design constraints such as the diameter and thickness of the walls of the strut and the limitations of stress in the material. These conditions can be written in the form of equations and the optimum size to yield the least weight can be determined.

Generally optimization problems involve long and tedious calculations and as such, manual computations are limited to simple problems comprising a few design variables. However, the development of high speed electronic digital computers[2,3] has revived the interest in complex optimization problems and significant advances have been made in solving various types problems in the field of structural engineering.

In fact, the real impetus to the growth of interest in optimization came only after the pioneering work of Dantzig[4] who developed the simplex algorithm for the solution of linear programming problems.

7.2 LINEAR PROGRAMMING

Linear programming[5,6] is a method of solving the type of problems in which two or more activities compete for limited resources. The allocation of resources is determined with objective of either maximizing or minimizing a linear objective function which is generally the profit or cost respectively.

A majority of the problems in various branches of human activity can be formulated as linear programming problems. There are several methods[7,8] of solving this type of problems. These methods are grouped as follows:

1. Graphical method

2. Trial and error method

3. Simplex method

Linear programming problems involving three or less competing activities are easily solved by the first two methods. If there are large number of activities, the more general and powerful method known as simplex method[9,10] is used.

The following examples illustrate the method of solving linear programming problems using different techniques.

7.3 SOLUTION OF LINEAR PROGRAMMING PROBLEMS

7.3.1 Graphical Method

Example 7.1

Solve the following linear programming problem graphically.

Maximize $Z = 4x_1 + 10x_2$ $\hspace{5cm}$ (1)

Subject to the constraints

$$2x_1 + x_2 \leq 50 \hspace{4cm} (2)$$

$$2x_1 + 5x_2 \leq 100 \hspace{4cm} (3)$$

$$2x_1 + 3x_2 \leq 90 \hspace{4cm} (4)$$

$$x_1 \geq 0 \text{ and } x_2 \geq 0$$

Solution

Considering Eq. (2), we have

$$2x_1 + x_2 = 50$$

When $\hspace{2cm}$ $x_1 = 0, x_2 = 50$

When $\hspace{2cm}$ $x_2 = 0, x_1 = 25$

This equation is plotted as shown in Fig. 7.1 and the lesser sign of inequaity is marked towards the origin.

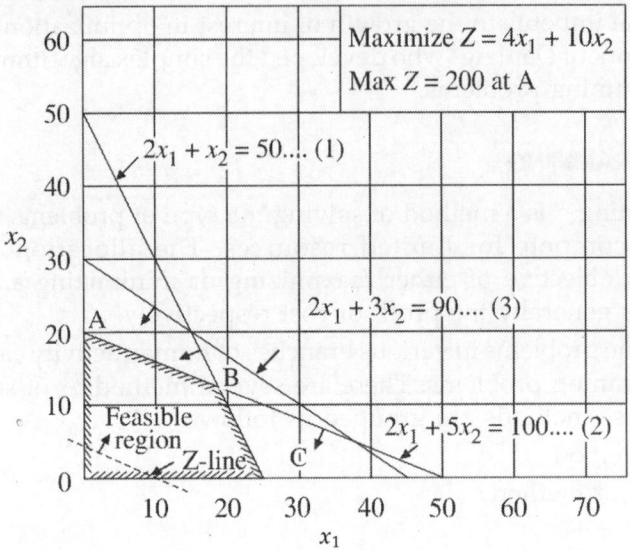

Fig. 7.1: Linear programming problem (general)

Similarly considering the Eq. (3), we have

$$2x_1 + 5x_2 = 100$$

When $\qquad x_1 = 0, x_2 = 20$

When $\qquad x_2 = 0, x_1 = 50$

Similarly considering the Eq. (4), we have .

$$2x_1 + 3x_2 \leq 90$$

When $\qquad x_1 = 0, x_2 = 30$

When $\qquad x_2 = 0, x_1 = 45$

Equations (3) and (4) are plotted as shown in Fig. 7.1.

Considering the Eq. (1), we have max. $Z = 4x_1 + 10x_2 = $ constant

$4x_1 + 10x_2 = 40$ (assumed)

When $x_1 = 0, x_2 = 4$

When $x_2 = 0, x_1 = 10$

By plotting the constraint Eqs (2), (3) and (4), the feasible region is marked as shown in Fig. 7.1.

The objective function line is moved parallel to itself to the outermost corner of the feasible region (A). It actually coincides with the boundary and hence infinite solutions exist. Any point on line AB gives the solution.

Hence we have the optimum solution as

$$Z = 4x_1 + 10x_2 = 4(0) + 10(20)$$

or $Z = 200$

Example 7.2

A firm produces two types of paints. The specific amount of material, labour and machinery hours required to produce each paint and the availability of each of the resources are given in Table 7.1

Table 7.1: Relevant data in the production of the paints

Type of resources	Paint A (tins)	Paint B (tins)	Availability (resources)
Labour	3.00	2.00	12.00 h
Machinery	1.00	2.30	6.9 h
Material	1.00	1.40	4.90 kg

Solution

If the profit for each tin of paint A is Rs. 20 and that for paint B is Rs. 15, formulate the problem as a linear programming problem and determine the optimum production schedule.

Let x_1 = Number of tins produced of paint A

x_2 = Number of tins produced of paint B

The given conditions are transformed into equations by the logic given below. If 1 tin of paint A requires 3 hours of labour, x_1 tins of paint A requires $3x_1$ hours of labour. Similarly x_2 tins of paint B requires $2x_2$ hours of labour.

Total labour hours $= 3x_1 + 2x_2$

Availability of resources = 12 hours

Therefore $3x_1 + 2x_2 \leq 12.00$ (1)

Similarly 1 tin of paint A requires 1 hour of machinery. Hence x_1 tins require x_1 hours of machinery. 1 tin of paint B requires 2.3 h of machinery. Hence x_2 tins of paint B require 2.3 x_2 h of machinery. Total machinery hours $= x_1 + 2.3x_2$ and the availability of resources is 6.90 h.

Therefore $x_1 + 2.3x_2 \leq 6.90$ (2)

1 tin of paint A requires 1 kg of material
x_1 tins of paint A requires x_1 kg of material
1 tin of paint B requires 1.4 kg of material
x_2 tins of paint B requires $1.4x_2$ kg of material
The availability of material is 4.9 kg.

Therefore $x_1 + 1.4x_2 \leq 4.90$ (3)

1 tin of paint A makes a profit of Rs. 20
x_1 tins of paint A makes a profit of Rs. $20x_1$

1 tin of paint B makes a profit of Rs. 15

x_2 tins of paint B makes a profit of Rs. $15x_2$

Total profit is $20x_1 + 15x_2$ which is maximized

Therefore Max. $Z = 20x_1 + 15x_2$ \hfill (4)

The linear equations (1) to (4) are plotted as shown in Fig. 7.2

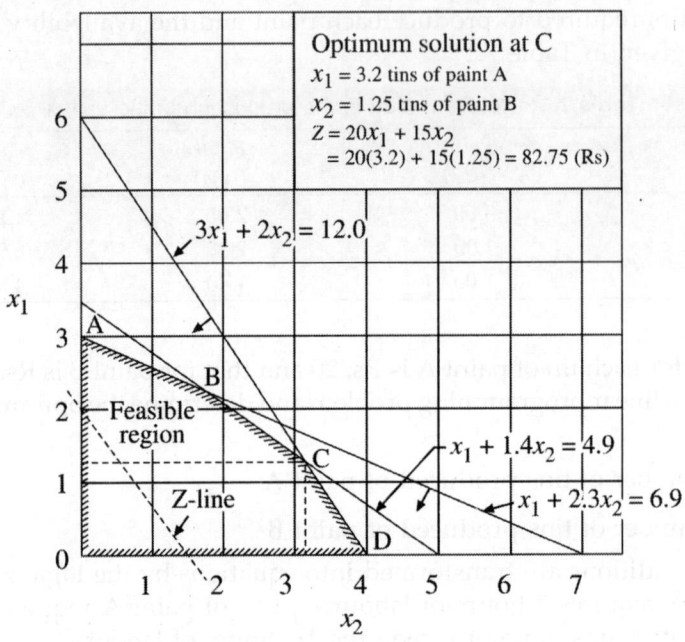

Fig. 7.2: Linear programming problem

The Z-line is moved parallel to itself o the outermost point of the feasible region OABCD to obtain the maximum value of Z corresponding to the point C is then obtained.

From the graphical method substituting the coordinates of C, we get the maximum profit $Z = $ Rs. 82.75 and the optimum production schedule is 3.2 tins of paint A and 1.25 tins of paint B.

Example 7.3

Two grades of paper x and y are produced on a paper machine. Because of raw material restrictions, no more than 400 tonnes of grade x and 300 tonnes of grade y can be produced in a week. There are 160 production hours in a week. It requires 0.2 and 0.4 hr to produce a ton of products of x and y respectively. The profits per ton of x and y are Rs. 20 and Rs. 50 respectively. Formulate the problem and find the optimum production schedule.

Solution

Let x be the number of tones of x grade and y be the number of tones of y paper produced. The first condition is

$$x \le 400 \hfill (1)$$

$$y \leq 300 \tag{2}$$

To produce a tonne of product x it requires 0.2 h

For x tonnes, the time required $0.2x$ is h

To produce a tonne of product y it requires 0.4 h

For y tonnes, the time required $0.4y$ is h

Total production hours is limited to 160 and hence we have the condition,

$$0.2x + 0.4y \leq 160 \tag{3}$$

1 tonne of product x gives a profit of Rs. 20

x tonnes of product x gives a profit of Rs. 20 x

1 tonne of product y gives a profit of Rs. 50

y tonnes of product y gives a profit of Rs. 50 y

Hence the condition is

$$\text{Max } Z = 20x + 50y \tag{4}$$

The linear equations are plotted as shown in Fig. 7.3.

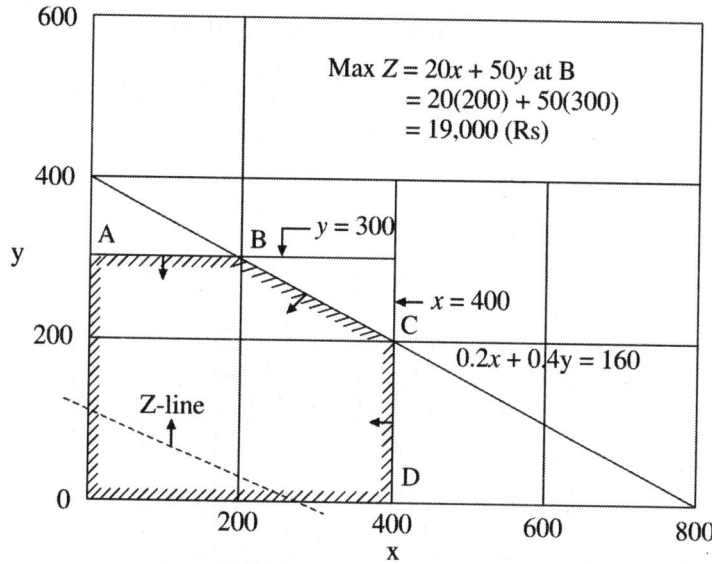

Fig. 7.3: Linear programming problem

From Fig. 7.3, the maximum value of Z occurs at point B, for which

$$x = 200 \text{ tonnes}$$
$$y = 300 \text{ tonnes}$$

Maximum profit is obtained as

$$Z = 20x + 50y$$

$$= 20(200) + 50(300)$$

$$= \text{Rs. } 19000$$

Example 7.4

Solve graphically the function given by

$$\text{Max. } Z = 500x_1 + 200x_2$$

Subject to the restraints

$$9x_1 + 6x_2 \geq 540$$

$$x_1 \geq 30$$

$$x_1 \leq 50$$

$$x_2 \geq 30$$

$$x_2 \leq 80$$

Solution

These equations are plotted graphically as shown in Fig. 7.4.

The optimal solution is when $x_1 = 50$ and $x_2 = 80$

The maximum value of Z is given by

$$Z = 500(50) + 200(80) = 41000$$

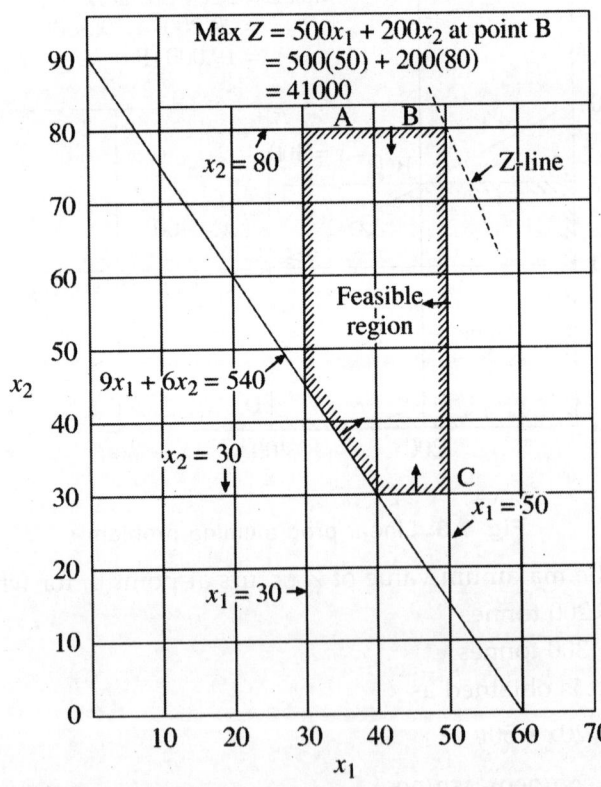

Fig. 7.4: Linear programming problem

Example 7.5

The owner of a dairy is trying to determine the correct blend of two types of feed. Both contain various percentages of four essential ingredients. With the data provided in Table 7.2, determine the least cost blend.

Table 7.2: Data of dairy feed quality and requirement

| Ingredient | Percentage per kg of feed | | Minimum requirement |
	Feed 1	Feed 2	(kg)
1	40	20	4
2	10	30	2
3	20	40	3
4	30	10	6
Cost in Rs/kg	5	3	

Solution

Let x_1 unit of feed 1 are taken and x_1 unit of feed 1 are taken. From the data given in Table 7.2, we have the following linear equations:

$$0.4x_1 + 0.2x_2 \geq 4 \tag{1}$$
$$0.1x_1 + 0.3x_2 \geq 2 \tag{2}$$
$$0.2x_1 + 0.4x_2 \geq 3 \tag{3}$$
$$0.3x_1 + 0.1x_2 \geq 6 \tag{4}$$

Minimize $Z = 5x_1 + 3x_2$

The four equations are graphically represented as shown in Fig. 7.5.

The optimum solution is represented by point B is given as (minimize)

$$Z = (5x_1 + 3x_2) = [5(20) + 3(0)] = 100$$

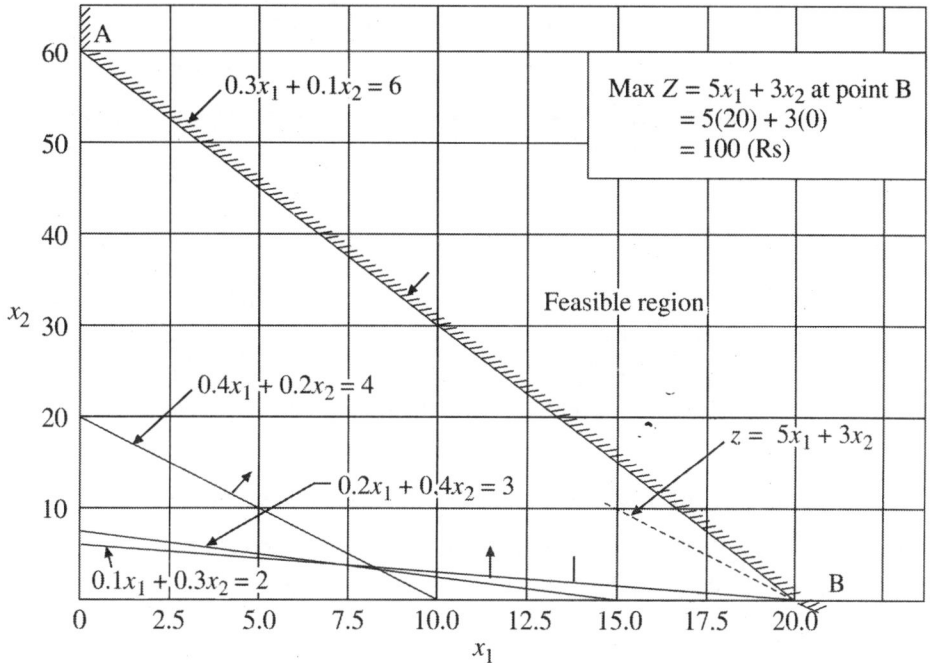

Fig. 7.5: Graphical representation of minimization problem

Example 7.6

A contractor is planning a job that will require a large amount of gravel and sand. There are two pits A and B from which he can obtain material and plans to haul from these pits. Analysis shows that the material at each pit has the composition as shown in Table 7.3.

Table 7.3: Percentage composition of aggregates

Material	Pit A	Pit B	Requirement (m^3)
Coarse gravel	20%	30%	2000
Fine gravel	15%	40%	3000
Fine sand	25%	20%	2000
Coarse sand	40%	10%	Nil

Solution

It costs him Rs. $10/m^3$ for material and transportation from pit A and Rs. $15/m^3$ from pit B. Formulate the linear programming model and determine the blend which results in minimum cost (Fig. 7.6).

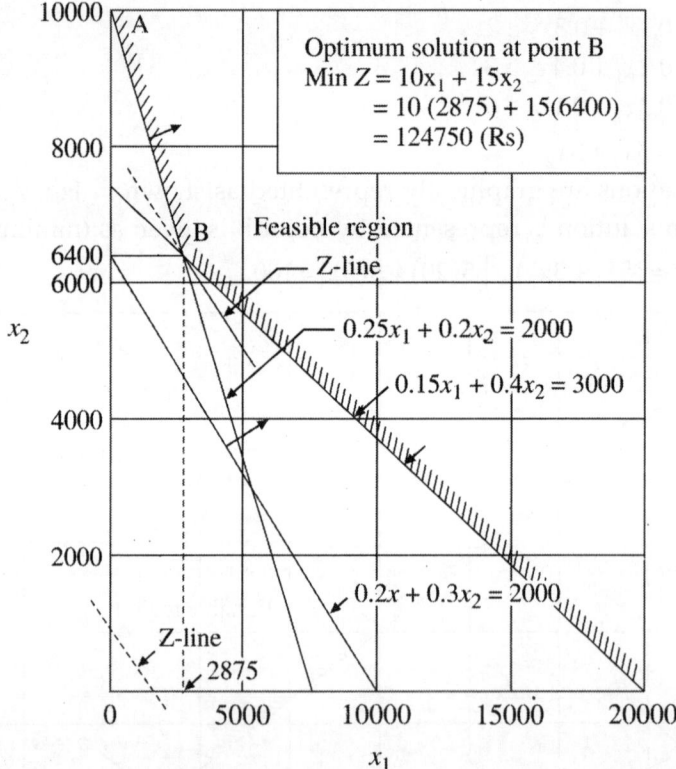

Optimum solution at point B
$$\text{Min } Z = 10x_1 + 15x_2$$
$$= 10\,(2875) + 15(6400)$$
$$= 124750 \text{ (Rs)}$$

Feasible region

Z-line

$$0.25x_1 + 0.2x_2 = 2000$$

$$0.15x_1 + 0.4x_2 = 3000$$

$$0.2x + 0.3x_2 = 2000$$

Z-line

Fig. 7.6: Graphical representation of minimization problem

Let x_1 be the units of material taken from pit A and x_2 from pit B. From the given data the following linear equations are formed.

$$0.2x_1 + 0.3x_2 \geq 2000 \tag{1}$$

$$0.15x_1 + 0.4x_2 \geq 3000 \tag{2}$$

$$0.25x_1 + 0.2x_2 \geq 2000 \tag{3}$$

Minimize $Z = 10x_1 + 15x_2$ $\tag{4}$

These equations are graphically represented as shown in Fig. 7.6.

The optimal solution is represented by the point B which results in

$$x_1 = 2875 \text{ m}^3 \text{ and } x_2 = 6400 \text{ m}^3$$

The minimum cost is obtained as

$$Z = (10x_1 + 15x_2) = \left[10(2875) + 15(6400)\right] = \text{Rs. } 124750$$

Example 7.7

A construction company has two different mines which produce the same ore. After crushing, the ores are graded as A, B and C grades. The company has contracted to supply 48 tonnes of A and 32 tonnes of B and 24 tonnes of C grade ore per month to a smelting plant. The company spends Rs. 1000 per day to run the first mine and Rs. 800 per day to run the second. The capacities are as listed in Table 7.4. How many days per month the mines should operate to fulfill the conditions economically?

Table 7.4: Production capacities of mines

Grade	Production per day (tones)		Supply
	Mine 1	Mine 2	
A	3	1	48
B	2	2	32
C	1	3	24

Solution

Let x_1 be the number of days the mine 1 runs and x_2 be the number of days the mine 2 runs then we have the following equations:

$$3x_1 + x_2 \geq 48 \tag{1}$$

$$2x_1 + 2x_2 \geq 32 \tag{2}$$

$$x_1 + 3x_2 \geq 24 \tag{3}$$

Minimize $Z = 1000x_1 + 800x_2$ $\tag{4}$

These Eqs (1) to (4) are graphically represented as shown in Fig. 7.7

The optimum solution is obtained corresponding to point B and the values of the variables are

$$x_1 = 14.8 \text{ days}$$

$$x_2 = 3.2 \text{ days}$$

Minimum cost $Z = 1000x_1 + 800x_2$

$$= 1000(14.8) + 800(3.2)$$

$$= \text{Rs. } 17360$$

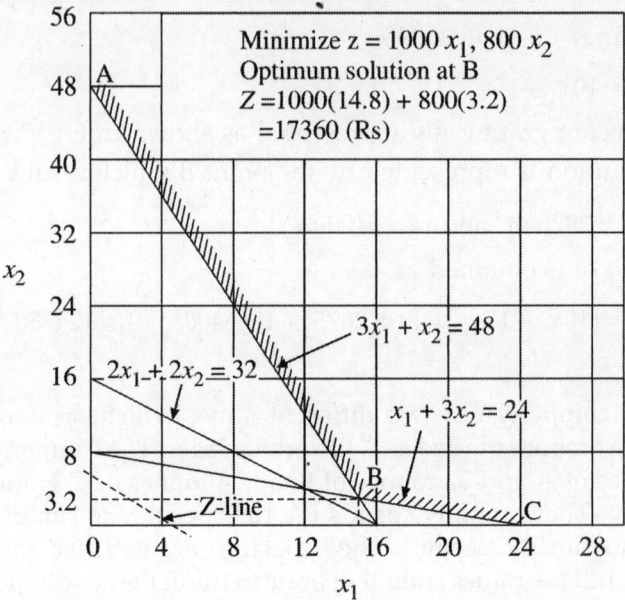

Fig. 7.7: Graphical solution of minimization problem

7.3.2 Trial and Error Method

Example 7.8

Solve the linear programming problem using the systematic trial and error method.

Max. $Z = 3x_1 + 2x_2$

Subject to the constraints

$$x_1 + 2x_2 \leq 430$$

$$3x_1 + 2x_2 \leq 460$$

$$x_1 \geq 0 \text{ and } x_2 \geq 0$$

Solution

Introducing the slack variables, the given equations are modified as

$$x_1 + 2x_2 + s_1 = 430 \tag{1}$$

$$3x_1 + 2x_2 + s_2 = 460 \tag{2}$$

From the Z-equation the largest coefficient of variable is 3

From Eq. (1), $x_1 = 430 - 2x_2 - x_1$

Eq. (2), $x_1 = 153.33 - 0.33x_2 - 0.33s_2 \tag{3}$

Substituting Eq. (3) in Eq. (1), we have

$$153.33 - 0.33x_2 - 0.33s_2 + 2x_2 + s_1 = 430$$

$$1.67x_2 + s_1 - 0.33s_2 = 276.67 \tag{4}$$

$$Z = 3\left(153.33 - 0.33x_2 - 0.33s_2\right) + 2x_2$$

$$= \left(460 - 0.99x_2 - 0.99s_2 + 2x_2\right)$$

$$= \left(1.01x_2 - 0.99s_2 + 450\right) \tag{5}$$

From Eq. (5), maximum positive coefficient occurs for variable x_2.

Considering Eqs (3) and (4) and setting $x_1 = 0, s_1 = 0$ and $s_2 = 0$, we have

$$0 = 153.33 - 0.33x_2 - 0$$

or
$$x_2 = 464.64$$

and
$$1.67x_2 + 0 - 0 = 276.67$$

or
$$x_2 = 165.67$$

Considering Eq. (4), we have

$$1.67x_2 = 276.67 - x_1 + 0.33s_2$$

$$x_2 = 165.67 - 0.598x_1 + 0.1976s_2 \tag{6}$$

Substituting Eq. (6) in Eq. (3), we have

$$x_1 = 153.33 - 0.33\left(165.67 - 0.598s_1 + 0.1976s_2\right) - 0.33s_2$$

$$= 98.66 + 0.1973s_1 - 0.3952s_2 \tag{7}$$

Substituting the value of x_2 from Eq. (6) in Eq. (5), we have

$$Z = 1.01\left(165.67 - 0.598x_1 + 0.1976s_2\right) - 0.99s_2 + 460$$

$$= 627.3267 - 0.6039s_1 - 0.79s_2$$

The resulting variables s_1 and s_2 being negative, they are assigned zero values and by back substitution in Eq. (6) and Eq. (7) the final values are obtained as:

$$x_1 = 98.66$$

$$x_2 = 165.67$$

$$Z = 627.3267$$

Example 7.9

Solve the following linear programming problem having three unknowns using trial and error method.

$$2x_1 + 3x_2 \le 8$$

$$2x_2 + 5x_3 \le 10$$

$$3x_1 + 3x_2 + 4x_3 \le 15$$

$$\text{Max. } Z = 30x_1 + 50x_2 + 40x_3$$

Solution

Rewriting the given equations using slack variables, we have

$$2x_1 + 3x_2 + s_1 = 8 \tag{1}$$

$$2x_2 + 5x_3 + s_2 = 10 \tag{2}$$

$$3x_1 + 3x_2 + 4x_3 + s_3 = 15 \tag{3}$$

$$30x_1 + 50x_2 + 40x_3 = Z \tag{4}$$

From Eq. (4), the largest positive coefficient of variables is 50; hence eliminate x_2

From Eq. (1) $\qquad\qquad x_2 = (8/3) = 2.67$

Eq. (2) $\qquad\qquad x_2 = (10/3) = 5$

Eq. (3) $\qquad\qquad x_2 = (15/3) = 5$

Considering Eq. (1)

$$3x_2 = 8 - s_1 - 2x_1$$

$$x_2 = 2.67 - 0.33s_1 - 0.67x_1 \tag{5}$$

Substituting Eq. (5) in Eq. (2)

$$5.34 - 0.66s_1 - 1.34x_1 + 5x_3 + s_2 = 10$$

$$-1.34x_1 + 5x_3 + s_2 - 0.66s_1 = 4.66 \tag{6}$$

Substituting Eq. (5) in Eq. (3)

$$3x_1 + 8 - s_1 - 2x_1 + 4x_3 + s_3 = 15$$

$$x_1 + 4x_3 - s_1 + s_3 = 7 \tag{7}$$

Substituting Eq. (5) in Eq. (4)

$$Z = 30x_1 + 50(2.67 - 0.33s_1 - 0.67x_1) + 40x_3$$

$$= -3.5x_1 - 16.5s_1 + 40x_3 + 133.5 \tag{8}$$

From Eq. (8), the largest positive coefficient of variables is 40 for x_3, hence eliminate x_3 from
Eqs (5), (6) and (7).

From Eq. (6), $\qquad\qquad x_3 = (4.66/5) = 0.932$

Eq. (7), $\qquad\qquad x_3 = (7/4) = 1.75$

Considering Eq. (6),

$$5x_3 = 4.66 + 0.66s_1 - s_2 = 1.34x_1$$

$$x_3 = 0.932 + 0.132s_1 - 0.2s_2 + 0.268x_1 \tag{9}$$

Substituting Eq. (9) in Eq. (7),

$$x_1 + 4(0.932 + 0.132s_1 - 0.2s_2 + 0.268x_1) - s_1 + s_3 = 7$$

or
$$2.072x_1 + s_3 - 0.472s_1 - 0.8s_2 = 3.272 \tag{10}$$

Substituting Eq. (9) in Eq. (8),

$$Z = -3.5x_1 - 16.5s_1 + 40(0.932 + 0.132s_1 - 0.2s_2 + 0.268x_1) + 133.5$$

$$= 7.22x_1 - 11.22s_1 - 8s_2 + 170.78 \tag{11}$$

From Eq. (11), the largest positive coefficient of variables is 7.22 for x_1 and hence x_1 is to be eliminated from Eqs (5), (9) and (10).

From Eq. (5), $x_1 = (2.67 / 0.67) = 3.985$

From Eq. (9), $x_1 = (-0.932 / 0.268) = -3.4776$

From Eq. (10), $x_1 = (3.272 / 2.072) = 1.579$

Considering Eq. (10),

$$2.072x_1 = 3.272 - x_1 + 0.472s_1 + 0.8s_2$$

$$x_1 = 1.5791 - 0.4826s_3 + 0.2278s_1 + 0.386s_2 \tag{12}$$

Substituting Eq. (12) in Eq. (5),

$$x_2 = 2.67 - 0.33s_1 - 0.67(1.5791 - 0.4826s_3 + 0.2278s_1 + 0.386s_2)$$

$$x_2 = 1.6120 - 0.4826s_1 + 0.323s_3 - 0.2586s_2 \tag{13}$$

Substituting Eq. (12) in Eq. (9),

$$x_3 = 0.932 + 0.132s_1 - 0.2s_2 + 0.268(1.5791 - 0.4826s_3 + 0.2278s_1 + 0.386s_2)$$

$$x_3 = 1.3552 + 0.193s_1 - 0.0964s_2 - 0.129s_3 \tag{14}$$

Substituting Eq. (12) in Eq. (11),

$$Z = 7.22(1.5791 - 0.4826s_3 + 0.2278s_1 + 0.386s_2) - 11.22s_1 - 8s_2 + 170.78$$

$$Z = 182.181 - 3.4843s_3 - 9.5753s_1 - 5.213s_2 \tag{15}$$

There is no positive coefficient for the variables in Eq. (15) and hence the final values of the variables are obtained as,

$$x_1 = 1.5791$$
$$x_2 = 1.6120$$
$$x_3 = 1.3552$$
$$Z = 182.181$$

7.3.3 Simplex Method

Example 7.10

Using simplex method, find the optimum value of the linear programming problem.

Max. $Z = 4x_1 + 10x_2$ subject to the constraints

$$2x_1 + x_2 \leq 50$$

$$2x_1 + 5x_2 \leq 100$$

$$2x_1 + 3x_2 \leq 90$$

$$x_1 \geq 0 \text{ and } x_2 \geq 0$$

Solution

Step 1: The inequalities are converted into equalities by adding slack variables.

$$2x_1 + x_2 + s_1 = 50$$

$$2x_1 + 5x_2 + s_2 = 100$$

$$2x_1 + 3x_2 + s_3 = 90$$

$$-4x_1 - 10x_2 + Z = 0$$

Step 2: The array numbers are written in the order shown below:

		x_1	x_2	
s_1	50	2	1	$(50/1) = 50$
s_1	100	2	5	$(100/5) = 20$
s_1	90	2	3	
Z	0	-4	-10	
			↑	

Step 3:

1. The (– ve) value most in the last row is marked.
2. The ratio of constant to the value in the marked column is determined.
3. The least positive ratio is marked.
4. The element at which these two arrows meet is considered as the pivot.

Step 4: The new array of numbers are written down using the following rules

1. The variables are interchanged.
2. The elements in the pivot row are divided by the pivot, except the pivot.
3. The pivot is replaced by its reciprocal.
4. The elements in the pivot column are divided by the pivot with the negative sign.
5. Any other element is replaced by the new value given by

$$= \left[\text{Previous value} - \frac{e_{\text{pivot row}} \times e_{\text{pivot column}}}{\text{Pivot}} \right]$$

$$= 50 - \left(\frac{100 \times 1}{5} \right) = 30$$

$$= 2 - \left(\frac{2 \times 1}{5}\right) = 1.6$$

$$= 90 - \left(\frac{100 \times 3}{5}\right) = 30$$

$$= 0 - \left(\frac{100 \times -10}{5}\right) = 200$$

$$= -4 - \left(\frac{2 \times -10}{5}\right) = 0$$

Step 5: The new array 2, obtained by using the rules mentioned above is recorded.

Array 2:

		x_1	x_2
s_1	30	1.6	−0.2
x_2	20	0.4	0.2
s_3	30	0.8	−0.6
Z	200	0	20

Step 6: The last row is examined. If the values are still negative, the procedure is continued until all the values are positive. The optimum values are obtained as:

$$x_1 = 0 \qquad x_2 = 20 \qquad Z = 200$$

Example 7.11

Solve the following maximization problem using simplex method

Max. $Z = 20x_1 + 15x_2$ subject to the constraints

$$3x_1 + 2x_2 \le 12.00$$

$$x_1 + 2.3x_2 \le 6.90$$

$$x_1 + 1.4x_2 \le 4.90$$

Solution

Introducing slack variables, the equations are rewritten with equality sign as,

$$x_1 + 2x_2 + s_1 = 12.00$$

$$x_1 + 2.3x_2 + s_2 = 6.90$$

$$x_1 + 1.4x_2 + s_3 = 4.90$$

$$-20x_1 - 15x_2 + Z = 0$$

Array 1

		x_1	x_2	
s_1	12	3	2	$(12/3) = 4$
s_2	6.9	1	2.3	$(6.9/1) = 6.9$
s_3	4.9	1	1.4	$(4.9/1) = 4.9$
Z	0	−20	−15	
		↑		

Array 2

		s_1	x_2	
x_1	4	0.33	0.67	$(4/0.67) = 5.87$
s_2	2.9	−0.33	1.64	$(2.9/1.64) = 1.77$
s_3	0.9	−0.33	0.73	← $(0.9/0.73) = 1.23$
Z	80	6.67	−1.67	
			↑	

Array 3

x_1	3.17	0.63	−0.92
s_2	0.88	0.41	−2.25
x_2	1.23	1.37	1.37
Z	82.06	5.29	2.29

Hence the optimum values are:

$$x_1 = 3.17 \qquad x_2 = 1.23 \qquad Z = 82.06$$

Example 7.12

Determine the optimal solution by the simplex method for the objective function given as,

Max. $Z = 10x_1 + 11x_2$

Subject to the following constraints:

$$3x_1 + 4x_2 \le 9$$
$$5x_1 + 2x_2 \le 8$$
$$3x_1 - 2x_2 \le 1$$
$$x_1 \ge 0 \text{ and } x_2 \ge 0$$

Solution

The equations are rewritten with equality sign using slack variables as,

$$3x_1 + 4x_2 + s_1 = 9$$
$$5x_1 + 2x_2 + s_2 = 8$$
$$3x_1 - 2x_2 + s_3 = 1$$
$$-10x_1 - 11x_2 + Z = 0$$

Array 1

		x_1	x_2	
s_1	9	3	4	← $(9/4) = 2.25$
s_2	8	5	2	$(8/2) = 4.0$
s_3	1	1	−2	−ve
Z	0	−10	−11	
			↑	

Array 2

		x_1	s_1	
x_2	2.25	0.75	0.25	(2.25/0.75) = 3
s_2	3.50	3.50	−0.50	← (3.5/3.5) = 1
s_3	5.50	2.50	0.5	(5.50/2.50) = 2.2
Z	24.75	−1.75	2.75	
		↑		

Array 3

		s_2	s_1
x_2	1.5	−0.21	−0.357
x_1	1	0.286	−0.143
s_3	3	−0.71	0.857
Z	26.5	0.5	2.5

Hence the Optimum values are:

$x_1 = 1$ $\qquad$ $x_2 = 1.5$ $\qquad$ $Z = 26.5$

Example 7.13

A firm produces 3 types of canvas say I, II and III. Three kinds of materials A, B and C are required. One unit length of I canvas requires 2 m of A and 3 m of C. One unit of II canvas 3 m of A and 2 m of B and 3 m of C. One unit of canvas III requires 5 m of B and 4 m of C.

Solution

The company has a stock of 8 m of A, 10 m of B and 15 m of C. The profits obtained from unit lengths of I, II and III are Rs. 30, 50 and 40 respectively. Formulate the linear programming problem and find the optimum units of production for maximum profit using simplex method.

		Material		
Canvas	A (m)	B (m)	C (m)	Profit (Rs)
I	2	0	3	30
II	3	2	3	50
III	0	5	4	40
Availability of resources	8	10	15	

Let $\quad x_1$ be the units of canvas made
$\qquad x_2$ be the units of canvas made
$\qquad x_3$ be the units of canvas made

Hence $2x_1 + 3x_2 \le 8$

$\qquad 2x_2 + 5x_3 \le 10$

$\qquad 3x_1 + 3x_2 + 4x_3 \le 15$

Max. $\quad Z = 30x_1 + 50x_2 + 40x_3$

Introducing slack variables, we have

$$2x_1 + 3x_2 + 0x_3 + s_1 = 8$$

$$0x_1 + 2x_2 + 5x_3 + s_2 = 10$$

$$3x_1 + 3x_2 + 4x_3 + s_3 = 15$$

$$-30x_1 - 50x_2 - 40x_3 + Z = 0$$

Array 1

		x_1	x_2	x_3	
s_1	8	2	3	0	← (8/3) = 2.67
s_2	10	0	2	5	(10/2) = 5.0
s_3	15	3	4	4	(15/3) = 5.0
Z	0	-30	-50	-40	
			↑		

Array 2

		x_1	s_1	x_3	
x_2	2.67	0.67	0.33	0	(2.67/0) = ∞
s_2	4.67	-1.33	-0.67	2	(4.67/2) = 2.385
s_3	7	1	-1	4	← (7/4) = 1.75
Z	133.33	3.33	16.67	-40	
				↑	

Array 3

		x_1	s_1	s_3
x_2	2.67	0	0.33	0
s_2	1.17	-1.83	-0.17	-0.5
x_3	1.75	0.25	-0.25	0.25
Z	203.33	13.33	6.67	10

Hence the optimum values are:

$$x_1 = 0, \qquad x_2 = 2.67, \qquad x_3 = 1.75, \qquad Z = \text{Rs } 203.33$$

Example 7.14

Using the simplex method, solve the following linear programming problem:

Max. $\quad Z = 5x_1 + 3x_2 + 2x_3$

Subject to the constraints

$$2x_1 + 6x_2 - x_3 \le 4$$

$$-x_1 + 5x_2 - 3x_3 \le 1$$

$$5x_1 + x_2 - 6x_3 \le 3$$

$$x_1, x_2 \text{ and } x_3 \ge 0$$

Solution

Introducing slack variables, we have

$$2x_1 + 6x_2 - x_3 + s_1 = 4$$
$$-x_1 + 5x_2 - 3x_3 + s_2 = 1$$
$$5x_1 + x_2 - 6x_3 + s_3 = 3$$
$$-5x_1 - 3x_2 - 2x_3 + Z = 0$$

Array 1

		x_1	x_2	x_3	
s_1	4	2	6	-1	$(4/2) = 2$
s_2	1	-1	5	-3	$(1/-1) = -1$
s_3	3	5	1	-6	$\leftarrow (3/5) = 0.6$
Z	0	-5	-3	-2	

Array 2

		x_1	x_2	x_3	
s_1	2.8	-0.4	5.6	1.4	$\leftarrow (2.8/1.4) = 2$
s_2	1.6	0.2	4.8	-4.2	$(1/6/-4.2) = -0.38$
x_1	0.6	0.2	0.2	-1.2	$(0.6/-1.2) = -0.50$
Z	3	1	-2	-8	

Array 3

x_3	2	-0.285	4	0.71	$(2/-0.285) = -7.02$
s_3	10	-1	21.6	3	$(10/-1) = -10$
x_1	3	-0.14	5	0.86	$(3/-0.14) = -21.42$
Z	19	-1.28	30	5.71	$(19/-1.28) = -14.8$

Since all the ratios are negative, unbounded solution exists.

Example 7.15

Solve the following linear programming problem using the simplex method:

Min. $Z = 1000x_1 + 800x_2$

Subject to the constraints

$$3x_1 + x_2 \geq 48$$
$$2x_1 + 2x_2 \geq 32$$
$$x_1 + 3x_2 \geq 24$$

Solution

A minimization problem can be converted into a maximization problem by introducing the dual problem as shown below:

The dual problem is obtained by considering the first and second column coefficients respectively of the primal problem with new variables a, b and c reversing the inequality signs.

Primal problem	Dual problem
$3x_1 + x_2 \geq 48$	$3a + 2b + c \leq 1000$
$2x_1 + 2x_2 \geq 32$	$a + 2b + 3c \leq 800$
$x_1 + 3x_2 \geq 24$	Max. $Z_1 = 48a + 32b + 24c$

Min. $Z = 1000x_1 + 800x_2$

Solution

The dual problem is solved by introducing the slack variables.

$$3a + 2b + c + s_1 = 1000$$

$$a + 2b + 3c + s_2 = 800$$

$$-48a - 32b - 24c + Z_1 = 0$$

Array 1

		a	b	c	
s_1	1000	3	2	1	← (1000/3) = 333.33
s_2	800	1	2	3	(800/1) = 800
Z_1	0	−48	−32	−24	
		↑			

Array 2

a	333.33	0.33	0.67	0.33	(333.33/0.33) = 1010
s_2	466.67	−0.33	1.33	2.67	← (466.67/2.67)
Z_1	16000	16	0	−8	
				↑	

Array 3

		x_1	b	x_2
a	275.65	−0.289	0.5056	−0.123
c	174.78	−0.123	−0498	0.374
Z_1	17398.26	15.01	3.985	2.996

Hence the optimum values are:

$x_1 = 15.01$ $x_2 = 2.996$ $Z_1 = Z = 17398.26$

The results are comparable to th solution obtained by graphical method presented in Example 7.7, where $x_1 = 14.8$ days and $x_2 = 3.2$ days and Z = Rs 17360

Example 7.16

Using the simplex method solve the minimization problem given by

Min. $Z = 1000x_1 + 800x_2$

Subject to the constraints

$$3x_1 + x_2 \geq 24 \tag{1}$$

$$x_1 + x_2 \leq 24 \tag{2}$$

$$x_1 + x_2 \leq 24 \tag{3}$$

Solution

To convert the inequality sign $\leq$ to $\geq$ multiply the Eq. (3) by –1. Then we have the following equations:

$$3x_1 + x_2 \geq 24$$

$$x_1 + x_2 \geq 16$$

$$-x_1 - x_2 \geq -24$$

The dual of the problem can be written as

$$3a + b - c \leq 1000$$

$$a + b - c \leq 800$$

Max. $Z_1 = 24a + 16b - 24c$

Introducing the slack variables,

$$3a + b - c + s_1 = 1000$$

$$a + b - c + s_2 = 800$$

$$Z_1 - 24a - 16b + 24c = 0$$

Array 1

		a	b	c	
s_1	1000	3	1	–1	$\leftarrow (1000/3) = 333.33$
s_2	800	1	1	–1	$(800/1) = 800$
Z_1	0	–24	–16	24	
		↑			

Array 2

		s_1	b	c	
a	333.33	0.33	0.33	0.33	$(333.33/0.33) = 1010$
s_2	466.67	0.33	0.67	0.67	$\leftarrow (466.67/0.67) = 696.5$
Z_1	8000	8	–8	16	
			↑		

Array 3

		s_1	s_2		
a	103.47	0.49	–0.49	0	
b	686.52	–0.50	1.50	–1	
Z_1	13572.18	4.06	11.94	8	

Hence s_1 corresponds to $x_1 = 4.06$ and s_2 corresponds to $x_2 = 11.94$

and $Z_1 = Z = 13572.18$

Example 7.17

Raj and Raj construction company has alternatives of building 2, 3 and 4 bedroom houses. The company wishes to establish the optimum number of these types yielding maximum profit for the company subject to the following conditions:

1) The total budget is limited to Rs. (360×10^6)
2) The total number of units must be at least 250 for the venture to be economically feasible.
3) The maximum percentage of each type of the flats based on market analysis is
   a) 2 bedroom units 60% of total
   b) 3 bedroom units 25% of total
   c) 4 bedroom units 15% of total
4) Building costs and profits by sales are as follows:

Units	Cost (Rs)	Net profit (Rs)
2 bedroom	8,00,000	80,000
3 bedroom .	10,00,000	1,20,000
4 bedroom	12,00,000	1,50,000

Formulate the problem as a linear programming problem.

Solution

Let x_1 be the number of 2 bedroom house constructed

Let x_2 be the number of 3 bedroom house constructed

Let x_3 be the number of 4 bedroom house constructed

Budget conditions

One 2 bedroom house costs—Rs. 8,00,000

x_1 2 bedroom houses cost—Rs. 8,00,000 x_1

One 3 bedroom house costs—Rs. 10,00,000

x_2 3 bedroom houses cost—Rs. 10,00,000 x_2

One 4 bedroom house costs—Rs. 12,00,000

x_3 4 bedroom houses cost—Rs. 12,00,000 x_3

Hence the total cost will be

$$8,00,000\,x_1 + 10,00,000x_2 + 12,00,000x_3 \leq (360 \times 106) \tag{1}$$

Condition for total number units

The total number of units should be at least 250. Hence the condition is

$$x_1 + x_2 + x_3 \geq 250 \tag{2}$$

Demand condition

Number of 2 bedroom houses = 60% of the total $= 0.6(x_1 + x_2 + x_3)$

Similarly, we have the conditions

$$x_1 = 0.6(x_1 + x_2 + x_3)$$
$$x_2 = 0.25(x_1 + x_2 + x_3) \tag{3}$$
$$x_3 = 0.15(x_1 + x_2 + x_3)$$

Profit condition

One bedroom house yields a profit—Rs. 80,000
x_1 2 bedroom houses yield a profit—Rs. 80,000 x_1
Similarly x_2 3 bedroom houses profit—Rs. 1,20,000 x_2
And x_3 4 bedroom houses profit—Rs. 1,50,000 x_3
Therefore the objective function maximizing the profit is **given** by

Max. $$Z = 80,000\, x_1 + 1,20,000\, x_2 + 1,50,000\, x_3 \tag{4}$$

The objective function (Eq. (4)) together with the constraint Eqs (1), (2) and (3) form the linear programming problem.

Example 7.18

Rajendra construction company has finances to build 50 two bed room houses, 100 three bed room houses and 80 four bed room houses. The company owns land in Bangalore and Mysore cities. The land at Bangalore is sufficient for 180 houses and that at Mysore for 120 houses. The profits are as follows:

Type of House	Bangalore	Mysore
2 bedroom house	Rs. 8,000	Rs. 7,200
3 bedroom house	Rs. 6,000	Rs. 6,000
4 bedroom house	Rs. 9,000	Rs. 7,500

Formulate the linear programming problem.

Solution

Let x_{2B} the number of 2 bedroom houses at Bangalore
Let x_{2M} the number of 2 bedroom houses at Mysore
Let x_{3B} the number of 3 bedroom houses at Bangalore
Let x_{3M} the number of 3 bedroom houses at Mysore
Let x_{4B} the number of 4 bedroom houses at Bangalore
Let x_{4M} the number of 4 bedroom houses at Mysore

Condition of construction of houses

The total number of 2, 3 and 4 bedroom houses constructed should satisfy the following conditions:

$$x_{2B} + x_{2M} \le 50 \tag{1}$$
$$x_{3B} + x_{3M} \le 100 \tag{2}$$
$$x_{4B} + x_{4M} \le 80 \tag{3}$$

Condition of total number of houses

$$x_{2B} + x_{3B} + x_{4B} \le 180 \tag{4}$$
$$x_{2M} + x_{3M} + x_{4M} \le 120 \tag{5}$$

The objective function maximizing the profit is given by the equation:

Max. $\quad Z = 8000x_{2B} + 6000x_{3B} + 9000x_{4B} + 7200x_{2M} + 6000x_{3M} + 7500x_{4M}$ $\qquad$ (6)

The objective function [Eq. 6] together with the constraint Eqs (1) to (5) form the linear programming problem.

Example 7.19

Suresh Company produces two types of products namely A and B. The raw material requirement, space required for storage and time requirement are given in Table 7.5. All products produced are shipped out of the storage area at the end of the day. Formulate the linear programming model using the given data.

Table 7.5: Requirement and availability of quantities

	Product A	Product B	Availability
Storage space (m²/unit)	4	5	1500 m²
Raw material	5	3	1575 kg
Production rate	60	30	8.5 h
Profit (Rs/unit)	15	12	

Solution

Let $\quad x_1$ be the number of products of type A produced

$\qquad x_1$ be the number of products of type B produced

Storage space restriction

$\qquad$ Product A requires 4 m² area

$\qquad x_1$ units of A require $4x_1$

$\qquad$ Product B requires 5 m² area

$\qquad x_2$ units of B require $5x_2$

$\qquad$ Total space available = 1500 m²

$\qquad$ Hence $4x_1 + 5x_2 \le 1500$ $\qquad$ (1)

Raw material restriction

$\qquad$ Product A requires 5 kg

$\qquad x_1$ units of A require 5

$\qquad$ Product B requires 3 kg

$\qquad x_2$ units of B require 3

$\qquad$ Hence we have the condition

$\qquad 5x_1 + 3x_2 \le 1575$ $\qquad$ (2)

Working hours condition

$\qquad$ Total number of working house available is 8.5 h

$\qquad$ 1/60 unit of product A requires a time of 1 h

$\qquad x_1$ units of product A requires $x_1/60$ h

$\qquad x_2$ units of product B requires $x_2/30$

Hence the condition can be expressed as
$(x_1/60) + (x_2/30) \leq 8.5$ (3)

Profit condition

Product A yields a profit of Rs. 15
x_1 units of product A yields a profit of 15
Product B yields a profit of Rs. 12
x_2 units of product B yields a profit of $12x_2$
Hence the profit condition is given by

Max. $Z = 15x_1 + 12x_2$ (4)

The objective function (4) together with the constraint Eqs (1) to (3) form the linear programming problem.

Example 7.20

The Bangalore brick company has three plants with capacities of 25, 30 and 35 units. It has plans to supply bricks to four customers in different locations. The demands together with transportation costs are given in Table 7.6. Formulate the shipping schedule as a linear programming problem.

Table 7.6: Transportation costs of bricks from different plants

Customer Plant	A	B	C	D	Capacity of Plants
I	100	140	80	150	25 units
II	120	110	150	90	30 units
III	130	100	120	140	35 units
Demand from Customer	15	30	20	25	

Solution

Let x_{1A} be the material from plant I to customer A
Let x_{2A} be the material from plant II to customer A
Let x_{3A} be the material from plant III to customer A
Similar notations have been used for materials to customers B, C and D.

Capacity condition

$$x_{1A} + x_{1B} + x_{1C} + x_{1D} \leq 25 \qquad (1)$$
$$x_{2A} + x_{2B} + x_{2C} + x_{2D} \leq 30 \qquad (2)$$
$$x_{3A} + x_{3B} + x_{3C} + x_{3D} \leq 35 \qquad (3)$$

Demand condition

$$x_{1A} + x_{2A} + x_{3A} \geq 15 \qquad (4)$$
$$x_{1B} + x_{2B} + x_{3B} \geq 30 \qquad (5)$$
$$x_{1C} + x_{2C} + x_{3C} \geq 20 \qquad (6)$$
$$x_{1D} + x_{2D} + x_{3D} \geq 25 \qquad (7)$$

Transportation cost condition

$$\text{Min.} \quad Z = 100x_{1A} + 140x_{1B} + 80x_{1C} + 150x_{1D}$$
$$+ 120x_{2A} + 110x_{2B} + 150x_{2C} + 90x_{2D}$$
$$+ 130x_{3A} + 100x_{3B} + 120x_{3C} + 140x_{3D} \tag{8}$$

Equations (1) to (8) form the linear programming problem.

Example 7.21

Solve the following minimization problem using the simplex (direct) method.

$$3x_1 + x_2 \geq 24$$
$$x_1 + x_2 \geq 16$$
$$x_1 + x_2 \leq 24$$
$$x_1 + x_2 \leq 32$$
$$\text{Min.} \quad Z = 1000x_1 + 800x_2$$

Solution

Introducing he slack variables s_1, s_2, s_3 and s_4 and artificial variables A_1 and A_2, the equations are rewritten in the following form:

$$3x_1 + x_2 - s_1 + A_1 = 24$$
$$x_1 + x_2 - s_2 + A_2 = 16$$
$$x_1 + x_2 + s_3 = 24$$
$$x_1 + x_2 + s_4 = 32$$
$$- 1000x_1 - 800x_2 + Z + P(A_1 + A_2) = 0$$

Array 1

		x_1	x_2	s_1	s_2	
A_1	24	3	1	−1	0	← (24/3) = 8
A_1	16	1	1	0	−1	(16/1) = 16
s_3	24	1	0	0	0	(24/1) = 24
s_4	32	1	1	0	0	(32/1) = 32
Z	0	−1000	−800	0	0	
$P(A_1 + A_2)$	40	4	2	−1	−1	
		↑				

Array 2

		A_1	x_2	s_1	s_2	
x_1	8	0.33	0.33	−0.33	0	(8/0.33) = 24.24
A_2	8	−0.33	0.67	0.33	−1	← (8/0.67) = 11.94
s_3	16	−0.33	0.67	0.33	0	(16/0.67) = 23.89
s_4	24	−0.33	0.67	0.33	0	(24/0.67) = 35.92
Z	8000	333.33	−466.67	−333.33	0	−ve
P	8	−1.33	0.67	−0.33	−1	−
			↑			

Array 3

		A_1	A_2	s_1	s_2
x_1	4.06	0.4925	−0.492	−0.492	0.4925
x_2	11.94	−0.49	1.492	0.49	−1.4925
s_3	8	0	−1	0	1.00
s_4	16	0	−1	0	1.00
Z	13572.18	103.47	696.52	−103.47	−696.52
P	0	−1	−1	0	0

Since there is no positive value I the last row, the procedure is stopped and the final values are:

$$x_1 = 4.06$$
$$x_2 = 11.94$$
$$Z = 13572.18$$

Example 7.22

Solve the following linear programming problem using the simplex method (direct method).

$$\text{Min. } Z = x_1 - 3x_2 - 2x_3$$

Subject to the constraints

$$3x_1 - x_2 + 2x_3 \le 7$$
$$2x_1 - 4x_2 \ge 12$$
$$-4x_1 + 3x_2 + 8x_3 \le 10$$

Solution

Introducing the slack variables and rewriting the equations, we have

$$3x_1 - x_2 + 2x_3 + s_1 = 7$$
$$2x_1 - 4x_2 - s_2 + A_1 = 12$$
$$-4x_1 + 3x_2 + 8x_3 + s_3 = 10$$
$$-x_1 + 3x_2 + 2x_3 + Z + P(A_1) = 0$$

Array 1

		x_1	x_2	x_3	s_1	s_2	
x_1	7	3	−1	2	1	0	← (7/3) = 2.33
A_1	12	2	−4	0	0	−1	(12/2) = 6
s_3	10	−4	3	8	0	0	−ve
Z	0	−1	3	2	0	0	−
Z	12	2	−4	0	0	−1	
		↑					

Array 2

		s_1	x_2	x_3	s_2
x_1	2.33	0.33	−0.33	0.67	0
A_1	7.33	−0.67	−3.33	−1.33	−1
s_3	19.33	1.33	1.67	10.67	0
Z	2.33	0.33	2.67	2.67	0
Z	7.33	−0.67	−3.33	−1.33	−1

Since there is no positive value of the variables in the last row, the procedure is stopped and the final values are

$$x_1 = 2.33$$
$$x_2 = x_3 = 0$$
$$Z = 2.33$$

Example 7.23

For the linear programming problem

Min. $Z = 1000x_1 + 800x_2$

Subject to the constraints

$$3x_1 + x_2 \geq 24$$
$$x_1 + x_2 \geq 16$$
$$x_1 + x_2 \leq 24$$

Prepare the optimal Tableau of the primal and dual problem and compare the solutions.

Solution

The solution of the primal problem presented in Example 7.21 and the solution of the dual problem presented in Example 7.16 are herewith compared in Table. 7.7.

Table 7.7: Comparison of primal and dual problem solutions									
Linear programming problem: Min. $Z = 1000x_1 + 800x_2$ subject to the constraints									
						$x_1 + x_2 \geq 24, x_1 + x_2 \geq 16, x_1 + x_2 \leq 24$			
Optimal tableau of primal problem						Optimal tableau of dual problem			
		A_1	A_2	s_1	s_2			s_1	s_2	c
x_1	4.06	0.49	−0.5	−0.49	0.49	a	103.47	0.49	−0.49	0
x_2	11.94	−0.50	1.492	0.49	1.50	b	696.5	−0.50	1.5	1
s_3	8.0	0	−1.00	0	1.0	Z	13572.18	4.06	11.94	8
Z	13572.18	103.48	696.52	−103.47	696.52					

The comparative analysis of Table 7.7 containing the solutions of the primal and dual problems indicates the following inter-relations:

1. Objective functions of the optimal tableau of both primal and dual problems give similar values
2. The values of and which are basic variables in the primal problem correspond to the values of the slack variables and in the dual problem.

3. The values of the slack variables with the negative sign in the primal problem correspond to the basic values in the dual problem.

EXERCISES

1. Solve the following linear programming problem by graphical method.

   Min. $Z = 1500x_1 + 1575x_2 + 420x_3$

   Subject to the constraints

   $$4x_1 + 5x_2 + x_3 \geq 13$$

   $$5x_1 + 3x_2 + 2x_3 \geq 11$$

   $x_1 \geq 0$ and $x_2 \geq 0$

2. A patient of limited means was advised by the physician to increase the consumption oftwo two foods. In each meal he must get vitamin A and B not less than 10 units and 8 units respectively from the combination. There are 2 units of vitamin A and 6 units of vitamin B per unit of food 1. Each unit of food 2 has 4 units of vitamin A and 2 units of vitamin B. The cost per unit of food 1 and food 2 is Rs. 5 and 2.5 respectively. What is the optimum combination at minimum cost? Adopt the graphical method.

3. In order to assure adequate stability under load repetitions, a soil mixture for basic and sub base Courses in the construction of a certain highway must have a liquid limit (LL) between the limits $21 \leq LL \leq 28$ and plasticity index in the range $4 \leq PI \leq 6$.

   Two types of soils A and B are available with the following properties:

	Soil A	Soil B
LL	35	20
PI	8	3.5
Cost (Rs)	120	180

   Assume LL and as linear functions of combination of two soils A and B.

   Formulate the problemas a linear programming problem and find out the optimum mixing proportions using graphical method.

4. Products A and B are produced in a factory involving three major operations such as cutting, folding and packing. The processing time in minutes for each of these operations for products A and B are as shown in Table 7.8. Find by the graphical method, the mix of product A and B which will yield the maximum combination.

Table 7.8: Process time by state of department

Department	Size (Units) A	B	Available time (Minutes)
Cutting	10.7	5.0	2705
Folding	5.4	10.0	2210
Packing	0.7	1.0	445
Profit contribution (per unit)	Rs. 10	Rs. 15	

5. A firm produces two types of plastic containers. Each of these containers must be processed through two different machines. The machine capacities, processing time and profit contribution per unit are given in Table 7.9.

Table 7.9: Requirements and capacities of various machines

Machine	Processing time per unit (min)		Available capacity per time period (min)
	Container A	Container B	
1	4	2	2000
2	3	5	3000
Profit contribution (per unit)	Rs. 20	Rs. 10	

Formulate the linear programming problem.

6. The following algebraic statements represent a typical production problem which can be solved by linear programming.

Max. $Z = 3x + 4y$ subject to the constraints,

$5x + 8y \leq 2000$

$3x + 10y \leq 1000$

$x \geq 0, y \geq 0$

Solve the problem by the graphical method and give some physical meaning to the algebraic Statements.

7. Solve the linear programming problem by trial and error method.

Maximize $Z = 6x + 4y$ subject to the constraints

$x + y \leq 4$

$x - y \leq 2$

$x \geq 0, y \geq 0$

8. Using the trial and error method, solve the linear programming problem

Max. $Z = 2x_1 + 5x_2$ subject to the constraints

$2x_1 + x_2 \leq 25$

$2x_1 + 5x_2 \leq 50$

$2x_1 + 3x_2 \leq 45$

$x_1 \geq 0, x_2 \geq 0$

9. Determine the optimal solution if the objective function is to be maximized using the the Simplex method.

Max. $Z = 10x_1 + 11x_2$ subject to the constraints

$3x_1 + 4x_2 \leq 9$

$5x_1 + 2x_2 \leq 8$

$x_1 - 2x_2 \leq 1$

$x_1 \geq 0, x_2 \geq 0$

10. Determine the optimum solution by maximizing the profit function using the simplex method.

Max. $Z = 10x + 15y$ subject to the constraints

$10.7\, x + 5.0y \leq 2705$

$5.4\, x + 10.0y \leq 2210$

$0.7\, x + 1.0y \leq 445$

11. The following algebraic statements represent a typical production problem which can be solved by linear programming.

Max. $Z = 3x + 4y$ subject to the constraints,

$5x + 8y \leq 2000$

$3x + 10y \leq 1000$

$x \geq 0, y \geq 0$

Solve the problem by simplex method and give some physical meaning to the algebraic statements.

12. Using the simplex method, solve the following linear programming problem.

Minimize $Z = 5x_1 + 7.5x_2$ subject to the constraints

$2x_1 + 3x_2 \geq 200$

$1.5x_1 + 4x_2 \geq 300$

$2.5x_1 + 2x_2 \geq 200$

13. A tile company manufactures two types of flooring tiles, regular and deluxe. The product is prepared in two plants. Regular tiles are manufactured in plant A and deluxe tiles in plant B. Due to limitations in production capacities of A and B, the daily production is limited to not more than 800 regular and 600 deluxe tiles. The production of both types of tiles requires chips of a particular variety which is in short supply and limited to 600 units per day.

The production of a regular tile requires 5 units of chips and deluxe tiles require 6 units of chips. The company has 160 hours of labour. To manufacture 10 regular tiles, it requires one hour. 10 deluxe tiles require 2 hours of labour. The profit for 100 regular tiles is Rs. 50, while that for deluxe tiles, it is Rs. 80. Formulate the linear programming problem.

14. A hard rock company provides gravel from its quarry pits for concrete mixing companies. Table 7.10 gives the sales costs and available time expected during the next 4 months. There is no gravel stock in the beginning of the first month and at the end of 4 months.. It takes 1.5 hours of production time to produce 1000 m^3 of gravel. It costs Rs. 50 to store 1000 m^3 from one month to the next.

The company wants a production schedule that does not exceed the production time limitations. Formulate the linear programming problem for optimum costs of operation.

Table 7.10: Sale, cost and available time for hard rock company

Month	1	2	3	4
Gravel required (m³)	1000	2500	2100	2900
Regular cost (Rs)	100	100	110	110
Over time cost (Rs)	110	116	120	124
Operation time (h)	240	240	240	240
Over time (h)	99	99	99	99

REFERENCES

1. Gallaghar RH and Zienkiwicz, *Optimum Structural design, Theory and Applications*, John Wiley Sons, 1973, pp. 7-17.

2. Pearson C, *Structural Design by High Speed Computing Machines, Proceedings of ASCE Conference on Electronic Computation*, Kansas City, Missouri, 1958.

3. Venkayya VB, *Design of Optimum Structural Elements, Computers and Structures*, Vol. 1 No.1/2, 1971, pp. 265-309.

4. Dantzig GB, *Linear Programming and Extensions*, Princeton UniversityPress, Princeton, New Jersey, 1963.

5. Srinath LS, *Linear Programming*, Affiliated East West Press Ltd, New Delhi, second Edition. 1982.

6. Richard Fox L, *Optimization Methods for Engineering Design*, Addison–Wesley, Reading, Massasuchets, 1971.

7. Kunzi HP, Tzchach HG and Sehnder CA, *Numerical Methods of Mathematical Optimisation*, Academic Press, New York, 1968.

8. Rajasekaran S, *Numerical Methods in Science and Engineering–A* Practical Approach, A.H. Wheeler & Co, Delhi, 1986.

9. Gass SI, *Linear Programming; Methods and Applications*, McGraw Hill, New York, 1959.

10. Paul Loomba N, *Linear Programming*, Tata McGraw-Hill, New Delhi, 1971.

REVIEW QUESTIONS

1. Explain clearly the basic purpose of optimization in engineering problems like analysis, design, and manufacturing plants.

2. Briefly list the various features of the optimization in engineering problems involving multitude of possible solutions.

3. Explain briefly with examples the three basic features of the optimization problems in the engineering domain.

4. What is linear programming? Briefly outline the various methods generally used in linear programming in solving engineering problems.

5. Explain the graphical method of solving maximization problems with several variables, mentioning its advantages.

6. Explain the terms a) Maximization b) Feasible region c) Optimal solution, with respect to the solution of linear programming problems using the graphical method.

7. Explain with examples: the trial and error method of solving linear programming problems involving several variables in engineering problems.

8. Briefly explain the simplex method of finding the optimum value in linear programming problems involving several variables.

9. What are slack variables? In what way they are useful in solving the linear programming problems using the simplex method.

10. Explain the terms a) Objective function b) Constraints c) Primal problem d) Dual problem with respect to the solution of linear programming problems using the simplex method.

OBJECTIVE TYPE QUESTIONS

1. Optimization is generally used in engineering problems having several solutions to
   a) analyze the various solutions
   b) find the best possible solution
   c) compare the cost of various solutions.

2. In the optimization problem of designing a hollow circular shaft subjected to axial load, the main aim of the design is to
   a) determine optimal size of the shaft
   b) minimize the weight and cost
   c) ensure maximum strength

3. The solution of optimization problems involving several variables gathered momentum only after The advent of
   a) various design procedures
   b) electronic computers
   c) ingenious mathematical techniques

4. For solving optimization problems involving 2 to 3 variables only, the ideal method to be used is
   a) moment distribution method
   b) matrix method
   c) graphical method

5. Graphical method of solving optimization problems can be used only in
   a) maximization problems
   b) minimization problems
   c) both maximization and minimization problems

6. In solving linear programming problems using the trial and error method, the solution is obtained by using
   a) slack variables
   b) back substitution
   c) the elimination method

7. The solution of linear programming problems with three unknowns using the trial and error method involves the
   a) elimination of the variable having the smallest positive coefficient
   b) elimination of the variable having the largest positive coefficient
   c) elimination of the variable having the largest negative coefficient

8. In the simplex method of solving liner programming problems, the inequalities are converted to equalities by introducing
   a) additional constants
   b) slack variables
   c) mathematical functions

9. In solving linear programming problems using the simplex method and generating the arrays, it is important to consider
   a) the most positive value in any of the rows
   b) the most negative value in the last row
   c) the most positive value in the first row

10. The simplex method can be conveniently used for converting the minimization problem into a maximization problem by introducing the
    a) inversion procedure
    b) dual problem
    c) objective function

8

Computer Programming

8.1 INTRODUCTION

8.1.1 Programming Languages

The application of numerical methods for solving the various types of engineering problems discussed in chapters 1 to 7 involves computations which are repetitive, cumbersome and time consuming with calculators. A digital computer[1,2] is ideally suited to perform these computations in a very short time when the problem is programmed and presented in a logical sequence using a definite programming language. Some of the early programming languages developed are the ALGOL, COBOL and FORTRAN followed by C and Java programming languages to cater to the needs of ever increasing demands of the commerce, science and engineering fields.

1. Fortran Programming Language

FORTRAN is considered as one of the oldest programming language in existence developed by a team of programmers at IBM led by John Backus in 1957. Its name derives as "FORmula TRANslation" is generally used for numeric and scientific computing. It is a general-purpose, imperative programming language. The first standard definition of this language was adopted in 1966 and a major revision was made in this standard in the 1970s, leading to the FORTRAN 77 and FORTRAN 90 in the year 1990. In its time FORTRAN was one of the most popular programming languages in the area of high performance computing and was developed "for execution on the IBM 704 computer". It opened the door to practical usage of computers by large numbers of scientific and engineering personnel.

2. C Programming Language

One of the most popular languages till date is the C programming language used by both novice and expert programmers. It was developed in 1972 by Dennis Ritchie and Ken Thompson at AT and T Bell Laboratories. Although a general-purpose programming language, its compact syntax and efficient execution characteristics have made it popular as a system programming language. C is an imperative (procedural) systems implementation language. It was designed to be compiled using a relatively straightforward compiler, to provide low-level access to memory, to provide language constructs that map efficiently to machine instructions, and to require minimal run-time support. A standards-compliant and portably written C program can be compiled for a very wide variety of computer platforms and operating systems with little or no change to its source code.

Among the various programming languages in use, FORTRAN[3,4] (formula translation language) is widely used by engineers throughout the world for engineering computations for the last several decades. C/C++ is a programming language[5,6] first introduced in 1972 with a powerful influence on the computer programming[7,8] domain despite its steep learning curve. The advanced high speed computers such as IBM-360, ICT-1909, DEC-10 and CDC-3600 use FORTRAN-IV and hence some salient features of FORTRAN-IV[9] are presented in the following section. Typical computer programmes using the FORTRAN language are used for most of the problems encountered in the engineering field are presented at the end of the chapter. Some salient programmes using the C–language as reported by Jain et al[10] are also included at the end of this chapter.

8.1.2 Flow Charts

Flow charts are diagrammatic representation of the various operations involved in the solution of a given problem. The operations and the paths to be followed are represented as a flow chart.

The flow chart helps to identify the various operations such a starting, processing, decision making and other items involved in a computer programme. The flow chart helps to decipher the logic to be followed in writing a correct programme and also helps the programmer to modify an existing programme.

The final preparation of a computer programme in a programming language is preceded by flow charting and coding of the given problem. Several symbols used for the various critical operations in flow charts are compiled in Fig. 8.1.

Symbol	Operation
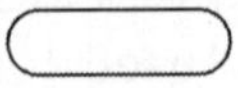	Start and stop terminals
	Processing annotation
	Decision
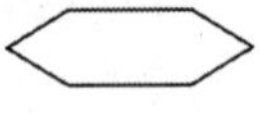	Predefined process
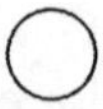	Connector
	Punched card

Fig. 8.1: Flow chart symbols

The start and stop symbols are used at the commencement and end of the programme.

The processing symbol is used for conducting the main mathematical operations and also for specifying instructions such as reading from a card or printing of results.

The decision symbol is used whenever there is a possibility of branching of the problem into two or more alternative paths.

The predefined process symbol is used for specifying the use of a subroutine which can be directly used in the main programme. The connector symbol helps to show the continuation of the flow chart without having a line to join the two portions of a flow chart.

Figure 8.2 shows a typical flow chart to compute the value of the moment of resistance M of a reinforced concrete beam using the formula, $M = Q \cdot B \cdot D^2$.

Figure 8.3 shows a flow chart to find the sum of 200 numbers.

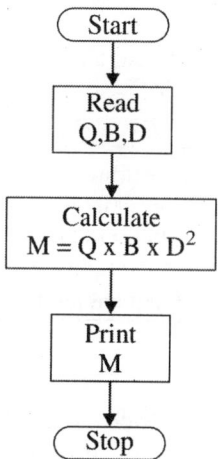

Fig. 8.2: Flow chart for calculating and printing moments from given formula

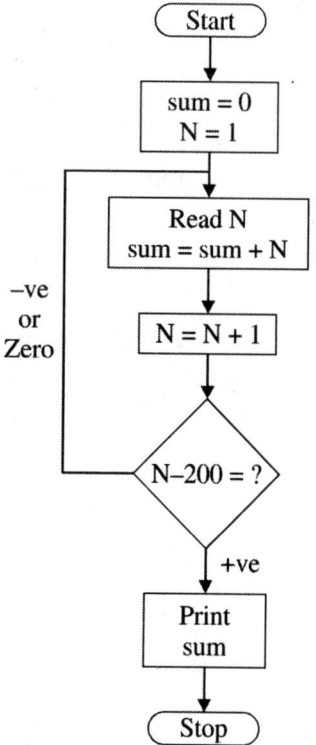

Fig. 8.3: Flow chart for finding the sum of 200 numbers

8.2 ARITHMETIC EXPRESSIONS AND STATEMENTS

8.2.1 Arithmetic Expression

The arithmetic expression involving the routine mathematical operations of addition, subtraction, multiplication and division and exponentiation, comprises a sequence of constants and variables separated by the appropriate arithmetic operation symbols.

Table 8.1 shows the various arithmetic operations symbols expressed in the FORTRAN language together with examples.

Table 8.1: Arithmetic expressions and operations

Name of symbol	Symbol	Operation	Mathematical statement	FORTRAN statement
Plus	+	Addition	$A + B$	$A + B$
Minus	–	Subtraction	$A - B$	$A - B$
Asterisk	*	Multiplication	$A \times B$	$A \times B$
Slash	/	Division	$A \div B$	A/B
Double star	**	Exponentiation	A^B	$A ** B$

8.2.2 Fortran Constants

A Fortran constant is any number which is used in computations without being changed during the execution of the programme.

(a) Fixed point or integer constant

Integer or fixed point constant is represented by whole numbers without a decimal point. The following rules are applicable for integer constants to be valid.

1. A fixed point constant should be written without a decimal point using the digits 0, 1, 2, 3, ..., 9.
2. A preceding –ve sign is essential and an unsigned constant is assumed to be positive.
3. The maximum number of digits permitted is 10.

Table 8.2 Gives some examples of valid and invalid integer constants

Table 8.2: Fixed point or integer constants

Sl. No.	Fixed point constant	Valid or invalid with reasons
1.	0	Valid
2.	1,469	Not valid, comma not allowed
3.	18.63	Not valid, decimal point is not allowed
4.	– 4863	Valid
5.	456 + 75	Not valid, the fixed point constant can never be an arithmetic expression.
6.	567898	Not valid, unless a parameter card is used. The integer should not exceed four digits in the absence of a parameter card.
7.	+ 9364	Valid
8.	84 * 18	Not valid, this is an arithmetic expression.
9.	0789	Valid

Contd...

Sl. No.	Fixed point constant	Valid or invalid with reasons
10.	$16\frac{1}{2}$	Not valid, Fractions are not permitted.
11.	₹ 120	Not valid, prefix symbol not permitted
12.	± 250	Not valid, conditional sign not permitted.

The following rules are applicable for floating point constants.

1. A floating point constant should be written with a decimal point using the digits 0, 1, 2, 3, ..., 9.
2. A preceding –ve sign is essential. An unsigned constant is considered to be positive.
3. When the constant is written with an exponent, the exponent together with its sign should be prescribed by the letter E.
4. The normal length of mantissa is 8 digits. The length of the mantissa can be prescribed by the programmer to contain 2 to 28 digits using a parameter card. The exponent should not have more than 2 digits. In fact, the exponent should be between – 99 and + 99.
5. If a mantissa of 25 digits is specified without a parameter card, then the first eight digits will be considered during calculations. Some examples of valid and invalid floating point constants are listed in Table 8.3.

Sl. No.	Floating point constant	Valid or invalid with reasons
		Table 8.3: Floating point constants
1.	20.35	Valid.
2.	– 52.67	Valid.
3.	0.005732	Valid.
4.	0.1567E + 4	Valid (0.1567×10^4)
5.	0.78567 E12	Valid, the sign of the exponent is assumed to be positive.
6.	0.4E24	Valid
7.	652.8E – 15	Valid
8.	465.3E – 4.5	Invalid, the exponent should not contain a decimal point.
9.	8.64E + 745	Not valid, the exponent should lie between
10.	78,534.66	Invalid, the special character like comma are not allowed.
11.	87E15	Invalid, the floating point constant should be written with a decimal point. The decimal point is missing.
12.	0.84E – 4	Invalid, the exponent should not be a floating point constant.
13.	0.846 + 3.5	Invalid, two decimals not permitted.
14.	143.2E	Invalid, field following exponent is blank.
15.	1.4E – 200	Invalid, the exponent should lie between
16.	56*E8	Invalid, star not allowed.

8.2.3 FORTRAN Variables

A FORTRAN variable can change its value during the different stages of the programme. Each variable is assigned a name for easy identification. The name of the variable used in Fortran refers to the address of the memory location in which the value of the variable is stored. Since the value of any variable can only be a constant, the Fortran variables are of two categories: (a) Fixed point or integer variables and (b) Floating point or real variables. The names of the Fortran variables should conform to the following set of rules.

(a) Fixed point or integer variables

(i) A fixed point variable should consist of alphabets, numerals or alpha-numeric characters, not exceeding 6 characters in all (i.e. alphabets A to Z and digits 0 to 9)
(ii) The first character should be either I, J, K, L, M or N.
(iii) No special characters are allowed in the name of a variable. Typical examples of fixed point or integer variables are:

J. KING, MAP, LINE, KUM, MAX, LAMDA, INDIGO, J123, Num 136.

(b) Floating point or real variables

(i) A floating point variable should comprise 1 to 6 alphanumeric characters.
(ii) The first character should be an alphabet other than the letter I, J, K, L, M, N.
(iii) Special characters are not allowed in the name of a variable. Some of the examples of real variables are:

FORCE, BINARY, AMOUNT, SYSTEM, SLOPE, SPEED, RATE, ABC.

Table 8.4 presents some of the typical valid and invalid real and integer variables.

Table 8.4: Floating point constants

Sl. No.	FORTRAN variables	Valid or invalid with reasons
1.	MOMENT	Valid integer variable.
2.	JOB 21	Valid integer variable.
3.	STIFF	Valid real variable.
4.	DEFLN	Valid real variable.
5.	AREA	Valid real variable.
6.	STRESS	Valid real variable.
7.	STRAIN	Valid real variable.
8.	NAX + MAX	Invalid, no special character allowed in a variable.
9.	INSIGHT	Invalid, the length of the variable should not exceed 6 characters.
10.	2 ADD	Invalid, since a variable should not start with a numeral.
11.	Y*3	Invalid, since a variable should not contain operation symbols.
12.	MASS/2	Invalid, since operation symbol not allowed.
13.	KLKLM	Valid integer variable.
14.	RAMP.	Invalid, since dot is not allowed.
15.	(XYZ)	Invalid, since characters are not allowed.

8.2.4 Operation Symbols

In writing FORTRAN expressions, care should be taken to see that mixed mode expressions are not used since they are not valid. The only exception to this rule is that any floating point quantity can be exponentiated by a fixed point constant or variable. In this case, the expression will be in the floating point mode. The following examples point out the valid and invalid modes.

1.	$A + M$	is in mixed mode and is not valid.
2.	$S + T + Z$	is in single mode(floating point mode) and is valid.
3.	$L * 5$	is valid since it is in the same mode.
4.	$R * 5$	Invalid since in a mixed mode.
5.	$B/2$	Invalid since in a mixed mode.
6.	$(B + C) ** 4$	Valid, floating point mode.
7.	$CLv ** 3$	Valid, floating point mode.
8.	$E ** J$	Valid, floating point mode.
9.	$I ** M$	Valid, fixed point quantity used to a fixed point power.
10.	$J ** A$	Invalid, fixed point quantity cannot be raised to a floating point power.
11.	$A + - B$	Invalid, two operation symbols should not be used in succession.
12.	$A + (- B)$	Valid
13.	$A/(- B)$	Valid
14.	PRESUR = FORCE/AREA	Valid
15.	FORCE = MASS * ACCEL	Invalid since MASS is a fixed point variable and ACCEL is a floating point variable and mixed modes are not valid.
16.	$I**2.5$	Invalid, integer cannot be raised to a floating point exponent.

8.2.5 Hierarchy of Arithmetic Operations

The hierarchy or the order of execution of arithmetic operations in a Fortran arithmetic expression is as follows:

Exponentiation	**first		
Multiplication or Division	*and/second		
Addition and Subtraction	+ and – Third		
Logical Operators	* GE *,	* GT *	Fourth
	* LT *,	* LE *	Fifth
	* NE *,	* EQ *	Sixth
	* AND *		Seventh
	* OR *		Eighth
	* EQV *,	* XOR *	Ninth

The expressions are evaluated from left to right

For example, in the expression given below:

$A/B + C + D**E*F - G$

The operations are carried out in the following order:

1. $D**$ is first computed (Exponentiation)
2. A/B is calculated (Division)
3. $E*F$ is computed (Multiplication)

4. *A/B* is added to (Addition)

5. The results of (4) and (3) added (Addition)

6. *G* is subtracted from (5)

8.2.6 Use of Parentheses

The use of parentheses in Fortran expression will over-ride the rules of hierarchy of arithmetic operations. For example in the Fortran expression $A/(B + C)$, the value of $(B + C)$ in the parentheses is evaluated first and the division operation will be performed in the second stage. The maximum number of nested parentheses used in Fortran is limited to 9 pairs. If there are more

Than one set of parentheses, all separated then the order of evaluation is from left to right.

For example in the expression, $(A + B)/(C + D)$

$(A + B)$ is evaluated first and then $(C + D)$ is evaluated and subsequently the division is performed.

8.2.7 Change of Modes

The Fortran expression can be formed in both modes. The variables in a given mode can be changed to another mode by adding a character preceding the variable.

Some examples of change of mode are:

1.	REAL	JREAL
2.	ARCO	KARCO
3.	APS	MAPS
4.	LOT	PLOT

Fortran language also provides explicit type conversions which enable the programmer to change from one mode to the next mode. These functions are called FLOAT and IFIX. The real expressions are converted into integer mode by using

IFIX (Real Name)

YELLOW —— IFIX (YELLOW)

The integer expressions are converted into real mode by using FLOAT (Integer name)

INDIGO FLOAT (INDIGO)

8.2.8 Library Functions

The standard library functions provided in FORTRAN IV are compiled in Table 8.5.

Table 8.5: Library functions	
Library function designation	*FORTRAN IV expression*
$\sin x$	SIN (X)
$\cos x$	COS (X)
$\tan x$	TAN (X)
$\sin^{-1} x$	A SIN (X)
$\tan^{-1} x$	A TAN (X)
$\cos^{-1} x$	A COS (X)
$\log_e x$	A LOG (X)

Contd...

Library function designation	FORTRAN IV expression
$\log_{10} x$	A LOG 10(X)
$\sqrt{x}$	SQRT (X)
$|x|$	ABS (x)
e^x	EXP (X)
$\sinh x$	SINH (X)
$\cosh x$	COSH (X)
$\tanh x$	TANH (X)
max value	AMAXI$(Y_1, Y_2, Y_3 \ldots\ldots Y_N)$
	MAXO $(J_1, J_2, J_3 \ldots\ldots J_N)$
Conversion	
Integer to real	FLOAT (J)
Real to integer	IFIX (Y)
Single precision to double precision	DBLE (X)
Double precision to single precision	SNGL (X)

8.2.9 Mathematical Equations and Fortran Expressions

Several common examples of mathematical equations generally used in engineering computations are expressed in the FORTRAN language as detailed in Table 8.6.

Table 8.6: FORTRAN expressions

Sl. No.	Mathematical equation	FORTRAN expression
1.	$M = Q \cdot b \cdot d^2$	EM = Q * B * D
2.	$M = A_{st} \cdot t(d - n/3)$	EM = AST * T * (D – EN/3)
3.	$P = \pi^2 EI/L^2$	P = 3.14 ** 2 * E * AI/(EL * EL)
4.	$P = C_p \cdot wh^2/2$	P = CP * W * H * H/2
5.	$h = 5.5\sqrt[3]{M/f_b}$	H = 5.5 *(EM/FB) ** 0.33
6.	$R = 1.25 - \dfrac{L_e}{48D}$	R = 1.25 –ALE/(48. * D)
7.	$C_p = \left(\dfrac{1 - \sin\phi}{1 + \sin\phi}\right)$	CP = (1 – SIN(PHI))/(1 + SIN(PHI))
8.	$t = (3w/b)\sqrt{A^2 - B^2/4}$	T = (3 * W/B) * SQRT(A * A –0.25 * B * B)
9.	$P = f_c \cdot A/(1 + (le/D)^c)$	P = FC * A/(1 + A * (ALE/D) ** C)
10.	$\phi = Ax^3 + Bx^2 + Cx + D$	PHI = A * X ** 3 + B * X ** 2 + C * X + D
11.	$n_m = 2nJ - 3$	NM = 2 * NJ – 3
12.	$M_x = a_x wLx^2$	EMX = ALFAX * W * ELX ** 2
13.	$BM = \dfrac{wLx}{6} - \dfrac{wx^2}{2}$	BM = 0.167 * W * AL * X – 0.5 * W * X * X
14.	$P = f\left\{1 - 1/3\left(\dfrac{l_e}{kd}\right)^4\right\}$	P = F * (1. 0.33 * (ALE/(AK * D)) ** 4
15.	$S = \left[\dfrac{4S_w l_w}{q} - l_w\right]$	S = (4 * SW * ALW/Q) – ALW

Sl. No.	Mathematical equation	FORTRAN expression
16.	$M = 0.87 f_y A_{st} \cdot d$	AM = 0.87 * FY * AST * D *
	$\left\{ 1 - \dfrac{A_{st} \cdot f_y}{bd \cdot f_{ck}} \right\}$	(1. – (AST * FY/B * D * FCK))
17.	$x_u \, max = \left\{ \dfrac{0.87 f_y A_{st}}{0.36 f_{ck} \, b} \right\}$	XUMAX = (0.87 * FY * AST)/(0.36 * FCK * B)
18.	$C = 0.36 f_{ck} \cdot x_u \cdot b$	C = 0.36 * FCK * XU * B
19.	$P = P_o \cdot e^{-(\mu\alpha + kx)}$	P = PO * EXP (–AMU * ALFA + AK * X)
20.	$f_c = (P/A + Pe^2/I)$	FC = (P/A) + P * E * E/AI
21.	$\varepsilon_{sh} = \dfrac{200 \times 10^{-6}}{\log_{10}(t+2)}$	ESH = (200 · E – 06)/ALOG 10 (T + 2)
22.	$\varepsilon_{sh} = \phi \cdot \alpha^e \cdot f_c$	ECR = PHI * ALFAE * FC
23.	$\delta = \dfrac{23 \, WL^3}{648 EI}$	DELTA = (23 * W * AL ** 3)/(648 * E * AI)
24.	$LCP = \varepsilon_{cc} \cdot f_c \cdot Es$	ALCP = ECC * FC * ES
25.	$LSLIP = \dfrac{E_s \Delta}{L}$	LSLIP = ES * DELTA/AL
26.	$S = \sqrt{s(s-a)(s-b)(s-c)}$	S = SQRT(S * (S – A) * (S – B) * (S – c))
27.	$v^2 = u^2 - 2as$	V = SQRT (U * U – 2 * A * S)
28.	$\phi = m\left(\dfrac{x^2}{a^2} - \dfrac{y^2}{b^2} + 1 \right)$	PHI = AM * (X * X/A * A) – Y * Y/ (B * B) + 1)
29.	$E = 2C(1 + \mu)$	E = 2 * C (1 + AMU)
30.	$\phi = \tan^{-1} \sqrt{\left(\dfrac{\mu}{\alpha}\right)^2 + 3\mu}$	PHI = ATAN (SQRT (AMU/ALFA) **2 + 3 * AMU
31.	$w = \dfrac{24 \, \mu m}{l_y^2 \tan^2 \phi}$	W = 24 * AMU * AM/(ALY * ALY * TAN (PHI) ** 2
32.	$\sigma_x = \dfrac{E}{(1-\mu^2)}(\varepsilon_x + \mu\varepsilon_y)$	SIGMAX = E * (EX + AMU * EY)/
33.	$\varepsilon = \varepsilon_x \cos^2\alpha + \varepsilon_y \sin^2\alpha$ $\gamma_{xy} \sin\alpha \cos\alpha$	E = EX * COS (ALFA) ** 2 + EY * SIN (ALFA) ** 2 + GAMAXY * SIN (ALFA) * COS (ALFA)
34.	$\gamma = 2/3\sqrt{(\sigma_1 - \sigma_2)^2 +}$ $\sqrt{(\sigma_2 - \sigma_3)^2 + (\sigma_3 - \sigma_1)^2}$	GAMA = 0.67 * SQRT (S1 – S2) ** 2 + (S2 – S3) ** 2 + (S3 – S1) ** 2)
35.	$t = \dfrac{3M_w h}{f(h^3 - 12dy^2)}$	T = 3. * AMW * H/(F * (H ** 3 – 12. * D * Y * Y))
36.	$K = d - \dfrac{ds}{2} + \dfrac{ds^2}{6(2n - ds)}$	AK = D – 0.5 * DS + 0.167 * DS * DS/(2. * AN – DS)

Sl. No.	Mathematical equation	FORTRAN expression
37.	$y_1 = g \cos \dfrac{\phi}{3} - \dfrac{p}{3}$	Y1 = G * COS (PHI/3.) – P/3)
38.	$\tau_{yz} = -\dfrac{\gamma_x}{\cos^2 \beta}$	TYZ = GAMAX/COS (BETA) ** 2q
39.	$C_1 = \dfrac{P}{\tan \tan \beta} - \dfrac{2\gamma}{\tan^3 \beta}$	C1 = P/TAN (BETA) – 2 * GAMA/TAN(BETA) ** 3
40.	$\Delta W = \dfrac{1}{2}\sigma_1 \cdot \Delta x \cdot \Delta y \cdot \Delta z$	DW = 0.5 SI * DX * DY * DZ
41.	$U = \dfrac{(1+\mu)\tau_y^2}{E}$	U = (1. + AMU) * TY * TY/E
42.	$\delta = (3/2\pi + 4L)\left(\dfrac{Pr^2}{EI}\right)$	DELTA = (1.5 * 3.14 + 4. * AL) * P * R /E * A)
43.	$R = \dfrac{3KWL^4}{8(3EI + KL^3)}$	R = 3. * AK * W * AL ** .4/
		(8. * (3. * E * AI + K * AL ** 3))
44.	$\delta = \dfrac{2\rho w^2 r^5}{Et^2}$	DELTA = 2 * RO * W * W * R ** 5 (E * T * T)
45.	$C = \left[\dfrac{\cot \alpha}{2} + \dfrac{\alpha}{\sin^2 \alpha}\right]$	C = 0.5 *1/TAN (ALFA)) + ALFA/(SIN (ALFA) ** 2)
46.	$\phi = \tan^{-1}\left(\dfrac{\gamma xy}{\varepsilon_x - \varepsilon_y}\right)$	PHI = ATAN(GXY/EX – EY))
47.	$y = 3(l^2 x - x^3)\, e^{-2x}$	Y = 3. *(AL * AL * X X ** 3)* EXP(2. **)
48.	$Z = \dfrac{e^{\sqrt{2}} \sin x}{\sqrt{2ax}}$	Z = EXP (SQRT (2.) * Sin (X)/ SQRT(2. * A * X))
49.	$w = \left(\dfrac{m\pi x}{a}\sin\dfrac{m\pi x}{a}\right)\left(\sin\dfrac{n\pi y}{b}\right)$	W = (AM * 3.14 * X/A) * SIN (AM * 3.14 * X/A)
		* SIN (AN * 3.14 * Y/B)
50.	$S = -\dfrac{R}{2L} + \sqrt{\dfrac{R^2}{4L^2} - \dfrac{1}{LC}}$	S = – 0.5 * R/EL + SQRT (R * R/4. * EL * EL)
		– 1./EL * C)

8.3 INPUT, OUTPUT AND FORMAT STATEMENTS

8.3.1 General

The input statement is essential to indicate the type of device from which the data are to be transmitted or read into the memory. It also specifies the number of variables and the order in which their values are to be used. The input operation also requires in addition to the input statement, a specification about the form and size in which the constants appear and their respective locations in the input device, which is referred to as a FORMAT statement in the source programme.

The result of the problem is obtained from the memory of the computer in a required form by writing an output statement and the corresponding FORMAT statement.

The common input devices are the (1) Punched card, (2) Paper tape, (3) Magnetic disk, (4) Magnetic tape and (5) Console typewriter.

The output devices include all the five forms of input device and also the printed paper. When the input is fed into the computer in the form of punched cards, the computer reds information and stores the same in the memory in its internal notation. During the output operation, the results are generally printed on paper. In general, computers equipped with line printers can print 132 characters per line.

8.3.2 Input/Output Statements

In Fortran IV, the general form of input statement is written as:

$$READ \ (k, n) \ list$$

where k 1 if the variables are to read from a punched card and k varies with the type of machine used; n is the statement number of the corresponding FORMAT statement. 'List' is the set of variables to be read into the storage.

The general form of output statement in FORTRAN IV is

$$WRITE \ (k, n) \ list$$

where $k = 2$ if the output is required in punched form, $k = 3$ if the output is required in printed from, also the number varies with the type of the machine.

'n' is the statement number of the corresponding FORMAT statement.

'List' is the set of variables to be punched/printed out.

Some FORTRAN IV compilers allow the input/output statements permitted in FORTRAN II where WRITE is replaced by PRINT.

8.3.3 FORMAT Statement

The computer refers to the FORMAT statement to decipher the physical arrangement in which the values of the variables are to be supplied by the input/output device. The FORMAT statement specifies the number and modes of values per card and also where these values are to be locatedin the card. The different types of FORMAT specifications are compiled in Table 8.7.

Table 8.7: Types of FORMAT specifications

Sl. No.	Type of variables	FORMAT specification	Code to be associated
1.	Fixed point variable	I - Type	IW
2.	Floating point variable (Value written without an exponent)	F - Type	$FW \cdot d$
3.	Floating point variable (Value written without an exponent)	E - Type	$EW \cdot d$

W = total width of field (The number of columns within which the value is to be punched)
d = number of decimal places

Typical examples of input, output and FORMAT statements in FORTRAN IV are as follows:

1. READ (1, 20) A, B, C   }
   20 FORMAT (3F 7.2)   }..............................Input

2. WRITE (3, 14) X, Y, Z   }
   14 FORMAT (3F 8.2)   }..............................Output

3. READ (1, 80) ALPHA, BETA
   80 FORMAT (F 10.2, F 10.6)

4. PRINT (3, 40) L, M, A, B, C
   40 FORMAT (16, 17, E 1'4.6, F 9.2, F 6.3)

For improving the readability of in input and output, the FORMAT statement can be designed to allow some spacing between the different numbers.

The letter x preceeded by an integer is introduced in the FORMAT statement. This is termed as blank field specification and is of the form '$W \cdot X$'.

Where 'W' is the width of the blank field the value of which should not exceed 49. A typical example of an output statement with blank field specification is written as

PRINT (3, 40) S, AREA

40 FORMAT (5X, F 12.4, 6X, F 16.8)

8.4 CONTROL STATEMENTS

8.4.1 Statement Numbers

In FORTRAN programming, assignment of an arbitrary number to a statement will result in the execution of the programme in a sequential order. The use of a control statement makes the computer deviate from the sequential order. The statement numbers are arbitrarily chosen by the programmer and no two statements can have the same number. The statement number appears to the left of the statements as shown in the following example:

4 B = 4.356

8 C = 83.15

100 A = 175.895

2 X = A * B + C * B ** 2

In these statements, the computer will execute the statements in the order 4, 8, 100, 2. The statement number should be an unsigned fixed point constant having a value from 1 to 9999 and it is punched between columns 1 and 5 of the punched card.

8.4.2 Control Statements

The control statements are broadly classified as:

  i. Unconditional Control Statements
  ii. Conditional Control Statements

The unconditional control statement is also referred to as 'GO TO' statement. When the computer executes an unconditional control statement, the control is transferred to the statement number referring to the control statement. The general form of the 'GO TO n' where 'n' is the statement number of the executable statement. The use of the Go To statement is illustrated by the following example:

```
10   READ (1, 20) A, B, C
20   FORMAT (3 F 8.4)
30   C = A + B
40   PRINT (3, 50) C
50   FORMAT (F 9.2)
60   Go To 10
70   C A * B ** 2
80   PRINT (3, 90) C
90   FORMAT (E 10.6)
```

In the case of conditional control statements such as 'IF' statement, the decision is made by the computer and then the control is transferred according to the decision.

The general form of the 'IF' statement is designated as

$$IF\ (n),\ a,\ b,\ c$$

Where 'n' is the arithmetic expression and 'a', 'b', 'c' are the statement numbers. The significance of the 'IF' statement is as follows:

If the value of 'n' is less than zero, the control is transferred to the statement numbered 'a'.

If the value of 'n' is equal to zero, the control is transferred to the statement numbered 'b'.

If the value of 'n' is greater than zero, the control is transferred to the statement numbered 'c'.

For example, when the control reaches the statement,

$$IF\ (A\ B)\ 50,\ 80,\ 90.$$

The value of $(A - B)$ is tested and if $(A - B) < 0$, the statement numbered 50 is executed.

$(A - B) = 0$, the statement numbered 80 is executed.

$(A - B) > 0$, the statement numbered 90 is executed.

8.4.3 Subscripted Variables

Subscripted variables are used when dealing with a group of variables of the same class. Let us consider an organization running 6 educational institutionsand the expenditure of the institutions are represented as R_i where R_i is the expenditure of the institution and i varying from 1 to 6. In Fortran language, suffixing of a variable is not permitted. Hence a subscript notation is used and the expenditures of the six institutions are expressed as

$$R(1),\ R(2),\ R(3),\ ...,\ R(6)$$

This is referred to as a 'one dimensional array' since each variable has a single subscript.

In a similar way a two dimensional array can be written if an organization is having six companies, selling 4 different types of products; the sales of the organization is written as SALES (K, L), where K varies from 1 to 6 and L varies from 1 to 4.

If the products are sold in 10 different cities, then a three dimensional array can be written as SALES (K, L, M)

Where K varies from 1 to 6

L varies from 1 to 4

M varies from 1 to 10

Hence SALES (4, 3, 6) means sale by the 4th company of the 3rd product in the 6th city.

8.4.4 DIMENSION and DO Statements

(a) DIMENSION Statement

The DIMENSION statement allocates the specified number of storage locations for the element of each of the arrays (subscripted variables) occurring in the programme. DIMENSION statement is necessary only when subscripted variablesare used in the source programme.

The general form of a Dimension statement is represented as

DIMENSION d, d, d, ...

where each 'd' is a fixed or a floating point variable subscripted with one, two or three unsigned fixed point constants. Any number of 'd's may be included in a DIMENSION statement.

A one dimensional array containing 50 elements is represented as

DIMENSION A (50)

A two dimensional array containing 100 elements in all is represented as

DIMENSION X (2, 50)

A three dimensional array comprising 150 elements in all is represented as

DIMENSION Y (3, 5, 10)

It is also possible to represent all the above three arrays ina single statement represented as

DIMENSION A (50), X (2, 50), Y (3, 5, 10)

(b) 'DO' statement

Whenever repetitive calculations such as iterations have to be executed, a 'DO'used keeps track of and executes a looping operation. The general form of a 'DO' statement is written as

DO n i = n_1, n_2, n_3

Where 'n' is the statement number

'i' is the index of the Do statement

n_1' Is the initial value of i

n_2' Is the final value of i and

n_3' Is the increment of i for each step.

If the increment 'n_3' is not specified, its value is taken as 1.

Consider the DO statement in a programme written as

        DO 10.1 = 30, 1

Here the computer evaluates the range of statements with the value of

        I = 1, 2, 3, 4, ..., 30

For the following statement,

        DO 10.1 = 1, 50, 3

The computer evaluates the range of statements with the values of

        1, 4, 7, 10, 13, ..., 43, 46, 49.

(c) CONTINUE statement

Since a Do loop cannot end with a control statement, a dummy statement such as CONTINUE statement is used as the last statement of a Do loop. A typical example is shown below:

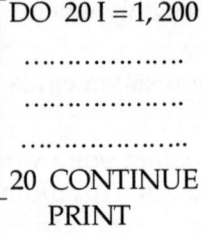

        DO 20 I = 1, 200

        ....

        ....

        ....

        20 CONTINUE

           PRINT

Nested DO loops are used if one or more Do statements are to be included within the range of a DO statement, as shown in the following example:

        DO   10 I = 10, 60, 2
        DO   20 J = 5, 20
        DO 30 K = 1, 10, 2
        30   CONTINUE
        20   CONTINUE
        10   CONTINUE

Although 'DO' loops can meet each other, they should not overlap or cut each other as illustrated in the following example:

        DO   10 I = 1, 20, 2
        DO   10 J = 1, 10, 2

                              ....Valid

        10   CONTINUE

        DO   10 I = 10, 50, 2
        DO   20 J = 15, 150, 5

                                ....Not Valid

        10   CONTINUE
        20   CONTINUE

8.4.5 Logical Statements

The Fortran symbols used for some of the common logical statements are as follows:

$> \cdot GT \cdot$	$= \cdot EQ \cdot$
$\geq \cdot GE \cdot$	$\neq \cdot NE \cdot$
$< \cdot LT \cdot$	$\& \cdot AND \cdot$
$\leq \cdot LE \cdot$	

A typical programme illustrating the use of logical statements will be as follows:

```
80   STOP
     END
```

8.4.6 STOP and END Statements

The STOP statement causes the computer to a halt after erasing the object programme from its memory. The stop statement is an executable statement. The last statement of a Fortran programme is the END statement. It indicates the physical end of the programme but it also instructs the compiler to translate the same programme into the machine language. If the END statement is not written in the source programme, the programme will not be compiled.

8.5 EXAMPLES OF COMPUTER PROGRAMMES USING FORTRAN LANGUAGE

Example 8.1

```
C     Write A program to find F(X) for a value of X ranging from
C     X = – 10 to 50 with increment of 2.
C     F(X) = AX ** 2 + BX + C IF X < 0
C     F(X) = AX ** 2 – BX – C IF 0 < = X < = 0
C     F(X) = – AX ** 2 + BX + C IF X > 20
C     ...............................................................................
C     PROGRAMME
C     ...............................................................................
      OPEN (1, STATUS = 'NEW', FILE = 'P1.OUT')
      WRITE (*, *)'ENTER VALUES OF A, B, C'
      READ (*, *) A, B, C
      WRITE (1, *)..........................................................
      WRITE (1, *) 'X                    VALUE OF FX'
      WRITE (1, *)..........................................................
      X = – 10.0
10    IF (X . LT . 0.0) FX = A * X * X + B * X + C
      IF (0.0 , LE , X) . AND . (X . LE. 20)) FX = A * Y ** 2 – B * X – C
      IF (X . GT. 20.0)) FX = – A * Y ** 2 + B * X + C
      WRITE (1, 25) X, FX
25    FORMAT (1X, F6.2, 14X , f14.4)
      X = X + 2.0
```

```
      IF (X . LE . 50.0) GOTO 10
      STOP
      END
C     ..................................................................................
ENTER VALUES OF A, B, C
9.3, 6.9, 3.1
STOP  Program terminated
```

X	Value of FX
− 10.00	864.1000
− 8.00	543.1000
− 6.00	296.5000
− 4.00	124.3000
− 2.00	26.5000
0.00	− 3.1000
2.00	20.3000
4.00	118.1000
6.00	290.3000
8.00	536.9000
10.00	857.9000
12.00	1253.3000
14.00	1723.1000
16.00	2267.3000
18.00	2885.9000
20.00	3578.9000
22.00	− 4346.3000
24.00	− 5188.1000
26.00	− 6104.3000
28.00	− 7094.9000
30.00	− 8159.9000
32.00	− 9299.3010
34.00	− 10513.1000
36.00	− 11801.3000
38.00	− 13163.9000
40.00	− 14600.9000
42.00	− 16112.3000
44.00	− 17698.1000
46.00	− 19358.3000
48.00	− 21092.9000
50.00	− 22901.9000

Example 8.2

```
C       ..................................................................................
C       Program to find roots of a quadratic equation 5x² + 3x + 18 = 0
C       ..................................................................................
C       PROGRAMME
C       ..................................................................................
        WRITE (*, *) 'ENTER VALUES  A, B, C'
        READ (*, *) A, B, C
        DISC = B * B – 4.0 * A * C
        IF (DISC) 10, 20, 30
10      WRITE (*, *) COMPLEX ROOTS'
        RPA = B/(2. * A)
        EMPA = SQRT (– DISC) / (2.0 * A)
        WRITE (*, *) 'REAL PART OF ROOT =' , RPA
        WRITE (*, *) 'IMAGINARY PART OF ROOT ' =, EMPA
        STOP
20      WRITE (*, *) 'EQUAL ROOTS'
        R1 = B / (2. * A)
        R2 = R1
        WRITE (*, *) 'R1 =',  'R2 =', R2
        STOP
30      WRITE (*, *) 'DISTINCT ROOTS'
        R1 = – B / (2. * A) + SQRT (DISC) / (2 * A)
        R2 = – B / (2. * A) SQRT (DISC) / (2 * A)
        WRITE (*, *) 'R1, 'R2 =', R2
25      STOP
        END
```

```
C       ..................................................................................
ENTER VALUES OF A, B, C
5.0,  3.0, 18.0
COMPLEX ROOTS
REAL PART OF ROOT = – 3.000000E – 001
IMAGINARY PART OF ROOT = 1.8735000
Stop – Program terminated.
```

Example 8.3

```
C       ..................................................................................
C       To find the square root of 2 by Newton Raphson method
C       ..................................................................................
        WRITE (*, *) 'ENTER NUMBER WHOSE SQUARE ROOT IS TO BE FOUND'
        READ (*, *) N
```

```
        WRITE (*, *) 'ENTER INTIAL VALUE OF X'
        READ (*, *) XO
10      X1 = (XO ** 2. + N) / (2. * XO)
        ACR = X1 – XO
        IF (ACR . LE . 1.OE O6) GOTO 25
        XO = XI
        GOTO 10
25      WRITE (*, *) 'SQUARE ROOT OF NUMBER ENTERED IS =', XI
        STOP
        END
C       .................................................................................................
ENTER NUMBER WHOSE SQUARE ROOT IS TO BE FOUND
2
ENTER INITIAL VALUE OF X
1.0
SQUARE ROOT OF NUMBER ENETERED IS 1.4166670
Stop – Program terminated.
```

Example 8.4

```
C       .................................................................................................
C       THE NEUTRAL AXIS OF A RECTANGULAR RCC COLUMN
C       SUBJECTED TO DIRECT LOAD AND MOMENT GIVEN BY
C       X ** 3 – 170 * X ** 2 – 1425 * X + 80456 = 0
C       WHERE X = DEPTH OF THE NEUTRAL AXIS. WRITE A
C       PROGRAM TO FIND THE ROOT NEAR 18 USING N – R METHOD
C       .................................................................................................
C       PROGRAMME
C       .................................................................................................
        WRITE (*, *) 'ENTER INTIAL VALUE OF X'
        READ (*, *) XO
10      A = ((XO ** 3) – (170 * XO ** 2) (1425 * X0) + 80456)
        B = ((3 * XO ** 2) – (340 * XO) 1425)
        X1 = XO – (A / B)
        ACR = XI – XO
        IF (ACR. LE. 1. OE – 06) GOTO 25
        XO = XI
        GO TO 10
25      WRITE (*, *) 'VALUE OF X =' , X1
        STOP
        END
C       .................................................................................................
ENTER INITIAL VALUE OF X
18
VALUE OF X 18.8334100
Stop – Program terminated.
```

Example 8.5

```
C     ..............................................................................................
C     WRITE A PROGRAM TO EVALUATE THE AREA BY USING THE TRAPEZOIDAL
      RULE USING THE FORMULA
```

$$C \quad A = \Delta x \left[\frac{y_1}{2} + \sum_{i=2}^{n-1} y + \frac{y_n}{2} \right]$$

```
C     ..............................................................................................
C     PROGRAMME
C     ..............................................................................................
      DIMENSION Y (15)
      WRITE (*, *) 'ENTER VALUE OF INTERVAL'
      READ (*, *) DX
      WRITE (*, *) 'ENTER NUMBER OF VALUES – N'
      READ (*, *) N
      WRITE (*, *) 'ENTER N VALUES OF Y'
      READ (*, *) (Y(I)), I = 1, N))
      SUM = 0, 0
      M  = N – 1
      DO 25 J = 2, M
      SUM SUM + Y(J)
25    CONTINUE
      A = DX * (Y(1) / 2.0 + SUM + Y (N) / 2.0)
      WRITE (*, *) 'AREA USING TRAPEZOIDAL RULE IS' , A
      STOP
      END
C     ..............................................................................................
ENTER VALUE OF INTERVAL
0.25
ENTER NUMBER OF VALUES – N
9
ENTER N VALUES OF Y
1
0.80
0.67
0.57
0.50
0.44
0.40
0.36
0.33
AREA USING TRAPEZOIDAL RULE IS   1.1012500
Stop – Program terminated
```

Example 8.6

```
C      .........................................................................
C      PROGRAMME TO FIND THE AREA BY SIMPSON'S RULE
C      .........................................................................
       DIMENSION  Y (25)
       WRITE (*, *) 'ENTER VALUE OF INTERVAL'
       READ (*, *) DX
       WRITE (*, *) 'ENTER NUMBER OF VALUES – N'
       READ (*, *) N
       WRITE (*, *) 'ENTER N VALUES OF Y'
       READ (*, *) (Y(I), I = 1, N))
       SUMEVN = 0, 0
       M = N – 1
       L = N – 2
       DO 25 J = 2, L, 2
       SUMODD =SUMODD + Y (J)
20     CONTINUE
       DO 25 K = 3, M, 2
       SUMEVN = SUMEVN  Y (
25     CONTINUE
       A = (DX / 3.0) + (Y(1) + 4.0 * SUMODD + 2 * SUMEVEN + Y(N))
       READ (*, *) AREA BY SIMPSON'S RULE IS', A
       STOP
       END
C      .........................................................................
ENTER VALUE OF INTERVAL
0.25
ENTER NUMBER OF VALUES – N
9
ENTER N VALUES OF Y
1
0.80
0.67
0.57
0.50
0.44
0.40
0.36
0.33
AREA BY SIMPSON'S RULE IS   9.758334E – 001
Stop – program terminated.
```

Example 8.7

```
C       ...........................................................................................................
C       A SIMPLY SUPPORTED BEAM OF SPAN 'L' SUPPORTS A UDL OF INTENSITY
        WKN/M OER THE WHOLE SPAN. WRITE A PROGRAMME TO PRINT OUT
        THE BENDING MOMENT AND SHEAR FORCE IN THE BEAM AT
        REGULAR INTERVALS OF 0.5METRE.
C       ...........................................................................................................
C       PROGRAMME
C       ...........................................................................................................
C       OPEN (UNIT = 1, STATUS = 'NEW', FILE = 'P8 . OUT'
C       EL = 5.0
C       W = 10.0
C       X = 0.0
        WRITE (1, *)' ...................................................................................
        WRITE (1, *) 'X              SF              BM'
        WRITE (1, *)' ...................................................................................
10      SF = (0.5 * W * EL) – (W * X)
        BM = (0.5 * W * EL * X) – (0.5 * W * X ** 2)
        WRITE (1, 15) X, SF, BM
15      FORMAT (1X, 3(F8.2, 2X))
        X = X + 0.5
        IF (X . LE . 5.00) GOTO 10
        STOP
        END
C       ...........................................................................................................
```

X	SF	BM
.00	25.00	.00
.50	20.00	11.25
1.00	15.00	20.00
1.50	10.00	26.25
2.00	5.00	30.00
2.50	0.00	31.25
3.00	–5.00	30.00
3.50	–10.00	26.25
4.00	–15.00	20.00
4.50	–20.00	11.25
5.00	–25.00	.00

Example 8.8

```
C       ...............................................................................................
C       WRITE A PROGRAM TO COMPUTE AND PRINT OUT THE PORTION
        WHERE THE RESULTANT PRESSURE CUTS THE BASE OF A MASONRY
        DAM HAVING TRAPEZOIDAL SECTION WITH U/S SIDE BEING
        VERTICAL. THE BASE WIDTH OF DAM IS 9.0 METRES AND TOP WIDTH
        IS 1.0 METRE.
C       ...............................................................................................
C       PROGRAMME
C       ...............................................................................................
C
        A        = 1.0
        B        = 9.0
        H        = 5.0
        H1       = 1.0
        GAMA     = 10.0
        AREA     = 0.5 * H * (A + B)
        W        = AREA * 1 * 24.0
10.     P        = GAMA * H1 * H1 / 2.0
        X        = 90.5 * A * A * H + 0.5 * (B – A) * H * (B + 2. * A / 3.0)) / AREA
        Z        = X + P * H1 / (3. * W)
        WRITE (*, *) 'VALUE OF H1 = ' , H1
        WRITE (*, *) 'VALUE OF RESULTANT FROM U/S', Z
        H1 = H1 + 1.0
        IF H1 = LE.5.0 GOTO 10
        STOP
        END
C       ...............................................................................................
```

```
VALUE OF H1 =          1.0000000
VALUE OF RESULTANT FROM U/S      7.8361120
VALUE OF H1 =          2.0000000
VALUE OF RESULTANT FROM U/S      7.8555560
VALUE OF H1 =          3.0000000
VALUE OF RESULTANT FROM U/S      7.9083340
VALUE OF H1 =          4.0000000
VALUE OF RESULTANT FROM U/S      8.0111120
VALUE OF H1 =          5.0000000
VALUE OF RESULTANT FROM U/S      8.1805560
Stop – Program terminated.
```

Example 8.9

```
C       ..............................................................................................
C       GIVEN THE VALUES OF THE TWO VARIABLES X AND Y WRITE A
        PROGRAM TO FIND LINEAR RELATIONSHIP BETWEEN X AND Y AND
        PRINT OUT THE CONSTANTS A AND B
C       ..............................................................................................
C       PROGRAMME
C       ..............................................................................................
        DIMENSION X (15), Y (15)
        SX      = 0.0
        SY      = 0.0
        SXX     = 0.0
        SXY     = 0.0
        WRITE (*, *)  'ENTER VALUE OF N'
        READ (*, *) N
        WRITE (*, *)  'ENTER VALUE OF 'X AND 'Y'
        READ (*, *) (X (1), Y (1), I = 1, N)
        DO 10 I = 1, N
        SX      = SX + X (I)
        SY      = SY + Y (I)
        SXX     = SXX + X (I)
        SXY     = SXY + X (I) + Y (I)
9       CONTINUE
        B = (N * SXY – SX * SY) / (N * SXX – SX ** 2)
        A = (SY / N) – (B * SX) / N)
        WRITE (*, *) 'CONSTANT A = ', A
        WRITE (*, *) 'CONSTANT B = ', B
        STOP
        END
C       ..............................................................................................
ENTER VALUE OF N
10
ENTER VALUE OF X AND Y
2.4
4.8
6.12
8.15
10.20
12.23
14.27
16.31
18.34
20.40
```

CONSTANT A = 6.666565 – 002
CONSTANT B = 1.9393940
Stop – Program terminated.

Example 8.10

```
C       ...............................................................................................
C       USING A DO STATEMENT WRITE A PROGRAM TO COMPUTE THE
        VALUES OF Y USING THE EQUATION
```

$$C \quad y = \left(\frac{x^2 - 3x + 3}{x - 3}\right) + \left(\frac{\sqrt{\sin x + 3}}{x - 3}\right)$$

```
C       FOR VALUES OF X VARYING FROM 1 TO 10 EXCEPT FOR X = 3
C       ...............................................................................................
C       PROGRAMME
C       ...............................................................................................
        OPEN (UNIT = 1, STATUS = 'NEW' , FILE = 'P11, OUT)
        WRITE (1, *) ' ...............................................................................................
        WRITE (1, *) ' X          Y'
        WRITE (1, *) ' ...............................................................................................
        DO 10 1X = 1, 10
        X = IX
        IF (X . EQ . 3.0) GOTO 10
        Y = (X * X – 3. * X + 3.) / (X – 3.) + SQRT (SIN (X) + 3.) / (X – 3.0)
        WRITE (1, 15) X, Y
15      FORMAT (1X, 2 (F8.2, 3X))
10      CONTINUE
        STOP
        END
C       ...............................................................................................
```

X	Y
1.0	– 1.48
2.0	– 2.98
4.0	8.50
5.0	7.21
6.0	7.55
7.0	8.23
8.0	9.00
9.0	9.81
10.0	10.65

Stop – Program terminated.

Example 8.11

```
C      .................................................................................................
C      IN THE DESIGN OF A TENSION MEMBER IN A ROOF TRUESS USING
       STEINMANN'S FORMULA
C      THE THICKNESS OF THE ANGLE IS TO BE DETERMINED FROM THE
       FOLLOWING  EQUATION
```

$$
C \quad (87.5 - 0.50t + (95 - 0.50)\, t \left\{ \frac{3\,[(87.2) - (0.5t)]}{3\,(87.2 - 0.5t) + (95 - 0.50)t} \right\} = 1200
$$

```
C      WRITE A PROGRAM TO DETERMINE THE VALUE OF T
C
C      .................................................................................................
C      T = 6.0
9      A1 = (87.5  0.5 * T) * T
       A2 = (95  0.5 * T) * T
       AK = (3. * A1) / (3. * A1) + A2)
       F = A1 + A2 + AK
       DIF = F - 1200.0
       IF (ABS (DIF) . LE . 1) GOTO 20
       T = T + 0.1
       GOTO 10
20     WRITE (*, *) 'THICKNESS = ' , T
       STOP
       END
C      .................................................................................................
THICKNESS = 7.9999980
Stop – Program terminated.
```

Example 8.12

```
C      .................................................................................................
C      USING DO STATEMENT WRITE A PROGRAM TO CALCULATE THE AVG
       MARKS OF A CLASS OF N STUDENTS AND PRINT OUT THE INDIVIDUAL
       AND AVERAGE VALUE OF MARKS SCORED SIDE BY SIDE
C      .................................................................................................
C      PROGRAMME
C      .................................................................................................
       CHARACTER * 20 NAME
       OPEN (UNIT = 1, STATUS = 'NEW', FILE = 'P12 OUT')
       READ (*, *) N
       WRITE (*, *) 'ENTER NAME AND MARKS SCORED BY EACH STUDENT'
       WRITE (*, *) 'IN THREE SUBJECTS FOR N STUDENTS'
       WRITE (1, *) .................................................................................
```

```
        WRITE (1, *) 'NAME      M1      M2      M3      TOTAL      AVERAGE'
        WRITE (1, *) ' .................................................'
        DO 100 1= 1, N
        TOTAL = 0
        AVG = 0
        READ (*, *)  NAME, M1, M2, M3
        TOTAL = M1 + M2 + M3
        AVG = TOTAL / 3
        CLASSTOT =  CLASSTOT + TOTAL
        WRITE (1, 10) NAME, M1, M2, M3, TOTAL, AVG
10      FORMAT (1X, A20,  2X, , 2X, F16.2, 4X, F6.2)
100     CONTINUE
        WRITE (1, *)
        WRITE (1, *)  'CLASS AVERAGE = ' , CLASSTOT / (N * 3)
        STOP
        END
C       .................................................................
ENTER VALUE OF N
4
ENTER NAME AND MARKS SCORED BY EACH STUDENT IN THREE SUBJECTS
FOR N STUDENTS
'SATHYA',  78, 76, 89
'SUNITHA', 95, 56, 78
'PRAKASH'. 45. 76, 65
'GOPALAKRISHNA', 67, 87, 90
Stop – Program terminated
```

NAME	M1	M2	M3	TOTAL	AVERAGE
SATHYA	78	76	89	243.00	81.00
SUNITHA	95	56	78	229.00	76.33
PRAKASH	45	76	65	186.00	62.00
GOPALAKRISHNA	67	87	90	244.00	81.33

```
    CLASS AVERAGE = 75. 1666600
```

Example 8.13

```
C       .................................................................
C       A SET OF NUMBRS ARE STORED IN A COMPUTER IN AN ARRAY A.
        WRITE A PROGRAM TO FIND THE BIGGEST OF ALL THE NUMBERS
C       .................................................................
C       PROGRAMME
C       .................................................................
```

```
       DIMENSION A (50)
       OPEN (UNIT = 1, STATUS = 'OLD', FILE = N'P13. IN')
       READ (1, *, END = 10) (A (1), = 1, 5
10     WRITE (*, *)'ENTER VALUE OF N'
       READ (*, *) N
       BIG = A(1)
       DO 25 = 2, N
       IF (A (I), GT, BIG) BIG = A(1)
25     CONTINUE
       WRITE (*, *).BIGGEST NUMBER IS =', BIG
       STOP
       END
C      ......................................................................
ENTER VALUE OF N
15
BIGGEST NUMBER IS = 99.9000000
Stop – Program terminated
30.0, 35.3, 35.6, 85.4, 4.58, 5.84, 77.7, 88.8, 99.9, – 0.005, – 0.007, – 0.056
1.02, 2.01, 0.056
```

Example 8.14

```
C      ......................................................................
C      THE MEAN VELOCITY OF FLOW  V ON THE UPSTREAM SIDE OF A GIVEN
       STANDING WAVE FLUME CORRESPONDING TO CERTAIN DISCHARGE
       IS DEFINED BY THE EQUATION
C      V³ – 3.86V + 1.95 = 0
C      WRITE A PROGRAM TO ETERMINE THE VALUE OF V CORRECT TO 2ND
       DECIMAL PLACE BY N – R METHOD. ASSUME THE APPPROXIMATE
       VALUE OF THE ROOT AS 0.50
C      ......................................................................
C      PROGRAMME
       ......................................................................
       WRITE (*, *) 'ENTER VALUE OF V'
       READ (*, *) VO
10     A          = ((VO ** 3) – (3.86 * VO) + 1.95
       B          = (3 * (VO ** 2)) – 3.86
       V1         = VO – A / B
       ACCR       = V1 – VO
       IF (ACCR. GE. 1.0E – 02) GOTO 25
       VO         = V1
       GOTO 10
```

```
20    WRITE (*, *) 'VALUE OF V1 = ', V1
      STOP
      END
```

```
C     ..............................................................................
ENTER INITIAL VALUE OF V
0.50
VALUE OF V1 = 5.44238E – 001
```

Stop = Program terminated.

Example 8.15

```
C     ..............................................................................
C     THE TORQUE T TRANSMITTED BY A SHAFT IS REPRESENTED BY THE
      EQUATION OF THE TYPE
```

$$C \quad T = \frac{C\theta I}{L}$$

```
C     WRITE A PROGRAM TO COMPUTE T FOR THE VALUES OF THETA
      VARYING FROM 0.10 TO 0.50
C     WITH A STEP OF 0.02
C     ..............................................................................
C     PROGRAMME
C     ..............................................................................
C     OPEN (UNIT = 1, STATUS = 'NEW' , FILE = 'P15.OUT')
      WRITE (*, *) 'ENTER VALUES OF C, LENGTH AND
      READ (*, *) C, EL, AI
      WRITE (1*) ' ..............................................................................
      WRITE (1*) 'THETA VALUE              TORQUE VALUE'
      WRITE (1*) ' ..............................................................................
      TETA = 0.1
15    TORQUE = C * TETA * A /EL
      WRITE (1, 20) 'TETA, TORQUE
20    FORMAT (1X, F16.8, 2X, F16.8)
      TETA = TETA + 0.02
      IF (TRTA  0.5) 15,  15, 30
      STOP
      END
```

```
C     ..............................................................................
ENTER VALUES OF C, LENGTH AND
1, 5000, 10000
```

Stop – Program terminated

Theta Value	Torque Value
.10000000	.20000000
.12000000	.24000000
.14000000	.28000000
.16000000	.32000000
.18000000	.36000000
.20000000	.40000000
.22000000	.44000000
.24000000	.48000000
.26000000	.52000000
.28000000	56000000
.30000000	.60000000
....	....
.50000000	1.0000000

Example 8.16

```
C       ................................................................................
C       FIND THE REGRESSION EQUATION IN THE FORM y = a + bx + cx² BY
        LEAST SQUARES BY
C       USING THE FOLLOWING DATA IN FILE
        ................................................................................
        DIMENSION X (50), Y (50), A (3,4), Z (3)
        OPEN UNIT = 1, STATUS = 'OLD', FILE = 'P16. IN')
        OPEN UNIT = 2, STATUS = 'NEW', FILE = 'P16.OUT')
        WRITE (*, *) 'ENTER NUMVER OF PAIRS OF X AND Y IN DATA'
        READ (*, *) N
        DO 5 I = 1, N, 1
        READ (1, *, END = 6) X (I), Y (I)
        WRITE (2*) X (I), Y (I)
5       CONTINUE
6       SY      = 0.0
        SX      = 0.0
        SXY     = 0.0
        SX2Y    = 0.0
        SX2     = 0.0
        SX3     = 0.0
        SX4     = 0.0
        DO 100 I = 1, N, 1
        SY      = SY       + Y (I)
        SXY     = SXY      + X (I) * Y (I)
```

```
          SX2Y  = SX2Y    + X (I) ** 2) * Y (I)
          SX    = SX       + X (I)
          SX2   = SX2      + X (I) ** 2
          SX3   = SX3      + X (I) ** 3
          SX4   = SX4      + X (I) ** 4
100       CONTINUE
          WRITE (2 *) SY, SXY, SX2Y, SX, SX2, SX3, SX4
          A (1, 1) = N
          A (1, 2) = SX
          A (1, 3) = SX2
          A (1, 4) = SY
          A (2, 1) = SX
          A (2, 2) = SX2
          A (2, 3) = SX3
          A (2, 4) = SXY
          A (3, 1) = SX2
          A (3, 2) = SX3
          A (3, 3) = SX4
          A (3, 4) = SX2Y
          N = 3
          DO 200 K = 1, N – 1
          DO 200 I = (K + 1), N
          U = A(I, K) / A( , K)
          DO 200 J = K, (N + 1)
          A (I, J) = A (I, J) – U * A (K, J)
200       CONTINUE
          Z (N) = A (N. N + 1) / A ( N, N)
          DO 300  = N1, 1, 1
          SUM = 0, 0
          DO 400 J = (1 + 1). N
          SUM = SUM + A ( , J) * Z (J)
300       CONTINUE
          Z (I) = (A(I, N + 1) – SUM) / A (I, I)
400       CONTINUE
          WRITE (*, *) 'VALUES OF REGRESSION COEFFICIENTS A, B, C, ARE'
          DO 500 I = 1, N. 1
          WRITE (*, *) Z (I)
500       CONTINUE
          STOP
          END
```

```
     1900.0,  22.1
     1910.0,  32.80
     1920.0,  36.40
     1930.0,  38.30
     1940.0,  41.20
     1950.0,  46.20
     1960.0,  48.10
     1970.0,  50.20
     1980.0,  56.30
     1990.0,  62.40
     2000.0,  68.10
     2010.0,  73.40
     ENTER NUMBER OF PAIRS OF X AND Y IN DATA
     12
     VALUES OF REGRESSION COEFFICIENTS A, B, C ARE
     48.7905900
     − 2.838177E − 004
     − 7.255620E − 008
```

Stop – Program terminated.

Example 8.17

```
C      ..............................................................................................
C      WRITE A PROGRAM TO READ A SET OF VALUES FROM THE DATA AND
       FIND NUMERICALLY
       LARGEST AND ALGEBRAICALLY LARGEST VALUE OF THE GIVEN SET
       OF DATA
C      ..............................................................................................
C      PROGRAMME
C      ..............................................................................................
       DIMENSION A (50)
       WRITE (*, *) 'ENTER VALUE OF N'
       READ (*, *) N
       WRITE (*, *) 'ENTER N VALUES'
       READ (*, *) (A (I), I = 1, N)
       BIGN = ABS (A (I))
       BIGA = A (1)
       DO 100 (I) = 2, 10
        IF A (I)) .GT, BIGA) BIGA = A (I)
        IF (ABS A (I). GT. BIGN) BIGN = (ABS A (I))
100    CONTINUE
       WRITE (*, *) 'LARGEST VALUE NUMERICALLY = ', BIGN
```

```
        WRITE (*, *) 'LARGEST VALUE ALGEBRAICALLY = ' , BIGA
        STOP
        END
C       ....................................................................
ENTER VALUES OF N
5
ENTER N VALUES
- 98
14
12
99
45
LARGEST VALUE NUMERICALLY = 99.0000000
LARGEST VALUE ALGEBRAICALLY = 99.0000000
Stop – Program terminated.
```

Example 8.18

```
C       ....................................................................
C       WRITE A COMPUTER PROGRAM THAT SOLVES THE DIFFERENTIAL
        EQUATION
```

$$C \quad \frac{dy}{dx} = 2 + \sqrt{xy}$$

```
C       BY USING THE RUNGE-KUTTA METHOD OF ORDER 4 GIVEN THAT Y
        (1) = 1 CALCULATE
C       Y (2) USING THE STEP SIZE H = 0.50
C       ....................................................................
C       PROGRAMME
C       ....................................................................
        WRITE (*, *) 'ENTER VALUE OF XO, YO, XLAST AND H'
        READ (*, *) XO, YO, XLAST, H
        X = XO
        Y = YO
10      AK1         = H*(2. + SQRT (XO * YO))
        AK2         = H*(2. + SQRT (XO + 0.5 * H) * (YO + 0.5 * AK1)))
        AK3         = H*(2. + SQRT (XO + 0.5 * H) * (YO + 0.5 * AK2)))
        AK4         = H*(2. + SQRT (XO + H) * (YO + AK3)))
        AK          = (1/6) * (AK1 + 2. * AK2 + 2. * AK3 + AK4)
20      WRITE (*, 30) X, Y
30      FORMAT (1X, 'X = ', F6.2, 4X, 'Y = ', F6.2)
        Y = Y + AK
        X = X + H
```

```
      IF (X – XLAST) 10, 10, 40
40    STOP
      END
```

C   ....

ENTER VALUES OF XO, YO, XLAST AND H

1, 1, 2.0, 0.50

X = 1.00	Y = 1.00
X = 1.50	Y = 2.75
X = 2.00	Y = 4.51

Stop – Program terminated.

Example 8.19

C   ....

C   WRITE A COMPUTER PROGRAM TO FIND THE AREA OF, CENTRE OF GRAVITY, MOMENT OF INERTIA ABOUT THE MAJOR AND MINOR AXIS, RXX AND RYY OF AN UNSYMMETRICAL I-SECTION

C   ....

C   PROGRAMME

C   ....

```
C     WRITE (*, *) 'ENTER BREADTH OF TOP FLANGE'
      READ (*, *) B1
      WRITE (*, *) 'ENTER DEPTH OF TOP FLANGE'
      READ (*, *) T1
      WRITE (*, *) 'ENTER WEB THICKNESS'
      READ (*, *) B2
      WRITE (*, *) 'ENTER WEB DEPTH'
      READ (*, *) T2
      WRITE (*, *) 'ENTER BREADTH OF BOTTOM FLANGE'
      READ (*, *) B3
      WRITE (*, *) 'ENTER DEPTH OF BOTTOM FLANGE'
      READ (*, *) T3
      AREA = B1 * T1 + B2 * T2 + B3 * T3
      Y1   = B3 * T3 * T3 / 2
      Y2   = B2 * T2 * (T3 + 0.5 * T2)
      Y3   = B1 * T1 * (T3 + B2 + 0.5 * T1)
      YBAR = (Y1 + Y2 + Y3) / AREA
      EI 1 = B3 * T3 ** 3 / 12. + B3 * T3 * (YBAR – 0.5 * T3) ** 2
      EI 2 = T2 * B2 ** 3 /12. + T2 * B2 * (YBAR – (T3 + B2 * 0.5)) ** 2
      EI 3 = B1 * T1 ** 3 / 12 + B1 * T1 * (T3 + B2 + 0.5 * T – YBAR) ** 2
      EIXX = EI 1 + EI 2 + EI 3
      EIYY = (T3 * B3 ** 3. + B2 + T2 ** 3 + T1 * B1 ** 3) / 12.
```

```
      RXX              = SQRT (EIXX / AREA)
      RYY              = SQRT (EIYY / AREA)
      WRITE (*, *) 'AREA =', AREA
      WRITE (*, *) 'CENTRE OF GRAVITY LOCATION = '. YBAR
      WRITE (*, *) 'MIXX = ', EIXX
      WRITE (*, *) 'MIYY = ', EIYY
      WRITE (*, *) 'RXX = ', RXX
      WRITE (*, *) 'RYY = ', RYY
      STOP
      END
C        ..............................................................................................
ENTER BREADTH OF TOP FLANGE
100
ENTER DEPTH OF TOP FLANGE
10
ENTER WEB THICKNESS
10
ENTER WEB DEPTH
380
ENTER BREADTH OF BOTTOM FLANGE
200
ENTER DEPTH OF BOTTOM FLANGE
10
AREA = 6800.0000000
CENTRE OF GRAVITY LOCATION = 113.2353000
MIXX = 68849900.0000000
MIYY = 52393330.0000000
RXX = 100.6230000
RYY = 87.7775700
Stop – Program terminated.
```

Example 8.20

C   ....

C   THE PRESTRESS IS COMPUTED BY THE FOLLOWING EQUATION

C $f_c = \dfrac{P}{A} + \dfrac{Pe^2}{I}$

C   WITH P VARYING FROM 20 TO 30 IN STEPS OF 2

C   WITH A VARYING FROM 0.20 TO 0.30 IN STEPS OF 0.01

C   WITH E VARYING FROM 0.03 TO 0.06 IN STEPS OF 0.01

C   WITH I VARUING FROM 0.01 TO 0.05 IN STEPS OF 0.01

C   WRITE A PROGRAM TO EVALUATE FC VALUES

```
C      ..........................................................................................................
C      PROGRAMME
C      ..........................................................................................................
       OPEN (UNIT = 1, STATUS = 'NEW', FILE = 'P20.OUT)
       WRITE (1, *)' ............................................................................................,
       WRITE (1, *) 'P              A                  E                              FC'
       WRITE (1, *)' ............................................................................................,
       DO 100 P = 20, 30, 10
       P = P/1
       DO 100 IA = 20, 30, 10
       A = IA / 100.
       DO 100 IE = 3, 6
       E = IE / 100.
       DO 100 II = 1, 5, 2
       XI = II/100
       FC = (P/A) + (P * E ** 2) / XI
       WRITE (1, 20) P, A, E, XI, FC
20     FORMAT (1X, 5 (F6.2, 4X))
100    CONTINUE
       STOP
       END
```

P	A	E	I	FC
20.00	0.20	0.03	0.01	101.80
20.00	0.20	0.03	0.03	100.60
20.00	0.20	0.03	0.05	100.36
20.00	0.20	0.04	0.01	103.20
20.00	0.20	0.04	0.03	101.07
20.00	0.20	0.04	0.05	100.64
20.00	0.20	0.05	0.01	105.00
20.00	0.20	0.05	0.03	101.67
20.00	0.20	0.05	0.05	101.00
20.00	0.20	0.06	0.01	107.20
20.00	0.20	0.06	0.03	102.40
20.00	0.20	0.06	0.05	101.44
20.00	0.30	0.03	0.01	68.47
20.00	0.30	0.03	0.03	67.27
20.00	0.30	0.03	0.05	67.03
20.00	0.30	0.04	0.01	69.87
20.00	0.30	0.04	0.03	67.73

P	A	E	I	FC
20.00	0.30	0.04	0.05	67.31
20.00	0.30	0.05	0.01	71.67
20.00	0.30	0.05	0.03	68.33
20.00	0.30	0.05	0.05	67.67
20.00	0.30	0.06	0.01	73.87
20.00	0.30	0.06	0.03	69.07
20.00	0.30	0.06	0.05	68.11
30.00	0.20	0.03	0.01	152.70
30.00	0.20	0.03	0.03	150.90
30.00	0.20	0.03	0.05	152.54
30.00	0.20	0.04	0.01	154.80
30.00	0.20	0.04	0.03	151.60
30.00	0.20	0.04	0.05	150.96
30.00	0.20	0.05	0.01	157.50
30.00	0.20	0.05	0.03	152.50
30.00	0.20	0.05	0.05	151.50
30.00	0.20	0.06	0.01	160.80
30.00	0.20	0.06	0.03	153.60
30.00	0.20	0.06	0.05	152.16
30.00	0.30	0.03	0.01	102.70
30.00	0.30	0.03	0.03	100.90
30.00	0.30	0.03	0.05	100.54
30.00	0.30	0.04	0.01	104.80
30.00	0.30	0.04	0.03	101.60
30.00	0.30	0.04	0.05	100.96
30.00	0.30	0.05	0.01	107.50
30.00	0.30	0.05	0.03	102.50
30.00	0.30	0.05	0.05	101.50
30.00	0.30	0.06	0.01	110.80
30.00	0.30	0.06	0.03	103.60
30.00	0.30	0.06	0.05	102.16

Example 8.21

C ....

C THE FLEXURAL STRENGTH OF A RCC BEAM IS EVALUATED BY THE EQUATION

C $M_U = 0.87 f_Y A_{ST} d[1 - (A_{ST}/bd)(f_Y/f_{CK})]$

C WRITE A PROGRAM TO COMPUTE MU FOR DIFFERENET PERCENTAGES OF STEEL P VARYING FROM 0.50 TO 4.0 IN STEPS OF 0.10

```
C       ............................................................................................
        PROGRAMME
C       ............................................................................................
        OPEN (UNIT = 1, STATUS = 'NEW' , FILE = 'P21.OUT')
        WRITE (1, *) '..................................................................................'
        WRITE (1, *) 'P        FCK = 15     FCK = 20     FCK = 25      FCK = 30
        WRITE (1, *) '...........................................................................'
        WRITE (1, *) 'ENTER VALUE OF FY'
        READ (*, *) FY
        DO 100 IP = 5, 40, 1
        P = IP / 1000
        WRITE (*, *) P
        WRITE (1, 10) P
10      FORMAT (F6.2, 4X)
        DO 200 FCK = 15, 30, 5
C XMU = MU/BD²
        XMU = .87 * FY * P * (1 (P * FY / FCK))
        WRITE (1, 20) XMU
20      Format (1X, F6.3, 2X)
200     CONTINUE
        WRITE (1, *)
100     CONTINUE
        STOP
        END
C       ............................................................................................
```

P	FCK = 15	FCK = 20	FCK = 25	FCK = 30
.005	1.556	1.618	1.655	1.680
.006	1.807	1.897	1.951	1.986
.007	2.038	2.160	2.234	2.283
.008	2.249	2.409	2.505	2.569
.009	2.440	2.643	2.764	2.845
.010	2.612	2.861	3.011	3.111
.011	2.763	3.065	3.246	3.367
.012	2.894	3.254	3.470	3.613
.013	3.006	3.428	3.881	3.850
.014	3.097	3.586	3.880	4.076
.015	3.168	3.730	4.067	4.292
.016	3.220	3.859	4.242	4.498
.017	3.251	3.973	4.406	4.694

P	FCK = 15	FCK = 20	FCK = 25	FCK = 30
.018	3.262	4.072	4.557	4.881
.019	3.254	4.155	4.696	5.057
.020	3.225	4.224	4.824	5.223
.021	3.177	4.278	4.939	5.379
.022	3.108	4.317	5.042	5.526
.023	3.020	4.341	5.134	5.662
.024	2.912	4.350	5.213	5.788
.025	2.783	4.344	5.280	5.905
.026	2.635	4.323	5.336	6.011
.027	2.466	4.287	5.379	6.307
.028	2.278	4.236	5.411	6.194
.029	2.070	4.170	5.430	6.270
.030	1.841	4.089	5.437	6.336
.031	1.593	3.993	5.433	6.393
.032	1.325	3.882	5.416	6.439
.033	1.037	3.756	5.388	6.476
.034	.728	3.615	5.347	6.502
.035	.400	3.459	5.295	6.518
.036	.052	3.288	5.230	6.525
.037	− .316	3.103	5.154	6.521
.038	− .704	2.902	5.065	6.508
.039	− 1.112	2.686	4.965	6.484
.040	− 1.540	2.455	4.583	6.451

Example 8.22

```
C    ............................................................................
C    WRITE A PROGRAM TO CALCULATE THE TIME FACTOR T WHICH IS A
     FUNCTION OF THE
C    DEGREE OF CONSOLIDATION U GIVEN BY THE RELATION
```

C   When $U \leq 60\% \quad T = \dfrac{\pi}{4}\left(\dfrac{U}{100}\right)^2$

$$U \geq 60\% \quad T = 0.9332 \log_{10}\left(1 - \dfrac{U}{100}\right) - 0.0851$$

```
C    ............................................................................
C    PROGRAMME
C    ............................................................................
     WRITE (*, *) 'ENTER PERCENTAGE OF DEGREE OF CONSOLIDATION'
     READ (*, *) U
     IF (U, LE. 60) THEN
```

```
        T = (3.1415926 / 4) * ((U/100) ** 2)
        ELSE
        T = - 0.9332 * ALOG10 (1 - U/100) - 0.0851
        ENDIF
        WRITE (*, *) 'VALUE OF TIME FACTOR T = ', T
        STOP
        END
C       ...........................................................................................
        ENTER PERCENTAGE OF DEGREE OF CONSOLIDATION'
        20
        VALUE OF TIME FACTOR T = 3.141593E - 002
        Stop - Program terminated.
        ENTER PERCENTAGE OF degree of consolidation
        80
        VALUE OF TIME FACTOR T = 5.671788E - 001
        Stop - Program terminated.
```

Example 8.23

```
C       ...........................................................................................
C       WRITE A PROGRAM THAT SOLVES THE DIFFERENTIAL EQUATION
C       (dy/dx) = 1 + y²
C       BY USING RUNGE-KUTTA METHOD OF ORDER 4, GIVEN THAT Y (0) = 0
        AND CALCULATE
C       Y (0.60) AT INTERVALS OF 0.10
C       ...........................................................................................
C       PROGRAMME
C       ...........................................................................................
        WRITE (*, *) 'ENTER VALUES OF X, Y, XLAST, H'
        READ (*, *) XO, YO, XLAST, H
        X = XO
        Y = YO
10      AK1 = H * ( 1 + Y ** 2)
        AK2 = H * ( 1 + (Y + 0.50 * AK1) ** 2)
        AK3 = H * ( 1 + (Y + 0.50 * AK2) ** 2)
        AK4 = H * ( 1 + (Y + 0.50 * AK3) ** 2)
        AK = (1/6)* (AK1) + (2 * AK2) + (2 * AK3) + AK4)
20      WRITE (*, 30) X, Y
30      FORMAT (1X, 'X = '. F 6.2, 4X, 'Y =' F8.4)
        Y = Y + AK
        X = X + H
        IF (X - XLAST), 10, 10, 40
        STOP
        END
```

```
C        .................................................................................................
ENTER VALUES OF X, Y, XLAST, H
0, 0, 0.60, 0.10
X = .00              Y = .0000
X = .10              Y = .1002
X = .20              Y = .2023
X = .30              Y = .3084
X = .40              Y = .4210
X = .50              Y = .5433
X = .60              Y = .6793
Stop – Program terminated.
```

Example 8.24

```
C        .................................................................................................
C        WRITE A PROGRAM TO CALCULATE THE REAL ROOT OF THE EQUATION
C        x² + 4 sin x = 0
C        CORRECT TO FOUR DECIMAL PLACES USING THE N – R METHOD
C        ASSUME APPROXIMATE SOLUTION AS – 1.90
C        .................................................................................................
C        PROGRAMME
C        .................................................................................................
         WRITE (*, *) 'ENTER VALUE OF X'
         READ (*, *) XO
         A          = (X0 ** 2) + (4 * SIN (X0))
         B          = (2 * X) + (4 * COS (X0))
         X1         = X0 – A/B
         ACR        = X1 – X0
         IF (ACR .LE. 1E – 04) GOTO 25
         X0         = X1
         GOTO 10
25       WRITE (*, *)'VALUE OF ROOT =' , X1
         STOP
         END
C        .................................................................................................
ENTER VALUES OF X
– 1.90
VALUE OF ROOT = – 2.0354830
Stop – Program terminated.
```

Example 8.25

```
C        .................................................................................................
C        A TESTING LABORATORY HAS MAINTAINED THE DATA OF THE
         COMPRESSIVE STRENGTH
```

```
C       OF CONCRETE CUBES OVER A PERIOD. ASSUME THE STRENGTHS ARE
        REPRESENTED BY
C       VARIABLES C (1) TO C (N). WRITE A FORTRAN PROGRAM TO
        CALCULATE THE MEAN AND
C       THE VARIANCE OF THE DATA.
C
C       .................................................................................................
C       PROGRAMME
C       .................................................................................................
        DIMENSION C (100)
        WRITE (*, *) 'ENTER NUMBER OF SAMPLES'
        READ (*, *) N
        WRITE (*, *) 'ENTER COMPRESSIVE STRENGTH OF N SAMPLES'
        SUM = 0.0
        DO 100  = 1, N
        READ (*, *) C (I)
        SUM = SUM + C (I)
100     CONTINUE
        AVER = SUM / N
        DSUM = 0.0
        DO 200 I = 1, N
        DSUM = DSUM + ((C (I) – AVER) ** 2)
200     CONTINUE
        VAR = SQRT (DSUM / N)
        WRITE (*, *) 'THE AVERAGE COMPRESSIVE STRENGTH IS' AVER
        WRITE (*, *) 'THE VARIANCE OF DATA IS' VAR
        STOP
        END
C.      .................................................................................................
ENTER NUMBER OF SAMPLES
4
ENTER COMPRESSIVE STRENGTH OF N SAMPLES
53
54
55
56
THE AVERAGE COMPRESSIVE STRENGTH IS 54.5000000
THE VARIANCE OF DATA IS 1.1180340
```

Stop – Program terminated.

Example 8.26

```
C       .................................................................................................
C       IT IS REQUIRED TO FIND THE FORCE TRANSMITTED FT TO THE
        FOUNDATION OF A MACHINE
```

C   WHICH IS SET TO VIBRATE. THE FORCE TRANSMITTEDFT IS GIVEN BY THE EQUATION

C $$F_t = \left[\frac{\sqrt{1 + 2w(w/w_n)^2}}{\sqrt{\left(1 - (w/w_n)^2\right)^2 + 2w(w/w_n)}}\right]F_0$$

C   WRITE A PROGRAM TO CALCULATE FT FOR ALL COMBINATIONS OF DAMPING RATIOS W

C   AND FREQUENCY RATIO W/WN VARYING W FROM 0 TO 2.0 IN STEPS OF 0.10 AND W/WN

C   FROM 0 TO5.0 IN STEPS OF 0.20 GIVEN THAT F0 = 112.50

C
C   ....

C   PROGRAMME

C   ....

```
OPEN (UNIT = 1, STATUS = 'NEW', FILE = 'P26.OUT')
F0 = 112.50
WRITE (1, *) ' W/WN                W              FT'
WRITE (1, *) ' ..........................................................................
DO 100IW = 0, 20, 5
W = IW / 10.
WRITE (*, *) W
DO 100 IWWN = 0, 50, 5
WWN = IWWN / 10.
XNUM = (SQRT (1 + (2 * W * (WWN ** 2)))) * F0
XDEN = SQRT ((( 1 – WWN ** 2) + (2 * W * WWN))
IF (XDEN .EQ.0) GOTO 100
FT = XNUM / XDEN
WRITE (1, 10) WWN, W, FT
10      FORMAT (1X, F6.2, 4XS, F6.2, 4X, F10.4)
100     CONTINUE
STOP
END
```

C   ....

W/WN	W	FT
.00	.00	112.5000
.50	.00	150.0000
1.50	.00	90.0000
2.00	.00	37.5000
2.50	.00	21.4286

W/WN	W	FT
3.00	.00	14.0625
3.50	.00	10.0000
4.00	.00	7.5000
4.50	.00	5.8442
5.00	.00	4.6875
.00	.50	112.5000
.50	.50	122.0234
1.00	.50	159.0990
1.50	.50	115.8927
2.00	.50	75.8475
2.50	.50	55.2470
3.00	.50	43.4625
3.50	.50	35.9074
4.00	.50	30.6520
4.50	.50	26.7781
5.00	.50	23.7986
.00	1.00	112.5000
.50	1.00	110.2270
1.00	1.00	137.7838
1.50	1.00	123.5186
2.00	1.00	93.6507
2.50	1.00	72.4370
3.00	1.00	58.6112
3.50	1.00	49.1564
4.00	1.00	42.3381
4.50	1.00	37.1993
5.00	1.00	33.1886
.00	1.50	112.5000
.50	1.50	103.6274
1.00	1.50	129.9038
1.50	1.50	127.1972
2.00	1.50	104.7318
2.50	1.50	84. 4335
3.00	1.50	69.6739
3.50	1.50	59.0407
4.00	1.50	51.1536
4.50	1.50	45.1097
5.00	1.50	40.3428

W/WN	W	FT
.00	2.00	112.5000
.50	2.00	99.3884
1.00	2.00	125.7788
1.50	2.00	129.3659
2.00	2.00	112.5000
2.50	2.00	93.5970
3.00	2.00	78.4958
3.50	2.00	67.0970
4.00	2.00	58.4253
4.50	2.00	51.6808
5.00	2.00	46.3116

Example 8.27

```
C       ..................................................................
C       THE SECOND MOMENT OF AREA OF A TEE BEAM IS GIVEN BY THE
        FOLLOWING FORMULA:
```

$$\frac{y}{D} = \left[\frac{\left\{\left(\frac{b_f}{b_w}\right)\left(\frac{D_f}{D}\right)\left(1-\frac{1}{2}\right)\left(\frac{D_f}{D}\right)+\left(1-\frac{D_f}{D}\right)^2/2\right\}}{\left(\frac{D_f}{D}\right)\left(\frac{b_f}{b_w}-1\right)+1}\right]$$

$$K = \frac{I_{xx}}{\left(\frac{b_w D^3}{12}\right)} = \left[\left(\frac{b_f}{b_w}\right)\left(\frac{D_f}{D}\right)^3 + 12\left(\frac{b_f}{b_w}\right)\left(\frac{D_f}{D}\right)\left(1-\frac{y}{D}-\frac{D_f}{2D}\right)^2 + \left(1-\frac{D_f}{D}\right)^3 + 12\left(1-\frac{D_f}{D}\right)\frac{1}{2}\left(1-\frac{D_f}{D}\right)\right]$$

```
C       ..................................................................
C       WRITE A PROGRAM TO CALCULATE THE COEFFICIENT K FOR
        DIFFERENT VALUES OF (Df/D)
        VARYING FROM 0 TO 0.4 AND (bf/bw) varying from 1 to 20.
C       ..................................................................
C       PROGRAMME
C       ..................................................................
C       GROSS MOMENT OF INERTIA OF TEE BEAMS
C       NOTATIONS
C       BFBW = bf/bw
C       Dfd = Df/d
        DO 10 IBFW = 1, 20
        BFBW = IBFW
```

```
      DO 10 IDFD = 10, 14
      DFD = (IDFS – 10.)/10
      Y1 = (BFBW * DFD * (1 – 0.5 * DFD)) = (0.5 * (1 – 0.5 * DFD) **2
      Y2 = DFD ** (BFBW – 1.) + 1.
C     YBARD = YBAR/D
      YBARD = Y1/Y2
      C1 = BFBW * DFD 8 ** 3
      C2 = 12. * BFBW * DFD (1. – YBARD – (0.5 * DFD)) ** 2
      C3 = (1. – DFD ** 3
      C4 = 12. * (1. – DFD) * (( 0.5 * (1. – DFD) – YBRD ** 2
      COEFF = Ig/(BW*d ** 3/12)
      COEFF = C1 + C2 + C3 + C4
      WRITE (10, 20) BFBW, DFD, YBARD, COEFF
20    FORMAT (F15.3, F15.3, F15.3, F15.3)
10    CONTINUE
      STOP
      END
```

b_f/b_w	D_f/D	y/D	$K = I_g/(b_w D^3)/12$
1.00	0.000	0.500	1.000
1.00	0.100	0.500	1.000
1.00	0.200	0.500	1.000
1.00	0.300	0.500	1.000
1.00	0.400	0.500	1.000
2.00	0.000	0.500	1.000
2.00	0.100	0.541	1.222
2.00	0.200	0.567	1.328
2.00	0.300	0.581	1.366
2.00	0.400	0.586	1.373
3.00	0.000	0.500	1.000
3.00	0.100	0.575	1.407
3.00	0.200	0.614	1.565
3.00	0.300	0.631	1.605
3.00	0.400	0.633	1.608
4.00	0.000	0.500	1.000
4.00	0.100	0.604	1.564
4.00	0.200	0.650	1.744
4.00	0.300	0.666	1.777
4.00	0.400	0.664	1.781
5.00	0.000	0.500	1.000
5.00	0.100	0.629	1.675

b_f/b_w	D_f/D	y/D	$K = I_g/(b_w D^3)/12$
5.00	0.200	0.679	1.885
5.00	0.300	0.671	1.916
5.00	0.400	0.685	1.921
6.00	0.000	0.500	1.000
6.00	0.100	0.650	1.015
6.00	0.200	0.700	2.000
6.00	0.300	0.710	2.017
6.00	0.400	0.700	2.040
7.00	0.000	0.500	1.000
7.00	0.100	0.669	1.747
7.00	0.200	0.710	2.095
7.00	0.300	0.725	2.197
7.00	0.400	0.712	2.146
8.00	0.000	0.500	1.000
8.00	0.100	0.605	2.000
8.00	0.200	0.733	2.176
8.00	0.300	0.737	2.115
8.00	0.400	0.721	2.224
9.00	0.000	0.500	1.000
9.00	0.100	0.700	2.053
9.00	0.200	0.746	2.246
9.00	0.300	0.747	2.253
9.00	0.400	0.729	2.555
10.000	0.000	0.500	1.000
10.000	0.100	0.718	2.100
10.000	0.200	0.757	2.506
10.000	0.300	0.755	2.206
10.000	0.400	0.735	2.421
11.000	0.000	0.500	1.000
11.000	0.100	0.725	2.225
11.000	0.200	0.767	2.500
11.000	0.300	0.762	2.375
11.000	0.400	0.740	2.500
12.000	0.000	0.500	1.000
12.000	0.100	0.736	2.285
12.000	0.200	0.775	2.400
12.000	0.300	0.769	2.485
12.000	0.400	0.744	2.585
13.000	0.000	0.500	1.000

b_f/b_w	D_f/D	y/D	$K = I_g/(b_w D^3)/12$
13.000	0.100	0.745	2.357
13.000	0.20	0.788	2.451
13.000	0.300	0.774	2.472
13.000	0.400	0.748	2.612
14.000	0.000	0.500	1.000
14.000	0.100	0.754	2.386
14.000	0.200	0.789	2.491
14.000	0.300	0.779	2.321
14.000	0.400	0.752	2.738
15.000	0.000	0.500	1.000
15.000	0.100	0.763	2.432
15.000	0.200	0.795	2.537
15.000	0.300	0.783	2.565
15.000	0.400	0.755	2.812
16.000	0.000	0.500	1.000
16.000	0.100	0.770	2.478
16.000	0.200	0.800	2.560
16.000	0.300	0.786	2.608
16.000	0.400	0.757	2.886
17.000	0.000	0.500	1.000
17.000	0.100	0.777	2.511
17.000	0.200	0.805	2.591
17.000	0.300	0.790	2.647
17.000	0.400	0.759	2.958
18.000	0.000	0.500	1.000
18.000	0.100	0.783	2.547
18.000	0.200	0.809	2.620
18.000	0.300	0.793	2.686
18.000	0.400	0.762	3.030
19.000	0.000	0.500	1.000
19.000	0.100	0.789	2.580
19.000	0.200	0.813	2.647
19.000	0.300	0.795	2.726
19.000	0.400	0.763	3.100
20.000	0.000	0.500	1.000
20.000	0.100	0.795	2.611
20.000	0.200	0.817	2.672
20.000	0.300	0.798	2.764
20.000	0.400	0.765	3.170

Example 8.28

```
C       ...................................................................................................
C       A SOLID CIRCULAR SHAFT IS SUBJECTED TO A BENDING MOMENT OF
        12500 N-M AND A
        TWISTING MOMENTOF 17000 N-M
C       IN A SIMPLE UNIAXIAL TENSION TEST FY = 800 N/MM2  ES= 200 GN/M2
        FS = 3. POISSON'S
C       RATIO = 0.25. ESTIAMTE THE DESIGN DIA USING THE FOLLOWING
        THEORIES
C       (1) MAXIMUM PRINCIPAL STRESS THEORY
C       (2) MAXIMUM SHEAR STRESS THEORY
C       (3) MAXIMUM PRINCIPAL STRAIN ENERGY THEORY
C       (4) TOTAL MAXIMU STRAIN ENERGY THEORY
C       (5) MAXIMUM ENERGY OF DISTORTION THEORY
C       ...................................................................................................
C       PROGRAMME
C       ...................................................................................................
C       MB, MT ARE GIVEN IN N-MM
        DIMENSION Z (5)
        DATA EMB, EMT, FE, FS, EM/1.25E + T, 300.0, 3.0. 0.25/FP = FE / FS
        MAXIMUM STRESS THEORY
        A = 16. / (3.14 * FP)
        B = SQRT (EMB ** 2 + EMT ** 2)
        C = 1. - (1. /EM)
        D = 1. + (1. /EM)
        Z (1) = A * (EMB + B) ** 0.33
C       MAXIMUM SHEAR STRESS THEORY
        Z (2) = (2. * A * B) ** 0.33
C       MAXIMUM PRINCIPAL STRAIN THEORY
        Z (3) = (A * (C * EMB + D * B)) ** 0.33
C       TOTAL MAXIMUM STRAIN ENERGY THEORY
        Z (4) = (A * SQRT (4. 8 EMB ** 2 + 2. * (D * EMT ** 2))) *8 0.33
C       DISTORTION ENERGY THEORY
        Z (5) = A * SQRT 94. * EMB ** 2 + 3. 8 EMT ** 2) ** 0.33
        WRITE (*, *) 'DIAMETER ACCORDING TO DISTORTION ENERGY THEORY'
        WRITE (*, 10) Z (5)
        WRITE (*, *) 'DIAMETER ACCORDING TO MAXIMUM STRESS THEORY'
        WRITE (*, 10) Z (1)
        WRITE (*, *) 'DIAMETER ACCORDING TO MAXIMUM SHEAR STRESS
        THEORY'
        WRITE (*, 10) Z (2)
```

WRITE (*, *) 'DIAMETER ACCORDING TO MAXIMUM STRAIN THEORY'
WRITE (*, 10) Z (3)
WRITE (*, *) 'DIAMETER ACCORDING TO MAXIMUM STRAIN ENERGY THEORY'
WRITE (*, 10) Z (4)
BIG = Z (I)
DO 14 I = 2, 5
DIA Z (1)
IF (DIA ,GT. BIG) BIG = DIA
14   CONTINUE
10   FORMAT (1X, F8.2)
WRITE (*, 8) 'THE BIGGEST DIAMETER IS' , BIG
STOP
END
C   ....
DIMETER ACCORDING TO DISTORTION ENERGY THEORY
        16.25
DIAMETER ACCORDING TO MAXIMUM STRESS THEORY
        15.52
DIAMETER ACCORDING TO MAXIMUM SHEAR STRESS THEORY
        122.95
DIAMETER ACCORDING TO MAXIMUM STRAIN THEORY
        143.92
DIAMETER ACCORDING TO MAXIMUM STRAIN ENERGY THEORY
        137.55
THE BIGGEST DIMETER IS   143.9166000
Stop – Program terminated.

Example 8.29
C   ....
C   WRITE A PROGRAM TO ANALYSE THE CONTINUOUS BEAM SHOWN BELOW (Fig. 8.4) USING
C   MOMENT DISTRIBUTION METHOD

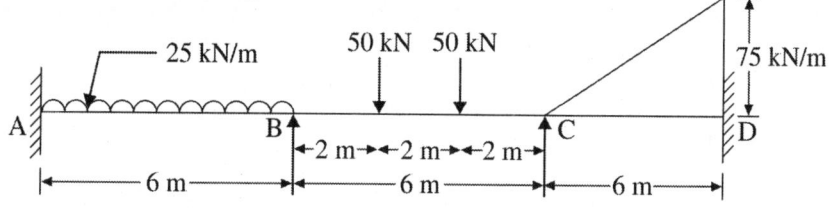

Fig. 8.4: Continuous beam of three spans fixed at ends

IMPLICIT REAL (I – N)
DATA U, W, L1, L2, L3, A/25.0, 59.0, 6.0, 6.0, 4.0, 2.0/

```
C       FIXED END MOMENT
        I = 1
        MFAB = U * (L1 ** 2) / 12.0
        MFBA = − MFAB
        MFBC = W * A * (L2 −A) / L2
        MFCB =  MFBC
        MFCD = 1.5 * W * (L3 ** 2) / 30.0
        MFDC = 1.5 * W * (L3 ** 2) / 20.0
C       CALCULATION OF STIFFNESS 'K' VALUES
        K1 = 1. / L1
        K2 = 1. / L2
        K3 = 1. / L3
C       DISTRIBUTION FACTORS − 'DF' VALUES
        DFAB = 0.0
        DFBA = K1 / (K1 + K2)
        DFBC = K2 / (K1 + K2)
        DFCB = K2 / (K2 + K3)
        DFCD = K3 / (K2 + K3)
        DFDC = 0.0
C       UNBALANCED MOMENT
        MUB = MFBA + MFBC
        MUC = MFCB + MFCD
C       BALANCED MOMENT
        MBAB = 0.0
        MBBA =(DFBA + MUB)
        MBBC =  (DFBC + MUB)
        MBCB = (DFCB + MUC)
        MBCD = (DFCD + MUC)
        MBDC = 0.0
C       MOMENT AT FIRST CYCLE
        MAB = MFAB + MBAB
        MBA = MFBA + MBBA
        MBC = MFBC + MBBC
        MCB = MFCB + MBCB
        MCD = MFCD + MBCD
        MDC = MFDC + MBDC
C       CARRY OVERS
100     MCAB = 0.5 * MBBA
        MCBA = 0.5 * MBAB
        MCBC = 0.5 * MBCB
        MCCB = 0.5 * MBBC
```

```
        MCCD = 0.5 * MBDC
        MCDC = 0.5 * MBCD
C       UNBALANCED MOMENTS
        MUB = MCBA + MCBC
        MUC = MCCB + MCCD
C       BALANCED MOMENTS
        MBBA = – (DFBA + MUB)
        MBBC = – (DFBC + MUB)
        MBCB = – (DFCB + MUC)
        MBCD = – (DFCD + MUC)
C       FINAL MOMENTS
        MAB = MAB + MCAB + MBAB
        MBA = MBA + MCBA + MBBA
        MBC = MBC + MCBC + MBBC
        MCB = MCB + MCCB + MBCB
        MCD = MCD + MCCD + MBCD
        MDC = MDC + MCDC + MBDC
        J = J + 1
        IF (J, .EQ. 6) GOTO 150
        GOTO 100
150     WRITE (*, 50)  MAB, MBA, MBC, MCB, MCD, MDC
50      FORMAT (3X, 'MAB =', F8.3/,
        1       3X, 'MBA =', F8.3/,
        2       3X, 'MBC =', F8.3/,
        3       3X, 'MCB =', F8.3/,
        4       3X, 'MCD =', F8.3/,
        5       3X, 'MDC =', F8.3/,
        STOP
        END
C       ...................................................................................
MAB = 75.793
MBA = – 73.421
MBC = 73.421
MCB = – 55.524
MCD = 55.524
MDC = – 52.236
Stop – Program terminated.
```

Example 8.30

```
C       ...................................................................................
C       WRITE A PROGRAM TO ANALYSE THE CONTINUOUS BEAM (Fig. 8.5)
        SHOWN BELOW USING THE MOMENT DISTRIBUTION METHOD
```

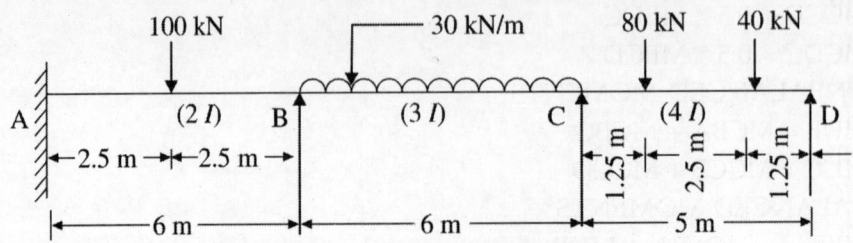

Fig. 8.5: Three span continuous beam

IMPLICIT REAL (I – N)

DATA U, W1, W2, W3, L1, L2, L3, A, E1, E2, E3/30.0, 100.0, 80.0, 40.0, 5.0, 6.0, 5.0,

1.25, 2.0, 3.0, 4.0/

FIXED END MOMENT

J = 1

MFAB = (W1 * (L1 / 2) * ((L1 / 2) ** 2)) / (L1 ** 2)

MFBA = – MFAB

MFBC = U * (L2 ** 2) /12

MFCB = – MFBC

MFCD = (W2 * A ((L3 – A) ** 2)) / (L3 ** 2) + (W3 * (L3 – A) * (A ** 2))) / (L3 ** 2)

MFDC = (((W2 * (L3 – A) * (A ** 2)) / (L3 ** 2)) + ((W3 * A * (L3 – A) ** 2) / (L3 ** 2)))

C   CALCULATION OF STIFFNESS 'K' VALUES

K1   = E1 /L1

K2   = E2 /L2

K3   = E3 /L3

C   DISTRIBUTION FACTORS – 'DF' VALUES

DFAB = 0.0

DFBA = K1 / (K1 + K2)

DFBC = K2 / (K1 + K2)

DFCB = K2 / (K2 + K3)

DFCD = K3 / (K2 + K3)

DFDC = 0.0

C   UNBALANCED MOMENT

MUB = MFBA + MFBC

MUC = MFCB + MFCD

C   BALANCED MOMENT

MBAB = 0.0

MBBA = – (DFBA + MUB)

MBBC = – (DFBC + MUB)

MBCB = – (DFCB + MUC)

MBCD = – (DFCD + MUC)

```
         MBDC = 0.0
C        MOMENT AT FIRST CYCLE
         MAB = MFAB + MBAB
         MBA = MFBA + MBBA
         MBC = MFBC + MBBC
         MCB = MFCB + MBCB
         MCD = MFCD + MBCD
         MDC = MFDC + MBDC
C        CARRY OVERS
100      MCAB = 0.5 * MBBA
         MCBA = 0.5 * MBAB
         MCBC = 0.5 * MBCB
         MCCB = 0.5 * MBBC
         MCCD = 0.5 * MBDC
         MCDC = 0.5 * MBCD
C        UNBALANCED MOMENTS
         MUB = MCBA + MCBC
         MUC = MCCB + MCCD
C        BALANCED MOMENTS
         MBBA =(DFBA * MUB)
         MBBC =  (DFBC * MUB)
         MBCB = (DFCB * MUC)
         MBCD = (DFCD * MUC)
C        FINAL MOMENTS
         MAB = MAB + MCAB + MBAB
         MBA = MBA + MCBA + MBBA
         MBC = MBC + MCBC + MBBC
         MCB = MCB + MCCB + MBCB
         MCD = MCD + MCCD + MBCD
         MDC = MDC + MCDC + MBDC
         J = J + 1
         IF (J, .EQ. 6) GOTO 150
         GOTO 100
150      WRITE (*, 50) MAB, MBA, MBC, MCB, MCD, MDC
50       FORMAT (3X, 'MAB =', F8.3/,
        1        3X, 'MBA =', F8.3/,
        2        3X, 'MBC =', F8.3/,
        3        3X, 'MCB =', F8.3/,
        4        3X, 'MCD =', F8.3/,
        5        3X, 'MDC =', F8.3/,
         STOP
         END
```

```
C        ..................................................................................................
MAB = 54.948
MBA = – 77.611
MBC = 77.611
MCB = – 86.434
MCD = 86.434
MDC = – 36.477
Stop – Program terminated.
```

Example 8.31

```
C        ..................................................................................................
C        WRITE A PROGRAM TO ANALYSE THE CONTINUOUS BEAM (Fig. 8.6)
         SHOWN BELOW USING
C        MOMENT DISTRIBUTION METHOD
```

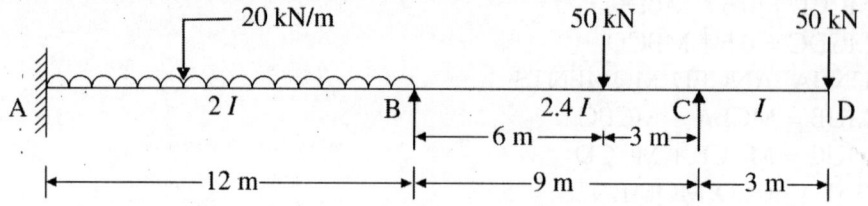

Fig. 8.6: Two span continuous beam with overhang

```
         IMPLICIT REAL (I – N)
         DATA U, W1, L1, L2, L2, A, E1, E2, EM/20.0, 50.0, 12.0, 9.0, 6.0, 2.0, 2.4, –150/
         WRITE (*, 10) U, W1, L1, L2, A, E1, E2, EM
10       FORMAT (5F 10.3)
C        FIXED END MOMENT
         J = 1
         MFAB = (U * (L1 ** 2)/12
         MFBA = – MFAB
         MFBC = (W1 * A ((L2 – A ** 2)) / (L2 ** 2)
         MFCB = ((W1 * (L2 – A) * (A ** 2)) / (L2 ** 2)) + EM
C        CALCULATION OF STIFFNESS 'K' VALUES
         K1 = E1 /L1
         K2 = E2 /L2
C        DISTRIBUTION FACTORS – 'DF' VALUES
         DFAB = 0.0
         DFBA = K1 / (K1 + K2)
         DFBC = K2 / (K1 + K2)
         DFCB = 0.0
C        UNBALANCED MOMENT
         MUB = MFBA + MFBC
         MUC = MFCB
```

```
C       BALANCED MOMENT
        MBAB = 0.0
        MBBA = - (DFBA * MUB)
        MBBC = - (DFBC * MUB)
        MBCB = 0.0
C       MOMENT AT FIRST CYCLE
        MAB = MFAB + MBAB
        MBA = MFBA + MBBA
        MBC = MFBC + MBBC
        MCB = MFCB + MBCB
C       CARRY OVERS
100     MCAB = 0.5 * MBBA
        MCBA = 0.5 * MBAB
        MCBC = 0.5 * MBCB
        MCCB = 0.5 * MBBC
C       UNBALANCED MOMENTS
        MUB = MCBA + MCBC
C       BALANCED MOMENTS
        MBBA = - (DFBA * MUB)
        MBBC = - (DFBC * MUB)
C       FINAL MOMENTS
        MAB = MAB + MCAB + MBAB
        MBA = MBA + MCBA + MBBA
        MBC = MBC + MCBC + MBBC
        MCB = MCB + MCCB + MBCB
        J = J + 1
        IF (J, .EQ. 6) GOTO 150
        GOTO 100
150     WRITE (*, 50) MAB, MBA, MBC, MCB
50      FORMAT (3X, 'MAB =', F8.3/,
        1       3X, 'MBA =', F8.3/,
        2       3X, 'MBC =', F8.3/,
        3       3X, 'MCB =', F8.3/,
        STOP
        END
C       ....................................................................
MAB = 233.500
MBA = - 12.821
MBC = 12.821
MCB = - 10.256
Stop - Program terminated.
```

Example 8.32

```
C       ........................................................................................
C       WRITE A PROGRAM TO ANALYSE THE BOX CULVERT (Fig. 8.7) SHOWN
        BELOW USING
C       MOMENT DISTRIBUTION METHOD
```

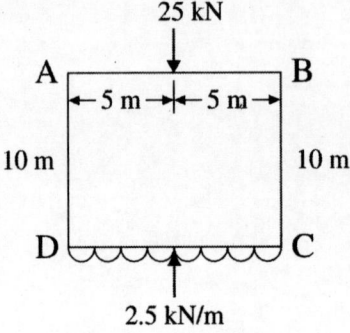

Fig. 8.7: Box culvert

```
C
        IMPLICIT REAL (I – N)
        DATA U, W1, W2, W3, L1, L2, L3, L4, A, /2.50, 25.00, 10.0, 10.0, 10.0, 5.0/
C       FIXED END MOMENT
        J = 1
        MFAB = (W1 * (L1 / 2) * ((L1 / 2) ** 2)) / (L1 ** 2)
        MFBA = – MFAB
        MFBC = 0.0
        MFCB = – MFBC
        MFCD = – (U * (W3 ** 2) / 12)
        MFDC = – MFCD
        MFDA = 0.0
        MFAD = 0.0
C       CALCULATION OF STIFFNESS 'K' VALUES
        K1      = 1.0 / L1
        K2      = 1.0 / L2
        K3      = 1.0 / L3
        K4      = 1.0 / L4
C       DISTRIBUTION FACTORS – 'DF' VALUES
        DFAB = K1 / (K1 + K4)
        DFBA = K1 / (K1 + K2)
        DFBC = K2 / (K1 + K2)
        DFCB = K2 / (K2 + K3)
        DFCD = K3 / (K2 + K3)
        DFDC = K3 / (K3 + K4)
        DFAD = K4 / (K1 + K4)
        DFDA = K4 / (K3 + K4)
```

C   UNBALANCED MOMENT
      MUA = MFAB + MFAD
      MUB = MFBA + MFBC
      MUC = MFCB + MFCD
      MUD = MFDC + MFDA
C   BALANCED MOMENT
      MBAB = – (DFAB * MUA)
      MBBA = – (DFBA * MUB)
      MBBC = – (DFBC * MUB)
      MBCB = – (DFCB * MUC)
      MBCD = – (DFCD * MUC)
      MBDC = – (DFDC * MUD)
      MBDA = – (DFDA * MUD)
      MBAD = – (DFAD * MUA)
C   MOMENT AT FIRST CYCLE
      MAB = MFAB + MBAB
      MBA = MFBA + MBBA
      MBC = MFBC + MBBC
      MCB = MFCB + MBCB
      MCD = MFCD + MBCD
      MDC = MFDC + MBDC
      MDA = MFDA + MBDA
      MAD = MFAD + MBAD
C   CARRY OVERS
100   MCAB = 0.5 * MBBA
      MCBA = 0.5 * MBAB
      MCBC = 0.5 * MBCB
      MCCB = 0.5 * MBBC
      MCCD = 0.5 * MBDC
      MCDC = 0.5 * MBCD
      MCDA = 0.5 * MBDA
      MCAD = 0.5 * MBAD
C   UNBALANCED MOMENTS
      MUA = MCAB + MCAD
      MUB = MCBA + MCBC
      MUC = MCCB + MCCD
      MUD = MCDC + MCDA
C   BALANCED MOMENTS
      MBAB = – (DFAB * MUA)
      MBBA = – (DFBA * MUB)

```
        MBBC = - (DFBC * MUB)
        MBCB = - (DFCB * MUC)
        MBCD = - (DFCD * MUC)
        MBDC = - (DFDC * MUD)
        MBDA = - (DFDA * MUD)
        MBAD = - (DFAD * MUA)
C       FINAL MOMENTS
        MAB = MAB + MCAB + MBAB
        MBA = MBA + MCBA + MBBA
        MBC = MBC + MCBC + MBBC
        MCB = MCB + MCCB + MBCB
        MCD = MCD + MCCD + MBCD
        MDC = MDC + MCDC + MBDC
        MDA = MDA + MCDA + MBDA
        MAD = MAD + MCAD + MBAD
        J = J + 1
        IF (J, .EQ. 6) GOTO 150
        GOTO 100
150     WRITE (*, 50) MAB, MBA, MBC, MCB, MCD, MDC, MDA, MAD
50      FORMAT (3X, 'MAB =', F8.3/,
        1       3X, 'MBA =', F8.3/,
        2       3X, 'MBC =', F8.3/,
        3       3X, 'MCB =', F8.3/,
        4       3X, 'MCD =', F8.3/,
        5       3X, 'MDC =', F8.3/,
        6       3X, 'MDA =', F8.3/,
        7       3X, 'MAD =', F8.3/,
        STOP
        END
C       ............................................................
MAB = 25.085
MBA = - 18.433
MBC = 18.433
MCB = 5.005
MCD = - 5.005
MDC = - 1.648
MDA = 1.648
MAD = - 25.085
Stop - Program terminated.
```

Example 8.33

C   ....

C   WRITE A PROGRAM TO ANALYSE THE PORTAL (Fig. 8.8) FRAME SHOWN
       BELOW USING MOMENT

C   DISTRIBUTION METHOD

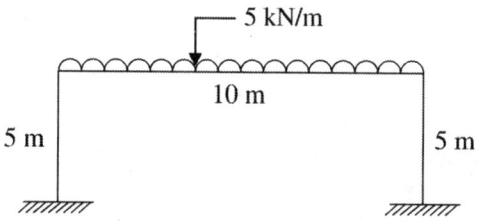

Fig. 8.8: Portal frame with fixed supports

```
C       IMPLICIT REAL (– N)
        DATA U, L1, L2, L3 / 5.0, 5.0, 10.0, 5.0/
C       FIXED END MOMENT
        J = 1
        MFAB = 0.0
        MFBA = – MFAB
        MFBC = U * (L2 ** A) / 12
        MFCB = – MFBC
        MFCD = 0.0
        MFDC = – MFCD
C       CALCULATION OF STIFFNESS 'K' VALUES
        K1      = 1.0 / L1
        K2      = 1.0 / L2
        K3      = 1.0 / L3
C       DISTRIBUTION FACTORS – 'DF' VALUES
        DFAB = 0.0
        DFBA = K1 / (K1 + K2)
        DFBC = K2 / (K1 + K2)
        DFCB = K2 / (K2 + K3)
        DFCD = K3 / (K2 + K3)
        DFDC = 0.0
C       UNBALANCED MOMENT
        MUB = MFBA + MFBC
        MUC = MFCB + MFCD
C       BALANCED MOMENT
        MBAB = 0.0
        MBBA = – (DFBA * MUB)
```

```
        MBBC = - (DFBC * MUB)
        MBCB = - (DFCB * MUC)
        MBCD = - (DFCD * MUC)
        MBDC = 0.0
C       CARRY OVERS
100     MCAB = 0.5 * MBBA
        MCBA = 0.5 * MBAB
        MCBC = 0.5 * MBCB
        MCCB = 0.5 * MBBC
        MCCD = 0.5 * MBDC
        MCDC = 0.5 * MBCD
C       UNBALANCED MOMENTS
        MUB = MCBA + MCBC
        MUC = MCCB + MCCD
C       BALANCED MOMENTS
        MBBA = - (DFBA * MUB)
        MBBC = - (DFBC * MUB)
        MBCB = - (DFCB * MUC)
        MBCD = - (DFCD * MUC)
C       FINAL MOMENTS
        MAB = MAB + MCAB + MBAB
        MBA = MBA + MCBA + MBBA
        MBC = MBC + MCBC + MBBC
        MCB = MCB + MCCB + MBCB
        MCD = MCD + MCCD + MBCD
        MDC = MDC + MCDC + MBDC
        J = J + 1
        IF (J .EQ. 6) GOTO 150
        GOTO 100
150     WRITE (*, 50) MAB, MBA, MBC, MCB, MCD, NDC
50      FORMAT (3X, 'MAB =', F8.3/,
        1        3X, 'MBA =', F8.3/,
        2        3X, 'MBC =', F8.3/,
        3        3X, 'MCB =', F8.3/,
        4        3X, 'MCD =', F8.3/,
        5        3X, 'MDC =', F8.3/,
        STOP
        END
C       ....................................................................
MAB = - 16.665
```

MBA = − 33.333
MBC = 33,333
MCB = 33.333
MCD = 33.333
MDC = − 16.665
Stop − Program terminated.

Example 8.34

```
C      ............................................................................................
C      THE LOAD ENHANCEMENT OF A RESTRAINED ONE WAY SLAB IS
       GIVEN AS
```

$$C \quad P/PY = 1 + \alpha \left[\frac{\alpha}{\alpha\beta} - \frac{\delta\tau_0}{4\beta M_u} \right] - \beta \left(\frac{\alpha}{\alpha\beta} - \frac{\delta\tau_0}{4\beta M_u} \right)^2 - \left(\frac{\alpha}{\alpha\beta} - \frac{\delta\tau_0}{4\beta M_u} \right) \frac{\delta\tau_0}{M_u}$$

$$C \quad \alpha = \left(\frac{h}{2d} - \frac{2.2\rho f_y}{f_{cu}} \right) / \left(1 - \frac{1.1\rho f_y}{f_{cu}} \right), \quad \beta = \left[\frac{1.1 - \rho f_y / f_{cu}}{1 - 1.1\rho f_y / f_{cu}} \right], \quad \tau_0 = \rho d f_y$$

```
C      MU = Pd²(1 − 0.59 fyρ) /0.8 fCU
C      WRITE A PROGRAM TO DETERMINE THE LOAD ENHANCEMENT
       FACTOR P/ PY FOR D/H
C      VARYING FROM 0 TO 1 IN STEPS OF 0.10 GIVEN THAT H = 150 MM, FCU
       = 35 N/MM2,
C      FY = 250 N/MM2, RHO = 0.004
       DATA H, D, FCU, FY, RHO/150 MM, 120 MM, 35, 250, 0.004/
       OPEN (UNIT = 1, STATUS = 'NEW', FILE = 'P35.OUT')
       WRITE (1, *) ' ............................................................................'
       DO 100 DH = 0, 10, 1
       DH = DH / 10.
       ALPHA 1 = ((H /(2 * D)) (2.2 *RHO * FY / FCU))
       ALPFA 2 = (1 (1.1 * RHO) * FY / FCU))
       ALPHA = ALPHA 1 / ALPHA 2
       BETA = (1.1 * RHO) * FY / FCU) / ALPHA 2
       MU = ((RHO * (D ** 2)) * FY) * (( 1  0.59 * RHO * FY) / (0.8 * FCU))
       TO = RHO * D * FY
       DELTA = DH * H
       PPY 1 = (ALPHA / (ALPHA / BETA))
       PPY 2 = ((DLET * TO) / (4 * BETA * MU))
       PPY 3 = 1 + ALPHA * (PPY1 PPY2)
       PPY 4 = BETA * ((PPY1 PPY2) ** 2))
       PPY 5 = (DELTA * TO / MU) *PPY1 PPY2)
       PPY = PPY3 PPY4 PPY5
```

```
        WRITE (1, 10) DH, PPY
10      FORMAT (1X, 2(F8.2, 2X))
100     CONTINUE
        STOP
        END
C       ........................................................................................................................
```

D/H Ratio	P/PY Ratio
.00	0.90
.10	1.27
.20	2.06
.30	3.26
.40	4.89
.50	6.93
.60	9.39
.70	12.26
.80	15.55
.90	19.26
1.00	23.39

Example 8.35

```
C       ........................................................................................................................
C       THE STATE EB CHARGES THE FOLLOWING RATES TO DOMESTIC USERS
        TO DISCHARGE
C       LARGE CONSMPTION OF ELECTRICITY
C       FOR THE FIRST 100 UNITS : 90 PS PER UNIT
C       FOR THE NEXT 200 UNITS : 150 PS PER UNIT
C       BEYOND 300 UNITS          : 270 PS PER UNIT
C       ALL USERS ARE CHARGED A MINIMUM OF RS. 25/-
C       WRITE A PROGRAM TO READ THE USER NO., THE NUMBER OF UNITS
        CONSUMED
C       AND PRINT OUT THE CHARGES WITH THE USER NOS.
C       ........................................................................................................................
C       PROGRAMME
C       ........................................................................................................................
        OPEN (UNIT = 1, STATUS = 'OLD', FILE = 'P36.IN')
        OPEN (UNIT = 2, STATUS = 'NEW', FILE = 'P36.OUT')
        WRITE (2, *) '........................................................................................................'
        WRITE (2, *) ' USERNO          UNITS               CHARGE'
        WRITE (2, *) '........................................................................................................'
10      READ (1, *, END = 100) USERNO, UNITS
```

```
        IF (UNITS .LE. 100) THEN CHARGE
                CHARGE = UNITS * 0.90
        ELSEIF ((UNITS .GT. 100) .AND. (UNITS .LT. 300)) THEN
                CHARGE = 90 + (UNITS  100) * 1.50
        ELSEIF (UNITS .GT. 300) THEN
                CHARGE = 90 + 300 + (UNITS  300) * 2.70
        ENDIF
        IF (CHARGE .LT. 25.0) THEN
                CHARGE = 25.0
        END
        WRITE (2, 20) USERNO, UNITS, CHARGE
20      FORMAT (1X, 14, 6X F8.2, 7X, F8.2)
        GOTO 10
100     STOP
        END
C       .........................................................................
```

USER NO	UNITS	CHARGE
1	10.00	25.00
2	50.00	45.00
3	75.00	67.50
4	100.00	90.00
5	125.00	127.50
6	140.00	150.00
7	180.00	210.00
8	200.00	240.00
9	325.00	457.50
10	500.00	930.00

Example 8.36

```
C       .........................................................................
C       WRITE A PROGRAM AND CLASSIFY THE GROUP OF N EMPLOYEES
        WORKING IN AN
C       ORGANISATION ACCORDING TO THEIR SALARIES LIG, MIG AND HIG.
        THOSE EARNING
C       LESS THAN RS. 2000/- PER MONTH FALL UNDER LIG AND BETWEEN
        2000/- AND 7000/-
C       UNDER MIG AND ABOVE 7000/- UNDER HIG
C       .........................................................................
C       PROGRAMME
C       .........................................................................
```

```
        CHARACTER * 20 NAME, CATEGORY
        OPEN (UNIT = 1, STATUS = 'OLD', FILE = 'P37.IN')
        OPEN (UNIT = 2, STATUS = 'NEW', FILE = 'P37.OUT')
        WRITE (2, *) '................................................................'
        WRITE (2, *) 'NAME OF EMPLOYEE      SALARY          CATEGORY'
        WRITE (2, *) '................................................................'
10      READ (1, *, END = 100) NAME,   SALARY
        IF (SALARY .LT. 2000) THEN
               CATEGORY = 'LIG'
        ELSEIF (SALARY .GT. 2000) .AND. (SALARY .LT. 7000) THEN
               CATEGORY = 'MIG'
        ELSEIF (SALARY .GT. 7000) THEN
               CATEGORY = 'HIG'
        ENDIF
        WRITE (2, 50) 'NAME, SALARY,    CATEGORY'
20      FORMAT (1X, A20, 4X F8.2, 4X, A5)
        GOTO 10
100     STOP
        END
C       ...........................................................................
```

NAME OF EMPLOYEE	SALARY	CATEGORY
PRAKASH	1200.00	LIG
SATYA	2500.00	MIG
SUNITHA	3500.00	MIG
AMBRISH	4500.00	MIG
MUNEEB	5000.00	MIG
PRAKASH N.S	8000.00	HIG
PUTTEGOWDA	9000.00	HIG
GOPALKRISHNA	10000.00	HIG

Example 8.37

```
C       ...........................................................................
C       WRITE A PROGRAM TO READ MARKS RECORDED BY TEN STUDENTS
        IN ONE SUBJECT
C       AND CALCULATE THE AVERAGE MARKS. ALSO COUNT THE NUMBER
        OF STUDENTS
C       GETTING MARKS
C       (A) LESS THAN 40
C       (B) GREATER THAN 60
C       (C) EQUAL TO 100
```

```
C      ..................................................................................................
C      PROGRAMME
C      ..................................................................................................
       DIMENSION A (10)
       WRITE (*, *) 'ENTER MARKS SCORED BY TEN STUDENTS'
       READ (*, *) (A (), = 1, 10)
       SUM = 0.
       DO 30 J = 1, 10
       SUM = SUM + A(J)
30     CONTINUE
       AVER = SUM / 10.0
       WRITE (*, *) 'AVERAGE' ='
       WRITE (*, 35) AVER
35     FORMAT (1X, F8.2)
       NL40 = 0
       NL60 = 0
       NL100 = 0
       DO 45 K = 1, 10
       IF (A (K) .LE. 40) NL40 = NL40 + 1
       IF (A (K) .GT. 60) NL60 = NL60 + 1
       IF (A (K) .EQ. 100) NL100 = NL100 = 1
45     CONTINUE
       WRITE (*, *) 'NUMBER OF STUDENTS WITH MARKS LESS THAN 40'
       WRITE (*, 50) NL40
       WRITE (*, *) 'NUMBER OF STUDENTS WITH MARKS GREATER THAN 60'
       WRITE (*, 50) NL60
       WRITE (*, *) 'NUMBER OF STUDENTS WITH MARKS EQUAL TO 100'
       WRITE (*, 50) NL100
       FORMAT (1X, 4)
       STOP
       END
C      ..................................................................................................
ENTER MARKS SCORED BY TEN STUDENTS
10, 25, 35, 40, 100, 100, 100, 75, 65, 78
AVERAGE = 62.80
NUMBER OF STUDENTS WITH MARKS LESS THAN 40 = 4
NUMBER OF STUDENTS WITH MARKS GREATER THAN 60 = 6
NUMBER OF STUDENTS WITH MARKS EQUAL TO 100 = 3
Stop – Program terminated
```

Example 8.38

```
C      ...........................................................................
C      WRITE A GENERAL FORTRAN PROGRAM TO EVALUATE THE RADIAL
       AND HOOP STRESS
C      IN A THICK CYLINDER SUBJECTED TO INTERNAL FLUID PRESSURE AT
       INTERVALS OF 0.10T
C      WHERE T = THE THICKNESS OF THE CYLINDER. USE SUITABLE
       FORMATS FOR INPUTS AND
C      PRINT STRESSES IN TABULAR COLUMN AT DISTANCES FROM THE
       CENTRE FOR THE RADIAL
C      AND HOOP STRESSES. THE EQUATIONS FOR THE RADIAL AND HOOP
       STRESS IN THICK CYLINDER
C      IN THE USUAL NOTATIONS ARE
```

$$
C \qquad \sigma_r = \frac{P d_I^2}{\left(d_O^2 - d_I^2\right)}\left[1 - \frac{d_O^2}{4r^2}\right], \qquad \sigma_t = \frac{P d_I^2}{\left(d_O^2 - d_I^2\right)}\left[1 + \frac{d_O^2}{4r^2}\right]
$$

```
C      INNER DIAMETER = 100, OUTER DIAMETER = 200, INTERVAL = 5 MM, P
       VARYING FROM
C      1.5 TO 3.5 IN STEPS OF 0.50
C      ...........................................................................
       DATA DI, DO/100.00, 200.00/
       OPEN (UNIT = 1, STATUS = 'NEW', FILE = 'P39.OUT')
       WRITE (1, *) '...........................................................................'
       WRITE (1, *) ' P RADIUS CONS C RADIAL HOOP'
       WRITE (1, *) '...........................................................................'
       DO 10 IP = 15, 35, 5
       P = IP/ 10.0
       R = IR
       DO 10 IR = 50, 100, 5
       C = (P * DI ** 2) / (DO ** 2 - DI ** 2)
       SR = C * (1. - (( DO ** 2) / (4. * R ** 2)))
       ST = C * (1. + (( DO ** 2) / (4. * R ** 2)))
       WRITE (1, 20) P, R, C, SR, ST
20     FORMAT (1X, 5F6.2, 2X)
10     CONTINUE
       STOP
       END
C      ...........................................................................
```

P	RADIUS	C	RADIAL	HOOP
1.50	50.00	.50	− 1.50	2.50
1.50	55.00	.50	− 1.15	2.15
1.50	60.00	.50	− .89	1.89
1.50	65.00	.50	− .68	1.68
1.50	70.00	.50	− .52	1.52
1.50	75.00	.50	− .39	1.39
1.50	80.00	.50	− .28	1.28
1.50	85.00	.50	− .19	1.19
1.50	90.00	.50	− .12	1.12
1.50	95.00	.50	− .05	1.05
1.50	100.00	.50	.00	1.00
2.00	50.00	.67	− 2.00	3.33
2.00	55.00	.67	− 1.54	2.87
2.00	60.00	.67	− 1.19	2.52
2.00	65.00	.67	− .91	2.24
2.00	70.00	.67	− .69	2.03
2.00	75.00	.67	− .52	1.85
2.00	80.00	.67	− .38	1.71
2.00	85.00	.67	− .26	1.59
2.00	90.00	.67	− .16	1.49
2.00	95.00	.67	− .07	1.41
2.00	100.00	.67	− .00	1.33
2.50	50.00	.83	− .50	4.17
2.50	55.00	.83	− 1.92	3.59
2.50	60.00	.83	− 1.48	3.15
2.50	65.00	.83	− 1.14	2.81
2.50	70.00	.83	− .87	2.53
2.50	75.00	.83	− .65	2.31
2.50	80.00	.83	− .47	2.14
2.50	85.00	.83	− .32	1.99
2.50	90.00	.83	− .20	1.86
2.50	95.00	.83	− .09	1.76
2.50	100.00	.83	0.00	1.67
3.00	50.00	1.00	− 3.00	5.00
3.00	55.00	1.00	− 2.31	4.31
3.00	60.00	1.00	− 1.78	3.78
3.00	65.00	1.00	− 1.37	3.37
3.00	70.00	1.00	− 1.04	3.04
3.00	75.00	1.00	− .78	2.78

P	RADIUS	C	RADIAL	HOOP
3.00	80.00	1.00	– .56	2.56
3.00	85.00	1.00	– .38	2.38
3.00	90.00	1.00	– .23	2.23
3.00	95.00	1.00	– .11	2.11
3.00	100.00	1.00	– .00	2.00
3.50	50.00	1.17	– 3.50	5.83
3.50	55.00	1.17	– 2.69	5.02
3.50	60.00	1.17	– 2.07	4.41
3.50	65.00	1.17	– 1.59	3.93
3.50	70.00	1.17	– 1.21	3.55
3.50	75.00	1.17	– .91	3.24
3.50	80.00	1.17	– .66	2.99
3.50	85.00	1.17	– .45	2.78
3.50	90.00	1.17	– .27	2.61
3.50	95.00	1.17	– .13	2.46
3.50	100.00	1.17	.00	2.33

Example 8.39

```
C      ...............................................................................
C      IT IS PROPOSED TO PREPARE A DESIGN TABLE FOR THE DESIGN OF A
       TRAPEZOIDAL
C      CHANNEL WHICH HAS THE DETAILS OF THE CROSS SECTION AREA
       A, HYDRAULIC MEAN
C      RADIUS R, WETTED PERIMETER P, BED WIDTH B, MEAN VELOCITY OF
       FLOW V AND
C      DISCHARGE Q. THE VALUES ARE TO BE CALCULATED FOR DIFFERENT
       VALUES OF BED WIDTH
C      AND DEPTH OF FLOW USING THE EQUATIONS
```

$$C \qquad A = (b + nd)d, \qquad P = b + 2d\sqrt{1+n^2} \qquad R = (A/P)$$

$$C \qquad B = (b + 2nd), \qquad V = KR^{2/3}S^{1/2} \qquad Q = AV, \qquad n = \text{SIDE SLOPE}$$

```
C      WITH B VARYING FROM 2 TO 12 METRES AND d VARYING FROM 3 TO 8
       METRES, K = CONSTANT
C      ...............................................................................
       DATA N, XK, S / 2, 10.80, 0.0002/
       OPEN (UNIT = 1, STATUS = 'NEW', FILE = 'P42.OUT')
       WRITE (1, *) '..............................................................................'
       WRITE (1, *) ' B      D      A      P      R      BE      V      Q'
       WRITE (1, *) '..............................................................................'
       DO 100 IB = 20, 120, 20
```

```
        B = IB / 10
        DO 100 ID = 30, 80, 10
        D = ID / 10
        A = (B + N * D) * D
        P = (B + (2 * D * SQRT (1.0 + N ** 2.)))
        R = A / P
        BE = B + N * D * 2
        V = (XK * (R ** (2. /3.)) * (S ** (1. /2. )))
        Q = A * V
        WRITE (1, 10) B, D, A, P, R, BE, V, Q
10      FORMAT (1X, 8 (F6.2, 1X))
100     CONTINUE
        STOP
        END
C       ....................................................................................
```

B	D	A	P	R	BE	V	Q
2.00	3.00	24.00	15.42	1.56	14.00	.21	4.92
2.00	4.00	40.00	19.89	2.01	18.00	.24	9.73
2.00	5.00	60.00	24.36	2.46	22.00	.28	16.71
2.00	6.00	84.00	28.83	2.91	26.00	.31	26.17
2.00	7.00	112.00	33.30	3.36	30.00	.34	38.40
2.00	8.00	144.00	37.78	3.81	34.00	.37	53.67
4.00	3.00	30.00	17.42	1.72	16.00	.22	6.58
4.00	4.00	48.00	21.89	2.19	20.00	.26	12.37
4.00	5.00	70.00	26.36	2.66	24.00	.29	20.50
4.00	6.00	96.00	30.83	3.11	28.00	.33	31.26
4.00	7.00	126.00	35.30	3.57	32.00	.36	44.94
4.00	8.00	160.00	39.78	4.02	36.00	.39	61.81
6.00	3.00	36.00	19.42	1.85	18.00	.23	8.30
6.00	4.00	56.00	23.89	2.34	22.00	.27	15.09
6.00	5.00	80.00	28.36	2.82	26.00	.30	24.39
6.00	6.00	108.00	32.83	3.29	30.00	.34	36.48
6.00	7.00	140.00	37.30	3.75	34.00	.37	51.64
6.00	8.00	176.00	41.78	4.21	38.00	.40	70.12
8.00	3.00	42.00	21.42	1.96	20.00	.24	10.05
8.00	4.00	64.00	25.89	2.47	24.00	.28	17.87
8.00	5.00	90.00	30.36	2.96	28.00	.32	28.37
8.00	6.00	120.00	34.83	3.45	32.00	.35	41.81
8.00	7.00	154.00	39.30	3.92	36.00	.38	58.46

B	D	A	P	R	BE	V	Q
8.00	8.00	192.00	43.78	4.39	40.00	.41	78.57
10.00	3.00	48.00	23.42	2.05	22.00	.25	11.83
10.00	4.00	72.00	27.89	2.58	26.00	.29	20.70
10.00	5.00	100.00	32.36	3.09	30.00	.32	32.40
10.00	6.00	132.00	36.83	3.58	34.00	.36	47.21
10.00	7.00	168.00	41.30	4.07	38.00	.39	65.38
10.00	8.00	208.00	45.78	4.54	42.00	.42	87.15
12.00	3.00	54.00	25.42	2.12	24.00	.25	13.63
12.00	4.00	80.00	29.89	2.68	28.00	.29	23.56
12.00	5.00	110.00	34.36	3.20	32.00	.33	36.49
12.00	6.00	144.00	38.83	3.71	36.00	.37	52.69
12.00	7.00	182.00	45.30	4.20	40.00	.40	72.39
12.00	8.00	224.00	47.78	4.69	44.00	.43	95.84

Example 8.40

```
C      ...............................................................................
C      WRITE A PROGRAM TO FIND THE VALUE OF SINH USING THE SERIES
```

$$C \quad SINH(X) = \left[X + \frac{X^3}{3!} + \frac{X^5}{5!} \ldots\ldots\ldots + \frac{X^n}{n!} \right]$$

```
C      TO AN ACCURACY OF 1.E-7
C      ...............................................................................
       REAL NUM. NDEM
       WRITE (*, *) 'ENTER VALUE OF X'
       READ (*, *) X
       IP = 1
       SUM = 0.0
       TER = 1.E - 07
40     NUM = X ** IP
       NDEM = 1
       DO 100 1 = 1, IP
       NDEM = NDEM * I
100    CONTINUE
       SUM = SUM + (NUM/NDEM)
       IF ((NUM/NDEM) .LT. TER)) GOTO 50
       IP = IP + 2
       GO TO 40
50     WRITE (*, *) 'VALUE OF X IS' , X
       WRITE (*, *) 'VALUE OF SINHX IS', SUM
       STOP
       END
```

C   ....

ENTER VALUE OF X

1

CALUE OF X IS 1.0000000

VALUE OF SINHX IS1.1752010

Stop – Program terminated

Example 8.41

C   ....

CWRITE A PROGRAM TO ARRANGE NUMBERS IN DESCENDING ORDER

C   ....

C   PROGRAMME

C   ....

```
       DIMENSION XN (50)
       WRITE (*, *) 'ENTER VALUE OF K'
       READ (*, *) K
       WRITE (*, *) 'ENTER K VALUES TO BE ARRANGED IN DESC ORDER'
       READ (*, *) (XN (I), I = 1, K
       L = K – 1
       DO 40 I = 1, L
       NEXT = I + 1
       DO 60 J = NEXT, K
       IF (XN(I).GE. XN(J) GOTO 60
       XKO = XN (I)
       XN (I) = XN (J)
       XN (J) = XKO
60     CONTINUE
40     CONTINUE
       WRITE (*, *)'NUMBERS IN DESCENDING ORDER ARE'
       WRITE (*, 50) XN (I) , I = 1, K
50     FORMAT (1X, F6.2, 2X)
       STOP
       END
```

C   ....

ENTER VALUES OF K

5

ENTER K VALUES TO BE ARRANGED IN DESC ORDER

1

2

3

4

5

NUMBERS IN DESCENDING ORDER ARE

      5.00

      4.00

      3.00

      2.00

      1.00

Stop – Program terminated.

Example 8.42

```
C       ..............................................................................
C       WRITE A PROGRAM TO ARRANGE NUMBERS IN ASCENDING ORDER
C       ..............................................................................
C       PROGRAMME
C       ..............................................................................
        DIMENSION XN (50)
        WRITE (*, *) 'ENTER VALUE OF K'
        READ (*, *) K
        WRITE (*, *) 'ENTER K VALUES TO BE ARRANGED IN ASC ORDER'
        READ (*, *) (XN (I), I = 1, K
        L = K – 1
        DO 40 I = 1, L
        NEXT = I + 1
        DO 60 J = NEXT, K
        IF (XN(I).LE. XN(J) GOTO 60
        XKO = XN (I)
        XN (I) = XN (J)
        XN (J) = XKO
60      CONTINUE
40      CONTINUE
        WRITE (*, *)'NUMBERS IN ASCENDING ORDER ARE'
        WRITE (*, 50) XN (I) , I = 1, K
50      FORMAT (1X, F6.2, 2X)
        STOP
        END
C       ..............................................................................
```

ENTER VALUES OF K

5

ENTER K VALUES TO BE ARRANGED IN ASC ORDER

5

4

3

2

1

NUMBERS IN ASCENDING ORDER ARE

     1.00

     2.00

     3.00

     4.00

     5.00

Stop – Program terminated.

Example 8.43

```
C     ..........................................................................................
C     WRITE A PROGRAM TO SOLVE THE SET OF SIMULTANEOUS
      EQUATIONS USING
C     GAUSS ELIMIATION METHOD
C
C     ..........................................................................................
C     PROGRAMME
C     ..........................................................................................
      DIMENSION A (20, 20, X(20)
      WRITE (*, *) 'ENTER THE NUMBER OF UNKNOWNS'
      READ (*, *) N
      WRITE (*, *) 'ENTER THE COEFFICIENTS OF SIMULTANEOUS EQNS'
      DO 100 I = 1, N, 1
      WRITE (*, *) 'ENTER THE COEFFICIENTS OF ROW NO', 1
      DO 100 J = 1, N + 1, 1
      READ (*, *) A (I, J)
100   CONTINUE
      DO 200 K = 1, N – 1
      DO 200 J = (K + 1), N
      U = A (I, K) / A (K, K)
      DO 200 J = K, (N + 1)
      A (I, J) = A (I, J) – U * A (K, J)
200   CONTINUE
      X (N) = A (N, N + 1) / A (N, N)
      DO 300 I = N – 1, 1, – 1
      SUM = 0.0
      DO 400 J = (I + 1), N
      SUM = SUM + A (I, J) * X (J)
400   CONTINUE
      X (I) = (A (I) = (A (1, N + 1) – SUM / A (I, I)
300   CONTINUE
      WRITE (*, *) 'VALUES OF X ARE'
      DO 500 I = 1, N, 1
      WRITE (*, *) X (I)
```

```
500    CONTINUE
       STOP
       END
C
```
....
```
ENTER THE NUMBER OF UNKNOWNS
3
ENTER THE COEFFICIENTS OF SIMULTANEOUS EQNS
ENTER THE COEFFICIENTS OF ROW NO      1
1
8
1
10
ENTER THE COEFFICIENTS OF ROW NO      2
1
1
7
9
ENTER THE COEFFICIENTS OF ROW NO      3
9
1
1
11
VALUES OF X ARE
       1.0000010
       9.999999E – 001
       9.999999E – 001
```
Stop – Program terminated.

Example 8.44

```
C
```
....
```
C      COMPUTE AND INTERPRET THE CORRELATION COEFFICIENT FOR THE
       DATA GIVEN BELOW:
```

C	X (HEIGHT)	12	10	14	11	12	9
C	Y (HEIGHT)	18	17	23	19	20	15

```
C      WRITE A PROGRAM TO INTERPRET THE CORRELATION BETWEEN
       EACH OF THE VARIABLES
C
```
....
```
C      PROGRAMME
C
```
....
```
       DIMENSION  X (15),  Y (15)
       WRITE (*, *) 'ENTER VALUES OF N'
       READ (*, *) N
```

```
      WRITE (*, *) 'ENTER N VALUES'
      READ (*, *) (X (I), Y (I), I = 1, N
      SX     = 0.0
      SY     = 0.0
      SXY    = 0.0
      SXX    = 0.0
      SYY    = 0.0
      DO 6I = 1, N
      X I    = X I
      Y I    = Y I
      SX     = SX + X (I)
      SY     = SY + Y
      SXY    = SXY + X )* Y
      SXX    = SXX + X ** 2.0
      SYY    = SYY + Y ** 2.0
6     CONTINUE
      AMX = SX / FLOAT (N)
      AMY = SY / FLOAT (N)
      R = (SXY – (FLOAT (N) * AMX * AMY))/ SQRT ((SXX – (FLOAT (N) * (AMX
      ** 2.0))) + (SYY – (FLOAT (N) * (AMY ** 2.0)))
      WRITE (*, 15) R
15    FORMAT (1X, 'CORRELATION COEFF =', F12.8)
      STOP
      END
C     .........................................................................................
ENTER VALUES OF N
6
ENTER N VALUES
12, 18
10, 17
14, 23
11, 19
12, 20
 9, 15
CORRELATION COEFFICIENT = .94737300
```

Stop – Program terminated.

Example 8.45

```
C     .........................................................................................
C     A BEAM OF LENGTH 'I' METRES IS SIMPLY SUPPORTED AT BOTH THE
      ENDS AND IT CARRIES
```

C   A CONCENTRATED LOAD OF 'P' at DIST 'C' FROM THE LEFT SUPPORT. THE ELASTIC CURVE

C   CAN BE REPRESENTED BY THE SERIES

C $y = \dfrac{2PI^3}{EI\pi^4} \displaystyle\sum_{n=1}^{8} \dfrac{\sin\left(\dfrac{n\pi c}{I}\right)}{n^4} \cdot \sin(2\pi/I)$

C   WHERE X IS ANY POINT ALONG THE BEAM AT WHICH THE DEFLECTION IS REQUIRED.

C   WRITE A FORTRAN PROGRAM TO DETERMINE THE ELASTIC CURVE OF THE BEAM OF

C   LENGTH 'I'. I = 3 M, C = 1.50 M WITH ACCURACY OF 0.10E-6. THE FOLLOWING VARIATIONS

C   OF I AND P ARE TO BE INCLUDED IN THE PROGRAMMING

C   I FROM 0.01 TO 0.02 IN STEPS OF 0.001

C   P FROM 4000 TO 5000 IN STEPS OF 100 KG

C   E FROM 1.2 E 6 KG/CM^2 OR 1.2 E 10 KG/CM^2

C   ....

C   PROGRAMME

C   ....

```
        OPEN (UNIT = 1, STATUS = 'NEW' , FILE = 'P49.OUT')
        DATA E, EL, S/1.2 E = 10, 3.0, 1.5/
        WRITE (1, *) '...................................................................................'
        WRITE (1, *) ' I          P          X          Y'
        WRITE (1, *) '...................................................................................'
        DO 10 I = 10, 20
        A I    = I /1000.0
        DO 20 IP = 4000, 5000, 100
        P      = FLOAT (P)
        C      = (2. * EL ** 2 * P) / (E * A * 3.1415 ** 4)
        X      = 0.0
25      EN     = 0.0
        SUM    = 0.0
30      EN     = EN + 1.0
        A      = SIN ((EN * 3.1415 * C / EL) /(EN ** 4))
        IF (A) 31, 30, 31
31      B      = SIN (2.0 * 3.1415 * X /EL)
        SUM    = SUM + A * B
        Z      = ABS (A * B)
        IF (Z  0.1E – 06) 21, 21, 30
21      Y      = C + SUM
```

```
X        = X + 0.1 * EL
         IF(X .LE. EL) THEN GOTO 25
         ELSE
         PX = X – 0.1 * EL
         WRITE (1, 40) A I, P, PX, Y
40       FORMAT (1X, F8.4, 2X, 8.2, 2X, E10.4, 2X, E10.4)
         ENDIF
20       CONTINUE
10       CONTINUE
         STOP
         END
C        ..............................................................................................
```

I	P	X	Y
.0100	4000.00	.3000E + 01	– .6654 E – 13
.0100	4100.00	.3000E + 01	– .6981 E – 13
.0100	4200.00	.3000E + 01	– .7326 E – 13
.0100	4300.00	.3000E + 01	– .7679 E – 13
.0100	4400.00	.3000E + 01	– .8040 E – 13
.0100	4500.00	.3000E + 01	– .8410 E – 13
.0100	4600.00	.3000E + 01	– .8788 E – 13
.0100	4700.00	.3000E + 01	– .9174 E – 13
.0100	4800.00	.3000E + 01	– .9569 E – 13
.0100	4900.00	.3000E + 01	– .9972 E – 13
.0100	5000.00	.3000E + 01	– .1038 E – 13
.0110	4000.00	.3000E + 01	– .5492 E – 13
.0110	4100.00	.3000E + 01	– .5770 E – 13
.0110	4200.00	.3000E + 01	– .6055 E – 13
.0110	4300.00	.3000E + 01	– .6346 E – 13
.0110	4400.00	.3000E + 01	– .6645 E – 13
.0110	4500.00	.3000E + 01	– .6950 E – 13
.0110	4600.00	.3000E + 01	– .7263 E – 13
.0110	4700.00	.3000E + 01	– .7582 E – 13
.0110	4800.00	.3000E + 01	– .7908 E – 13
.0110	4900.00	.3000E + 01	– .8241 E – 13
.0110	5000.00	.3000E + 01	– .8581 E – 13
.0120	4000.00	.3000E + 01	– .4615 E – 13
.0120	4100.00	.3000E + 01	– .4848 E – 13
.0120	4200.00	.3000E + 01	–.5088 E – 13
.0120	4300.00	.3000E + 01	– .5333 E – 13

I	P	X	Y
.0120	4400.00	.3000E + 01	− .5584 E − 13
.0120	4500.00	.3000E + 01	− .5840 E − 13
.0120	4600.00	.3000E + 01	− .6103 E − 13
.0120	4700.00	.3000E + 01	− .6371 E − 13
.0120	4800.00	.3000E + 01	− .6645 E − 13
.0120	4900.00	.3000E + 01	− .6925 E − 13
.0120	5000.00	.3000E + 01	− .7210 E − 13
.0130	4000.00	.3000E + 01	− .3932 E − 13
.0130	4100.00	.3000E + 01	− .4131 E − 13
.0130	4200.00	.3000E + 01	− .4335 E − 13
.0130	4300.00	.3000E + 01	− .4544 E − 13
.0130	4400.00	.3000E + 01	− .4758 E − 13
.0130	4500.00	.3000E + 01	− .4976 E − 13
.0130	4600.00	.3000E + 01	− .5200 E − 13
.0130	4700.00	.3000E + 01	− .5428 E − 13
.0130	4800.00	.3000E + 01	− .5662 E − 13
.0130	4900.00	.3000E + 01	− .5900 E − 13
.0130	5000.00	.3000E + 01	− .6144 E − 13
.0140	4000.00	.3000E + 01	− .3390 E − 13
.0140	4100.00	.3000E + 01	− .3562 E − 13
.0140	4200.00	.3000E + 01	− .3738 E − 13
.0140	4300.00	.3000E + 01	− .3918 E − 13
.0140	4400.00	.3000E + 01	− .4102 E − 13
.0140	4500.00	.3000E + 01	− .4291 E − 13
.0140	4600.00	.3000E + 01	− .4484 E − 13
.0140	4700.00	.3000E + 01	− .4681 E − 13
.0140	4800.00	.3000E + 01	− .4882 E − 13
.0140	4900.00	.3000E + 01	− .5088 E − 13
.0140	5000.00	.3000E + 01	− .5297 E − 13
.0150	4000.00	.3000E + 01	− .2953 E − 13
.0150	4100.00	.3000E + 01	− .3103 E − 13
.2000	5000.00	.3000E + 01	− .2596 E − 13

Example 8.46

C   ....

C   A BEAM OF LENGTH 'I' METRES IS SIMPLY SUPPORTED AT BOTH THE ENDS AND IT CARRIES

C   A CONCENTRATED LOAD OF 'P' AT A DISTANCE 'C' FROM THE LEFT SUPPORT. THE ELASTIC

C   CURVE CAN BE REPRESENTED BY THE SERIES

C $\quad y = \dfrac{4I^4 q}{\pi^5 EI} \cdot \sum\limits_{1,3,5} \dfrac{1}{n^5} \sin(n\pi x/I)$

C WHERE X IS ANY POINT ALONG THE BEAM AT WHICH THE DEFLECTION IS REQUIRED. WRITE

C A FORTRAN PROGRAM TO DETERMINE THE ELASTIC CURVE OF THE BEAM OF LENGTH 'I',

C I = 3 M, C = 1.50 M WITH ACCURACY OF 0.10 E-6. THE FOLLOWING VARIATIONS OF I AND

C P ARE TO BE INCLUDED IN THE PROGRAMMING

C I FROM 0.01 TO 0.02 IN STEPS OF 0.001

C P FROM 4000 TO 5000 IN STEPS OF 100 KGS

C E FROM 1.2 E 6 KG/CM^2 OR 1.2 E 10 KG/CM^2

C ....

C PROGRAMME

C ....

```
OPEN (UNIT = 1, STATUS = 'NEW' , FILE = 'P49.OUT')
DATA E, EL, S/1.2 E = 10, 3.0, 1.5/
WRITE (1, *) '..........................................................................'
WRITE (1, *) 'I          P            X              Y'
WRITE (1, *) '..........................................................................'
DO 10 I = 10, 20
A I = I /1000.0
DO 20 IP = 4000, 5000, 100
P     = FLOAT (IP)
Q     = P / EL
C     = (4. * EL** 4 * Q) / ( 3.1415 ** 5 *  E * A I)
X     = 0.0
25      EN  = 1.0
SUM = 0.0
30      EN  = EN + 2.0
31      B   = SIN (EN * 3.1415 * X /EL) / (EN ** 5)
SUM = SUM + B
Z     = ABS (B)
IF (Z  0.1E – 06) 21, 21, 30
21      Y    = C +  SUM
X    = X + 0.1 * EL
IF(X .LE. EL) THEN GOTO 25
ELSE
PX = X – 0.1 * EL
WRITE (1, 40) A I, P, PX, Y
```

```
40      FORMAT (1X, F8.4, 2X, 8.2, 2X, E10.4, 2X, E10.4)
        ENDIF
20      CONTINUE
10      CONTINUE
        STOP
        END
C       ..................................................................................
```

I	P	X	Y
.0100	4000.00	.3000E + 01	− .1019 E − 11
.0100	4100.00	.3000E + 01	− .1045 E − 13
.0100	4200.00	.3000E + 01	− .1070 E − 13
.0100	4300.00	.3000E + 01	− .1096 E − 13
.0100	4400.00	.3000E + 01	− .1121 E − 13
.0100	4500.00	.3000E + 01	− .1147 E − 13
.0100	4600.00	.3000E + 01	− .1172 E − 13
.0100	4700.00	.3000E + 01	− .1198 E − 13
.0100	4800.00	.3000E + 01	− .1223 E − 13
.0100	4900.00	.3000E + 01	− .1249 E − 13
.0100	5000.00	.3000E + 01	− .1274 E − 13
.0110	4000.00	.3000E + 01	− .9268 E − 12
.0110	4100.00	.3000E + 01	− .9499 E − 12
.0110	4200.00	.3000E + 01	− .9731 E − 12
.0110	4300.00	.3000E + 01	− .9963 E − 12
.0110	4400.00	.3000E + 01	− .1019 E − 11
.0110	4500.00	.3000E + 01	− .1043 E − 11
.0110	4600.00	.3000E + 01	− .1066 E − 11
.0110	4700.00	.3000E + 01	− .1089 E − 11
.0110	4800.00	.3000E + 01	− .1112 E − 11
.0110	4900.00	.3000E + 01	− .1135 E − 11
.0110	5000.00	.3000E + 01	− .1158 E − 11
.0120	4000.00	.3000E + 01	− .8495 E − 12
.0120	4100.00	.3000E + 01	− .8708 E − 12
.0120	4200.00	.3000E + 01	− .8920 E − 12
.0120	4300.00	.3000E + 01	− .9133 E − 12
.0120	4400.00	.3000E + 01	− .9345 E − 12
.0120	4500.00	.3000E + 01	− .9557 E − 12
.0120	4600.00	.3000E + 01	− .9770 E − 12
.0120	4700.00	.3000E + 01	− .9982 E − 12
.0120	4800.00	.3000E + 01	− .1019 E − 11
.0120	4900.00	.3000E + 01	− .1041 E − 11

I	P	X	Y
.0120	5000.00	.3000E + 01	− .1062 E − 11
.0130	4000.00	.3000E + 01	− .7842 E − 12
.0130	4100.00	.3000E + 01	− .8038 E − 12
.0130	4200.00	.3000E + 01	− .8234 E − 12
.0130	4300.00	.3000E + 01	− .8430 E − 12
.0130	4400.00	.3000E + 01	− .8626 E − 12
.0130	4500.00	.3000E + 01	− .8822 E − 12
.0130	4600.00	.3000E + 01	− .9018 E − 12
.0130	4700.00	.3000E + 01	− .9214 E − 12
.0130	4800.00	.3000E + 01	− .9410 E − 12
.0130	4900.00	.3000E + 01	− .9606 E − 12
.0130	5000.00	.3000E + 01	− .9802 E − 12
.0140	4000.00	.3000E + 01	− .7282 E − 12
.0140	4100.00	.3000E + 01	− .7464 E − 12
.0140	4200.00	.3000E + 01	− .7646 E − 12
.0140	4300.00	.3000E + 01	− .7828 E − 12
.0140	4400.00	.3000E + 01	− .8010 E − 12
.0140	4500.00	.3000E + 01	− .8192 E − 12
.0140	4600.00	.3000E + 01	− .8374 E − 12
.0140	4700.00	.3000E + 01	− .8556 E − 12
.0140	4800.00	.3000E + 01	− .8738 E − 12
.0140	4900.00	.3000E + 01	− .8920 E − 12
.0140	5000.00	.3000E + 01	− .9102 E − 12
.0150	4000.00	.3000E + 01	− .6796 E − 12
.0150	4100.00	.3000E + 01	− .6966 E − 12
.0150	4200.00	.3000E + 01	− .7136 E − 12
.0150	4300.00	.3000E + 01	− .7306 E − 12
.0150	4400.00	.3000E + 01	− .7476 E − 12
.0150	4500.00	.3000E + 01	− .7646 E − 12
.0150	4600.00	.3000E + 01	− .7816 E − 12
.0150	4700.00	.3000E + 01	− .7986 E − 12
.0150	4800.00	.3000E + 01	− .8156 E − 12
.0150	4900.00	.3000E + 01	− .8325 E − 12
....	....	....	....
....	....	....	....
.2000	5000.00	.3000E + 01	− .6372 E − 12

Example 8.47

WRITE A PROGRAMME FOR MULTIPLICATION OF MATRICES A (3 × 3),
B (3 × 3) AND PRINT THE PRODUCT MATRIX C (3 × 3) GIVEN

$$[A] = \begin{bmatrix} 3.100 & 1.300 & 4.300 \\ 4.500 & 5.400 & 6.000 \\ 10.100 & 11.400 & 10.600 \end{bmatrix} \text{ AND } [B] = \begin{bmatrix} 1.000 & 2.000 & 3.000 \\ 4.000 & 5.000 & 6.000 \\ 7.000 & 8.000 & 9.000 \end{bmatrix}$$

```
        USE SUITABLE FORMAT STATEMENTS
C       PROGRAMME FOR MATRIX MULTIPLICATION C (L, N) = A (L, M) B (L, N)
        DIMENSION A (10, 10, B (10, 10), C (10, 10)
        OPEN (UNIT = 9, FILE = 'GAURI5, OUT')
        READ (*, *) L, M, N
        READ (*, *) ((A (I, J), J = 1, M), I = 1, L)
        READ (*, *) ((B (I, J), J + 1 = 1, N), I = 1, L)
        WRITE (9, 5)
5       FORMAT ('************MATRIX A**************')
        WRITE (9, 6) ((A (I, J), J = 1, M), I = 1, L)
        WRITE (9, 7)
7       FORMAT ('************MATRIX B**************')
        WRITE (9, 6) ((B (I, J), J = 1, N), I = 1, L)
        FORMAT (3(F10.3))
        DO 100 I = 1, L
        DO 100 J = 1, N
        C (I, J) = 0,0
        DO 100 K = 1, M
100     C (I, J) = C (I, J) + A (I, K) * B (K, J)
        WRITE  (9, 10)
10      FORMAT ('***********MATRIX C************')
        WRITE (9, 11) ((C (I, J) , J = 1, N), I = 1, L)
8       FORMAT (3 (F10.4))
        STOP
        END
        ****** MATRIX A ******
                3.100    1.300    4.300
                4.500    5.400    6.000
               10.100   11.400   10.600
        ****** MATRIX B ******
                1.000    2.000    3.000
                4.000    5.000    6.000
                7.000    8.000    9.000
        ****** MATRIX C ******
                38.4000    47.1000    55.8000
                73.7000    90.4000   107.1000
               137.9000   178.0000   218.1000
```

Example 8.48

WRITE A COMPUTER PROGRAMME TO DETERMINE X_1, IN TERMS OF X_2 AND X_3 OF THE FORM,

$$X_1 = a + bX_2 + CX_3$$

GIVEN

X_1	64	71	53	67	55	50	77	57	56	51	76	68
X_2	57	59	49	62	51	50	55	48	52	42	61	57
X_3	8	10	6	11	8	7	10	6	12	9	–	–

USE MULTIPLE REGRESSION ANALYSIS AND PRINT THE VALUES OF a, b and c.

```
C       PROGRAM TO DETERMINE X1 IN TERMS OF X2 AND X3
        DIMENSION X1 (15), X2 (15), X3 (15), A (10, 10), B (10), XX (10)
        READ (*, *) N, (X1 (I), X2 (I), X3 (I), I = 1, N)
        WRITE (9, 5) N
5       FORMAT (15)
        WRITE (9, 6) (I, X1 (I), X2 (I), X3 (I), I = 1, N)
6       FORMAT ('X1 (', 12,') = 'F8.5, 5X, 'X2 ('12,') = ', F8.5, 5X
        ,'X3 (', 12') = ', F8.5)
        SX1 = 0.0
        SX2 = 0.0
        SX3 = 0.0
        SX22 = 0.0
        SX2X3 = 0.0
        SX32 = 0.0
        SX1X2 = 0.0
        SX1X3 = 0.0
        SX12 = 0.0
        DO 10 I = 1, N
        SX1 = SX1 + X1 (I)
        SX2 = SX2 + X2 (I)
        SX3 = SX3 + X3 (I)
        SX22 = SX22 + X2 (I) ** 2
        SX2X3 = SX2X3 + X2 (I) * X3 (I)
        SX32 = SX32 + X3 (I) ** 2
        SX1X2 = SX1X2 + X1 (I) * X2 (I)
        SX1X3 = SX1X3 + X1 (I) * X3 (I)
        SX12 = SX12 + X1 (I) ** 2
10      CONTINUE
        WRITE (9, 8) SX1, SX2, SX3, SX22, SX2X3, SX32, SX1X2, SX1X3, SX12
```

```
8       FORMAT (// 'SX1 = ', F10.3, 3X, SX2 = ', F10.3, 3X, //,'SX3 = ', F10.3, 3X, SX22
        = ', F10.3, 3X, //,'SX2X3 = ', F10.3, 3X, 'SX32 = ', F10.3, 3X, 'SX1X2
        = ', F10.3, 3X, SX2 = ', F10.3, 3X, //,'SX1X3 =',F10.3 3X, 'SX12 = ', F10.3)
C       ****************************************************
C       TO CALCULATE MEAN OF X1, X2 AND X3
C       ****************************************************
        AMX1 = SX1/N
        AMX2 = SX2/N
        AMX3 = SX3/N
        WRITE (9, 9) AMX1, AMX2, AMX3
9       FORMAT (// .AMX1 =', F10.4, 3X, 'AMX2 = ', F10.4, 3X, 'AMX3 = ', F10.4)
C       ....................................................................................
C       TO CALCULATE THE ADJUSTED TERMS
C       ....................................................................................
        AIX22 = N * AMX2 ** 2
        AIX2X3 = N * AMX2 * AMX3
        AIX32 =N * AMX3 ** 2
        AIX1X2 = N * AMX1 * AMX2
        AIX1X3 = N * AMX1 * AMX3
        AIX12 = N * AMX1 ** 2
        WRITE (9, 11) AIX22, AIX2X3, AIX32, AIX1X2, AIX1X3, AIX12
11      FORMAT (// 'AIX22 = ', F10.4, 3X, 'AIX2X3 = ', F10.4, 3X, 'AIX32 = ', F10.4, 3X,
        // 'AIX1X2 = ', F10.4, 3X, 'AIX1X3 =', F10.4, 3X, 'AIX1X2 = ', F10.4)
C       ....................................................................................
C       TO CALCULATE THE ADJUSTED TERMS
C       ....................................................................................
        ASX22 = SX22 – AIX22
        ASX2X3 = SX2X3 – AIX2X3
        ASX32 = SX32  AIX32
        ASX1X2 = SX1X2 – AIX1X2
        ASX1X3 = SX1X3 – AIX1X3
        ASX12 = SX12 – AIX12
        WRITE (9, 12) ASX22, ASX2X3, ASX32, ASX1X2, ASX1X3, ASX12
12      FORMAT (// ' ASX22 =', F10.4, 3X, 'ASX2X3 =', F10.4, 3X, 'ASX32 =F10.4, 3X,
        //,'ASX1X2 =', F10.4, 3X, 'ASX1X3 =', F10.4, 3X, 'ASX12 = ', F10.4)
        A (1, 1) = 1.0
        A (1, 2) = AMX2
        A (1, 3) =AMX3
        A (2, 1) = 0.0
        A (2, 2) = AXS22
        A (2, 3) = ASX2X3
```

```
        A (3, 1) = 0.0
        A (3, 2) = ASX2X3
        A (3, 3 ) = ASX32
        B (1) = AMX1
        B (2) = ASX1X2
        B (3) = ASX1X3
        CALL GAUSS (A, B, XX, 3)
        WRITE (9, 13) XX (1), XX (2), XX (3)
13      FORMAT (//, 5X, 'A = ' F10.4, 3X, 'B = ' F10.4, 3X, 'C = 'F10.4)
        STOP
        END
C       ..............................................................................................
C       SUBROUTINE TO SOLVE A SET OF SIMULTANEOUS EQUATIONS BY
        GAUSS
        ELIMINATION METHOD
C       ..............................................................................................
        SUBROUTINE GAUSS (A, B, X, N)
        DIMENSION A (10, 10), B (10), X (25)
        DO 110 I = 1, N
110     PRINT *, (A (I), J = 1, 3) B ()
        M = N – 1
        DO 11 I = 1, M
        L = I + 1
        DO 11 J = 1, N
        IF (A (J, I) 12, 11, 12
12      DO 13 K = L, N
13      A (J, K) = A (J, K) – A (1, K) * A (J, I) / A(I, I)
        B (J) = B (J) – B (I) * A (J, I) / A(I, I)
11      CONTINUE
        X (N) = B (N)/A (N, N)
        DO 30 I = 1, M
        K = N – I
        L = K + 1
        DO 2 I J = L, N
21      B (K) = B (K) – X (J) * A (K, J)
        X (K) = B (K) / A(K, K)
30      CONTINUE
        RETURN
        END
        N = 12
```

DATA		
X1 (1) = 64, 00000	X2 (1) = 57.00000	X3 (1) = 8.00000
X1 (2) = 71.00000	X2 (2) = 59.00000	X3 (2) = 10.00000
X1 (3) = 53.00000	X2 (3) = 49.00000	X3 (3) = 6.00000
X1 (4) = 67.00000	X2 (4) = 62.00000	X3 (4) = 11.00000
X1 (5) = 55.00000	X2 (5) = 51.00000	X3 (5) = 8.00000
X1 (6) = 50.00000	X2 (6) = 50.00000	X3 (6) = 7.00000
X1 (7) = 77.00000	X2 (7) = 55.00000	X3 (7) = 10.00000
X1 (8) = 57.00000	X2 (8) = 48.00000	X3 (8) = 9.00000
X1 (9) = 56.00000	X2 (9) = 52.00000	X3 (9) = 10.00000
X1 (10) = 51.00000	X2 (10) = 42.00000	X3 (10) = 6.00000
X1 (11) = 76.00000	X2 (11) = 61.00000	X3 (11) = 12.00000
X1 (12) = 68.00000	X2 (12) = 57.00000	X3 (12) = 9.00000

RESULTS		
SX1 = 753.000	SX2 = 643.000	SX2 = 106.000
SX22 = 34843.000	SX2X3 = 5779.000	SX32 = 976.000
SX1X2 = 40830.000	SX1X3 = 6796.000	SX12 = 48139.000
AMX1 = 62.7500	AMX2 = 53.5833	AMX3 = 8.83333
AIX22 = 34454.0800	AIX2X3 = 5679.8330	AIX32 = 936.3333
AIX1X2 = 40348.2500	AIX1X3 = 6651.5000	AIX12 = 47250.7500
ASX22 = 389.9180	ASX2X3 = 99.1670	ASX32 = 39.6667
ASX1X2 = 481.7500	ASX1X3 = 144.5000	ASX12 = 888.2500
A = 3.6514	B = .8546	C = 1.5063

Example 8.49

WRITE A COMPUTER PROGRAMME TO COMPUTE THE MOMENT OF RESISTANCE OF AN R.C.C BEAM GIVEN b = 400, d = 700, c = 7, t = 230, A_{ST} = 1000 (20) 2000 where b and d ARE BREADTH AND EFFECTIVE DEPTH OF BEAM IN MM, c AND t ARE PERMISSIBLE STRESSES IN MPa AND A_{ST} IS THE AREA OF TENSILE STEEL IN MM^2.

THE FORMULAS USED IN COMPUTATIONS ARE AS FOLLOWS:

$$m = \text{Modular ratio} = (280/3c) \tag{1}$$

$$\left(\frac{b.n^2}{2}\right) = mA_{st}(d-n) \quad \text{where n = depth of neutral axis} \tag{2}$$

$$n_1 = \text{critical neutral axis factor} = \left[\frac{280}{(280+3t)}\right] \tag{3}$$

$$n_c = \text{critical neutral axis} \tag{4}$$

$$Q = \text{Moment of resistance factor} = \frac{1}{2}cn_1\left(1-\frac{n_1}{3}\right) \tag{5}$$

If $n < n_{c'}$

$$MR = A_{st}\, t\left(d-\frac{n}{3}\right) \tag{6}$$

$$n = n_c$$

$$MR = Qbd^2 \tag{7}$$

$$n > n_c \qquad MR = \frac{bnc}{2}\left(d - \frac{n}{3}\right) \qquad\qquad (8)$$

where MR is the moment of resistance of the section.

A typical flow chart of this problem is shown in Fig. 8.9

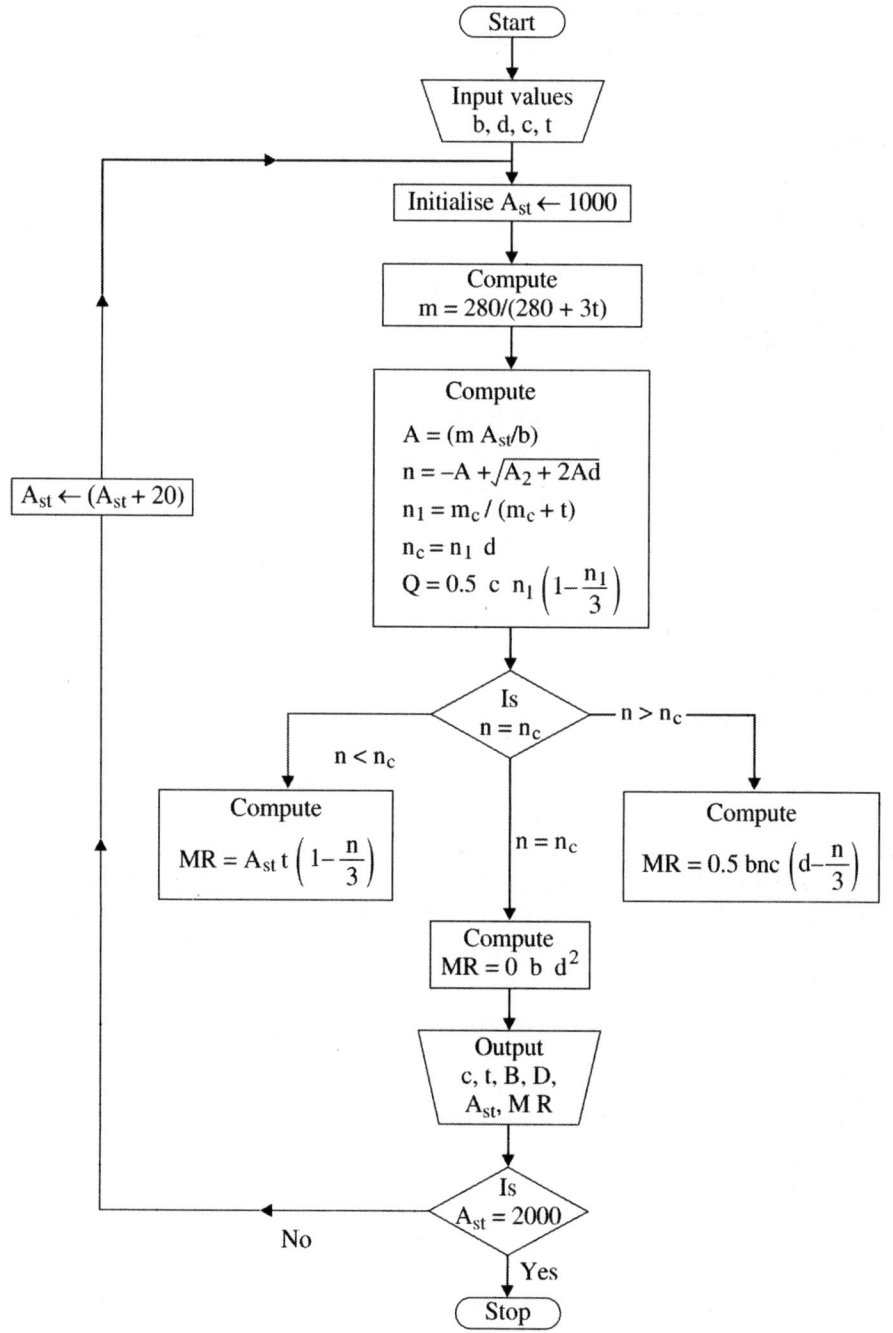

Fig. 8.9: Flow chart for the computation of moment of resistance of an RCC beam

MOMENT OF RESISTANCE OF SINGLY REINFORCED CONCRETE BEAM

Notation Explanation

B = Breadth of beam in mm
D = Effective depth of beam in mm
c = Compressive stress in concrete in N/mm^2
t = Tensile stress in steel in N/mm^2
MR = Moment of resistance in N.mm

Programme

```
      DATA B, D, C, T/400.0, 750.0, 7.0, 230.0/
      AST = 1000.0
      EM = 280.0 / (280.0 + 3. * T)
      A = EM * AST / B
      EN1 = EM * C / (EM*C + T)
      ENC = EN1* D
      Q = 0.5 * C * EN1 * (1 – 0.33 * EN1)
      IF (EN.GT.ENC) MR = B * EN * C * (D – (EN/3.))/2.
      IF (EN.EQ.ENC) MR = Q * B * D * D
      IF (EN.LT.ENC) MR = AST * T * (D – (EN/3.))
      WRITE (*, 40) MR, B, D, C, T, EM, AST
40    FORMAT (13X, 'MR =', F3.2, 3X, 'B =', F10.5, 3X, 'D =', F10.5/13X, 'C = ',F10.5, 3X,
      'T = ', F10.5/13X.
      AST = AST + 20.0
      IF (AST.LE. 2000.0) GO TO 40
      STOP
      END
```

Example 8.50

THE APPLICATION OF FINITE DIFFERENCE SCHEME ON A SIMPLY SUPPORTED SQUARE THIN PLATE SUBJECTED TO UNIFORMLY VARYING LOAD DUE TO HYDROSTATIC PRESSURE, RESULTED IN THE FOLLOWING SET OF EQUATIONS:

$$\begin{bmatrix} 20 & -16 & -8 & 4 & -8 & 4 \\ -8 & 20 & 2 & -8 & 2 & -8 \\ -8 & 4 & 19 & -16 & 1 & 0 \\ 2 & -8 & -8 & 19 & 0 & 1 \\ -8 & 4 & 1 & 0 & 19 & -16 \\ 2 & -8 & 0 & 1 & -8 & 19 \end{bmatrix} \begin{bmatrix} W_1 \\ W_2 \\ W_3 \\ W_4 \\ W_5 \\ W_6 \end{bmatrix} = \begin{bmatrix} 0.5 \\ 0.5 \\ 0.75 \\ 0.75 \\ 0.25 \\ 0.25 \end{bmatrix} \left(-\frac{Qh^4}{D} \right)$$

WRITE A COMPUTER PROGRAMME (USING MATRIX INVERSION) AND PRINT THE FOLLOWING

(a) COEFFICIENT MATRIX
(b) CONSTANT MATRIX
(c) INVERSE OF THE COEFFICIENT MATRIX
(d) DEFLECTION AT NODAL POINTS

```
C       ......................................................................................................
C       PROGRAMME
C       ......................................................................................................
        DIMENSION A (6, 12), B (6, 1), C (6, 6), W (6, 1)
        WRITE (*, 5)
5       FORMAT (1X, 'ENTER THE VALUES IN ROWWISE')
        *    1X. ('### ## ###   ## ### ## ### ## ###   ## ### ##')
        READ (*, 10) (( A(,
10      FORMAT (6 (6F7.2/))
        WRITE (*, 30)
30      FORMAT (15X, 'THE GIVEN MATRIX'/15X,'......................................')
        *  /15X, '[A] = ')
        Do 40 I = 1, 6
        Write (*, 35) A (1, I), A (2, I), A (3, I), A (4, I), A (5, I), A (6, I)
35      FORMAT (18X, '1', F7.2, 3X, F7.2, 3X, F7.2, 3X, F7.2, 3X, F7.2, 3X, F7.2, ' : ')
40      CONTINUE
        WRITE (*, 42)
42      FORMAT (/17X, '[K] = :0.5 : '/23X, ' : 0.5 :(QH⁴/D)'
        *    /23X, ': 0.75 : ' /23X, ' : 0.75 : ' /23X, ' : ' 0.25 : ' /23X, ' ; 0.25'
        *    /18X , ' [W] = [A⁻¹] [K]' )
        B (1, 1) = 0.5
        B (2, 1) = 0.5
        B (3, 1) = 0.75
        B (4, 1) = 0.75
        B (5, 1) = 0.25
        B (6, 1) = 0.25
        DO 65 I = 1, 6
        Do 65 J = 7, 12
        IF (J .EQ. I + 6) THEN A (I, J) = 1.0
        GOTO 65
        END IF
        A (I, J) = 0.0
65      CONTINUE
        WRITE (*, 2)
        FORMAT (////)
        WRITE (*, 75)
```

```
75      FORMAT (15X, 'THE INVERSE MATRIX' /15X,' .............................')
        DO 80 J = 1, 6
        DO 80 M = 1, 6
        IF (M .EQ. J) GOTO 80
        F = A (I, J) / A (J. J)
        DO 90 N = 1, 12
        A (M, N) = A (M, N) – A(J, N) * F
90      CONTINUE
80      CONTINUE
        DO 95 I = 1, 6
        DO 95 J = 1, 6
        C (I, J) = A (I, J + 6)/A (I, I)
95      CONTINUE
        WRITE (*, 100) ((C (I, J), I = 1, 6, J = 1, 6)
100     FORMAT (6 (17X, ' : ' , 6F7.4, ' : '/))
        WRITE (*, 105)
105     FORMAT (15X, 'THE DEFLECTIONS AT THE NODALK POINTS ARE')
        DO 110 I = 1, 6
        DO 110 J = 1, 1
        W (I, J) = 0.0
        DO 110 K = 1, 6
        W (I, J) = W (I, J) + C (I, K) * B (K, J)
110     CONTINUE
        DO 140 I = 1, 6
        W (I, 1) = – 1.0 * W (I, 1)
140     CONTINUE
        DO 130 I = 1, 6
        WRITE (6, 120) I, W (I, 1)
120     FORMAT (15X, 'W', I 1, ' = ' , F7.4, 'QH⁴/D)')
130     CONTINUE
        STOP
        END
```

Results

The given matrix

$$[A] = : \begin{matrix} 20 & -16 & -8 & 4 & -8 & 4 \\ -8 & 20 & 2 & -8 & 2 & -8 : \\ -8 & 4 & 19 & -16 & 1 & 0 \\ 2 & -8 & -8 & 19 & 0 & 1 \\ -8 & 4 & 1 & 0 & 19 & -16 : \\ 2 & -8 & 0 & 1 & -8 & 19 \end{matrix}$$

[K] =:   0.5   :
    :   0.5   :
    :   0.75   : $(- QH^4/D)$
    :   0.75   :
    :   0.25   :
    :   0.25   :

[W] = [A − 1] [K]

The Inverse matrix is obtained as:

: 0.2188	0.2500	0.1250	0.1563	0.1250	0.1563 :
: 0.1250	0.2188	0.0781	0.1250	0.0781	0.1250 :
: 0.1250	0.1563	0.1553	0.1658	0.0635	0.0842 :
: 0.0781	0.1250	0.0829	0.1553	0.0421	0.0635 :
: 0.1250	0.1563	0.0635	0.0842	0.1553	0.1658 :
: 0.0781	0.1250	0.0421	0.0635	0.0829	0.1553 :

The Deflections at the nodal points are

$W1 = -0.3750 \ QH^4/D)$
$W2 = -0.5156 \ QH^4/D)$
$W3 = -0.3066 \ QH^4/D)$
$W4 = -0.4184 \ QH^4/D)$
$W5 = -0.2403 \ QH^4/D)$
$W6 = -0.3316 \ QH^4/D)$

Example 8.51

WRITE A COMPUTER PROGRAMME TO DESIGN A CANTILEVER RETAINING WALL

TO SUIT THE FOLLOWING DATA:

HEIGHT OF WALL ABOVE GROUND LEVEL = 6 M

DEPTH OF FOUNDATION FROM GROUND LEVEL = 1.5 M

UNIT WEIGHT OF SOIL = 18 kN/m³

UNIT WEIGHT OF CONCRETE = 25 kN/m³

ANGLE OF REPOSE = 30 degrees

SAFE BEARING CAPACITY OF SOIL = 180 kN/m²

COEFFICIENT OF FRICTION = 0.4

PERMISSIBLE STRESS IN CONCRETE = 5 N/mm²

PERMISSIBLE STRESS IN STEEL = 230 N/mm²

CHECK THE STABILITY OF THE RETAINING WALL AGAINST OVERTURNING AND SLIDING.

Notation Explanation

DSC   = DENSITY OF CONCRETE kN/m³

H1   = HEIGHT OF STEM ABOVE THE ROUND IN METRES

W   = DENSITY OF SOIL IN kN/m³

DSOIL = DEPTH OF FOUNDATION IN METRES
FY   = ANGLE OF FRICTION IN DEGREES
SBC   = SAFE BEARING CAPACITY OF SOIL IN kN/m^2
AMU = COEFFICIENT OF FRICTION
C   = COMPRESSIVE STRESS IN CONCRETE IN N/mm^2
T   = TENSILE STRESS IN STEEL IN N/mm^2
AM   = MODULAR RATIO

Programme

```
IMPLICIT REAL (I – N)
DSC = 25.0
H1 = 6.0
DSOIL = 1.5
DATA W, FY, SBC, AMU, C, T, AM
/18.0, 30.0, 180.0, 0.4, 5.0, 230.0, 19.0/
F I IS CONVERTED TO RADIANS
F I = FY * 3.14/180.0
CP = (1.0 – SIN (F I)/(1 + SIN (F I))
CA = 1./CP
DESIGN OF STEM: TW = TOP WIDTH IN METRES
TW = 0.2
H = H1 + DSOIL
EFFCS = 4.0
TB = 0.1 * H
HSTEM = H – TB
MXX = (CP * W * HSTEM ** 3/6.0) * 1.E + 05
N1 = C/(C + (T/AM))
Q = (0.5 * C * N1 * (1.0 (N1 /3.))) * 100.0
DREQ = SQRT (MXX / (Q * 100.))
BWST = (DREQ + EFFCS) / 100.
AST = MXX /(T * 100 * (1. (N1/3.)) * DREQ)
S20 = ((3.14 * 2.0 * 2.0/4.)AST) * 100
ADS = .12 * 100. * ((BWST + TW)/2.) * 10.0/100.
S10 = ((3.14 * 1.0 * 1.0/4.)/ADS) * 100.0
WRITE (*, 25) TW, H, TB, HSTEM, BWST
```
25   `FORMAT (/5X, 'TW = ', F8.4, 2X, 'H = ', F8.4 3X, 'TB =', F8.4, 3X,`
        `'HSTEM =', F8.4, 3X, 'BWST =', F8.4)`
        `J = 1. – (N1/3.)`
C   `CURTAILMENT OF MAINSTEEL: CURTAILMENT IS DONE`
C   `AT 1/3 HEIGHT AND 2/3 HEIGHT FROM TOP`

```
        D11 = (TW + (1./3.) * 'BWST – TW)) * 100.
        EFD11 = D11 – EFFCS
        D22 = (TW + (2./3.) * (BWST – TW)) * 100.
        FD22 = D22 – EFFCS
        M22 = (8./27.) * MXX
        AST22 = (M22/(T * 100 J * EFD22))
        C2 = ((3.14 * 2.0 * 2.0/4.)AST22) * 100
C       CURTAILMENT OF STEM MAIN AT H/3 FROM TOP
        M11 = MXX/27.
        AST11 = (M11/(T * J * 100 * EFD11))
        C1 = ((3.14 * 2 * 2./4.)/AST11) * 100.
        WRITE (*, 35) S20, C1, C2
35      FORMAT (/5X, 'S20 =', F8.4, 3X, 'C1 = ', F8.4, 3X, 'C2 = ', F8,4)
C       DESIGN OF BASE SLAB AND STABILITY CALCULATIONS FOR 1 METRE
        RUN
        BASE = 0.6 * H
        TOE = BASE/3
        HEEL = BASE – TOE – BWST
        WSI = TW * HSTEM * 1. * DSC
        WS2 = 0.5 * HSTEM * (BWST – TW) * 1. * DSC
        WB = BASE * TB * 1. * DSC
        WSHEL = HSTEM * HEEL * 1. * W
        WTSOIL = TOE * (DSOIL – TB) * 1. * W
        SUMW = WS1 + WS2 + WB + WSHEL + WTSOIL
        DS1 = HEEL + .5 * TW
        DS2 = 1./3. * (BWST – TW) + TW + HEEL
        DB = BASE/2
        DHSOIL = HEEL/2.
        DTSOIL = BASE – 0.5 * TOE
        SUVM = WS1 * DS1 + WS2 * DS2 + WB * DB + WSHEL * DHSOIL + WTSOI
        * DTSOIL
        HSMOM = CP * W * H ** 3./6.
        SUMM = SUVM + HSMOM + TSMOM
C       RESULTAMT DISTANCE IS DENOTED AS 'Z'
        Z = SUMM/SUMW
        E = Z – BASE/2
        PMAX = SUMW * (1. + (6. E/BASE))/BASE
        PMIN = SUMW * (1. – (6. E/BASE))/BASE
        IF (E .LE. (BASE/6.)) GOTO 100
        GOTO 500
```

```
100    IF (PMAX .LE. SBC)GOTO 200
       GOTO 500
200    WRITE (*, 300)
300    FORMAT (//5X, 'IT IS STABLE')
       WRITE (*, 325) Z, E, PMAX, PMIN
325    FORMAT (/5X, 'Z = 'F8.4, 3X, 'E = 'F8.4, 3X, 'PMAX = ', F8.4, 3X, 'PMIN = ' , F8.4)
C      DESIGN OF TOE REINFORCEMENT
       P1 = PMIN + (HEEL + BWST)/BASE) * (PMAX – PMIN)
       P2 = PMIN + (HEEL / BASE) * (PMAX – PMIN)
       WTOE  = TOE * TB * 1. * DSC
       URECT = P1 + TOE + 1.0
       UTR    = 0.5 * (PMAX – P1) * TOE
       DTOE  = 0.5 * TOE
       EFFB   = 6.0
       DSOT  = 0.5 * TOE
       DRECT = 0.5 * TOE
       DTR    = (2./3.) * TOE
       MX1X1 = WTSOIL * DSOT + WTOE * DTOE – URECT * DRECT – UTRI * DTRI
       ASTOE = (MX1X1 * 1.E + 0.5)/T 8 100. * J * (TB * 100. – 6.0))
       TO16   = (3.14 * 1.6 8 1.6/4.) * 100 /ASTOE
       DIST   = (0.12/100.)  8 100 * TB * 100.0
       TO10   = (3.14 * 1.0 * 1.0/4.0 * 100. /(DIST)
C      DESIGN OF HEEL REINFORCEMENT
       SHEEL    = HEEL * HSTEM * 1.0 * W
       WHEEL    = HEEL * TB * 1.0 8 DSC
       UHREC   = PMIN * HEEL * 1.0
       UHTRI    = 0.5 * HEEL * (P2 – PMIN)
       DSHEEL  = HEEL / 2.
       DWHEEL = HEEL / 2.
       DHREC   = HEEL / 2.
       DHTR     = HEEL /3.
       MX2X2    = SHEEL * DSHEEL + WHEEL * DWHEEL – UHREC * DHREC –
       UHTRI * DHTRI
       ASHEL    = (MX2X2 * 1. E + 0.5)/(T * 100. * J * (TB * 100. – 6.0))
       HE16     = (3.14 * 1.6 * 1.6/4.) * 100./ASHEL
C      CHECK AGAINST SLIDING
       NETP = (05 * W * CP * h ** 2)  (CA * 0.5 * W * DSOL ** 2.)
       MUW = AMU * SUMW
       IF (NETP .LE. MUW) GOTO 700
       WRITE (*, 750)
```

750	FORMAT (//5X, 'IT IS NOT SAFE AGAINST SLIDING')
	STOP
700	WRITE (*, 775)
775	FORMAT (//5X, 'IT IS SAFE AGAINST SLIDING')
500	STOP
	END

Results

TW	= 0.2000	H	= 7.5000
TB	= 0.7500	HSTEM	= 6.7500
BWST	= 0.7231	S20	= 14.4683
C1	= 191.2177	C2	= 36.3664
IT IS STABLE			
Z	= 2.5476	E	= 0.2976
PMAX	= 142.5219	PMIN	= 61.5476

IT IS SAFE AGINST SLIDING

8.6 EXAMPLES OF COMPUTER PROGRAMMES USING C LANGUAGE

In this section, some typical computer programmes using the C language is presented to benefit the students to understand the method writing programmes using the C language. The commonly used numerical methods such as Gauss–Seidal, Regula–Falsi, Newton–Raphson and Runge–Kutta are presented in the C-computer language as reported by M.K Jain etal[10].

Example 8.52

```
/* PROGRAM GAUSS–SEIDAL METHOD
```
Write a Program to solve a system of equations using Gauss–Seidal iteration method.Order of the matrix is n, maximum number of iterations is niter, error tolerance is eps and the initial approximation to the solution vector x is oldx. If the system of equations is larger than 10 × 10, change the dimensions in float.   */

```c
#include <stdio.h>
#include <math.h>
main()
  {
  float   a[10][10], b[10], x[10], oldx[10], sum, big, c;
  float   eps;
  int     n, niter, i, j, ii, jj, k, l;
  FILE    *fp;

  fp = fopen("result","w");

  printf("Input the order of matrix : n\n");
```

```
printf("Input the number of iterations : niter\n");
printf("Input error tolerance : eps\n");
scanf("%d %d %e", &n, &niter, &eps);
fprintf(fp,"n = %d, niter = %d, eps = %e\n", n, niter, eps);
printf("Input augmented matrix row-wise\n");
fprintf(fp,"Elements of the augmented matrix\n");
for (i = 1;  i <= n; i++)
{ for (j = 1; j <= n; j++)
{ scanf("%f", &a[i][j]);
fprintf(fp,"%f   ", a[i][j]);
        }
scanf("%f", &b[i]);
fprintf(fp,"      %f\n", b[i]);
      }
printf("Input initial approx. to the solution vector\n");
fprintf(fp,"Initial approx. to solution vector :\n");
for (i = 1;  i <= n; i++)
{ scanf("%f", &oldx[i]);
fprintf(fp,"%f ", oldx[i]);
      }
fprintf(fp,"\n");
for (i = 1;  i <= n; i++)
x[i] = oldx[i];

/* Compute the new values for x[i]   */
  for (ii = 1;  ii <= niter; ii++)
  { for (i = 1; i <= n; i++)
  { sum = 0.0;
    for (j = 1;  j <= n; j++)
  { if((i - j) != 0)
  sum = sum + a[i][j] * x[j];
              }
  x[i] = (b[i] - sum) / a[i][i];
          }
  big = fabs(x[1] - oldx[1]);
  for (k = 2; k <= n; k++)
  { c = fabs(x[k] - oldx[k]);
  if(c > big)
  big = c;
          }
  if(big <= eps)
```

```
       goto 110;
       for (l = 1;  l <= n; l++)
       oldx[l] = x[l];
           }
     printf("ITERATIONS NOT SUFFICIENT\n");
     fprintf(fp,"ITERATIONS NOT SUFFICIENT\n");
     goto 120;
110:  fprintf(fp,"Number of iterations = %d\n", ii);
     fprintf(fp,"Solution vector\n");
     for(i = 1; i <= n; i++)
     fprintf(fp,"  %f ", x[i]);
     fprintf(fp,"\n");
     printf("\nPLEASE SEE FILE 'result' FOR RESULTS\n\n");
120:  return 0;
       }
/*************************************************************/
n = 4, niter = 30, eps = 1.000000e-06
Elements of the augmented matrix
3.000000  4.000000  2.000000  2.000000  6.000000
2.000000  5.000000  3.000000  1.000000  4.000000
2.000000  2.000000  6.000000  3.000000  3.000000
1.000000  2.000000  4.000000  6.000000  6.000000
Initial approx. to solution vector :
0.100000  0.100000  0.100000   0.100000
Number of iterations = 28
Solution vector
1.000000   0.500000  -0.500000   1.000000
/*************************************************************/
```

Example 8.53

```
/* PROGRAM REGULA–FALSI METHOD
```

Finding a simple root of f(x) = 0 using Regula–Falsi method. Read the end points of the interval (a, b) in which the root lies, maximum number of iterations n and the error tolerance eps. */

```
#include <stdio.h>
#include <math.h>

float f();

main()
  {
  float       a, b, x, eps, fa, fb, fx;
  int         i, n;
  FILE        *fp;
```

```
        fp = fopen("result","w");
        printf("Input the end points of the interval (a, b) in");
        printf("which the root lies");
        printf("n: number of iterations\n");
        printf("eps: error tolerance\n");
        scanf("%f %f %d %E", &a, &b, &n, &eps);
        fprintf(fp,"a = %f  b = %f  n = %d", a, b, n);
        fprintf(fp," eps = %e\n\n", eps);
/* Compute the value of f(x) at a & b and calculate the new
   approximation x and value of f(x) at x.           */
        for (i = 1;  i <= n; i++)
      {  fa = f(a);
         fb = f(b);
         x = a - (a - b) * fa / (fa - fb);
         fx = f(x);
         if(fabs(fx) <= eps)
/* Iteration is stopped when abs(f(x)) is less than or equal to eps.
Alternate conditions can also be used.          */
                  goto l1;
                  if((fa * fx) < 0.0)
                     b = x;
                  else
                     a = x;
        }
     printf("\nITERATIONS ARE NOT SUFFICIENT");
     goto l2;
l1: fprintf(fp,"Number of iterations = %d\n", i);
     fprintf(fp,"Root = %10.7f, f(x) = %e\n", x, fx);
     printf("\nPLEASE SEE FILE 'result' FOR RESULTS\n\n");
l2: return 0;
     }
/***********************************************************/
float f(x)
   float   x;
     { float fun;
         fun = cos(x) - x * exp(x);
         return(fun);
     }
/***********************************************************/
a = 0.000000  b = 1.000000  n = 20 eps = 1.000000e-04
```

Number of iterations = 9

Root = 0.5177283, f(x) = 8.832585e-05

```
/**********************************************************/
```

Example 8.54

```
/* PROGRAM NEWTON–RAPHSON METHOD
```

Finding a simple root of f(x) = 0 using Newton–Raphson method.
Read initial approximation xold. Maximum number of iterations
n and error tolerance eps.   */

```
#include <stdio.h>
#include <math.h>

float f();
float df();

main()
    {
    float       xold, eps, fx, dfx, xnew;
    int         i, n;
    FILE        *fp;

    fp = fopen("result","w");
    printf("Input value initial approximation xold\n");
    printf("n: number of iterations\n");
    printf("eps: error tolerance\n");
    scanf("%f %d %E", &xold, &n, &eps);
    fprintf(fp,"Input value initial approximation xold\n");
    fprintf(fp,"number of iterations n,");
    fprintf(fp," error tolerance eps\n");
    fprintf(fp,"xold = %f  n = %d  eps = %e\n\n", xold, n, eps);
/* Calculate f and its first derivative at xold    */
    for(i = 1;  i <= n; i++)
        { fx = f(xold);
          dfx = df(xold);
          xnew = xold - fx / dfx;
          fx = f(xnew);
          if(fabs(fx) <= eps) goto 110;
/* Iteration is stopped when abs(f(x)) is less than or equal to eps.
    Alternate conditions can also be used.         */
                            xold = xnew;
        }
    printf("\nITERATIONS ARE NOT SUFFICIENT");
    goto 120;
```

```
110:
    fprintf(fp,"Iterations = %d", i);
    fprintf(fp,"   Root = %10.7f,  f(x) = %e\n", xnew, fx);
    printf("\nPLEASE SEE FILE 'result' FOR RESULTS\n\n");
120: return 0;
      }
/*****************************************************************/
float f(x)
   float   x;
     { float     fun;
       fun = cos(x) - x * exp(x);
       return(fun);
     }
/*****************************************************************/
float df(x)
   float   x;
     { float     dfun;
       dfun = - sin(x) - (x + 1.0) * exp(x);
       return(dfun);
     }
/*****************************************************************/
Input value initial approximation xold
number of iterations n, error tolerance eps
xold = 1.000000  n = 15  eps = 1.000000e-04
Iterations = 4  Root =  0.5177574,  f(x) = 2.286344e-08
/*****************************************************************/
```

Example 8.55

/* RUNGE–KUTTA CLASSICAL FOURTH ORDER METHOD

Program to solve the IVP, $dy/dx = f(x,y)$, $y(x0) = y0$ using the classical Runge–Kutta fourth order method with steps h and h/2 and also computes the estimate of the truncation error. Input parameters are: initial point, initial value, number of intervals and the step length h. Solutions with h, h/2 and the estimate of truncation error are available as output. The right hand side $f(x,y)$ is computed as a function subprogram.   */

```
#include <stdio.h>
#include <math.h>
float f();
main()
  {
  float      u[20], v[40], x0, y0, h, k1, k2, k3, k4;
```

```
float       h1, v1, te, x1, u1;
int         n, i, m, nn, ij;
FILE        *fp;

fp = fopen("result","w");

printf("Input initial point x0, initial value y0,\n");
printf("number of intervals n and step size h\n");
scanf("%f %f %d %f", &x0, &y0, &n, &h);
fprintf(fp,"Initial point x0 = %f, initial ", x0);
fprintf(fp,"value y0 = %f\n", y0);
fprintf(fp,"Number of intervals = %d,\n", n);
x1 = x0;
for (m = 1;  m <= 2; m++)
    { if(m == 1)
       { nn = n;
         u[0] = y0;
       }
else
    { nn = 2 * n;
      h = h / 2.0;
      v[0] = y0;
      }
for (i = 1;  i <= nn; i++)
  { if(m == 1)
    { u1 = u[i-1];
      h1 = h / 2.0;
      k1 = h * f(x0, u1);
      k2 = h * f(x0 + h1, u1 + 0.5 * k1);
      k3 = h * f(x0 + h1, u1 + 0.5 * k2);
      k4 = h * f(x0 + h, u1 + k3);
      u[i] = u1 + (k1 + 2.0 * (k2 + k3) + k4)/6.0;
      x0 = x0 + h;
    }
    else
        { v1 = v[i-1];
        h1 = h / 2.0;
        k1 = h * f(x1, v1);
        k2 = h * f(x1 + h1, v1 + 0.5 * k1);
        k3 = h * f(x1 + h1, v1 + 0.5 * k2);
        k4 = h * f(x1 + h, v1 + k3);
        v[i] = v1 + (k1 + 2.0 * (k2 + k3) + k4)/6.0;
```

```
            x1 = x1 + h;
          }
        }
    }
  te = 16.0 * (v[nn] - u[n]) / 15.0;
  fprintf(fp,"Step = %4.2f\n", 2.0*h);
  fprintf(fp,"Solution at nodal points\n");
  for (i = 1;  i <= n; i++)
  fprintf(fp,"%11.7f ", u[i]);
  fprintf(fp,"\n");
  fprintf(fp,"Step = %4.2f\n", h);
  fprintf(fp,"Solution at nodal points\n");
  for (i = 1;  i <= 2 * n; i++)
  {
      if(i == n + 1)
      fprintf(fp,"\n");
      fprintf(fp,"%11.7f", v[i]);
  }
  fprintf(fp,"\n");
  fprintf(fp,"Estimate of truncation error at ");
  fprintf(fp,"xf = %12.5e\n", te);
  printf("\nPLEASE SEE FILE 'result' FOR RESULTS\n\n");
  return 0;
  }
/*************************************************************/
 float  f(x, y)
   float     x, y;
     { float    fun;
       fun = - 2.0 * x * y * y;
       return(fun);
     }
/*************************************************************/
Initial point x0 = 0.000000, initial value y0 = 1.000000
Number of intervals = 5,
Step = 0.10
Solution at nodal points
 0.9900990   0.9615382   0.9174306   0.8620682   0.7999992
Step = 0.05
Solution at nodal points
 0.9975063  0.9900990  0.9779951  0.9615384  0.9411764
 0.9174311  0.8908685  0.8620689  0.8316008  0.8000000
Estimate of truncation error at xf = 7.62939e-07
/*************************************************************/
```

8.7 LIST OF COMPUTER PROGRAMMES

A comprehensive list of computer programmes covered in this monograph along with the page numbers are compiled in Appendix.

EXERCISES

1. Write a FORTRAN programme to read in pairs of positive numbers of X and Y and print out the smaller, or if the numbers are equal print the words 'numbers equal'.
2. Write a computer programme to find the sum of odd numbers from 1 to 500.
3. Write a complete FORTRAN programme to evaluate the equation,

$$Y = e^{-3x} + 0.09\ x^2 + 0.02$$

   for $x = 0\ (0.001)\ 0.05$ and Y should be printed with 6 significant figures in separate columns.
4. Write a computer programme to compute and print the function

$$f(x) = 6x^3 + 4x^2 + 2x \quad \text{for } 3.0 < x < 6.0$$
$$= 5x^2 + 6x \quad \text{for } 6.0 << 9.0$$

   A simply supported beam of span L supports a concentrated load P at the centre of span.
5. Write a computer programme to print out the bending moment and shear force in the beam at regular intervals of 1 m.
6. Write a programme to find the sum of numbers from 1 to 5000 using a Do statement.
7. A testing laboratory has maintained data of the compressive strength of concrete cubes tested over a period. Assuming the strengths are represented by the variables $C_1, C_2, C_3, \ldots\ldots\ldots C_{500}$, write a Fortran programme to calculate the mean and variance of the set of data.
8. The correlation coefficient between two sets of variables X and Y are given by the relation

$$r = \left\{ \frac{\sum(XY) - N\,(M_x)(M_y)}{\sqrt{\left[\sum X^2 - N(M_x)^2\right]\left[\sum Y^2 - N(M_y)^2\right]}} \right\}$$

   Where r is the correlation coefficient, N is the number of observations, X and Y are the two groups of observations, M_x and M_y are the mean values of the two groups respectively. Write a FORTRAN programme to evaluate the correlation coefficient and print out the results. The programme should provide 100 pairs of observations.
9. Write a function sub-programme to evaluate the root of the function

$$f(x) = e^x - 3x = 0 \quad \text{near } x = 0.4$$

   using Newton–Raphson's method.
10. Write a programme to tabulate the function

$$f(x, y) = (x^2 + y^2 + 2xy)\ /\ (x^2 + y^2 + 8xy)$$

   for a set of values given by

x	0	2	4	6	8	10	12
y	−10	−8	−6	−4	−2	0	2

Use 'do loop' in the programme.

11. Write a computer programme to evaluate the determinant,

$$D = \begin{bmatrix} 4 & 3 & 1 & 5 \\ 1 & 2 & 2 & 3 \\ 3 & 1 & 2 & 1 \\ 1 & 3 & 4 & 0 \end{bmatrix}$$

12. Write a programme to multiply the matrices,

$$A = \begin{bmatrix} 1 & -2 & 3 \\ 2 & 3 & -1 \\ -3 & 1 & 2 \end{bmatrix} \text{ and } B = \begin{bmatrix} 1 & 0 & 2 \\ 0 & 1 & 2 \\ 1 & 2 & 0 \end{bmatrix}$$

Use suitable format statements for READ and PRINT statements.

13. Write a computer programme to find the trace of 6 × 6 matrix. (Hint: Trace is the sum of the diagonal elements)

14. Write a computer programme to determine $y(0, 8)$ bu Milne's predictor and corrector formula for the differential equation

$$\left(\frac{dy}{dx}\right) = y - x^2 \text{, given } y(0) = 1, y(0.2) = 1.2186$$

$$y(0.4) = 1.4682 \text{ and } y(0.6) = 1.7379$$

15. Write a computer programme to evaluate the function $\int_1^2 \frac{dx}{(1+x^3)}$ using

a) Gauss–Legendre three point formula
b) Trapezoidal rule and
c) Simpson's rule

16. Write a FORTRAN programme to compute

$$S = \int_{n=1}^{10} \frac{(-1)^n x^{n/2}}{n(n+1)}$$

17. Fifteen randomly selected bricks have seven days compressive strength in N/mm² as 7.10, 8.53, 7.92, 6.54, 9.14, 10.35, 8.73, 5.40, 10.98, 9.95, 5.68, 6.29, 7.51, 8.33, 7.71. Write a computer programme to determine the mean and variance.

18. A cantilever of span L supports a linearly varying load of intensity zero at the free end and W at the fixed end. Write a computer programme to evaluate the bending moment and shear force at intervals of 1 m.

19. Write a computer programme to evaluate the second moment of the area of the hollow circular section of internal diameter d and thickness t about
a) The centroidal axis in its own plane
b) The centroidal axis perpendicular to the plane of the section.

20. The deflection of a simply supported beam under two point loads is expressed by the relation

$$\delta = \left(\frac{23WL^3}{648EI} \right)$$

where W = concentrated load
L = span of the beam
EI = flexural rigidity

Write a programme to evaluate the deflection for
W = 20.0 (2.0) 30.0
L = 4.0 (0.5) 8.0

21. A cantilever beam of uniform section is subjected to a parabolic varying load of intensity

$$w_x = w_0 \, (L^2 - x^2)/L^2$$

$x = 0$ at the free end. Write a Fortran programme to determine the total load on the beam, using
a) Simpson's rule and
b) Gaussian quadrature formula.

22. A simply supported beam AB of span carries a distributed load which varies from w kN/m. At A to $2w$ kN/m at B. The second moment of area is $= 350 \, (10)^6$ mm^4 and modulus of elasticity E = 200 GPa. The double integaration method gives

$$EI\left(\frac{dy}{dx} \right) = -30x^2 + 1.67x^3 + 0.08x^4 + 362.7$$

and $y(0) = 0$. Write a computer programme to compute $y(4)$ using a numerical method.

23. The metal thickness of a pressure vessel subjected to internal pressure is obtained from Rankine's yield criteria as

$$\left[\frac{30(100)^2}{\{(100 + t)^2 - 100^2\}} \right] + \left[\frac{30(100 + t)^2}{\{(100 + t)^2 - 100^2\}} \right] = 120$$

Write a computer programme to evaluate t.

24. The state of stress at a point is characterized by the stress tensor

$$S = \begin{bmatrix} 4 & 0 & 2 \\ 0 & 8 & 0 \\ 2 & 0 & -12 \end{bmatrix}$$

Write a computer programme to determine
a) principal stresses and directions
b) maximum shear stress
c) the stresses on an octahedral plane
d) the principal strains given $E = 200$ kN/mm^2 and $\mu = 0.2$

25. A spherical dome is under the action of its own weight q per unit area. The membrane forces per unit length of principal sections are given by

$$N_\phi = \frac{-aq}{(1+\cos\phi)}$$

$$N_\theta = aq\left[\frac{1}{(1+\cos\phi)} - \cos\phi\right]$$

where a is the radius of the sphere. Write a computer programme to print N_ϕ and N_θ for $\phi = 0$ (10) 90°. The input contains a and q. Tabulate the results and determine the value ϕ of where N_θ is zero.

26. The membrane analogy solution for the torsion problem of a rectangular section $2b \times 2a$ where $b > a$ is given by the relation,

$$\tau_{max} = k\,(2\,G\theta a)$$
$$M_t = k_1 G\theta\,(2a)^3\,(2b)$$

where

$$k = 1 - \frac{8}{\pi^2}\sum_{n=1,3,5}^{\infty}\left(\frac{1}{n^2\cosh\left(\dfrac{n\pi b}{2a}\right)}\right)$$

$$k_1 = \frac{1}{3}\left[1 - \frac{192}{\pi^5}\left(\frac{a}{b}\sum_{n=1,3,5}^{\infty}\frac{1}{n^5}\right)\tanh\left(\frac{n\pi b}{2a}\right)\right]$$

and $\quad k_2 = (k_1/k)$

Write a computer programme to prepare a table of constants k, k_1 and k_2 for $(b/a) = 1$ (0.5) 10.0.

27. Write a Fortran programme to evaluate (b/R) and (pR^2/M_2) for values of $(M_1/M_2) = 1.00$ (0.25) 2.00, given

$$\left(\frac{p^2}{M^2}\right) = \frac{2[(M_1/M_2)-1]}{(b/R)^2}$$

$$\left(\frac{pR^2}{M^2}\right) = \left\{\frac{6\left[(M_1/M_2) + \dfrac{1+(b/R)}{1-(b/R)}\right]}{1+(b/R)+(b/R)^2}\right\}$$

Print the results as (M_1/M_2), (b/R) and (pR^2/M_2) in the same order with suitable formula.

28. A portal frame ABCD fixed at A and D has rigid joints at B and C. The columns AB and CD are 4.5 m long and the transom BC is 3 m and supportsa load of 50 kN/m. Write a computer programme to determine the moments at the joints using Kani's method.

29. Write a computer programme to construct the influence line diagram for the following reactions in the continuous beam ACB.
    a) Vertical reaction at A
    b) Vertical reaction at C

c) Moment at C

d) Shear at right of support C

e) Bending moment at centre of span F

Assume the flexural rigidity *EI* is constant.

30. The finite difference scheme applied to a simply supported skew plate subjected to a uniformly distributed load of intensity p_0 resulted in the following two sets of expressions:

$$\begin{bmatrix} -6 & 4 & 2 & 0 \\ 1 & -5 & 1 & 1 \\ 1 & 2 & -6 & 0 \\ 0 & 2 & 0 & -6 \end{bmatrix} \begin{Bmatrix} M_1 \\ M_2 \\ M_3 \\ M_4 \end{Bmatrix} = \frac{-3p_0h^2}{2} \begin{bmatrix} 1 \\ 1 \\ 1 \\ 1 \end{bmatrix}$$

and

$$\begin{bmatrix} -6 & 4 & 2 & 0 \\ 1 & -5 & 1 & 1 \\ 1 & 2 & -6 & 0 \\ 0 & 2 & 0 & -6 \end{bmatrix} \begin{Bmatrix} w_1 \\ w_2 \\ w_3 \\ w_4 \end{Bmatrix} = \frac{-3h^2}{2D} \begin{bmatrix} M_1 \\ M_2 \\ M_3 \\ M_4 \end{bmatrix}$$

Where $D = \dfrac{Et^3}{12}(1-\mu^2)$

Write a computer programme to evaluate the bending moments M_1, M_2, M_3, M_4 and determine the deflections w_1, w_2, w_3 and w_4 given

$E = 25000$ Mpa, $t = 50$ mm, $\mu = 0.15$, $h = 150$ mm, $p_0 = 0.01$ MPa.

31. The load enhancement factor ë of a thin circular plate is derived as

$$\lambda = (1+\alpha^2 A - \beta A^2) + (\alpha B - 2\beta AB)(R/2) - (T\delta/4M)(A + BR/3) - (7\beta BP^2/24)$$

Where $\alpha = \left[\dfrac{0.5\,(D/d) - 1.5t}{1 - 0.75t} \right]$

$\beta = 0.75t/(1 - 0.75t)$

$A = (\alpha/2\beta) - (\mu T/2\beta M)$

$B = \delta T/(4\beta RM)$

$t = (A_s f_y)/(b_d f_c)$

$\mu = (\delta/2)$

Write a programme to compute λ for

$(\delta/d) = 0.5\ (0.1)\ 1.0$

$100(As/bd) = 0.15\ (0.1)\ 0.65$

Given $f_c = 25, f_y = 415, R = 700, D = 50, d = 35, (T/M) = 1.25$.

32. The details of earthwork of a road work are as follows:

Distance (m)	Section Area (m²)
0	1200
30	1400
60	1800
90	1600
120	1500
150	900
180	600

Write a FORTRAN programme to calculate the volume of the earth work by trapezoidal rule.

33. A, B and C are three visible stations in a hydrographic survey. Outside this triangle (and nearer to AC) a station D is established and its position is to be found by three point resection at A, B and C. Write a computer programme to determine the distances DA and DC. The distances AB, BC and CA and the angles ADB and BDC are given as input.

34. The horizontal angles of a quadrilateral ABCD with a central point E have been measured in a triangulation survey. Write a computer programme to adjust the quadrilateral using the method of least squares. The input is twelve measured angles, viz, central angle, left hand side angles and right hand side angles measured in triangles AEB, BEC, CED and DEA respectively.

35. Ten consecutive readings wewre taken with a level and leveling staff on a continuously sloping ground at a common interval of 20 m. The reduced level of the first point was 205.325 m. Write a computer programme to print out a page of level field book and compute the reduced levels of the points by
    a) Rise and fall method and
    b) Height of instrument method. Also calculate the gradient of the line joining the first and the last point.

36. Write a computer programme to find the time required to lower the water level from 3 m to 2 m in a reservoir of 75 m by 75 m by a notch of length 2 m. C_d = 0.60. Compare the results if it is replaced by aright angled V notch.

37. A masonry dam is of trapezoidal section and its water face is vertical. Write a computer programme to determine
    a) the minimum width of the base of the dam, so that there is no tension anywhere at the base.
    b) maximum stresses at the base and
    c) factor of safety against sliding. The height, top width and the unit weight of masonry are given as input.

38. Water flows over the spill way of a dam at a depth 2.75 m over it. The difference of elevation between spillway crest and down stream bed level is 30 m. If the discharge coefficient of the spillway is 0.75, determine the water depth after the hydraulic jump. Write a general programme for different depths of flow over the spillway for finding out the depth after the hydraulic jump.

39. For a given discharge data corresponding to different heads over a weir, write a programme to determine the constants a and b for general discharge equation for the weirgiven by $Q = ah^b$.

40. The annual peak flood data for N years is given. Write a programme to estimate the magnitude of floods having frequency equal to M_1 years by Gumbel's probability method with known table of frequency factor (K) for different sample size (N) and frequency in years.

41. It is required to select a suitable pipe diameter for a sewer by considering the velocity and economic factor. The population and per capita water supplyare known. The dry weather flow is in litres/day can be taken as 80 percent of total quantity of water. The maximum flow in the sewer is taken as three times the dry weather flow. Six varieties of pipes are available viz. (1) salt glazed stone ware (2) cement concrete (3) cast iron (4) brick unglazed (5) asbestos Cement and 6. P.V.C. Manning's coefficients for them are N (1) = 0.012, $N(2)$ = 0.013 $N(3)$ = 0.012, $N(4)$ = 0.013, $N(5)$ = 0.011, $N(6)$ = 0.011 respectively. For all the pipes a minimum self cleaning velocity 0.8 m/sec is considered. The maximum velocities are Max $V(1)$ = 3.0 Max $V(2)$ = 2.4, Max $V(3)$ = 3.5, Max $V(4)$ = 1.5, Max $V(5)$ = 2.5, Max $V(6)$ = 2.0. The dimeter varies from 200 (50) 450. Design the sewer using manning's formula,

$$\text{Max } V(1) = = \left(\frac{R^{2/3}S^{1/2}}{N} \right)$$

where V = Peak velocity and N = Manning's coefficient
        R = Hydraulic gradient and S is the slope and

$$\text{Maximum flow in pipe/sec} = \left[\frac{\text{Maximum flow in the pipe}}{(1000)\,24\,(60)\,(60)} \right]$$

Input to be given are: the population, amount of water used per head in litres and the slope.

The output should be (1) material of the pipe (2) slope (3) quantity (4) diameter and (5) velocity use suitable formats.

42. Write a computer programme to construct nomograms to determine the area of steel for singly, doubly reinforced and tee beams. Use limit state method as per IS: 456-2000. The input should contain the concrete grade, steel grade, dimensions of the cross section and the design ultimate moment.

43. Write a computer programme to compute the cracked moment of inertia of a reinforced Concrete T-beam section given (b_f/b_w) = 1 (2) 20; (D_f/d) = 0.1 (0.1) 0.4; $(A_{st}/b_w d)$ = 0.01 (0.01) 0.04; f_{ck} = 15 (5) 30, where b_f, b_w are the breadth of flange and web respectively. D_f, d, D are the depth of flange, effective depth and total depth. A_{st} = area of steel and f_{ck} = grade of concrete.

44. The safe load carrying capacity of a timber column is given by the relation,
$$P = f_c A \text{ if } (L_e/d) \le 11$$
$$= f_c [1 - (L_e/kd)^2]A \text{ if } 11 < (Le/d)$$

$$= \left[\frac{0.329EA}{(L_e/d)^2} \right] \text{ if } (L_e/d) > k$$

where $k = 0.702 \sqrt{(E/f_c)}$

Using the above equations, write a computer programme to determine the safe axial load of a timber column 200×150 mm size. $L_e = 3000, 4500, 6000$ mm, $f_c = 100$ MPa, $E = 10000$ Mpa.

45. Write a computer programme to determine the tensile strengthof a roof truss diagonal connected to the gusset plate by one leg only in one line along the length of the member given

$$A_1 = (L_1 - 0.5t)\, t - dt$$
$$A_2 = (L_2 - 0.5t)\, t$$
$$k = 3A_1 / (3A_1 + A_2)$$
$$T = (A_1 + A_2 k)\, 0.6 f_y$$

For $L_1 = 90\ (10)\ 200$
  $L_2 = 60\ (5)\ 150$
  $t = 12\ (3)\ 18$
  $d = 21.5, f_y = 250$

46. A concrete beam with a rectangular section 100 mm wide and 300 mm deep is stressed by three cables each carrying an effective prestressing force P. The spn of the beam is 10 m. The first cable is parabolic with an eccentricity of 50 mm below the centroidal axis at the centre of span and 50 mm above the centroidal axis at supports. The second cable is parabolic with zero eccentricity at the supports and an eccentricity of 50 mm at the centre of span. The third cable is straight with a uniform eccentricity of 50 mm below the centroidal axis. If the beam supports a uniformly distributed live load of w kN/m and $E_c = 38$ kN/mm^2, write a computer programme to estimate the instantaneous deflection at the following stages:

a) prestress + self weight of beam and

b) prestress + self weight + live load

Input contains $P = 200\ (10)\ 250$ kN

$w = 2\ (1)\ 5$ kN/m

47. It is proposed to prepare design tables for one-way and two-way slabs. Write a computer programme for the preparation of design tables. The table should be such that for the calculated bending moment, one should be able to get the spacing of the reinforcement for the selected bar diameter.

(1) Grade of concrete; M-15, M-20 and M-25

(2) Grade of steel: Fe-415, Fe-500 and Fe-550

(3) Available reinforcement bar diameter: 6, 8, 10, 12 and 16 mm

(4) Spacing of bars with spacing increments of 10 mm and not less than 75 mm and not greater than $3d$ or 450 mm.

(5) Bending moment in the range of 5 (1) 30 kNm

(6) Slab depth 100 (250 $\times$ 250)

(7) Clear cover to reinforcement to be 15 mm

48. Write computer programme to determine the ultimate moment of resistance of a reinforced concreteTee beam for the following data:

Sl.No	b_f (mm)	b_w (mm)	D_f (mm)	d (mm)	A_{st} (mm²)	f_{ck} (N/mm²)	f_y (N/mm²)
1	1200	450	120	600	3040	20	415
2	1200	300	100	600	4845	15	250
3	1500	300	150	600	3930	15	415
4	1500	300	200	750	5972	15	250
5	1800	450	120	580	2500	20	415
6	1800	450	120	580	2500	15	415
7	2000	300	150	1000	9000	15	250

Use limit state method of analysis for design.

49. Write a computer programme to design areinforced concrete counterfort type retaining wall to retain earth 6 m above ground level. Good foundations are available at a depth of 1.5 m below ground level. The density of soil at site is 18 kN/m³. The safe bearing capacity of soil is 150 kN/m². Angle of shear resistance is 30 degree. Spacing of counterforts is 3 m. Adopt M-15 grade concrete and Fe-415 grade HYSD bars.

50. Write a computer programme to construct axialforce-moment interaction curves for a rectangular concrete column with 3 percent steel distributed equally on two faces. M-20 grade concrete and Fe-415 grade HYSD bars are available for use. The programme should include the possibilities
    a) When eccentricity is less than the minimum eccentricity.
    b) When neutral asix lies outside the section.
    c) When neutral axis lies within the section.

51. The values of shear parameters C and ϕ of a soil determine the type of soil as follows:
    If $C = 0$; the soil is cohesionless
    If $\phi = 0$; the soil is pure clay
    If $C \neq 0$ and $\phi \neq 0$; the soil is general clay.
    Given a random set of shear parameters, it is required to group them into three groups as per the above criterion. Write a computer programmeto classify the type of soil.

52. The shear strength of soil is calculated by the following equation:
    $$t = (C + \sigma \tan \phi)$$
    Where C and ϕ, together known as shear parameters are the unit cohesive strength and friction angle respectively. Write a computer programme to determine the shear parameters of soils given two experimentally observed values of corresponding to two chosen values of σ.

53. The process of determining the required size of a square footing, based on shear failure criterion, reduces to the solution of the following cubic equation in terms of size B in metres.
    $$B^3 + 48.4 B^2 = 200$$

Write a computer programme to determine the value of B with an accuracy of 0.05 m.

54. Brinch Hansen's bearing capacity factors are computed by the following equations:

$$N_q = \tan^2\left(45 + \frac{\phi}{2}\right)e^{\pi \tan \phi}$$

$$N_c = (N_q - 1)\cot\phi$$

$$N_r = 1.8\,(N_q - 1)\tan\phi$$

Write a computer programme to calculate and tabulate the values of N_c, N_q and N_r for values of angle ϕ from 0 to 50 degrees insteps of 5 degrees.

55. The radial and circumferential stress distribution around a circular holein an infinite plate Subjected to uniaxial tensile stress σ_x is given by the following equations:

$$\sigma_\theta = \frac{\sigma_x}{2}\left(1 + \frac{a^2}{r^2}\right) - \frac{\sigma_x}{2}\left(1 + \frac{3a^4}{r^4}\right)\cos 2\theta$$

$$\sigma_r = \frac{\sigma_x}{2}\left(1 - \frac{a^2}{r^2}\right) + \frac{\sigma_x}{2}\left(1 + \frac{3a^4}{r^4} - \frac{4a^2}{r^2}\right)\cos 2\theta$$

where σ_x = uniaxial stress

r = Distance of any point from centre of the hole

a = Redius of the circular hole

θ = Angle measured from the X-axis along which the tensile stress σ_x acts.

Write a computer programme to print out the values of the circumferential and radial stresses for values of the distances $r = a$, $2a$ and $3a$ and of angle θ at intervals of 10 degrees varying from zero to 90 degrees.

REFERENCES

1. James ML, GM Smith and JC Wolford, *Applied Numerical Methods for Digital Computation with FORTRAN and CSMP*, 2nd Edn, IEP-A, Dun-Donnelley Publications, New York, 1977.

2. Kuo SS, *Computer Applications of Numerical Methods*, Addison-Wesley, Reading, Massasuchets, USA, 1972.

3. Rajaraman V, *Principles of Computer Programming*, Prentice-Hall, India, New Delhi, 2nd Edn, 1980.

4. Terrence W Pratt, Marvin V Zelkowitz and Tadepalli V Gopal, *PROGRAMMING LANGUAGES, Design and Implementation*, 4th Edn, Pearson, 2001. Keshav Biswa et al, / (IJCSIT) *International Journal of Computer Science and Information Technologies*, Vol. 7 (2), 2016, 1004-100.

5. Ramani S, NV Koteshwara Rao and Nagarajan R, *A Text Book on Computer Programming*, 2nd Edn, C.B.S. Publishers & Distributors, New Delhi, 1983.

6. Rajaraman V, *Computer Oriented Numerical Methods*, Prentice-Hall, India, New Delhi, 2nd Edn, 1982.

7. Right EW, *Structural Design by Computer*, Van Nostrand, London, 1976.
8. Rajasekaran S, *Numerical Methods in Science & Engineering*—A Practical Approach, A.H. Wheeler & Co, Delhi, 1986.
9. Moseley WH and WJ Spencer, *Micro-Computer Applications in Structural Engineering*, Macmillan, London, 1984.
10. Jain MK, Iyengar SR and Jain RK, Numerical Methods for Scientific and Engineering Computations, New Age International Publishers, 6th Edn, New Delhi, 2012.

REVIEW QUESTIONS

1. Briefly explain the various programming languages used in the analysis of complex problems in the domain of civil and structural engineering.
2. What are flow charts? What are the advantages ofusing these charts in the analysis of civil engineering problems?
3. Briefly explain the terms
   a. Arithmetic expression
   b. Fortran constants
   c. Fortran variables
4. What are the typical Input/output statements used in FORTRAN programming? Specify with examples.
5. Explain with typical examples the use of dimension and do statements in FORTRAN programming.
6. What are logical statements and where do you use them? Specify their use in solving problems in structural analysis and design.
7. Write a brief note on
   a. Subscripted variables
   b. Do loops
   c. Stop and end statements used in FORTRAN programming.
8. Prepare a flow chart for the computation of the second moment of area of an unsymmetrical I-section.
9. Specify the various steps to be followed in writing a FORTRAN program for analyzing the moments and shear forces in a two span continuous beam with simple supports and supporting uniformly distributed load.
10. Write a FORTRAN program to determine the maximum deflection in a simply supported beam of span L supporting concentrated loads of magnitude W at quarter span points. Assume uniform flexural rigidity for the beam.

OBJECTIVE TYPE QUESTIONS

1. The programming language most widely used in solving engineering problems is
   a) ALGOL
   b) FORTRAN
   c) C/C++

2. In using the FORTRAN programming language the maximum number of digits permitted in the fixed point or integer constant is limited to
   a) 6
   b) 8
   c) 10

3. The valid fixed point or real variables in a FORTRAN language programme should comprise of alpha numeric characters not exceeding
   a) 2
   b) 4
   c) 6

4. In the hierarchy of arithmetic operations in FORTRAN the first operation to be executed is
   a) Addition
   b) Division
   c) Exponentiation

5. The first character in a floating point variable should be an alphabet other than the letter
   a) P, Q, R, S, T, U
   b) I, J, K, L, M, N
   c) A, B, C, D, E, F

6. The correct standard library function in FORTRAN IV language is represented as
   a) COS X
   b) A TAN (X)
   c) SINHX

7. In Fortran IV language the square root of a function is represented as
   a) $\sqrt{xy}$
   b) SQRT (XO * YO)
   c) SQRT X Y

8. The correct Dimension statement in FORTRAN language is expressed as
   a) Dimension (A.50)
   b) DIMENSION (A, FIFTY)
   c) DIMENSION A (50)

9. In Fortran computer programmes, the unconditional control statement is represented as
   a) Print (3, 50) C
   b) G0 T0 10
   c) FORMAT (F 9.2)

10. The Input statement in a FORTRAN IV programme is usually expressed as
    a) Print (3, 40) A, B, C
    b) READ (1, 20) A, B, C
    c) DO 25 K = 3, M, 2

Appendix

List of Computer Programmes

Index

Author Index